Making and Unmaking the Carolingians

Making and Unmaking the Carolingians

751–888

Stuart Airlie

BLOOMSBURY ACADEMIC
LONDON • NEW YORK • OXFORD • NEW DELHI • SYDNEY

BLOOMSBURY ACADEMIC
Bloomsbury Publishing Plc
50 Bedford Square, London, WC1B 3DP, UK
1385 Broadway, New York, NY 10018, USA

BLOOMSBURY, BLOOMSBURY ACADEMIC and the Diana logo
are trademarks of Bloomsbury Publishing Plc

First published in Great Britain 2020
Paperback edition published 2022

Copyright © Stuart Airlie, 2020

Stuart Airlie has asserted his right under the Copyright,
Designs and Patents Act, 1988, to be identified as Author of this work.

For legal purposes the Acknowledgements on p. x constitute an
extension of this copyright page.

Cover image: Page from *Stuttgart Psalter*, Württembergische Landesbibliothek,
Stuttgart, Cod. bibl. fol. 23, folio 13v (illustration of Psalm 11)

All rights reserved. No part of this publication may be reproduced or
transmitted in any form or by any means, electronic or mechanical, including
photocopying, recording, or any information storage or retrieval system,
without prior permission in writing from the publishers.

Bloomsbury Publishing Plc does not have any control over, or responsibility for,
any third-party websites referred to or in this book. All internet addresses given
in this book were correct at the time of going to press. The author and publisher
regret any inconvenience caused if addresses have changed or sites have
ceased to exist, but can accept no responsibility for any such changes.

Every effort has been made to trace copyright holders and to obtain their
permissions for the use of copyright material. The publisher apologizes for any errors or
omissions and would be grateful if notified of any corrections that should be
incorporated in future reprints or editions of this book.

A catalogue record for this book is available from the British Library.

Library of Congress Cataloging-in-Publication Data
Names: Airlie, Stuart, author.
Title: Making and unmaking the Carolingians, 751-888 / Stuart Airlie.
Description: London ; New York : Bloomsbury Academic, 2020. |
Includes bibliographical references and index.
Identifiers: LCCN 2020035919 (print) | LCCN 2020035920 (ebook) |
ISBN 9781788317443 (hardback) | ISBN 9781350189003 (paperback) |
ISBN 9781786726407 (epub) | ISBN 9781786736468 (ebook)
Subjects: LCSH: Carolingians–History. | France–Kings and rulers. |
Monarchy–France–History. | France–History–To 987. | Europe–History–476-1492.
Classification: LCC DC70 .A525 2021 (print) |
LCC DC70 (ebook) | DDC 944/.014–dc23
LC record available at https://lccn.loc.gov/2020035919
LC ebook record available at https://lccn.loc.gov/2020035920

ISBN:	HB:	978-1-7883-1744-3
	PB:	978-1-3501-8900-3
	ePDF:	978-1-7867-3646-8
	eBook:	978-1-7867-2640-7

Typeset by Integra Software Services Pvt. Ltd.

To find out more about our authors and books visit www.bloomsbury.com
and sign up for our newsletters.

To Robyn, finally.

Contents

Preface		ix
Acknowledgements		x
Abbreviations		xii
Maps		xv
Family Trees		xvii
1	A ruling family	1
	Weighing the legacy of the Carolingians	1
	The illusion of natural authority	4
	Frankish royalty as inheritance	9
	Carolingian specialness	13
	Portraying Carolingian specialness	18
	Fate of a child, fate of a dynasty	23
2	Building Carolingian royalty 751–68	27
	Roots of Carolingian royalty	27
	The royalty of Pippin III: 751	34
	How Pippin III stayed royal	43
3	A house and its head: The reign of Charlemagne 768–814	53
	Casting Charlemagne's shadow	53
	Focusing on Charlemagne's line: 768–92	60
	Problems of success and succession: Pippin the Hunchback 792	66
	A father under pressure: 792–806	71
	Gambling on futures: 806–14	78
4	Child labour 751–888	93
	Born rulers	93
	Sons royal by name and nature	102
	All boys together	109
5	Louis the Pious and the paranoid style in politics	121
	Louis the Pious as new imperial centre	121
	817: Godly empire and earthly families	130

	Years of pressure: 823–30	138
	Permanent tension: 831–9	146
	Disintegration: 839–43	161
6	Lines of succession and lines of failure 843–79	173
	Dividing an empire and rebuilding kingdoms	173
	Keeping it in the family: Rule by brothers	179
	Rule by fathers	184
	Kingdoms after 843: The middle kingdom	187
	Kingdoms after 843: The eastern kingdom	190
	Ending a line: Aquitaine	192
	Radical options: The western kingdom after 843	205
7	Universal Carolingians: Masteries of time and space 751–888	217
	One-way street: Genealogies towards the future	217
	Peopling the realm with Carolingians: The wider ranges of kinship	224
	Praying for a Carolingian future	233
8	Women's work	243
	The marrying kind: Incomers and women as treasures	244
	'The whole crowd of women'	254
	Royal women at work amongst the aristocracy	260
9	The loss of uniqueness: 888 and all that	273
	The incredible shrinking dynasty?	273
	Western kingdom, eastern kingdom and the reunited empire of Charles the Fat	279
	Charles the Fat and towards 888	287
	888 and the breaking of the dynastic spell	292
	Ending	310

Notes	319
Bibliography	387
Index	427

Preface

This is a book about a family and the empire that it ruled in what seems like a very remote world, the world of early medieval Europe. Like many royal families, the Carolingian family was a many-headed monster whose members could prey on each other even while they fought against outsiders who might envy or challenge their unique status as rulers. For a long time, from 751 to 888, this family alone provided the rulers of the kingdoms. This book looks at this royal family as a family and not just as a sequence of men who were rulers. The women of the family, those who married in and those who were daughters of kings, play a prominent role in this book, as they did in the realm. Children also appear on its stage. These women and children are important enough to deserve chapters of their own and they duly receive them, in the thematic Chapters 4 and 8, though they are not just confined to these sections. Illegitimate and seemingly marginal members of the family also get their own chapter, Chapter 7. These thematic chapters are not self-contained but are part of my overall argument and analysis and I have placed them where they can deepen the argument and enrich the picture of the dynasty's achievements and problems. The book thus offers a broad view of the political culture of the period where gender and the life-cycle are as prominent as the assemblies where rulers and ruled came together. At the heart of the vast Frankish realm was a family.

While medieval Europe can seem remote from us, I have tried to ask questions in this book that have a wider resonance for political culture and communication. Why do people obey authority? How far do people who believe that the authority that they obey is natural actually realize that they are in fact the ones who construct that authority which is, of course, far from natural? If a family is the source of authority, how does it make itself look more special than other families, and how does it convey and maintain that specialness in a pre-modern world without the communications and armies that help maintain authority of dynasties (political, criminal) today?

I hope that these threads will help guide the reader through the maze of the monster with all its endlessly repeated royal names. These names were part of the magic spell of royal charisma that this book seeks to explain, evoke and take apart.

Acknowledgements

This book has been a long time in the making and I have accumulated many debts in its writing. The fact that I completed it during the COVID-19 pandemic has brought home just how important co-operation is to any individual work. Those mentioned below will know how much I owe to their advice, criticism, support and work, more than can be conveyed in a list. Those whom I may have neglected to mention will also know my debt to them and I hope that they can overlook any forgetfulness on my part here.

The whole book was read by Jinty Nelson and Julia Smith and I am very grateful for their detailed critique and ultimate enthusiasm. Jinty Nelson read several chapters twice and she would doubtless have improved more chapters if I had kept sending them to her, but the book had to be finished. John Hudson read several chapters and I profited from his incisive comments. Various chapters were read by Mayke de Jong, Simon MacLean, Helmut Reimitz, Andrew Roach and Ian Wood and I thank them all for their support and advice. Over many years, Matt Strickland and Andrew Roach have listened patiently, I think, to ever-changing outlines of the book's argument and concepts, and I thank them for their wisdom and their friendship. David Ganz has tested me on historical matters for a long time and is more responsible for the book's argument than he knows.

Many of the ideas and arguments in this book were tested in meetings of various research groups that I had the good fortune to attend, and I am very grateful for these encounters, critical in every sense for the book's development. The meetings of the research group on Staat and Staatlichkeit were key to the conceptualizing of the book's arguments and I am immensely indebted to the core members of the group, particularly Matthias Becher, Hans-Werner Goetz, Jörg Jarnut, Mayke de Jong, Régine Le Jan, Steffen Patzold, Walter Pohl, Helmut Reimitz, Bernd Schneidmüller and Ian Wood. That group's various incarnations and afterlives also enabled me to benefit from discussions with Philippe Depreux, Max Diesenbeger, Stefan Esders, Sören Kaschke, Rutger Kramer, Janneke Raaijmakers, Irene van Renswoude and many others. The seminar rooms and cafes of Vienna and Utrecht have helped mightily in the making of this book. The research networks led by John Hudson and Ana Rodriguez on comparison of institutions in the Christian and Islamic Middle Ages were immensely stimulating. An invitation to deliver a paper to a research group based at the Netherlands Institute for Advanced Study Wassenaar resulted in rigorous critique from Mayke de Jong, David Ganz, Rosamond McKitterick, Helmut Reimitz and Els Rose that proved invaluable. A steady stream of books and offprints, as well as advice, from the members of all these groups helped me work on a European empire while based in the west of Scotland. Some chapters were delivered as papers at Münster and Mainz, and I thank Gerd Althoff and Ludger Körntgen and their colleagues and students for their responses. I have learned much from conversations with Patrick Geary, Eric Goldberg, Jennifer Davis and Geoff Koziol, as well as from their own work.

I benefited from institutional support from the AHRC which awarded me a Fellowship (AH/I002464/1) which enabled me to finalize the form of the whole book, and I am very grateful for that support. As the book neared completion, I learned much from the members of my research network on The Castle and the Palace, funded by an Arts and Humanities Network Award from the Royal Society of Edinburgh. I have spent most of my professional life at the University of Glasgow and have on occasion found the workings of the institution to be challenging, but I have been extremely fortunate in my colleagues and friends at History in Glasgow. Lynn Abrams, Karin Bowie and Callum Brown provided very welcome support and practical help in the final stages of completion, as did the School of Humanities and the College of Arts, and I am grateful to them. Steve Marritt has been consistently generous with time and advice, and Mathilde von Bülow and Phil O'Brien, with other Glasgow colleagues and friends, have been warm in their encouragement. I owe much to the students of Glasgow, particularly those who have taken my Special Subject on Charlemagne over the years.

Bloomsbury Academic waited patiently for this manuscript to emerge and I thank them for that, as well as thanking the anonymous reader for their report.

I started thinking about this book many years ago, and was lucky enough to be able to discuss my initial ideas with the teacher who opened my eyes to the world of early medieval Europe, Patrick Wormald.

In the final stages of completion, and not only then, Mark Thompson's warm encouragement helped me make progress.

My family has lived with this book for a very long time, and I owe my family more than I can say. My brother John has always believed that I could finish it while expressing impatience at the time I was taking to do so. He has been a generous supporter throughout. My daughter Madeleine has grown up with this book and will not miss it when it has gone, but her happiness in seeing its end hove into view helped me through its final stages, and she has consistently reminded me of the wider joys of the world away from the desk. My wife Robyn has supported the author of this book with love throughout its making, nicely balanced with terse encouragements to him to just get on with it. In the last stages, she worked hard and selflessly to prepare the manuscript and to bring coherence to what often must have looked like primal chaos. I am forever grateful to her for that, and much else.

June 2020

Abbreviations

AB	*Annales de Saint-Bertin*, ed. F. Grat, J. Vielliard, S. Clemencet and L. Levillain (Paris, 1964)
AF	*Annales Fuldenses*
AMP	*Annales Mettenses priores*
ARF	*Annales Regni Francorum*
Ann. Xant.	*Annales Xantenses*
Astronomer, *VH*	Astronomer, *Vita Hludowici imperatoris*, ed. E. Tremp, MGH SRG 64 (Hannover, 1995)
AV	*Annales Vedastini*
BM	J. F. Böhmer and E. Mühlbacher, eds, *Die Regesten des Kaiserreichs unter den Karolingern 751–918* (2nd edition, Innsbruck, 1908)
Cap.1	*Capitularia Regum Francorum*, vol. 1, ed. A. Boretius, MGH Legum Sectio 2, Capitularia (Hannover, 1883)
Cap.2	*Capitularia Regum Francorum*, vol. 2, ed. A. Boretius and V. Krause, MGH Legum Sectio 2 (Hannover, 1897)
ChLA	*Chartae Latinae Antiquiores*
Cod Dip. Fuld.	*Codex Diplomaticus Fuldensis*, ed. E. F. J. Dronke (Kassel,1850)
Cod. Lauresh.	*Codex Laureshamensis*, ed. K. Glöckner, 3 vols (Darmstadt, 1929–36).
Cont. Fredegar	*The Fourth book of the Chronicle of Fredegar with its continuations*, trans. J. M. Wallace-Hadrill (London, 1960)
DA	*Deutsches Archiv für Erforschung des Mittelalters*
Dhuoda, *LM*	Dhuoda, *Liber Manualis*, Dhuoda, *Manuel pour mon fils*, ed. P. Riché, trans. B. de Vregille and C. Mondésert, Sources Chrétiennes 225 (Paris, 1975)
Dip. A	*Die Urkunden Arnolfs*, ed. P. Kehr, MGH Diplomata Regum Germaniae ex stirpe Karolinorum, 3 (Berlin, 1940)

Dip. Karol. 1	*Pippini, Carlomanni, Caroli Magni Diplomata*, ed. E. Mühlbacher, MGH Diplomata Karolinorum, 1 (Hannover, 1906)
Dip. Lo. I, Dip. Lo. II	*Die Urkunden Lothars I. und Lothars II.*, ed. T. Schieffer, MGH Diplomata Karolinorum 3 (Berlin and Zürich, 1960)
Dip. CF	*Die Urkunden Karls III.*, ed. P. Kehr, MGH Diplomata Regum Germaniae ex stirpe Karolinorum, 2 (Berlin, 1937)
Dip. Karlmann	*Die Urkunden Ludwigs des Deutschen, Karlmanns und Ludwigs des Jüngeren*, ed. P. Kehr, MGH Diplomata Regum Germaniae ex stirpe Karolinorum, 1 (Berlin, 1934)
Dip. Louis G.	*Die Urkunden Ludwigs des Deutschen, Karlmanns und Ludwigs des Jüngeren*, ed. P. Kehr, MGH Diplomata Regum Germaniae ex stirpe Karolinorum, 1 (Berlin, 1934)
Dip. Louis Y.	*Die Urkunden Ludwigs des Deutschen, Karlmanns und Ludwigs des Jüngeren*, ed. P. Kehr, MGH Diplomata Regum Germaniae ex stirpe Karolinorum, 1 (Berlin, 1934)
Dip. Louis P.	*Die Urkunden Ludwigs des Frommen*, ed. T. Kölzer, MGH Diplomata Karolinorum, 2, 3 vols (Wiesbaden, 2016)
Dip. LC	*Die Urkunden Zwentibolds und Ludwig des Kindes*, ed. T. Schieffer, MGH Diplomata Regum Germania ex stirpe Karolinorum, 4 (Berlin, 1960)
Dip. Louis II	*Die Urkunden Ludwigs II.*, ed. K. Wanner, MGH Diplomata Karolinorum, 4 (Munich, 1994)
Dip. Rudolf	*Die Urkunden der burgundischen Rudolfinger*, ed. T. Schieffer, MGH Regum Burgundiae e stirpe Rudolfina Diplomata et Acta (Würzburg, 1977)
Dip. Zwentibold	*Die Urkunden Zwentibolds und Ludwig des Kindes*, ed. T. Schieffer, MGH Diplomata Regum Germania ex stirpe Karolinorum (Berlin, 1960)
Ep. KA	MGH Epistolae Karolini Aevi
Ermold	Ermold, *Poème sur Louis le Pieux et épires au roi Pépin*, ed. and trans. E. Faral (Paris, 1964)
Flodoard, *HRE*	Flodoard, *Historia Remensis Ecclesiae*, ed. M. Stratmann. MGH SS 36 (Hannover, 1998)
FMSt	*Frühmittelalterliche Studien*
Lib. Pont.	*Le Liber Pontificalis*, ed. L. Duchesne, vol. 1 (Paris, 1886)

Nithard	Nithard, *Historiae*, ed. and trans. P. Lauer, *Histoire des fils de Louis le Pieux* (Paris, 1964)
Notker, *GK*	Notker, *Gesta Karoli imperatoris*, ed. H. F. Haefele, MGH SRG, nova series 12 (Berlin, 1959)
PL	Patrolgiae cursus completes, series Latina, ed. J.-P. Migne, 221 vols (Paris, 1841–64).
PLAC	MGH Poetae Latini Aevi Carolini
Recueil Aquitaine	*Recueil des actes de Pépin Ier et de Pépin II, rois d'Aquitaine, 814–848*, ed. L. Levillain (Paris, 1926).
Recueil Charles II	*Recueil des actes de Charles II le chauve, roi de France*, ed. G. Tessier, 3 vols (Paris 1943–1955).
Recueil Charles III	*Receuil des actes de Charles III le Simple, roi de rance, 893-923*, ed. F. Lot and P. Lauer (Paris, 1949).
Recueil Eudes	*Recueil des actes d'Eudes, roi de france, 888–898*, ed. G. Tessier and R.-H. Bautier (Paris, 1967).
Recueil Provence	*Recueil des actes des rois de Provence (855–928)*, ed. R. Poupardin, Chartes et diplômes relatifs à l'histoire de France (Paris, 1920).
Recueil Louis II	*Recueil des actes de Louis II le Bègue, Louis III at Carloman II, rois de France, 887–884*, ed. F. Grat, J. de Font-Réaulx, G. Tessier and R.-H. Bautier (Paris, 1978).
Recueil Robert et Raoul	*Recueil des actes de Robert Ier et de Raoul, rois de France (922–936)*, ed. R.-H. Bautier and J. Dufour (Paris, 1978).
Regino, *Chron.*	Regino, *Chronicon cum continuatione Treverensi*, ed. F. Kurze, MGH
	SRG in usum scholarum separatim editi, 50 (Hannover, 1890).
SRG	MGH Scriptores rerum Germanicarum
SS	MGH Scriptores
Thegan, *GH*	Thegan, *Gesta Hludowici imperatoris*, ed. E. Tremp, MGH SRG 64 (Hannover, 1995)
UB St Gallen	*Urkundenbuch der Abtei Sanct Gallen*, ed. H. Wartmann, 3 vols (Zürich, 1863–66).

Maps

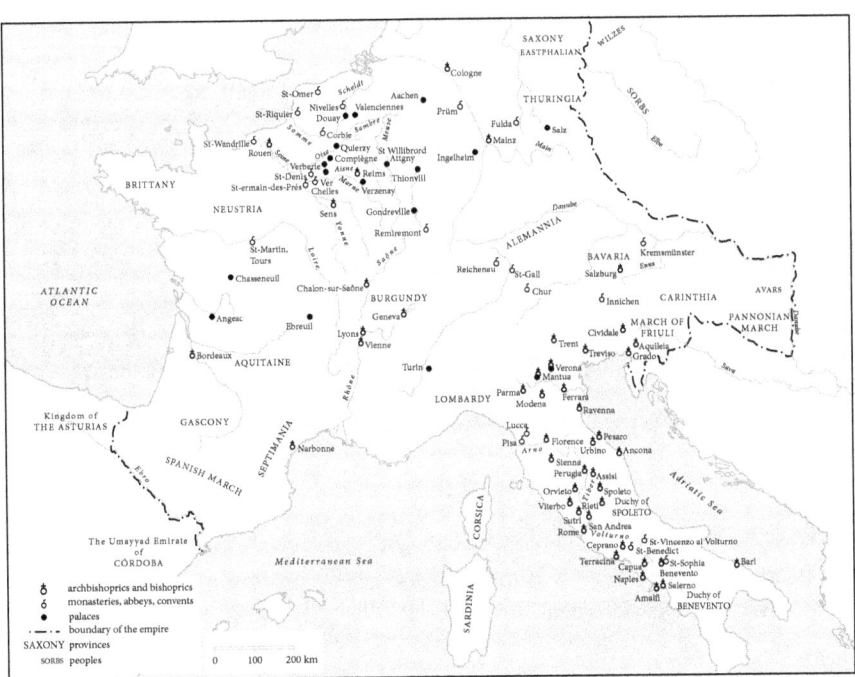

Map 1 The Empire of Charlemagne.

Map 2 The Carolingian Kingdoms after 843.

Family Trees

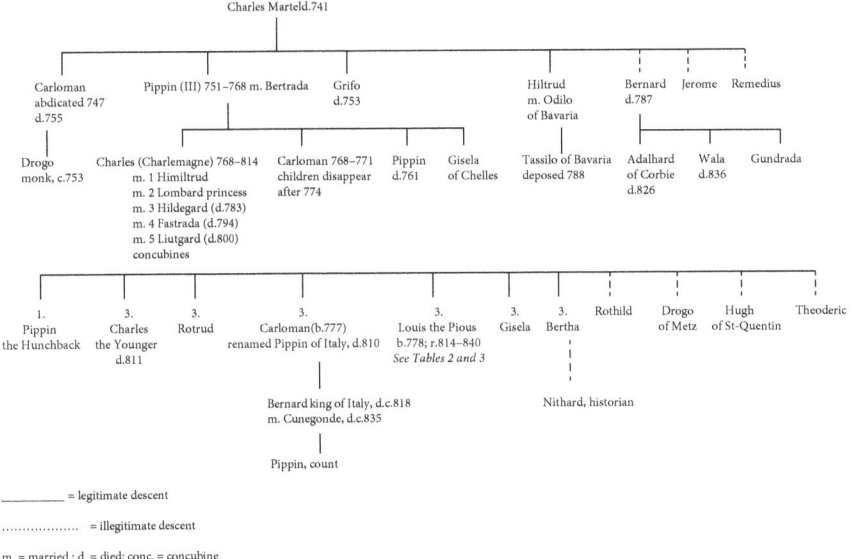

Family Tree 1 Pippin III and Charlemagne (simplified).

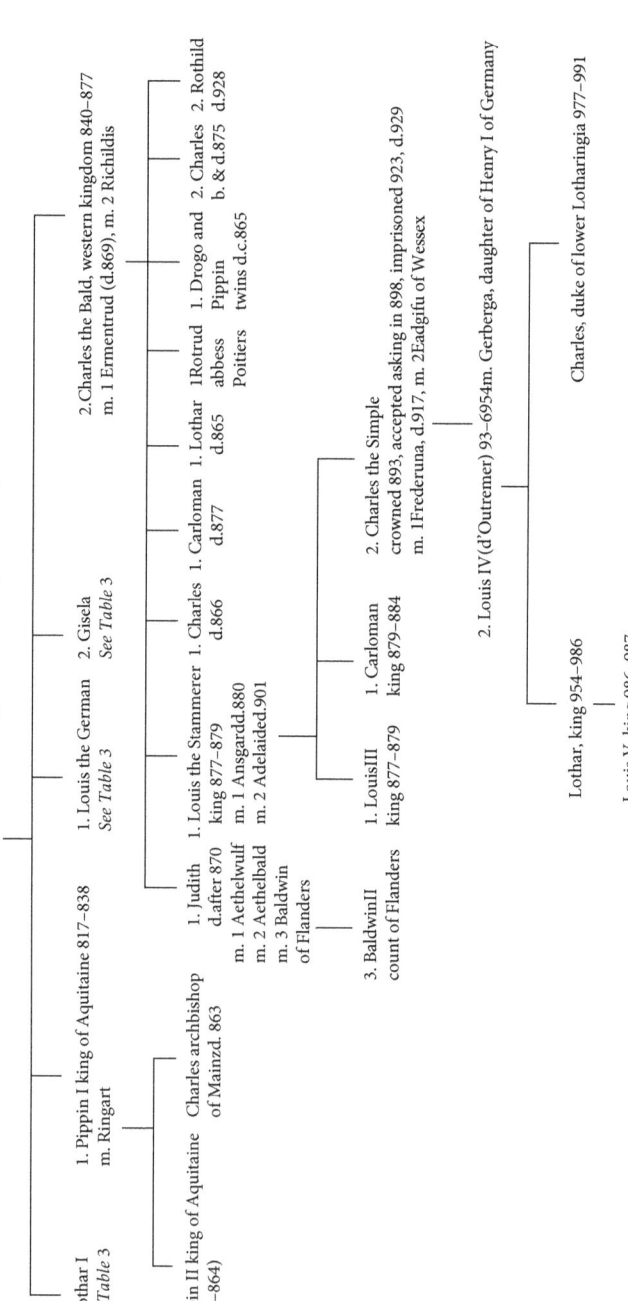

Family Tree 2 Louis the Pious and his descendants (1). Western Kingdoms (simplified).

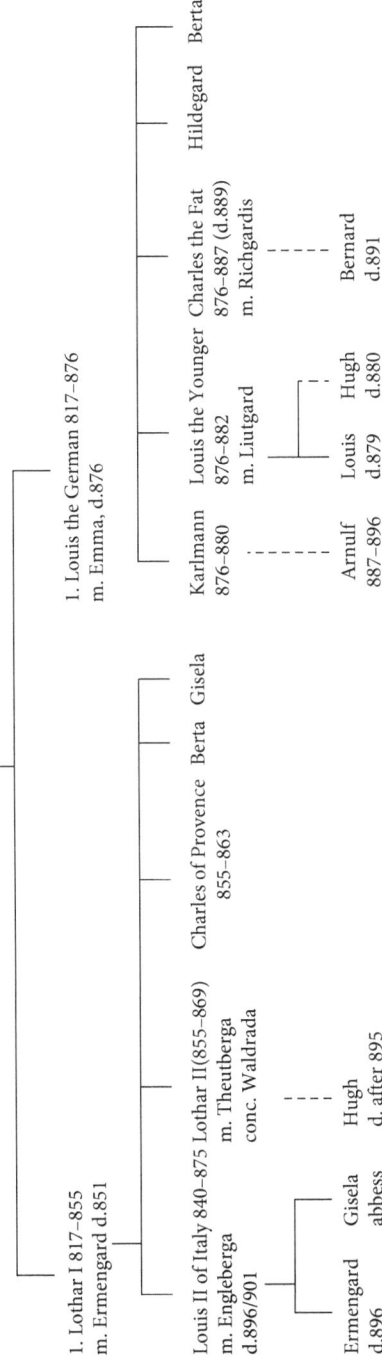

Family Tree 3 Louis the Pious and his descendants (2). Eastern and Middle Kingdoms (simplified).

1

A ruling family

Weighing the legacy of the Carolingians

The magnificent aura of the great medieval king and emperor Charlemagne (768–814) and of his family, the Carolingians, has dazzled Europeans for centuries. The very name of the king evokes grandeur: Charles the Great, in Latin Carolus Magnus, hence the now generally adopted (French) Charlemagne. In the Middle Ages, the kings of France proclaimed their attachment to the Carolingian royal line while a king of Germany, Frederick Barbarossa, went one better by having him proclaimed a saint in 1165. The great chandelier that Frederick granted to the church at Aachen for the cult of the now saintly Charlemagne survives as visible testimony to the medieval investment in the remembrance of Charlemagne and his dynasty, just as the tombs of his western descendants in the abbey of St-Denis to the north of Paris were intended to be a visible focus for reverence towards the French crown.[1] The church of Charlemagne at Aachen still stands and can provide for those visitors with sufficient imagination 'a history lesson more vivid than any book can offer'.[2]

One visitor with more than enough imagination was the French writer Victor Hugo, whose novel *Notre Dame of Paris* testifies to his lively sense of the Middle Ages. On his visit to Aachen in 1840, Hugo fell into a sort of trance and saw, as in a vision, the gigantic figure of Charlemagne himself lumber to his feet and stand as a vast shadow on the horizon. For Hugo, Charlemagne and the Carolingian empire seemed to offer a blueprint for the union of France and Germany; that has been the role that Charlemagne and his family were called upon to play in the political imagination of western Europe after 1945. In this respect the title of a book by the French scholar Pierre Riché – *The Carolingians: A Family That Made Europe* – is suggestive, as is the fact that it has been translated into other European languages.[3] Nor are such notions of the Carolingians as the progenitors of modern (western) Europe confined to university professors, as shown by the great Charlemagne-centred exhibitions held in Aachen in 1965 and in 1999 in Germany, Spain, Italy and Croatia.[4] Furthermore, the city of Aachen now awards an annual prize to individuals who have served the cause of European unity. Unsurprisingly, recipients have tended to be political grandees, including British prime ministers such as Winston Churchill and Tony Blair.[5]

The fact that is now impossible to imagine a British prime minister being awarded this prize shows that Charlemagne and his line should not be imagined as harmless puppets in the service of blandly harmonious Euro-speak. While Europe after the fall of communism in 1989 looks bigger than the post-1945 western grouping that tended to look back to Charlemagne, it also looks smaller in a world in thrall to globalization. Historians now fret over Charlemagne's dwindling stature: was he a 'global player'?[6] European identity, however, remains as complex and problematic as that of individual European states. Charlemagne could not always be invoked as a universally acceptable father-figure. Thus, the attempt to place a large equestrian statue of Charlemagne outside Notre-Dame cathedral in Paris in the late nineteenth century provoked strong opposition from secular republicans on the grounds that Charlemagne personified absolute royal power and imperial aggression.[7] Charlemagne's legacy could be drawn on for dark purposes, as in Nazi Germany where it was invoked in attempts to foster a sense of European unity in the struggle against Bolshevism. In our own time, the battle between Charlemagne's grandfather and Muslim Arab forces in 732 has been evoked by the far right as an example of a 'clash of cultures'.[8]

Given this weighty heritage, it can be difficult for us to realize that the Carolingians were not always looked on with awe and respect. In fact, Charlemagne's ancestors were simply one aristocratic family among others in the struggles for power that engulfed Frankish kingship in the late seventh and early eighth centuries. At this time the kingship was held by the family of the Merovingians who had been kings of the Franks since time out of mind. The attempts by the Carolingians to muscle in on the supreme power cost them dear. One of Charlemagne's ancestors, Grimoald (I), prepared a coup d'état in 656 but was ambushed by his enemies who imprisoned him before torturing him to death, a bleak testimony to the horror his ambitions had aroused. The name Grimoald seems to have been ill-starred, for Grimoald (II), another of Charlemagne's ancestors, was assassinated in 714 despite, or probably because of, the political power of his father Pippin. The stabbing of this Grimoald and the rising of his father from his sickbed to unleash vengeance on the assassins show how deeply involved the early Carolingians were in the feuds and resentments of Frankish power politics. They had no privileged status that lifted them out of that mire and pro-Carolingian sources reflect the family's anger and unease. The name Grimoald did not recur in the family. Some of Charlemagne's ancestors were too awkward to be remembered.[9]

Thus we must not project the later glories of Carolingian royalty back on to the family's pre-royal past. As powerful aristocrats, Charlemagne's ancestors were respected by contemporaries but were not seen as uniquely awe-inspiring figures. Even after it was elevated to the throne in 751, the new royal Carolingian dynasty did not always get the respect which it believed that it deserved. After Charlemagne's conquest of much of Italy in the 770s, in one monastery an abbot refused to join in prayers for the king, snarling that if it weren't for the fact that he wanted to keep his post as abbot he would treat Charlemagne like a dog. This, however, together with other vividly anti-Frankish remarks, was reported back to Charlemagne who took a very dim view of it. North of the Alps, the situation was not always much better. In 785, a conspiracy was hatched against Charlemagne and when the conspirators were seized, one of them boldly told the king to his face that if the plotters had only held together then Charlemagne would never have crossed the Rhine alive. The desperate utterances of Duke Tassilo of Bavaria, who said that he would rather die than continue to buckle under Charlemagne's escalating demands for his submission, reveal further resistance at the end of the 780s to Charlemagne's claims to western European hegemony.¹⁰ Rather than seeing Charlemagne as 'the father of Europe', as his court poets styled him, we should remember Michael Wallace-Hadrill's characterization of the rulers of this period as 'Barbarian chieftains who quarrelled fiercely among themselves ... and who were commonly despised outside their own territory'.¹¹

If Carolingian rule had to be imposed in the face of such stiff opposition and resentment, this only makes the Carolingians becoming the acclaimed legitimate masters of Europe all the more striking. Towards the end of the ninth century, Europe itself was a term that simply meant the Carolingian realms: 'Europe, that is the kingdom of Charles [the Fat, 876–887]'.¹² This book does not offer a comprehensive survey of the nature of this dynasty's power, but its sheer scale ought to be recalled. The idea of empire in the west was revived, famously, in Charlemagne's coronation by the pope as emperor in Rome in 800. At a less rarefied level, Carolingian government sought to become involved at a very practical level in people's daily lives. Such aspirations are clearly visible in Carolingian legislation, particularly in the reign of Charles the Bald, king of west Francia (840–77). The Edict of Pitres, for example, is a vast document stemming from a royal assembly which Charles held there in 864, and it contains regulations on coinage, weights and measures, markets, and labour-services on building of roads and bridges, together with payment of royal rents.¹³

While Carolingian rulers did busy themselves with all levels of society, this book is rather more elitist. My concern is the royal family itself. The 888 reference to Europe cited above has for its focus the Carolingian ruler. 'Europe is the kingdom of Charles', that is, Charles the Fat. The Carolingian dynasty, in fact the Carolingian family at large, was prominent in the landscape of this world. Conflicts and struggles within this 'notably quarrelsome' family were the stuff of politics and were closely watched by contemporary political observers. Struggles for power within the family between 830 and 834 (when the emperor Louis the Pious was locked in conflict with his three oldest sons) were reflected in a letter of Einhard, friend and biographer of Charlemagne, enquiring as to the exact balance of power between the emperor and his sons as well as in more humble documents such as property transactions in Brittany, far from the centres of Carolingian power, but whose inhabitants nevertheless felt sufficiently brushed by the ruling family's quarrels to date their documents by the years of rival members of that family.¹⁴

It was not only in the political arena that kings and their doings had an impact. They also intruded into more private spaces. A remarkable book has survived written up by abbot Hartbert between 864 and 879 while he was in the abbey of Corbie in what is now northern France. Both the 'shorthand' script and the contents of this book reveal that it was a personal object. In it, Hartbert records the precise time of death of monks and nuns in a variety of monastic communities, which suggests that he officiated as priest for the last rites. He also noted his dreams, including dreams about his sister. Amidst such spiritual and intimately personal concerns, we also find references to the deeds of Carolingian kings. Hartbert was not writing a chronicle but compiling a mixture of personal memories, liturgical material and historical dates. The historical notes have a terse quality. Charles the Bald's invasion of the eastern Frankish kingdom is noted thus: 'Charles came to Aachen on Sunday in the year of Our Lord 876'. Hartbert does not give him his royal title; that was hardly necessary; Charles was a royal name, borne exclusively by members of the ruling family. Many people would have visited Aachen that year, but the royal visit of a Charles was something special, and the name alone would have identified it as such.[15] We thus find Carolingian kings in a personal text and can conclude that they loomed large in the consciousness of figures such as Hartbert. Indeed a variety of texts from the period purport to record the dreams of their subjects about the Carolingian rulers; the dreams of monks and humble women were populated by the great kings of the day. Nor was it only the kings that made an impact. The death of a Carolingian princess in 925 was seen by a poet as evoking mourning across all Europe. The holy Carolingian woman Saint Gertrud of Nivelles was called upon by the possessed in their agony.[16] The Carolingian family was deeply integrated into imaginations of this world, as well as into its political structures.

The illusion of natural authority

The depth of the dynasty's integration can perhaps be most fully grasped at the point of its dissolution. In 888, the Carolingian dynasty entered political crisis. Charlemagne's great-grandson, the ailing Charles the Fat, who had re-united Charlemagne's empire under the rule of a single figure, was abandoned by his supporters in the winter of 887–8 to die in obscurity. This was the signal for new challengers to emerge. A well-known account of all this is offered by a contemporary, Regino, who wrote up his *Chronicle* some twenty years after the event. Abbot of the great abbey of Prüm, which was closely linked to the Carolingian family, Regino structured his account of the decade leading up to 887–8 as a story of dynastic crisis: the Carolingians were running out of suitable heirs to inherit royal authority. In fact, as we shall see in the final chapter of this book, the process was more complicated than that, but the pattern that Regino perceived retrospectively is important testimony to contemporary understanding of Carolingian claims to rule. Key here is the following well-known passage:

> After [Charles the Fat's] death the kingdoms which had been subject to his rule, deprived of a legitimate heir, dissolved into separate parts, and each of them, rather than waiting for its natural lord, chose a king from its own guts. This was the cause of great wars; not because the Franks lacked leaders with the nobility, courage and wisdom necessary to rule over kingdoms; rather the equality of ancestry, rank and power magnified the discord, since none of them was so outstanding that the others could accept submission to his control.

Another contemporary shared Regino's perspective, describing these new rulers as mere 'kinglets'.[17]

We will look at what actually happened in 887–8 in my last chapter. For now I focus on a paradox of Regino's text: while much of the scholarly comment it has provoked has seen it as providing a perceptive explanation for much of the political instability of subsequent decades, it also casts a searching light backwards, into the very nature of Carolingian authority before its disintegration.[18] In showing what happened when the Carolingian dynastic system crashed, it shows how that system worked. It is thus a guide through the labyrinth of that system to the very heart of Carolingian authority.

Regino's account of the challenge to the dynasty's exclusive right to rule is the climax to his story of Carolingian decline. That account does not seem, at first sight, to be characterized by originality. Regino probably drew on the *Consolation of Philosophy* by the sixth-century Roman writer Boethius, a text that has much to say on the role of fortune in the vicissitudes of human life. It is certain that, like many medieval writers, he drew on an account of the reign of the Greek ruler Alexander the Great preserved in the text of Justin, who possibly compiled his work in the second or third century AD. Justin's influence on Regino's text here was deep but was also truly creative and did not imprison Regino in an antiquarian vision. Rather, it helped him, and us, to understand the shifts in power of his own age. Creative originality need not mean creating something out of nothing.[19]

Why was the story of Alexander the Great of such importance to Regino? The section of Justin upon which he drew here dealt with the problems of the succession to Alexander, with the famous story of how Alexander's anxious companions asked him on his deathbed whom he wanted to have as his successor. 'The best' was Alexander's enigmatic reply. It is with this prospect of an empire up for grabs that Justin begins his Book XIII describing the merits of Alexander's leading warriors as the possible successors. This is the section that Regino found so useful, and no wonder. Justin does not belittle Alexander's warriors as unworthy to fill the great man's boots. Instead, he claims that they were of such high quality that one might think each one of them deserving of the title of king, but they were fatally equal. Their great qualities made it impossible for one of them to yield to another and fortune decreed that they should turn against each other. Surely this was the dilemma and self-image of Frankish aristocrats themselves in 888.[20]

While the parallels with the situation of winter 887–8 are not exact, they gave Regino a way of articulating his own essential points about the emergence of the 'kinglets'. Like Justin, but more urgently, Regino was dealing with the problems posed by the death of a leader who had been acknowledged as such by all under him. Nor was Regino alone in knowing of Alexander the Great as a powerful but problematic figure of a ruler. Towards the end of the eighth century, Alcuin's poetic response to the Viking attack on Lindisfarne had taken Alexander as part of its cataloguing of the transience of earthly glory. In the ninth century, Gerward, librarian of Louis the Pious and friend of Einhard, possessed a copy of Justin, as did abbeys in northern Francia as well as St-Gall and other abbeys in the south-east of the empire. The story of Alexander's death and the subsequent squabbles over the succession was also told in the *History of Alexander* by Quintus Curtius, a copy of which seems to have been made for a great lay aristocrat, Count Conrad, in the late ninth century.[21]

For Regino, the Carolingian ruler's claims to leadership were of a different order from those who came after. He was a 'natural lord'; 'each kingdom, instead of waiting for its natural lord chose a king'. By 'natural lord' Regino was referring to the senior able-bodied Carolingian male, Arnulf, nephew of Charles the Fat. The implication is that though Charles the Fat left no legitimate heir, a Carolingian was the 'natural lord'. Without that lord, there was disintegration into separate parts. In anatomizing the break-up of Carolingian hegemony, Regino actually pays tribute to its strength. The power of a ruling dynasty is of course far from natural. Such power is *made*. But when a dynasty or institution is successful in maintaining its claims to hegemony, then the effort required to maintain such power becomes veiled and the power becomes part of the natural landscape as accepted authority.

Carolingian hegemony was not in fact effortlessly maintained even before 888. Regino necessarily uncovers its workings at the very moment of its being challenged so that he can show the deadly nature of that challenge. But its maintenance had required work throughout the entire Carolingian period. It is worth recalling here a couplet from an intense meditation on political power and authority by the seventeenth-century poet Andrew Marvell: 'The same arts that did gain / A power must it maintain' ('An Horatian Ode ...'). Carolingian authority, seemingly part of the very fabric of the natural world, had to be maintained. It was training, not instinct, that made the possessed cry out to Carolingian saints for help. As E.P. Thompson put it, referring to a very different period, 'Once a social system has become "set", it does not need to be endorsed daily by exhibitions of power ... What matters more is a continuing theatrical style.' One answer to Giorgio Agamben's question why power needs glory is that power needs glory so that it can appear as authority.[22] This book is less concerned with 'coercive' power than with 'symbolic' power, that is, that which 'shapes people's desires so that they want to do what you want'.[23] Of course, such a distinction between coercive and symbolic power is artificial: after 751, Carolingian royalty still deployed force; before 751, Carolingian mayors of the palace relied on claims to legitimate lordship as well as on force.

Regino grasped the drastic consequences of the evaporation of Carolingian charisma; he and his contemporaries understood 'coercive' and 'symbolic' power, though these are not terms that they used. In considering royalty, authority and power in the Carolingian world, I naturally will pay close attention to that world's values and practices but I have found the work of some modern thinkers particularly helpful and illuminating in making my main argument. The Carolingian dynasty could not relax; it did not reach a plateau where authority was securely self-perpetuating through some political perpetual motion contraption. It had to be made to look natural through 'strategies of distinction'.[24] Seeing rule and power as legitimate authority comes through the social construction of reality, a process deftly summed up in Rogers and Hammerstein's little song about racism ('You've Got to Be Carefully Taught') from their 1949 musical *South Pacific*.

In any discussion of consent to authority, the work of Antonio Gramsci (d.1937) remains active. Which historian does not thrill to Gramsci's assertion that everyone is a philosopher, or ruefully acknowledge that 'we are all conformists of some conformism or other'? Gramsci's exploration of hegemony – the success of dominant classes in presenting their way of seeing the world as the natural way of seeing the world, a way accepted 'spontaneously' by the population – put values and beliefs centre-stage and opened up ways of understanding consent to authority as more than merely passive, cowed subjection. Gramsci's understanding that levels and intensity of consent to a given authority would vary within society is a historical understanding. The link between thought and action was a problematic one for Gramsci and he sought to unite thought and action so that capitalist hegemony could be exposed and challenged. Gramsci was thus concerned about broader and deeper social forces than the authority of a medieval dynasty, but his dazzling insights help us see that values that we might think of as imposed from above to suit the purposes of those in authority can be 'genuinely' held by those subject to that authority, and that these values contribute to the actions of our historical subjects. Such values, an ideology, a culture, thus have social force. Medievalists' interest in the significance of rituals of kingship in pre-modern political culture, to choose an example relevant to this book, does resonate with Gramsci's political concern with cultural values.[25]

In discussing social groups' acceptance of authority, he wrote:

> A group has, for reasons of submission and intellectual subordination, adopted a conception which is not its own but is borrowed from another group; *and it affirms this conception verbally and believes itself to be following it* because this is the conception which it follows in 'normal times' (my emphasis).[26]

Now, I am not suggesting here that in 751 the wily Carolingians simply managed to fool gullible Franks into accepting them as kings and that the Franks were thenceforth their ideological puppets. That would not be a Gramscian view; it would be Voltaire's cynical eighteenth-century view of the self-interested cunning of monarchs and priests working together in the illusory splendour of the coronation ritual of 751.[27] Gramsci's importance for this book is his great insight that belief in authority is all the more potent when it seems to be natural, internalized. Frankish aristocrats came to believe that the Carolingians were the rightful ruling family, even as they resented and despised individual kings who had mistreated them.

Gramsci is also relevant to us here in his insistence on how much work it takes to maintain a system of thought and practice as the norm, as the orthodoxy in which people have faith. The Catholic Church, an even more majestic edifice than Carolingian royalty, would be an example here:

> Religion, or a particular church, maintains its community of faithful ... in so far as it nourishes its faith permanently and in an organised fashion, indefatigably repeating its apologetics, struggling at all times and always with the same kind of arguments, and maintaining a hierarchy of intellectuals who give to the faith, in appearance at least, the dignity of thought.[28]

It is that kind of ceaseless work that is the subject of this book. It takes a lot of pressure to generate authority that seems normal and natural.

In exploring concepts and mechanisms of distinction (Carolingian exclusive claims to royalty) and the reproduction of that distinction (the maintaining of Carolingian royal distinction across space and time), I am also indebted to work by the sociologist and anthropologist Pierre Bourdieu. Bourdieu explored how 'the dominated apply categories constructed from the point of view of the dominant to the relations of domination, thus making them appear as natural'. One answer to this is the *habitus* which is the result of intense social processes, of 'a process of inculcation which must last long enough to produce a durable training, that is, a *habitus*, the product of internalization of the principles of a cultural arbitrary capable of perpetuating itself after pedagogic action has ceased and thereby of perpetuating in practice the principles of the internalized arbitrary'.[29] We might read Bourdieu's 'cultural arbitrary' here as Carolingian inborn and exclusive royal distinctiveness. Admittedly, Bourdieu was concerned with deeper structures than the political authority of a royal dynasty, and the keen-eyed reader will have seen that the second quote above refers to the ceasing of 'pedagogic action' while this book focuses on unceasing action to teach/ maintain Carolingian authority. Nonetheless, Bourdieu's concept of the *habitus* and his work on social and cultural reproduction has been very suggestive for my framing of my analysis, though I would not want to suggest that a rigid 'habitus' completely determined thought and action in the Carolingian world; my approach remains historical.

This book looks at Carolingian authority as a discourse that, through social practices and texts, continually articulated the natural legitimacy of Carolingian rule. And this discourse was bigger than the Carolingians themselves, who were not the only actors and authors in it. Carolingian authority was sustained by the work of many non-Carolingian actors and authors invested in it, which was both a massive advantage for the dynasty, and a disadvantage in that this discourse was not under the dynasty's control. Here we encounter our third presiding deity, Michel Foucault. Foucault's work forms a recognizable body of thought, though it is various and not consistent, and it is open to many criticisms, not just from historians; one thoughtful analyst of power has characterized Foucault's generalized ideas as both 'commonplace' and 'extravagant'.[30]

Nonetheless, Foucault's thinking is helpful to me and thus, I hope, to the reader. For Foucault, to give a rather crude summary, power is not something that exists in a box to which the powerful alone have access and which they can then unleash on passive recipients. Rather, it is everywhere and it works through networks. For example, 'state power' is not something separate and pure standing outside the social realm:

> The state can only operate on the basis of ... an already existing power relation. The state is superstructural in relation to a whole series of power networks that invest the body, sexuality, the family, kinship, knowledge, technology and so forth, ... the state consists in the functioning of a whole range of power relations that render its functioning possible.[31]

Foucault's salutary evocation here of a number of relatively informal, private sites, subjects and groupings ('the body, sexuality, the family', etc.) as essential elements in power networks points us towards the richness of the Carolingian culture of authority; such elements played key roles in that culture, as we shall see. Nor is power simply repressive; rather, it is creative: it 'traverses and produces things, it induces pleasure, forms knowledge, produces discourse. It needs to be considered as a productive network that runs through the whole social body.' Although Foucault's thought is very different from Gramsci's, it usefully parallels for us here Gramsci's ideas on consent, in its understanding of power as something that 'operates "through" individuals rather than "against" them'. Equally important here is the point that, if power is dispersed, percolating through networks that actually constitute it, then a single point, a centre, cannot contain it.[32]

That means, among other things, that the Carolingian family was not always able to control a system of authority and power relations from which it benefited. Not all definitions of Carolingian-ness were made by the rulers. Some members of the royal kin itself challenged rulers' definitions and decisions; marginalized Carolingian men (and some women) resisted being pushed aside. Above all, aristocrats could help construct Carolingian identity and authority, or challenge it, by accepting or rejecting claims to rule. The existence of dispersed power networks does not mean, however, that rulers were unable to deploy constraint and violence. Rulers were prepared to unleash force on their own relatives and on aristocrats who rose against them or who flitted too often between competing claimants to royal authority. Charlemagne's urgent advice in 806 to his adult sons not to wilfully kill or maim their own relatives speaks volumes; as does Charles the Bald's execution of the great aristocrat Bernard of Septimania in 844, a grim contrast to the visions of mutual respect and faithfulness among rulers and followers recently articulated by Bernard's wife Dhuoda.[33]

Frankish royalty as inheritance

Some of this Carolingian power and authority was new, as the dynasty-making rituals of 751 and 754 may have been (see Chapter 2). Some of it was a more intense development of features of Frankish politics of the Merovingian period. After all, it was the Merovingian kings who Pope Gregory the Great was referring to when he said c.600 that 'in the kingdom of the Franks kings succeed by the family line'. The Carolingian Charles the Bald was happy to publicly cite this phrase centuries later in support of the well-known 'venerably old' Frankish custom of hereditary kingship, a practice that now bolstered him and his line.[34] The hereditary kingship of the Frankish world was thus a very distinctive and deeply rooted feature of that world and was not invented by the Carolingians. It was known in Byzantium as a Frankish characteristic. Such was the Frankish attachment to the traditional royal dynasty that even young children could be kings, something that was 'inconceivable in any other European state of that time'.[35] The Carolingian takeover of the royal house in 751 marked a re-energizing of the traditional Frankish political structures and so Carolingian power was not simply 'power possessed by one faction ... but a complex set of activities and relationships that created previously unsuspected resources'.[36] The bonds between the Carolingians and their followers, bonds of consensus, created a powerful political force that carved out and maintained a massive empire in relentless wars and governance. The Franks themselves were a 'holy people, a royal priesthood', while one of the glories of the hereditary line of rulers was precisely that it stemmed from the 'most Christian people of the Franks'.[37]

The Frankish kingdoms are not unique in having hereditary rulers. As a modern specialist in dynastic history has put it, 'power in the pre-modern world was based on kinship'. Not that this realm was primitive, or underdeveloped, or simply a patrimonial form of rule, in the influential terminology of the early twentieth-century sociologist Max Weber. Carolingian kings did not enjoy the 'unlimited power of the patriarchal master limited only by tradition and custom' which Weber saw as forming the basis for patrimonial rule. Weber himself did not intend his categories to be used rigidly. As he himself pointed out, 'Historically, there has never been a purely patrimonial state'.[38] The point to grasp is that the royal family was at the heart of Frankish politics, that is to say, at the heart of competition for power and it was one of the modalities and structures through which such struggles took place, conditioning their shape and nature.[39] Such struggles might appear rather different if we viewed them through other lenses focusing on, say, the role of material resources or the nature of communications, and we will look at such elements. But, however we look at this period, the role of the Carolingian family remains essential to the formation and maintenance of the ruling elite as well as to its splits and fissures.

I tend in this book to refer to the Carolingian family generally as a dynasty. In some ways, this is a term that works better for periods such as the later Middle Ages or the early modern era, when distinctive lines with famous names (the Habsburgs, the Bourbons, the Jagiellonians, the Romanovs) exercised hereditary rule over time through a clearly defined family line and crystallized their identity and authority at courts and through clearly delineated hierarchy. The Carolingians seem much less well developed.[40] But after Pippin III seized the Frankish throne in 751, his family had an exclusive claim to rule, though not every member could realize their claim. The fact that some family members from obscurer branches of the larger kin-group also played important roles in maintaining and representing the royal line's authority means that I sometimes stretch the term 'dynasty'. But as a shorthand, it is evocative in senses that are very relevant and helpful for my picture.

In other ways, however, this was a diffuse family which contemporaries could find hard to define. The term 'Merovingian' does appear in the Merovingian period itself and was clearly understood as referring to a special family, a line of kings descended from kings. Einhard deployed it at the very start of his *Life of Charlemagne* as a way of signalling the sharp dynastic break of 751. But he did not then go on to refer to 'Carolingians'. In fact, 'Carolingian' really only appears in our sources after that family had lost its exclusive hold on the kingship after 888. It seems that contest revealed the Carolingian family as distinct, that is, as needing to be distinguished from other royal lines that challenged it. Thus, the Saxon writer Widukind of Corvey in the 960s referred to the struggle between 'the family (*stirps*) of the Charleses and the descendants of Odo' in west Francia, though the plural 'Charleses' is still not an equivalent of Merovingian and the word 'Carolingian' was not to appear till later.[41]

This does not mean that contemporary sense of Carolingian identity was weak, though it does suggest that it was not always sharply focused, making the more linear term 'dynasty' rather problematic. But it remains applicable to a dominant family that had an exclusive right to the throne and which transmitted this right over time within itself. A Carolingian ruler, the emperor Louis II, articulated an impressive sense of collective family identity in a letter of 871 to the Byzantine emperor Basil I. Basil had shrewdly noted that the Carolingians ruled over different kingdoms, with different royal lines in charge of each kingdom, and that Louis had no share of Francia, the heartland. But Louis brushed this aside: Basil should know that Louis did rule in Francia as he was of the same flesh and blood as the rulers there.[42]

Contemporaries knew that king's sons were more special than other Carolingians, but the sense of family was broad (see chapter on genealogies). And precisely because of that, contemporaries, including kings, queens and their offspring and relatives, could not be absolutely sure who would turn out to be the most special. Study of terminology, of the vocabulary of kinship, is thus not necessarily the best way into this dynamic structure as it suggests a precision that can mislead. Susan Reynolds's thought-provoking formulation is relevant here: 'of the trio, word, concept and phenomenon, the least significant for the historian of society is the word'.[43] Contemporaries do not transmit to us a consistent or complete picture of the broad Carolingian family, and probably did not have such a picture themselves, not least because there were so many family members, not all of whom were equally prominent. Since contemporaries did not consistently flag up Carolingian-ness, we cannot have a total picture of it or its significance. They knew more than we did, and some of them probably knew more than others. For all our genealogical savvy, we cannot allocate bishop Franco of Liège to a specific place in the Carolingian family, but a well-connected poet in the 860s knew him to be a 'Karolides', a word that surely means here that he was Carolingian, rather than that he was 'a son of [a particular] Charles'.[44]

The Carolingians themselves did work to ensure that they retained tight control of dynastic identity. In the Merovingian period, uncertainty over the parentage of claimants to the throne and accusations that some royal figures did not have royal parentage show that the Merovingian dynastic structure and family were looser and more porous than the Carolingian equivalent. That is to say, members of the aristocracy could manipulate it with dangerous creativity. The Carolingians policed the frontiers of their royal line more tightly. No outside candidate was able to bluff their way in. No Carolingian royal son had to confront accusations that his father was a gardener. Questions might be raised over the marital status of a son's mother but that is a different problem from those faced by the loose baggy monster that was the Merovingian family. Only when the Carolingian exclusivity was faltering was the status of royal sons challenged in a way reminiscent of the Merovingian era.[45]

Franks knew that they had a line of kings, though more thoughtful Franks knew that hereditary kingship was neither universal nor necessarily the best form of rule. Around 860 archbishop Hincmar of Reims was driven by some contemporary royal problems to reflect on the variety of ways in which men could become kings (such as heredity, election, violence), not all of them approved by God. Hincmar drew here on Roman histories as well as the Bible and concluded that while heredity was acceptable, what really mattered was that a son should possess his father's good qualities; a father's true power passed to his son by virtue, not merely by birth: a good father could have bad sons. Hincmar urged the relevance of this for every king, and in particular for the king at whom he was writing, Lothar II, whose spectacular divorce case had triggered Hincmar's arguments. Hincmar saw his own views on kings as urgently relevant and, even though this particular text of his did not circulate, he was responding to contemporary debate on this theme.[46]

Reflections such as Hincmar's were of course informed by Christian morality; a true king had to follow God's law. Such reflections could be polemical, ad hoc responses to particular problems and situations. This does not limit their value for us as expressions of contemporary ideas: quite the reverse. They could be generated by political pressures and be part of a game with high stakes, as in the divorce case of Lothar II, for example. We should beware of freezing them as clear expressions of a coherent body of thought. Some statements were very clear. In 829, amidst famine and military defeats, clear signs of God's anger with the realm, bishops gathered in great councils at Paris and elsewhere and pointedly told their rulers that their kingdom came from God, not from their ancestors. Bishop Jonas of Orléans, who wrote up the proceedings of the assembly at Paris, included this statement a couple of years later in a text actually written for a king, Pippin I of Aquitaine, a son of the emperor Louis the Pious. Some modern commentators have seen this as evidence for contemporary emphasis on kingship as a Christian office, marked out by obedience to God's commands rather than by birth.[47]

Such stress on kingship as office and the need for rulers to be worthy of it was a massive presence in a series of admonitions directed by bishops at Carolingian kings.[48] Yet these very same churchmen were not anti-dynastic; they knew that birth mattered. In their culture, a king was the son of a king; a royal father had kingly sons. Bishops not only knew this, they worked to make it so. The bishops at Paris in 829 may have discounted royal ancestry as qualification for rule, but these same bishops commanded that the entire people were to pray for the life of the ruler, his wife and his children so that the storm-tossed realm might be secure. The whole realm was to think of the ruler's children as part of the divinely approved order.[49] At the heart of the realm was a family. Bishop Jonas did indeed repeat Paris's austere views on ancestry to king Pippin of Aquitaine, but he also highlighted Pippin's distinguished family as one of his outstanding qualities. In referring to the emperor Louis the Pious, Jonas could not help but refer to him as Pippin's father while going on to cite biblical injunctions on the honour due to a father from his sons. This was a family like any other, subject to Christian norms. For this family, however, these norms had enormous public importance. Harmony in the ruling family was vital for preserving harmony in the kingdom. In addressing Pippin, Jonas referred to the emperor Louis as 'our lord, your father' and to Pippin's brothers as 'your brothers, our lords', thus indicating a family origin and identity for Pippin's own rule. It was conflict within this family, Jonas reminded Pippin that had brought discord to the whole realm in 830. Bishops knew that Christian teaching on the importance of the family mattered as much as Christian teaching on kingship as office. The Lord's many precepts on the need for sons to honour fathers were widely available through divine laws, the Evangelists and the Apostles.[50]

This was no marginal element in contemporary churchmen's thinking on office, and while there may have been tensions between this and ideas of kingship as office, there was no essential opposition. A prayer composed around 800 for the blessing of a king as part of a coronation ritual implored God to bless the king's reign with abundant harvests, peace, protection for churches, victory over enemies and also prayed 'may kings come forth from his loins through succession of future times to rule this whole realm'.[51] The king's (and queen's) fertility mattered immensely and churchmen prayed for it as keenly as aristocrats hoped that their womenfolk would become a royal wife.

Aristocrats were not passive figures, in subservient thrall to the royal family. They knew that aspiring rulers needed their support, and rulers were keenly aware of this, as were bishops and abbots who were themselves aristocrats. A king was not simply born a king. This was particularly true of the very first Carolingian king, Pippin III, who deposed his Merovingian predecessor in 751 and had to work hard to convince the aristocracy to accept him as true king, as we shall see in the next chapter. But some time after the king-making ceremonies of the 750s, a writer at the abbey of St-Denis imagined that the pope, after anointing and blessing Pippin, his wife and his sons, forbade the Franks from having a king from the loins of anyone but Pippin.[52] Carolingians were thus created kings and were also kings by birth.

Carolingian specialness

Ecclesiastical concepts of kingship as office formed a pillar upon which the majestic edifice of Carolingian rule rested and another one was aristocratic support for kings (and the great churchmen were themselves aristocrats). Both have been the subject of substantial scholarship.[53] My focus here is different. Some of the most important work on this subject has tended to stress consensus among the political elite, co-operation between Carolingian rulers and their aristocratic followers, and has traced in some detail the formation of such networks of co-operation within the localities of that empire.[54] This book draws on such work; indeed, it could not have been written without it, but it argues that we must not lose sight of the centrality of Carolingian authority in this world. Carolingians were very much the senior partners. We need to give the familial element in Carolingian rule greater prominence, and a more distinctive profile if we are to grasp contemporary realities.

It was not that the aristocracy was generally opposed to the Carolingians. On the contrary, Franks wanted kings. Aristocrats depended on royal patronage as much as kings relied on aristocratic support. The Frankish realm, like many others in the Middle Ages, was not split between mutually antagonistic royal and aristocratic powers but was 'governed by largely co-operative oligarchies'.[55] The term 'aristocracy' may suggest too much institutional stability and coherence within these groups of elite men and women; there was no Frankish constitution with a House of Lords (though that very British institution is not exactly aristocratic). But it is a convenient term to use, and contemporaries could, and did, conceive of a group identity for this elite. In the late ninth century, the archbishop of Reims referred to the 'generality of the aristocracy as a whole' (*generalitas universorum maiorum*). He did so, significantly, in the context of assemblies, gatherings where individuals could actually see themselves as forming part of a larger group, including the king, concerned with the condition of the whole realm.[56]

In this book, I argue that such consensus was indeed fundamental for the success of Carolingian royal authority: the aristocracy came to believe in the naturalness of Carolingian family rule. Aristocrats themselves believed in hereditary transmission of family qualities as well as of property claims.[57] This is the positive flipside of kings not having all the power and where Foucault's concepts of power are particularly helpful for us. Kings did not have to do all the work to make themselves special. The discourse of Carolingian authority was bigger than them. This does mean that I also argue that we need to pay attention to the differences between kings and aristocrats: kings were special and aristocrats saw that, and worked to make it so. Count Gerard of Vienne clashed with various Carolingian rulers but he acted as foster-father (*nutritor*) for a young king, and when he and his wife Bertha founded abbeys in Burgundy around 860, they requested that the monks and nuns there pray for the royal family as well as for Gerard and Bertha. Most of the aristocrats who appear in this book are, like Gerard and Bertha, from the elite level, a small proportion of a broader group that had differing levels of status and resource within it. What marks out magnates such as these is their closeness to rulers and the wide extent of their lands and offices, though even they did not spend all of their time with rulers.[58]

The Carolingian empire's total population was perhaps 15 million. The high elite was small: Philippe Depreux's register of the entourage of the emperor Louis the Pious from 781 to 840 lists 280 individuals, only two of whom are women. But we are dealing with a bigger cast of characters than these figures suggest. Depreux himself set clear and stringent limits on his selection of people, and actually includes in an appendix another score or so figures including one more woman (Theuthild). His cast list may also be socially broader than we might anticipate. Because his criteria for inclusion include closeness to the ruler, some figures appear in it because of that, but they were not themselves grand figures: the cleric Launus would be an example, as would Coslus, keeper of the king's horses, whom a contemporary source describes as not top-drawer.[59] It was not just a gilded elite that had direct contact with rulers; behind the magnates was a larger crowd that also could participate in gatherings with kings. At the great assemblies marking the treaty of Verdun in 843, the bishop of Freising and a prominent secular noble concluded a deal on sale of lands, a deal witnessed by almost 100 individuals, a few of whom were very prominent figures, but others were people of only regional Bavarian importance pulled towards Verdun because of the scale of the political negotiations taking place there. Around a thousand aristocrats may well have been present at Verdun that year. Carolingian palaces and assembly sites in early medieval Europe expected and could cope with large numbers, particularly since assemblies could take place in the open air.[60]

In some ways, kings did not have an alternative form of power available; they had to work with the aristocracy whose values they shared anyway. Of course kings could manipulate that aristocracy in various ways to suit their own purposes. On the other hand, while aristocratic culture embraced faithfulness to royal lords, aristocrats in regions distant from kings did not spend all their time looking back over their shoulder at rulers.[61] Rulers did have substantial material resources and did work hard to ensure that their authority was communicated across their realm, even if not with the same intensity at all times and in all places, and this book will discuss these important topics, though I am all too conscious of how much more work needs to be done in these areas and of how indebted I am to significant work already done here.[62] But Carolingian kings were not simply aristocrats writ large. This was the claim of Professor Johannes Fried in a thought-provoking attempt in the 1980s to cut Carolingian kingship down to size, arguing that royal rule was not hierarchically ordered above aristocratic rule within an overarching concept and system of authority. The value of this argument was its sharp warning not to imagine a Carolingian state as a manifestation of some timeless historical essence of the fully institutionalized state. Overall, however, its extreme claims failed to convince other historians and Carolingian kingship still looks to us like big stuff, as it did to its contemporaries. While Fried was right to highlight the inconsistencies and gaps in the political terminology of our sources, and to warn us that the Carolingian kingdom was a pre-modern state and should not be imagined as being conceptually like the states of the modern western world, public institutions did exist, along with a sense of public authority vested in the king. Kings regulated the coinage, claimed control over the building of fortifications and asserted overwhelming rights of jurisdiction. As Janet Nelson has said, 'Even if Carolingian power was mediated in practice through the aristocracy, it was exercised through institutions – courts, musters of the host – vested with public authority.'[63]

Nonetheless, this was a Carolingian realm. Keith Hopkins's devastatingly simple question for the Roman world brings this book's concerns and arguments into sharp focus: 'How did the Romans know that they were living in the Roman Empire?'[64] This book seeks to pose that question about Carolingian political culture. One distinctive resource that rulers did possess was the special aura of royalty and in Frankish culture that specialness was confined to one family: the Merovingians and then the Carolingians. In this book, my analysis follows three intertwined implications that all stem from this centrality of the Carolingian royal family. First, the 'specialness' of the Carolingians themselves: Carolingian rule was legitimated, that is, it was 'normalized', through presenting the royal family's members as being of special status; the family to which kings belonged could be no ordinary family. Secondly, since this family was special, the rhythms of family life formed the shape of politics among the elite. The life-cycle of the ruling family, including women as well as men, could set the pace and shape the form of politics. Thirdly, if Carolingians were special, some were more special than others and the problems in controlling definitions of rank and expectation within the royal family fed into ambitions and fears of the high aristocracy. Ultimately, members of this aristocracy came to challenge the exclusivity of Carolingian claims to rule. When this was done, the nature of politics was changed; much of the Carolingian world's structure remained in the tenth century but the disappearance of Carolingian monopoly of kingship marked the end of an era.

The Carolingian family is the central concern of this book because I believe it to be a central defining institution of the realms it ruled. Occasionally, I will use the term 'charisma' loosely to indicate the aura, the specialness, of members of the royal dynasty. I also refer occasionally to Carolingian blood. This is not to evoke some dark and murky belief in Germanic sacral blood, but is another convenient shorthand to remind the reader of the centrality of the royal kin to this world. Families are of course cultural as well as biological and I hope that I treat this particular family historically and not as some natural phenomenon effortlessly radiating an inborn charisma to dazzle passive observers. Charisma, to work as a term, is to be seen as not objective but as something believed in by those who bear it as well as by those upon whom it works. Charisma and specialness can be socially constructed from pre-existing social and cultural elements, and that means that all sorts of people and institutions were able to decide which Carolingians were special or not very special at all.[65]

The articulating of that dynastic specialness took place in social practices that included the writing of a wide variety of texts, themselves providing key evidence for the wider practices. Texts are hardly transparent windows onto the reality that they themselves construct but that is precisely what makes them valuable as evidence. They enable us to perceive and analyse key aspects of contemporary political culture. Sometimes this is relatively simple; texts, including those on coins and inscriptions as well as chronicles, feature the royal names of the dynasty, the endlessly, and confusingly, repeated names of Charles, Louis, etc. This points to a historical reality. The consistent use of a restricted pool of names exclusive to some of the men of the dynasty is a historical fact. I argue in this book that this is a significant practice that was understood as such; that is an interpretation that may or may not be accepted by others. This book does sometimes analyse texts in detail but I have tried to relate that analysis to contexts, as my focus is on political culture and its structures.

One important aspect of the Carolingian context is that this was a manuscript culture. Contemporaries did not encounter texts such as Einhard's *Life of Charlemagne* in the fixed editions that we use; Einhard himself seems to have made various versions of his text and different versions of it circulated.[66] Contemporaries' historical writings are indeed central to my concerns and will play a prominent role in the book, but my selection of evidence is more eclectic. I am lucky enough to be able to draw on important scholarship on historical texts from the Carolingian era. Such scholarship shows that the explosion in historical writing that characterizes this period produced narratives that depicted the rule of Carolingian kings, in partnership with the Franks, as the natural order of things, even if individual rulers and magnates were rebuked.[67] It may be that modern historians who, as professional academics are peculiarly specialized in their interests, take some texts more seriously than the Franks did. Did anyone in the ninth century read Einhard's *Life of Charlemagne* with the level of attention that we do?[68]

And yet the charged silence of some historical texts on contentious political events such as the aristocratic conspiracy against Charlemagne shows that the writers thought and worried about contemporary response to their writings. Writers such as Einhard, biographer of Charlemagne, and Thegan, biographer of Louis the Pious, expected and hoped that rulers would read their work. Contemporaries were also bombarded by many kinds of texts. The revolt against Louis the Pious in 833 featured hostile armies marching across the realm, but it also generated the 'massive production of authoritative documentation' to justify Louis's deposition by God-fearing bishops. The fact that only one of these bishops' versions of a key text has survived shows how sensitive and how important these documents were; shrewder bishops did not preserve incriminating texts once Louis surged back to power in 834.[69]

Such texts were the products of a manuscript culture, not of a centralized government publishing house. They are thus not the products of a single centre, but of many centres, some of course more important than others. The potential value of Foucauldian ideas of power for this book is thus apparent. If the royal family was a centre of authority, that authority was broadcast and articulated by many voices, not simply by the king's voice shouting from his palace. After all, kings did not write their own charters, mint their own coins, build their own palaces, compose their own prayers for the safety of the royal family or paint the impressive manuscript pictures of rulers in majesty that adorn the covers of so many modern books on this period. All these items, however, are invaluable sources about the nature of royal authority.[70] That authority, however, had to be exercised and transmitted in the face of the challenges posed by time, space and fluctuating resources.

Of course, material resources were involved in this. Rulers possessed great estates, and we will see how they utilized them in subsequent chapters. Their palaces were also symbols of rule as well as actual places of government. Coins carried the names of kings. Rulers possessed precious crowns that they wore to mark their status and which they took care to pass on to specified heirs and successors.[71] Royal women wore fine robes, as did kings, who also wore swords; but aristocrats could also dress sumptuously and noble men also wore swords as sign of high status. The lavishing of gold, silver, silks, etc. on followers was a theatrical display of royal generosity as well as a necessary royal recognition of service, and it could also recognize successful collective triumph of king and aristocrats, as in the sharing out of the Lombard treasures among the Frankish army in 774. There was an element of obligation in this gift culture. Royal rule rested on this collective political culture, but kings had a central and distinctive place in it and people knew this through repeated experience. A wonderfully vivid account of a dispute in Istria in northern Italy shows the workings of the rhythm of royal exactions in a region far from Aachen. These particular exactions had been exploited by the local duke and after an enquiry that mobilized dozens of people, Charlemagne subsequently commanded that when horses were sent as 'gifts' to the king, they must have the genuine donor's name attached. Thus centre and region looked at each other; the singular name of the ruler encountered the myriad of local names.[72] The presenting of the 'annual gifts' from the aristocracy and high churchmen to the ruler, usually at assemblies, demonstrated to all the ruler's key position within the collective setting of the assembly and helped perpetuate that position by funnelling economically valuable items to him. When King Lothar usurped his father's throne in 833, he held an assembly and the 'bishops, abbots, counts and all the people there formally presented him with the annual gifts and promised him their loyalty'. The previous autumn, such gifts had been presented to this father. Lothar thus tested and deployed his claims to rule in a traditional setting that testified to the changes in politics as well as providing a framework for the performance of Carolingian continuity. He also gained a welcome bonus in the form of the 'annual gifts'. Not that this did him any good in the feverish climate of the 830s.[73]

My argument in this book is that such practices and resources formed a discourse of the uniqueness of Carolingian royalty. Here again I am indebted to Foucault whose ideas of discourse have been clearly summarized by Wendy Brown: 'discourse embraces a relatively bounded field of terms, categories and beliefs expressed through statements that are commonsensical within the discourse … discourse never merely describes but, rather, creates relationships and channels of authority though the articulation of norms'. Alert readers of Foucault will notice that I deviate from the master in leaning towards the concept of hegemony, a concept that tends to dissolve in the pure beam of Foucauldian light, a light that 'replaces an image of power governing a social totality with an image of power suffusing the present with an array of historically freighted discourses that do not harmonize or resolve in a coherent, closed system'.[74] This book tends to stress the coherence of the discourse of Carolingian royalty, arguing that the unique distinction of the Carolingian family was a key 'natural' element in the constructing and maintaining of the political culture of the Franks and their realm from 751 to 888. Rule by a Carolingian was what was thinkable.

But rule by non-Carolingians was also thinkable in some ways. After 751, people could still remember the Merovingians. And when aristocrats revolted against Charlemagne in 785, they did not seem to have plans to replace him with a Carolingian. In 879 Boso, a powerful magnate related by marriage to the Carolingians, made a bid for a crown in Provence and thus became the first non-Carolingian king in over a century; this predated the crisis of 888. Between 751 and 888, the natural rule of Carolingians and the contingent historical nature of that rule were both thinkable. Hence, there was the need for the continuing stress on naturalness of rule; this discourse of natural Carolingian rule shone all the more brightly for being shadowed.

Portraying Carolingian specialness

The effort made by the Carolingians and their supporters to portray the dynasty's rule as part of the natural order of things was necessary because while contemporaries could believe this, and indeed proclaim it, they were also aware that it was in fact a product of history and as such subject to challenge, change and decay. Such thoughts appear in a range of texts stretching from the eve of the crisis of 887–8 backwards, that is, into the days of unchallenged hegemony. Notker, a monk of the abbey of St-Gall in what is now Switzerland, wrote a biography of Charlemagne, the *Deeds of Charles*, between 884 and 887. Notker was a dyed-in-the-wool Carolingian loyalist in a monastery that had close links with the Carolingian line, as well as to the nobles of the region (Alemannia). For Notker himself, the glory of the Carolingians was something of an obsessive concern that could emerge in unlikely places; the smooth surface of one of his other prose works, a summary of patristic sources, is disrupted when the great figure of Charlemagne appears unexpectedly.[75] Addressed to the emperor Charles the Fat, the *Deeds of Charles* is steeped in Carolingian dynastic thinking and displays pride in the dynasty's glorious history as well as anxiety about its future.

It contains an instructive story about Pippin III (751–68), the first Carolingian king and father of Charlemagne. According to Notker, after expeditions to Italy Pippin discovered that the leaders of his army scorned him behind his back. These uppity magnates were to be taught a stark lesson. Pippin had a wild bull released and then set a ferocious lion on it. As the lion grappled with the bull, Pippin invited his magnates to separate the beasts or kill them. His appalled audience stammered that such a feat was impossible. Rising from his throne, Pippin drew his sword, sliced through the pair, sheathed his weapon, resumed his position on the throne and asked his magnates whether they now thought that he deserved to be their lord. Abasing themselves, they loudly proclaimed his superiority. More is at stake here than muscular heroics (though such muscularity would have impressed contemporaries). Long ago, Georg Waitz shrewdly recognized that Notker's story underlines the throne-worthiness of Pippin's line by highlighting its sheer strength and vitality, in contrast to the tottering Merovingians. Pippin is king, though his magnates sneer at him. He cannot take respect or loyalty for granted but must compel it through superhuman effort. Notker was a literary artist and he charges his little story with the imagery of Carolingian right to rule. Chords of royal lordship resound throughout. Pippin's magnates address him as lord and, mightily impressed, they reply that only a madman would fail to recognize his lordship. The props of sword and throne are pregnant with royal authority for Notker.[76]

In an earlier chapter, Notker tells another story of the mastering of a lion as an index of strength of Frankish royalty. This echoes a tale about Alexander the Great and Alexander, together with the biblical David, is specifically invoked by Notker's lion-slaying Pippin as an example of a king's harsh authority over his followers. Alexander's overwhelming strength could strike a Carolingian audience as dangerous. He appeared in the paintings of Ingelheim palace in the series of grimly powerful pagan rulers from the classical past, and, close in time to Notker, the archbishop of Reims warned young Carolingian rulers that Alexander may have conquered worlds, but never learned to master himself.[77] It seems unlikely that the historical Pippin III would have compared his magnates to Goliath or to the subdued followers of Alexander. Such worrying comparisons, from the magnates' point of view, are much more likely to express Notker's fearful view of challengers to the Carolingians. Notker associated his story with material and figures (Alexander the Great and David) which were the stuff of medieval royalty. This was not an isolated monastic fantasy confined to St-Gall. It pops up in a tenth-century Metz version of the *Life of St Arnulf*, the ancestral holy man of the Carolingians. The story also appears to have been known in the western monastery of Ferrières, which claimed to have been the site of the action, possibly in the ninth century; perhaps Notker had got it from there. When King Carloman, Charlemagne's brother, died in 771, he was buried at Reims in a late Roman sarcophagus that depicted a Roman general spearing a lion. Images of the biblical David as lion-killer appear in sculptures and pictures across the early medieval world, from the lands of the Picts to the Byzantine empire.[78] Of course, aristocrats could ride with real kings on real hunts. But such images may have shadowed these real hunts. And perhaps this sort of tale, and its attendant lesson on the need to obey a potent ruler, was evoked in the mind of a great magnate such as Eckhard of Macon when he contemplated his treasures, which included a collection of engraved gems, one of which depicted a man killing a lion.[79]

Notker had introduced his story about Pippin by evoking the majestic dynastic aura of the Carolingians, addressing the emperor Charles the Fat directly: 'Let me insert here in the history of your namesake [Charlemagne] an incident in the life of your great-grandfather Pippin: which perhaps some future little Charles or Louis may imitate'. The dynastic pivot here is Charles the Fat. Behind him loom the noble ancestors, Pippin and Charlemagne; stretching into the future are more Carolingians as yet unborn, destined to bear the resoundingly royal names of Louis and Charles. Pippin's fiercely confident demonstration of authority is intended for them. But this bright picture is flaking away in the acid of uncertainty over the dynasty's future. Charles the Fat had no legitimate children; Notker's little Louis and little Charles were merely hopeful projections. A void was opening up; it had to be filled.[80]

Notker was trying to re-assure Charles the Fat and also perhaps trying to re-assure himself and the community of St-Gall and indeed the wider community of Alemannia. Notker understood that empires were transient. His text opens with an image of an empire, that of the Romans, passing away under God's dispensation to be followed by the Christian empire of Charlemagne. But was there any guarantee that it would last? Notker also knew of the fate of the Merovingians, as a contemptuous reference to Childeric III shows.[81] Even the special status of the Carolingian dynasty, which Notker saw as possessing an inherent right to rule, under God's dispensation, could be challenged. The intensity of Notker's anxiety over this makes itself felt throughout his text. He believed that the Carolingian right to rule had been challenged in the very heyday of the dynasty, claiming that, after the death of the emperor Louis the Pious in 840, arrogant giants arose who scorned the Carolingian line. They were like those sinister Biblical figures descended from the daughters of Cain or like the people of Israel who turned away from the line of David. Only loyalty to the line (*progenies*) of Charlemagne could crush such rebellion. Notker's story reflects, not realities of the 840s but worries of the 880s over possible challenges to that line by aristocratic descendants of female Carolingians.[82] Notker believed, however, that such a challenge could have come at any time to threaten Carolingian status, the lynch-pin of the kingdom. Such status was therefore vulnerable and had constantly to be asserted.

Even before the crisis of 887–8, Notker shows that the Carolingians were not always seen as the 'natural lords' of their world. Their claims had to appear as self-evident truths in a world that recognized them simultaneously as truths but also as mere claims. The perspective receding backwards from Regino reveals keen awareness of transience in what looks to us like the 'secure' period of Carolingian royalty. Such awareness reaches us even in utterances purporting to come from the dynasty itself. The spectre of the end of the line was abroad long before 887–8. Some time in the 860s or 870s a text, the *Vision of Charlemagne*, was written by someone at Mainz with links to the royal court. Here Charlemagne appears as an uneasy dreamer disturbed by a figure come from heaven to hand him a sword. On the sword were mysterious inscriptions and Charlemagne was urged to memorize them as they were prophecies, one of which he interpreted to mean the end of his dynasty (or end of the world – the same thing for a Carolingian?). These were no cloistered musings – they were probably written for a Carolingian, Louis the German, who also received instruction from his bishops on the meaning of biblical prophecies on the fall of King Belshazzar.[83]

Louis the German was not the only Carolingian who received sombre instruction in the fall of kingdoms. Back in the 820s, the young prince Charles (Charles the Bald) received a work of history from Freculf, bishop of Lisieux. In a letter accompanying the text sent to Charles' mother, the empress Judith, Freculf said that Charles would be able to look into the text as into a mirror and could thus learn which courses of action to follow and which to avoid. Freculf's modern editor sees his text as 'loaded with warnings and encouragements'. While Freculf's letter celebrated the dynasty, acclaiming the young Charles as the renewal of his grandfather (Charlemagne), his history's stark lesson was the transience of empires and ruling lines, whether in ancient Rome or in Israel.[84] This historical text revealed a bleakly Augustinian view of dynasties coming and going in the ebb and flow of history. All that really mattered was to be pleasing to God.

It is in this light that we can see some of the significance of the most famous picture of the Carolingian takeover of the throne, that of Einhard in his *Life of Charlemagne*, written sometime in the 820s. Einhard's image of the later Merovingian kings, impotently trundling around the realm in their ox-carts, is striking in several respects. It has been massively influential in shaping a perception of inevitable Merovingian decline and equally inevitable Carolingian ascent. As such it has attracted criticism from modern historians anxious to restore the historical picture.[85] What is truly remarkable, however, is not that Einhard gives the Merovingians such a hard time as that he refers to them at all. Neither of the other two royal biographers in the next decade or so – Thegan and the so-called Astronomer – in their accounts of the reign of Charlemagne's son Louis the Pious, makes such reference to the older dynasty, though they had read Einhard. Einhard's focus is dynastic but distinctively so. Thegan went on to open his biography of Louis with dynastic elements, but he zeroed in on the sacred figure of Arnulf, the holy ancestor of Carolingian kings. This tracing of the Carolingian line back to a remote and numinous figure parallels, not Einhard, but the projected ancestry of other early medieval dynasties. The Merovingians themselves, for example, were thought to be descendants of the coupling of a sea-monster and a Frankish queen and this may have given them a glowing supernatural aura. Outside the Frankish realms, Anglo-Saxon kings were also represented as rich in ancestors. Alfred of Wessex (871–99) shared many of the political and cultural concerns of his Carolingian contemporaries, not least the problem of Viking attacks, but he was incomparably better endowed with royal ancestors. The great genealogy with which Asser opens his *Life of Alfred* stretches back all the way to the founder of the royal house of Wessex, Cerdic, and goes on through Woden to Adam. Asser knew Thegan's text but the royal heritage of Wessex enabled him to improve on it as far as ancestors were concerned.[86]

Carolingian royalty's roots look shallow beside this. Thegan's attempt to conjure up an impressive genealogy fails to measure up to the stately series of Alfred's ancestors or the murkily deep past of the Merovingians. Ancestors mattered to Carolingians and their followers; Thegan referred to his knowledge of Carolingian genealogy as stemming from oral testimony and many written sources; interest was widespread.[87] Einhard, however, like the author(s) of the more elaborate version of Merovingian decline and Carolingian ascent in the so-called earlier Annals of Metz, compiled a decade or so before his own text, concentrates on the historical process by which the new royal dynasty came to power. But his de-mystified account necessarily reveals that the Carolingians had not always been kings, and in showing the Merovingians ceasing to be kings as their dynasty disintegrates he offers a warning: dynasties could fail and they could be replaced. Einhard's Merovingians uncannily foreshadow the end of the Carolingians themselves in tales of the wretched Charles the Fat's becoming dependent on his bishops and supplanter for sustenance.[88]

If Einhard vividly depicted the end of Merovingian royalty, he also cannily pushed back Carolingian specialness into the Merovingian era. He spotlit the early Carolingians in their role as mayors of the palace, an office that he presented as the exclusive inheritance of a streamlined and conflict-free version of the Carolingian line.[89] These mayors of the palace thus turn out to have been a royal family all along. The odd man out in Einhard's 751 is the man with truly royal ancestors, the Merovingian Childeric. Amidst all these Pippins and Charles, his very name proclaims him as a non-starter. Other writers, such as Paul the Deacon in his *Deeds of the Bishops of Metz* written *c*.784, also tended to project Carolingian royalty back into the past; the family had thus always been special, its line had always been worthy of royalty. Kingly status was not a transformation, but a confirmation of the family's royal identity.[90] In explicitly evoking Charlemagne as his foster-father, Einhard bathes his text in the warm glow of the bonds of the royal household. He can speak here for the aristocracy to which he belonged, but he was unique in repaying his debt to his royal patrons by writing a vision of their legitimacy which became a widespread text. Among those who received it were members of that family itself who could now, if they wished, contemplate the history of their authority as seen by one of their shrewdest servants.[91] We can find other early ninth-century texts that take an equally dim view of Merovingian feebleness, texts moreover that engaged with audiences outside of the monasteries where they were composed.[92]

Texts were flexible and fluid and views could be too. But these differing views were themselves responses to the same problem: how to conceptualize and guarantee legitimacy and its reproduction? Kings did not want people to learn the wrong lesson from 751, that is, that Carolingian rule could be replaced just as Merovingian rule had been. In 862, threatened by unruly sons and rebellious magnates while being assailed by Vikings, Charles the Bald held an assembly at Pîtres, near Rouen. In the late 850s, some of Charles's western magnates had risen against him and had maintained resistance without having an alternative Carolingian as a front man, an unusual and unnerving phenomenon.[93] We can hear Charles's voice asserting royalty's distinctive place through the capitulary associated with the meeting composed by his trusted counsellor archbishop Hincmar of Reims. Here Charles, evoking a landscape devastated by sinners, proclaimed 'We cannot all be kings', referring sombrely to the ambitions of the devil and his followers who were once angels in heaven. They had refused, however, to accept their subordinate status and, scorning rightful equal subjection to divinely constituted authority, had become God's enemies and subject to the devil. Charles seems to pre-echo Regino in warning of the grim consequences of rejecting hierarchy.[94]

We have gone down a fairly long corridor from Regino's tenth-century view of the dynasty's 887–8 crisis to Einhard's 820s account of its triumph in 751 but, in doing so, we have returned to our starting point. The tensions in Regino's text were also apparent in Einhard's, and indeed in a whole series of other texts. The Carolingian dynasty was simultaneously glorious and vulnerable. Contemporaries experienced Carolingian dynastic rule as natural but could also understand it to be historical. In other words, we must not imagine that the dynasty 'arrived' in 751 and ran into trouble in 887–8, but that between these dates it could relax and take its authority for granted. That is why the discourse of Carolingian legitimacy worked to contain everybody in its spell.

We have to be able to pick up Carolingians on our radar and gauge their significance. This is what contemporaries had to do, and the stakes were higher for them. Again, Notker of St-Gall has an instructive anecdote. He says that Charlemagne had a young relative who sang at a church festival; Charlemagne proudly remarked to a watching bishop that the young man had done well. But the bishop had not recognized the young man as the king's relative and replied that any country bumpkin could sing like that. The outraged king punched the bishop to the ground. People had to be alert to Carolingian presence; Carolingians had to check that they were being seen as special.[95]

Fate of a child, fate of a dynasty

The ways in which individual members of the Carolingian royal house meshed with the political and conceptual structures of their world form the subject of this book and I end this chapter with a specific example of how examination of a particular individual can illuminate such structures. Chroniclers report violent upheavals across western Europe in 879: Vikings burning fields, killing and enslaving the people; Christian armies slaughtering the very populations they were supposed to protect; usurpers challenging Frankish kings, etc. Yet away from these headlines and the great anguish that they suggest, for the vast majority of the population life would have continued to grind on in accordance with the essential rhythm celebrated in an Irish text of the eighth or ninth century: the working of the land, the tending of herds and flocks, and the women's work of embroidery continued to be 'the three slender things that best support the world'. Human communities could weather the storms unleashed by warriors and potentates.[96]

As well as these grand dramas, there were of course individual tragedies and sorrows. In what is now southern Germany a two-year-old boy had a fatal accident in his house; he fell from an upper window, plunging his parents and household into grief. We know this boy's name, the place where he died, the names of his parents and we can catch the resonance of this sad event. For this boy was called Louis, a royal name; he was the son of a king and a queen; he belonged to a very special family, the Carolingians.

The fullest account of the fate of this child comes from the chronicle of Regino of Prüm, who wrote some twenty years or so after the event. Regino tells how the east Frankish king Louis the Younger fell ill and died at Frankfurt in 882, and was buried beside his father in the monastery of Lorsch. By his wife Liutgard this king had one son, to whom he had given his own name. The king's death prompted Regino to flash back to this child's death. While this king Louis had been visiting Bavaria (in 879) in the hope of gaining his brother's kingdom, he stayed at Regensburg and 'this little boy fell from the palace window, broke his neck and died on the spot; this untimely and dishonourable death brought the greatest grief not only to the king and queen but to the whole royal household'.[97]

For Regino, the death of this boy was a public tragedy. The royal household was shattered, emotionally and politically. Writing a couple of years after the death of the boy Louis, Notker of St-Gall presented his death as part of the rising tide of dynastic problems facing the royal line.[98] Regino wrote with hindsight; he knew that the dynasty was to have serious trouble reproducing itself as the 880s wore on. But the death of the child Louis would still have had a profound impact on contemporaries in late 879. He bore the royal name of Louis, a public marker of his distinction from his babyhood. It is surely him that a markedly dynastic charter of Louis the Younger refers to affectionately in early 877. It is likely that the young baby and his mother were with the king at the palace of Frankfurt where the charter was issued (perhaps the boy had just been born there), and aristocrats would have seen the boy as incorporating the future of their king's line.[99] A political settlement made between west and east Frankish kings in 878 named this infant as the future successor of his father; this would have been a message aimed at the kings and their followers who had gathered to make this treaty.[100] Writing a thousand years after Regino, the historian Ernst Dümmler saw the accident as a tragedy for Germany. His nineteenth-century category of the nation-state would not have been recognized by Regino, but both observers saw the same importance in the event. This is a lot of weight for a baby to bear.[101]

The child could bear this weight because he was, from birth, an element in a larger system of communication and exercise of authority, a system that had been built over time. The name Louis was not originally a Carolingian family name but was borrowed in the late eighth century from the first dynasty of Frankish royalty to add lustre to the second. Regensburg, where the boy died, had been a stronghold of a rival dynasty to Charlemagne's, the Agilolfing dukes of Bavaria. With the collapse of Duke Tassilo's power in 788, Regensburg had been absorbed into the Carolingian empire and had become a favoured residence of east Frankish monarchs. It was thus a key Carolingian site where Carolingian majesty could be displayed and acclaimed, something we can glimpse in the ceremonial prayers composed by bishop Baturich of Regensburg for the rulers Louis the Pious and Louis the German in 820s: '*domnum nostrum Hludwicum imperatorem/ ... Domnum nostrum Hludwicum regem*'.[102] The Carolingian resonance of the name Louis in Regensburg was the product of such effort. Such effort continued in death; the child appears to have been buried in Regensburg, in St-Emmeram. His tomb was among the 'tombs of the rulers' pointed out to King Conrad I on his visit there in 918. In death, the child kept a permanent Carolingian presence in Regensburg.[103] The fact that the community of St-Emmeran went on to creatively recast this Louis as the later king Louis the Child shows how death did not freeze members of the dynasty and how malleable community memory could be.

This child died with his royal future unfulfilled and that makes him obscure to us. But it was precisely that shut down future that drew contemporaries' attention. Alive, his future was of interest to the elite community of the rulers and their great aristocrats. If the child was present at Frankfurt in early 877, then his existence would be known to several of the great magnates of the realm of his father such as the Saxon Counts Brun and Otto. Since Brun was the queen's brother, we may assume that he took an interest in his royal nephew and would have been a channel for relaying the significance of the latter's birth to Saxony and elsewhere. Also present at Frankfurt in early 877 were magnates of the West Frankish court who had established good relations with Liutgarda, the boy's mother.[104] As we have seen, the child was explicitly referred to in the 878 treaty as his father's intended successor. His death therefore mattered. Of course it was not front-page news in a world saturated by mass communications. It is not even reported in such major narrative sources as the *Annals of St Vaast* or the *Annals of Fulda*. Notker of St-Gall knew of the child's death but was unsure of the exact manner of it. Notker does say, however, that the death of Louis gave rise to many stories, and seems rather uneasy about this. Regino thought that the child's death in an accident was somehow dishonourable, unworthy of a Carolingian. We catch echoes of how this accident resonated.

Our starting point, Regino's account of the boy's fatal accident, is artfully placed in a narrative of death and destruction and Regino's literary artifice conditions our reading of him. He selects the boy's accident as an element in a picture designed to convey an image of transience, particularly the transience of Carolingian royals, and the care with which he paints his picture recalls the skill of those storytellers of the modern period whose death-haunted narratives so fascinated Walter Benjamin.[105] The death of Louis in 879 would not have had quite the meaning for contemporaries that it was to have later for Regino. Regino's narrative, however, has helped us uncover some of the range of meanings that Louis's death had at the time and has also helped reveal how we can see it as an element in a system. If Regino is not simply representative, he is richly instructive. The system to which he points us, in his account of the death of a child in 879 and the crisis of a dynasty in 888, is the subject of the rest of this book.

2

Building Carolingian royalty 751–68

Roots of Carolingian royalty

The beginnings of Carolingian royalty in 751 are glowingly recounted in one of the most prominent sources from the eighth century, the so-called *Royal Frankish Annals*. This tells us how two eminent Frankish churchmen journeyed to Rome to ask the pope a highly charged political question about the nature of royal power in Francia, namely whether the office of king should be held by someone who was king only in name or by someone who had real power. The pope gave the correct answer, commanding that Pippin, the Carolingian mayor of the palace, should be made king and he was duly anointed in Soissons by archbishop Boniface, the awe-inspiring Anglo-Saxon holy man, while the feeble Merovingian king Childeric had his hair shorn for a monastic tonsure and was packed off to a monastery.[1] This is the classic picture of the fall of one dynasty, clinging on to royal status long after losing royal muscle, and the rise of another, potently vigorous and bound to acquire the royal status it so richly deserved. It is a picture of inevitability and consensus: apart from the wretched Merovingian Childeric III, everyone could see that Pippin was destined to be king. The pope saw this particularly clearly and his counsel brought about the great ceremony with holy oil at Soissons.

This event cast a long shadow. Four centuries later, the dynamic Pope Gregory VII evoked the events of 751 as justification for papal power over kings.[2] In political history, the elements of holy oil, churchmen, royalty and sacred sites reappear constantly in coronations in places as diverse as Reims and Scone while they evoke the glorious ritual splendours of the Middle Ages in vivid imaginative fictions as diverse as *The Prisoner of Zenda* and Tintin's adventures in *King Ottakar's Sceptre*.[3] To read the annals for 751 and then to watch the film of the coronation of the young Elizabeth II in 1953 is to feel that the events of 751 were indeed among the 'beginnings of western political thought'.[4]

Historians have been enthralled by these events, lavishing critical attention on holy oil, the liturgical exaltation of kingship, the drama of the last of the long-haired kings being tonsured, etc.[5] That attention, however, has become ever more critical and the gorgeous fabric of Pippin's ceremony has melted away. There are three essential problems with seeing the events of 751 as the ritualized expression of the triumph of Carolingian royalty. First, our evidence for these events now looks very shaky indeed. Long-held suspicions about the reliability of the *Royal Frankish Annals* have now hardened into outright rejection of its testimony as being too distant from the event (the annals were composed decades later) and too tendentiously pro-Carolingian to be safe.[6] There is one narrative source that is closer in time to 751, the continuation of the chronicle of Fredegar. This was written under the aegis of Pippin's uncle count Childebrand and the latter's son count Nibelung and may have been composed, in the section going up to 751, for the coronation of that year. It makes no explicit reference to anointing, saying only that Pippin was consecrated by the bishops. Furthermore, we cannot be absolutely sure that this Childebrand chronicle is contemporary (though we cannot be sure that it is not).[7]

Even if it was written in or around 751, would it be reliable? This takes us to a second problem. Historians' preference for sources produced closer in time to the events to which they relate is understandable but is in some ways a rather crude criterion of reliability. Such a source is still a representation and does not offer direct access to the historical phenomenon itself, a point particularly relevant to accounts of rituals. Rituals themselves could be polysemic and texts describing them could try and impose an interpretation that other texts or observers could challenge.[8]

Students of medieval ritual would do well to read Samuel Pepys's wonderful description of the coronation of Charles II in 1661 which vividly recounts his admiration of the colourful robes and solemnity of the participants, his frustration at not being able to hear or see much of the ceremony itself, his anxious need for a toilet break amidst all the splendour and his enthusiastic participation in drinking deep.[9] Pepys's experience of the day was rather different from the king's. The splendours of a king-making could not obliterate all complexity. This takes us to the third problem and it is a fundamental, historical one. The *Royal Frankish Annals*' reference to Merovingian feebleness makes Merovingian decline and Carolingian ascent look inevitable: by 751, the Merovingians had run out of time because the Franks had run out of patience. These annals were not the only text written in the late eighth century and early ninth to see Carolingian royalty as an inevitable development.[10] This view is seriously misleading. The Carolingians could not simply wait for the breeze of historical inevitability to waft them onto the throne. Behind 751 lay a long struggle for power and, as we shall see, the person who was running out of time in 751 was not the Merovingian Childeric III but the Carolingian Pippin III.

To understand Pippin's power and problems in 751, we need to look at some of the previous history of his family and the Frankish world. Rule by a hereditary line of kings, the Merovingians, was a hallmark of Frankish political identity, the Franks themselves here being the political elite of the kingdom. The ancestors of Pippin were Frankish aristocrats from the central and eastern part of the Frankish world, Austrasia. Modern historians tend to label Pippin's ancestors as 'Arnulfings' or 'Pippinids' after two prominent family members, bishop Arnulf of Metz (died around 640) and Pippin I (d.639) and only to use the term 'Carolingian' for the later period, since it derives from the name of Pippin's father Charles Martel (d.741). For simplicity, I use the term 'Carolingian' throughout, though this may mask some complexities of identity and descent.[11]

Pippin I was a powerful aristocrat who held the office of mayor of the palace which meant that he was a key figure in the royal entourage. (Our Pippin, the king of

751, was the third office-holder in his family's history to bear that name and is thus known to historians as Pippin III even though he was the first Carolingian king.) As mayor of the palace, this Pippin I was a major player in the political conflicts of his time. These conflicts were essentially struggles for influence and power within the Frankish kingdom. Such struggles were hardly new but what was new was that from the mid-seventh century on the Merovingian kings themselves were not the dominant actors in them but were caught up in the conflicts of the great aristocrats of the rival powers of Neustria in the west and Austrasia in the east. Pippin's family, based in Austrasia, was prominent but was only one of the actors in this drama and did not dominate the scene as effortlessly as later pro-Carolingian sources would have us believe.[12] In the 650s, Pippin's son Grimoald put his own son on the throne and this certainly shows the family's power; but Grimoald was quickly overthrown and tortured to death. The Franks were not ready for a new dynasty. The fact that Grimoald's son bore the Merovingian name of Childebert and may at one stage have been adopted by a Merovingian king shows how the old dynasty still provided a framework for politics.[13]

Neither the Merovingian kings nor the Frankish aristocracy believed that the Carolingian family was destined to dominate. Grimoald's nephew (via the female line, interestingly), the formidable Pippin II, had to publicly agree to a royal judgement against his own son's claims to some monastic property in 697, a scene doubtless relished by the king and the other magnates present. Pippin II did manage to spread his power west into Neustria but his death in 714 unleashed more opposition to his family, a family that was itself spilt by internal power struggles.[14] A resplendent victor emerged from these storms; as a later fawning Carolingian source put it, Charles Martel ('the Hammer') 'the most worthy heir of Pippin began to shine forth as a mighty defender before a people suffering and almost despairing of hope'.[15] Between 714 and his death in 741, Charles fought hard to crush opposition, to establish himself and his sons Carloman and Pippin (the Pippin of 751) as supreme figures in Francia and to re-assert Frankish dominance over the 'peripheral' duchies that had slipped out of the orbit of Frankish power during the second half of the seventh century. That latter activity brought Charles to Poitiers in the far west of Gaul in 732 where he crushed the hostile Arab forces which had attacked Aquitaine. This great victory is the most famous event of Charles's rule and has given him a sinister aura in our own day as a champion against perceived threats from Arabs and Islam. In fact, one reason for Charles's appearance at Poitiers is that he was in north Aquitaine mounting a campaign against the (Christian) duke of Aquitaine before the latter made a panicky appeal for help.[16] Charles's main enemies were not the hosts of Islam but the dukes on the edges of Frankish kingdom and aristocrats within that kingdom.

If the scale of the power that he and his sons held was clearly visible, their legitimate authority looked misty. Charles's position was described in a variety of ways: 'leader', 'prince', etc. If his formal title to rule was his being mayor of the palace, whose palace was it? When king Theuderic IV died in 737, Charles did not bother to wheel out another Merovingian to succeed him but went on to make succession arrangements by dividing the kingdom as a king would do. When Charles himself died in 741, his sons Carloman and Pippin also decided that they could do without a Merovingian on the royal throne. But life without a Merovingian turned out to be difficult and so they made Childeric III king in 743.[17]

This was the paradox of success. Charles Martel, his sons and their supporters were fighting to recreate the centre of the kingdom as a potent political force, but that centre could still only be understood by the Franks as one ruled by kings. Even in the years without a Merovingian king's presence, the old dynasty had not vanished. Thus, at the centre, Charles Martel himself continued to have charters dated by the years after the death of Theuderic IV and though his sons daringly abandoned this and dated simply by their own rule, this could not last and they dated their charters by Childeric III's years once he became king.[18] Meanwhile, on the periphery of the Frankish world, the abbey of St-Gall had played safe by dating its charters by the years since the death of Dagobert III who had passed away in 715. Perhaps the composer of these charters did not know exactly what was going on at the Frankish court, which would suggest that political communications were not fully functioning. Or perhaps he knew only too well that radical ambiguity was the order of the day at the centre and so plumped for an authoritative Merovingian ruler to lend authority to his charters. Once Childeric III appeared, charters tended to be dated by his years.[19]

All this indicates that contemporaries were aware that a portentous something was happening, but if the situation was not entirely clear to them it is pretty obscure to us. This is partly due to the dearth of source material but it is also due to the tendentious nature of the material that does survive. The Childebrand/Nibelung chronicle simply does not mention either the death of Theuderich IV or the eventual succession of Childeric III. This too points to a nervy self-consciousness. The spotlight was to be kept on 'the famous pair of brothers' Carloman and Pippin.[20]

But all this just shows that the Merovingians still mattered. After all, Carloman and Pippin themselves went to the trouble of finding one, Childeric III, in 743. We do not know for certain who Childeric's father was; perhaps it was his predecessor Theuderic IV; perhaps not. Childeric's own claims to the throne may thus have been rather iffy; Merovingian claimants could sometimes be manufactured if the political community needed them. This 'malleability' of the Merovingian family here helped the Carolingians and their Frankish supporters for the last time by giving them a candidate who could be agreed upon by everyone as an acceptably Merovingian king. Even in the later age of Carolingian supremacy, compilers of king-lists were struck by all this.[21] There even seemed to be a prospect of the Merovingian dynastic line continuing: Childeric had fathered a son and that son bore an indisputably Merovingian royal name.[22] Merovingians mattered to contemporaries who still needed to see them as uniquely royal. The clear implication is that the Franks did not see the Carolingians as distinctive enough to be kings. Even Charles Martel and his sons had seen this. Of course, we should not lose sight of the fact that Charles Martel and his line were now the most powerful family in the Frankish realm. But they could not simply bide their time, waiting for the kingship to fall into their lap. The grisly fate of Grimoald in the 650s was long remembered, though the political context of the later era was rather different.[23] The middle years of the eighth century were in fact a time of political experimentation in which the Carolingian mayors were restorers of the Merovingian line rather than usurpers. They must have exercised tight control over the Merovingians in waiting. It was Carloman and Pippin who pulled Childeric III out of the hat when he was needed. None of their opponents had been able to produce a spare Merovingian to embarrass the Carolingian mayors of the palace. If the Merovingian line of succession was indeed malleable, there were limits to that and these limits were policed by the Carolingians.

If the Merovingians remained politically indispensable, they were not powerful. Stridently pro-Carolingian sources, written long after the events of 751–4, paint a notoriously negative picture of Merovingian political impotence, with representatives of the once proud dynasty bumbling aimlessly around the realm in ox-carts or living quietly under a form of house arrest apart from the rare days when they were wheeled out to perform their ancient functions in public in a tightly scripted piece of political theatre. Important scholarly work has shown just how tendentiously misleading such a picture is as an image of the realities of the later Merovingian period.[24]

But Merovingian kings actually were in trouble and one did not need to be a supporter of the Carolingians to see that. Writing in the 720s, the author of the *Liber Historiae Francorum* was a traditional Merovingian loyalist but even he could see that the history of the previous fifty years was one in which the dominant actors were the aristocratic mayors of the palace, and he is surprisingly open about the questionable Merovingian identity of Chilperic II (715–21): 'On the throne, the Neustrians placed, in fact, Daniel, a former cleric, having allowed the hair of his head to grow, and they named him Chilperic.'[25] Perhaps this Daniel/Chilperic really was a genuine Merovingian but the author seems as unconvinced by this claim as he was convinced of the necessity of having a Merovingian on the throne. From the late seventh century right up to 751, the Frankish political establishment, including the Carolingians, still found Merovingian kingship to be a necessary fiction.

This did not make for a settled Frankish world. The great dukes and princes outside the core of the kingdom in places such as Alemannia and Bavaria saw opportunities for more independence.

> At that time and afterwards [*c.* 700], Gotfrid, duke (*dux*) of the Alemanni and the other dukes (*duces*) round about refused to obey the leaders (*duces*) of the Franks because they could not now serve the Merovingian kings as they had been accustomed to do previously. And so each of them held himself apart until, eventually, after the death of Gotfrid Charles [Martel] and the other leaders/princes (*principes*) of the Franks sought to gradually win them back by whatever means they could.[26]

For all that it was written down about a century's distance from the historical situation that it describes, this text sounds a historically convincing note. Its explicit concern with the Merovingian kings as the apex of the political order that contained the dukes is echoed in an earlier Alemannian text, the Law of the Alemanns, issued *c.*724 under duke Lantfrid. It is suggestive that the text of the Breviary of Erchanbert, which tells us of the duke's refusal, appears in a manuscript containing a version of that lawcode.[27] The same political order is proclaimed in a legal text from Bavaria, also on the periphery of the Frankish world: 'This was decreed before the king and his princes (*principes*) and before the whole Christian people who dwell within the kingdom of the Merovingians.'[28] As K. F. Werner has shown in a classic article, the dukedoms were not autonomous, ethnically distinct entities, but were very much part of the political order of the Frankish world. The dukes wanted, not independence as such, but to play the prominent role to which their rank entitled them within a Frankish realm under Merovingian authority.[29]

This means that if the dissolution of Merovingian power was posing problems for the centre, it would also do so for the dukedoms. All these problems were linked. We should not think that early Carolingians simply focused on building up their power in the Frankish heartlands and only then unleashed their Frankish followers on the unruly dukes of the periphery. They could not separate these sets of problems which were linked by a compelling political logic. The rulers and aristocracies of the peripheral dukedoms had all sorts of links, familial, economic and political, with those at the Frankish centre. The Carolingians could not successfully dominate the centre without also dominating the 'periphery'. Thus, Charles Martel's fierce campaigns in Burgundy and Provence were a continuation of a struggle against a powerful family whose roots were in the far north, in Neustria.[30] Similarly, Bavaria provided a refuge for the great aristocrat Rupert, an opponent of the Carolingians from the Rhineland. One reason for Bavaria's welcoming Rupert is that he appears to have been related by marriage to the ducal family, the Agilolfings. When the Carolingians became engulfed in conflict as Charles Martel tried to claim his inheritance in 714, Rupert was able to return from Bavaria.[31]

The tentacles of the duchies even reached into the heart of the Carolingian family itself in the confusion following the death of Charles Martel in 741. Charles's daughter Hiltrud escaped the control of her brothers and married the duke of Bavaria. This failure to prevent the spread of the Carolingian blood-line was a blow to the dynasty and helps explain something of the subsequent Carolingian obsession with subduing Bavaria, as well as the dynasty's caution in letting daughters marry. Such women had high dynastic value.[32] Carloman and Pippin were also confronted with the prospect of dealing with their half-brother Grifo, who claimed a share of the kingdom on their father's death and who could draw on significant support within the kingdom.[33] As Paul Fouracre has observed, the upheavals on Charles Martels' death show that he had not created a new political order but had simply inspired a terror that evaporated on his death. Carloman and Pippin scrambled for all the help they could get and thus pushed Childeric III, blinking in the unaccustomed limelight, on to the throne; both of them needed a Merovingian to shore up their position at home and abroad.[34]

War played a key role in this reconfiguring of the Frankish realm. Charles Martel had built his rule on relentless military campaigning and his sons followed suit.[35] Carloman and Pippin spent the years of their joint rule (741–7) campaigning hard in Francia to subdue their brother Grifo and outside Francia to subdue everybody else. These conflicts were intense; years when the army was not summoned for campaigns were seen as worthy of comment.[36] They were expensive, requiring upheavals in military organization and property-holding, and churches felt the ripples. They were also destructive and painful: in the south-east death and dispossession may have been the fate of much of the aristocracy of Alemannia in 746; in the south-west, the landscape of Aquitaine was burnt and ravaged in a grimly extended series of campaigns.[37] All this was fiercely resisted; it took three generations of Carolingian rulers to subdue Aquitaine.

Despite all this, these campaigns were not simply a struggle of a centre against the periphery. We have already seen that centre and periphery were linked. Certainly Frankish centres benefited from the tightening of links and the (re-) imposition of harsher norms of control. By the 760s, churches such as Reims, Trier and Verdun had regained their properties and privileges in Aquitaine, thanks to Pippin's pressure.[38] The Carolingians took care, however, to ensure that profits were distributed widely, if not evenly. When they broke up the independent power of the bishop of Auxerre, they distributed some of the property to aristocrats from Bavaria.[39] The assertion of Frankish-Carolingian authority thus offered opportunities as well as threats to regional aristocracies. Sometimes, these opportunities were simply tough political choices that had to be made: Frankish pressure led the uncle of the duke of Aquitaine to defect to Pippin who showered him with gifts but when he tried to renege on his agreement with Pippin he was caught and hanged.[40]

The man who hanged him was count Chunibert of Bourges who had also been caught up in conflicting loyalties between the duke of Aquitaine and the ruler of the Franks. But Chunibert's story shows that more than brute force was deployed in building a Frankish empire. Force certainly played a key role. Bourges was a key point between the lands of the northern and southern rulers and Chunibert had joined the latter in a raid into Burgundy in 761 that had brought down the wrath of the former. In 762, Pippin took Bourges and captured Chunibert and others. Pippin made them swear oaths to him, kept them in his custody and forced their wives and children to walk to Francia.[41] Such was the traffic in human misery generated by these wars. The arrival of such men, women and children in Francia would have boosted the pride and self-consciousness of the Franks as builders of an evolving empire but hostages and prisoners could themselves profit from this lesson and be turned into agents of the empire.[42] If Chunibert travelled back to Francia in Pippin's custody, he would have been exposed to a ruler and entourage intoxicated with the scale of their God-given victories and may well have glimpsed something of the far horizons of Pippin's court with envoys arriving from distant locations such as Rome.[43] Doubtless such re-education at the Frankish court was impressive, not least because of the prospect of rewards for those who participated in it. The upshot of all this was that Chunibert kept his oath to Pippin and thus his own position in the south while Pippin later promised to preserve traditional institutions in Aquitaine.[44] The Carolingians and the Franks needed these regional aristocracies; only their co-operation could remake the Frankish world.

The intensifying relationship between centre and periphery dialectically changed all parties, including the Franks themselves. The Carolingians were not solitary actors and when historians refer to Carolingian activities and campaigns we often deploy the term 'Carolingian' synecdochically. This screens out the role of the supporters of the Carolingians, those aristocrats whose wealth and warriors gave the dominant family its victories. Carolingian leadership provided opportunities for enrichment and social status for the aristocracy but it was that aristocracy's power and resources that permitted the Carolingians to launch such campaigns in the first place.

All this suggests that the processes of empire-building were more complex than saddling up and riding out to snatch as much plunder as you could carry, to simplify an immensely important article by the late Tim Reuter.[45] Yet treasure did matter hugely to contemporaries. Though it is hardly unique in this, the chronicle of Childebrand and Nibelung displays an almost obsessive interest in giving and receiving of gifts (which might include land), tribute, plunder and treasure. The Franks and their rulers are thus bathed in a glow of riches.[46] Individual Franks are sometimes, though rarely, identified as winning plunder but more often it is the Franks as a group who receive gifts and tribute.[47] Yet the key figure in the vast majority of these cases is the Carolingian ruler; it is he who presents great gifts to others and it is to him that gifts are presented and that plunder and tribute flow: 'He [Pippin] received many gifts from the Franks and his magnates.'[48] The term 'Frank' itself was changing at this time. Writings of the early eighth century such as the *Liber Historiae Francorum* use the term in a restricted sense to refer to the Neustrians of the north-west rather than to all Franks. In the Childebrand-Nibelung chronicle, the term refers to a broader community of the Franks between the Seine and the Loire and thus seeks to show that 'the rise of the Carolingians and the establishment of Frankish lordship are bound together' and later historical writings and compilations were to continue to treat this term dynamically.[49]

The royalty of Pippin III: 751

The developments that we have been surveying provide a context for the transformation of the Carolingians into a royal family but they do not explain the replacement of the Merovingian dynasty. Why did this key change come about when it did? What do we actually know about this change? We can state with confidence that Pippin's king-making ceremony was a Christian one that grew out of the deeply Christian nature of Merovingian kingship and Frankish identity.[50] Much about the ceremony and its background, however, remains elusive. The clear statement in the *Royal Frankish Annals* that the Franks turned to Pope Zacharias for advice and that he commanded that Pippin be made king is no longer taken at face value. The Franks knew enough about king-making without having to ask a pope about it, and the language of these annals on Frankish anxieties over disturbances in the order of things and the role of papal authority reflects thinking of the time of the annals' composition in the late 780s, not the 750s.[51] Furthermore, Rome may not have grasped the radical nature of the step that Pippin was proposing to take; papal sources are silent on the events of 751 and some people in the papal entourage may have thought that Pippin's family was already royal, as suggested by the casual reference to Charles Martel as king in the biography of Zacharias.[52] Perhaps popes were not quite as absorbed by the nuances of Frankish politics as the Franks thought.

The Franks, however, may have turned to the pope because they were heading into uncharted waters and needed guidance. The pope appeared as a figure of sufficient spiritual authority to free them, including Pippin, from their oath of loyalty to the reigning Merovingian, Childeric III, and this mattered. Childebrand's chronicle does say that Pippin contacted Rome and a later Byzantine source reports that the pope released Pippin from his oath, though the pope in this account is Stephen II, Zacharias's successor and it would surely have made more sense for the Franks to have had papal resolution on this problem in 751, that is, from Zacharias.[53]

Childebrand's chronicle is contemporary evidence for Franks contacting Rome on the eve of 751 and we know that Zacharias had been in contact with Frankish bishops and magnates on spiritual matters at the end of the 740s.[54] Overall, while we remain suspicious of the language and details of the *Royal Frankish Annals'* account of the consultation with Rome, we can be fairly confident that Pippin and his supports did indeed contact Rome on their plans and worries, and that they did so because they needed as much help as possible in their risky enterprise.

One might think that the actual ceremonies of 751 would also be designed to make Pippin look as special as possible in order to compensate for his lack of royal blood. Even in Byzantium, a chronicler knew that the Franks had a hereditary royal family and that in 751 it was not Pippin's.[55] Earlier generations of scholarship saw the ceremonies of 751 as very special indeed, as epoch-making ceremonies that introduced the anointing of the king with holy oil into the political bloodstream of the medieval west and historians have sought roots of this in the Old Testament and in practices in Ireland and Visigothic Spain. More recently, historians have looked to ecclesiastical practices such as baptism, confirmation, together with papal interest in anointings as a context for 751.[56]

Unfortunately, we cannot be certain that Pippin actually was anointed in 751. Again, the clearest testimony comes from the all too eloquent *Royal Frankish Annals* which not only explicitly tell us that Pippin was anointed but also by whom: 'anointed by the hand of archbishop Boniface of holy memory'.[57] This reference to Boniface makes clear that the entry was written after Boniface's death as a Christian missionary in 754. His appearance in the annal for 751 has more to do with the annalist's desire to associate Pippin with a holy martyr than with the desire to record who actually performed the ceremony. Historians now tend to think that Boniface was too much of an outsider to be chosen for such a sensitive role and that the most likely candidate for it was Chrodegang, bishop of Metz and member of a powerful Frankish family.[58] The contemporary chronicle of Childebrand does not use the term 'anointing', instead referring to Pippin's 'consecration' (a term that can, in the Latin Bible, be associated with anointing, as historians who are keen to find evidence of anointing in 751 have pointed out).[59] Nor need we think that Pippin was crowned, as coronation with a crown does not seem to have become part of Frankish royal ceremonies until 781, where the pope, again, played a key role.[60]

We cannot even be sure that the ceremony of 751 was a radical break with previous Frankish practice. Perhaps Pippin and his followers would have deployed some new form of ritual in order to distinguish the new dynasty from its predecessor.[61] Or perhaps the last thing that Pippin would have wanted would have been any more disturbance at a tense time and so he may well have followed Merovingian precedents; as Childebrand's chronicle says, it all happened 'as the rules of ancient tradition required'.[62] One element, however, was new: the consecration of a woman, Pippin's wife Bertrada, and we shall return to the significance of this.[63] Unsurprisingly, historians tend now to be cautious, arguing quite rightly that, without the all too clear and explicit testimony of the *Royal Frankish Annals*, we simply cannot be sure that Pippin was anointed in 751.[64] Of course, we cannot be sure that he was not.

All this uncertainty is very different from the confident judgements of earlier generations of scholarship which labelled the events of 751 as 'the beginnings of western thought on the state'.[65] This uncertainty is more than mere academic quibbling. It stems from honesty about the fragmentary nature of our sources as well as scepticism about the master-narrative given by the *Royal Frankish Annals*, now to be understood as very unreliable in all their retrospective tendentiousness as an account of the period, but to be valued all the more, precisely because of these negative qualities, as an example of the ceaseless work of legitimating Carolingian rule and the new Frankish order.[66]

But the historian also has to paint a bigger picture. This means focusing on essentials in order to grasp how 751 turned out to be enormously important for contemporaries. The year 751 was certainly the time of change. Dating evidence from charters points to the autumn or winter of 751 as the time of Pippin's king-making, with Christmas day as a possibility, though we cannot be certain of the location, with Soissons, Reims or Metz as possibilities.[67] Magnates and bishops attended upon him and were no passive audience. They swore fidelity to him as king and the bishops enfolded him in a sacred aura and signalled the establishing of a new dynasty by consecrating him as king and Bertrada as queen. Childebrand's chronicle emphasizes the traditional nature of all this, as well as the role of the Franks, whose advice, consent and choice were active factors in the raising of Pippin. Childebrand and Nibelung were members of Pippin's family who had done well out of backing him, but they were Franks as well. In witnessing Pippin's transformation, the Franks also saw themselves transformed into a new collectivity.[68]

A new era meant the disappearance of an old one: the Merovingian king was made to vanish in 751 and the old dynasty continued to be humiliated in a variety of texts written later. The best known image of the later Merovingians as feeble figures in an inevitable decline is the one produced by Einhard in the 820s, but that is the culmination of a series of such images composed and circulated from the 780s onwards.[69] The fact that the Greek chronicler Theophanes, writing in the early ninth century, saw the Merovingians as feeble gluttons suggests that the Carolingians and their supporters had actively spread this image: Merovingian feebleness justified Carolingian royalty.[70]

But the Merovingians were not always mocked. In fact for some readers, Einhard's picture seems to have been too extreme. One manuscript compilation (Vienna ÖNB cod.473) cuts his opening sections in favour of texts highlighting continuity of royal rule in (western) Francia. This compilation was made around 869 by people very close to King Charles the Bald, a king who had a copy of Einhard's text complete with the anti-Merovingian sections.[71] The Merovingians were not always remembered with disdain after 751. Charlemagne himself gave sons Merovingian royal names (Lothar and Louis) in 778 and some genealogies composed in his lifetime tried to attach the new rulers to the Merovingan family.[72] After 751, contemporaries could see the new royal family as part of a continuous sequence of Frankish rulers smoothly following on from the Merovingians. For example, a law manuscript composed in Lyon in the 790s contains a list of Frankish rulers where Pippin III fits into a line of (Merovingian) predecessors without causing any ripples. But this sequence of names is not neutral; the list itself shows the change. 'Pippin' is not among the Merovingian names that precede him; his name stands out among the older royal repertory, and the scribe dated the completion of the manuscript by a prominent reference to the rule of Charles (Charlemagne), another newly royal name.[73]

Frankish history was continuing, but one of the justifications for the coup in 751 must have been that Frankish history would continue ever more gloriously under new management. This is the message of the account of that coup in the chronicle produced by Pippin's uncle, count Childebrand, close to 751: 'In accordance with that order anciently required, he [Pippin] was chosen king by all the Franks, consecrated by the bishops and received the homage of the great men.'[74]

Nonetheless, some Franks were now much more special, newly special, than others. This very chronicle celebrates reinvigorated Frankishness but keeps a spotlight on one particular family, the very family to which its authors (Childebrand and his son Nibelung) belonged. These authors did not trouble themselves with continuing the story of Merovingian kings that they had found in their sources for their own work, or whose reigns they themselves had experienced. After a mention of King Theuderic IV (721–37), this Carolingian house chronicle does not refer to any of the subsequent Merovingian kings, but spends pages glorifying Pippin III, his brother and their father.[75] People did not need to read history books to know that the royal line had changed. The great aristocrats caught up in the political conflicts from the 740s onwards had themselves participated in that change; they helped make it happen. They witnessed whatever inauguration ceremony for Pippin took place in 751; it would have been some of them who whisked the reigning Merovingian, Childeric III along with his son, to monastic exile; they witnessed Pope Stephen II bless the new royal family of Pippin, his queen Bertrada and their young sons.[76]

Nothing is known of the details of the deposition and tonsuring of the last Merovingian. Perhaps Pippin had it done publicly at a great assembly, the same one that witnessed his own king-making, in order to demonstrate as clearly as possible that the old order had passed and to involve the Franks in the transition to the new order. But perhaps it was wiser to do this offstage and simply report it to the Franks as a *fait accompli*. Pippin surely had Childeric tonsured in order to mark his passing from royal status to monastic retreat rather than because he wished to cancel any 'sacral' quality in the famous long hair of the Merovingians. We do not know if Childeric was given the opportunity to 'volunteer' for a monastic life as a form of penance, nor do we know of any accusations made against him of anything that he might have needed to be penitent about.[77] It is more likely that he was turned into a passive victim, not a monastic enthusiast. Pippin was the active figure and, unlike his father, he aimed to cancel the Merovingian future. He had to do this in order to secure his own line. That line faced threats from closer quarters than the Merovingians.

Pippin ensured the disappearance not only of Childeric but also of the latter's son.[78] This was particularly important as it simultaneously defined the shape of the Merovingian royal line and obliterated it. And Pippin succeeded. Neither Childeric nor his son ever emerged from monastic confinement, as far as we know. This contrasts with the later fate of Tassilo, duke of Bavaria, deposed in 788 by Charlemagne who found it necessary a few years later to permit him to emerge temporarily from monastic confinement in order to re-affirm his family's loss of the dukedom.[79] Nor did any other Merovingian claimants subsequently emerge from the woodwork; there was no repetition of the careers of Merovingian pretenders such as Gundovald, or Daniel/Chilperic whose iffy claims to Merovingian blood and inheritance had mobilized important support.[80]

Pushing the Merovingians off the stage was a remarkable achievement and marked a real change in the political history of the Franks who turned out to be prepared to accept it as part of the re-ordering and restoration of the Frankish kingdom. But the definitive despatching of the old dynasty was not a result of the potency of the ceremonies of 751 or of Pippin's unchallengeable strength. The failure of the Merovingians to act as a focus for opposition to Pippin is partly due to the fact that another family was better able to do that: his own. Phrases such as 'the rise of the Carolingians' obscure the fact that not all the Carolingians rose to royal power in 751 and that Pippin was much more threatened by the enemy within than our sources dare to say. Pippin was one of six brothers by various mothers; four of these brothers had been excluded from succession by their father Charles Martel in 737.[81] Three of them accepted their relatively subordinate status and worked for the interests of the privileged line of the family; one of them was only nine years old when he copied out a version of the life of the family saint, Arnulf of Metz; reproduction of distinctiveness relied on dynastic child labour, as we shall see in a later chapter.[82]

Not all worked so selflessly. Towards the end of Charles Martel's rule one brother, Grifo, advanced claims for a share of power and fought hard to realize these claims on Charles's death in 741. Our sources are uneasily silent or tendentious on Grifo's activities but it is clear that he was a real contender who won significant aristocratic support, possibly from within the broader pool of Carolingian kin. Structurally, Grifo's trouble-making worked for the Carolingian family by channelling aristocratic competition within the rivalries of the ruling family.[83] Pippin and his full brother Carloman, however, could not take this detached academic view. They subdued Grifo and had him imprisoned by the time they produced Childeric III as king in 743, doubtless in the hope that this would bring about consensus in a divided kingdom.

In 747, Carloman abandoned office for monastic retreat in Italy. Again, our sources are significantly reticent on the details of this; family tensions required discretion or tactful piety in later representation of Carolingian triumph.[84] Shifts in the constellation of the Carolingian family meant that difficult choices crowded in on Pippin in these crucially important years. Negotiating the arrangements for Carloman's retirement was so fraught and complex that the brothers had no time to mount the usual military campaigns that season.[85] Carloman's 747 abdication still left on the scene his son, Drogo, whom he had associated with himself in public display and who was expected by the aristocracy to take over some or all of his father's power in a settlement that the childless Pippin had accepted.[86] Aristocrats uneasily weighing up this new balance of power within the Carolingian family soon had to cope with two disturbing developments. Grifo escaped from confinement; Pippin's attempts to buy him off failed and he was soon making trouble for Pippin.[87] Then in 748, Pippin's well-connected wife Bertrada bore him a son, Charles, the future Charlemagne; a later source's recalling of the intense fervour with which his parents had prayed for such a blessing gives us a vivid glimpse of the couple's dynastic anxieties[88] With a son, who bore the resonant name of the mighty grandfather Charles, Pippin now had a line of his own and his relationship with his brothers Carloman and Grifo and his nephew Drogo was changed.

All this helps explain why Pippin made his royal move when he did. Nothing had changed within the Merovingian family to trigger that move; Childeric III was no more feeble in 751 than he had been in any other year. It was Pippin's own family who threatened him. His brother Grifo's hostility played into the hands of Pippin's aristocratic and ducal rivals on the periphery of the kingdom. Pippin's deal with his nephew Drogo now looked much less shrewd in the light of the appearance of his son Charles and even if Pippin had already managed to push Drogo to the sidelines, the latter's father Carloman was taking a dangerously keen interest in Frankish politics from his monastic retreat in Italy precisely in 750–1.[89] Grifo, Drogo and Carloman were still formidable figures around whom Pippin's opponents could gather. Even if Pippin were to make a deal with his brothers and nephew that would threaten any plans he now had for his own heir Charles. Such pressures could only intensify when Bertrada fell pregnant again and gave birth to a second son some time in 751.[90] Sharks were circling round Pippin's own line; insecurity and challenge as well as ambition now drove him and he had to find a way of trumping his opponents, including members of his own family. This explains the timing of his move to the kingship.[91]

It also highlights the nature of his move; it was dynastic in that Pippin and his wife and thus their children were raised on high, not his brothers or nephew. These relations seem to have been much less impressed by the ceremonies of 751 than generations of historians have been. Grifo continued his resistance, but perished in battle in 753.[92] Carloman now made a sensational return to the Frankish scene. One reason for this was his involvement in Italian politics and his desire to dissuade the Franks from taking action against the Lombards. But we can be sure that he would also have hoped to salvage some position for his sons in Pippin's new order. He was too late. Another figure had also been driven north of the Alps by Italian politics. This was Pope Stephen II whose historic journey to the new Frankish king was a mission to try and persuade the Franks to counter a Lombard threat to Rome. The pope sealed Pippin's new status in 754 by anointing him and his two young sons and consecrating Bertrada as well. Carloman reached Francia after this had happened and was too late to stop his sons being tonsured by Pippin who now felt confident enough to finally suppress that close branch of the family.[93] Carloman himself, with his unsound views on the Lombards and his still dangerously potent dynastic status, was kept in honourable custody by Pippin and died in 754 under the watchful eye of Bertrada herself. Even those monks who had accompanied him were kept in custody by Pippin, whom no detail escaped.[94]

By the end of 754, Pippin was splendidly alone; his troublesome brothers were dead; his nephews were in monasteries, as were the last Merovingians. The papal ceremonies of 754 had made this very clear to the Franks. This encounter between the new Frankish king and the Roman pontiff unfolded as part of the complex manoeuvres amongst pope, Franks and Lombards that were to have such fateful consequences.[95] These concern us less here than the dynastic aspect of 754. Even this, however, is a complex topic, not least because Frankish and papal sources, keen to show their respective heroes in the best light, give very different views of what actually happened. There is also the usual medievalists' problem of a source (*Clausula de unctione Pippini*) that temptingly offers a full and coherent account of events but which is too problematic to be safely relied on.[96]

Nonetheless, the big picture is clear. The visit was a spectacular multi-faceted event with encounters between king and pope stage-managed at showplaces such as the palace of Ponthion and the abbey of St-Denis.[97] The successor of St Peter arrived laden with cultural treasures that would impress his Frankish hosts, whether in the form of liturgical musical knowledge whose impact was long remembered or in the impressively visual and tangible form of the remarkable porphyry columns which he gave to Pippin and which we can still gaze upon in the Louvre in Paris.[98] Pippin sent his five-year-old son to welcome and escort the pope, a gesture whose dynastic accent would have been unmissable for contemporaries. This little boy represented the future of the dynasty and of the Franks and Pippin's deploying him in this highly visible role was designed to teach the Franks precisely that.[99] The pope underlined and broadcast this in early 754 when he anointed Pippin and his sons, aged five and three, as kings at St-Denis and also consecrated Bertrada.[100] The Merovingian past, so palpable at St-Denis, was now seen to yield to a Carolingian present and future.

Contemporaries may not have realized that this was the definitive end of the Merovingians but they would know that 751–4 marked a new beginning. This upheaval and change touched the aristocracy as a body. The suspension of military campaigns during the preparations for Carloman's abdication and for Pippin's king-making is a visible sign of the widespread tensions these affairs involved. The reticence of narrative sources on these years also testifies to such tensions and probably opposition to Pippin at that time.[101] Once Pippin became king, the ancient office of the mayor of the palace disappeared, changing the structure of the Frankish court, focusing attention directly on the new king and ensuring that there was no institutional reminder of the Carolingians' erstwhile subordinate status. As king, Pippin now had more resources in his unchallenged grasp of the fiscal estates that his family had for some time been seeking to control.[102]

Aristocrats would also have noted fundamental changes in the rhythms of time and space. Pippin moved the annual spring assembly from March to May, possibly to lessen the chances of war occurring in Lent but certainly a shift that would have affected the Frankish warriors and it was a change that provoked comment.[103] People could see changes. Whereas even Charles Martel seems to have been too cautious to reside in the royal palace of Compiègne after the death of his Merovingian front-man Pippin now made use of such royal sites as Compiègne and Ponthion as well as of Carolingian family estates such as Quierzy and Ver. Coins in people's hands changed. Magnates in late Merovingian Francia could issue coins in their own name. But as king, Pippin re-asserted royal control over the coinage and ensured that his name and royal title appeared on coins in the form of RP (*rex Pippinus*: king Pippin), a very public strengthening of claims to royal authority that has a parallel in contemporary Anglo-Saxon Northumbria.[104]

The impact of the papal visit itself was felt far outside Francia. In Bavaria, charters were dated by reference to it and Pippin's kingship; in Italy the Lombards marvelled at a fireball in the heavens that announced the pope's journey.[105] Strangely enough, the Childebrand-Nibelung chronicle says nothing about the anointing at St-Denis, though it does report the pope's visit. Such silence is hard to interpret. Perhaps these Franks thought that the ceremony of 751 was definitive and no top-up was needed in 754, though later Frankish sources were happy to see 754 as a second anointing and biblical references to David being anointed twice may be relevant here (if Pippin actually was anointed in 751).[106] But the ceremonies of 754 mattered very much in Francia, not least because the Franks, including Pippin and his family, were told that they did by the popes themselves. The bond between Pippin and the successors of St Peter was an important spiritual one.[107] It was also, however, a public political bond whose significance was performed throughout Pippin's reign.

On the earthly level, the bond was maintained by envoys travelling between Rome and Francia bearing news and letters. Narrative sources say very little indeed on such envoys but the importance of their work is clear, thanks to the survival of some of these letters in a document called 'The Book of Charles (Charlemagne)' (*Codex Carolinus*). This is a collection of papal letters to Frankish rulers compiled at Charlemagne's court in 791; as such it is an edited selection of texts, and a one-sided one at that, and we should be properly critical in our use of it.[108] The Franks probably did not pore over these letters as modern scholars have done; their detailed contents may not have been well known.[109] But these were not private documents. Papal letters would have been delivered to the king by richly dressed envoys whose arrival was an event. Envoys also carried gifts, including on one occasion precious rings for the ten-year-old Charlemagne and seven-year-old Carloman, publicly marking them out as very special boys indeed.[110] Envoys would also have announced and commented on the letter's contents as was standard medieval practice and as can be vividly seen in Boniface's remarkable letter to a priest advising him on the dangerous task of delivering a letter of rebuke to an Anglo-Saxon king. In this papal correspondence, we find explicit instructions to envoys to do this and since one of the relevant letters is actually addressed to the Frankish magnates, we can assume that such speeches could be very public.[111]

In fact several letters were addressed to the Frankish magnates, clerical and lay. Pippin's aristocratic supporters were deeply involved in the delivery, arrival and performance of these messages.[112] Escorting the pope northwards in 753 fostered connections between count Ruthard and abbot Fulrad of St-Denis. Abbot Fulrad's contact with the papal court was so assiduous that the pope gave him residential properties and stables in Rome.[113] The papal letters and the *Book of the Pontiffs* reveal an extensive supporting cast of envoys, including high-ranking Frankish warriors and churchmen, and also featuring Pippin's half-brothers whose relationship with the king was known.[114]

Sometimes these envoys delivered very substantial gifts, as when Pippin gave an altar-table (*mensa*) to the pope in 761; they would have witnessed the pope's solemn reception of their lord's gift and would have heard him celebrate mass for the king as well as the chanting of the hypnotic royal blessings and acclamations, the *laudes*.[115] They were thus instructed in the special majesty of their king. Smaller objects could also work to this end. In 757/8, Abbot Wulfard of St Martin's Tours carried the baptismal shawl of Pippin's baby daughter Gisela to her godfather the pope who, in the sight of a rejoicing crowd, placed it within the splendidly decorated church of St Petronilla, an important saint to the Carolingians who, like other contemporaries, saw her as the daughter of St Peter himself.[116] Abbot Wulfard was a substantial figure who undertook several missions to Rome and also ensured that Tours provided troops for Pippin's campaigns in Aquitaine.[117] In Rome, in 757/8 he was working to honour a baby girl and thus learning to deepen his own and others' respect for the new dynasty that his diplomacy and troops also helped to secure.

For their part, popes regularly told the Frankish court that they called down blessings from God on this little girl.[118] To Frankish ears, this would have sounded intensely dynastic; which other Frankish girl received such treatment? Papal letters to Pippin's court honoured the Franks in general but also regularly called down blessings on the young Charlemagne and Carloman as well as their royal mother and father.[119] Pope Stephen II addressed Charlemagne and Carloman as kings when they were seven and four, respectively.[120] He himself knew that they were young and he knew that they were kings because he had met and anointed them. And popes took care to remind Pippin and his sons that God and St Peter had reached out to them via the papal anointing.[121] Queen Bertrada was also revered and prayed for in these letters; their respectful references to her indicate that she had also been blessed by Pope Stephen in 754.[122] No sooner did Pope Paul hear that Pippin had a new son in 759 (and someone must have brought this news to Rome) than he requested the privilege of standing as godfather to the infant whom he referred to as a 'new king from your loins (*visceribus*)'; this baby seemed to be instantly a king. This little boy was only one link in a dynastic chain for which popes desired a glorious future, praying for the prosperity of Pippin's seed.[123] If the text *On the Anointing of Pippin* cannot be cited as contemporary with the events of the 750s, though some historians do believe that it has an 'essential authenticity', it certainly echoes the key message that popes repeated to Pippin, his family and his followers, namely, 'never to presume in future to elect a king begotten by any men other than those whom the bounty of God has seen fit to raise up and has decided to confirm and consecrate by the intercession of the holy apostles'.[124]

Perhaps not every word of the sonorous papal Latin of these letters was fully understood or closely read by everyone at Pippin's court, but, as we have seen, these letters are only the surviving part of a whole series of acts of communication that touched Frankish aristocrats as well as popes and the royal family. On the eve of his visit in 753, Pope Stephen II had appealed to the Franks to support Pippin and they continued to be exposed to resolutely dynastic messages from Rome throughout the rest of Pippin's reign.[125] Popes of course had their own reasons for reminding Pippin and the Franks of the great ceremonies of 754. They wanted the Franks to remember their obligations to the successor of St Peter as he faced threats from Lombards and Greeks. To that extent, Pippin and his family were themselves the target audience.

And the reiteration of these messages taught them who they were. Like Wulfard on his journey with little Gisela's shawl, they too had to learn that the Carolingians were special, that they were a royal dynasty.

The aura of the sacred that graced Pippin and his line was not entirely new for the family. Charles Martel was prayed for as 'prince' (*princeps*).[126] Before he became king, Pippin made a grant to the monastery of Flavigny in Burgundy, a grant recorded on elegant ivory tablets, while requesting that the monks prayed for him and 'all my offspring present and future'.[127] Prayers were prayers. Rulers such as Charles Martel, Carloman and Pippin inherited and developed the duties of Christian rulership from the Merovingians and thus acted as patrons of holy men such as Boniface as well as of more conventional bishops such as Chrodegang of Metz. Neither Boniface's concern with the spiritual purity of the Frankish palace nor Chrodegang's efforts to unite Frankish churchmen, as seen in the great prayer-bond of 762 established at Attigny, were intentionally designed to enhance Carolingian rule. Nonetheless they were bound to enhance its aura as Christian leadership.[128]

How Pippin III stayed royal

Pippin also had to win over secular aristocrats. The partnership between Carolingian rulers and the aristocracy was an indispensable element in Carolingian success. And it was a partnership. The Carolingians did not create this aristocracy; they were dependent on it. Despite upheavals and casualties in the struggles for power during the late seventh and eighth centuries, regional aristocracies survived.[129] Some aristocrats, for example Wulfoadus at Verdun, defied Pippin and his family and he cannot have been alone, but much of the history of such opposition is unsurprisingly obscure.[130] In fact the fragmentary nature of eighth-century evidence means that we do not have too many details even about Pippin's aristocratic supporters but Josef Semmler has traced groups of supporters in the west, in Burgundy, as well as east of the Rhine, in Alemannia and elsewhere. Pippin was able to draw on members of his own family who were safely not in line for a throne such as his uncle Childebrand, his son Nibelung and Theodericus, who may have been related to Pippin's wife.[131]

Such aristocrats were not mere instruments in Pippin's hands nor did they operate as officials in some impersonal system of bureaucracy that smoothly carried out the king's will on the ground.[132] Much of Pippin's power rested on the power that such families already possessed. Among his followers before he became king, we find Gerard (Gairhardus). By 752, he was count of Paris and held that post till 778/9. He had thus experienced Pippin's transformation into a king and seen the transmission of this new Carolingian royalty to the next generation. This service to the new regime is all the more striking since he belonged to a family that had long held power around Paris and which had opposed Pippin's ancestors in the late seventh and early eighth centuries.[133] It was precisely such families that Pippin had to win over and he successfully did so in this case. Gerard also seems to have been connected to a branch of the Carolingian family by marriage. As count of Paris, he almost certainly witnessed the royal anointings by Pope Stephen in 754. But he had his own connection with the pope; his son was called Stephen, and this suggests that the pope had stood godfather to the boy; such Franks, like the new royal family, could see new horizons. Gerard's family held on to the county of Paris for the next hundred years.[134] The Carolingians had to make sure that the claims and appetites of such families were satisfied and offices and marriage connections helped do so. Without such figures, Pippin and his line could not rule. But such figures also had to learn that the Carolingians were a royal dynasty.

Great magnates brought resources that rulers needed and rulers rewarded their services well and offered further opportunities to enhance their resources and prominence. Thus, abbot Fulrad of St-Denis served Pippin well in maintaining relations with Rome, as we have seen. As an aristocrat with properties in Alsace and Alemannia, Fulrad helped bind these regions to the Carolingians and his service brought him useful contacts with Pippin's right-hand man in Alemannia, count Ruthard. Fulrad saw that his abbey profited from this; for example, the property of the rebel Wulfoad ended up in the hands of St-Denis. But profits that Fulrad and Ruthard made in Alemannia came at the expense of some local landholders there.[135] The complex balance of reward, service and self-interest (royal as well as aristocratic) meant that the aristocracy was not monolithic. Nor was it merely an instrument in the hands of the Carolingian ruler. As Matthew Innes has observed, this period saw local elites bound into a 'pyramidal' system connected to the centre via patrons such as Fulrad and Ruthard rather than the imposing of a network of office-holding counts 'directly responsible to the king for their individual counties'. Such developments came later, in the reigns of Charlemagne and Louis the Pious.[136]

In such a world, Pippin's becoming king was only one stage in the work of building the special status of the new dynasty. We can see something of his work and the resulting legacy to his successors of achievement and endless labour to maintain it in his patronage of two dynastically important monasteries. One of them lay in territory that the Carolingians had to win over while the other lay in their own heartlands but the dynasty had to cultivate both. These abbeys are St-Denis and Prüm; Pippin's relationship with them illuminates Carolingian royalty.

Among the great saints who brooded, undead and watchful, over the kingdom of the Franks, few were more important to the Merovingians than St Denis, the 'special patron' of the kings, as a series of royal charters put it. To desecrate the shrine of so powerful a saint was to bring misfortune on the kingdom and guarantee a blasted historical reputation for any king foolish enough to commit such an act.[137] Occupying as it did a key position in an economically active area, the great abbey offered material, political and spiritual resources that could still serve grateful Merovingian rulers of Neustria. As Charles Martel struggled to assert his own authority after the death of his father in 714, the Merovingian Chilperic II lavished privileges and grants on the abbey, channelling resources from as far away as Marseille into its coffers. The moving power behind such grants was the Neustrian mayor of the palace, Charles Martel's enemy, but it was the king's voice in the charters that requested prayers for the 'stability of our kingdom'.[138]

It is thus unsurprising to see that Charles took particular care of St-Denis as his authority in the west grew after his second victory over Chilperic in 718. He appointed his nephew Hugo as abbot who was succeeded in the mid-720s by a loyal follower of Charles's family, Godebaldus. Charles himself was generous to the abbey, deployed one of its monks as his envoy to the pope in 739, and made a grant to it on his deathbed and was buried there.[139]

Charles's decision to have his young son Pippin educated in this Merovingian centre some time in the 720s was a significant act of a dynast. Presumably, Charles wanted that education to be a fitting one for a future ruler. But the monks would also be educated. They were to see Pippin learning to be a ruler and they would grasp the dynastic fact of this seven-year-old's presence in St Denis. Here the servants of the 'special patron' of the Merovingian kings attended upon the young son of the new ruler; they nourished the future of what was to be a new dynasty. And the education was mutual. Some forty years later, Pippin could still recall his childhood experience of the rhythm of the life of the abbey, a memory that led him to judge a case in the abbey's favour.[140]

Cultivating this great abbey meant that its saint would help Pippin and his family in the heavenly realm but there was also an earthly dimension. As we have seen, the abbey had a close association with the Merovingians, and it did not sit in a geographical or social void; local aristocrats established close and lasting links with it.[141] The Carolingians had to work hard to insert themselves here in this important Neustrian site. The burial of Charles Martel in the abbey choir near the altar was a declaration of dynastic intent. There was an even clearer dynastic declaration on the very eve of Pippin's king-making, when his charter of restoration for the abbey proclaimed that St Denis was now his 'special patron', and that the abbey was to pray for Pippin and his sons as well as for the stability of the kingdom of the Franks; this was presumably part of the preparations for the king-making.[142] As abbot of St-Denis Fulrad served Pippin and his line well, taking charge of the palace chapel, travelling as envoy to Rome, negotiating episcopal appointments and maintaining useful links with Alsace and Alemannia, while the fate of Wulfoald and his property around Verdun shows something of how Pippin and Fulrad worked with each other.[143]

The fact that so much of our surviving evidence for the period comes from St-Denis may raise suspicions that our perspective is skewed but this evidence itself lets us see that in the relationship with this abbey Pippin could perform his royalty to a politically important audience. In 753, Pippin confirmed a variety of privileges for the abbey in a charter that placed him in a series of Merovingian rulers but which also included his ancestor Grimoald II (d.714), whom the monks of St-Denis had resisted, as well as referring to Charles Martel. Pippin requested prayers for the stability of the kingdom of the Franks as well as for himself and for his sons who were thus spotlit as the dynastic future of that kingdom on the eve of the anointing ceremonies of 754.[144] Members of the Frankish nobility were witnesses to all this. The charter names some fifteen 'faithful men' who had judged in St-Denis's favour and who by virtue of their involvement in this case formed the audience for the articulation of dynastic past, present and future. Several of these men featured in other transactions of Pippin with the abbey, including the time before he became king. Such activities fostered aristocratic group identity as followers of Pippin and taught aristocrats the meaning of Pippin's new royal and dynastic status. They could see that the new dynasty was to be enfolded in the great saint's benevolence.[145] St-Denis's preservation of original documents lets us see that humdrum land transactions involving landowners with no particular closeness to Pippin were now dated by the years of the Carolingian king.[146]

These activities – hearing disputes, making judgements, writing documents – were routine but that is precisely their importance. It was through taking part in such activities that people learned the nature of the Carolingian dynastic status that they were constructing. But St-Denis was also a site of more self-consciously symbolic acts of patronage that honoured God and his saints while visibly demonstrating Carolingian royal status. Pippin showered land and treasure on the abbey. The complexity of the relationship of textual and archaeological evidence is a problem in interpreting building activities at St-Denis in this period. Nonetheless it is clear that rebuilding of the abbey began under Pippin, was completed under his sons and resulted in a substantial basilica, of some sixty metres length, but lavishly decorated and above the doors adorned in silver and gold an inscription hailed the efforts of the royal patrons: Dagobert, Pippin, Charlemagne and Carloman.[147] The new dynasty thus had itself associated with the great patron of the abbey from the old dynasty.

When Pippin's final illness came upon him, he struggled to the sacred sites of the realm, praying anxiously at St-Martin's Tours, showering clergy and paupers with gifts as a Christian king should, but he then travelled to St-Denis to die there.[148] His father Charles Martel was buried there but Pippin was a king and his tomb now made a new royal dynasty present at the abbey and this gave Charles Martel a certain retrospective royal quality. Charles Martel, Pippin and Bertrada were all buried at St-Denis and their tombs would seem to have been decorated with their images or sculptures, to judge from an inscription for St-Denis written after 800 which refers to 'images of kings'.[149] Death recruited Pippin and his wife into further dynastic service. As royal dead, they repaired ruptures of the past, bringing Charles Martel within the royal aura of the new dynasty in the sacred place of the old one, and of the present, by taking up permanent resident in this important landscape and thus providing visible ancestral legitimation for their sons and descendants.

One of the important audiences for all this was the Carolingian royal line itself. Pippin's sons had to learn that they were the sons of a king. Pippin also took care to patronize another abbey in this region, St-Germain, and presided over a great ceremony in 755 there when the saint's body was ceremonially placed in a new tomb. The young Charlemagne was present and later in his life he recalled this event, not least because he had lost a tooth while playing there. As Janet Nelson has observed, Charlemagne's memory is one of shared experience of himself, his father and the attending Frankish aristocracy in their devotion to the saint.[150] Charlemagne would surely also have retained some memories of the great ceremonies at St-Denis in 754 in which he and his brother played leading roles as children. It is surely Carolingian house tradition, at once exalted and humble in its association with the great saint, that we can see in a remarkable letter written by Pippin's grandson, the emperor Louis the Pious in 835, some eighty years after Pope Stephen's visit. There seems little reason to doubt that Louis had been told some of this by Charlemagne himself. Other people, such as the abbot of St-Denis, had doubtless also told Louis about the abbey. In a flush of gratitude for his restoration after the crisis of 833–4 (see Chapter 5), Louis's devotion to the saint reached new heights and he wrote to the abbot asking him to gather material on the saint. His letter preserves 'the authentic voice' of a Carolingian ruler and what we hear in this voice is a tone of wondering pride as Louis recounts the benefits showered on his dynasty by its connection with the saint. Among these benefits was his dynasty's rise to power. His mind ranged over the dynasty's potent connection with the saint in his abbey, recalling the precise location of the burial there of his grandfather Pippin III, evoking the papal-royal ceremonies of 754. Louis had been well schooled in his family's sense of awe at the role of St Denis in the making of the new royal dynasty.[151]

Our second example, the great abbey of Prüm, was a different case as it did not have associations with the Merovingians. Unlike St-Denis, this was a Carolingian family monastery that helped in the expressing of the new royal status of that family. Prüm lay in the east, in the Ardennes, where the Carolingian family held sway. But that family did not hold exclusive dominance and Prüm was not in fact an original Carolingian foundation. It was established in 721 by the grandmother and father of Bertrada, Pippin's wife, and this should remind us of the indispensable support and alliance provided by members of the aristocracy for Pippin and his house, as well as the role of women here.[152] Nonetheless, Prüm stood in a central zone of Carolingian power and authority; it did not need to be won over from another allegiance or from a non-Carolingian history; it did not lie in a peripheral region. But successful structures of power and authority do not neglect their centres; quite the reverse. Pippin lavished attention and property on the abbey soon after he became king, taking care to associate Bertrada with his generosity. In 762, he and his wife showered Prüm with more largesse, ensuring that it was endowed with rich estates but also with an awesome collection of holy relics, including the very sandals of Christ. Charlemagne recalled his parents as having effectively re-founded the abbey.[153]

The donation of 762 and its context repay examination.[154] In 762, Pippin and the Franks, for the third year running, had been campaigning in the south-west, attempting to impose their authority on duke Waifar of Aquitaine. This year Pippin, in a campaign on a rather grander scale than usual, gained a spectacular success, with an impressed contemporary observing how he took the town of Bourges after an elaborate siege, gathered up prisoners and swept them back to Francia while their wives and children were compelled to trudge northwards on foot. Pippin's return north had the characteristics of a triumphal procession. Accompanied by prisoners, he and the booty-laden army of the Frank returned home under the guidance of Christ.[155] The prayers and hopes of the Franks and the successor of St Peter in Rome for victories had been answered, and Pippin's great donation to Prüm was a thank-offering to the God of battles.[156]

The donation, as revealed in the royal diploma, is intensely familial. Pippin refers to estates which he recalls being given to him by his father Charles Martel just as he refers to estates given to his wife Bertrada by her father Heribert. In fact, the diploma's reference to the royal couple's holdings reveals that they shared a common ancestor. Pippin, together with Bertrada, was making grants from their property. The donation was intended to be for the benefit of the soul of Pippin, his wife and their heirs. A striking feature of the document is that, unlike typical royal charters, it has a witness-list, and the now-mature royal sons Charlemagne and Carloman (who had been on the Aquitaine campaign) were among those named as consenting. Normally, the word and will of the king were sufficient and it was only 'private' charters that needed the authentication that witnesses provided, making the 762 document anomalous, but this may reflect its deep familial essence.[157]

It is undoubtedly a royal document. It follows the great victory. In its (re-) founding and dedicating of a great house and its bringing donations together, the charter reflects an intensely religious ceremony characteristic of Christian rulership and is thus, in Herbert Zielinski's words, 'an act of state representation'.[158] The document is shot through with the imagery of Christian rulership and gives an impression of Pippin self-consciously reflecting on his kingship:

> And since it is clear to us that divine providence has anointed [us] to the throne of the kingdom, it is right to exercise these things in God's name, in so far as we may be able to follow the grace and will of the most high. And since kings reign from God and he has entrusted nations and realms to us.[159]

It would appear that among those most impressed by the ceremonies of 751–4 was Pippin himself.

Kings of course did not write their own charters any more than most modern politicians write their own speeches. But we can surely catch their voices and thus something of their views in such charters, even if the elaboration of these views in the stylized Latin of charters stems from the royal entourage. The man who composed the charter was Baddilo, one of the chief ideologues, for want of a better phrase, of the reign. He can be found in Pippin's entourage from 757 onwards and is responsible for several of Pippin's charters as well as for a remarkable series of documents from Pippin's reign. These include, as well as the Prüm charter, the prologue to the proceedings of the synod of Ver and the well-known prologue to the ancient Frankish law-code, *Lex Salica*, re-issued by Pippin in 763/4. This famous text does not celebrate Pippin himself at all but glories in the splendid qualities of the Franks, devoted Christians and fierce warriors. Traditional Frankish law was the possession of all the Franks, not just their king, and so there was no occasion to exalt Pippin here.[160] Nonetheless, this text's references to the Franks as devoted cultists of the Christian martyrs may recall Pippin's own lavish granting of sacred relics of the saints to the great house abbey of Prüm.

For all the dynastic character of the Prüm charter it too, like the prologue to *Lex Salica*, was concerned with the community of the Franks. Pippin was no autocrat; he was king of the Franks (*rex Francorum*) as his charters, including this 762 charter, proclaimed. He did not speak into a void. Lying behind this document was a public ceremony, and, if it was just the royal entourage that received its message, that was an audience that counted. The list of witnesses lets us see the royal family together with aristocrats and bishops present as a group understanding Prüm as a holy place patronized by a victorious king and his family whose devotion would call forth benefits from it (dynastic prayers). The twenty witnesses were now part of the new world of Carolingian royalty. Several of them had been in Pippin's service since at least 753 and could probably remember a time when he was not king.[161] Let us take two of these witnesses, a bishop and a secular aristocrat, as examples of the transforming of the aristocracy into followers of a Carolingian king.

Bishop Gauziolenus of Le Mans belonged to a family which had thrown its weight behind Charles Martel in his struggle to control the west of the Frankish realm; in fact, Gauziolenus's grip on Le Mans dated back to the 720s. At some stage, possibly around the time of Pippin's coronation in 751, he may have wobbled in his loyalties and backed Grifo, triggering a harsh re-action from Pippin.[162] The trouble caused by this prominent figure shows how tricky the situation was for Pippin in 751 and reminds us once again that the coronation was a gamble. But bishop Gauziolenus accepted Pippin's rule. He had backed the Carolingians since the 720s and had thus seen them hold power under the mantle of Merovingian kings and then go on to depose the last of them in 751. A series of documents preserved in a dossier of the church of Le Mans shows how these changes were quietly tracked in the titles and dating formulas used to record everyday transactions. In them Gauziolenus and his contemporaries can be seen to move from a world where legal and administrative documents were suffused with references to Merovingian ancestors and dated by Merovingian regnal years to one where the king, for the first time in Frankish history, bore the name Pippin. Pippin may have had to crack down hard on Gauziolenus in 751–2 but, on the important, if less dramatic, level of property rights and claims, the transition to a Carolingian royal authority can be seen to have gone smoothly in the far west of the realm, a region remote from Pippin's traditional stamping-ground.[163]

The invoking of Pippin's name and dates in such documents did not merely reflect his authority; it helped disseminate and maintain it. To revert to the political level, Gauziolenus's presence among the witnesses of the 762 Prüm charter shows his firm commitment to Pippin and his line. Gauziolenus was of a generation that could remember a time, not just when the Carolingians were not even kings, but when they had to struggle against stubbornly uncompliant Merovingians backed by other formidable mayors of the palace.[164] Pippin had to convince such members of the aristocracy that he and his line were authentically royal and his fanfare of 762 affirming his own kingly status and the royalty of his dynasty would speak eloquently to such a man. Gauziolenus lived to see Pippin's sons succeed.[165] Six of the eight bishops in the 762 charter also appear in the prayer bond of Attigny (762) which expressed and helped create a united Frankish episcopal identity as the Prüm ceremony also did, but with a clearer stress on serving the new dynasty.[166]

The twelve lay aristocrats who appear in the charter (five of whom also appear in Pippin's 753 charter for St-Denis) would also have been exposed to Pippin's self-representation as generous donor to God's house in the tradition of Moses and Solomon as well as to the dynastic significance of the prayers for the king, his wife and his children, all in attendance.[167] They were not simple warriors, and, after all, Pippin's victories in Aquitaine lay behind his great offering to Prüm.[168] Perhaps some of them had served in that campaign. They are a mixed bunch, including prominent magnates and humbler figures but here they could all view and understand themselves in their relationship to the new dynasty. They did not thus lose their own identity and become only Pippin's faithful men. It was precisely their own identity, that is, resources of property and familial power that made them attractive to Pippin, just as he could offer them something on their own ground. Our example here, count Welantus/Wegelenzo, illustrates this very well, thanks to the work of Matthew Innes. Welantus was an aristocratic landowner in the Rhineland and, with two others (one of whom, Baugulf, was also listed in Pippin's charter), had given land to Pippin who had then granted it to Prüm in that very charter. Welantus, his son Warin and Baugulf, also a member of their family, all appeared in Pippin's charter and thus witnessed how what had been their land was now connected to the royal abbey. It was the local presence and connections of Welantus and his son Warin in the Rhineland that made them so useful to Pippin, while royal granting of an estate to them helped them to enhance that local eminence. The fact that Welantus's son eventually lost this royal estate to his kinsman Baugulf shows how kings could go on to mould these local connections for their own ends.[169]

Connections with the king gave aristocrats such as these broader horizons than their local powerbases. The gaze of such aristocrats was directed to the dynasty and thus to a Carolingian future. This was the significance of the presence of Bertrada (whose own property was important for Prüm) and the two royal sons. Prüm itself was to remain as a permanent place in the landscape radiating royalness, educating its inmates on royalness and weaving local landowners into a royal monastic web.[170]

But this Prüm grant was only one of Pippin's activities that made his sons present in the political landscape and thus focused aristocratic minds on a Carolingian future. In 760, he had taken the abbey of St. Calais in the diocese of Le Mans under his protection and also associated his son Charlemagne with this. Pippin was extending his reach into the west of Neustria, an area that needed to be secured and Charlemagne was to play a role in this. He was now twelve and mature enough to be deployed here. Pippin urged the monks to pray for the stability of the kingdom for himself and for Charlemagne and it may be that Pippin was thus seeking to establish his son there as ruler.[171] The charter does not refer to Charlemagne as king, but the Merovingian-era formula on which it is based has the king allocating the duty of protection for the monastery to the mayor of the palace. Pippin's diploma obviously makes no reference to the mayor; instead the duty of protection is allocated to the king's son and the whole flavour of this transaction thus becomes dynastic.[172] Charlemagne took part in the Aquitaine campaign of 761; this would have given him military experience but would also have displayed him to the aristocracy and army as leader of the future.[173] Both sons were displayed as such in the Prüm grant of 762 as we have seen.

Thus, all actors in Francia learned their parts. The new royal line was to stretch into the future. Prayers and blessings found in the sacramentary of Gellone, produced 790–800 but surely containing texts earlier than that date, call for a royal successor from the king's loins, for the royal seed to flourish, prayers that were to be repeated in the great benediction for royal inauguration, 'Look down, omnipotent God (*Prospice*)', written down in 800.[174] This was the liturgical expression of the meaning of the ceremonies that had taken place in 751 and 754: Pippin, his wife and his sons were raised up as a new dynasty, for whose continuation God was to be beseeched.

The chronicle of Childebrand-Nibelung gives a glowing account of the end of Pippin's reign: the king's military triumphs in Aquitaine, his pious donations to the great churches of the realm, a death-bed at St-Denis attended by the magnates of the Franks who approved harmonious division of the realm between two royal sons while their royal mother looked on.[175] Essentially this is a true picture, though we may speculate, as contemporaries doubtless did, about tensions between the sons. We may also wonder why the chronicler failed to get the symbolically important date of the young kings' coronation right, another troubling indication of contemporary failure to perceive all the import of ritual.[176] But much of Pippin's effort is invisible here and that is precisely its significance. Only the result, the achievement is represented: the new natural political order. St-Denis appears as the burial site of the new dynasty; there is no reference to the old one. Pippin, his wife and sons appear as the new dynasty. Nibelung and his father Childebrand had accepted their status as prominent aristocratic supporters of Pippin, members of the royal kin, but safely confined (from Pippin's point of view) to branch-line status. More dangerous members of the family, Pippin's brother Carloman and nephew Drogo, had died or vanished. His troublesome brother Grifo had been long dead. His other brothers, Remedius and Jerome, had held ecclesiastical office under him and served him as king. He had come close to seeing his daughter Gisela marrying a Byzantine emperor but when that had fallen through he did not let her marry a Frankish aristocrat; women could carry Carolingian blood, as Pippin's fury over his sister's marriage to the duke of Bavaria showed and that blood was to be rationed.[177] But Carolingian blood was to be reproduced; he had arranged for his sons to marry (see next chapter). He had overthrown an ancient dynasty and created a new one. But this was only a start.

3

A house and its head: The reign of Charlemagne 768–814

Casting Charlemagne's shadow

The reign of Charlemagne brought about a massive extension of the Frankish realm and of Carolingian royal authority. Charlemagne did not do all this on his own but he riveted people's attention. Before he was born, his existence was prayed for; after his death, he haunted people's dream visions. In between, he came to dominate western Europe, travelling across more of that area than any other ruler until Napoleon.[1] These journeys were not always easy; his army was badly mauled in its retreat from Spain in 778, an event so shameful that some contemporaries flinched from mentioning it. More often, however, contemporaries marvelled at their ruler's travelling unopposed on open roads through beaten Saxony, or penetrating the fearsome Alpine landscape to conquer Italy, or rushing northward in his sixties to challenge an aggressive Danish king. The fact that the latter was unable even to journey to confront Charlemagne merely highlighted Charlemagne's ubiquitous energy and menace.[2]

Of course, he did not travel alone. The ruler's wars mobilized hundreds of men to journey on his service from the Rhine to the Elbe, from the Loire to the Pyrenees, while his victories forced hostages and captives to tramp long distances into Francia.[3] But Charlemagne's presence was felt not only on the ground. He was also in people's minds. The Anglo-Saxon scholar Alcuin knew better than anyone how irresistible was the gravitational pull of the king's presence and patronage; in England, a holy man had foretold that he would serve Charlemagne.[4] Paradoxically, it is because Alcuin spent so much time away from Charlemagne's palace that he wrote so many of his letters, requesting and transmitting news about the ruler through his own impressive network of friends. They are a particular source from a particular time, and the examples here come after Charlemagne had been ruling for a quarter of a century, but they are generally illuminating on how a Carolingian royal aura was maintained across the vast realm.

Alcuin's testimony is exceptional in its richness, but his experiences were not unique. Charlemagne's movements dictated others'. If the king was away harassing Saxons, Alcuin could not reach him for the necessary permission to travel to York. Advance knowledge of meeting the king, or uncertainty over his whereabouts in the coming year (in which of his many palaces would he spend the winter?) shaped the year for Alcuin and his correspondents.[5] Despite such uncertainties, key features loomed up clearly enough: people knew that the king travelled, but this was balanced by an understanding of 'palace' as an institution, a site and focus of specifically royal authority. When Alcuin referred to the 'whole palace' being in a good mood, to 'the young men of the palace' and to the 'Davidian palace' (using the courtly nickname of Charlemagne, David being the glorious biblical king of Israel), he meant any and every palace. The palace was specific (e.g. Aachen) and abstract; people understood and experienced it as a community, centred round the ruler; the palace was a place and a form of royal rule.[6] Charlemagne's palace thus loomed as large in the minds of the elite as it did in the landscape. All these enquiries about itinerary, location, etc., reveal the existence of networks of communication. Alcuin was a very active agent in such networks and continued to be so while he was actually in the palace. Information and news came to it and radiated out from it. While at Aachen, in 796 Alcuin was able to send word to the archbishop of Salzburg about a royal decision on Salzburg's properties.[7]

The messages that Alcuin sent through such networks were social acts. He transmitted gifts as well as news, sometimes on very grand scale, as in his 796 letter in Charlemagne's name to King Offa in England accompanying ostentatious gifts from the Avar treasure. Sometimes the gifts were more intimate, as, for example, the gold arm rings sent on by Alcuin to a bishop in Italy from queen Liutgard, or the cloak sent to Alcuin himself by Gisela.[8] Liutgard was Charlemagne's wife and Gisela was his sister; for Alcuin and others, the palace and kingdom were populated by many bearers of Carolingian-ness, not just the king. Being Carolingian made such women special. Alcuin took care to stay in contact with Carolingian women, who had inherited the 'earthly nobility' of high birth, as well as with women who married into the royal family, as in a letter to Liutgard of 794, one that was preserved as part of a group of royal family letters.[9] Alcuin also looked outward, telling one count to remember to be 'faithful to the lords that God has given you', these lords being Charlemagne and his son Louis.[10]

Alcuin was not simply a sycophant or paid mouthpiece for Carolingian rule. His letters cover a wide range of topics and he was more than a letter writer; he was intensely concerned to secure Christian belief and culture in a dangerous world. Royal authority was valuable because it promised help. In fact Alcuin could be critical of royal decisions when they undermined Christian goals, as in his uneasy reflections on the counter-productive harshness of wars of conversion against Saxons and Avars. And he took action, urging friends, including the lay aristocrat Megenfrid, to advise the king to change his ways here.[11] In 801, he wrote to the newly imperial Charlemagne criticizing his decision to attack Benevento, a campaign involving his son Pippin, but he also lamented the death in that campaign of Megenfrid, whom he described as 'your faithful man (*fidelis*) and our most dear friend'. In distant Tours, Alcuin was receiving news from Italy, news that prompted him to expressions of community, one in which the king was lord; Alcuin was Megenfrid's friend but the king was his master.[12]

Alcuin's letters reveal a self-conscious Christian elite who watched the king's movements and whom the king drew to him; encounters took place in assemblies and palaces which acted as nodal points in networks of communication that were rooted in the authority of kingship gripped by one special family. These letters are not so much a sign that the Carolingians had arrived so much as evidence of the work, by the Carolingians and their followers, that constructed Carolingian royalty. This chapter's focus is on some aspects of that work rather than a comprehensive survey of the reign. The struggles for status and power that are the focus of this book tended to affect only an elite to any depth, though ripples from such struggles, and actions of the king's rule, could indeed touch a wider society. There is not, however, space to cover such topics. The wonderful case of the sly duke John in Istria who passed off as his own the horses dutifully yielded up to the distant Charlemagne by his trustingly faithful men cannot detain us, even with its lessons about communication between ruler and regions, and about justice, one of the key functions of rulership.[13] Nor will I do more than touch on the intense movement of renewal of Christian culture that was in many ways what Carolingian rulership was actually for and which was expressed with supremely severe clarity under Charlemagne in the *General Warning* of 789.[14] Rather, this chapter seeks to explore some of the ways in which Charlemagne's reign saw a deepening of the dynastic rule of the new royal family and how that process resulted in problems stemming from its very success: insoluble conflict over status and claims within that family itself. Like his father, though on a vaster scale, Charlemagne was aware of the need to keep building the dynasty. Neither he nor his contemporaries could know that he was the legendary Charlemagne.[15]

He and they were aware, however, that they had achieved extraordinary things. One of the most striking features of the reign, for them and us, was the massive expansion of territory under Frankish control. Einhard proudly recorded the inscription on Charlemagne's tomb in Aachen: 'he gloriously increased the kingdom of the Franks'.[16] In establishing his power in newly subjected lands, Charlemagne deployed the tactics of patronage and punishment of any intelligent ruler. Thus, after conquering the Lombard kingdom of Italy in 774 he shrewdly appointed a Lombard as duke of Friuli and, with equal shrewdness, killed him when he revolted a year or so later.[17] But he was also very conscious of the need to define, communicate and maintain that authority as legitimate as well as fearsome. After some time and consideration, he added the title 'king of the Lombards' to his Frankish title, acknowledging the status of the Lombards as a people, that is, as a political group, but also trying to cancel any hopes of restoration of a Lombard line. While Lombard kingship was not impregnated with dynasticism as Frankish kingship was, it mattered that a son of the conquered king had escaped to Constantinople. The *Royal Frankish Annals*' account of this as marking his descent into political twilight is far from the truth; he was able to cause trouble when he popped up in Lombardy a decade and a half later, an event that shows the importance of the annals' silence and of the Lombard fanfare of Charlemagne's new royal title.[18] As part of his settlement with the duchy of Benevento in southern Italy in 788, Charlemagne insisted on having his name on the coins and charters issued by the duke, just as the latter rejected the Carolingianization of his coinage when he turned against Charlemagne in 791; the dukes of Benevento had a fine sense of their own hereditary glory. When rumours reached Charlemagne that the Lombard abbot of San Vincenzo al Volturno had snapped in 783 and, scorning the Franks, had refused to take part in his community's prayers for Charlemagne and his offspring, alarm bells went off and the ruler insisted on investigation. Such failings of the norm always had to be policed.[19]

The more homespun world of the Saxons may have lacked the evolved media of coinage and liturgy but they also experienced the self-conscious articulation of new and violently intrusive royal authority. In 777, Charlemagne boldly transplanted the Franks' annual assembly to Saxon territory, at Paderborn, where he received submission from groups of prominent Saxons whose baptism as Christians displayed Charlemagne's Christian lordship, even as the arrival of Arab envoys from Spain broadcast to the assembled Franks the military reputation of their king and themselves. Imposing buildings, a fortified palace complex and church, were to imprint Frankish power and Carolingian royalty on this landscape; it was to be grandly named as Charlestown (*urbs Karoli*) and Saxons swore fidelity not only to Charlemagne but to his sons, if we can believe the retrospective annals. The Saxons' future was to be Carolingian and Frankish.[20]

Of course, such actions were not always successful. The opportunistic intervention in Spain led to defeat in 778 while the Saxons took advantage of the king's absence to devastate Paderborn. But effort continued; Charlemagne held the assembly at Paderborn again in 782 and a majestic palace and church did duly rise up there.[21] It is difficult to believe that these wars were part of a master-plan rather than opportunistic pursuit of what had been traditional Frankish interests. The king, like many of his aristocratic followers such as William (of Gellone) and Witiza, was of a generation that grew up while Pippin was continuing Charles Martel's work to reassert Frankish hegemony over a wide area. But the mastering of these territories was not simply achieved through the brutal simplicity of war. Charlemagne took care to stage his mastery. Particular pressures played on him. From 771 to 774, the Lombard king held a potential ace in the form of Carolingian royal children, Charlemagne's nephews, who had fled to him (see below and chapter on children). The duke of Bavaria was not only a potent warrior and patron of Christian culture whose presence challenged the Frankish ruler; he was Charlemagne's cousin and the failure of Charlemagne's father and uncle to prevent Tassilo's father from possessing a Carolingian woman haunted the dynasty. Charlemagne broke the duke of Bavaria in 788 through a spectacular mix of hard and soft power, mobilizing armies against him and subjecting him to a great show-trial in palatial Ingelheim, before forcing him to vanish into the political non-being of Christian penance, a penance that reflected the light of righteous Christian order that bathed the rule of Charlemagne.[22]

The great wars of conquest were won neither by Charlemagne on his own nor for his exclusive benefit. But they quickly transformed the entire political landscape of western Europe by massively extending the reach of the royal family. Previously, disgruntled Franks who had lost out in competitions for power and status could seek consolation in foreign courts, as Charlemagne's uncle Grifo had done in the previous generation in Aquitaine, Bavaria and Lombardy. After Charlemagne's brother Carloman died in 771, the Lombard king in Italy had sheltered dangerous exiles who escaped from the wreckage of Carloman's court.[23] All these exits were closed by Charlemagne who now cast a much longer shadow than any of his predecessors and most of his successors. Charlemagne's palace became the only game in town.

Alternatives now became Carolingian spaces. In 781, Charlemagne's sons Louis and Pippin were proclaimed as kings of Aquitaine and Italy, respectively. This king-making took place in Rome where the pope anointed the sons as kings. Dazzling ceremonies centred on this family. Charlemagne's daughter Rotrud was also publicly betrothed here to Constantine, the eastern emperor. And these were not simply political rituals; these were religious events. The boy Carloman was baptized by the pope with his name being changed to Pippin; the Godescalc Evangelistary, the magnificent holy book commissioned by his royal parents, survives as a remnant of the doubtless spectacular events of this social and Christian ritual. On his return journey to Francia, Charlemagne had his daughter Gisela baptized by the archbishop of Milan.[24] Pippin was four, Louis was three, Gisela was a wee baby while Rotrud was about six. These children had travelled with the king and his fertile wife so that their youthful presence could proclaim to their escorts and audience just how special this family was. Who else's children would get a Roman holiday like this? Gathered in the holy city of Rome, the watching aristocrats saw the successor of St Peter once again anoint young Carolingians as kings just as in 754. But this time, the ceremonies took place far from Francia and touched non-Frankish kingdoms. The horizons of that aristocracy had widened and the proclamation of children as kings opened up opportunities for that aristocracy as governors. But these new horizons were to be filled with Carolingians.

If Charlemagne and his family filled space, they also annexed time. Amongst the elaborate mechanisms deployed against Tassilo of Bavaria in 788 was the charge that he had been a disloyal vassal to his masters, Charlemagne and his royal father. This case was fully written up as a key part of a larger historical narrative (and prosecution dossier?) in a text known to us as the *Royal Frankish Annals*, the 'original' version of which was compiled in court circles around the time of Tassilo's fall. Court circles may here include such loyalist centres as the abbey of St-Denis. This text survives in various versions, none of which is the actual original but that term is used to distinguish earlier versions of the text from a revised version compiled later, possibly as late as 829. This widely disseminated historical narrative is part of an extraordinary flowering of historical writing in Charlemagne's reign and later, most of which provides a legitimating narrative of Carolingian and Frankish power.[25]

It is still not entirely clear how such writing was composed and compiled, and in classifying it as a legitimating historical narrative we may sometimes simplify it. It is not propaganda in the modern sense.[26] This is not least because, for all the dissemination of such (Latin) texts, they did not act as modern mass media do. Perhaps more people witnessed Charlemagne and his family at an assembly, or splashed in the baths of Aachen with the king, than read the texts that we as historians value so highly. Nor did contemporaries simply read these texts passively, in hypnotized thrall to their contents; they could rework them, treat them creatively.[27] Carolingian glory remained undimmed in such reworkings, as it did even in history writings that criticized individual rulers but some history writings preserve perspectives that are more various than the court's (see below on the Hardard revolt). Such writing was not quite as monolithic as it appears.

Some of this writing insists so strongly on the Carolingian nature of past Frankish history that it simultaneously reveals the triumph of the dynasty – even the past was subject to it – alongside an inability ever to declare the work of telling that tale of triumph as safely achieved. Even after the imperial coronation of Charlemagne in 800, after the building of the magnificent palace complex of Aachen, after the sensational winning of the Avar treasures, some people still had to work to give Carolingian greatness deeper historical roots than it actually had. Compiled around 805, the so-called *Earlier Annals of Metz* celebrate the Franks but focus on their leaders, bringing the curtain up in the 680s, not so much on the collectivity of the Franks, but on the glorious individual figure of Pippin II, bearer of a name that stretched even further back into a projected magnificent Carolingian past as it had been borne by his grandfather, source of the name and of power. Pippin was also strong in the virtues of the biblical David and was master of the Franks 'whom his glorious father had fostered and formerly elevated with highly honoured positions'. The past had to have been like that because the present had to be like that.[28]

Imposing Carolingian authority on non-Frankish areas such as Lombardy and Bavaria called for special measures, but rulers could not take for granted control over their own lands and their own aristocracies. They thus had to monitor the foundations of royal authority. Material resources were of fundamental importance here. Tim Reuter's work has ensured that the best known resource for the ruler is plunder and treasure, acquired through conquest and domination and artfully distributed amongst an acquisitive aristocracy to maintain its loyalty. External and internal domination were bound together.[29] Much of Reuter's picture remains attractive. Contemporaries marvelled at Charlemagne's snatching of the Lombard treasure and were thrilled at the spectacular arrival at court of the massive treasure plundered in the Avar campaigns: 'Human memory cannot record any war against the Franks that left them richer', according to Einhard who may well have been at Aachen when the treasure arrived there in many wagons. We ourselves can still gaze at examples of this treasure whose display in the capitals of Austria and Hungary has touched on modern political sensitivities.[30]

Nonetheless, Reuter gives only a partial account of the wars or indeed of rulers' resources and his thesis awaits the rigorous testing that he himself would have wanted. Land was the basis of wealth in this world; distribution of office was a more potent tool of royal patronage than distribution of treasure; safeguarding an economically important artery such as the Rhine was an important motivation for the Franks' attacks on the Saxons. The glitter of treasure was only one element in patterns of competitive production and consumption and thus should not completely mesmerize us. The Frankish weapons that won treasure and which were themselves precious heirlooms depended on the work of iron production.[31] The motivations of Frankish warriors were complex, as was the organizing of armies, and the immense social phenomenon of these wars of conquest still needs fuller investigation.[32] The strains of the endless Saxon wars created dangerous tensions for Charlemagne, as we shall see.

The granting and circulating of office and land were the real fuel for maintenance of power relations between ruler and aristocrats. The ability to award offices such as countships which brought profit and honour to their holder, as their generic term *honores* suggests, gave the ruler real powers of patronage.[33] As royal lords in an overwhelmingly rural world, rulers paid attention to their own resources. Significant documentation on royal estate management in Charlemagne's reign reveals royal concerns to maximize income from estates and to tighten control over the stewards in charge of them. This does not mean that Charlemagne had an 'economic policy'; it would be anachronistic to think of the Carolingians in such terms. But he was self-conscious about managing his resources, as the estate documents show, and as a ruler he knew that such resources underpinned his power. These documents may date from the 790s when he was building the extraordinary palace at Aachen, an expensive deployment of royal resources in construction and maintenance.[34]

Kings were not just canny landlords; their resource management had to have a political dimension in its maintaining good relations between them and their aristocrats. Charlemagne's instructions to his son Louis in the 790s on the artful management of estates recommended combining prudence with generosity to the magnates so that Louis might preserve royal honour without wasting royal substance. Louis was to learn how to maintain royal palaces without excessively burdening the local population. That all this was worthy of comment in a later biography of Louis shows that it was understood as a facet of royal wisdom.[35]

True royal wisdom knew that the unique distinctiveness of royal authority also had to be maintained and monitored within the realm, where it seemed a 'natural' part of the political landscape, as much as with the coinage in distant Benevento mentioned above. This had a fundamental impact on Frankish society at large. In 793/4, Charlemagne reformed the coinage, introducing larger, heavier coins. This was part of the ruler's office to ensure that weights and measures were fair and accurate for his people across his realm.[36] But this was also an assertion and demonstration of royal authority in a very specific way. Charlemagne proclaimed before a large audience in Frankfurt that the new coinage was to bear 'the monogram of our name', and it was so. The name Charles, with all its aura of royal personality, which had appeared on the old coins also appeared on the new coins which circulated in vast numbers across the realm, though they were not ubiquitous. Penalties for refusing the new coinage were stiff and evidence from coin-hoards shows that the new coins did effectively replace the old; contemporaries now casually referred to the weight and value of 'the new coinage of the king' when trying to indicate the scale of treasure.[37] While these new coins now identified Charlemagne as 'king of the Franks', and Ildar Garipzanov is surely right to stress this element as a recognition of the Frankish source of royal power, I myself would place more weight on the prominence of the royal name. It now monopolized the coinage in contrast to the earlier part of the reign when coins sometimes bore the names of powerful aristocrats such as Roland, and Charlemagne continued to tighten up royal control of the minting of coins.[38]

His successors went on to insist that coins bear their name. As Charles the Bald proclaimed in 864: 'One side of our new coins is to have our name in a circle and the monogram of our name in the centre.' Numismatists' difficulty in distinguishing between coins of Charles the Great and Charles the Bald may be suggestive of contemporary perceptions. Ninth-century Carolingian rulers had their names on coins and the repeated and exclusively royal names of Charles, Carloman, Pippin, Louis and Lothar thus circulated widely across society, reaching far beyond the political elite. Such money testified to Carolingian prosperity and spoke of a distinctively Carolingian royalty, while the rare portraits of Charlemagne and Louis the Pious on the coins acquired a magical significance far outside the Frankish world, testimony to the power of these personal royal images.[39]

Focusing on Charlemagne's line: 768–92

These great piles of coins bearing the royal names monopolized by the dynasty were not yet available, however, to help the twenty-year-old Charlemagne in 768 when his father died. He and his younger brother Carloman faced the challenge of reproducing the Carolingian royalty inaugurated by their father less than twenty years previously. The death of a ruler was always a tense occasion, a rupture in the fabric of political life. In 768, the death of the new dynasty's first king might have triggered a challenge from real or impersonated Merovingians. As far as we know, not a peep was heard from that quarter, or from anywhere else. The Frankish political elite found itself gathered at St-Denis, a centre of Frankish royalty under the old dynasty, but which now enfolded the new kings in its saintly aura. These aristocrats were not simply a passive audience for the staging of Pippin's edifying death there, but would have bargained and lobbied while the dying ruler divided up the realm.[40]

The key actors, however, were Pippin and his immediate family. The Franks had seen young Charlemagne and Carloman assume royal prominence before 768: they had both been anointed in 754, they witnessed their parents' great gift to Prüm in 762 and the Aquitanians had had to swear oaths to Pippin and to his two sons in the late 760s.[41] Pippin's queen Bertrada was also visibly active; she had played an important political role in the late 760s and her high status in 768 as wife of the king and, remarkably, afterwards as his widow and mother of the new kings provided re-assuring continuity in clearly dynastic terms.[42] Her prominence shows the dynastic effort that was needed. The succession of the two brothers was one of the most peaceful in Carolingian history. Carefully planned and staged events displayed to the aristocracy a sublime continuity of the new royal line at this potentially difficult time of transition. After their father's funeral at St-Denis, the twenty-year-old Charlemagne and his seventeen-year-old brother Carloman made their separate ways to their own kingdoms to prepare for their king-making. These two ceremonies took place in different locations in each ruler's own kingdom, Charlemagne's in Noyon and Carloman's in Soissons. Both ceremonies took place on the same day, 9 October, which testifies to common planning and agreement between the two kings: the locations were only about forty kilometres apart; the new rulers and their followers could keep a watchful eye on each other's proceedings and ensure that the reigns began simultaneously.[43] The date was the feast day of Saint Denis (Dionysius) whose heavenly patronage thus shone down on the kings at the start of their reign as it had done so on their father at the end of his. Disconcertingly for those of us who study medieval rituals, the chronicle of count Nibelung, one of the aristocrats at whom these rituals were partly aimed, gets this carefully chosen date wrong.[44]

To some extent, the new kings acted as co-operative brothers, seeking to convince themselves and their followers that divided kingdoms need not signify divisions within the family of the late Pippin. Pippin had given each of them a share in Aquitaine; both had links with the papacy; both displayed devotion to the abbey of St-Denis, with Charlemagne in January 769 expressing a wish to be buried there. The fact that the abbey actually lay in his brother's kingdom shows how clearly both young kings visibly pursued a common dynastic cult. Bertrada, now a widow visibly dedicated to God, remained exceptionally active, undertaking diplomatic missions in Italy and Bavaria, residing at Charlemagne's court but maintaining contact with Carloman.[45] All this kept attention focused on the royal family that Pippin had built.

But Pippin had built all too well. Both his sons were special; each deserved and received a kingdom. This created opportunities and problems for aristocrats who had to choose which brother to back but who could also exploit tensions between the brothers to advance their own interests. This was a problem that the Carolingians were never to solve; the uncertainties of divided kingship were to be a permanent feature of the political landscape until the end of Carolingian hegemony. Rosamond McKitterick has rightly argued that we need not see the brothers as permanent enemies. Nonetheless, the realm was divided; competition for resources was bound to cause friction. The kings could act in common but there is clear evidence that Pippin's division gave each king a separate kingdom. Contemporaries knew that relations between the kings could be very strained. In a genealogical arms race, each brother pointedly named their son Pippin after their own father in a claim to royal heritage.[46]

Aristocrats had to watch their footing amidst such royal rivalries. Count Cancor, a wealthy landowner with estates in the border regions of the two kingdoms, made a grant to his family abbey of Lorsch in 770 that was dated by the years of both kings even though it lay in Carloman's kingdom.[47] Other aristocrats committed themselves to one king. Carloman seemed to contemporaries to be as good a bet as Charlemagne. Autchar, a senior follower of Pippin, had staked so much on Carloman that, on Carloman's unexpectedly early death in 771, he had to flee to Italy with the latter's widow Gerberga and their children.[48] The fact that Gerberga raced to get her sons away from their royal uncle clearly illustrates fault-lines in the royal family, sharpened by rivalries within the aristocracy. In telling Charlemagne a few years later that his brother's early death was a blessing and making no reference at all to Carloman's children, the Anglo-Saxon counsellor Cathwulf was not simply saying what the king wanted to hear. He was reflecting the icy zero-sum realities of the contests between rulers of the royal family: one's gain had to be another's loss, the truth that Einhard's tendentious account of these events later sought to soften. Some seventy years after Cathwulf, another royal watcher made the same observation about Louis the Pious's exultant reaction to the death of his last surviving kingly brother: 'hope of gaining the whole inheritance rose up within him'.[49]

Family was also an asset. The death of his brother in 771 gave Charlemagne control of Carloman's fiscal estates and inheritance, though his failure to seize his nephews before they fled to the Lombard court was a serious blow. He soon resolved this problem when he conquered Italy in 774 and made these boys disappear. Like his father, Charlemagne could now make his own line the only royal line and, again like Pippin, was able to draw on the talents of his kin as subordinate agents of this more exalted and more circumscribed royal line.[50] The descendants of Childebrand and Nibelung held office under him; his paternal uncle Bernard and his more distant kinsman Theoderic led campaigns for him in the 770s and 780s; the pious warrior William of Gellone was also a relative. Contemporaries' knowledge of these figures' relation to the king reveals their awareness of the royal kin. There were hiccups: Charlemagne's cousin Adalhard had backed Carloman and lost favour when Charlemagne took over in 771, but he later bounced back and enjoyed prominence under the ruler. Such figures' status advertised the grandeur of the royal kin and, through their subordination to their kinsman ruler, helpfully underlined the specialness of the narrow royal line itself.[51]

The extinction of Carloman's line gave Charlemagne a monopoly of aristocratic loyalty, though he had to work to keep it. The aristocracy was not a coherent power bloc. At times, however, we glimpse assertions of collective aristocratic political and class interests, as in the brakes put on Pippin's hostility to the Lombards in the 750s by 'the bishops and nobles of the Franks', and in Charlemagne's deciding in 802 not to 'send out his poorer vassals from within the palace to do justice', since, according to an optimistic observer, such figures were more likely to accept bribes whereas the great ecclesiastical and secular magnates 'no longer needed to receive gifts' and were thus better candidates.[52] We also catch glimpses of aristocratic resentment at the prominence of royal kin as in 782 when some army commanders jealously feared that the prestige of any victory over the Saxons would go to a kinsman (*propinquus*) of Charlemagne, count Theoderic. They joined battle without waiting for him and his forces and duly perished at Saxon hands. This, however, testifies to the success of Carolingian publicity: Theoderic was probably descended from a sister of Charlemagne's great-grandmother, so the fact that these aristocrats and/or the annalist knew that he was related to the king is impressive.[53]

Theoderic had been a royal vassal and such men could have close direct ties with the king but did not constitute a completely separate group, closed off from the aristocracy.[54] Charlemagne, like his successors, worked with aristocrats as his partners; he had no choice but to rely on them for the governing of his realm. Royal envoys (*missi*) could be recruited from the areas that they visited, but this gave them traction there and thus enabled the king's will to be transmitted, if not always obeyed. There was no built-in clash of interests. Count Stephen of Paris was a *missus* for the Paris area in 802; as descendant of an aristocratic family that monopolized this countship, Stephen was the kind of man who Charlemagne needed to reward with office and favour. In his turn, Stephen ensured that changes to laws made at the palace were proclaimed in his localities.[55]

A king with resources of patronage and with a sharp eye for opportunities could turn quarrels within aristocratic kins to his own advantage. Tensions between relatives of the founders of the great Rhineland abbey of Lorsch resulted in an appeal to royal justice in 772 that ended with Lorsch becoming a royal abbey. This was not an act of royal power that was somehow independent of structures of aristocratic power and connections: Charlemagne did not sit alone in judgement but heard the case with a group of counts and his vassals. And Lorsch prospered; in 773, Charlemagne gave it a royal estate at Heppenheim, but his taking this out of circulation among counts was another aspect of royal patronage changing a landscape. Royal patronage and intervention, particularly through strong-arm tactics of diverting some aristocratic land towards churches, seem to have been particularly active in the 770s and early 780s.[56]

Gifts of office and favour made the palace an attractive place for aristocrats. Failure to attend the great assemblies held by the king drew unwelcome royal attention; in a capitulary of 803, Charlemagne's eye fell on those 'bishops, abbots and counts who did not come to our assembly [*placitum*]'.[57] Such assemblies were the venue for the promulgation of the legal texts known as capitularies. That label covers a wide variety of texts, not all of which may have stemmed from assemblies, but it is fair to see in them 'the public reason of the Franks', as Michael Wallace-Hadrill phrased it. The 779 capitulary of Herstal is the record of decisions made, not only by the king but also by the 'bishops, abbots, distinguished men and counts' and a century later scribes could title a capitulary collection as 'capitularies of bishops, kings and especially all the noble Franks'.[58] Capitularies were thus not the expression of autocratic royal will, but products of a world of co-operation between kings and aristocrats. Nonetheless, what made them significant to contemporaries who heard, read, copied, preserved and sometimes obeyed them was their royal quality: 'I have collected together the capitularies written (*descripta*) by the order of the rulers (*principes*)', wrote abbot Ansegis in the preface to his great capitulary collection of 827.[59]

Wars may have brought profit and glory to an aristocracy that relished both, but part of that glory was the honour of fighting and falling in the king's service. Eggihard, a victim of the 778 defeat at Roncesvalles, was remembered in a poetic epitaph that recalled his noble origins but that also celebrated his high place in the king's palace.[60] The endless campaigns in Saxony may have brought glory for some aristocrats but they subjected others to storms and stresses. Something much darker than jealousy over his showy relatives threatened Charlemagne a few years later in 785-6, a full-blooded conspiracy in east Francia aiming to kill him led by an aristocrat called Hardrad. This plot was so serious that original versions of the *Royal Frankish Annals* did not dare mention it, a testimony to chroniclers' sensitivity to audience. Many modern historians have worked hard to piece together the plot from what evidence does survive and have noted that annals connected with the monastery of Murbach in Alsace refer, not to east Franks and Hardrad, but to disaffected Thuringians, leading at least one historian to conclude that there were two separate conspiracies.[61] This is possible but the sources may be giving us two perspectives on one complex event rather than reporting two rebellions. Our own uncertainty on this is part of a broader uncertainty over what precisely caused this revolt. It is difficult to uncover the full range of aristocratic attitudes to Charlemagne at this time, including resentment. Murbach annals may also permit us a valuable glimpse into that abbey's history of adjusting to Carolingian lordship in Alsace.[62]

There are three points to highlight here. First, this appears to have been an anti-Carolingian conspiracy. The rebels did not have any member of the Carolingian family as their front-man and this distinguishes them from all other aristocratic rebellions of the following ninety years. Their aim was to kill Charlemagne and there is no evidence that they planned to replace him with any of his young sons, though there is also no evidence that they planned to extirpate the new dynasty.[63] But the plotters' independence clearly shows that the new dynasty had not yet managed to channel all resentments against the ruler through its own dynastic system.

Secondly, the conspiracy had a clear eastern dimension. One rebel's defiant claim that Charlemagne's crossing the Rhine (i.e. to the eastern side) would have been his death warrant is consistent with sources' references to the conspirators as east Franks and Thuringians; this was an eastern plot.[64] If some of the conspirators had proclaimed an identity as Thuringians rather than east Franks, they stood more clearly for opposition to a Frankish king and may well have conjured up memories of the former ducal dynasty of an independent Thuringia, the Hedenen. These dukes had fallen from power some six decades previously, in the era of Charles Martel. But their memory was still sufficiently dangerous to the Carolingians for the dukes to be retrospectively and falsely accused of having been soft on paganism in various texts from the 760s on. Authors of these texts, supporters of the godly line of Frankish kings, sought to rob these dukes of their status as righteous rulers. The rising of a group of Thuringians was thus a return of the repressed. This part of the realm was not yet fully Carolingian.[65]

But Carolingians worked hard to make it so. Charlemagne himself was careful to make no references to the Hedenen when he granted to Fulda in 777 the estate of Hammelburg; this had originally been granted in 717 to the Anglo-Saxon missionary Willibrord by duke Heden II, no pagan sympathizer he. Now it came to Fulda through Charlemagne's generosity, advertised there by royal vassals in an elaborate ceremony of transfer a few months later.[66] In return, Fulda was to pray for Charlemagne, for the security of the kingdom and for the ruler's wife and for the continuity of the Carolingian line. Thus was the landscape made ever more Carolingian. It was not, however, exclusively so; the ruler was only one figure amidst other networks. The conspirators themselves had hoped to find a safe haven in Fulda when their plot came to right. They were mistaken.[67]

The rebels were not simply traditionalists, but were figures in a landscape undergoing the stress of change. And this is the third point. The conspirators' action was a response to wider changes taking place in the east of the Frankish world. Under Charlemagne, Frankish royalty's centre of gravity shifted eastwards away from the Seine-Oise area to the Rhine-Main region with stays at sites such as Worms and the development of new palace sites in the 790s such as Frankfurt and Aachen.[68] To some extent, the wars in Saxony explain this eastward shift. But the shift was also a matter of choice, of decisions to forge alliances across the Frankish world and this offered opportunities to some fortunate aristocrats. Charlemagne's wives between 771 and 800 all had eastern family connections and contemporaries knew this. Charlemagne married the east Frankish Fastrada in 783 and the revolt followed only two years later; perhaps Fastrada or her family had stepped on too many toes.[69] Members of these successfully married families and their associates could benefit from the Carolingian connection just as others could find profit in the ever more tightly woven net of service, patronage and control that Charlemagne had constructed by muscling in on centres such as Lorsch, Hersfeld and Fulda in the 770s and 780s.[70]

But if there were winners, there had to be losers. It is striking that among the property holders connected with Fulda who had lost out to the king's grasping agents in the area was a man called Hardrad. This may not be the same man as the rebel of 785 but the name at least suggests kinship with him and, as Janet Nelson argues, the fate of this man's properties illustrates the deepening of the Carolingian shadow over this landscape.[71] It is also significant that another of the rebels turned against Charlemagne by rejecting a marriage arranged between his daughter and a Frank. Exchanges of women arranged or approved by the ruler could benefit favoured male aristocrats. But not all marriage alliances were welcome; where some benefited, others such as this man saw themselves as losing honour and status and protested violently. This was not a general eastern revolt. Some prominent figures connected to Hardrad were close to Charlemagne, just as some descendants or followers of the Hedenen of Thuringia managed to do well under the Carolingians.[72] Rather, this was a desperate step taken by losers before it was all too late.

Perhaps they did not realize how desperate their step actually was. Charlemagne seems to have caught wind of the conspiracy before the rebels could do very much. It was Charlemagne who went in hard; his followers' laying waste the rebels' estates caused the latter to panic and seek refuge in Fulda, hoping that they could negotiate a deal with the king.[73] This suggests that they thought that there was room for manoeuvre. Sources give us some glimpse of their case, possibly statements uttered at a trial. Remarkably, they claimed that they had not sworn an oath to be faithful to the king. This, however, did not get them off the hook. Rather, it un-nerved Charlemagne who was now confronted with gaps in his authority and his anxiety and his anger would have been intensified by the fact that the rebels *had* sworn an oath, but to each other, not to him.[74]

Charlemagne took this seriously. His problem was not that too few people were taking oaths, but that too many people were taking the wrong kind of oath. Mutual bonds, often cemented by a sworn oath, linked members of Frankish society together but such horizontal bonds could obscure or cut into the vertical ones that should bind Franks to their king. This was not some bloodless political abstraction. Associations formed for mutual help mattered in everyday life. And ensuring that people were bonded to the king was an urgent business. Military defeats and the grim spectre of famine in 778–9, signs of a reign that needed God's favour, were the backdrop to Charlemagne's command in the 779 capitulary of Herstal that people were not to form 'armed followings' or 'sworn associations'.[75]

Charlemagne was no dictator; it would be absurd to imagine that he wanted to snap existing social bonds that were underpinned by oaths. His 779 capitulary explicitly approved of associations for mutual help in the distributing of alms, dealing with fires and shipwreck, and he himself urgently commanded charitable work to be organized in the crisis of 778–9. He was determined, however, that such associations should not be formed by swearing an oath because that represented a social power that could be dangerously uncontainable, one whose momentum could threaten the king. Oaths should instead turn people's hearts and minds upwards, towards the ruler.[76] As late as 805, Charlemagne was still proposing very harsh penalties (death, flogging, mutilation) for those who dared to make 'conspiracies' by oath, that is, not plots against the king but sworn associations.[77]

Such sworn associations were not necessarily anti-Carolingian. In fact, the strongly Carolingian flavour to some of them was equally worrying to Charlemagne. In 789, he cracked down, prohibiting those 'sworn associations' (*coniurationes*) that men were making in the name of St Stephen, or of Charlemagne himself or his sons.[78] This clause's references to drunkenness and to winter festivities (St Stephen's day is 26 December) have led some historians to see here the survival of pagan practices of midwinter ritual drinking centred on the supernaturally sacral blood of the royal family. Such intriguing views are no longer fashionable, or necessary; the Christian Christmas season could generate drunkenness on its own. What worried the king was that oaths taken in his name might be used by the taker to challenge his own lord while oaths taken in the name of one or other of the king's sons could detonate tensions within the royal family.[79]

The existence of such oaths shows how deeply the names of the royal family had penetrated social discourse, but Charlemagne had to steer such charismatic power in the right direction. Thus, the 789 condemnation of these oaths was accompanied by commands for the swearing of the proper sort of oaths, in which the royal sons were indeed prominent. The oath of fidelity had to be taken, not only to Charlemagne but also to his sons, and that meant all his sons, the young kings of Italy and Aquitaine as well as the older sons who were not yet kings. What mattered was that they were sons of the king.[80] These were oaths to a line and the same dynastic concerns shine through Charlemagne's forcing the wretched conspirators of 785–6 to swear fidelity to him and his sons. His gaining the imperial title in 800 led Charlemagne to introduce a new oath two years later and this too had a dynastic character even though it did not refer to his (non-imperial) sons; people were now to swear fidelity to 'the most pious lord emperor Charles, son of king Pippin and queen Bertha'. Charlemagne wanted every male over the age of twelve to swear this oath and there is evidence that his wishes were carried out.[81]

All this took a huge effort and was not done by Charlemagne alone. His aristocratic envoys travelled round the realm, summoned people together, expounded the oaths and then presided over them being taken in the name of the ruler.[82] These aristocrats were thus relentlessly exposed to the formulae of Carolingian rule even as they dragooned others into taking these oaths. But all this was not one-sided. The oath-takings were staged in local assemblies which would have experienced them as a collectivity where horizontal bonds thus remained and were even enhanced, and as a collectivity that sought re-assurances from the ruler's envoys that customary rights be preserved and that the envoys would relay complaints to the palace. Lords may not always have heeded or transmitted such messages, nor could they always ignore them, as the Istria case of 804 showed. This was part of their involvement in the making of a just Christian society that was the whole point of Carolingian rule.[83]

Problems of success and succession: Pippin the Hunchback 792

If aristocrats looked up to the ruler, they expected much in return: wealth, power and the fruits of office (*honores*). Their grip on *honores* enabled favoured aristocrats to stand above rivals, including their own kin, and this fact gave rulers valuable levers of patronage.⁸⁴ But here lay an insoluble problem for aristocracy and ruler. Gazing upon the ruler and his sons, aristocrats could not know which of them was the best bet for a secure hold on their status and *honores* in the future, a future that loomed larger as the ruler aged. Nor could the king and his sons be sure that aristocrats would not switch loyalties if pressures came to bear. In Charlemagne's reign from the mid-790s onwards, royal daughters also came to play a role in such calculations and formations.

The second conspiracy that Charlemagne faced illuminates this problem. This was the rising in 792 of his oldest son Pippin, known as the Hunchback. It is Einhard, writing some thirty years after the event, who tells us that this Pippin was 'handsome but deformed by a hunchback'. Some scholars have thought that Pippin may have suffered from scoliosis and that as his condition worsened he became visibly less suitable for rule. Pippin may have had problems but it is also likely that Einhard was using physical quality to indicate moral flaw. Physical beauty, appropriately gendered, was a prized characteristic of the ruling elite, particularly kings. Perhaps Einhard invented this physical feature for Pippin. Hypnotized by the Carolingian charisma that he himself articulated so forcefully Einhard took care to say that Pippin was 'handsome'. Only a flawed figure would have dared to rise against the hero of Einhard's biography.⁸⁵ Einhard also says that Pippin was the son of a concubine but this too is a device to make him look rightly marginal. It is very unlikely that Charlemagne's father, king Pippin, would have let his sons contract anything other than full marriages in the 760s as the dynasty was rawly new and needed to produce unchallengeable heirs; a contemporary papal letter indicates that both sons were married.⁸⁶

In itself, the status of his aristocratic mother Himiltrud did not guarantee Pippin anything, and Charlemagne abandoned her early in his reign. But Einhard's image of Pippin as illegitimate and physically ill-favoured is a baleful hypnotic suggestion making us think that the inevitability of Pippin's exclusion and fall was obvious to his contemporaries. To think like this is to fundamentally misunderstand the complex dynamics of power relations within the royal family and between it and the aristocracy. (I am afraid, however, I shall refer to him as Pippin the Hunchback to distinguish him from other Pippins; Einhard is a tough man to beat.) Even if Pippin did lack physical grace, it is unlikely that aristocrats saw that as definitively excluding him; after all, he found support in 792. Even if some people did become worried about the status of his mother, being the son of a concubine was not in itself enough to be automatically unworthy of royal inheritance.⁸⁷

Pippin's status became problematic as his father's reign wore on. His mother Himiltrud may have belonged to the aristocracy of Alsace or Alemannia but it is unclear if any of her kin retained status when Charlemagne abandoned her very early in his reign. When Charlemagne made two of his sons kings in 781, he selected the young sons of his third wife Hildegard, giving Aquitaine to the three-year-old Louis and Italy to the four-year-old Carloman. The expansion of the Frankish realm had made such territories available and the youth of the kings testified to the very special status of royal sons. Neither Hildegard's oldest son, the nine-year-old Charles, nor Himiltrud's Pippin, probably aged twelve, received a kingdom and that may have looked to everyone that Francia itself was being held back for them. But it is hard to believe that Charlemagne made a definitive announcement on their succession in 781, not least because he quickly married again after Hildegard's death in 783 and could not know that this marriage would produce only daughters, not sons.[88]

All this, however, depressed Pippin's stock. The new queen Fastrada allied with the sons of Hildegard. Carloman of Italy's being re-named Pippin in 781 may have been understood by watchful aristocrats as a slighting of his older brother Pippin the Hunchback, the new Pippin cancelling out the old. But it may not have been. And if Pippin's mother was no longer the king's wife, that did not necessarily mean that her son was rejected by the king. After all, Hildegard's family remained high in royal favour after her death.[89] Pippin does appear, however, as a marginal figure in a text, the *History of the Bishops of Metz*, commissioned by the bishop of that city, Angilram, probably when he became head of the royal chapel in 784. Its author, Paul the Deacon, pays due respect to Pippin as son of a 'noble girl' and makes no reference to any physical blemish but says that this union took place before the king's 'legal marriage' and he throws the spotlight fully on the sons of Hildegard, who was herself buried at Metz, as were other Carolingian women. Paul's text surely reflects the efforts by Angilram, and presumably others, to ally with Hildegard's sons. Angilram can hardly have been alone in such downgrading of Pippin. The fact that Paul knew the name of Pippin's mother and called her 'noble' suggests that she had not vanished completely from the political scene and she and her family may well have been hovering in the background as supporters.[90]

The sketchy and tendentious nature of our sources here is actually helpful in some ways: our efforts to understand the shifting shapes of the royal family parallels contemporaries' efforts to do the same, though for them the stakes were much higher. The royal potential of kings' sons was constructed or whittled away by contemporaries who were active observers of royalty. His royal birth did not make Pippin invincible. But attempts to conjure away Pippin's throneworthiness were bound to hit a rock because his individual qualities stemmed from general qualities of Carolingian royalty. People were caught in the mesh of the Carolingian charisma-paradox: Carolingians worked hard to convince themselves and their followers that they were special, but that specialness took on a life of its own that prevented individuals such as Charlemagne from controlling it. The discourse of Carolingian exclusiveness was not exclusively controlled by Carolingians but acted a diffused power network of the sort familiar to us from the work of Michel Foucault (see below). Thus, Paul the Deacon explicitly pointed out the royal associations of the name of Pippin for 'his' Pippin (Pippin of Italy) and did not do so for Pippin the Hunchback. But in doing this for the Pippin of Italy, he inevitably evoked that same cluster of royal associations working for the other Pippin, the Hunchback. The discourse of Carolingian royalty forced both Pippins to be given top billing: 'a second Pippin [of Italy], the namesake of his brother [the Hunchback] and grandfather [king Pippin]'. The repeated names and the vocabulary of kinship show that Paul understood this royalty as a family affair, and we may recall here that one of Paul's sources for the Carolingian family past was Charlemagne himself. Carolingians were too special to be put back in a box, even by themselves.[91]

Paul's text is a trace of the pressures deployed by aristocrats and royals at court and elsewhere to advance their own interests at the expense of Pippin. But we also have traces of activities maintaining Pippin's royal identity. In liturgical entries from sites as far from each other as Salzburg around 784 and Soissons between 788 and 792, we find his name being acclaimed in its proper place, at the head of the sons of Charlemagne.[92] Behind the appearance of these names in these important locations lay transmission and circulation of knowledge of the names and rank of the king's sons. The royal family could thus be present across the realm and the voices that chanted, the ears that heard and the eyes that read these names learned its distinctiveness even as they helped create it in writing and performing acts of prayers and commemoration of which these surviving name-lists are only a trace. Like Paul the Deacon's Metz history, these are signs of activities in the social world, plotting and veneration.

When Charles the Younger finally received at the age of eighteen or thereabouts what looks like his own kingdom in Neustria in 789 or 790, all the sons of Hildegard now had territories to rule while the mature Pippin the Hunchback did not.[93] But he remained a revered son. Kings needed their followers to honour their sons and that made it difficult for Charlemagne just to snuff out a royal son. The charisma of the royal house was at stake. Nor can we be certain that Charlemagne wanted to downgrade Pippin who had supporters. Perhaps Charlemagne actually intended Pippin's position to be ambiguous. The public promoting of the sons of Hildegard placated their supporters while Pippin's continued position at court re-assured his. But not even Charlemagne could maintain such a delicate balancing act indefinitely. Some admittedly late evidence suggests that young Charles was growing increasingly impatient to marry after he was given rule in Neustria.[94] It is hard to imagine that the wifeless and kingdomless Pippin would have been stoical as he faced political death by inches.

The conquest of Bavaria in 788 must have ratcheted up familial tensions even while seeming to offer a potential solution to them. Surely this new territory attracted the gaze of Pippin and his supporters, just as the acquisition of new territory was to kindle the hopes of Charles the Bald's son Carloman almost a century later.[95] The campaign against the Avars had brought Charlemagne to this newly acquired south-eastern principality. He held court at the old ducal centre of Regensburg throughout 792, presiding over great assemblies that struck down heresies that menaced the Christian people. Members of the royal family were there, including queen Fastrada, and some of the royal daughters and sons. Perhaps these majestic gatherings wondered if Charlemagne would proclaim Pippin as king over the newly acquired territory, while yet more bad news of heavy Frankish defeats in Saxony may have fuelled aristocratic unease.[96] Some Bavarians seem to have welcomed the prospect of having a king of their own. Evidence from Freising in Bavaria points to Pippin being called king there in 792. Whether this reflects Charlemagne's will, Pippin's jumping the gun or a (mis-)reading of the situation by the Freising community is unknown. But if Charlemagne, or only Pippin himself, thought that Bavaria was the solution, they were wrong. Hildegard's sons and supporters could not tolerate this and Pippin of Italy had his eye on Bavaria.[97] With a kingdom of his own so temptingly close but with enemies' hands closing off his political oxygen, Pippin had to act. He launched a serious plot to kill his father and brothers only to see it fail and his followers rounded up and punished.[98]

This was a Carolingian plot, not merely a regional one. It had a Bavarian dimension, but the reason for its staging in Regensburg is that the royal family was there, far from its usual haunts. Charlemagne and his immediate family were the key players and targets. So if they were in Bavaria, that is where the plot had to be and Bavarians were almost certainly among the plotters. But so too were the bishop of Verdun and count Theodold who held office near Paris. Resentful and ambitious figures from across a wide geographical area now backed a dissident royal son, in a sharp contrast to the conspiracy of 785 which had no Carolingian frontman. The Carolingians could now channel aristocratic rivalries into their own family rivalries and king's sons were the leaders of this. Even ambitious members of the wider royal kin fell into line behind such princely leaders; Charlemagne's cousin Wala, son of the king's uncle Bernard who had led armies in the 770s, was involved in Pippin's plot.[99] The Carolingian family was now central to the politics of protest and conspiracy in a way that it had not been only a few years previously.

This, however, was of little comfort to Charlemagne. His calibrated reactions to the plot show the imposing of the ruler's discipline. A gathering of aristocrats at Regensburg presided over by him condemned Pippin and his followers to death, but Charlemagne modified this collective decision. He spared Pippin's life. Some other plotters also escaped death, suffering exile and degradation, but a contemporary observer explicitly links Pippin's survival to his father's actions. Kings had to mark out the special status of royal sons even in rebellion.[100] Charlemagne was, however, relentless towards his disobedient son. Pippin was redefined as a cleric and was eventually sent to the abbey of Prüm. This had close links with the royal family and may not have been too uncomfortable a billet but no contemporary pretends, as they had done with Tassilo, that Pippin volunteered for this as penance. Pippin was never to re-emerge; he died off-stage in 811.[101]

Charlemagne saw the plot as dangerously extensive among the aristocracy and went out of his way a year later to spectacularly display the restoration of order in the very place where it had been challenged. In the majestic setting of Regensburg, and on the eve of the great Avar campaigns, aristocrats experienced again their collective identity as faithful men of the king. He soothed discontent by showering 'gold, silver, silk and numerous gifts' on those magnates 'who did not support Pippin in that wicked plot', but only after he had checked up on their loyalty.[102] The bishop of Verdun only regained Charlemagne's grace in 794 in a public ceremony of the ordeal after being humiliated in full view of the vast gathering at Frankfurt that year where he found that no one was prepared to swear on his behalf to his loyalty. That is to say, two years later he still appeared to other aristocrats as dangerously contaminated by disloyalty and royal disfavour, and the church of Verdun remembered his loss of the king's favour as a scarifying experience. Count Theodold also regained the king's favour, likewise through the ordeal, but may have had to wait four years to do so and he thought it wise to give some of his returned property to the abbey of St-Denis, probably to keep it safe.[103]

Shockwaves from Pippin's actions thus took years to subside. The fact that the so-called original *Royal Frankish Annals*, apart from one version, say nothing about the conspiracy suggests that for some well-connected figures it was too controversial to write about in the 790s, which strongly implies that history writers expected their texts to be read or known. Only later did a reviser of these annals feel free to refer to it.[104] One contemporary annalist, however, did not hold back and compared Pippin to the biblical figure of the wicked Abimelech who had plotted the death of his father and brothers. He did not need to go on to describe Abimelech's ultimate fate: Abimelech was hit by a rock hurled by a woman and had to beg one of his own followers to finish him off lest he incur the disgrace of dying at a woman's hand. This vindictively contemptuous view of Pippin exposes the resentments that seethed among rival Carolingians and their followers.[105]

A father under pressure: 792–806

Even if Hildegard's sons were now the only obvious candidates for the succession, fear and loathing did not vanish from the political scene along with Pippin. Professor Nelson takes an optimistic view of the years after 792, stressing the undeniably striking fact that none of Charlemagne's other sons ever went on to rebel against him, in sharp contrast to later reigns.[106] Contemporaries, however, could not have known that. If the royal sons did not dare to turn against their father, they did not necessarily think that father knew best. Queen Liutgard had been Charlemagne's wife since the mid-790s and after she died in spring 800 he never married again (it is not certain that he was actually married to her, though it seems likely). He did not lose his worryingly intense interest in fertile women: he went on to have three sons by a series of mistresses (though not all his mistresses may post-date 800). Avoiding marriage and taking care to give these sons what look like non-royal names (see Chapter 4 on children) reflect a strategy of limiting the pool of heirs to the sons of Hildegard. There were to be no more throne-worthy sons.[107]

This bright idea may not have been just Charlemagne's. In the spring of 800, he travelled west to pray at the shrine of St Martin at Tours. This was part of the spiritual preparations for the journey to Rome and the imperial coronation but it was also part of the intense discussions among the court over the significance of these looming events. Remarkably, all three sons attended upon their father at Tours, an unusual site for such a concentration of royalty, normally to be found on eastern campaigns or in the great palaces to the east. A united dynasty proclaimed a Carolingian future as it travelled. But what was the shape of that future? Even Charlemagne could not control that. Queen Liutgard was visibly ill and died there.[108] It is no stretch of the imagination to think that the sons and some of the aristocracy here saw a chance to insist on no more marriages for the father. Controlling access to women was the dynastic strategy here. Such decisions could be collective, though Charlemagne remained dominant.

Another item on the family agenda was presumably the planned elevation of the oldest son, Charles, who was to be crowned king at Rome in December 800 in the wake of his father's imperial coronation. Charlemagne and Charles the Younger himself were doubtless the drivers of this decision in the summer of 800, but this too would have been the result of wider discussion within the royal family and the elite. All three sons had been at Aachen in the summer of 799 for a family gathering, including Charlemagne's trusted sister Gisela. We cannot be sure that every detail of the Rome coronations was planned then but we can safely assume that the family there tried to thrash out a resolution of the claims of the sons, now all over twenty. Perhaps Gisela acted as honest broker and peace-weaver, seeking to cool tensions. She certainly displayed her exalted status in the grand surroundings of the palace built by her brother; only a Carolingian woman could have a charter witnessed by three kings, as the royal sons did for their aunt in a show of harmonious royal familial accord in worthy purposes.[109]

Such actions and gatherings may have calmed aristocratic anxieties and ambitions that focused on any tensions within the family. Of course, the elite did not spend all its time worrying about shifting favour and status within the royal line. These were also years of glamorous encounters and happenings when members of the elite could marvel at wonders such as the arrival at court of sacred relics, envoys from Jerusalem and an elephant from the caliph at Baghdad; they themselves travelled to exotic destinations such as Constantinople, seeing palaces that no Carolingian ever witnessed.[110] Even in localities where the weight of royal governance could be felt, such as Dienheim in the Rhineland, landowners would spend more time checking the boundaries of their estates and coping with pressures from their powerful neighbour, the abbey of Fulda, than casting the political horoscopes of royal sons. Nonetheless, these everyday transactions in Dienheim were dated by the regnal years of the ruler.[111]

The realm knew that Charlemagne was its master. After the imperial coronation of December 800, the voices of all males over twelve across the empire were to utter his name in a loyalty oath. Envoys were mobilized and travelled the realm to reiterate the fact that Charlemagne was lord. All this was part of the structure of royal/imperial rule but the dynastic element of that rule was also made explicit. The new oath was to 'the most pious lord emperor Charles, son of king Pippin and queen Bertrada', and that oath was indeed administered and taken everywhere, from Neustria to Bavaria to Italy.[112] Dynasty spoke and was spoken. For all its unctuous inventiveness, a later poetic account of speeches made at Louis's assemblies in Aquitaine is credible in its vision of king and magnates referring to Charlemagne as their common master and Louis's father, and thus as familial source of Louis's kingship.[113]

Louis and his brothers, however, were now mature and active rulers; by 802, young Charles was around thirty, while Pippin of Italy and Louis were in their mid-twenties. Their father had become king when he was twenty. Charlemagne dominated the scene but was not alone. Women, including his sister, daughters and mistresses, enjoyed a notorious eminence; they could not harangue the assembled magnates at assemblies but perhaps the increasingly regular settlement of the court at Aachen, particularly over the winters, gave them more opportunities for exercising informal power. Far from court, Alcuin knew that Charlemagne's cousin Gundrada, sister of Adalhard and Wala, would be occupied with palace business. Adalhard himself was often busy at the palace in these years and was soon to be joined there by his brother Wala, now trusted intimately by his imperial cousin after his rash involvement in Pippin's 792 revolt.[114] There was thus a cluster of royals, including members of the branch-lines of the kin, at court.

Away from the court, the regular prayers for the ruler could be extended to his family. In 801/2, the bishop of Liège instructed all the priests of his diocese to pray for the 'life and rule of the lord emperor and of his sons and daughters'. Liège was not too far from Aachen but the daughters were also explicitly included in similar instructions issued by the archbishop of Salzburg in distant Bavaria between 806 and 811. Charlemagne himself insisted on due reverence being paid to his family, requesting the monks of Aniane in 799 to pray for him and 'for our sons and daughters and for the whole group of our house(hold)', terms that pointed to a broad group of Carolingian generations. The abbot of Aniane, Benedict, had grown up at the court of Charlemagne's father and mother, that is, the figures evoked for everyone in the oath of 802, and now his community was to pray for Charlemagne and his offspring. Past, present and future were dynastic.[115]

Of course, not all the dominant figures around Charlemagne were only members of his family. Of the thirty magnate witnesses to his will in 811, only one (Wala) was. But this reinforces a central point: Charlemagne was not a solitary actor. He had to reckon with his own illustrious kin and with aristocrats, as prominent individuals and *en masse* at the assemblies and royal hunts.[116] And they had to reckon with a still vigorous but ageing ruler; over fifty, his hair was white with age. He and the disturbingly difficult-to-read constellation of his family mesmerized aristocratic attention as they travelled west to Tours in that spring of 800. His followers there yearned that he might visit them.[117]

Princes knew that they were subjects of observation and speculation; Pippin of Italy probably did not need to be told by Alcuin that 'the eyes are the spies of the mind' or that the 'word is the betrayer of the mind/soul'.[118] Aristocrats observed, speculated, invested and disinvested in the ruler's sons in a political stockmarket. A story told by Ermold in his poem on Louis the Pious (written in the mid-820s) offers a vivid glimpse into these watchful aristocratic imaginations. Ermold deployed flattery and hindsight, and a story in the *Life of Alcuin*, also written in the 820s and also flattering to Louis, parallels it, but if both stories are moralizing fictions, they breathe the atmosphere of speculation among observers who did not know what the future might bring.[119] Any appearance of all three sons together as in 799–800 would have riveted aristocratic attention. According to Ermold, bishop Paulinus of Aquileia was attending Charlemagne's court and, while praying in church, encountered the three sons of Charlemagne entering in sequence. The first two, Charles and Pippin, ignored Paulinus, but Louis's tearfully emotional outburst of prayer at the altar electrified the bishop who prophesied that Louis would be the successor.[120] In imagining Charles and Pippin as surrounded by an important entourage, Ermold gets it exactly right: the heirs are attended by followers who had staked their own future on the prospects of their chosen leader and we too should imagine such princes as being part of a crowd in their entire political existence, though perhaps not with the escort of 100,000 men that poets dreamed up.[121] Nor were aristocrats merely passive observers; a prophecy such as Paulinus's was a spiritually transposed version of political lobbying for prominence.

We should be thinking here not so much of firmly established distinct households for the king's sons, though there is in fact some evidence for that.[122] Rather, millions of strange shadows did upon them tend. These young men were carefully watched by an aristocratic audience which would monitor any quarrels or bad blood among them. A later source vividly, and plausibly, describes an angry clash between young Charles and Pippin (probably the Hunchback) in the 790s. Aristocrats would watch such outbursts and probably take part in them. They had to weigh up the significance of the sons' varying prominence when they visited their father's court.[123] Poetic descriptions of that court, written between 794 and *c*.800, celebrate the sons' presence there as a sign of hope for the future dynastic continuation of past glories: Charles the Younger as 'hope of the kingdom', Pippin 'called by the name of his grandfather'. The central position of a harmonious royal family, including its women, in these poems is significant; they place a particular view of Charlemagne's family at the apex of the court hierarchy and at the core of the court community. Royal family members are not the only figures in such poems: people such as Einhard appear among the supporting cast as do the Franks themselves, but by this date Charlemagne had sons and daughters to fill the poetic picture, in contrast to the earlier group portrait featuring only him and his Franks in the poem on the fall of Tassilo.[124]

To sing this harmonious vision was not just to preach to the converted. Such poems were not neutral descriptions. Royals, as well as aristocrats, needed to be told whom to respect. It is notoriously difficult to know how widely these not always securely dated poems were performed, read or understood, or how long they were remembered, if at all. Perhaps the familiar royal names stood out clearly as the names of familiar characters do in opera arias sung in a foreign language. If the sons were actually present at court when these poems were presented, then on such occasions the absent son would be very absent indeed.[125]

But the royal sons and their relation with their father could never be absent from the mind's eye of the truly thoughtful observer. In writing to Charles the Younger, Alcuin could not help referring to his brother Louis. Writing to Charles before and after his royal coronation in Rome in 800, Alcuin urged him to model himself on his father. Alcuin also knew that his own men from Tours were staying in Italy for a while after the imperial coronation with king Pippin; he rebuked these men for not making sufficient use of good communication lines from Rome. The royal constellation on the Tiber was visible from the Loire, and presumably also from elsewhere in Francia.[126]

All three sons, doubtless armed with their own and their followers' demands, joined their father at the palace of Thionville in the winter of 805–6 for their first joint meeting since 799–800. Even Pippin the Hunchback may have been listening in on proceedings as the abbot of Prüm, where Pippin was confined, attended the great assembly. Or perhaps the abbot's prominence was a theatrical way of displaying Pippin's definitive exclusion; on the very eve of the assembly, Charlemagne requested Prüm to pray for his children.[127] But by now Charlemagne was not the only kingly father; Louis of Aquitaine and Pippin of Italy had children, and as we have seen, Charles the Younger chafed at his single state.

Contemporaries understood that the main business of the assembly was to establish and maintain peace among the royal sons, which clearly implies that there was publicly known tension. But all this took place while the realm was suffering famine and was haunted by the spectre of conspiracies. Charlemagne urged all to beg God for help, and threatened conspirators with death, flogging, facial disfigurement. It was a tense winter meeting.[128] For all his vigour (he had been hunting that autumn), as well as his carefully staged majesty at diplomatic receptions at Thionville, Charlemagne was not the sole actor at Thionville. He willed the succession settlement, but he was not its only creator. It has come down to us in a rich document, known as the *Division of the Kingdoms*, whose provisions have been pored over by historians as keenly as by contemporaries. Some of these historians have focused on the favoured position of the oldest son, Charles the Younger, who was promised all of the realm's heartlands, Francia, which was to remain undivided in contrast to 741 and 768.[129]

Some contemporaries would have shared the views of these historians. In a poem written for Charles between 800 and 811, bishop Theodulf of Orléans singled him out as the 'hope and glory of the kingdom' and could well have produced it to enhance Charles's prospects rather than merely as a reaction to the *Division*.[130] We may also hear the siren voices of contemporaries boosting Charles in a historical text, the so-called *Earlier Annals of Metz*. Professor Nelson has argued that this text, composed around 805–6, articulates the views of Charlemagne's sister Gisela, abbess of Chelles, who shaped it to tell a story of the dangers of a divided realm and thus backed the first-born Charles as heir to a united Francia. This is temptingly persuasive; Gisela was politically prominent, but we cannot be certain that this text was composed in Chelles; and so we cannot be sure that it reflects Gisela's views, whatever they were, nor how far such views were shared.[131] And while these annals do give Charles a good press, they are not fixated on him to the exclusion of his brothers. The fact that he was the first-born son (of Hildegard's sons) did not mean that he had an impersonally institutional supreme status. Three decades previously Cathwulf had hailed Charlemagne as 'first-born', citing biblical approval for this status; but he had also compared Charlemagne to Jacob, the younger twin of Esau. The *Division* did refer to Charles the Younger as 'older by birth' (*maior natu*, that is, first-born), but only in a neutral descriptive statement and in different language, perhaps less highly charged, from that of the *Annals*, and certainly did not pick out the oldest son as Louis the Pious was to do in his settlement of 817.[132]

The writer of this chronicle text, which found an audience in the ninth century, was not simply a partisan of Charles the Younger but had a keen interest in the Carolingian family in general, including its women.[133] The author found history to be a helpful genre for thinking about the royal family around 806. This, like Theodulf's poem, reveals contemporary concerns with the manoeuvrings of the succession and was also part of such manoeuvrings. But she or he revered all great rulers and approved the division of the realm between 'legitimate heirs' in 741 and the 'equal shares' of 768. All the king's sons deserved something and therefore deserved watching. The settlement of 806 forced that watching to become more intense. East of Chelles, a monk of Lorsch compiled a chronicle around 807 to counter the Chelles view, paying close attention from the perspective of a well-connected community to the shares of each son in the division. Bets were being placed; soon chips would be cashed.[134]

Such observers would have noticed one startling feature of Charles the Younger's royalty in 806: as far as we know, he was not married nor did he have children. This was a glaring contrast with his brothers whose own sons were now approaching maturity. Perhaps Charles had to be seen to cancel his own dynastic future as the price for the prospect of inheriting Francia and this may well have been decided at the previous meeting of all the sons in 799.[135] But such a trade-off was more likely to postpone potential explosions than neutralize them. Agreements to queue patiently for the succession tended to evaporate as time lapsed and inheritance pressures built up, as examples from the eighth-century kingdom of the Asturias in northern Spain and ninth-century Wessex show. And the *Division* refers to the possibility that all three sons could have children; perhaps that was a slip; perhaps not. The assembly and text of 806 only showed aristocrats a future as through a glass darkly.[136]

The settlement of 806 was the outcome of tough negotiations and could only be a truce. Magnates would have played a key role in bringing everyone to the table and in pushing the interests of themselves as well as of their patrons; we can hear their many voices behind the emperor's words of authority in the *Division*.[137] The *Royal Frankish Annals*' statement that the emperor and magnates at Thionville worked to establish and maintain peace among the royal sons rings true and is echoed in the *Division*'s horror at the prospect of 'confusion and disorder ... controversies, strife and disputes'. Perhaps the annalist read the text of the *Division* or attended the Thionville assembly.[138]

Hard work by the political elite continued after the text was completed. The magnates had sworn to uphold the settlement and Charlemagne laboured to make it stick, commanding that the whole realm was to promise to accept what he had decided in order to preserve peace and harmony among his sons.[139] Such oaths would have been extracted by members of the aristocracy travelling round the kingdom as *missi*, a group composed of such distinguished figures as abbots Fulrad of St-Denis and Adalhard of Corbie and count Unroch. Thus rulers and magnates effortlessly sought to bind each other to the settlement. Some, such as Adalhard, may even have had their own copies of the text of the *Division* and were probably expected to broadcast it further while another prominent courtier, Einhard, may have had a hand in drafting it. Einhard himself, a trusted intimate of the emperor, was sent to Rome with a copy of the *Division* for the pope to approve. The *Division* was better known than the few surviving copies of it may suggest.[140]

This struggle for peace sought to contain pressures of rivalry and uncertainty. Young Charles did indeed win the jackpot in 806 with the promised inheritance of an undivided Francia, and he continued to be prominently visible beside his father.[141] But this was a snapshot, not a frozen map. The settlement proclaimed so publicly at Thionville was equally public in acknowledging its own fragility: if Charles the Younger were to predecease his brothers, they would get to divide up Francia between themselves. Furthermore, Charlemagne explicitly reserved the power to alter the settlement in future, though his tact on this contrasts sharply with the attitude of Louis the Pious a generation later. Young Charles received Francia as his kingdom because his brothers already had kingdoms. Contemporaries could in fact see all three sons as having a share in the 'kingdom of the Franks'. Young Charles's position was less awe-inspiring than some historians have thought.[142]

The truly awe-inspiring feature of the political landscape unveiled in the *Division* was the Carolingian royal line itself, radiating into past, present and future of the gathered political collectivity of the Franks, themselves now understood in broad, even imperial terms. The *Division* was a particularly elaborate attempt to regulate royal succession in writing, and this document was creatively structured as a formal combination of diploma and will, its polish contrasting with many other capitulary texts.[143] Such marmoreal documentary solemnity could not stop manoeuvrings for power but could rivet the attention of the settlement's many participants on the Carolingian family. Four Carolingian rulers were at Thionville and were probably joined by other members of the family such as Charlemagne's daughters, his constant court companions in these years, his cousins Wala and Adalhard and possibly his sister Gisela. We may hear the voices of the daughters themselves in the *Division*'s insistence that they be allowed to marry after the emperor's death. Again this suggests something of the pressures building up within the family, pressures that the emperor could only try and dam for his own lifetime.[144]

The *Division* itself is heavily populated with Carolingians, referring to seven rulers, whose familial names (three Charles, two Pippins) form chains of dynastic association across the generations. The familial language of Carolingian royalty dominates the text as it must have dominated the Thionville assembly with references to sons, daughters, sisters, brothers, father, uncle, grandfather and grandsons.[145] These were the relationships that bound the realm together and which defined it as a Carolingian world. The assembly and the text depicted for their followers a world governed by the Carolingian family and its familial norms: royal nephews were to respect their fathers and uncles 'with all the deference which is fitting in such blood-relationship' while the subjection of the young kings to their imperial father paralleled subjects' relation to their ruler: 'we are to enjoy the obedience of our beloved sons … and of our people … with all the submission shown to a father by sons and to an empire and king by his peoples'.[146]

In urging deference to senior generations/members of the family, Charlemagne evoked general cultural norms shared by the aristocracy. The grandson of Charlemagne's old companion William of Gellone cannot have been the only young aristocrat instructed to honour his father, not simply as a virtue, but as a condition for continuation of the family line, a condition spelled out in biblical texts.[147] The political world operated under the sign of these royal kinship ties, not because it was an underdeveloped patrimonial polity, but because the Carolingian family was now the royal line and hereditary kingship was the central political institution. Pointedly omitting his illegitimate sons and Pippin the Hunchback, Charlemagne proclaimed his having three sons to be a sign of God's blessing on the realm as part of the order of generations, a statement duly echoed by the poet Ermold a generation later.[148] Thus, Charlemagne's command that Carolingians respect each other was not simply an echo of general social norms on generational relations, but a specific reminder that senior Carolingians deserved respect from everyone.

Junior Carolingians were also special. Their Carolingian blood was so valuable that it had to be respected precisely because its very value made it dangerous; hence, Charlemagne's sombre clause forbidding his sons to kill, mutilate or tonsure their nephews 'without lawful trial or inquiry'.[149] This, however, would not only be a mechanism for mercy to emerge but also a way of giving the charisma of vulnerable Carolingians a reality. That social meaning of Carolingian specialness was not easy for the Carolingians themselves to regulate. Charlemagne seems to have thought that only one grandson would succeed each of his royal sons, but also wished all actual and potential grandsons to be honoured.[150] While no king's son had a guaranteed future, the special status of kings' sons in Carolingian discourse, including this very document, meant that it would have been difficult to circumscribe such descendants. It had certainly been difficult to cancel Pippin the Hunchback, and Charlemagne himself referred in 806 to the aristocracy's role in the accepting of such (grand)sons as successors. As Alcuin had said in a letter to Charlemagne in 798 'may your power and rule (*regnum*) be blessed, and your sons and the sons of your sons unto the eternal generations'. Charlemagne was duly grateful for such prayers for his offspring (*progenies*). Carolingian followers' belief in dynastic specialness meant that the dynasty would find it hard to narrow the chances of its members.[151]

Gambling on futures: 806–14

The historian knows which sons' futures did not materialize. Contemporaries did not have this knowledge and in trying to understand their historical situation we have to remember the possible futures that lay before them, as threat or promise. Examining the kingship of Pippin of Italy is a particularly valuable way of doing this. Of course we could do also this for Louis the Pious in these years, but modern historians have done this, as indeed the authors of the *Royal Frankish Annals* seen to have done so. Focusing on Pippin means that Louis is perhaps a fainter presence in the picture I give here, but he should not be forgotten. The cluster of aristocrats visible around Louis in a charter of 794 did not make that mistake.[152] Contemporaries did not know that Pippin was to die in 810. He was thus a factor in their calculations and he must be the same in ours. Members of the aristocracy had interests and justifications for backing their own favoured royal son.

Pippin's future looked good and his promise was not confined to Italy. He did rule his Italian kingdom in the shadow of his father; capitularies for Italy stemmed from Charlemagne though they could bear Pippin's name. But Pippin's own grip on his kingdom tightened as he matured. He was a king; he was anointed; contemporaries did not use the term 'sub-king', they simply called him 'king', though often with a specifically Italian dimension.[153] He issued (now lost) diplomas; he had distinguished figures around him: bishop Ratold of Verona and Angilbert, lover of Pippin's own sister. He was remembered as a legislator in the great compilation of laws made for duke Eberhard of Friuli around 830, pictured with sword and staff beside Charlemagne and described as ' glorious king Pippin his [Charlemagne's] son'. Aristocrats were not to forget him as king and king's son.[154] He displayed his authority in settings such as Verona, subject of an eloquent contemporary poem in its praise, one that pictured the residence of the 'most pious king Pippin' there as one of that town's outstanding features. He was to be buried in Verona. Pippin's court was a cultural centre, associated with an impressive range of texts, possibly including such a well-known work as Paul the Deacon's *History of the Lombards*. He was an active military campaigner and his 810 attack on Venice shows that he was still vigorous in the year of his death. His passing must have shocked contemporaries.[155]

Pippin was not purely an Italian figure. Italy itself attracted interest in ways that Louis the Pious' kingdom of Aquitaine did not. A steady stream of pilgrims, for example, flowed into Italy and it is no surprise to find Alcuin writing to Pippin asking him to look after a priest on his journey there. In this letter, Alcuin takes care to praise Pippin's exalted origins and the fact that he is worthy of them, citing the biblical book of Proverbs on a wise son being the glory of his father.[156] The sensational Frankish victories over the Avars in the 790s shone a spotlight on him. Although Charlemagne and his Franks planned these campaigns and aristocratic leaders such as Eric, duke of Friuli, won the key victories, it was Pippin, king of strategically important northern Italy, who travelled from Pannonia to Aachen to bring Avar treasures to his father.[157]

Pippin forged connections with regions and power holders north of the Alps, particularly in Alemannia. In his 796 campaign against the Avars, his forces included troops from Bavaria and Alemannia while he also commanded Bavarian troops on his 797 campaign against the Slavs. Shared experiences on military campaigns established bonds between men.[158] But the generosity of Pippin's court was not confined to warriors, nor were men the only people there. Among his guardians in his childhood years as king was an Alemannian called Waldo, who administered the bishopric of Pavia from 785/7 to 795. Waldo was also abbot of Reichenau and had been abbot of St-Gall; once back in Alemannia, he remembered the generosity of Pippin's Italian court. Preserved in a late medieval source is the record of how Waldo brought books to Reichenau: 'in particular an antiphonary given to him by the queen, Pippin's wife'.[159] The crassly modern term 'networking' hardly covers the gift of a Christian book, but networking was what Pippin's wife did here. We know almost nothing about her and this glimpse of her generosity in this reverential memory sheds valuable light on her as an active agent in the disposal of books and patronage at the court of Pippin. Waldo remembered her while Albgar, count in Alemannia, was to retain vivid memories of his service as guardian of Pippin's daughters a decade or more afterwards. Generous or vulnerable, Pippin's women made Pippin remembered. Waldo went on to become abbot of St Denis, which, incidentally, held extensive properties in Italy. Other important office-holders in Pippin's kingdom also had roots in Alemannia.[160]

Alcuin wrote to all three sons in the 790s, but his 796 letter to Pippin is of particular interest. Here he prays that God would extend Pippin's kingdom and his line. In the course of giving the young man advice on how to be a good king, Alcuin urged him to 'rejoice with the wife (*mulier*) of your youth and do not let others be your companions so that the blessing given you by God may result in a series of descendants stretching long into the future'. Alcuin's reference to Proverbs 5.18 here may suggest that Pippin had a wandering eye but, more important, points to Pippin as married. Historians' view that he was not stems from their knowledge of later accusations against his son's status. Alcuin's letter may not be conclusive evidence, but contemporary perceptions of marriage and offspring could be fluid.[161] What Alcuin was clear about was his encouragement of dynastic thinking on Pippin's part, and here he was not alone. The king's own followers in Italy exulted in his achievements and an Italian poem celebrating Pippin's triumphs over the Avars looked to a glorious future for his line: 'Long may he reign, grow old and beget sons/who shall preserve his palaces in his lifetime and after his death.'[162]

Observers north and south of the Alps agreed on Pippin's present glory as foreshadowing a future for his line. They understood him to be one ruler in a

Carolingian sequence. Alcuin's references to the posterity of a wife are important. In 794 or 795, Pippin's brother Louis the Pious had just been given a wife by Charlemagne from a powerful family, a wife who was to replace Louis's mistress and who gave Louis a legitimate son in 795. If Louis was now married, celebrations of Pippin's line were therefore timely, and pointed: young Charles now enjoyed the lonely prominence of being unmarried.[163] Taking an interest in Pippin did not mean losing interest in his royal brothers. Angilbert, who had served as a sort of regent for the youthful Pippin in Italy, celebrated the arrival of the mature warrior Pippin in Aachen in 796, but took care to lavish praise on Charles the Younger and Louis the Pious too. In fact, Angilbert's celebration of all the brothers' affection for each other sounds suspiciously excessive; smiles were forced.[164]

As we have seen, in the summer of 799 all three sons were at their father's court, but this was the momentous summer that saw the pope suffer assault in Rome and travel north to seek Charlemagne's help. It was Pippin of Italy who had the honour of meeting the pope and leading him to Charlemagne's presence at Paderborn in a splendid procession of many warriors.[165]

Much to his chagrin, one imagines, Louis was absent from the great gathering in Rome at Christmas 800. Louis's own circle was keen to stress that Charlemagne had originally planned for Louis to be there but that the military responsibilities of the frontier meant that he had to stay and that he and his father were in friendly contact over all this.[166] This is perfectly possible. In fact, Charlemagne may have wanted to keep one son in Francia so that a kingly Carolingian presence remained north of the Alps. Louis was, so to speak, the designated driver for 800. It is not surprising that he quickly sought to advertise his own military glory by sending the captured governor of Barcelona as a prize to Charlemagne in the summer of 801. The escorting of the prisoners from Barcelona into Charlemagne's presence by one of Louis's closest followers was a way of reminding Aachen, and Louis's supporters, of Louis's kingship. Out of sight could not be allowed to mean out of mind.[167]

Louis in fact seems to have been one of the few members of Charlemagne's immediate family not present in Rome in 800. Young Charles was crowned there, as king, and Charlemagne's sister Gisela was also there, as were at least some of Charlemagne's daughters and Pippin himself.[168] But was this gathering necessarily a harmonious one? Was Pippin there with his wife (queen) and his own children? What would young Charles and his followers have made of that? Did all Charlemagne's daughters agree that young Charles was the man of the future? One daughter, Bertha, was the lover in the 790s of Angilbert who retained Italian connections. Charlemagne's cousin Adalhard may have been in Rome in 800 and he had connections with Pippin and Angilbert.[169]

The year 800, however, marked promotion for only one of the sons: Charlemagne had underlined the status of young Charles. This was the message broadcast to the royal family and its attendants in Rome as well as its followers north of the Alps. Furthermore, Charlemagne's lengthy presence in Italy, where he 'dealt with the affairs of the whole of Italy', commanding Pippin to go on campaign in Benevento, demonstrated to all that he was the ruler of the empire and that Pippin was his son and subordinate.[170] But, once Charlemagne returned north, Pippin sent a captured hostile governor to him in 801, just as Louis the Pious did. This acknowledgement of an imperial father's superior status was also a reminder of an absent son's military achievement. Both captives were ushered into Charlemagne's presence on the same day as a demonstration to the centre of Frankish imperial power on the frontiers but this also doubtless offered opportunities to aristocrats in Aachen to compare and recall these distant sons of the emperor.[171]

Pippin now assertively pushed his links with Alemannia. Some time between 806 and 810, he and bishop Ratold of Verona visited the Alemannian shrine of Schienen, itself the foundation of a count Scrot who had connections with Italy and Alemannia, and with abbot Waldo. Pippin's pushing into Alemannia can also be seen in transactions there. A group of charters from the great abbey of St-Gall between 807 and 809 are dated by the regnal years of Pippin (as well as of Charlemagne).[172] It appears that some people in Alemannia were acknowledging Pippin. Pippin was quick off the mark to make his presence felt in a region with which he had long-standing connections, a region to which he was entitled by the promises in the *Division* but which was to be a border-zone between himself and his older brother Charles.[173] Not every aristocrat here spent every moment of every day thinking about the tensions within the ruling family. We can see one count, Hunfrid, busy on a winter's day in this region some time between 806 and 808 presiding over a relatively humdrum property dispute where participants' focus was on the boundaries of local estates. Even if this particular case did involve some pressures on old regional structures to accommodate more royal power, the people involved in it did not on that day brush against the dynastic tensions that we have been analysing. But the count's family and his local subordinate were themselves to be exposed to the heat of dynastic tensions when Pippin's son Bernard rose against Louis the Pious in 817–18.[174]

By 806, Pippin was king of Italy, with a son, and he also enjoyed a high-profile north of the Alps. He does not look like a man ready to meekly accept the lofty status of his brother Charles the Younger. Nor does Charles's status seem to have cut much ice with Louis the Pious and his followers. He sent a messenger to stop Charles in his tracks when the latter was sent by an anxious Charlemagne to help Louis face frontier trouble in 802. For a wide section of the aristocracy Pippin looked a good bet. So did Louis the Pious. So did Charles the Younger. But in July 810 Pippin, 'brilliant offspring of a noble line', suddenly died.[175] All bets were off. What happened to the momentum Pippin had generated?

Pippin's death was only one of four deaths among Charlemagne's children over an eighteen-month span in 810–11, including a daughter, Rotrud.[176] These were accompanied by unnerving disturbances in the cosmic order. Looking back, Einhard saw these eclipses as clear signs of the approaching end of the old emperor himself. Contemporaries may well have been worried at the time and the 810 death of Charlemagne's elephant, that most spectacular of the imperial trappings, doubtless deepened their gloomy mood. They may, however, have been equally impressed by such positive news as the collapse of the threat posed by the Danish king Godefrid, seeing it as a sign of Charlemagne's continuing *felicitas* in his wars.[177]

But they were anxious. In 811, Charlemagne himself wrote to the community of St-Denis, where Waldo was abbot, demanding an explanation of the heavenly phenomena. The learned monk Dungal replied reassuringly, explaining that eclipses were natural happenings. We need not imagine that the emperor and his court relaxed entirely. Einhard explicitly says that the eclipses struck not just the emperor but also others as threatening signs, and Charlemagne's son Louis in his turn, marvelling at Halley's comet in 837, was to brush aside the re-assurances of his astronomical expert and preferred to understand comets as a warning.[178] Such stories are retrospective, but even Dungal and the community of St-Denis may not have been as calm as his cosmological observations suggest. If veterans such as abbot Adalhard of Corbie could still recall the reign of Charlemagne's father Pippin, many aristocrats would have known only Charlemagne as ruler and any eagerness for a new era was balanced by fear of the unknown. Dungal ends his letter with prayers that Charlemagne should live on for many years and also prays that God would preserve the emperor's 'sacred offspring'. Dungal's abbot was Waldo, that staunch supporter of Pippin of Italy who could now see how vulnerable the royal line was. These prayers expressed real wishes for stability in a world shadowed by eclipses and royal death.[179]

These deaths did not freeze speculations and political calculations on the market of royal futures. Indeed family politics moved to an ever quicker tempo. Pippin's death meant that Charlemagne now had his children moved from Italy to Aachen, the senior source of family power. Boys or girls, they were precious children of a Carolingian king, and were not to be left to fend for themselves in a faraway realm. This was a public demonstration of Charlemagne's masterful but anxious control of a royal house that now included many grandchildren. Women could not rule but their honoured presence in the palace could re-assure all that the royal family remained healthily numerous. Bringing them north kept them all under Charlemagne's eye, but his gaze would not have been the only one that fell on them. Their aristocratic escorts from Italy remembered them, as we have seen. Einhard recalled the names of all five of Bernard's sisters and notes the connections that they made with Charlemagne's own daughters at court. Bernard himself probably spent time at Charlemagne's court before being sent to the monastery of Fulda for his education.[180] Fulda was no remote backwater; Einhard himself had come to the court from Fulda in the 790s. Charlemagne was well informed about the disputes within the monastic community there at precisely this time and had sent the archbishop of Mainz there to investigate them in 809. At Fulda, Bernard was part of a community that was bound into dynamic local aristocratic networks but which also looked back at the court: it prayed for the emperor and his children every day, as the monks themselves reminded Charlemagne in 812. In Bernard's time of trial in 817–18, such connections went live: monks at Fulda were to intercede for him then.[181] Pippin's death paradoxically had made his family more visible at the centre of power than ever and these young children could now develop new connections.

Charlemagne's control meant that he took Italy into his hands, re-routing to his own presence envoys from Constantinople who had travelled to Pippin. Between 810 and 812, people in Italy dated charters by the reign of Charlemagne. It was Charlemagne at Aachen who made grants to the church of Aquileia and dealt with the dispute between it and Salzburg.[182] There is no evidence that either of his surviving kingly sons, young

Charles or Louis the Pious, had any role to play in Italy at this time. They and their followers doubtless recalled the promises of the 806 *Division* that they would share Italy if their brother Pippin predeceased them, but Charlemagne himself was still clearly in charge.

He also drew up a will in 811, having it witnessed by thirty prominent magnates whose interests spanned the empire, not exactly a way of keeping his intentions secret. This will did not regulate the succession; he was trying to disperse a storm-cloud of disputes gathering over the glittering treasures he bequeathed, including 'royal ornaments' (*ornatus regius*), but his reference to the possibility of his abandoning the world for a monastery could only have stoked further uncertainty about the future among the court.[183] The fact that this will was not comprehensive and that the emperor was known to be planning further inheritances for his daughters and his children by concubines would have also fuelled speculation about the pecking order in the royal family, and these children would have striven to influence their father and his intimates.[184] Questions of inheritance were circulating. These daughters and sons were not in line for a throne but the emperor's own actions reflected and heightened the tensions gathering within the royal family and the aristocracy over the looming succession.

Death now brutally simplified the situation: young Charles died in 811 (as did Pippin the Hunchback, an odd coincidence). The exact dates of the deaths of 810–11, including Rotrud's, were recorded in the annals, perhaps for commemoration purposes. The special status of exalted individuals, the ruler's children, was thus manifested and these entries themselves depended on communication networks.[185] But such networks could also carry fevered speculations and enquiries about the succession. Brothers were happier with zero-sum games than fathers could be.

An envoy from Louis to Charlemagne now encountered powerful magnates instructing him to urge Louis to come to the palace now and support his grieving and ailing father. The Astronomer's account of this is retrospective and moralizing in its depiction of Louis as dutifully preferring to wait for his father to send for him, but there is no reason to doubt either its essence or details.[186] This is a glimpse of the intrigues sited at the palace and which obsessively pivoted on the royal line and relationships within it, though we also see the active role of the magnates: they worked behind the ruler's back; their message to Louis was a 'private' one, not something relayed from the emperor. In some ways, there was no distance between Aachen and Aquitaine; the magnates at the palace turned to Louis because he was the emperor's son no matter how far away he was. But distance nonetheless existed in real time and space and communication was vital; it was envoys such as Louis's falconer Gerricus galloping between Aquitaine and Aachen who helped keep father and son in the aristocracy's picture of the royal line.[187]

Louis certainly had supporters at his father's court. Einhard appears to have been keen on his succession. Louis's followers in Aquitaine included men such as count Bego who had powerful connections in Francia itself, and there was steady traffic of envoys between the two rulers. Nor need we think that supporters of Charles the Younger such as bishop Theodulf of Orléans had much difficulty switching their loyalty to Louis;

supporters of Pippin of Italy could also now back Louis.[188] We should imagine some of these figures pushing the old emperor to proclaim Louis as successor. But why would they need to push? Who else could succeed?

The most striking aspect of Charlemagne's behaviour towards Louis at this time is inactivity. He did not summon his son northwards. None of the deaths of 810–11 resulted in Louis appearing at his father's palace. Not until the autumn of 813 did Louis come to Aachen to be proclaimed as the imperial successor; he had not been there since early 809.[189] Out of sight was hardly out of mind. But not all palace minds were favourably disposed to Louis. The thick cluster of royals in his father's entourage did not whole-heartedly support Louis and he knew and resented that. Under Charlemagne, the senior Carolingian male at court was Wala and Louis's prospects cast a shadow over him. Some of this tension was due to the peculiar circumstances of Charlemagne's last years; his daughters may not always have been with him but had a high profile in his palace.[190] They were, however, vulnerable as they depended exclusively on their father's favour and Louis, with a wife of his own to queen it over the court, would not need them. Charlemagne's control had been a hard bargain for them. Only as the reign had worn on did he curtail marriage prospects for them (see above on Rotrud, an engagement actually mentioned by Einhard), but he balanced this with their importance in the palace and permitting them to have sexual liaisons with important magnates, liaisons that produced male children. In 813, these children were still young, possibly around thirteen or so, their mothers were not married, and the surviving mothers could not rule. The old emperor had been smart. But, as 'their' clause in the *Division* shows, the daughters had also been thinking of a future without father. They were not passive and they could now see that time was not on their side.[191]

These figures were bound to work to hamper Louis's progress towards the throne. Nor could all members of the aristocracy switch easily to Louis; some had invested too deeply in alternative lines and Louis had followers of his own to reward and promote.[192] The disappearance of competitive brothers left the spotlight on Louis. The picture was clearer, but that now brought the precise nature of its challenges into sharp focus. Louis's biographer later claimed that Louis selflessly lobbied his father for Bernard in Italy. As a claim, this is incredible, but as a retrospective glimpse into the world of urgent messages and bargaining at that time it is as valuable as the same source's remark that Charlemagne feared 'internal conflicts' within his realm.[193]

This tense jockeying for power and influence across a wide section of the ruling elite was important but was more than merely manoeuvrings of court cliques. We see here some of the problems stemming from the massive expansion of the Frankish realm as aristocrats from across its extent struggled to ensure their continued access to a ruler who could feed them the rewards, *honores*, etc., that maintained their status. The prosperous Carolingian kingdom of Italy needed more than rule by remote control. Charlemagne himself had had to go there five times in his reign. For most of the Carolingian period, Italy required a king of its own: Pippin (781–810), Bernard (812–17) were followed by Lothar I (a special case but often present in Italy in the 820s and 830s) and Louis II (839–75). This is in sharp contrast to the Ottonian dynasty's pattern in the tenth century, when the northern ruler himself spent extended periods of time in the peninsula. The Carolingians gave Italy a specific ruler to focus on.[194]

Aristocrats had invested deeply in the empire and its ruling family. Individual Carolingians were enormously important in this empire; Pippin and young Charles dramatically demonstrated this in the impact of their death. But their individual importance did not mean that kings and their sons were all-powerful actors of untrammelled agency. Charlemagne could not escape the need to work with the reality of aristocratic power, nor was he free to shape his own family. An insightful study of the reign has recently argued that Charlemagne made use of creative ambiguity and tensions to keep political options among the political elite and to ensure that the elite focused on him as ringmaster.[195] But there were now too many uncertain options.

The system of exclusive Carolingian familial royalty was bigger than its individual members. This was true on the surface level, an important one, of events, that is, the growth of the royal family. Charlemagne fathered some twenty children, including nine sons who survived into adulthood; he married five times; by the time of his death in 814, he had around a dozen grandchildren. Keeping his daughters unmarried, the differentiated naming of sons (legitimate sons alone were given 'royal' names), and promoting branch-line kin such as Adalhard and Wala to high positions but not to thrones all show his masterful gradation of shape and status within the family. His 'capture' of the Italian grandchildren shows his ability to supervise his line even into the next generation, but the grandchildren in Aquitaine, the sons of Louis the Pious, were not under his eye in the same way and as Louis's sons grew, their claims and potential also grew, generating new pressures. Two of Charlemagne's daughters had liaisons with powerful magnates, and had had sons by them, and so yet another line of Carolingians was growing up.[196]

In some ways, time was very much on the Carolingians' side; as time passed, their royalty deepened as son succeeded father and names such as Charles and Louis gained more royal lustre in the eyes of the aristocracy and the kings themselves. In other ways, time ensured that the royal line would become more complex to manage as sons, and daughters, grew and multiplied. Above all, rulers such as Charlemagne became ever more deeply enmeshed in a dynastic charisma paradox. Here the career of Pippin's son Bernard of Italy, physically much closer to the emperor's court than Louis between 810 and 812, is very instructive.

Charlemagne himself had grasped the importance of the youthful Bernard's Carolingian qualities as his bringing him north shows. The existence of these qualities, that is to say, the fact that they were socially recognized, means that Charlemagne's room for manoeuvre here was limited if he had thought of denying Bernard a throne. Historians, however, have tended to be impressed by Charlemagne's control of the situation and to underplay Bernard's inborn status, arguing that Charlemagne had no intention of giving the boy a throne in 810 and that it was only with the death of Charlemagne's oldest son by Hildegard, Charles, in December 811 that Bernard's prospects improved.[197] While Charles the Younger was alive, neither he nor his brother Louis the Pious nor their followers would have had much enthusiasm for Bernard succeeding.

Charlemagne certainly held the initiative here. Neither Bernard nor any potential supporters of his could take the prospect of his succeeding his father for granted. But Charlemagne himself was not a free agent in 810. Perhaps he and his two surviving legitimate sons were not much troubled by the clause of the *Division* that stated that if any of the sons had a son then he could succeed in the relevant kingdom, though they would have remembered that the magnates had sworn to accept the 806 settlement. And that settlement itself spoke of the role of the aristocracy (*populus*) in such a succession. Political pressures were real. Sons needed aristocratic backing to activate their claim; rulers could not ignore such aristocrats.[198] This means that Charlemagne alone could not define Bernard's value. The specialness of the Carolingians was not constructed by some single-minded Carolingian high command that then issued top-down instructions on who was in and who was out. Rather, that royal specialness was constituted in complex relations between partners, the Carolingians and the aristocracy (including churchmen), a type of web of power relations as 'an ensemble of actions', a concept familiar from the work of Michel Foucault. Thinking of Carolingian royalty in such terms helps us understand that even a ruler as powerful as Charlemagne was caught up in such a web. He was not able to stand outside such relations and direct them. If he was to continue to benefit from the system of Carolingian royalty, he had to fulfil what that system demanded. As Chris Wickham puts it, kings 'were to an extent prisoners of the expectations of their audiences in [a] sort of uncontrollable power network'.[199]

Foucault argued that relationships of communication should be distinguished from relationships of power though they could overlap. Charlemagne's actions towards Bernard communicated his own power but could not help but communicate that Bernard too had power, had Carolingian status. Bernard's claims became active as soon as his father died in 810; he did not need to wait till his uncle died in 811 to become a contender. But what he did need was some form of recognition of his potential and Charlemagne's bringing him north of the Alps was precisely this. Charlemagne's actions recognized Bernard's explosive royal status and in seeking to stabilize it could only serve to construct it further in the eyes of aristocratic observers who in their turn ascribed more value to it. Carolingian specialness was too dynamic a force for Charlemagne to control. He himself was subject to pressures even as he generated them.[200]

Charlemagne waited. He did not send Bernard to Italy until 812, but he sent an expert on the Italian scene down there in late 810, only a few months after Pippin's death. This was his kinsman abbot Adalhard of Corbie, who had already played a key role in Italy in the 780s while Pippin was young; he now returned as the trusted envoy of Charlemagne.[201] Adalhard's family connection to Charlemagne doubtless gave him status in Italy, just as it did for his brother Wala in Saxony, entrusted with important tasks there in 811. Experienced and skilful, these men displayed the royal kin in far-away lands but their service to Charlemagne and his line also manifested the hierarchy within that kin-group. And kings ruled kingdoms within this far-flung empire. Aquitaine had a king; Italy was going to have one. Figures such as Adalhard in Italy and Wala in Saxony were not regal.[202]

This means that the presence in Italy of Adalhard, for all his competence, could only underline the fact that the kingdom still awaited a king. That need not have meant that that king had to be Bernard. But he was the obvious candidate. One source, written by a monk who knew Adalhard, states explicitly that he was working in Italy only until Bernard grew up and could come into his inheritance: 'he was entrusted with the important task of having to govern the kingdom of the Lombards until Pippin's son Bernard grew up'. This text was written some time after 836.²⁰³ Its view is thus a retrospective one. The author knew that Bernard had become king of Italy and assumed that his succession was inevitable because he was the son of the previous king. But this is itself a demonstration of deep conviction in dynastic reproduction. This Saxon monk in the monastery of Corvey, hundreds of kilometres from Italy and indeed Aachen, proud of Adalhard's Carolingian blood, here articulated the learned natural pattern of Carolingian succession in the case of Pippin and Bernard.

Obviously, as the historical procession of Carolingians succeeding each other grew longer, such a perspective had deepened. But this view was already contemporary with Bernard himself. A chronicle written in Lorsch explicitly emphasizes the father-son relationship as an aspect of Bernard's succession: 'Bernard the son of Pippin was established in his father's place (*constituitur pro patre suo*) in the kingdom of Italy', and this text was written close in time to the events it describes.²⁰⁴ Even a chronicle such as this one was written after the events it describes and may thus present Bernard's succession as more seamless than it actually was. On the level of representation, however, that serves only to illustrate the authoritative nature of Carolingian dynastic discourse, a discourse that this chronicle participated in and enhanced, intended as it was for a wider audience than the monks of Lorsch. Other chronicles echoed its formulation. Writers who wanted to stress the role of Charlemagne in making Bernard king still found themselves pointing out who Bernard's father was.²⁰⁵ Writers looking at events after the catastrophic end of Bernard's career found themselves unable to avoid delineating his Carolingian descent, whether giving it straight, as Einhard did, or trying to accentuate his relationship to Louis the Pious, the senior family member and thus just judge of his errant nephew, as Thegan and the Astronomer did.²⁰⁶

Older connections also mattered. Adalhard went to Italy as Charlemagne's envoy but he had worked there for Bernard's father and, as we shall see, his and Bernard's branches of the royal kin seem to have been particularly close. The monk of Corvey was not merely projecting back his later knowledge when he wrote that Adalhard was sent to govern Italy until Pippin's son grew up. People recognized that his father's death made Bernard a player and acted accordingly, thus making him more of a player. Carolingian-ness was now a necessary condition for ruling a kingdom within the massively expanded realm; that gave status and importance to Bernard. Carolingian-ness was not in itself, however, sufficient to guarantee Bernard a throne. Backers had to activate his Carolingian identity by supporting his claims to kingship. But such backers believed that Carolingian-ness was necessary and so their own self-interest in backing Pippin's line coincided with a deep belief in the entitlement of that line to rule. Highly placed figures round Charlemagne knew the Italian line. Angilbert had served in Italy, was the lover of the emperor's daughter Bertha and knew Adalhard well; like Adalhard, he was a witness to Charlemagne's will of 811. Adalhard had served Pippin and his return to Italy was a signal that Pippin's line would have a future. His brother Wala was to escort Bernard to Italy in 812, and contemporaries' knowledge that Wala's father was called Bernard suggests that they understood the closeness between these figures.²⁰⁷

Young Bernard was not marginal. He was a possible future open to contemporaries. The fact that we know that some futures were closed helps us in all analyses of historical developments but it can also distort our historical vision. Our vision of Bernard in particular is further distorted because some ninth-century evidence seems to point to him as not quite a top-drawer Carolingian. In the 830s, Thegan described him as the son of a concubine, but this could well be only the same sort of retrospective sneering that we have already seen directed against Pippin the Hunchback. Bernard's appearance in a list of rulers that dates from c.812, that is, before his fall, has led some historians to claim that his illegitimacy is 'beyond doubt' since his name appears within a sub-group of illegitimate Carolingians. Such certainty, however, is illusory; other historians have argued with equal conviction that if we see the list of rulers as arranged chronologically, then Bernard appears in his rightful place as a grandson and not as illegitimate.[208] Various aspects of this list remain puzzling and we cannot use it as hard evidence of Bernard's illegitimacy. What we can use it for will become apparent below.

Bernard's name, however, is a puzzle. It is not a royal name, though it is one that appears in the wider Carolingian family (Charlemagne had an uncle with this name). In a world of competitive royals, kingly fathers gave their sons potent names to boost their chances. Louis the Pious had a son by a concubine and had called him Arnulf, an indubitably Carolingian name, but not a kingly one; Louis was marking out this boy as not quite the full heir. This Arnulf was Bernard's exact contemporary, so this naming style was current.[209] Even if Bernard were of illegitimate birth, did it matter to contemporaries? After all, it was only later, in the reign of Louis the Pious, that a ruler insisted that only legitimate sons could succeed and this was an exceptional declaration. If Bernard was illegitimate, that might have been a factor in the calculations of family members and aristocrats, but in 810–11 they were not rigidly bound by ecclesiastical thinking or imperial norms to exclude him. Charlemagne's distinguishing between his legitimate children and those by concubines at precisely this time did not rob these boys of special status as royal sons. Boundaries of legitimacy could be fluid, and thus useful to contemporaries.[210]

The royal deaths of 810–11 had triggered actions that were communicated across a stage that stretched from Italy through Francia to Aquitaine. The court was not the only place that counted. What happened and was decided there had to be communicated. These actions were communication aimed not at a passive audience but at players. The aged Charlemagne, the newly ambitious Louis and the young Bernard were not alone on stage. Rulers dominate narrative discourses like this because they dominated politics. But if a young man like Bernard had a future because he had charisma (he was a king's son), that charisma needed a creatively responsive audience. His father Pippin had built up sufficient political momentum for his support to outlast his death. The scale of that support, and how it constrained and enabled the rulers' own manoeuvres, is often masked or invisible in narrative sources.

Here we are lucky. We can catch a tantalizing glimpse of the nature and extent of the wider political community involved in the politics of succession after 811 from an enigmatic piece of contemporary evidence, evidence that is all the more valuable to us as it does not itself come from the court. It is an entry in the confraternity book of the abbey of St-Gall in Alemannia, the very region that Pippin had been cultivating.

Such books listed names of people to be prayed for or commemorated in the abbey and who thus had some sort of connection with it. It consists of the names of some eighty-three individuals, some living, some dead, and probably dates from shortly before Charlemagne's death in 814, possibly around 812. The people named, who are all men, consist of members of the Carolingian family and the high aristocracy together with names from the lower ranks. We can divide them up into three groups: (1) kings and sons of kings; (2) members of the high aristocracy, including members of the broader Carolingian kin; (3) over fifty counts and office-holders from Alemannia.[211] That figure is worth pausing over; it is not even a comprehensive list of the Alemannian aristocracy but it lets us see something of the scale of groups involved in the political manoeuvrings. That scale is much less visible in the narrative sources, at least for Charlemagne's reign. The *Royal Frankish Annals*, for example, refer to a total of around fifty individual aristocrats (four of whom belonged to the Carolingian kin-group) for the whole of that reign. Rulers dominated but were not as isolated or free as narrative sources for this period suggest.[212]

Important aspects of this entry remain debatable, not least its date, the identification of key individuals in the royal group and the circumstances of its being entered into the St-Gall book. The primary function of this list was not political but was liturgical and commemorative, to recall the names of people appearing in prayers in a holy place (some of the people listed were dead). It also reveals contemporary perceptions of political relations among the great men of the realm and some fundamental points are clear. Whoever composed/entered the list understood that the Carolingian royal line stood above the ranks of even the greatest aristocrats: the first group includes young children such as Theoderic, whose status as (illegitimate) son of a king gave this seven-year-old boy precedence here above the experienced warriors and governors in the other parts of the list.[213] Kings and their sons also ranked higher than branch-lines of the royal kin as the appearance of exalted figures such as Adalhard and Wala in the second group rather than the first shows. And the composition of the list fixes its gaze on the teenage Bernard of Italy. His name closes the first group and indeed that group culminates in him in that he is identified as 'son of Pippin' and the name Pippin thus opens and closes this group as well as appearing more frequently than any other royal name in it. Seven of the second group's twelve names can be associated with Bernard and the kingdom of Italy.[214] This group includes Adalhard and Wala who may have been particularly close to Bernard's branch of the family. The list (groups 2 and 3) also reveals that Pippin of Italy's push into Alemannia had borne fruit as some figures on it had very precise connections with him. It includes count Gebhard of Treviso (d.c.800) and Count Scrot of Florence who were both involved in the honouring of the relics of St Genesius whose resting place at Schienen in Alemannia had been visited by Pippin.[215] Udalrich and Richuin, two of the counts in locations where St Gall charters had been dated by Pippin's rule between 806 and 810, also appear in it. Bernard had potentially wide support beyond Italy.[216]

We should not assume, however, that this is a list of die-hard supporters of Pippin's line. While it contains Eckideoh, count of Camerino, who did indeed support Bernard when he eventually rebelled against Louis the Pious in 817, it also contained Richuin, the Thurgau count whose indirect brush with the earlier Alemannian claims of Pippin, Bernard's father, did not prevent him from mopping up the messy aftermath of that rebellion there.[217] But such splits among its personnel actually give us a valuable clue to the interpretation of the list. Dark clouds of conflict now loomed over the men in this list. If conflict between Bernard and the senior ruler was to break out, then choices of loyalty would have to be made. This list suggests that such hard choices were precisely what many Carolingian aristocrats dreaded and sought to avoid. If this list preserves the traces of a group that lobbied for Bernard in the last years of Charlemagne's rule, that group was doing so precisely to ward off a clash with Louis and his supporters.

The list also contains names of supporters of Louis, men who had nothing to do with Italy or Alemannia, and this also reveals something of the lobbying and negotiating that may lie behind it. These men, Stephen and Leuthard, belonged to a Neustrian aristocratic family that dominated the county of Paris; members of this family were serving Louis in Aquitaine and it is very unlikely that this family had any sympathy with Bernard's claims; they were Louis's men. Their brother Bego, along with Louis the Pious's wife Ermengard, was an enemy of Bernard.[218] But in these last years of Charlemagne, aristocrats and royals had to try and make a compromise in their claims and interests. Professor Fried's claim that the list gives the names of the men who actually negotiated a deal resolving tensions between Louis and Bernard and their supporters is unprovable but very suggestive.[219]

The royal deaths of 810 and 811 had quickened the pace of political activity over the succession. The old emperor's last years were punctuated with calls for harmony amongst the elite, heard, for example, in the great church councils that he commanded to meet across the realm in 813.[220] This list takes its place amidst all this as the trace of tense negotiations on the royal status of Bernard of Italy. Far from being simply a dry list of names, it offers a vivid glimpse of the hopes and fears of those who did not know the future but were keen to head off conflict. And, perhaps most importantly, it highlights the fact that Carolingian protagonists, even *Carolus imperator*, could not and did not act alone. Other players projected on to them hopes and fears for the future, and they were enmeshed in specific associations and links with the aristocracy. The fact that this list was written down in St-Gall is itself suggestive. What was being played out between Aquitaine, Aachen and Italy registered on the seismographs of sensitive spots of the empire.

Bernard's Carolingian charisma, his status as son of a king, was recognized by too much of the aristocracy and his own family to be cancelled; his claims were active because they found sufficient traction with this group. The result was that Charlemagne at an assembly in Aachen in 812, a few months after the death of his son Charles, publicly sent Bernard into Italy. Bernard had probably been escorted to Aachen from Fulda by prominent magnates and he was accompanied to Italy by Wala. The *Royal Frankish Annals* highlight the Carolingian familial colouring in all this.[221] This source does not tell us, however, that Bernard was proclaimed as king in Italy, though that now looked inevitable. For that, Bernard had to wait until 813 when he returned to Aachen and Charlemagne established him as king of Italy at the great assembly there, where the primary business was Charlemagne's personally crowning Louis as his imperial successor.[222] In other words, Bernard had gone to Italy in 812 to establish his rule there in advance. The emperor had not let Louis come to Aachen before he could present him with a *fait accompli*.

We possess several lengthy accounts of Louis's crowning in 813 and while we cannot distinguish one as more reliable than another we can surely accept their stress on the importance of the acclamation by the assembly that Louis should indeed succeed to the empire. There was no other candidate; this was not an election, but the imperial title, in contrast to the assembly of 806, was now in play. The rulers of the Frankish realm were welcomed into their office by the aristocracy. We can also be sure that the familial element was very prominent. Not only do the sources stress, in varying ways, the succession of father by son, they also, in differing degrees, tell how Charlemagne made Louis promise to honour all his relatives. These authors wrote after Louis had spectacularly broken this promise; the ironic twinge in their writing is less historically significant than their sense that this was the right promise to request and give: family first.[223] It is hard not to believe that the old emperor's surviving daughters and his young illegitimate children were there, as well as Bernard and Wala, etc. as a living diagram of the high but varied and conflicted status of that group.

Charlemagne then sent kingly Bernard back to Italy and, more surprisingly, imperial Louis back to Aquitaine. It seems that Aachen was not yet ready to embrace Louis. But concern over the royal line was not confined to Aachen. The year 813 also saw Charlemagne command church councils to meet to discuss church reform. Numbers of churchmen had duly assembled across the realm, in Arles, Reims, Mainz, Chalons-sur-Saone and Tours. As they worked to improve God's church, they also implored heaven to preserve the emperor, his children and his line (*proles*).[224] But the old emperor's time was running out. Unlike his father, he entered upon his final illness without his successor present. No one seems to have summoned Louis. If Charlemagne's death in January 814 confronted some of his family with tough options, as we shall see, it brought the prospect of change to the world that he had ruled. In the monastery of Bobbio in northern Italy someone composed a lament for the late emperor. We have no way of confirming its claims that children and bishops alike wept for him, but the claimed universal nature of the impact of his death is certain. In Bobbio, this writer knew or imagined that the emperor was buried in Aachen.[225] The palace stood in this distant writer's mind as the site of rule as it had in Alcuin's. This centre, even though now vacant, still acted as a centre. Whereas, when Charles Martel had died in 741 and even when Pippin III had died in 768, disturbances had rocked the 'peripheral' regions such as Aquitaine, and Charlemagne had opened his reign by travelling with warriors to Aquitaine, now these regions were firmly locked into a Frankish centre. Indeed, Aquitaine had a Frankish king who now set out for Aachen, the palace of his father, to grasp his Carolingian legacy.

4

Child labour 751–888

In 1638, Anne of Austria, wife of the French king Louis XIII, gave birth to a son, the future Louis XIV. The long-awaited appearance of an heir to the throne of France was the signal for national celebrations and the kingdom echoed to the explosion of fireworks, the pealing of church bells and the intoning of the Te Deum while writers expatiated on the significance of the infant's arrival. Similarly, though on a slightly less lavish scale, the birth of the future Philip Augustus in 1165 was the trigger for riotous celebrations in Paris.[1] The Carolingian age had neither the system of primogeniture common to the Capetians and Bourbons nor the elaborate media of communication and commemoration which articulated the representation of the Sun King. Carolingian palaces had no equivalent of the Porphyra, the purple chamber of the imperial palace in Constantinople, the setting for the birth of future emperors. Nor is the appearance of children in leading political roles an infallible sign of the primacy of dynastic thinking. The surprising prominence of child emperors in the late Roman world had as much to do with changing structures and concepts of the imperial office as with fond fathers' dynastic ambitions.[2] Not every son of a Carolingian king could be absolutely sure of inheriting a throne; the birth of a legitimate royal son did not have quite the same meaning for the Carolingian world as the birth of Louis XIV and Philip Augustus had for their contemporaries. Nonetheless, Carolingian political reproduction depended upon the birth of sons, and kings' sons were understood as special from their birth, royal even before they assumed office.

Born rulers

The birth of a royal son is not always noted in our sources but this does not mean that we can deduce that contemporaries saw this as 'a political non-event'.[3] In a dynastic kingdom, male children mattered from the start, and boys shall be the focus of this chapter. The testimony of the aristocratic mother Dhuoda from the early 840s shows her recalling the date of birth of her new son born in 841 as well as that of his brother from 826.[4] There has been important work on the relations of royal fathers and sons within the Carolingian world but much of it has tended to focus on the formal stages by which sons reached royal office. I draw on that work gratefully here, but my focus is more specifically dynastic, as in J. Duindam's magisterial recent account of the early modern world.[5] In fact, Carolingian royalty started at birth and this chapter will explore some of the more informal but real ways in which this royalty was created and announced, and how even young children could incorporate dynastic identity and demonstrate it to an aristocratic audience. The birth of a royal son was a special event and one of enormous potential significance. The queen's pregnancy would have been a factor in the political calculations of courtiers, a factor that was all the more difficult to define given that until the birth no-one could be sure if the child would be a boy and even after the birth no-one could be sure that the child would survive.[6]

But this did not mean that contemporaries were stoically indifferent to the birth of royal children or that they waited calmly for the importance of the child to be unveiled through time. It is true that hindsight often shapes our sources accounts' of the birth of sons. Writing in the 840s, the Astronomer, the anonymous biographer of Louis the Pious (born 778), mentioned that Louis was one of twins and that his brother died in early infancy but does not bother to report the name of that brother. For the Astronomer's contemporary, Nithard a noble of Carolingian blood, the important birth was that of Charles (the Bald) in June 823, son of Louis the Pious and Louis's second wife Judith, since Nithard was writing a history commissioned by that Charles. In contrast, Louis's other biographer, Thegan, writing in the 830s but keen to support another of Louis's sons, was stonily silent on Charles's birth.[7]

The perspectives of these texts remind us that followers tended to focus on 'their' Carolingian and screen out others. But such perspectives are misleading if they obscure from us the full impact on contemporaries of the birth of such sons when they happened.[8] Take the cases of Louis the Pious and of Charles the Bald. Neither Hildegard, the mother of Louis, nor Judith, the mother of Charles, was discreet off-stage figures in the last stages of their pregnancy. In 778, Hildegard accompanied her husband Charlemagne and the army as far south as the villa of Chassseneuil in Aquitaine. Charlemagne was on his way even further south, to launch what turned out to be the ill-fated expedition into Spain where the Franks suffered a defeat later immortalized in the *Song of Roland*. Prominent members of the aristocracy would have been at Chasseneuil when the king celebrated Easter there before heading off to war. They would thus have been aware of the imminence of the birth. As for Judith, she spent the last winter of her pregnancy with her husband Louis the Pious in the grand surroundings of the refurbished palace of Frankfurt. In that winter of 822–3 there, Christmas was celebrated and assemblies met, gatherings attended by a host of the aristocracy of the empire.[9]

The men and women who observed these heavily pregnant queens approaching their time could not know for certain that the queens would produce boys nor that these boys were to grow up to be kings. After all, Charlemagne already had two sons in 778 and Louis had three legitimate sons in 823. It is unlikely that their birth was greeted with the sort of self-conscious announcement that Froissart depicts at the birth of the future Richard II in 1367.[10] But members of the aristocracy would have been foolish to bet against the chances of these boys. Baby boys such as these would have made an impact on observers because they were very quickly placed by their fathers in a system of representation and definition for Carolingian royalty.

When Charlemagne returned from his Spanish adventure and found that Hildegard had given birth to twin boys, he chose potent names for them. The boys were called Lothar and Louis. The numbing familiarity of the name Louis to students of French royalty should not blind us to the fact that these names were new to the Carolingian family. They were in fact the property of the displaced Merovingians and Charlemagne's bestowing of them on his sons marked a further stage in the enhancement of the Carolingians as the new royal family of the Franks. The year 778 was a tough year for the Carolingian king. The defeat in Spain was matched by trouble in the east as the Saxons took advantage of the king's absence and rose in revolt, unleashing turmoil along the Rhine. Charles responded with force, but in naming his sons Louis and Lothar he was specifically evoking the names of Merovingian rulers who had wielded power in Aquitaine and Saxony in the sixth century, Clovis and Chlothar I. He thus hoped to associate his children and the new royal dynasty with a usefully glorious past, and people noted this association.[11]

A contemporary source tells us that Charlemagne chose the name of Lothar for one of the twins because of his 'deep love of the ancient kings'. This is a rather different attitude from Charlemagne's own eloquent silence on his Merovingian predecessors in his charters from 775 onwards; the legacy of the Merovingian dynasty, which Charlemagne might himself have remembered, was a complex one.[12] This positive view of the 'ancient kings' comes from an epitaph for Lothar who died in 779 or 780. This text is itself significant. While the surviving twin, Louis, was to be pressed into royal service at the tender age of three as king of Aquitaine, Lothar died too soon to be even a child king. In death, however, Lothar could be drafted into representational service for the dynasty. His epitaph describes him as 'sprung from a famous line, of royal blood' before going on, as we have seen, to associate his name with the Merovingians. This epitaph balances mourning for Lothar with reference to the surviving twin together with references to the boy's parents, Charlemagne and Hildegard, parents of future kings. The author of this substantial poem was Paul the Deacon, who also recalled the boy in his history of the bishops of Metz, written in the 780s. The memorializing of this small child shows the role that royal sons could play in the legitimation of the new dynasty in its third decade of royal status.[13]

As for Louis's own son born in 823, he was given the resonant name of Charles. This would have been the decision of Louis himself and it was a significant one. The potential importance of the birth of a legitimate son to a reigning king or emperor was signalled in the boy's name. Charles was the name of Louis's own royal father and brother; it was a name of kings. This new Charles was still very young when contemporary observers were linking him to his great namesake: 'glowing … with the great name of his grandfather'.[14] Charles's position within the royal family was further secured by Louis having Lothar, his eldest son from his first marriage, become Charles's godfather. It is hard to imagine that Louis had this done quietly. The bond between godfather and godson was meant to ensure that Lothar and Charles and the political community understood the mutual respect and obligations that bound them. The fact that this bond, even though it failed, was later remembered testifies to the impact of its making.[15] Charles's mother also worked on behalf of her infant son. As Charles himself recalled years later: 'In the very hour of my birth, my mother Judith sent a ring to Ebo.' Ebo was the archbishop of Reims and Judith sent this ring as a gift accompanying her request that the archbishop pray for the boy. She may have sent similar gifts to all the great churchmen of the empire. From 'the very hour of birth', the existence of Charles was news to be broadcast and his health was a matter of more than private concern.[16]

Babies such as Charles or Louis the Pious's short-lived brother had to work within the grand system that articulated Carolingian royal status. This system exploited child labour and that exploitation began at birth. Pope Paul I's letter of 770/1 to Charlemagne and his brother Carloman stating that they had been blessed by God in their mother's womb shows royal identity could actually start even earlier than birth; another contemporary assured Charlemagne around 775 that his mother had prayed anxiously for his birth.[17] Such biological facts as pregnancy (or failure to conceive) and birth are what they are but they also belong to the world of culture. Judith's actions in 823 may not so much reflect her infant's intrinsic status as reveal how that status had to be constructed. Pope Paul knew that the royal brothers had been blessed in the womb because he was looking back from the present reality of their royal status. But these retrospective views reveal pre-birth speculations and show how the prospect and event of birth drew attention. Pauline Stafford has commented perceptively on how historians need to distinguish between biological birth and social birth and on the importance of understanding childhood within precise historical contexts. The Carolingian context brings these points into sharp focus. But that focus reveals that for sons of kings, biological birth could be effectively their social birth; there was hardly any gap between the two; contemporaries did not see royal childhood 'negatively' as only the 'period before full social participation'. As soon as the pope heard that Pippin III had a new son in 759, he wrote to congratulate him on having fathered a 'new king'.[18]

Writing in the 820s, almost eighty years after his hero had been born, Einhard tells us that he knew nothing of these early stages in the life of Charlemagne, of his birth, infancy or boyhood, since 'nothing was written down'. Einhard's ignorance here is actually reticence stemming from his unwillingness to touch on tensions of Charlemagne's childhood.[19] In referring to 'infancy' (*infantia*) and 'boyhood' (*pueritia*), Einhard was referring to his culture's stages of childhood. In infancy (*infantia*), sons were probably brought up under the care of the queen but their upbringing and education were in the hands of guardians and tutors. At about six, boyhood (*pueritia*) saw the start of serious education and gendered activities such as hunting and riding, the pastimes of the ruling elite for centuries. This phase of boyhood could last till about fifteen and adolescence (*adolescentia*).[20] But for royal sons, the stages of this life-cycle were different phases of the performing of a royal identity.

Einhard's silence does not imply that Charlemagne's childhood, and by extension that of other Carolingian boys, had been uneventful, or uninteresting to observers. Childhood of rulers was certainly covered in Einhard's model, the imperial biographies of the Roman writer Suetonius. Einhard did in fact believe that Carolingian childhoods were important. He devotes much space to an idealized account of how Charlemagne raised his children and grandchildren; the sons, when they reached the 'right age', were trained to ride in the Frankish fashion, to fight and to hunt while his daughters learned to work with wool.[21] Charlemagne himself seems to have remembered his childhood, indeed his own transition from infancy to boyhood in an anecdote he told about how he lost his first tooth aged seven while playing 'like a boy' during a solemn religious ceremony involving his father the king. If this anecdote can be trusted, it not only sheds valuable light on a king's self-perception of his childish self, it also reveals the participation of young boys in public events and gatherings where aristocrats could see them (Charlemagne's four-year-old brother also attended the ceremony).[22]

Childhood also mattered to the three other royal biographers of the ninth century. The Astronomer, writing around 841, described the miniature royal outfit of the infant Louis the Pious. Louis's other biographer, bishop Thegan writing 836–7, stressed how Louis's good qualities shone out already from his 'infancy'.[23] Writing in the 880s, the fourth biographer, Notker, did not include any stories about Charlemagne's childhood and thus intertextually replicated the silence of Einhard, one of his sources. But his own text has several references to youthful Carolingians, including a very instructive story about the young Louis the German, as we shall see.[24] This may seem to echo hagiography, which often focused on saints' precocious demonstration of their holy qualities. Saintly demonstrations, however, were in defiance of childhood norms; the child who is destined to be a saint rejects the pleasures of childhood, displaying the wisdom and restraint of an old head on young shoulders, an old man cut down ('*puer senex*').[25]

Significantly, Carolingian texts that criticized the Merovingians for their weakness as rulers did not criticize Merovingian child rulers as such. Neither the Royal Frankish Annals nor Einhard nor Notker makes any reference to Merovingian ineffectiveness being the result of Merovingian rulers being children. The vivid account of the ten-year-old Merovingian king Sigibert III crying because he had lost so many men in battle is perhaps less a criticism of the boy king than an acknowledgement that royal boys in all their youthfulness had a place in politics as well as royal men.[26] The innocence of a young child could in fact be a card to play, if rather desperately, in support of Carolingian legitimacy when the whole system came to be challenged after 888, as we shall see in the final chapter.

Royal children could play the part of miniature adults, but their very childishness undercut the adult pose and drew attention to the fact of dynastic rule. When Charlemagne had the three- or four-year-old Louis (the Pious) sent to Aquitaine as king in 781, the fact that Louis was a child could not be ignored. He travelled in a cradle ('push-chair'); on reaching Orléans, he was given 'weapons suitable for his age' and put on a horse and thus entered his kingdom. When Louis travelled to an assembly held by his father in Paderborn in Saxony in 785 he was dressed up with weapons and in an Aquitanian costume as were the young boys who accompanied him.[27] As king in Aquitaine, Louis had to represent the Frankish royal line there just as he presented the far-flung corners of the Frankish realm to its centres, as in his trip to Saxony, and in this we might see him as impersonating an adult. But his cradle, his boyish companions and his little weapons could only underscore that fact that he was a child, not an adult. What was special about Louis was his future but he was already performing it in his childish way. His contact with weapons marked a publicly visible gulf between his experience and his potential. Such junior weapons did exist and were signs of status, of the authority that these children would go on to wield but were also props that showed that a young prince was already acting his part. A young son of Charlemagne could be a king and thus he had to carry weapons. And he did this as a child; it was only later, on reaching 'adolescence' at thirteen, that Louis was formally girded with a sword by his father.[28]

Such miniature weapons pointed to the high status of a child, but may not always have carried precise connotations of office holding. In 826, at the age of three, Louis's own child Charles (the Bald) took part in a stylized version of a royal hunt in which he struck at a deer with little weapons that were just the right size for his tender age. The poet Ermold depicts this junior huntsman in the midst of a crowd, including his mother, his tutor and hunting attendants.[29] Charles was not a king, but his father and mother had plans for him and sought to broadcast such plans; as a three-year-old son of the emperor he had access to weapons and to opportunities to be represented in handling them. These opportunities were also necessities. Like aristocratic children, little royal boys had to learn how to be men.[30] But royal boys' childish antics took place in public.

Of course neither royal fathers nor their aristocratic followers could be sure that royal babies would survive. Nor was the Carolingian context an unchanging one. The *Ordering of the Empire* of 817, one of the two great Carolingian written statements on royal succession, proclaimed that, in some circumstances, sons of kings could only become kings when they reached the age of majority. In fact, it warned that not every son of a king would become a king and here it echoed the earlier generation's statement on succession, the *Division of the Kingdom* of 806.[31] The *Ordering of the Empire* also explicitly disqualified sons of concubines from the succession.[32] But, for all their impressiveness, these documents did not mesmerize contemporaries. The settlements of 806 and 817 could not dent the belief that all (legitimate) sons of a king had a claim to the throne. Indeed, illegitimate sons continued to have, and take, their chances in the ninth century.[33] Neither legislation of their great-grandfather and grandfather, nor the heavy hand of their own fathers, prevented the royal cousins Louis the Stammerer and Louis the Younger from explicitly proclaiming in 878 that *all* their sons were to succeed them, including a little one year old, who, like the others, was to be helped to 'hold their father's kingdom peacefully and by hereditary right'.[34]

This had some roots in the older Frankish idea of the special status of all royal sons; in the sixth century bishop Gregory of Tours wrote that 'all boys born of kings are called king's sons'.[35] For Carolingian sons, the decisions of the father and the role of the magnates in determining these sons' prospects were certainly important.[36] But royal fathers could find it very difficult indeed to disinherit legitimate sons; fathers could not suppress the dynastic charisma upon which they themselves depended. Aristocrats were taught to revere royal sons from their birth and they learned this lesson well. The political culture of dynastic authority was bigger than individual rulers. Sons could have their own followings, could be protectors of monasteries, oaths of fidelity could be taken to them, etc., and churchmen saw the office of under-king (which is a modern term, not a contemporary one) as being held directly from God and so did not distinguish the under-king from the over-king in his office.[37]

On the other hand, even when they came to maturity such sons could remain under the control of their father as seen, for example, in the relatively late age at which Carolingian fathers permitted their sons to marry. On average, Carolingian princes tended to marry later, at twenty-six, than Merovingian ones had done, at fifteen, though some sons were too impatient to wait.[38] (The term 'prince' is not contemporary and I only use it here as shorthand for legitimate son of a reigning king, and would not claim for it even the validity of the contemporary Anglo-Saxon term *aetheling*.[39]) Even mature princes could be overshadowed by their father and their royal power did not always match their royal status. But the mirror image of this is also true: they did not need to be mature to have authority and indeed did not need to be installed in a kingdom to have status; being the recognized sons of their father gave them exceptional status.

Ceremonies such as weapons-giving were socio-cultural rather than legal. If young sons became kings, their authority, as expressed in charters, etc., was not depicted as limited; for Carolingians, there was no institutionalized concept of regent even if in fact they needed minders.[40] Historians have tended to look to ceremonies of coming of age or of king-making as solid indications that royal sons' potential was to be fulfilled. But the great magnates with access to court would have started watching sons much earlier, from their infancy. Slighting references to young royals as childishly incompetent are isolated and tendentious.[41] Royal children had to be taken seriously from the start; courtiers projected a future on to these young boys. In 829, court poet Walahfrid Strabo saw the six-year-old Charles the Bald as a potential father who would continue the dynastic line to which his birth and name so gloriously associated him. Walahfrid was not simply reflecting the boy's status; his poem helped construct it, though a poem could not construct everything.[42]

The various stages of the young royal life-cycle mattered and formal recognition of, or investment with, authority mattered very much to contemporaries, who were also, however, more aware of the bigger picture than we might be. Eric Goldberg has argued plausibly that, since Louis the German began his personal rule in Bavaria in 825–6, he was probably born in 810 as 825–6 would mark his coming of age. Goldberg further suggests that Louis's father presided over a formal coming-of-age ceremony for his son, where the teenage prince received the sword belt, sign of maturity and masculinity.[43] But other historians have noted that ceremonies such as weapon-giving were part of a repertoire of meanings, social-cultural as well as legal and were not tied to specific ages. There is a danger of circularity in assuming that the prince needed to be of age in 825–6 and thus deducing that he was born in 810. Carolingian fathers could send out very young sons to rule kingdoms (e.g. the three-year-old Louis Pious in Aquitaine) while sons who had come of age could still be subject to tutelage.[44] The young Louis the German's royal qualities pre-dated his assuming rule in his eastern kingdom in 825–6; that date mattered: his charters were dated from then and he may well have been crowned in a solemn ceremony in Bavaria.[45] But Louis was kingly before that date. The settlement of 817 had allocated him a kingdom and even if he did not take it up until 826 it had proclaimed that he and his brother Pippin were to be called kings.[46] After this, but before he went to Bavaria, he led an army against the Bretons in 824. Of course, he had a very senior aristocratic minder and when a veteran of this campaign looked back on it, he noted Louis's youth but this only underscored Louis's Carolingian identity: he was the son of his father ('You, Louis, as a boy wage the wars of your father') and father and son shared the same name, thus mirroring each other's royalty.[47]

Louis was not the only son of a king to see action while young. Charlemagne accompanied his father on campaign in Aquitaine when he was about twelve, but he had already been anointed and had an assured kingly status; war was part of a process to prepare him and the aristocracy for a defined future.[48] Amidst the savagery of the civil wars of 840–3, we catch a glimpse of a royal child that seems to offer a different perspective. In 841, after the terrible battle of Fontenoy against his brothers, Lothar I withdrew east to regroup and summoned his young son Lothar to meet him at Speyer. Professor Kasten has noted how this boy had taken no part in the battle and had in fact been kept in safe hands far away from the combat zones; she has also noted that Lothar had already proclaimed his older son as king in Italy but had given no indication of a kingly future for the little boy who came to Speyer. Perhaps Lothar I had plans for only his older son to inherit a royal title.[49] This view is too black and white. The young boy was about five when he travelled to his father at Speyer, and our source knows that he was very young, 'just a little boy' (*parvulus*). Would the travels of any other five-year-old have been reported at this time? As a royal son, the little boy was special, certainly too special to have been with the army in battles that got out of control, but also special enough to be escorted from Saxony to be present at the wedding of his sister in a dynastic set-piece at Worms. Worms and Speyer were key centres in an important region that Lothar I was trying to control at this precisely this time.[50] The warriors (and nursemaids?) who escorted the boy in 841 would have seen a royally named boy already participating in the political dramas of the Frankish world. The boy's very youth expressed the importance of royal parentage and presaged a royal future. Such actions by kings and aristocrats helped announce and construct a royal identity that started early without formal office.

Put more positively, this means that dynastic charisma started at birth. Royal status was constructed socially but the construction of this status started very early indeed. The birth of a royal son was news. Carolingian kings may not have let off fireworks to celebrate like Louis XIII in 1638; they may not even have matched their Merovingian predecessors who freed servants on the birth of a royal heir.[51] Nonetheless, the birth of a royal son was part of the news that travelled out from the royal court. The abbot of Lobbes is said to have greeted the news of the birth of Pippin, son of Charles Martel, in 714 or 715 with a prophecy of the boy's glorious future destiny as king. We may temper our respect for the holy man's prophetic powers with the knowledge that the source that tells us this was written after Pippin became king, but the story points to news of royal births as part of the information that spread out from royal courts. The news of the birth of a new son to king Pippin in 759 swiftly reached the pope.[52] King Pippin himself was also subject of another retrospective prophecy of royal glory in Alcuin's late eight-century account of the child's baptism by St Willibrord.[53] These later prophecies suggest that, for some at least of the post-751 followers of the Carolingians, Pippin's gaining of the throne in 751 was merely the fulfilment of a destiny announced by his birth.

The full significance of the birth of a royal son could only unfold under the harsh sky of early medieval power politics and mortality rates and, as we have seen, not all such births were noted in the historical record. But perhaps we should be surprised that there are as many references as there are. And some of the silences, for example on the birth of Charles the Bald in 823 or on that of Charles the Simple in 879, were loaded rather than ignorant.⁵⁴ While Einhard claimed that he knew nothing about Charlemagne's birth, some of his contemporaries knew that the great man's birthday was April 2nd.⁵⁵

The prospect of a royal birth would compel attention. We have already seen that Charles the Bald's birth at the palace of Frankfurt in 823 immediately triggered networking efforts by his mother. In fact, it looks as if the court had already prepared for a significant birth. A set of annals from the abbey of Weissenburg in Alsace tells us that Charles's birth was also a big day for Drogo, half-brother of Charles's father Louis the Pious. In 823, 'on the Ides of June, Charles, son of Judith, was born. On the same day Drogo was ordained [as a priest]', and also in the same palace of Frankfurt. This was a prelude to Drogo's being made bishop of Metz. This may simply have been a coincidence as the date for such a ceremony could have been fixed in advance and the court cannot have known that Judith would give birth to a son. Nonetheless, the juxtaposition of the two events is striking. After all, Louis had only recently (in 821–2) restored Drogo to favour after a spell out in the cold, and now any tremors rumbling through the royal kin on the birth of a new heir had to be suppressed. The death of the incumbent bishop of Metz in September 822 meant that Louis could now promote his dangerously talented half-brother out of harm's way.⁵⁶ Having him ordained as priest on the same day and in the same palace as his son was born enabled Louis to demonstrate that any royal road that may have been open to Drogo was now closed while a new royal journey, that of the infant Charles, had begun.

The significance of all this, and its central pivot, the birth of a royal son, was not lost on the audience in Frankfurt or indeed beyond the palace walls. The information in the Weissenburg annal probably stems from Drogo himself. Drogo thus seems to have got Louis's point and to have impressed influential people within his own circle with the importance of juxtaposing the birth of a new Carolingian son with the entry of another Carolingian into divine service.⁵⁷ Thus, ceremonies and texts defined the shape and burnished the aura of the Carolingian family. The appearance of this potential heir was a marked out event from the start.

Memories such as Drogo's could only come into full play if the child lived and went on to have a royal career. Pippin III, Charlemagne, Louis the Pious, Charles the Bald and Louis the Younger all experienced the death of one or more sons.⁵⁸ A combination of death rates and the whirligig of political favour meant that the birth of some royal sons could be the announcement of a potential that withered. Charlemagne's father Pippin had a son in 759 and gave him the royal name of Pippin. This may have caused the eleven-year-old Charlemagne, his younger brother Carloman and the aristocracy a few anxious moments as the succession took on a more complex aspect but the boy died a couple of years later.⁵⁹ Similarly, there was to be no royal career for the boy Carloman born almost a century later to the emperor Lothar I and his mistress Doda in 853. We do not know whether this is because Lothar was austerely following the precepts of the great imperial decree of 817 which excluded illegitimate sons from power, or because the boy died young, or because the boy's older brothers ruthlessly sidelined him, though the latter scenario is surely more likely.⁶⁰

This little boy would not have been as obscure to contemporaries as he is to us, as seen in the fact that his name was reported in a contemporary chronicle. What were

Lothar's plans for this boy? The birth of a son to the ageing emperor who already had grown-up sons may have triggered much furrowing of worried brows among Lothar's sons and followers. But Lothar's actions may in fact have been finely judged. His wife had died in 851 after thirty years of marriage. Taking a low-status mistress was not a Merovingian-style assertion that he could father future kings on any woman. Sara McDougall has argued recently that illegitimacy in itself did not cancel a Carolingian royal son's potential, but that having a lowly mother meant that such sons could not build sufficient support to make a convincing claim.[61] Lothar here was showing that he was still virile enough to consort with women and father a child, but not rash enough to trigger protests from his sons by his marriage. Doda's low status was an insurance policy. But Lothar also took care to make her prominent at court; his dignity was unimpaired. It is clear that the west Frankish bishop who reports the union of Lothar and Doda despised her as a mistress from the servant class but in fact she enjoyed a prominent status at Lothar's court and continued to appear in the royal entourage after his death.[62] In naming his son Carloman, Lothar was probably not promising him a kingdom, but was trying to shore up this child's status, as a good dynast had to do.

Sons royal by name and nature

Lothar's deliberate gift of a royal name for Doda's child points towards a political currency specific to royal childhood: the naming and baptizing of these children. The importance of name-giving for the identity of early medieval families is well known. Contemporaries were probably aware of a name's actual meaning and its function, in Regine Le Jan's words, as 'a personal totem'. We can see this in a poet of the 820s glossing the name of Louis the Pious (Hludo-wicus) as deriving from the Frankish elements 'Hluto' (famous) and 'Wicgh' which referred to Mars and war; the name that his parents chose for him was a portent (*prodigium*) foretelling what he would be.[63] But what seems to have really counted for contemporary royal name-watchers was less the etymological meaning of the name than its relation to other names in a name system. Although the importance of name-giving for the sense of identity of aristocratic families in the Frankish world should not be over-rated, the giving of entire names (i.e. not the combining of different name elements that we find so often among the aristocracy) was a deliberate and meaningful strategy to be found in royal families such as those of the Franks and the Lombards. The Carolingian system of name-giving for sons of rulers developed under Charles Martel, that is, even before the Carolingians take over the royal throne in 751, and became strictly patrilineal and agnatic. After the dynastic crisis of 888, changes can be detected in the system, as we shall see at the end of this book.[64]

It is hard to believe that anyone but the kingly father chose the names. We have the poignant testimony of an aristocratic mother on fathers' role here. Writing in the 840s, Dhuoda describes how her far-away husband had commanded that his newly born son be brought to him and so she did not even know the baby's name. There is a counter-example to this in the case of St Willibrord (born 657 or 658), whose name was chosen by his mother; the fact that modern historians have found this hard to believe tells us more about their assumptions than about contemporary realities.[65] But where we have explicit evidence, it tends to tell us that kings themselves named their sons and this shows how important the system of naming actually was. Pippin III himself gave his own name to his son born in 759, just as we are told that Louis the Pious (b.778) owed his name to his father Charlemagne and that later it was Louis's decision to call his son born in 823 by the luminous name of Charles.[66] Such evidence points not only to a pattern of behaviour but also to a pattern of expectations among the dynasty's followers: they expected kings to take the active part in naming their sons.

The isolated examples of royal sons being given names by their mothers are exceptions that prove this rule. Charles the Simple, born in 879, was given his name by his mother in order to associate him with previous bearers of that most illustrious name but we are explicitly told that she only did this because her husband (king Louis the Stammerer) had died before the child was born. Perhaps she was carrying out her late husband's wish, or perhaps she herself had a keen awareness of how this game was played.[67] Looking back from the 880s to the previous century, Notker of St-Gall claimed that Charlemagne's son Pippin the Hunchback was given his potent name by his mother. It is difficult to imagine Charlemagne allowing her such latitude but the point of Notker's story is that Pippin's mother was not Charlemagne's wife at all and that Pippin was a bad son. As he puts it: '[Charlemagne] was nearly captured and put to death by his son, whom a concubine had borne to him and who had been called by his mother by the ill-omened name of the glorious Pippin'.[68] Notker is attributing to Pippin's shadowy mother, rather than to Charlemagne, the mistake of giving the great name of Pippin to a disobedient son. Basically, father knew best.

Naming a royal son was an important act. How soon after his birth did a royal son receive his name? The general interest in baptism in Carolingian culture 'highlights childhood as a period of socialization into the Christian life'.[69] Carolingian churchmen, unlike their counterparts elsewhere in the Christian world, seem to have taken a relatively leisurely approach to baptism, urging that it take place at Easter or Pentecost rather than imposing a strict timetable by which it had to be carried out. Dhuoda's son who had been born in March had not yet been baptized by November of that year.[70] The baby born to the empress Richildis in early October 876 was not baptized with the royal name of Charles until after Christmas and this may only have been because the infant had become mortally ill. In general, however, it is hard to believe that kings lost much time in naming their sons or that they always waited until Easter or Pentecost before baptizing them. Charlemagne named his twin sons by Hildegard and had them baptized as soon as he returned from campaigning in Spain in the late summer of 778.[71] In the early years of the dynasty, popes rushed to volunteer to act (usually by proxy) as godfather to newly born royal sons. Louis the Pious probably acted quickly to have Charles the Bald named and baptized in the summer of 823.[72] In the effectively post-Carolingian world of tenth-century France, the birth of a royal son was still important enough to trigger the immediate decision to call the child Charles as part of the urgent preparations for his baptism. The very passivity of the child in baptism enhanced his role as symbol of an unknown future, as P. Cramer has pointed out.[73]

Fathers could use these occasions to make alliances and strengthen bonds. That is to say, their child could almost instantly become a political instrument. The baptizing of his son Pippin *c*.716 gave Charles Martel the opportunity at a critical time in his career to cement relations with Abbot Willibrord of Echternach who baptized the boy.[74] Such alliances might not always last but bonds established early could hold. In 893, Archbishop Hatto of Mainz and Bishop Adalbero of Augsburg baptized Louis, son of king Arnulf, and both men served him loyally when he came to the throne as a child seven years later, Adalbero being described as his guardian or foster-father (*nutritor*).[75] Bishops, abbots, popes and members of the secular aristocracy were all involved in the giving of names to royal sons.[76]

A Carolingian baby boy was not, however, merely a father's instrument but became himself politically active through his naming. The annalist recording the birth and baptism of Arnulf's son Louis (the Child) in 893 states that he bore the name of his grandfather Louis, that is, Louis the German (d.876), the great king of east Francia who had built that kingdom.[77] As a royal son, the baby embodied the future for contemporaries: the line of great kings called Louis would continue. But he also pointed backwards, to the great Carolingian past, the legitimating roots of that hoped for future. One wonders whether Arnulf or the bishops made the pointed reference to Louis the German during the ceremony itself. The fact that the annalist refers to the dynastic associations of the name certainly shows us that contemporaries fully understood the charge of meaning that an infant could carry. The power and meaning of a royal boy's name meant that his social birth was close to his biological birth.

Such names signalled inborn royal status. Two clear naming patterns are as visible to us as they would have been to contemporaries. The first one gave the Carolingians and their followers a clear message of distinction. Only sons of Carolingian kings or princes could bear the exclusively royal names such as Charles, Louis, Lothar, Carloman or Pippin. There are trifling, if surprising, exceptions to this rule. (One ought to pay tribute here to the late Donald Bullough's eagle-eyed spotting of a humble dependent of the Italian abbey of Farfa in the 820s bearing the exalted name of Pippin.) The main point, however, holds. These names resounded again and again in the Carolingian world. Karl Ferdinand Werner has studied the distribution of names among some forty legitimate descendants of Charlemagne and his figures show that the name Louis was used twelve times, Charles ten times, Lothar and Carloman five times each, Pippin four times.[78] Such repetitions drove the point home to the Franks who were to be taught that they were now ruled by kings who bore such names and that only the sons of kings were permitted to be called by them. Also, with very few exceptions, Carolingian daughters did not transmit these exalted names to any sons they might have. These names, which included names from the old Merovingian dynasty, remained under the control of the royal male Carolingians who alone could bestow them. These names were badges of distinction and rank that marked a line that the aristocrats would not cross until they had to in the late ninth century.

But not all sons of Carolingian rulers bore such potent names and this brings us to a second pattern. Names worked to create and demonstrate distinctions within the royal family itself. The names discussed above were the royal names par excellence. Illegitimate sons of rulers were given names from another stockpile. They bore names such as Arnulf, Hugo and Drogo.[79] Admittedly, the whole question of how illegitimacy was defined and how it mattered politically at this time is problematic, not least because its significance changed across the Carolingian era and because members of the aristocracy did not always agree with kings' definitions of some sons as unthroneworthy. Kings' definitions, and it was their definitions that mattered rather than the proclamations of churchmen, were not always clear or consistent. Charles the Bald gave his twin sons the names Pippin (a very royal name) and Drogo (not a clearly royal name), but this need not mean that he saw only one of these children as throneworthy. Inconsistency and ambiguity gave kings and aristocrats some flexibility in political manoeuvres around sons, and must also have created some uncertainties.[80] Nonetheless, with the exception of Bernard of Italy, every single Carolingian king from Pippin III (751–68) to Charles the Fat (deposed 887) was called Louis or Charles or Lothar or Carloman or Pippin. This suggests that some self-fulfilling gradations of distinctions within the royal family did exist, for royals and aristocrats. In the dynastic crisis of 887–8, the illegitimate Arnulf became king and contemporaries celebrated the resonance of the name that his father had chosen for him (from the saintly Arnulf of Metz) but even observers who supported him had yearned for princes called Charles and Louis.[81]

Sometimes these illegitimate sons came from sexual liaisons that princes had contracted in their youth. Régine Le Jan has noted this pattern for ninth-century sons of rulers.[82] Sons born from such liaisons tended to be given names from the less kingly stockpile and this could suggest that princes realized that these informal unions were not destined to produce heirs to the throne.[83] Professor Le Jan's picture of royal life-cycles can be modified. Charles the Fat, for example, fathered an illegitimate son, but this was while he was married; the sons of Charles the Bald defiantly married young rather than opting for mistresses chosen with their father's approval.[84] But the pattern of name-giving remained consistent amidst these unruly royal life-cycles. Charles the Fat ruefully recognized his marriage, though it was childless, by giving his illegitimate son the less royal name of Bernard, while Charles the Bald's son clearly asserted the positive status of his marriage by calling his children by the royal names of Louis and Carloman.[85] Charlemagne reversed the life-cycle pattern of his descendants by opting for mistresses in his old age rather than in his youth, but he too chose non-kingly names for his sons by them.[86]

If kings spoke through the names of their sons, their followers listened closely to this discourse and grasped its nuances. This is true of even the relatively early days of the royal dynasty. Theodulf's court poetry of 795 saw Charlemagne's name as recalling that of his grandfather (Charles Martel).[87] As the dynasty's history deepened, people saw richer patterns in the associations of royal names. Consider comments made in the 880s by Notker of St-Gall on Bernard, son of Charles the Fat, comments addressed to that king himself. Notker looked on Bernard with favour, but saw that Bernard's name clearly reflected his status as son of Charles by a concubine. Notker's references to Bernard reveal his ability to place the boy's name in a Carolingian hierarchy of value. While gloomily lamenting the dynasty's dwindling stock of male heirs, Notker singles out little Bernard as one of the few twigs left on the family tree.[88] But he immediately follows this with a story about the first Carolingian king, Pippin III, and he announces that story with a veritable fanfare of legitimate Carolingian names: 'And so something about your great-great-grandfather Pippin should be put into this history of your namesake [Charlemagne], something which some future little Charles or Louis of yours might imitate if merciful heaven permits it.'[89] The great Carolingian names ring out like bells in Notker's text but the names of the wished-for Louis and Charles, being, as we have seen, the most common royal names, have a deeper resonance than that of the illegitimate Bernard.

For Notker, the truly magical names were the legitimate ones such as Charles, Louis or Pippin and this is apparent elsewhere in his text, a text haunted by the spectre of challenges to Carolingian exclusivity.[90] In uttering these names, Notker was not merely repeating the discourse of Carolingian legitimacy that had mastered him; he was in his turn actively working at the endless effort of repeating it even as it stuttered in the crisis years of the 880s. These names enabled Notker to emphasize, and pray for, dynastic continuity. History could thus be simultaneously celebrated and abolished. Names could evoke the glories of the past while collapsing the distance between past and present. This is what the repetition of names asserted, whether these names were repeated in the name-giving practices of the royal family or in texts such as Notker's. Notker could link Charles the Fat directly and immediately to his great-grandfather Charlemagne ('in this history of your namesake').[91] In a previous generation, the young Charles of Provence (born c.845), son of Lothar I, was hailed by the poet Sedulius Scottus in these terms: 'Here is a new Charles, from the seed of the great Charles [i.e. Charlemagne]: / Let us all rejoice, here is a new Charles.'[92]

Even after the Carolingians' exclusive claim to the throne had been challenged in 888, their followers evoked the aura of their names. Writing c.890, the Saxon Poet celebrated the name of Arnulf, the east Frankish ruler whose name was that of his saintly ancestor from seventh-century Metz. The poet understood very well how these special dynastic names distinguished and unified the rulers and how ancestral depth should support a glorious future, for the Carolingians and the Franks. Saint Arnulf had blessed his glorious line as the biblical Jacob had blessed Judah and that line should continue to wield the sceptre into a future where the ruler was another Arnulf.[93] After the evaporation of dynastic exclusiveness, this poet could still weave history, prophecy and prayer into an assertion of Carolingian specialness, a quality that shone out through the very names of rulers.

Knowledge of such names, not simply as individual counters, but as a group, as a sequence, circulated widely among the aristocracy. Writing in the 830s, Thegan displayed his genealogical knowledge of the royal family with all its Pippins and Charleses at the beginning of his biography of Louis the Pious. Strikingly, he also mentioned how he knew this information: 'as we learned from stories told by our own fathers (*paterno relatu*) and as many histories testify'.[94] Oral and written materials thus circulated to teach the aristocracy which names and name-bearers it had to respect and obey, and knowledge of these materials was part of aristocratic identity. In his youth, William, son of Bernard and Dhuoda, was instructed by his mother in the 840s that the king (Charles the Bald) was of very noble descent and there is some early medieval evidence for the role of women in transmitting knowledge of ancestors.[95]

Some fifty years after Thegan and Dhuoda, the Saxon Poet referred to popular poems that celebrated the ancestors of Charlemagne: 'As is well known, popular poems (*vulgaria carmina*) celebrate with great praises his grandfathers and great-grandfathers, singing of the Pippins, Charleses, Clovises, Theodorics, Carlomans and Chlothars.' The specific identities of these ancestors matter less than the simple plural names which suggest a mass of legitimately named royals looming up behind Charlemagne who basks in their glory even as he goes on to outshine them in his own spectacular career, thus providing in his turn ancestral glory for those who come after him.[96] Matthew Innes has warned that we cannot know for certain whether the 'songs' referred to by the Saxon Poet and earlier writers were in Latin or the vernacular but he has also stressed that such 'orally transmitted material' was 'royal, dynastic and Frankish'.[97] All this material points to active channels of communication, oral and literary, through which the aristocracy would be sensitized to the meanings of Carolingian names.

Because names were given to kings' sons very early on in their 'careers', these royal infants spoke in the system. The child did indeed trail clouds of glory. We can see this very precisely in the picture of the three-year-old Charles the Bald in Ermold's epic poem *In Honour of Louis [the Pious]*, written between 826 and 828. This was written for Louis, and Ermold, out of favour and in exile, was keen to please the emperor. The picture of the latter's son Charles as a worthy descendant of Charlemagne could only enhance Louis's own sense of dynastic self-worth. The Carolingians had to be as deeply hypnotized as their aristocracy into believing in the inevitability of Carolingian right to rule. Ermold surely intended his poem to have a court audience and it was to them as well as to Louis that he addressed the image of wee Charles, celebrating the boy as royally named son and grandson.[98] The audience is thus reminded of the place that this three-year-old has in the dynastic scheme of things. His boyhood is indeed glorious, as Ermold asserts.[99] The message carried by Charles's name was transmitted to a writer far from court who then bounced it back, magnified and elaborated, to a court audience in a poetic text, one of the channels of communication for an important message. The message that Ermold received for transmission was that even a young child who was not yet a king could resemble Charlemagne through the almost magical powers of the exclusive name. Once a boy such as Charles actually became king, the resonance of his name increased as there was now another king bearing the glorious name of the past.

Connoisseurs of the history of the Carolingian family, which was, by definition, the history of the empire, could zoom in very sharply on aspects of that history via names. When Louis the Pious marked the coming of age of Charles the Bald in 838 by granting him Neustria, territory between the rivers Seine and Loire that was outstandingly rich in royal estates, he was appointing Charles to a territory that had been held by distinguished Carolingian princes, including Louis's father Charlemagne and his brother Charles. That contemporaries got this point we know from a biography of Louis written shortly after his death in 840. This says that 'the lord emperor granted to his son Charles … the part of the kingdom *which his namesake Charles had*' (my emphasis). Not all sources described this grant in these terms and so we can see that individual courtiers could choose to use very precise terms of reference. Perhaps Charles of Provence, born in 845 as son of Lothar I, was given that name to echo the name of Lothar's half-brother and erstwhile rival the west Frankish king Charles the

Bald, with whom Lothar was enjoying a rapprochement around the time of the boy's birth. As we have just seen, however, a court poet channelled the associations of the boy's name backwards towards the mighty shade of his great-grandfather Charlemagne rather than sideways towards his western uncle.[100]

This means that it is probably more accurate to say that contemporaries evoked and telescoped history through names rather than that they could simply abolish it. Names had power but that power had to be socially recognized. When Charlemagne went to Rome in 781, he took his young sons Louis (the Pious) and Carloman with him. A set of annals, probably contemporary with the events it recounts, tells us that 'his [Charlemagne's] son was baptized there, he whose name was Carloman. This was changed and he was named Pippin by Pope Hadrian'. The re-naming of this little boy, born in 777, was news. One reason why this name-change was news is that it was bound up with a major political ordering of the realm. For the pope not only baptized the boy, he anointed him and his even younger brother Louis (the Pious) as kings of Italy and Aquitaine, respectively.[101] The name Pippin had positive overtones in Rome due to the bond between Charlemagne's father (Pippin III) and the papacy and must have been chosen for the boy with an eye to the fact that he was to rule in Italy. While the pope thus probably approved the new name, the decision to change it was Charlemagne's; the ceremonies at Rome were only the final stages of a process that had begun a year previously when an assembly of Franks had agreed to the setting up of kingdoms for these two children.[102]

The naming of small boys was part of the public business of the realm. Something of the effort and trappings that accompanied such boys, their father, their mother and the aristocracy in these journeys and ceremonies is still visible in the magnificently luxurious manuscript commissioned by Charlemagne and Hildegard, the boy's mother. This is the Godescalc Gospel lectionary, created in connection with the baptismal events of 781 and which it commemorates in a dedicatory poem and whose spiritual significance is evoked in its painting of a symbolic fountain of life.[103] Further ceremonies that year in Rome and Milan highlighted the status of Charlemagne's young daughters who were thus also pressed into service to demonstrate the specialness of the royal family.[104]

Naming a royal child was neither a casual nor a private matter. If such names were signs of royal distinctiveness and status, they were signs that had to be read. The re-naming of little Pippin in 781 would have triggered much speculation about the fate of his older brother Pippin the Hunchback, as we saw in Chapter 3. Names worked on a general level as a sequence marking out Carolingian exclusivity and proclaiming Carolingian continuity, but they also worked on a micro-level of political choices and conflict. Just as the Astronomer in his biography of Louis the Pious evoked a great namesake of Charles the Bald to depict this favoured son of Louis in a flattering light, so other observers of Louis's family picked other names to serve their purposes. Thegan of Trier ignored the young Charles but drew pointed attention to the fact that his own favourite among Louis's sons, Louis the German, bore the same name as his father. For Thegan, this equivalence was meaningful and he also suggested that the equivalence of name between father and son meant that there would be an equivalently exalted royal destiny for the son, his own favoured royal candidate.[105]

The overall picture is clear. The birth of a son to a ruler was nearly always a tremendous fact and this has not always been sufficiently perceived by historians.[106] Silence in contemporary sources on the birth of children does not mean that such births did not matter to contemporaries, and such births were in fact sometimes recorded.[107] The giving of a kingly or a non-kingly name took place very early in a child's life, activating a royal status for that child, though the realizing and defining of the full potential of that status could only come later. The child could thus help generate Carolingian distinctiveness while still a child, indeed through being a child. Children contributed to the present in which they themselves existed as well as guaranteeing a future. All this is intensely dynastic. Observers of the political scene had to cultivate an 'appreciation of the efforts of toddlers'.[108] Lack of fully comparative source material makes generalization insecure, but we are surely right in thinking that royal children, specifically sons, entered the social world sooner than other children did.

All boys together

Young princes needed tutors and minders. These attendants personified the moral concerns and political expectations that were the very atmosphere in which the boys existed. Early on in their lives, they were enmeshed in moral and political connections. To look at these princes is to see them amidst a supporting cast that helped create the Carolingian royalty it served and benefited from. Royal boyhood was relentlessly social.

Royal education had a distinctive moral quality The stakes were higher for princes than for their aristocratic playmates; the fate of the whole realm itself depended on what a prince could learn from his royal father in his 'house', which was the palace. As Alcuin wrote to Charlemagne's son Charles:

> Show justice and mercy among your Christian people. ... You have not far to look for good examples, for you have the finest examples of virtue in the house (*domus*) in which you were brought up. You may be quite sure that you will be blessed like your excellent and noble father ... if you strive to copy his noble, good and disciplined character ...[109]

Alcuin's text for another of Charlemagne's sons, *Dialogue of the Royal and Most Noble Youth Pippin with Master Alcuin*, was probably intended for other schoolboys and not simply for Pippin alone but it was modelled on a dialogue between the Roman emperor Hadrian and a philosopher. This imperial model would have had a particular resonance for Pippin; only he, among the boys at whom the text might be aimed, was destined for a throne.[110]

What princes experienced while they were still young was seen to be of general importance. In the late ninth century, confronted with the prospect of young kings coming to the throne, Archbishop Hincmar of Reims brooded on the dangerous lessons that the young Alexander the Great had learned from his dissolute tutor Leonidas, whose 'faults the young boy absorbed from him like bad milk'. The result was that 'in adulthood ... although Alexander conquered all kingdoms, he was unable to conquer himself'.[111] As a mature king in 862, Lothar II assumed that his bishops knew that his 'infancy and boyhood' were spent predominantly in the company of women. It was this youthful exposure to what Lothar probably intended his contemporaries to understand as loose women that made him, he said, keen to avoid vice and contract a legitimate marriage.[112] Lothar's earnest account of his quest for sexual virtue would acquire darkly ironic overtones for his contemporaries, but for now it is worth noting his own stress on his early upbringing as a formative experience that was relevant to his life as king. It is also significant that Lothar thought that the fact that he had been brought up in woman's company was worthy of comment. In other words, the expected norm was a heavily masculine presence. Allen Frantzen has claimed that the Anglo-Saxon lord in his hall presided over 'an all-male community that is as strongly same-sexed as a monastery'. Royal courts were more complex spaces. Famously, Charlemagne's daughters were an important presence at their ageing father's court, as were his granddaughters. Queens and aristocratic women would also have been present at other Carolingian courts and were neither invisible nor passive there. Wet nurses also had a role to play.[113] But as royal boys and their aristocratic peers moved from infancy to boyhood and learned to be men, the tone and experiences became increasingly masculine, something that we can observe in princely youth in many historical cultures.[114]

Some of that education was telling a prince that he was special. Education was part of the social construction of royal status. Princes were born but had to become what they were in their own eyes and in those of the people around them. Mothers could play a role here. In 829/30, bishop Frecul of Lisieux sent the second volume of his world history to the empress Judith for the instruction of her six-year-old son Charles (the Bald). Judith herself may have commissioned this volume. This text might have been connected with the granting of Alemannia to Charles in the summer of 829 and can thus be linked with the acquiring of office. Tellingly, however, Frecul urges Judith to educate her son as the biblical Bathsheba taught her son Solomon, who then went on to say of himself, 'For I was my father's son'. And Frecul did not fail to associate the boy's name with that of his grandfather Charlemagne.[115] If a six-year-old boy could not yet read this massive Latin text, what Frecul and Judith were giving to Charles were self-knowledge and self-definition about an essential identity as a royal son. In his education, which included the grand court processions and ceremonies, as recounted by Ermold in his poem a couple of years previously, a child such as Charles could be a spectator of his own royal status.[116] Presumably, it was Judith who told Charles the story of the ring she had sent to archbishop Ebo. Perhaps not all mothers fed this sense of self-worth as Judith may have fed Charles's (though Alfred of Wessex and his mother are another example), and Judith was a second wife who had to back her own son against existing sons. But this evidence suggests that it would be wrong to imagine that princes existed in a political vacuum while they were young enough to be close to their mothers. Royal beginnings tended to look more solid in retrospect but among the very first people to be taught the special status of a Carolingian son was that son himself.[117] Charles the Bald's own sons were to be rudely disappointed here but the general point still holds.

A story from the late ninth century in Notker's *Deeds of Charlemagne* indicates that the followers of the Carolingians expected royal children to know their identity and worth from an early age. Notker tells how Charlemagne's son Louis the Pious took his six-year-old son (Louis the German) to the court of Charlemagne. When Charlemagne found out who the little boy was, he had him brought to him, kissed him and sent him back to his place. But the boy now 'knew his own rank' and moved to stand beside his father in a place of honour. Notker deploys hierarchical vocabulary to delineate the political order which is part of his subject.[118] The essence of this story, however, is the self-knowledge of the young Carolingian. The boy's youth and his own sense of his value make a re-assuring story of the precocity of a youthful but fully Carolingian boy. Notker himself lived far from court, though he had actually experienced a visit of a Carolingian father (Louis the German) and his sons to St-Gall and had thus witnessed the ordering of royal family hierarchy.[119] His imagination, however, stretched into the heart of the royal family, visualizing a comforting dynastic scene. Back in the 820s, Einhard saw similar scenes, imagining queen Bertrada's pleasure at seeing grandchildren at her son Charlemagne's court. Charlemagne himself gathered grandchildren to his palace, as did Louis the German.[120]

A dynastic system automatically generated clusters of people around royal children well before they were ready for office.[121] Born royal, they needed tutors, guardians and attendants who witnessed and helped construct the social meaning of royal childhood. In fact, these royal male children, as children, were a nodal point for the formation of a specifically Carolingian aristocracy. This operated in several ways. First, the kings had to keep their young sons close. This then required a significant clustering of helpers at court for these children. Third, the cultural formation of young aristocrats themselves, or at least those of high status, meant that they spent part of their youth (in both the biological and the sociological sense of that term) at the royal court, with the Carolingian ruler as a second father, a *nutritor*.

First of all, royal boys had to be kept secure, close to a royal centre; they themselves could be a royal centre, but not secure on their own. Kings and their aristocratic followers knew this. Charlemagne's efforts to gain control of the sons of his brother Carloman show the high value of young royal sons. When Carloman died unexpectedly in 771, his widow fled with their sons and some aristocratic supporters to the Lombard king Desiderius in Italy which seemed a safer place than the court of their uncle. But their presence there helped pull Charlemagne into invading Italy in 774.[122] His attempt to avert war by offering the Lombard king the vast sum of 14,000 gold solidi which may have included 'the price of two princes' reveals Charlemagne's worries here. These boys were enormously valuable. The Lombards treated them as a form of treasure, shutting them up behind the walls of Verona, though this did not save them from falling into Charlemagne's hands and into historical oblivion in 774. Charlemagne's later command to his own sons not to have any nephews killed or blinded may recall the fate of these all too precious children.[123]

Looking back on this episode Einhard affected bafflement at Gerberga's flight, but this is a shudder of fear underneath the smooth surface of his prose.[124] Two young Carolingian boys had not only slipped out of the control of their uncle, the head of the family, they had gone to a non-Frankish court. This was the last time such valuable contraband would leave Carolingian control until the dynasty itself came under threat from the late ninth century onwards. The young sons of this dynasty were contained within a tightly Carolingian system that was rather different from that of the Lombards, for example. According to Paul the Deacon, a contemporary of Charlemagne, 'it is not the custom among [the Lombards] that the son of the king should eat with his father unless he first receives his weapons from the king of a foreign people'. This is a variant of 'adoption by weapons, as practised by the barbarians, [which] created bonds of artificial fatherhood between two individuals of different age but equal power'.[125] Charlemagne's own father Pippin had experienced such an adoption and Paul tells us that, in the 730s, 'Charles [Martel], ruler of the Franks, dispatched his son Pippin to Liutprand that the latter should take his hair according to custom. And the king, cutting his hair, became a father to him and sent him back to his father greatly enriched with many royal gifts'. This ceremony was only one of many in the barbarian west that turned on the symbolic value of hair.[126] It was, however, the last ceremony that involved a Carolingian prince growing up at a foreign court.

One reason for this is that the Carolingians, in their rise, had eliminated many 'foreign' courts. By 788, Gascony, Aquitaine, Lombard Italy and Bavaria had been eliminated as worthy alternative courts and the political chessboard was bare. Furthermore, while modern historians have stressed that bonds of artificial or spiritual kinship such as those created through adoption or godparenthood created bonds of friendship and alliance, such connections also created a hierarchical relationship.[127] It was this aspect that the Carolingians sought to avoid after Pippin's Italian trip in the 730s. Once they had gained the kingship, they were to be beholden to no one, apart perhaps from Saint Peter, and experiences such as Pippin's were replaced by ones with narrower horizons. Of course, young Carolingian boys still had godparents and these could be members of the aristocracy but they were 'home-grown' and belonged to the following of the ruler, that is, the father of the boy concerned. When outsiders were sought, they had transcendent spiritual authority, not the dangerous allure of an alternative princely court. Popes fitted the bill here.[128]

Rather than Carolingian children travelling to the court of an alien ruler to forge bonds of artificial kinship or to learn the ropes of rulership, it was children of other rulers who were drawn into the orbit of a Carolingian father. The young sons of Breton rulers became godsons of Charles the Bald in 851 and 863 and thus gained a new father in the Carolingian ruler, just as adult pagan princes did when they accepted baptism at Carolingian urging.[129] Sometimes, rulers did not even look outside of their own family for potential godparents. Louis the Pious had Lothar, a son of his first marriage, stand as godfather to Charles (the Bald), the son of his second marriage, while Charles the Bald went on, at the age of about eight, to stand as godfather to a little nephew (Charles, son of Pippin I of Aquitaine) and later had his brother-godfather Lothar become godfather to his (Charles the Bald's) daughter(s).[130] Such internal recruitment of godparents was not unique to the royal family; we find it practised among the high aristocracy as in Theoderic being both kinsman and godfather to Dhuoda's son William.[131] But the stakes for the royal family were uniquely high. Its distinctiveness and exclusiveness had to be guaranteed and could not be allowed to leak away at the baptismal font or at any other stage of the royal boyhood.

The few exceptions to this pattern only confirm its potency. The exotic name of Zwentibold appears in the royal family at the end of the ninth century. It was given to an illegitimate son of Arnulf, himself the illegitimate son of the east Frankish prince Karlmann, and it was taken from the boy's Slav godfather, Zwentibold (Svatopluk) of Moravia. This probably happened in 871 when even Karlmann himself did not yet hold the title of king, so little Zwentibold was low down in the pecking order of this line.[132] Only a relatively lowly Carolingian boy could be spared to be given a godfather and name of this sort. The young Zwentibold's name may have pointed to the world of Slav princes but there is no reason to suppose that the boy was brought up anywhere else than at a Carolingian court.

When we find young Carolingian princes making involuntary stays outside these courts, we can be sure that the dynasty was in trouble. Charles the Simple was a posthumous child; his father had died before he was born in 879 and he spent much of his boyhood being bandied about from one non-Carolingian centre to another in southern France and Burgundy. The fact that this boy escaped the control of senior members of the dynasty indicates the scale of the dynastic crisis of 888.[133] When Charles himself, as king, was captured and imprisoned in 923 by his nemesis Herbert of Vermandois, his wife, who was a princess of the royal house of Wessex, spirited their two-year-old son, dynastically priceless, back to her father's court.[134] This rather desperate tactic served a broader strategy: the boy born to be king could now be brought up by his royal uncle Athelstan, and his distinctiveness was thus preserved and enhanced; that is, he had a chance to return to the game. But this cannot disguise the fact that the great shelter of the Carolingian house was shaken. This case casts retrospective light on how effectively that shelter had protected the dynasty's children in the past.

Royal boys had to be secure. But they also had to be socialized and that means that their youth was usually, or predominantly, lived in the palace. In the early 720s, Charles Martel's son Pippin had been educated by the monks of St-Denis and later royal children may possibly have had a monastic education at some stage of their lives. Generally, however, after Pippin, royal children seem to have been brought up in a royal court rather than a monastery.[135] The presence of young aristocrats at the palace meant that they could share some of the same education as princes. Princes had to be prepared for a special future but their actual experiences in their youth overlapped with those of young aristocrats. Charlemagne and his young cousin Adalhard shared teachers. Charlemagne's sons learned to ride to the hunt because that was what all young Frankish (aristocratic) boys did.[136] We need not assume that royal princes had a better education than their aristocratic contemporaries. Dhuoda's text reveals the seriousness of moral education that could be available to aristocrats and it is hard to imagine that a prince would experience anything more intense than that. By the ninth century, aristocrats' libraries contained works of history, potentially as edifying to a young aristocrat as Freculf's world-history was meant to be for young Charles the Bald.[137] In learning to ride a horse, Charlemagne's young sons were following Frankish custom, rather than behaving in an exclusively royal way.[138]

The royal life-cycle provided job opportunities for aristocrats. Louis the Pious sent out the 'master of our little ones' (*magister parvulorum*) from the palace to investigate a property dispute.[139] The childhood and youth of princes were thus 'networking' opportunities for the royal family and the aristocracy alike and this could be partnership. As a very young child ruler in Aquitaine after 781, Louis the Pious was an apprentice; he could only learn the arts of ruling from the great aristocrats around him and from his distant father. He could hardly be master of his own court. Louis was attended by 'fitting servants' and a guardian (*baiulus*) carefully selected and appointed by Charlemagne, who continued to keep a watchful eye on the running of his son's kingdom, even when Louis had reached his teens.[140] Nonetheless, Louis was the king; the pivot on which such relationships turned was a Carolingian one.

Those who had charge of a prince's upbringing and education in his boyhood and adolescence, to telescope these ages, are usually labelled as guardian or mentor (*nutritor, baiulus* or *pedagogus*) in our sources, and such terms could carry warm emotional overtones. The same powerful bonds existed between aristocratic families. This was a familiar relationship.[141] Princes could revere such mentors. There is no reason to disbelieve the sincerity of the respect towards the royal *nutritor* (count Gerard of Vienne) found in the charters of the young king Charles of Provence in the 850s and 860s, or similar expressions in the charters of Louis the Child to his *nutritor* bishop Adalbero of Augsburg, even though these may not be the kings' own words. There is a correspondence between the reverence and gratitude which an aristocrat such as Einhard felt towards his kingly *nutritor*, Charlemagne himself, and what a king felt towards his aristocratic guardian.[142] These were two-way bonds of upbringing and association. Lothar II (855–69) brought up the young aristocrat Wicbert, who reverently recalled that king's fatherly behaviour and went on himself to look after Lothar's own son Hugh.[143]

On the other hand, there is equally no reason to doubt that some princes resented being placed under guardians and chafed at a supervision experienced as an extension of the heavy paternal hand. This was certainly the case with Charles the Bald's son Louis the Stammerer, who seems to have found it particularly galling to be assigned a new guardian in 861 just as he turned fifteen.[144] Close bonds could curdle and a particularly stark example of princely resentment of a guardian appears in the fact that Lothar II's son Hugh eventually turned against his protector, count Wicbert, and killed him in 883.[145] It was precisely because such aristocrats could be so close to young royals that the relationship could be so highly charged. A thoughtful observer wrote to Charles the Bald in 843 warning him of the dangers of *baiuli* deflecting the limelight from the young ruler to themselves.[146]

Tutors and guardians were chosen for princes by their fathers, with mothers possibly helping to choose tutors, and princes may not always have wanted to maintain close contact with such men when they grew to maturity and independence. We have no evidence that Louis the German stayed close to his Bavarian *pedagogus* Egilolf. Charles the Bald did not stay close to his *baiulus* Atto, an aristocrat from the Rhineland who had been picked for him in 838 by his father Louis the Pious; subsequent political upsets put Atto on a different path.[147]

Atto, however, was remembered by contemporaries as having been close to Charles and they expected Charles himself to remember him. Thus, a monk wrote to Charles, some time after the separation from Atto, reminding him of the time when his father had appointed Atto as his *baiulus* as a way of recalling a particular transaction to Charles's memory.¹⁴⁸ The phenomenon of the *baiulus* was widely known; contemporaries observed such relationships closely. There was a lot to observe; this was a complex set of relationships. The figures who watched over young Carolingian boys could be socially various. Atto and Bernard of the Auvergne, the *baiuli* of Charles the Bald and Louis III in 838 and 879 respectively, were already great secular magnates with an important role in high politics before they were assigned to these royal youths.¹⁴⁹ But the tutor of Lothar I was a priest called Clemens, and he was no Frankish magnate, but a scholar from Ireland.¹⁵⁰ This variety reflects the range of different social functions that such men were called upon to perform. The *baiuli* were to help a young prince in the task of governing and so they needed to be men with political muscle or to possess particular administrative skills. Scholarly tutors did not need to be so well connected politically. But both kinds of men clustered round young royals.

Some of the figures we have been surveying attended upon the sons when the latter had been effectively nominated for rule, but potential royal identity started even before this with tutors and guardians. Royal sons performed aspects of royalty from the very start. One famous example shows the transforming power of connections with a royal infant. This is the career of Ebo, archbishop of Reims. Ebo was neither tutor nor guardian to the young Louis the Pious but the bonds between him and Louis were forged at a very early age indeed. A tenth-century source says that Ebo was Louis 'milk-brother', that is, that Ebo's mother was the young Louis's wet-nurse. The basic task of nourishing the young Louis had been given to a woman of servile status on a royal estate (though she bore the name Himiltrud, the same name as a wife of Charlemagne). Ebo was thus socially far below his royal foster-brother but he was brought up and educated alongside him and flourished in the palace of Charlemagne, who spotted his intellectual talent. He accompanied Louis to Aquitaine and went on to a glittering career as archbishop of Reims.¹⁵¹ Much about Ebo is exceptional. His lowly social origins provoked some snobbish hostility, though perhaps not as much as we might expect, and these origins may have been exaggerated.¹⁵² We should not imagine that young Carolingian princes would normally form lasting bonds with lowly foster siblings in some nursery of democracy, but Ebo's association with Louis does show that a very early stage of childhood was, for a future ruler, highly social. The storms of the 830s, however, shattered the bonds between Ebo and Louis (see Chapter 5).

Memories formed in royal childhoods could be important for kings and their guardians and tutors and this found public expression. In the 750s, king Pippin cast his mind back a quarter of a century to recall his education in St-Denis while settling a case in the abbey's favour; in the 850s, Charles the Bald's affectionate memories of his old tutor from two decades ago helped maintain bonds with the great Carolingian abbey of Prüm.¹⁵³ In 817–18, the monks of Fulda remembered that Charlemagne's grandson Bernard had been educated with them and pleaded for mercy for him when he fell foul of his imperial uncle.¹⁵⁴

Aristocratic members of the Carolingian entourage could come to structure their own memories according to moments of the Carolingian life-cycle. This can be seen in a record of a property dispute in northern Italy between 823 and 840. Here Alpcarius, a count from Alemannia and a member of a prominent aristocratic family, was claiming back property that had been illegally taken over by a local deacon.¹⁵⁵ There was nothing royal about this dispute in itself. But it was the demands of royal service that had led Alpcarius to take his eye off his properties and what is particularly significant here is Alpcarius's definition of the time when he bought the properties in question. The charter reports his direct speech: 'In the time of the lord king Pippin [i.e. son of Charlemagne], while I was *baiolus* of Adelaid, daughter of the same king Pippin' and 'by the order of the lord king Pippin I travelled to Francia with the aforementioned Adelaid to the lord emperor Charles'. This is very probably an accurate report, albeit in a Latin version, of what Alpcarius actually said.[156] He dated the relevant transaction, the buying of property, with reference to a significant part of his life, his time spent as *baiulus* to a child of a king. Alpcarius expected this reference to be significant to his audience. He could expect them to be familiar with Pippin, who had been king in Italy, and thus, in referring to him, Alpcarius was referring to Italian time. But it is his reference to Pippin's child that is particularly illuminating. Alpcarius had been *baiulus* of the king's daughter, Adelaid, and in pronouncing her name in the basilica of San Nazario of Milan he was not only recalling her name at least a dozen years after he escorted from Italy, he was also instructing his hearers in the specialness of the Carolingians, whose young daughters were important enough to be brought into public discourse and to be preserved in it. They were also, of course, important enough to have *baiuli* and to be taken to Francia like a precious treasure for safe-keeping, but we shall see more of the specialness of daughters in Chapter 8.

The only pattern of royalty for Carolingian boys and the aristocracy was a Carolingian one. Carolingian sons were to stay in a Carolingian orbit and sons of other aristocratic families were to be drawn into it. The travel of sons was to be strictly one-way. Fosterage and pro-parenting in general were important in the upbringing of medieval children and the path to the Frankish royal court was a familiar one to noble boys.[157] The Merovingian court had been a magnet for the sons of the aristocracy and by the era of Charles Martel (715–41) young nobles were getting an education and making contacts at what had now become a Carolingian court. This process can only have gained momentum when Pippin III became the first Carolingian king and he and his queen took charge of the education of young nobles such as the Visigoth Witiza, an example of the centripetal function of the court.[158] Young members of the 'branch-lines' of the Carolingian family were also drawn to Pippin's court; Pippin had his nephew Adalhard brought up there.[159] Many of the young men who streamed towards the Carolingian court doubtless looked to expand their intellectual and social horizons. The best known illustration of this is probably William (born 826), son of Bernard of Septimania and Dhuoda. Dhuoda urged him to serve his king faithfully and to learn all he could from the 'big house' that he was about to join along with many other similar companions. In joining a royal court while he was still young, William was following a pattern that was common across medieval Europe; king Alfred of Wessex, Charles the Bald's contemporary, had aristocratic sons brought up in his household.[160] The young aristocrat Aldric came to Charlemagne's court when he was twelve and it was there, in the great church at Aachen, that he underwent a spiritual experience and decided to leave the service of the world and serve God, a decision which the youth had to clear with the ruler. But many would also have simply looked forward to having a good time in such an exciting place, where they could 'hunt hard, drink hard, fight hard' with the king.[161]

All this was an end in itself. There was also an element of service. Towards the end of the ninth century, Hincmar of Reims spoke of the court's need for 'young men' among its servants, and some of these were servants of servants; the palace attracted, and needed to attract, a broader social spectrum than merely the high-born.[162] Contemporaries tended to refer to the 'palace' rather than the 'court'. Around 800 Aldric had been 'taken to the palace by his father'; two decades later, a future bishop of Auxerre had his youthful education 'in the palace'.[163] The palace was thus understood not simply as a specific place but as a more abstractly and objectively conceived centre of the realm, site of a complex of cultural, spiritual and political experiences unfolding in a royal space, experiences that were a normal part of the education of the elite as the conventional references to the palace demonstrate. The term 'court' may be more fitting for the High and Later Middle Ages, but it remains a useful term for this period too, in its sense of a defined community pivoting on the ruler's patronage but also having its own self-aware identity.[164]

In the war-dominated years of the later eighth century, many of the young men who came to the palace came to be warriors and the king's vassals.[165] Some of these young men may have been very young indeed when they arrived. Angilbert, father of the historian Nithard, is described as 'having been brought up in [Charlemagne's] palace almost since infancy', and this term refers to early childhood.[166] It is important to realize, however, that the youth of these men at the court had a social meaning as well as a simply biological one. In a letter that highlights the network of contacts that facilitated the introducing of young men to the palace, bishop Frothar of Toul (813–47) asked a courtier to introduce the son of a count to king Lothar I. He refers to the son as 'boy' (*puer*) but this term probably refers to his junior status rather than to his actual age; he was a 'boy' because he was now going to be one of the lads at the palace, a dependant of the great lord that was the ruler.[167] The young men at the court were young because they had not yet settled down, had not yet married and had not yet acquired land and responsibilities.

Even if the youths who went to court did not always do so as children, and even if there were some veterans among them, many of these men must have been biologically young, going through 'a longer transitional stage [than girls did], falling between the age of 12 and 20'. Dhuoda's son William was around fifteen when he went to the king. This could give such young men a sense of themselves as a generation with a 'prince' of their own. The seven-year-old Louis the Pious at his father's court in Paderborn in 785 was accompanied by 'boys of his own age'.[168] There is no reason to disbelieve ecclesiastical contemporaries who described the palace as a place where people could learn scholarly as well as military skills, but many of these youths learned to be men of a particular masculine cast, through fighting, carousing and hunting, literally through horseplay.

Sometimes this could go badly wrong, as in 864 when young Charles, son of Charles the Bald, came back from a day's hunting with his companions, who were all young. Unfortunately, their clowning around resulted in his being severely wounded in the head by a sword wielded with more exuberance than care by Albuin, one of these companions. Hunting accidents were common and were not confined to high-spirited youths; that same year 864 also saw two senior Carolingians, aged about fifty-four and thirty-nine, badly hurt while out hunting.[169] But the wounding of young Charles was a severe malfunctioning of the system. Hunting should have provided a showplace for the display of qualities of leadership and should have provided opportunities for the forging of bonds of comradeship in danger. Instead, young Charles was 'dishonoured by his injury' and Albuin, instead of being able to use his contact with the royal court to shed further lustre on his own noble connections, now had to invoke these connections to soften the impact of his appalling blunder.[170]

Such connections must have provided pathways to court for all the young men who tend to appear only as a group in our sources. Their youth and their common experiences gave them a common identity; they learned to be 'companions (*comilitones*: a New Testament term) within the royal palace'.[171] Presumably such memories of a common identity survived after the youths had matured and left court for office and tasks elsewhere.[172] The court also educated these men in the ways of hierarchy as well as fellowship. They had to learn to respect their betters. Dhuoda saw this as a key lesson. Her son William was to learn respect for the king and his family as well as his seniors among the great magnates. Such respect did not always survive the twists and turns of politics, as William's later career of rebellion was to show.[173] Often, however, such lessons were well learned. Einhard offers eloquent testimony here. He was probably about twenty when he went to Charlemagne's court; he already had experience in the service of the abbey of Fulda and he had shown his intellectual quality in his education there. He was no raw youth when he went to court but he saw his time there as an essential part of his upbringing. In the Preface to his *Life of Charlemagne*, he refers reverently to Charlemagne as his 'foster father' and states that the 'foster care that Charlemagne bestowed on me' is one of his motives for writing the biography. Einhard also adduces, as a motive for writing, the bond of 'consistent friendship I had with Charlemagne and his children after I began living at his court (*aula*)' and he thus got to know the younger Carolingian generation which would have been closer to him in age than the great king himself.[174] There is a parallel to this in the now-lost account of Louis the Pious's reign in Aquitaine by a noble contemporary of Louis who was brought up with him.[175]

Einhard's emphasis on the court as the place where he formed this 'consistent friendship' is noteworthy. In fact, for much of Einhard's time there these children were not always present at the court. This shows that the court as concept could exist as separate from the fluctuations of an actual historical court: 'early medieval courts were mental constructs as well as social microcosms'.[176] Actual courts in historical space and time did of course matter to contemporaries who were jockeying for position there, as they should matter to us who study them. Donald Bullough noted how the young warriors who thronged Charlemagne's court in the 760s and 770s were later supplemented with, though not replaced by, young men with broader intellectual horizons, while the 790s saw a new stage in the court's evolution as it settled amidst the new buildings of Aachen.[177] Among those buildings would have been residences for the queen (or mistress?) and the royal sons (and daughters) and that brings the historical Aachen nicely into line with Einhard's perception of Charlemagne's children as being at court.[178]

This chapter has tended to speak of the Carolingian centre as if it was a constant element. From 781, there were separate kingdoms and historical factors such as rivalries among the sons of Charlemagne and of Louis the Pious and the creation of new kingdoms after 843 meant that for nearly all of our period there was not one Carolingian court but several. Furthermore, not all these royal courts would have contained adolescent princes with whom young nobles could bond. In 856, Charles the Bald established his nine-year-old son Louis (the Stammerer) in a sub-kingdom in the west of the realm to match the southern sub-kingdom of his other son Charles, who was seven, while his other sons were destined for the church. Charles the Bald presided over his own palace as a mature ruler in his thirties.[179] But the young nobles who streamed to Charles's court still had opportunities to rub shoulders with princes of their own age. It was in his father's hunting-grounds near Compiegne, far from his own sub-kingdom of Aquitaine, that the young Charles had his terrible accident and young men of his father's court were surely among the party. The fact that Albuin, the young man who so badly injured the son of Charles the Bald, had highly placed relatives in the eastern kingdom reminds us that the boundaries between the kingdoms were still permeable (this was some two decades after the Treaty of Verdun which created the separate kingdoms).[180]

The young nobles who went to the court of individual rulers went to courts that were historically distinct from one another and they thus had differing experiences. It is, however, possible to talk of the court in general terms. After all, this is what Dhuoda did in the early 840s. She wrote at a time of open warfare among the sons of Louis the Pious; she was not sure who would be king over the region where she lived and wrote, a region far from the traditional centres of Carolingian power. Yet the authority and attractiveness of the concept of the court were so deeply rooted in her that she disregarded this temporary historical crisis and retained her sense of 'the big house' as the appropriate venue for her son to complete his moral education as a member of the aristocracy, as we have seen.[181] She understood the abstract, objective character of the royal palace as site of moral and political education. But Dhuoda, like other aristocratic women, had seen a real royal palace; she tells her son William that she was married 'in the palace of Aachen' and this took place just a year after the birth of Charles the Bald; perhaps she had seen him, his nurses and minders.[182] It was political expediency that led William's father to send him to Charles the Bald, but William's mother had internalized a strong cultural tradition of the royal court's place in a young noble's education. In articulating that for her son, she reproduced exactly what the Carolingians wanted and needed. Furthermore, she assumed, and this is exactly what a ruling dynasty had to have its followers believe, that there would be plenty of young Carolingians for William and his descendants to serve in the future. At the time of her writing, Charles the Bald had no children but Dhuoda refers confidently to the continuity of the royal line.[183] When the royal court of the Carolingians ceased to be a magnet for the young nobility, as it did at the end of the ninth century, the dynasty was indeed in trouble.[184]

5

Louis the Pious and the paranoid style in politics

One terrible night in 874, King Louis the German was tormented by a dream in which he saw his father, the emperor Louis the Pious, suffering in the afterlife and begging his son for prayers that would release him. The son duly commanded the great mechanisms of prayer across his kingdom to help his father.[1] Historiographically, Louis the Pious has also spent much time in a place of shadow and condemnation. As a ruler who lost this throne to his rebellious sons and whose legacy was conflict, Louis has all too often languished in the shadow of Charlemagne and appeared as 'the great father's lesser son'. The past few decades have seen concerted effort by historians to do justice to Louis and his times and this has highlighted the complexity and richness of the period. A portrait of a capable Louis in a time that was not simply one of failure and crisis now exists, and the recent edition of the emperor's diplomas will deepen this picture's texture.[2]

This chapter, however, focuses on storm and stress. It does so, not to turn away from the new assessments of the reign but because this book's concern with the dynasty inevitably takes us into a world of conflict. This period's generation reaped the whirlwind of dynastic success. Too many Carolingians with convincing claims overloaded the system of Carolingian legitimation. From this perspective, Louis's reign appears as peculiarly problematic. The very opening of Louis's reign demonstrates this. He was the only legitimate son of Charlemagne left when the old emperor died in Aachen in January 814. Louis, however, was not the only adult Carolingian on stage and he was not actually in Aachen when his father died, but far away in his own kingdom of Aquitaine.

Louis the Pious as new imperial centre

Aachen was a special place. Even if it was still a building site in the early 800s, contemporaries marvelled at the scale and lavishness of the palace complex there. And many contemporaries would have visited it as it became Charlemagne's favoured, though not exclusive, residence in his later years.[3] It contained a truly substantial amount of treasure; it is reasonable to conclude that the chamber referred to in Charlemagne's will of 811 as containing gold, silver and precious stones was in Aachen, and that was certainly where Louis the Pious was to find it when he arrived there in 814. Charlemagne's death gave Aachen a new precious possession: his body.[4]

Death, even when expected, is always a shock and it had been over forty years since the elite had had to cope with the death of a senior king. No kingly son was by

Charlemagne's side; Louis was far away in Aquitaine. None of our sources say that Louis was sent for before his father's death. Decades later, Louis was to send urgent messages from his own death-bed to his distant son Lothar, but no one says that the old emperor had commanded a rider to gallop from Aachen to Louis while he lay dying.[5] Perhaps no message was necessary. After all, Charlemagne had proclaimed Louis as his successor in a grand ceremony at Aachen in September 813. But even such a settlement might capsize under the pressure generated by the dreaded but desired death of the ruler.

Off-stage in Aquitaine, Louis and his entourage were very probably receiving updates from contacts in Aachen about Charlemagne's declining health in that winter of 813–14. Louis spent that winter in Doué-la-Fontaine; this was one of four palaces that served as winter quarters for him, but he surely selected this one as it was his most northerly palace, perched on the very edge of Francia. Looking back from 840, Louis's biographer the Astronomer wrote that Louis had summoned an assembly to meet there 'as if by some presentiment' of his father's death. This, however, was no accident; Louis was, quite literally, positioning himself to move into Francia.[6]

Equally striking, however, is the fact that he, the declared successor, stayed there, unable to move towards Aachen while his father lived. Charlemagne was dying without Louis, but his other children were present. Surely no palace in the dynasty's history was ever to shelter as rich a cluster of resident Carolingians as Aachen did at this time, and that was another of Aachen's treasures. A long life and, in contrast to later generations, unchallenged access to a series of partners meant that Charlemagne had more children than any other Carolingian king, though Charles the Bald (840–77) was to run him close. Einhard's claim that Charlemagne never dined or travelled without his sons and daughters hardly matches realities (Louis and Pippin ruling in Aquitaine and Italy) but does evoke the lived reality of a populous nest of the ruler's children at Aachen.[7] In 814, Charlemagne had six surviving daughters, one of whom was an abbess and may not always have been present, as well as three sons by concubines. It is reasonable to assume that these nine or ten were at the palace, along with the four surviving daughters of Pippin of Italy. The three sons of Charlemagne's daughters were possibly also present, and his daughter Bertha's two boys were approaching maturity.[8] Magnates could thus see a new generation of male Carolingians at the central palace while Louis was stuck in Aquitaine. A branch line of the family also had a high palace profile in these years: Charlemagne's cousin Wala was a dominant figure; his sister Gundrada was also at the palace; their brother Adalhard's duties in Italy re-inforced their own family connection with young king Bernard there, ensuring that neither Adalhard nor Bernard would be forgotten in Aachen.[9]

Above all, the prominence of Charlemagne's unmarried daughters made his palace distinctive. If they were their father's favourites, they were also his instruments, utterly dependent on him.[10] Fully adult, unlike their illegitimate half-brothers, these women were neither passive nor blind. We have seen how, as early as 806, they were manoeuvring for security in a fatherless future, and that surely involved them in alliances with aristocrats; perhaps the two men, Warnar and Tullius, who perished when Louis finally grasped Aachen, were part of a group associated with the daughters.[11] Watching their father's body fail in that winter was to see their own power evaporate. But if their grip on Aachen was slipping and their time was running out, they deployed a brilliant manoeuvre to turn space and time to their advantage.

When Charlemagne died on 28 January 814, his daughters were his only adult children present at Aachen and they, together with magnates including Wala, asserted control of his funeral while Louis was hundreds of kilometres distant. And they mastered time too, having their father buried in haste, on the very day of his death, a speed that suggests advance planning, as Jinty Nelson observes.[12] The deathbed of a ruler was a scene of crisis theatre. The serene tableau of Pippin's dying in 768 was exceptional. Louis the Pious (840), Lothar II (869), Charles the Bald (877) and Louis the Stammerer (879) died far from their sons; Louis II of Italy (d.875) had no son. The disturbing impact of such deaths and ensuing disputes on an audience gazing upon the dissolution of a Carolingian is vividly caught in accounts such as those by Andreas of Bergamo and the Astronomer.[13] When Louis the Pious's son Pippin I of Aquitaine died in 838, he was buried in the place that he himself had chosen, an important sacred and political site in Poitiers, testifying to a successfully staged deathbed probably supervised by supporters of his sons who were there. But Pippin's succession plans quickly unravelled when his father's long arm reached into Aquitaine, as we shall see.[14] The death of a ruler activated competitive claims among sons, brothers, uncles and this confronted aristocrats with tough choices. Taking control of the funeral was one way of guiding aristocratic attention to a successor in a very public manner. When Louis the German died in 876 at Frankfurt, only one of his three sons was present and he rushed his father's body to the abbey of Lorsch for burial so that he could broadcast messages in his favour to his brothers as well as to his acquisitive uncle Charles the Bald. The highly charged manoeuvring by magnates to control the journey of Otto III's body towards burial in 1002 is illuminating here.[15]

Most of the actors in the previous paragraph are male, and the daughters' exceptional status, as well as their potential vulnerability, stands out clearly. These women needed men to help them in their struggle to remain potent in the palace; they had them. Count Wala, Charlemagne's cousin, was a key figure at Aachen, and his high status and Carolingian blood may have made him look kingly. Bertha's two sons in young manhood may have been at Aachen; certainly one of them later recalled Aachen in 814 as a place that was far from solidly loyal to Louis.[16] The Astronomer also gives us the names of two men, obscure to us, but sufficiently notorious in 814 for Louis to have identified them as potential troublemakers before he even arrived in the palace.[17] Louis's gaze was thus fixed on the palace, focusing on potential enemies within, men and women. All this supports Professor Nelson's claim that 'to control Aachen was to run the empire'.[18]

This claim, however, may give Aachen too much intrinsic value. Aachen was not in itself the political centre. Its significance depended on its place amidst a variety of elements. And one of these elements was Louis himself who was glaringly absent from Aachen. Even as Louis visualized distant Aachen, Aachen was dominated by thoughts of him. After all, who else but he could be Charlemagne's successor? Louis's claim to rule was unassailable. Wala cast a portentous shadow over the palace elite; perhaps he and his siblings did look like 'an alternative ruling family'.[19] But Wala was not the son of a king. Bernard of Italy was a king's son but he was south of the Alps. The Frankish elite not only understood the distribution of authority and status within the Carolingian family but actively participated in performing that distribution. As the author of the *Royal Frankish Annals* made clear, Bernard was Charlemagne's grandson, but Louis was his son and shared in his imperial title. There is no reason to doubt that Einhard felt the same reverence for a broad selection of the royal family in 814 that he displayed in his *Life of Charlemagne*, written in the 820s. But his deep respect for the daughters of Charlemagne and the line of Pippin of Italy did not diminish his sense of the rightness of the succession of Louis, 'the only survivor of the sons of Hildegard'. And Einhard knew all about the rightful claims of Hildegard's sons; he himself had taken the text of the 806 *Division* from the assembly at Thionville to Rome. It was Einhard who spoke publicly for the magnates in 813 in urging Charlemagne to name Louis as his successor.[20]

Whether Einhard and those magnates of 813 were sincere or not does not matter here, and nor does the retrospective nature of these sources. How could a mature and capable son of Charlemagne and Hildegard not be the successor? According to Ermold, Charlemagne's address to the assembled Franks in 813 linked their collective destiny to the divinely approved hereditary succession of Carolingian son to father: 'Christ has not deserted you, Franks, for he has still preserved from our offspring the pleasing child [Louis].'[21] Writing about a dozen years after this event, and writing for Louis, Ermold was retransmitting the dynasty's own publicly expressed and acclaimed views back to itself. Charlemagne's invented speech in the poem echoes his official voice in the 806 *Division* speaking of it being God's will that Charlemagne was blessed with sons to preserve the kingdom of the Franks.[22] The point to grasp here is that Charlemagne's fatherly pride and relief were not his alone, but were shared by the Franks. Thus, the so-called Chronicle of Moissac, composed around 818, has Charlemagne gratefully addressing God on Louis's coronation of 813: 'Blessed be the Lord God, you who have given me to see with my own eyes this day a son of my line sitting upon my throne' (3 Kings 1.48).[23]

Sons inheriting from fathers was not the only form of royal succession that the Franks could find in the Bible but its accounts of hereditary succession supported and reinforced Frankish practice. Echoes from biblical succession stories sound in the Moissac text of Charlemagne's speech and also in its report on Louis's 814 accession: 'he sat upon the throne of his father' (3 Kings 2.12). Over twenty years later, the Astronomer drew on an intensive biblical meditation on father-son relations (Ecclesiasticus/Sirach, 30.4) to encapsulate his understanding of Louis's reproduction of his father: 'The just man is dead and yet is as if he is not dead, for he has left behind a son like himself as an heir.'[24] All this does not mean that contemporaries understood succession of sons to be a smooth process. The Astronomer's vision of ruptureless reproduction was written while Louis's own sons were slugging it out amongst themselves in 840–3 for their inheritance. Biblical accounts of struggles between David's sons Adonijah and Solomon may have been a bleak reassurance for the Franks of the normality of familial dispute within hereditary systems, but they were not news to them.

These representations of Louis's filial succession form part of the discourse of the natural dynastic rule. These representations appeared after Louis had succeeded, an act that deepened Carolingian naturalness and which thus affected these representations. Louis therefore could not be the full beneficiary of all this precisely when he needed it most in the winter of 813–14. But, as we have seen, figures such as Einhard were already caught up in this language of Carolingian filial succession, a language uttered by Charlemagne at Thionville in 806 and at Aachen in 813. While it is difficult to be sure of what Charlemagne did say to and about his son in the 813 ceremonies, he surely deployed father-son language as he had done in 806. Thegan's account of the ceremony, written some twenty years later, is saturated with familial language and while that may well reflect Thegan's own concerns in writing a history of sons, the bishops assembled in judgement upon Louis in 833 claimed to remember 'his father's admonition and terrifying exhortation' of 813. If such memories were affected by the intervening crises of the 830s, the Moissac chronicle of 818 predates these storms but is similarly soaked in familial language.[25] Perhaps Charlemagne really did explicitly thank God that he had lived to see a son of his upon the throne; his diplomas show clearly that the language of fatherhood was well-nigh inescapable whenever he referred to his kingly sons such as Louis or Pippin of Italy.[26]

This staging of son succeeding father in our texts and in the rituals whose traces we find there was not solely about the Carolingian family. As Philippe Buc has argued, the roles of David and Solomon in the Moissac chronicle point to broader contemporary concerns with kingly and priestly modes of installing rulers.[27] But what matters here is the existence of a discourse of hereditary succession to rulership, and that this discourse supported Louis in 813–14. This was not a weightless abstraction but existed in the minds of historical actors and appeared in public in the great ceremonies staged at Aachen by Charlemagne in September 813. The declaring of consent to Louis's emperorship there by the aristocrats of the realm highlights the collective nature of Frankish political culture, but these aristocrats also watched themselves as a group binding itself to accept the son of Charlemagne and Hildegard. Horizontal bonds of a collective aristocratic identity actively co-existed with vertical bonds stretching up to the family of rulers.[28]

All this did not make Louis's accession problem-free in early 814. The Astronomer's account of Louis's slow-motion journey to Aachen surely preserves the atmosphere of frantic calculation that enveloped the key actors that winter. But no one else could match Louis's Carolingian qualifications. And by his side in Aquitaine, Louis had powerful magnates such as count Bego whose reach and connections extended into Francia.[29] His Carolingian blood and the general recognition of his claim to office in 813 made Louis himself a centre. Without him, Aachen was a lock without a key and could not have a full objective existence as a centre. The Carolingian world had many centres and Louis and his entourage were one of them, poised to become dominant on Charlemagne's death. Communication was thus critically important here. From Aachen, a messenger called Rampo rushed to Louis with the urgent news of his father's death, covering the distance from Aachen to Doué-la-Fontaine in about a week.[30] If people in Aachen were trying to shut Louis out, it seems odd that such a swift messenger was dispatched, and one wonders who sent this messenger. If Aachen was the realm's centre, the longer Louis could be kept away from it, the more open the royal future might be. But it was not possible to muffle the news of Charlemagne's death. A lament composed in the north Italian monastery of Bobbio evokes universal grief for Charlemagne, spanning Francia and Italy and saddening men, women and children.

This is an imagined vision of what must have been a more dry-eyed spreading of the news across the empire. The great magnates had to be told. A swift messenger tracked down abbot Adalhard in Rome to break the news to him.[31] Aachen could not impose a news black-out.

This news had an immediate impact on its recipients. As soon as abbot Adalhard of Corbie heard it, he abandoned his mission in Rome and returned to his abbey in Francia; his diplomatic credentials, so to speak, were no longer valid and he had to await decisions of the new ruler. As for Louis, this news made him king. He did not need to possess Aachen in order to activate his royal office. Receiving in Doué-la-Fontaine the news of his father's death on the second of February meant that that day, the feast of the Purification of the Virgin Mary, was the start of his rule. Much later, in 831 and 835, Louis was to choose this date of solemn festivity to re-consecrate his reign after troubled times; he and contemporaries understood this as an attempt to propitiate God as well as a proclamation of Louis's legitimate rule. If possessing Aachen was not in itself essential for Louis to become ruler, he did need the acclamation of his aristocratic followers. Philippe Depreux rightly points out that Louis's dating the start of his reign from February 2nd, not from the date of Charlemagne's death on 28 January, shows that neither the rights of inheritance nor Charlemagne's crowning of Louis in 813 was enough in themselves to automatically make Louis king. He had to be recognized by magnates. Similarly, Charlemagne and his brother Carloman dated the start of their reigns in 768 by the date of their public king-making ceremonies and not by the death of their father a fortnight earlier.[32] But Louis saw himself as king before he reached Aachen.

As Louis approached Orléans, its bishop, Theodulf, 'very quickly' sent a messenger out to him to ask whether he should come out to meet Louis or greet him in the city. Theodulf's hesitation was not, as some historians have suggested, a sign of potential disloyalty to Louis from one of the old guard around Charlemagne (and Wala). Rather, realizing that Charlemagne had died, Theodulf was unsure of protocol for greeting the son who was no longer merely king but now the supreme ruler. The arrival on their doorstep of the un-nerving figure of a ruler and his warriors could disconcert bishops anxious to do the right thing; in 774, Charlemagne's unexpectedly swift arrival in Rome forced Pope Hadrian to improvise a suitable welcome ceremony modelled on that for the Byzantine exarch. Theodulf was not questioning Louis's authority; he was seeking the right way to participate in constructing it. Contemporary poems from Orléans give some idea of the elaborate greetings prepared for a ruler's arrival.[33] Louis's commanding Theodulf to come to him cast the bishop as another extra in the swelling crowd of messengers and petitioners who were now swarming to the new emperor. Even if he was an eye-witness to all this, Ermold's account of people swimming across the wintry river Loire in their enthusiasm to reach Louis is surely poetic hyperbole. But it vividly evokes Louis's magnetic force as the new ruler, drawing people towards him who wanted to ingratiate themselves as soon as possible. And Louis gave the required response, displaying to everyone 'an abundance of good will, each in his rank', that is, reassuring these new followers of his favour.[34]

The much later account of the Astronomer may well be coloured by his knowledge of the rushing of messengers after Louis's own death in 840 but that is no reason to doubt his picture of Louis encountering one messenger after another while at Orléans, and this suggests that they knew where to find him.[35] The messengers and petitioners hurrying towards Louis tilted the empire to the south-west, simultaneously recognizing and creating Louis's person, wherever he happened to be, as the new centre of royal authority. Louis kept building this authority as he moved relentlessly north-east. As he grew bigger, Aachen grew smaller. Aachen mattered; powerful people resided there. But the towering figure of Louis narrowed their options as people there knew that he was swiftly bearing down on them.[36]

Moving north-east from Orléans, Louis was taking possession of territory with fiscal lands and mints and thus rich in economic resources, but also in spiritual ones, with its great abbeys such as St-Germain-des-Prés and St-Denis each populated by around 100 well-connected monks and controlled by loyal servants of Charlemagne, abbots Irmino (like Theodulf, a witness to the emperor's will) and Waldo. The count of Paris was Stephen, another witness to Charlemagne's will, and brother to Bego, Louis's right-hand man. Arriving as lord and pilgrim, Louis thus mobilized the support of earth and heaven.[37] More specifically, at St-Denis Louis was able to inscribe himself in the series of legitimate rulers of the Franks. St-Denis was a shrine but was also a kingly place; there was a palace there and it was the burial site of many kings. For Louis now it was above all the resting place of his great-grandfather, his grandfather and his grandmother as well as the location for the anointing of his father and uncle in 754. The monks of St-Denis, together with Louis' entourage, must have been acutely aware that the aura of his royal ancestors enfolded Louis in this sacred place. The very name of count Stephen of Paris testified to that noble family's awareness of Pope Stephen's consecration of Louis's forebears at St-Denis in 754. And those who were not aware of that ancestral presence would have been made so; we know that churchmen were keen to point out tombs of their ancestors to royal visitors. Aachen now held Charlemagne's body but St-Denis possessed a whole series of royal tombs, and Louis himself understood the importance of St-Denis as royal site and as shrine to a saint whose patronage of the dynasty protected its throne.[38] Louis was convincing himself, as well as others, that he was the legitimate ruler. Like the mythical Antaeus, he grew stronger as he touched the landscape.

If Louis's kingship was dynamic and expanding, Aachen's potential was stalled. Louis and his entourage may indeed have feared Wala's intentions but it is more than likely that Wala and his supporters were just as unsure of their own options. Wala's political prominence under Charlemagne, his Carolingian blood, his alliance with the royal women of the palace: all this spelled potential, but for what? He was not the son of a king; no king had nominated him as acclaimed successor; he was hardly the only aristocrat to have Carolingian blood. Such potential could not crystallize into royal distinctiveness; Wala's clouds of glory dissolved in the light of Louis's rising sun. He could make trouble, but could he launch a credible bid for a throne? It turned out that Wala was at his most powerful when he gave up his power. He hurried to meet Louis, thus acknowledging the latter's superior status before even meeting him. His submission to the emperor triggered a rush of 'all the magnates of the Franks' to Louis, striving to out-do each other in their eagerness to impress Louis with their loyalty. The Astronomer's account pays tribute to the importance of

Wala, whose ability to deliver aristocratic support was a bargaining counter that he doubtless hoped would ensure that he gained Louis's favour.[39] But it also reveals the overwhelming relief felt by the aristocracy that ambiguities were now resolved. There was little appetite for conflict in 814. Wala's potential was unrealizable. Only sons of kings became kings.

One final obstacle remained: Aachen itself. Buttressed by all this aristocratic recognition, Louis nonetheless did not go straight to Aachen. He halted his progress at the palace of Herstal which was about only a day's journey from Aachen; this was a deliberate stop.[40] Aachen was not yet safe for Louis; a hardcore of figures who had irrevocably bet against him remained there and Louis sent a group of magnates including Wala to Aachen to round them up for judgement and punishment. This exquisite stroke proclaimed that Wala was now merely an instrument in Louis's hands to be turned against his own erstwhile supporters. If Aachen was insecure, it now represented only a local problem for Louis; it was not a capital fortified against him (it was not even a walled site); it could not be a centre of power until he entered it. It was, however, still a dangerous place. Louis's supporters encountered stiff resistance, violence got out of control and some of Louis's men perished in confused fighting along with the malcontents. Only the Astronomer tells us this; sources written closer in time to the events are silent on it, saying only that Louis entered Aachen as his father's successor. The Astronomer is careful to tell us that all the violence in Aachen took place before Louis arrived there; thus, he too presents Louis's actual arrival in Aachen as a smooth entry of an unchallenged ruler into the palace.[41] Aachen mattered, but Louis mattered more. It gave his sisters, Wala and their associates potential but Louis himself was the accepted and constructed centre.

Once he was safely in Aachen, he was able to take retrospective control of his father's funeral by paying the expenses for it (from the treasure), supervising bequests, etc., going on to stamp his own imprint on Aachen. Indeed, he spent much of his first year of rule at Aachen drawing the empire's aristocracy to him as the new centre.[42] He then asserted control over the dynastic future, exiling 'the whole female crowd from the palace' but kept his half-brothers close to him at court. With Carolingian women sealed up, Louis blocked any future leakage of dynastic charisma, the nightmare that had happened sixty years previously when Charles Martel's daughter escaped her brothers, a nightmare that still haunted ninth-century imaginations. Feasting with his brothers in his palace kept them under his eye and proclaimed the specialness of being a son of Charlemagne. His dangerously talented and well-connected kinsmen Wala and Adalhard found it wise to abandon the palace for the monastic life, leaving the spotlight on Louis.[43]

In asserting his own authority at the start of a new reign, Louis neither possessed nor desired carte blanche. Rulers needed to work with powerful aristocrats. Some magnates who had been close to his father lost prominence under Louis, though they may not have lost his favour. This is true of Hildebold, archbishop of Cologne and archbishop Leidrad of Lyons.[44] The 814 fighting in Aachen and the banishment of Carolingian women as well as of Wala and Adalhard meant that some important members of the elite now felt a very chill wind. Louis brought his own followers to Aachen and promotion for them could mean loss for others. Such figures, however, were not strangers to existing central elite networks. Count Bego's greedy enjoyment of the fruits of patronage did not endear him to everyone but he was no exotic southerner; he belonged to a Frankish aristocratic family focused on Paris. Abbot Benedict of Aniane, a Goth, journeyed from Aquitaine to advise Louis on spiritual reform for the whole empire, but he had attended upon Carolingian rulers since the days of Pippin III.[45] Louis's accession did not flood the palace with exotic new figures from Aquitaine. Philippe Depreux's prosopographical survey of Louis's entourage has, at a rough count, some forty-five men (including Louis's brothers and Bernard of Italy) holding office or position at court under Charlemagne (not including men holding office in Aquitaine under Louis himself). Of these men, thirty-five survived Louis's immediate accession.[46] We could probably increase that figure as I have erred on the side of caution in identifying such survivors, and we could consider other figures such as bishop Walcaud of Liège (810–31) not included by Depreux in his formal prosopographical register.[47] Like all Carolingian rulers, Louis had to work with established partners.

Louis, however, stamped his authority upon his house very firmly in 814. In removing Carolingian women and kinsmen such as Wala and Adalhard from court and keeping his brothers in a tight embrace, he asserted his own eminence. The venomous language directed at these women in pro-Louis sources is a grudging acknowledgement of their status. A quarter of a century later, the Astronomer shuddered to think that they might have married outside of Louis's control.[48] Louis's nephew Bernard remained king in Italy and was graciously received by Louis at an assembly in August–September 814. That assembly also saw Louis establish a new kingdom of Bavaria for his eldest son, the nineteen-year-old Lothar, and he appointed the seventeen-year-old Pippin as king of Aquitaine; the youngest son Louis the German remained with his father. Bernard and everyone else saw emperor Louis's Carolingian future cover their world.[49]

This book's focus on the dynasty means that its picture of that world cannot include its cultural fertility and variety, not to mention the sheer ordinariness of agricultural toil for the vast majority of its population. Furthermore, this focus on the dynasty gives a prominent place to tension and conflict, yet Louis's reign was not entirely dominated by trouble and he was not a weak ruler overshadowed by a mighty father.[50] But Louis's reign did come to be wracked by intense conflict. Some of that surely stemmed from the winding down after 800 of the gloriously profitable wars of conquest that had kept the Frankish elite happy in clearly defined roles. Scholars have yet to explore in detail the nature and full significance of this end of imperial expansion but it was an important backdrop to Louis's reign.[51] If the elite turned inward that could make the realm stronger, the creative imagining of the purpose of this Christian empire and the roles of its governors is a striking feature of Louis's reign, as are the refinements of capitulary texts, the enhancement of palaces, etc.[52] And at the centre of the vast realm lay one family which turned out to be all too successful at making itself special. The competing claims of king's sons generated tensions and conflicts that demanded solutions, but neither political coups, battles nor intense scrutiny of biblical precedents was to help the Carolingians and their followers out of the dynastic dilemma.

817: Godly empire and earthly families

Why did Louis arrange the succession in 817, a mere three years after his accession? He was no ageing King Lear. At thirty-nine, he was roughly the same age as his father Charlemagne had been when he mastered Tassilo. On the eve of the assembly at Aachen that was to unveil the 817 succession plans, Louis had been hunting, an ostentatious demonstration that a nasty fall in the palace had not impaired his virile fitness.[53] Perhaps the impetus came from the younger generation. His sons Lothar and Pippin were now twenty or over and, with their followers, may have been pushing for advancement. Although Lothar was indeed to be promoted by the new arrangement and the young Louis the German was named to a kingdom for the first time, 817 left real power in the father's hands.[54] What really drove Louis was the urgent need to reform society in a God-pleasing way, including the continued existence of peace in the realm, a prominent concern in the councils held by the ageing Charlemagne in 813. Heirs to this endless task, Louis and his advisers knew that pleasing God mattered much more than catering to royal sons' wishes for territories. Recent scholarship on the carefully crafted document on the succession arrangements, the *Ordinatio Imperii* (*The Ordering of Empire*) has grasped that what distinguished 817 from previous succession plans was its explicit submission to the will of God rather than to earthly considerations such as love of a father for his sons. Louis's reference to the fragility of human life in an address to the assembly was more of a general reflection on human dependence on God than to his own earlier accident in the palace.[55]

The atmosphere of this assembly in the majestic site of Aachen was intense. Twelve years later, archbishop Agobard still remembered the three days of fasting, praying and giving alms which transported participants into readiness to hear the will of God. He cannot have been alone in his memories.[56] For the *fideles* were visibly active at Aachen that summer, requesting discussion of the succession, possibly at the prompting of ambitious royal sons. Their consent to the settlement was very important; Louis later had aristocrats swear to abide by it at two separate assemblies in 821, and this shows how anxious he was to remind them of what had been agreed in the exalted atmosphere of 817, and to lock them into it.[57] Aristocrats did not spend their every waking hour thinking about the Carolingian family. Those counts, bishops and abbots who petitioned Louis for favours in the summer of 817 had their own concerns. But whether these interests lay in Alemannia in the east, or Cruas by the Rhone, or Tours in the north-west, the ruler's patronage, co-operation and intervention were necessary. And, in evoking his father and grandfather, Louis reminded these aristocrats of his special status as descendant of kings.[58]

Rulers such as Louis thus tried to keep aristocratic eyes on the royal family. What the aristocracy saw at Aachen, however, was a dramatically shrinking royal line. Brazenly amplifying the distinctions between legitimate and illegitimate children articulated in Charlemagne's will of 811, the *Ordinatio* formally proclaimed that only legitimate sons were to succeed. This was a public cancelling of royal futures for his dangerously charismatic brothers, who were doubtless highly visible at Aachen and who had reached maturity (Hugh was seventeen, while Drogo was around sixteen). Louis gave the aristocracy a vivid demonstration of what this meant, appointing his own illegitimate son Arnulf as count of Sens, thus simultaneously recognizing him and reducing him to the non-kingly ranks.[59] While this stress on legitimate offspring was consistent with Louis's moral purification of the palace in 814, it also had the more worldly advantage of shrinking the line of succession to Louis's own sons by the empress. As a bonus, it cast a shadow over Bernard of Italy, possibly already seen by some contemporaries as offspring of an illegitimate liaison.

Aachen proclaimed other measures to shrink the circle of royal inheritance. Even those sons who were legitimate now had to wait to be old enough to succeed. The *Ordinatio* radically deployed traditional Frankish laws to now say that a king's son had to wait till maturity (their fifteenth year) before he could succeed. For Louis and his advisers, in 817 Carolingian royal identity was no longer enough to let children toddle onto a throne; deepening conceptions of kingship as an office demanded that they be mature. This, however, was easier said than done. In fact Louis did not do what he said. The assembly witnessed the designation of his youngest son Louis (the German) as a king. Even if the latter did not take up his kingdom until some years later, aristocrats at Aachen witnessed a boy of ten (or possibly as young as seven) defined as a king by the very man who claimed that children should wait.[60] People would have drawn their own conclusions.

If the political elite understood kingship as an office, it also understood that that office was held by members of a special family and family claims were unignorable. If not, how could that family still be special? For a ruler such as Louis to try and limit Carolingian family charisma was to risk sawing off the very branch of the tree on which he was so loftily perched. But concern for harmony in the realm, and perhaps also an awareness of resources being finite, led Louis to try to do so. He was not alone. Contemporaries thought hard about how the high office of kingship could hold the realm together and this supreme good could trump family claims. People in the ninth century could conceive of a world of downgraded Carolingian sons. A poem by bishop Theodulf of Orléans sang of the peace that flowed from rule by one brother, while others enjoyed an honoured but less exalted place in the 'senate'. We cannot be sure when this poem was written but even if it dates from jostlings over the succession in 806 rather than 817, that does not lessen its significance. After all, even Charlemagne, in the *Division* of 806, may have thought that kingdoms were not to be subdivided among all sons. The *Ordinatio*'s more explicit utterance on this clearly implied for those with ears to hear that even fully grown legitimately born royal sons could be denied a kingdom and would thus effectively join the ranks of the magnates, not of princes. The realm was thus to be preserved against that love for his sons (*amor filiorum*) that might make a royal father disturb peace willed by God.[61]

Love of sons was, however, an indispensable feature of dynastic rule. Bishop Theodulf's song of a son in solitary eminence is drowned out by a chorus of contemporary celebration of many sons and descendants as part of the aura of royal glory. Writing ten years or so after 817, a poet depicted the pope blessing Louis in 816 with the words 'May almighty God, who increased the seed of Abraham, … double and triple your descendants' before heaping gifts on Louis, the empress and, of course, their children. Rulers longed for descendants. Charlemagne's mother Bertrada experienced a dynast's satisfaction in living long enough to see her son's house full of grandchildren.

Charlemagne proclaimed the fact that he had three sons deserving of a kingdom to be a sign of God's mercy to the realm, relieving him from 'fears of … oblivion' (though Pippin the Hunchback was no longer to be seen as a blessing). Contemporaries knew that Charlemagne mourned the premature death of two of his sons. As we shall see, King Charles the Bald in the 860s yearned for more sons even as he was locked in conflict with his existing ones.[62]

Love of sons was not necessarily a matter of affection, but of structures. Dynasts needed sons; how many could ever be enough? And sons all expected to have a future, as the aristocracy knew. Rulers urged people to look to a future of Carolingian descendants and we must assume that they did so (see chapter below on prayers). In their struggles with their father, all three of Louis's mature sons kept their eye on the future of their own line. Pippin of Aquitaine, Lothar and Louis the German issued diplomas in 829, 830 and 837 respectively, all urging their recipients in Aquitaine, Friuli and Bavaria to pray for them, their wife and their offspring.[63] Louis himself could hardly be immune to this; dynastic drives were too strong. In 816, for example, he issued a diploma for the abbey of St-Mihiel near Verdun, requesting that the monks there pray for himself, his wife and their offspring. The abbot of St-Mihiel, Smaragdus, was a highly placed member of Louis's entourage and this diploma was issued at Aachen.[64]

This does not mean that all sons were automatically guaranteed a kingdom, or that kingdoms had to be endlessly divided. As we have seen Louis and supporters had a clear vision of single son succession to undivided kingdom. But Carolingian specialness was too big to be put into the confining boxes of 817. Pressures of expectation for thrones for sons were too strong. And 817's measure to deal with that future pressure was itself problematic. Lothar was to tower over his brothers. The younger brothers' share of the empire was much less than had been allocated to Charlemagne's younger sons in 806, a fact so clear that these young men and the aristocracy, many of whom surely remembered 806, did not need to pore over the text of the *Ordinatio* to grasp it. But Lothar's future eminence as eldest brother was pushing the seniority of an older brother much further than it could go, even though the *Ordinatio* tried to elide that seniority into a fatherly authority. Being the older brother, however, was no trump card among a family of kings. Louis the Pious himself had been a younger brother; contemporaries knew this and also knew that God sometimes favoured the younger brother over an older who had failed to please heaven. There seems little reason to doubt retrospective sources that refer to the younger brothers' outrage at Lothar's status.[65] The arrangements of 817, despite insisting in almost every clause on the role of the eldest brother, were not based on any intrinsic quality that an older brother possessed; what counted was God's approval.

Overblown status of an older brother was a real change to Carolingian family norms and brotherly harmony was difficult to achieve anyway. An older brother did have status in Frankish familial culture, but royal brothers were hardly likely to concede him a father's dominance.[66] Louis's own memories would have told him that. Aristocrats were not passive witnesses to such tensions. They knew that conflict between royal brothers was always likely and strove to lessen its impact in divisions of the realm. Abbot Smaragdus of St-Mihiel, whom we have seen above receiving instructions to pray for the emperor and his line, was all too aware that the sons he prayed for were likely to fall out. He had warned Louis himself of precisely this in a book of advice on kingship (the *Via regia*), drawing his attention to the dangers of malice and envy among brothers. Smaragdus pointed to biblical examples such as Cain and Abel, and Esau and Jacob. This was not cloudily pious sermonizing. It was sharp advice. Smaragdus, like everyone else, knew that the royal family did not have its troubles to seek.[67]

The year 817 created expectations and anxieties and tightened the screw on them by withholding what it promised to give: Louis sought to hold onto his own powers while promoting his sons.[68] And yet in some ways, Louis and his counsellors spelt out the meaning and significance of 817's *Ordinatio* all too well. The three days of fasting and prayer at the Aachen assembly in July revealed that favouring Lothar was the best way of fulfilling God's will that unity be preserved. This unity signified the harmony within the ruling family and the governors of the realm rather than a territorially unified empire; God cared more for righteousness than geography.[69] To change these arrangements would be to expose oneself to charges of flouting God's will by following human wilfulness; such an open embrace of earthly mutability was to shock people such as archbishop Agobard of Lyons in the 830s.[70] Of course, Louis can hardly be blamed for not knowing the future; if only Smaragdus's warnings on familial malice and envy had been louder.

The great settlement of 817 was to trigger immediate family tension. With its allocation of Italy to Lothar, it threatened to choke Bernard. With Charlemagne's death in January 814, the climate had chilled for the young king of Italy. Adalhard and Wala, together with their siblings, had fallen from favour and were exiled from court, depriving Bernard of support in a palace now populated by aristocrats such as count Bego and queen Irmingard who had no love for him.[71] Louis did summon Bernard to Aachen and showered him with gifts, possibly a share of Charlemagne's treasure, thus acknowledging Bernard's status but also very publicly demonstrating his own superiority over a subordinate nephew.[72] Within Italy itself, people knew that Louis's shadow fell over Bernard; charters in Farfa, for example, were dated by the years of Louis as well as, sometimes, of Bernard.[73] Bernard remained a king and acknowledgement of Louis's superiority in 814 did not lessen this despite later claims by Louis's supporters. Bernard may not have issued charters but he did issue capitularies, and a surviving illustration in a manuscript copy of them depicts him as a ruler prayed for by the church.[74] And Bernard was creating a royal line. Adalhard had found a wife for him before Charlemagne died.[75] Some historians have thought that Bernard was not formally married to this woman, Cunigunda, noting that in her will she refers to herself simply as survivor or widow (*relicta*), not queen, and to Bernard as her 'lord' (*senior*), not husband, and concluding that she was thus no queenly dynastic partner.[76] But it is risky to put so much weight on such terms (Dhuoda referred to her husband as *senior*); contemporaries may well have seen her as queen, as that is the term used in the text written by Adalhard (mediated to us by the much later author Hincmar of Reims) as a guide for Bernard's rule, and they would have known that she belonged to a powerful Frankish noble family with connections north of the Alps.[77] She produced a son, probably in 815, to whom his parents gave the kingly name of Pippin, a clear statement of intent: Bernard was now head of an alternative royal line within the Carolingian family.[78] In summoning Bernard regularly to his court, Louis could not help but remind his own followers of this other line's existence as well as giving Bernard access to magnates north of the Alps.[79]

Bernard's kingship thus put some pressure on Louis. The emperor, however, could return the favour. The intensifying of the bond between Louis and the papacy lessened any standing Bernard had in Rome.[80] At some stage in 817, Louis formalized this in a document promulgated at an assembly and which refers to the bond between the papacy and Louis's great-grandfather, grandfather and father and which was subscribed by Louis's three sons, but which passed over Bernard and his father in silence. Louis probably promulgated this at the same great assembly at Aachen where he solemnly proclaimed the arrangements for the succession in the *Ordinatio Imperii*.[81] This likewise only spoke of Louis's line: the very public arrangements for the succession made no reference to Bernard at all, but did announce that Italy was to be subject to Louis's eldest son Lothar on his accession 'just as it was to our father and as it is subject to us, God willing, at the present time'. We might not see this as a threat.[82] Bernard could not afford to take such a detached view. For the first time since Louis succeeded, Bernard had not been summoned north and this great family settlement had been made without him, as everyone saw; what sort of future now stretched ahead for him and his son? One contemporary thought that it was the news of the Aachen assembly that triggered Bernard's revolt.[83]

It is hard to say exactly what form his revolt took. The same source that links his revolt to the Aachen assembly states that he rose against Louis and his sons and that he wanted to usurp their rule, a claim echoed in a later pro-Louis source.[84] This catches the hostility between the two royal lines but it is hard to believe that Bernard thought that he could replace Louis. Louis was safely tucked up in Aachen, far from Italy; Bernard did not have his rivals in his grasp as Pippin the Hunchback had at Regensburg in 792. He may have hoped that what support he did have outside Italy would blaze up. Contemporaries themselves could not be certain about Bernard's motives as rumours and disinformation swirled around Italy and the northern court.[85] Perhaps Bernard only closed the Alpine passes and compelled Italian towns to take an oath to him, a defiant act to be sure, but hardly a direct attack on Louis and more of a defensive move from Bernard's perspective. A 'bloodless' revolt would signal Bernard's anger at the *Ordinatio* and, after this show of strength, Bernard headed north to negotiate with his uncle.[86]

Open defiance, however, had raised the stakes for every player. Outraged honour and threatening rumours left little room for calm reflection in this world, as the rebellious Hardard had found to his cost in the 780s. A rattled Louis mobilized warriors, sending out urgent messages urging them to prepare to attack Italy where Satan had lured Bernard into rebellion, and he himself led the army south. Nor were Louis and Bernard the only actors on stage. Powerful aristocrats around Louis had no love for a Bernard whose existence threatened their investment in Louis and his line.[87] Aristocrats in Italy split, with some prominent figures rushing north to paint Bernard's actions in the worst light while others stuck by him. We have the names of two or three bishops and five secular aristocrats who backed Bernard, and there were surely more.[88] Carolingians fuelled the tensions that aristocrats generated and vice versa. Self-interest combined with respect for Carolingian blood meant that aristocrats did not always know who was in the right when the royal family quarrelled. This would only intensify as the century wore on and the number of throne-worthy royals expanded.

Bernard's actions activated the old links between Italy and Alemannia. A charter issued by Louis at Aachen in June 818 for that abbey reports how estates given to St-Gall by one Isimgrim had been seized by the fisc when his properties were confiscated after he had perished as a traitor (*infidelis*), surely a reference to Bernard's rising. Fighting and death came to this area.[89] Such upheaval had consequences; in this case, St-Gall lost property until an enquiry under count Richuin established the abbey's rights, rights confirmed by Louis. This Richuin appears in the St-Gall list discussed above in Chapter 3; he was count in Thurgau and is mentioned in a St-Gall charter of 808 that was dated by the reign of Pippin of Italy, Bernard's father.[90] We see here something of the splits and the tensions that must have racked the Alemannian establishment when Bernard rose. Richuin and Isimgrim had had to make choices. Although Richuin fits the profile of a potential Bernard supporter, he turned out to be Louis the Pious's man, sufficiently so to be entrusted with the 'normalization' of the situation in the disturbed Thurgau. Isimgrim had made another choice and had paid the ultimate price for it. The abbey of St-Gall and other regional powers must have watched all this with deep unease.

The rivalries that seethed amongst the aristocracy of this region fed into the equally poisonous rivalries and resentments in the royal family which in turn fed back into these regional tensions. That St-Gall list of 812/13 includes one Adalbert, a name that points to the 'Hunfrid' family, and also the names Rodbertus and Odlarich, names that point to the rival 'Ulrich'/Udalrich' family.[91] A tenth-century source has encouraged historians to trace clashes between these groups stretching from Rhaetia to Istria, clashes that intersected precisely in 817/18 with the tensions between Louis the Pious and his nephew.[92] Bernard's revolt was a complex phenomenon that could not be entirely shaped by him and his imperial uncle. Other actors could exploit this situation.

These were not clearly defined factions with a continuous existence and consistent goals. As bishop of Verona, Ratold held office in the heart of Bernard's kingdom, indeed in the very town that had celebrated its connection with Pippin in poetry; he himself came from Alemannia and had been a close associate of Pippin. All this might suggest that Bernard would be his Carolingian when trouble broke out. But Ratold was in fact one of the Italian magnates who rallied to Louis the Pious.[93] Painstaking prosopographical research can reveal to us patterns of potential loyalty, but contemporaries, whose research on this was urgent, knew that several patterns existed, with potentially various futures. That was the problem. In an aristocratic world such as this one people's connections were well known, and that included their ancestry. One of Bernard's close associates in rebellion was count Reginhar, a grandson of the treacherous Hardrad. Contemporaries knew this and Louis's supporters took a sour pleasure in seeing him suffer his grandfather's fate. This, however, was an opportunistic blackening of Reginhar's reputation, not a revelation of some innate anti-Carolingian opposition in Reginhar's blood. Siding with Bernard was hardly an anti-Carolingian move. While it is significant that contemporaries remembered his grandfather after so many decades (and it is also interesting that they traced Reginhar's descent through the maternal line), they also would have known that Reginhar's father had been close to Charlemagne.[94]

Punishments for rebellion did not blast an entire family. Hardrad's daughter had made a good marriage; the expansion of Carolingian rule gave her son high office in Italy. Bernard and his companions may have thought that they had made their protest and that negotiations would follow. One source says that Bernard was captured but it looks as if he and his allies travelled in winter all the way to Chalon-sur-Saone to disarm themselves and surrender in December to Louis, who had reached that point on his own punitive journey southwards.[95] Un-manning themselves might evoke a merciful counter-move from the emperor.

Louis then celebrated Christmas at Chalon, scene of their surrender and his triumph.[96] But the rebels' fate then unfolded at a curiously slow tempo. After returning to Aachen, Louis waited till the spring of 818 before dealing with them; possibly he did not want to unleash his anger in the holy season of Lent. Delay need not mean lack of urgency; discussion of the Bernard case would have been agitated. Bernard's response to 817 triggered panic amongst Louis's circle and various prominent figures who do not seem to have had anything to do with Bernard were rounded up: Louis's half-brothers Drogo, Hugh and Theoderic as well as bishop Theodulf of Orléans all fell from favour.[97]

Perhaps time was needed to identify everyone thought to be guilty and to calm the political elite. Above all, getting agreement on Bernard's fate would have taken time as Louis faced differing demands and petitions. The monks of Fulda, where Bernard had been educated, pleaded for clemency. Bernard was no marginal figure of only Italian interest; the monks of Fulda had learned that Carolingians were special. And Louis would surely have recalled his father's explicit 806 injunction against blinding or mutilating the royal line, a warning solemnly repeated in front of witnesses in 813. But the 806 *Division* had also enjoined royal nephews to show familial obedience to their uncles and had only forbidden mutilation without a fitting investigation first.[98]

Those who resisted the dazzling figure of the ruler were cast by him into darkness, as those who had defied Charlemagne or Louis had discovered. Blinding had become a fitting punishment for rebels as it expressed outraged royal majesty, while its sparing the traitor the death he so richly deserved displayed the ruler's Christian mercy.[99] But how were rulers to punish royal rebels? Charlemagne's assembly pronouncements in 806 and 813 against harming members of the royal line publicly proclaimed the specialness of that line. Pippin III had been lucky with Grifo; his troublesome brother's death in battle in 753 saved him from having to punish him. The condemnation and punishment of Pippin the Hunchback took place in the broad light of day at an assembly, thus demonstrating to the Franks the fall in Pippin's status; his father's determination to spare his life, while permitting aristocrats to be executed, then demonstrated Pippin's continuing royal identity. Bernard was not only a Carolingian, he was a king. People at Aachen in 818 now thought that both these factors counted against him: as king, he had sworn oaths to Louis and as a nephew he should have been 'obedient towards [his uncle] as is fitting in such a blood-relationship', as the *Division* of 806 insisted.[100] Louis was outraged as ruler and as senior family member: office and family intertwined. We do not know if Bernard underwent any ceremony of deposition from office and it is unlikely that he did, despite the provisions of 806, no such clear procedure actually existed, a lack that was to be seriously felt later in Louis's reign. Instead, while the guilty bishops seem to have been deposed by the judgement of their fellow bishops, Bernard, still referred to as 'king' in the *Royal Frankish Annals*, was lumped in with the secular aristocrats and, like them, condemned to death by the assembled Franks. Contemporary and later sources saw that Louis's order that the guilty merely be blinded was merciful.[101]

It may not have been an easy decision to make; Bernard, a king and the son of an anointed king, was the first Carolingian royal rebel after 751 to suffer corporal punishment, as far as we know. We do not know if Louis and his councillors had intended the result: three days after being blinded, Bernard died, as did his similarly punished ally Reginhar. Whether this was the Carolingian equivalent of 'shot while trying to escape', or desperate double suicide, as historians have wondered, is not something we can know at this distance.[102] As we shall see, contemporaries were very disturbed by Bernard's fate. His death, however, simplified the political landscape. Louis had marginalized his brother's line just as his grandfather and father had done so in their time. The fallen figures of unfortunate nephews littered the byways of Carolingian authority. The fate of Pippin the Hunchback and Bernard showed contemporaries that not all king's sons had a guaranteed royal future. But their risings showed that marginalized sons and nephews could nonetheless mobilize significant support for claims that were very hard to extinguish. After Hardrad's revolt, discontented aristocrats now rallied behind such Carolingian figures or manipulated them in their quarrels with other Carolingian rulers. The Carolingians had been very successful in focusing aristocratic loyalty upon themselves, on stages stretching from Italy to Bavaria to Francia. The aristocracy accepted that the Carolingians were special, but how was this to be maintained, and how were some Carolingians to make themselves more special than others?

For the first ten years of his reign, Louis was the master of such problems. As we have seen, he exerted stern mastery over the wider royal kin, expelling his sisters from the palace, keeping his brothers under his eye there, subordinating Wala and eventually tonsuring and exiling his brothers while finishing Bernard. Bernard's son, who bore the royal name of Pippin never made a bid for a throne, as far as we know, despite playing a prominent part in the conflicts of the 830s and 840s. This clearly demonstrates Louis's political strength; he permanently reduced a royal son to the ranks, compensating him through artful patronage. But this Pippin's fate also shows us that there were limits to the resources available to sons of kings; there were no vacant thrones for this Pippin, even though contemporaries knew that he was a king's son.[103] Louis also knew when to ease up on the pressure. At assemblies in Thionville in 821 and Attigny in 822, he restored his own brothers to favour, while still confining them to clerical status. He also recalled Wala and his brothers, and relented towards Bernard's surviving supporters such as Amingus of Alemannia who had his property restored. In witnessing such benevolence and particularly Louis's own plea for heaven's forgiveness at Attigny, these assemblies witnessed Louis as God-fearing and magnanimous ruler but also as master of his family, a point that Louis underscored by his marrying his eldest son to the daughter of the prominent aristocrat count Hugh of Tours. The presence at Thionville of papal envoys bearing exotic gifts and of warriors fresh from triumph on the empire's frontiers could only have burnished Louis's aura of masterful authority.[104]

In fact, however, people at assemblies were not simply uncritical audiences; the ruler was not the only speaker there; people were not always dazzled by imperial theatrics. Some later churchmen came to see the Attigny penance as an unconvincing performance on Louis's part, and his harsh treatment of Bernard was to be cast up against him in the troubles of the 830s.[105] The darkness of Carolingian family conflict was so intense and its disturbance of cosmic order so fearsome that not only the elite was touched by it. Even a wretchedly poor woman was haunted by a vision of heaven's anger at Louis's court and its treatment of Bernard, or so an artful text from Alemannia tells us.[106] By the end of the 820s, bigger troubles were to engulf the realm and to give conflict in the royal family an ever-sharper edge.

Years of pressure: 823–30

Louis's reign consisted of more than dynastic troubles. And these troubles were in some ways unexceptional; Louis was not the only ruler to try to hold onto power while assuaging the claims of growing sons. Nor should Louis's marriage to Judith in 819 after the death of his first wife be seen as a final straw for Louis's sons. This was only one element in the big world of contemporary politics where pleasing a loving but wrathful God and managing the patronage of aristocrats counted for more than Judith's arrival at court. In fact, Louis's marriage to Judith enhanced his reach into aristocratic networks in the south-east of his realm.[107] The fact that Judith bore Louis a son in 823 and that this son was given the resonantly royal name Charles must have disturbed Louis's sons by his first marriage. Louis and Judith obviously saw a future for Charles, who did indeed reign gloriously as Charles the Bald. But the future was a long way off and only emerged after a truly fiery crisis.

An older historiography tended to see Louis's granting of territories in Alemannia and Burgundy to the six-year-old Charles at an assembly at Worms in August 829 as the culmination of his scheming mother's dominance of her weak husband and as the trigger for the crises of the 830s. Now, however, historians tend to downplay the significance of this grant as the retrospectively partisan nature of many our sources distort the picture.[108] Perhaps, for example, Louis's forcing the grant through 'by edict', as Nithard tells us, gives us a vivid glimpse of the assembly's resistance to the opening of Pandora's box.[109] Nithard, however, was looking back with increasing bleakness from ten years later. On the other hand, perhaps Louis's act was much less peremptory, indeed one of 'brilliant subtlety', since one well-informed source says that Louis made Charles 'duke' (*dux*) and could thus have been reassuring his sons and the magnates that Charles was neutralized, destined for a subordinate position.[110]

But evidence from before the 830s storm shows that young Charles was not neutralized; he was a time-bomb. Louis and Judith had activated him, starting with his kingly naming in 823. His winsome cameo role in Ermold's 826/8 poem for Louis does not mean that all contemporaries saw him as destined for royal greatness, but Ermold was saying what Louis wanted to hear.[111] Charles was still a child but in 829 he had what few other boys in the whole empire had: royal parents and a royal name.

Walahfrid's celebration of this in his odd 829 poem about Aachen is illuminating in its parallelling wee Charles with Charlemagne; this of course was wishful thinking as the six-year-old had nothing in common with grandfather but his name. That, however, was the point; the link with the dynastic past promised the boy a royal future. Louis's evident favour for his son and Judith's skilful networking (the seventeen-year-old Louis the German married her sister in 827) sought to guarantee that prospect.[112]

Walahfrid's Aachen poem did so too. It was not merely a description of realities of the royal family and court. It sought to shape reality, lightly warning Pippin of Aquitaine to look to his reputation, trying to still any anxieties felt by Louis the German over the extent of his territories and, in praying that Charles would, like his grandfather, be blessed with 'loyal offspring', signalling that the boy would in turn generate a kingly line.[113] This suggests that the poem was written on the very eve of the grant to Charles, possibly as part of a softening-up exercise to prepare the elite to accept the will of Louis the Pious, hailed here by Walahfrid as tamer of wild beasts. We do not know how many people listened to Walahfrid's artful song (and it survives in only one manuscript) or were persuaded by it, but it was not the only manifesto for Charles at this important time. Bishop Freculf of Lisieux explicitly if metaphorically referred to the boy as a king in the letter he sent to Judith in 829 accompanying a presentation of his Chronicle. Einhard may very well have been composing his *Life of Charlemagne* at this time as a guide to rulership for this special child.[114] Charles's status was in 829 surely unambiguous: he was a son of the ruler and his imperial consort and he would be king. Giving him a royal name and making Lothar the godfather of this little brother showed how hard his parents had worked from his birth to proclaim his specialness.[115] Louis the Pious and Judith played to an audience that was watchful. Count Matfrid of Orléans was present at Frankfurt for Charles's birth in 823 and also witnessed the child's antics at Ingelheim in 826; he was thus immediately aware of the danger this child posed to his investments in Lothar.[116]

This audience was also active. Ermold (from Aquitaine), Walahfrid (from Alemannia), Freculf (bishop in the far west) and the well-connected courtier Einhard knew how to read the signs transmitted to them and they re-transmitted them, actively constructing Charles's royalty which in turn depended on their response. The fact that some charters from Alemannia which recognize Charles as king there get his regnal years wrong is less significant than the fact that these scribes were writing out what they believed to be the Carolingian truth: Charles was their king. They, and they would not have been alone in this, inscribed this Carolingian authority in their territory, registering the drastic changes in the royal family. The scribe Gozbert, who noted Charles's first year as king in a charter of April 830 that survives in a contemporary copy, had also produced a charter in August 829 dated by the years of Louis the Pious and Lothar.[117] Not a member of the high elite, not a courtier, Gozbert was a scribe of the important Alemannian abbey of St-Gall but it was actions by relatively humble men like him that gave the upheavals of royal politics a reality away from the centre. Contemporaries were very aware of this, as Agobard's outraged reaction to Louis's stripping Lothar's name from imperial documents shows.[118] Similarly, a supporter of Lothar expressed his resentment of Louis the Pious by deleting the emperor's name from a collection of legal texts some time in the 830s.[119]

Charles's royal destiny was far from unstoppable, but once it was activated Charles and his supporters could draw on forces bigger than a six-year-old. Charles probably visited Alemannia in 829–30, to imprint himself on his new realm. Walahfrid's poetic celebration of his arrival at the great monastery of Reichenau hailed him as the 'holy offspring of kings' in whom 'our land' greeted all the current Carolingian rulers ('In you, our land receives the father and brothers'). Charles's brothers would not necessarily have shared this enthusiasm, but they could hardly deny the truth of what Walahfrid sang. After all, they too benefited from this discourse of familial royalty. Walahfrid repeated this identification of the individual ruler with his family in a poem for Lothar, and in his poem on Aachen, he saw Louis the German's bearing his father's name (*nomen ... paternum*) as an important facet of his royalty and a bond between father and son, a theme that the younger Louis's supporter Thegan was to labour in the bitter 830s.[120] For his brothers to challenge Charles was to challenge themselves and to bring contradiction and tension into representations and practices devotedly crafted and performed by the very people on whom rulers depended.

On a more concrete level, Charles's position in Alemannia was to be anchored through a dense network of contacts with aristocrats and churchmen, but this would have meant some disturbance to existing networks. The 829 giving of Alsace and other territories to Charles certainly did so, and this affected aristocrats aligned with his brothers, as it would have disquieted the brothers themselves.[121] No-one was going to shrug off actual and potential losses, especially as there was no guarantee that Charles would stay confined to that region. Perhaps Louis would expand his youngest son's territories, or even swap kingdoms around; Lothar himself had started his kingship as king of Bavaria in 814 before being elevated to an imperial title in 817 and ceding Bavaria to his brother Louis. Charles's elevation was not some muted event relating to a quiet corner of the realm.

From the point of view of his brothers and their followers, it was the culmination of a growing menace. No wonder that the bishops gathered at the council of Paris in May 829 called on the rulers to instil mutual love and fraternal love among their sons, a plea that could only have gained in urgency when bishops repeated it, this time just to Louis, as they probably did in the thunderous atmosphere of the very assembly at Worms that witnessed the fateful grant to Charles. Walahfrid too, in his Aachen poem, stressed the importance of concord for the sons. The bishops we hear through Jonas of Orléans, who composed the council texts, were anxiously aware of the crucial importance of familial relationships within the dynasty, for all their stress on royal office as a post derived ultimately from God, not the ruler's ancestors.[122] The bishops grasped that the security of the realm depended in large part on the security of the royal line, and this truth was to be generally understood. The bishops at Paris had urged everyone to ward off divine anger from the kingdom by fervent prayers, including prayer for the emperor Louis, his wife and offspring (*proles*) and the realm.[123] Some time after the Worms assembly but before the storm broke over Louis in 830, archbishop Agobard of Lyons wrote to the emperor lamenting the tensions that were disturbing the relationship of father and sons, and urging Louis, before it was too late, to strive for the father-son harmony that his father and grandfather had enjoyed.[124]

Agobard's vision of the past harmony within the royal family may have been a rosy one, but he correctly saw the scale of threat generated by family tensions. Louis's very public creation of a kingdom for Charles in 829 while commending him to the care of count Bernard, recently promoted to high office in the palace, ratcheted tensions up and thus had an impact far outside Charles's Alemannian territories. Since, as we have seen, this is clear from evidence dating before the explosions of the 830s, there is little reason to doubt retrospective sources such as Thegan (writing 836/7) and Nithard (writing 841–3) when they tell us that Charles's royal status was a major problem and that giving him a kingdom made all three older brothers feel indignant and perhaps also dishonoured. Charles's problematic status transcended geographical boundaries. In the rebellion of 830, Lothar kept Charles under his watchful eye, a tribute to his importance.[125] The silence of the *Royal Frankish Annals* on Louis's 829 grant to Charles may be a sign that the grant was baffling, too hard to talk about. The next decade would bring even tougher dynastic questions.

By 829, the elite was in fact very worried. A series of military defeats on the frontiers, predicted by un-nerving cosmic signs, fears of poor harvests and sickness among cattle led to urgent self-examination by the ruler and his counsellors as to how best to ward off the wrath of God. A demon from hell uttered the disturbing truth: 'There are … an almost endless number of sins committed every day by the people themselves and their rulers.' Councils of bishops met in Lyons, Toulouse, Paris and Mainz to formulate responses. Identifying and correcting sin so as to avoid falling unrepentant into the hands of the living God was the essential task of the Carolingian elite.[126]

Failure in office, however, also had an earthly cost. Counts Matfrid and Hugh, who had failed on the Spanish frontiers, could no longer enjoy the emperor's grace, while count Bernard, the heroic defender of Barcelona, was rewarded. In the fevered atmosphere of 828–9, there was a political and moral logic to this, but Louis's dismissal of Matfrid and Hugh from office created more upheaval. Both men were exceptionally well-connected; Matfrid had deployed his access to favour at the centre to build up a network of clients, while Hugh was father-in-law to Lothar. Their disgrace was public and shaming. A pro-Louis writer later gloated that Hugh's own retinue made up songs about their master's cowardice.[127] This was a political culture possessed by honour and reputation and where royal favour underpinned magnates' prosperity; Hugh and Matfrid had to strike back. The fact that they remained important figures despite no longer being counts tells us something about aristocrats' own personal and inherited power; the fact that they could initiate the 830 rebellion against Louis himself tells us even more.

By the end of 829, Louis had not only broken some magnates, he had raised up new ones in the person of count Bernard and his kin and had given Judith's young son a kingdom. He went further and demoted Lothar from the co-emperorship, sending him off-stage to Italy. This may have been a bold pre-emptive move to prevent Lothar corralling the discontent of aristocratic losers and directing it against his father. But it only added fuel to the fire. Louis revealed himself to aghast observers as all too human. The downgrading of Lothar appeared simply as human wilfulness on Louis's part, a very public flouting of the will of God as unveiled very publicly in 817.[128] All this ungodly chaos in the palace meant that the palace itself, instead of irradiating the realm with virtue, now threatened to pollute it. Perhaps some of those shocked by all this, such as archbishop Agobard, thought that Louis himself had merely been misled. But if wickedness existed in the palace it had to assume some human form, and gender casting put the empress Judith in that role for critics.[129]

Matfrid was a hard man to break. Losing Louis's favour and his offices was a severe blow, but his status and power were not solely dependent on office. After his fall in 828–9 he, along with his ally count Hugh of Tours, dominates accounts of the troubles of the 830s as the chief instigator of disturbances, though blaming Matfrid may have been a way for some writers to avoid criticizing the royal sons too harshly. But Matfrid's resources and patronage network remained formidable enough after his fall for him to be able to loom up over any royal son, even if he did not seem to have much association with him, as with Louis the German in 832.[130] Archbishop Agobard of Lyons' warning of 827–8 to Matfrid not to abuse his high position to shelter wrong-doers casts as much light on Matfrid's client network as does the effort which Louis the Pious had to make to dismantle it in 829.[131]

Despite this, Matfrid needed office for the prestige and income it gave him. This was generally true for the high aristocracy of the Carolingian world. Such offices helped their holders to rise above their aristocratic competitors. Matfrid's stylish reception of Louis in his county of Orléans in 818, like duke Boso's entertaining King Louis the Stammerer in his house in Troyes in 878, shows how rank gave settings for official contact with rulers; a high place in the hierarchy advertised closeness to the ruler. For all his association with Lothar, Matfrid was also very much a man of Louis the Pious; his wide span of power and influence stemmed from his high position under Louis, a position made splendidly visible in the circlet which he, like other ninth-century holders of high office, wore on great court occasions, as we ourselves can see pictured in contemporary manuscripts.[132] Louis's dismissing Matfrid and Hugh from eminence, while bringing Count Bernard of Barcelona from the deep south to the palace and giving Bernard's cousin Odo the now vacant county of Orléans, shows that the Carolingian system of empire-wide patronage was working effectively. Like his rival Matfrid, Odo was an incomer to the west; he was from the Rhineland and is visible in Louis's entourage at the palace of Ingelheim in the 820s. Only the ruler could move people across such distances by placing them in a secure berth of office such as a county. The political clashes of the 830s do not reveal royal weakness; rather they show how effective and desirable royal favour was.[133]

Aristocrats such as Odo were not passive chess pieces dependent on royal grand masters for all their moves. Aristocratic familial resources and connections played their part. The fact that Odo was a cousin of Bernard's may have boosted his status in Louis's eyes just as it was to damn him in the eyes of his rivals. This, however, was only part of Odo's aristocratic identity. When Odo moved west, he was able to build on bonds with the family of the Adalhards, one of whom, Adalhard the seneschal, was to enjoy a high political profile for decades. Even Odo's death in 834 did not break these bonds; in 842, Adalhard arranged for Odo's daughter Irmintrud to marry king Charles the Bald, deepening already existing familial connections between this aristocratic grouping and the royal line. In building Odo up, Louis had made it possible for Odo's family to reach back into the royal family. Vertical bonds of royal patronage meshed with aristocratic bonds of kinship and alliance and this enabled the Carolingian world to function as a large-scale realm.[134]

This was not a frictionless system. Odo really needed royal patronage; we know that his father had died by 821 when Odo was probably young and this may have hindered him in the Rhineland, forcing him to search for pastures new. Odo exploited his Orléans office harshly for profits, according to a snarlingly hostile local account written a generation later. It was not just basic human greed that drove Odo. The rewards of office, *honores*, were what lifted aristocrats above competitors.[135] Odo was thus as determined to hold on to Orléans as Matfrid was to get it back. A priority for the rebels against Louis the Pious in 830 was a trip to Orléans to eject Odo, replace him with Matfrid and then, a few weeks later at an assembly at Compiègne, to publicly strip Odo of his weapons as a public sign of his loss of office and status, and bundle him off to exile.[136] When Matfrid in his turn fell into exile in 831, the way was open for Odo to return to Orléans where he faced Matfrid yet again in 834. This was after the great upheavals of 833 when Louis's sons drove their father from his throne only to fall out among themselves and see Louis return to imperial authority by March 834 (see below). Amidst troubles at the centre, Odo and Matfrid had kept a steady eye on the west and staged a bloody show-down there in May 834. Significantly, no ruler took part in this; these magnates may have fought in the name of their particular Carolingian patron but they clearly had their own agenda. Odo mobilized local levies of warriors (a vivid illustration of the power available to holder of an *honor*) but in the May 834 battle, Odo and his brother William perished, and it is significant that William, from the Rhineland like Odo, was fighting in the west where he too held a county (Blois).[137]

This was not the end of troubles in the west; we find descendants of one of Matfrid's supporters (Lambert) still locked in combat with rivals there in the 840s. This western region may have been a particularly unstable area and need not be representative of the realm as a whole even during the peak of the crises of 830–4. After all, there were no set-piece battles between the rival rulers and their followers in these years, unlike the brutal encounters of the royal brothers' war of 840–3.[138]

Contemporaries, however, could not know that the armed posturing of 830–4 would not result in explosions of violence. News of Matfrid's victory in 834 triggered his royal patron Lothar's grim executions of opponents at Chalon-sur-Saone, including that of a woman, Gerberga. This was a targeted cruelty as Gerberga was a sister of Bernard of Septimania. But there was hysteria in the air; opponents of Louis the Pious had painted his palace as a place of witchcraft and dark magic and fearfully believed their own accusations. Gerberga was drowned because she was found to be a witch and this verdict was pronounced by the wives of Lothar's leading counsellors at Chalon. Violence reached out to more than just the warriors; at Chalon women were victims and agents, while the later commemorating of Gerberga (along with other family victims of 830–4) by her sister-in-law Dhuoda, who may herself have had a narrow escape from Lothar's grip, shows how far the ripples of violence could reach.[139] Furthermore, the early 830s' struggles and manoeuvrings for favour and prominence disturbed the security and distribution of landed estates behind the lines. In the Orléans region, the abbey of Fleury and the church of Orléans suffered in the Matfrid-Odo conflict. Further east in the Rhineland, networks of local landholders were shaken. As Matthew

Innes has argued, Dhuoda's sense of 'dizzying insecurity' reflected a more widespread unease among local landholders over the disturbances that rocked the high elite and sent aftershocks to wider social groups.[140] Much of this lay in the future, but we can now see why aristocrats played the key role in initiating rebellion against Louis the Pious in 830.

Looking back on 829–30 from a distance of ten and twenty years respectively, the Astronomer and Radbert vividly depicted a world of secret plots spreading like cancer, hidden wounds festering and vast, all-powerful conspiracies visible only to a persecuted minority of the righteous. All this marks the entry of the paranoid style into Carolingian politics.[141] Not everyone succumbed to this fever at the time. As Professor de Jong points out, Agobard of Lyons, an implacable opponent of the emperor in 833, still thought in 830 that he and Louis could communicate via a 'shared moral high ground'. For Agobard, and he cannot have been alone, 829–30 was a time for warning the misguided emperor, not a time for turning on him as the main source of the problems. But Professor de Jong is also correct in saying that, once the revolt broke out in 830, the empress Judith was right to fear for her life. She was the target of a torrent of accusations of spectacular sexual misbehaviour, of committing adultery with the hated count Bernard in a palace transformed into a brothel by the hideous glamour of witchcraft. Such accusations served a precise political purpose: they discredited Judith and Bernard simultaneously and reduced Louis the Pious to an innocent dupe who needed rescuing before an outraged God unleashed punishments on the realm.[142]

The rebels were thus compelled to act in order to save the empire. But such accusations raised the political temperature to boiling point. The Frankish political elite had not previously experienced anything like this under Carolingian rule. Some six years after 830, bishop Thegan could hardly bring himself to repeat some of the accusations. As Bernard's sister was to discover in 834, accusations of witchcraft could lead to hideous death. Frankish queens had been killed before. Factional fury at favouritism and exclusion at the court of king Childeric II drove aristocrats to murder him and his pregnant queen Bilichild in 675 in the forest of Bondy of sombre legend. Neither royal aura nor the dazzling splendour that clothed Merovingian queens, so evident in the archaeological record, could save them. Kings and queens were hardly ever killed in the Carolingian era, but they surely knew that pent-up resentments created tensions that rulers could not always control.[143]

Rulers were certainly not in complete control of events in 829–30. Count Bernard had hardly had time to build up the sort of networks that Matfrid had, though his presence in a grant of Louis's for a *fidelis* in Narbonne shows that he was trying, and Narbonne may have been in the orbit of Bernard's father. But Bernard was a dominant figure in the palace and his prominence in narrative sources is instructive.[144] Hostility to him outlasted his tenure of the chamberlain's office. As late as the 860s, archbishop Hincmar of Reims characterized him as a 'tyrant'; perhaps Hincmar was remembering his experiences as a young monk in St-Denis during the rebellions. A text written there in the early 830s tells the story of how the young seventh-century prince Dagobert clashed with the (fictional) magnate Sadregisel. Some scholars have thought that Dagobert and Sadregisel represented Lothar and Bernard, and the parallels are indeed striking (though the tensions between them are also all too typical of the seventh century). What is certain is that the text catches the sulphurous atmosphere of resentment and jealousy that flourished in the small society of the Carolingians and their great men. We get a lively account of how Dagobert/Lothar perceives the arrogant and treacherous nature of Sadregisel/Bernard at table; drink and insults flow and the young prince assaults the over-reacher.[145]

Anger also curdled into fear. Decades later, Radbert shuddered to recall Bernard's diabolical scheme to eliminate Louis and his sons, to marry Judith and to rule the realm. It is tempting to write off this extreme accusation as the product of an imagination too long marinated in bitterness, but Agobard of Lyons also made a similar accusation in 833.[146] And contemporaries knew that Bernard was a member of the royal kin (*stirps regalis*). He was thus a dark mirror image of Radbert's hero Wala himself (both men were descendants of Charles Martel) dangerously charismatic members of a branch line of the royal house around whom supporters and dissidents could cluster.[147]

Killing the ruler was imaginable in Carolingian political culture. In 792, Pippin the Hunchback had allegedly planned to kill his father Charlemagne as well as his half-brothers (the sons of Hildegard); Wala, and presumably others still alive in 830, had been brushed by this conspiracy.[148] Unlike Pippin, however, Bernard was not the son of a king. If contemporaries really were thinking that he was planning to strike down or marginalize Louis and his sons by his first wife and perhaps rule through the young Charles the Bald, then Bernard's Carolingian blood would hardly have been enough to lift him above the challenges that would have erupted. A coup such as this would have shattered the Carolingian line; the ruler and his sons would have ceased to be the channels through which aristocratic ambitions and fears ran. The foundering of dynastic hegemony would have exposed Frankish kingship to open competition as was to happen in 888.

This may be speculative, but the testimony of Agobard and Radbert suggests that people did speculate along these lines. And there is clear evidence that, for all their anger with their father, Louis's sons were not the prime instigators of the revolt of 830. Things were slipping out of dynastic control. Several sources stress that it was a group of aristocrats who banded together and unleashed hostilities against Louis, Judith and Bernard in early 830. Part of this picture comes from partisan efforts to minimize the activeness of Louis's sons, whether to exculpate them, or to blacken them as feeble and unfilial.[149] Thus, the Astronomer's scornful reference to the 33-year-old Pippin of Aquitaine as a 'youth' (*iuvenis*) was a way of saying that he was a mere puppet of the sinister Matfrid of Orléans but was also a way of denigrating Pippin's own line, an urgent task at the time of writing in the early 840s.[150] But the fact that one of the first stops for the rebels, once Pippin had joined them, was Orléans where Odo (Bernard's cousin) had to yield his office to Matfrid shows how the magnates were in fact setting the pace, as does chronology: trouble broke out in early March but Lothar himself only arrived north from Italy towards the end of April.[151]

The sons thus had to join the rebels in order to retain their own political credibility with supporters and to channel it within a Carolingian framework. Of course, fear over loss of their father's favour was also a powerful driver. Lothar would have been just as shocked by his own downgrading as Agobard was, and as desperate to regain status as was Hugh of Tours; Pippin doubtless resented Louis's meddling in Aquitaine.[152] North of the Alps, aristocrats knew about Lothar's brooding fury in Italy. In a letter to him from early 830, Einhard pleaded with Lothar not to turn against his father. This was not just self-interested worry over the difficult choice of loyalties that such a conflict would pose for aristocrats. Most aristocrats tend to be traditionalists and Carolingian Christian culture taught the duty of sons to obey fathers, as Einhard urgently reminded Lothar.[153] We should not assume that the actors of the 830s were untroubled by such concerns. Family relationship gave the political conflict between these rulers an inescapable and insoluble moral dimension (how to render due obedience to a father who was unjust), but as the 830s wore on that made the conflict all the more intractable, as we shall see. Although aristocrats took the first steps in rebelling in 830, they did need the royal sons to join them. Only rulers such as Lothar and Pippin could provide the deep territorial security for the immuring of Judith and her brothers in Aquitaine, or Bernard's brother in Italy and only Pippin, as a king, could preside over Matfrid's restoration to the countship of Orléans, though this was a challenge to his father's prerogatives.[154]

These activities in Orléans and the west should not obscure the key point that the rebels focused clearly on the centre of the realm as well as the regions. The regional element in 830 was much less important than it had been in the risings of Hardrad in Thuringia or Pippin the Hunchback in Bavaria. Flight and banishment transformed the centre; when Bernard fled the palace for distant Septimania in the south-west, he was safe but ceased to matter for the moment. Once Lothar had arrived north from Italy, the purging of Louis's court and proclamation of the new regime took place at an assembly at the palace of Compiègne, a key royal location. Rebels now included a wide range of Louis's office-holders such as the abbot of St-Denis and the bishop of Amiens, that is, not just those who had lost out in the west or Alsace.[155]

And it was at an assembly at Nijmegen in the autumn of 830 that the emperor was able to turn the tables on his opponents. He had managed to select the site, Nijmegen, as that was accessible for his supporters in the east of the realm. In an account so vivid, if tendentious, that it reads as by an eye-witness, the Astronomer depicts Louis as calling the rebels' bluff and majestically asserting paternal and imperial authority. After all, what could sons and magnates actually do to a legitimate ruler? Assemblies in palace sites of Aachen and Ingelheim in early 831 witnessed Louis dispensing justice and mercy to rebels in instructive doses. If the rebellion had opened horizontally, with conspiracy among the aristocracy, it quickly went vertical with the royal sons and father as lead actors and assemblies as the site where it would be made and broken.[156]

Permanent tension: 831–9

After 830, political and conceptual coherence broke down. The imperial palace, far from being the moral centre of its world, is attacked as a centre of pollution that threatens to engulf the realm. Fathers and sons assail each other instead of supporting each other. The aristocracy, far from harmoniously sharing in the ruler's *ministerium*, fights among itself for office and favour and foments rebellion of sons against father.

The guardians of the religious moral-political order try to re-assert norms in a storm of texts that fiercely argue conflicting cases.[157]

Such texts were intended to operate in the public arena but that space was now also filled with ceremonies and rituals where competing and incompatible claims were dramatically staged and articulated. And with these ceremonies, we are certainly able to witness 'contested interpretations', the centrality of which to ritual and ceremony Philippe Buc has rightly emphasized.[158] For ritual and ceremony, the 830s are a time of dizzying inflation. It is easy to overlook this, to be lulled into visualizing the 830s as a time of phoney war in which sons could rebel, a father could lose his throne and then everyone would kiss and make up according to the rules in carefully stage-managed rituals. But we are in fact looking at ceremonies that were ad hoc, improvised and tense, ceremonies that seldom imposed or generated consensual meaning, and whose intended meanings did not stick. The 830s offer a striking contrast with the penance of Attigny in 822, a controlled experiment in consensus that pulled participants into its field of meaning.[159] Admittedly, some of the staged scenes of the 830s did succeed. Louis the Pious's 830 restoration at Nijmegen was a brilliantly successful piece of improvisation at an assembly, 'live' theatre without rehearsal or an agreed script. The elaborate restoration of Louis in 834–5 also won good reviews and political acceptance. Here new rituals countered the new kind of 'tragedy' that had overwhelmed Louis in 833: 'unheard of things'.[160]

Certainly the events of 833 had been difficult to stage-manage. The removal of Louis from office via the penance imposed at Compiègne and Soissons was another intelligently creative, if radical, development of ritual, including performance and texts. But its very novelty and extremity left it open to challenge and dissent.[161] Writing in its immediate aftershock, Hraban Maur revealed that not all the participants had been of one mind: some had acted out of malice, but some had done so out of fear while others had acted out of weakness. This was echoed later by the Astronomer who starkly illuminates the making of consensus in the 830s in his claim that after the bishops had judged Louis in 833 'a few people challenged this, some more agreed to it, but the majority, as is usual in such cases, made a show of agreeing, so as not to annoy the magnates'. Lothar himself took a different line. Confronted in 834 with demands for the release of Louis, he pointed out that he had not acted alone in the recent 'calamity' of his father, those who now wanted his release had also betrayed him, and the bishops had judged him.[162] Lothar was trying to make 833 stick, for everyone, even as agreement on it crumbled. Or so the Astronomer makes him say. But the fact that the Astronomer, writing after Louis's death in 840, and Thegan, writing c.837, still devoted so much space to 'un-doing' the events of 833 shows that 833's ceremony of penance, even though it was now to be understood as politically instrumentalized in the extreme, had to be countered, argued against, just as it had been in its immediate aftermath.

The rituals of the 830s could not close wounds, could not settle cases. The carefully planned and staged return of Judith to court in 831 was designed to display her innocence of the sexual crimes that she had been accused of in 830. At an assembly held amidst the splendours of Aachen around the symbolically charged time of the feast of purification of the Virgin Mary Judith 'in the sight of the lord emperor and his sons …

declared her willingness to purge herself on all the charges levelled against her'.[163] There was nothing spontaneous or uncontrolled about this declaration. With Louis the Pious back in the saddle, no-one would now volunteer to maintain the accusations against the empress, and the royal sons' presence at the assembly declared to the audience that they accepted her innocence. But even though he had guaranteed this happy outcome in advance, Louis had to act carefully, punctiliously. His court annalist tells us that Judith had been 'ordered' to attend the assembly and Nithard's later testimony that Judith was not admitted 'to the royal bed' until she had cleared herself of the charges must refer to a very public exclusion of her from the private chamber of Louis.[164] The accusations against Judith had been shrewdly targeted: Louis's own kingship and the purity of his palace were thus called into question and his rule destabilized. Caught up in the concepts of Christian rule, Louis had to be seen to be demonstrating that he understood the gravity of such concepts while also denying the validity of the charges. Hence the caution with which Judith was re-introduced to the royal bed which was at the heart of the palace and thus of the realm; the role of bishops in presiding over Judith's return would have been important here.[165]

But all this care could not prevent bishop Agobard of Lyons in 833 thundering against Judith, repeating the accusations of *lascivia* made in 830 and going on to denounce her failure to control herself after she had been re-admitted to the palace, something that had only happened because of the 'excessive indulgence of the sons'. The 831 ceremony was now a dead letter and did nothing to blunt Agobard's attack. In 837, Thegan was *still* furiously denying the charges of adultery made against her in 830 and his fervour suggests that he felt that he had to do so. The actors at Aachen in 831 had not had the last word.[166]

In 831, Louis had arranged another public ceremony to clear the name of Bernard of Septimania, the aristocrat who had been Judith's alleged partner in the sexual scandal. At an autumn assembly presided over by Louis with his sons Lothar and Louis the German in attendance, Bernard appeared ready to defend his impugned honour in armed combat. The fact that nobody could be found to challenge him and that he was able to clear his name by taking an oath clearly indicates that Louis the Pious had stacked the deck; no accusers would dare to show their face.[167] While all this suggests that Louis wanted to broadcast to the political community that Bernard was back, Louis seems to have been unconvinced by his own rituals. Within a year, he had turned against Bernard. If the impact of his own stagings on Louis himself was only temporary, how likely were they to convince anyone else? Louis, now deeply fearful of Bernard's connection with his son Pippin, had Bernard accused of treachery (*infidelitas*) at a gathering at Jouac in Aquitaine. Again, no-one dared to come forward to challenge Bernard, but this time round Louis took this as proof of Bernard's guilt and deprived him of his *honores*.[168] Louis thus contributed to the devaluation of the currency of such displays while his determination to impose contradictory readings of identical procedure in both cases (the failure of challengers to step up against Bernard) revealed him to be a ninth-century Humpty-Dumpty: '"When I use a word", Humpty Dumpty said in a rather scornful tone, "it means just what I choose it to mean."' Or, as contemporaries would have put it, the only thing that counted now was the ruler's will (see below). And Louis's volatile wilfulness was to be a key factor in the difficulties of the decade.

If some rituals failed to carry conviction and thus could not resolve tensions, others were designed to exacerbate problems. Sometimes, the ceremonies that closed conflict were designed by Louis to be frightening, humiliating. In February 831, those members of the aristocracy who had risen against Louis in the previous year were condemned to death at an assembly. The *Annals of St-Bertin* say that this sentence was pronounced 'first by [Louis'] sons and then by all those present'; a few years later Nithard explicitly recalled that Lothar had had to condemn his own followers to death.[169] Rebels were thus reminded that Carolingian rulers held the whip hand while Louis's sons were reminded in their turn who was their master. Could these aristocrats have been absolutely certain that they would be spared? People could remember the fate of Bernard and Reginhar in 818; we should think of Dostoevsky's mock execution of 1849 rather than of some calmly staged performance where everyone knew that it was all a pretence. Louis ostentatiously commuted the death sentence to exile but his decision, a few months later, to forgive these exiles at a great assembly at Ingelheim may not have cleared the air. Perhaps the Astronomer's stress on Louis's exceptionally merciful nature was protesting too much.[170]

Where the events of the 830s did foster a solidarity, they fostered a divisive one, defined *against* others. The daring adventure of a heroic youth called Ruadbern, in rescuing Judith back from her Italian captivity in 834, was celebrated in a poem by Walahfrid Strabo: 'the king and queen … and all their faithful retainers, filled with gratitude, shall exalt your reputation in ever higher praise'. But Ruadbern's enemies are also in the poem, that is, Lothar's men (though Lothar is not mentioned by name); to celebrate Ruadbern's heroism was to celebrate oppositional community: Ruadbern labours for the king and queen with the support of the magnates of the west and he thus struggles against 'fierce treachery' and guards around Lake Como.[171] Ruadbern was showered with praise by Walahfrid but those who had supported Judith and Louis in Italy lost property there at the hands of Lothar and this bedevilled politics after the restoration of 834, as we shall see.

The other side also had its own heroic escapades to celebrate. Perhaps Pippin of Aquitaine's night-time escape from his father's custody at Aachen in the depth of winter in 831–2 was sung by those followers who had bravely sprung him. The fact that the author of the (contemporary) entry in the *Annals of St-Bertin*, a courtier of Louis, noted the exact date and time of Pippin's escape as well as Louis the Pious's incredulity at the event reveals something of its sensational quality. The fact that Pippin managed to escape twice from his father's custody also shows something of the status of kings' sons; who could dare confine a king's son too closely? Carolingian charisma was an awkward fact for senior Carolingians such as Louis.[172] On both occasions, Pippin escaped in the company of 'his own men'; such adventures were bound to lead to bonding in opposition.

Both Louis and his sons could draw upon the support of loyalists such as Ruadbern and Pippin's escape team. But many members of the aristocracy would be unsure who to support. Fundamentally, this was because there were three adult kings, all legitimate sons of the emperor and established in rule by him; the existence of Charles the Bald only added to this problem. For uncertainty and tension were not the result of this alone. Uncertainty was institutionalized by Louis the Pious himself, as we can see in an extraordinary plan of his for the division of the realm in 831. This plan survives as a capitulary text preserved in only one manuscript but it was a public plan addressed to all the faithful men of the realm; we can assume that this was proclaimed or at least discussed in public, possibly at Aachen in February 831, one of three assemblies in that busy year; aristocrats would certainly have been aware of it.[173] To some extent, this projected settlement built calmly on existing foundations, working outwards from the kingdoms that Pippin, Louis the German and the young Charles already held (Aquitaine, Bavaria, Alemannia). This would reassure the followers of Pippin and Louis the German that their kingdom was stable and signalled that Alemannia was to be the core of Charles's future. The fact that Lothar was to retain Italy also offered some stability.

Overall, however, this was a very disturbing plan that can only have further ratcheted up the very tensions that had produced it. It was disturbing because neither Lothar nor the future of the imperial title was mentioned in it. Lothar's future in Francia was cancelled. The imperial project of 817 was scrapped and the text of 831 was based on the *Divisio* of 806 not on the *Ordinatio* of 817. Contemporaries could not be sure that this might be only something designed to frighten Lothar rather than a definitive settlement. Those members of Louis's entourage who took part in composing it would have encountered some of the skeletons in the Carolingian family cupboard. The family strife of 830–1 drove people back to the settlement of 806 but that text, in its reference to Louis's sisters and to grandsons (i.e. Bernard of Italy), must have triggered uneasy twinges of memory: to look at 806 in 831 was to recall the family troubles of 814 and 817–18. Of course, the gaze of Louis's courtiers in 831 was as focused on the family dynamics of the ruling dynasty as was that of the courtiers of 806 and 817 and this means that, on one level, the great discourse of Carolingian centrality and legitimacy continued to be uttered over again. The line of Louis's ancestors was updated in 831 from the original text of 806.[174] The passing of time benefited the Carolingians as the sequence of dynastic succession continued to stretch out from an ever deeper past.

But none of this was much comfort for the actors caught up in the tensions of the 830s. For them, Carolingian legitimacy simply meant that there were more princely competitors for power among whom it was difficult to choose. And Louis's plans did nothing to ease such tensions. Patched together from the 806 *Divisio*, the 831 text does not convey any sense of negotiated agreements. The lack of detail surely shows watchful wariness; Louis the Pious was not planning any further ahead than he had to. At this point, greater consensus was not possible. Where Louis does add detail to his model, he only reveals and creates more anxiety as in his explicit command to these three sons that none of them are to try and tempt any of the emperor's followers 'away from his oath to us or anyone else and draw them to himself'.[175]

Amidst such provisional and jittery arrangements, one thing now mattered above all: the will of Louis himself.

> If any of these three sons of ours, seeking through greater obedience and good will to please almighty God and us, deserves so by their good behaviour ... we wish that, as remains in our power, we may increase his rule and honour and power from the share of his brother who has not taken pains to please us, and we shall make him what he has shown he deserves to be.

Threat and promise resound together here. Sons are urged to please Louis and are promised rewards for doing so. But this is a zero-sum game as such profit will be at the expense of the son 'who has not taken pains to please' his father. Uncertainty of tenure is here elevated to a political principle. The settlement of 831 thus explicitly threatened to take away what it promised to grant and could only generate deep unease among the young kings and their followers. What constituted good or bad behaviour on the part of the sons? Would they win or lose honour and prestige or territory as well? No one could know for sure.[176] All would be decided by the will of the father.

That simply meant more uncertainty because that will was unstable. The combination of open-ended promises and threats in the emperor's planned division of 831 is emblematic of the confused contemporary hopes and fears over which son (and supporters) would hold Louis the Pious's slippery favour. The disturbances of 830–1 had created resentful and powerful losers such as Matfrid who could not be placated by Louis's relaxation of some punishments such as exile. We may associate Matfrid with the countship of Orléans, the loss of which he felt keenly, but his family lands were in the Rhineland and that helped him make contact with Louis the German; Louis's fears over his own father's intentions about dividing the empire made him welcome Matfrid, still powerful even without office, as support in rebellion against the emperor in 832. One can understand why such actions made the father ever more changeable but strong-willed in his responses to his sons. He cowed Louis the German with a large army, and also took care to outbid his son as patron of aristocrats in east Francia: although the abbey of Lorsch experienced a visit from the younger Louis and his warriors, it continued to date documents in 832 by the emperor's reign. In the west, reports of closeness between Bernard of Septimania and Pippin of Aquitaine deeply disturbed the emperor. His response was to deprive Bernard of favour and to summon Pippin north for a spot of moral re-education in filial obedience. One source tells us that Louis the Pious commanded Pippin to bring his wife and children with him, a sign that Pippin's entire line might be about to be effaced from an Aquitaine that could now be given to the nine-year-old Charles in a division of the empire with Lothar, who was inching his way back into paternal favour.[177] The importance of young Carolingians in this is a noteworthy sign of dynastic focus for contemporaries.

The emperor worked hard to impose his will and this work covered a large area. The year 832 saw an exceptional number of assemblies summoned by Louis ranging from traditional sites such as Aachen to more unusual and far-flung areas (Mainz; Augsburg in Bavaria; in the west: Orléans, Jouac and Tours). We do not know the numbers of those who attended such assemblies, but we must not think that only Louis and a few advisers did so. Philippe Depreux has identified by name 275 people who attended at least one assembly in the reign of Louis.[178] And Louis's arm extended to those who may not have attended assemblies. Einhard's correspondence bears the traces of the emperor's mobilization of supporters in the Rhineland against the ambitions of Louis the German.[179] Louis could transmit his intentions far and wide. But since his intentions seemed to be so variable (boosting Louis the German in 831, menacing him with warriors in 832) that could only increase uncertainty over what he planned. Nor did Louis have a monopoly of communication or Carolingian authority. Pippin of Aquitaine found it remarkably easy to escape (again) from custody and was able to travel around Aquitaine as he pleased, transmitting his Carolingian charisma and resentment of his father to all and sundry.[180] All this meant that too many people in too many places thought that they had something to lose.

The result was the astounding sequence of events in 833–4 where all three adult sons rose against Louis with support on such a scale that Louis's own supporters lost their nerve completely. When both sides met in 833 on a field near Colmar in Alsace, Louis's supporters bent their oaths of loyalty to him and went over to the rebels or slipped away to await better days. If anger and guilt led Louis's supports to characterize that location as the 'field of lies', the rebels saw the dissolution of Louis's army as a judgement of God on the emperor's conduct. Louis yielded himself to the custody of his sons, who had the empress Judith whisked off-stage to Italy and the young Charles the Bald to internment in the Carolingian house abbey of Prüm. Lothar and his brothers divided up the realm amongst themselves. What to do with the old emperor in a political culture that had no machinery for deposition from royal office? Lothar and a group of bishops attempted to make Louis disappear permanently from the political scene by staging a ritual of penance that moved Louis from the royal palace of Compiègne to the sacred abbey of St-Medard at Soissons and into an oblivion of un-manned un-royal penance. Separated from his wife, being made to ungird his sword-belt and thus abandon the two key signs of secular male identity, commerce with women and weapons, the weeping Louis was to vanish from the world. But neither this radical ritual nor Lothar's grasping hands on power could build consensus. The tide flowed back in the emperor's favour as Pippin of Aquitaine and Louis the German turned against their older brother. The years 834–5 saw new manoeuvrings and rituals of restoration as Louis the Pious returned to the throne, embraced Judith and Charles, beamed upon Louis the German and Pippin and sent Lothar and company off to confinement in their Italian kingdom.[181] These were extraordinary events, but Louis's restoration after them solved nothing and did not bring stability.

The scale of the political crises of the 830s is impressive. They touched the aristocratic elite across the whole realm. Of the 280 figures listed by Philippe Depreux in his study of Louis's entourage, we can identify some sixty-seven as affected in some way by the troubles.[182] That proportion, almost a quarter, would in fact be higher than it seems, as 30 of Depreux's 280 died before the troubles broke out, and that 30 is probably an under-estimate.[183] The number of known people touched by the troubles becomes higher if we include significant figures such as archbishop Agobard of Lyon, bishop Jesse of Amiens and count Olioba of Carcassone, none of whom form part of Depreux's prosopography.[184]

The conflicts' tremors extended far and wide. Wala's supporter Radbert recalled warriors and envoys disturbing the calm of his monastery with demands that Wala join with Lothar in 833, and he remembered his own anxious journey to Lothar that spring across a landscape patrolled by soldiers and watchers. Einhard's letters vividly illustrate the twists and turns of an aristocracy trying to safeguard properties in places such as Tournai, Geneva and east Francia while the kings struggled in the central places of the realm. They also reveal aristocrats' urgent efforts to get solid information on where rulers were actually meeting and how the realm was to be divided, as well as showing equally determined efforts to make sure that their rivals were not bad-mouthing them in the palace.¹⁸⁵ Far from the great palaces of Francia, people in Brittany were unsure whether Louis the Pious or Lothar was in power in the winter of 833–4, and Frankish refugees who reached Brittany may not have been able to tell them.¹⁸⁶ The dramas of 830–4 thus did not play out only in central theatres such as Compiègne, Nijmegen, Soissons and Aachen.

Those who were directly involved in the drama worked hard to communicate it much more widely. Set-pieces such as Louis's Aachen judgement on rebels in the presence of his sons in 831, or his spectacular penance at Compiègne and Soissons of 833, or his splendid restoration and crowning at St-Denis and Metz in 834–5 were designed to impress and convince spectators and participants. The directors of these wanted them to be properly interpreted, remembered and disseminated and so they were accompanied by a blizzard of texts. The bishops who judged Louis in 833 wrote up an account of the penance and signed it, though of all the individual summaries that they were to make, only Agobard's has come down to us. When the bishops and abbots who condemned the penance and its imposers as unjust re-proclaimed Louis the Pious as rightful ruler in 835 they too wrote up an account of this judgement, signed it and sought to disseminate it.¹⁸⁷ Such texts did indeed circulate and may not have always lost their potency even when they were overtaken by events. In the second half of the 830s, Thegan and Walahfrid were still grappling with the bishops' account of 833 as a dangerous text. In 853, chronicle accounts of 835's documentary productivity were still pored over by bishops tracking the reverberations of the 830s.¹⁸⁸ The events of the early 830s mobilized a large cast: the crowds of people reported as gathering in Francia, Burgundy, Aquitaine and the east to express their disturbance at Louis' fall; the messengers sent by Louis across the whole realm to proclaim his release in 834. Not all these crowds were men: as we have seen, aristocratic women condemned Count Bernard's sister Gerberga to a witch's death at Chalon in 834.¹⁸⁹

Many people were touched by the events of the early 830s; they were unlikely to forget what had happened. As we shall see, the impact of these years continued to be felt after the restoration of Louis the Pious in 834–5. In some ways, people presented this as a new beginning. Louis's own diplomas now stated that he ruled through the reconciling quality of divine mercy. But his sons also now asserted a new status and independence in their own diplomas. Louis the German, for example, no longer titled himself 'king of the Bavarians', but 'king by the favour of divine grace', that is, a pure king, not bound by geography; he also displayed this in a new seal for his diplomas, one that visually associated him with his father and grandfather.¹⁹⁰ If the shock of 833–4 made it unlikely that contemporaries would try for a third time to restrain Louis' rule, his restoration still left them facing the very problems that had provoked the troubles.

Thoughtful contemporaries now tried to articulate norms of family order, hierarchy and harmony in order to counter the chaos that had been unleashed by the failure of such norms to constrain the ruling family. They understood that rulership consisted of more complex concepts and realities than patrimonial elements. The criticisms of Louis in 833 focused on oaths, for example, and the chaos following from Louis's wilful imposing of contradictory promises. But familial thinking was fundamental in this society and to think about families was to think about norms, laws and customs.¹⁹¹ In Carolingian society, this inevitably meant thinking in Christian terms. Contemporaries certainly understood the problems of the 830s as dilemmas turning on office and claims, but also as challenges of Christian life under God's eye. Eternal wisdom, however, did not provide a key.

Hraban Maur, abbot of Fulda, wrote an eloquent letter to Louis on this in 834. Written in the immediate aftermath of crisis, Hraban's text was part of the effort to make sense of what had happened and to ensure that it did not happen again. It reveals to us, as it must have done to a rueful Hraban himself, that solutions were not to be found. At the heart of the political community that had to be rebuilt were the royal father and his sons. In reassuring Louis that confession of sins could bring pardon and grace rather than punishment, Hraban was not only cancelling the forced penance of 833, he was speaking the discourse of the constant succession of the Carolingian family. He urged Louis to recall the biblical David who had acknowledged his sin but who, rather than losing his kingdom, had gained authority and confirmed royal authority for himself and his sons *perpetualiter*. Such ideas were at the very centre of Hraban's thought here as they were at the heart of the divine plan for human society. Hraban focused on this familial element, the bond between parents and children, not just because it was of central conceptual importance but because it was so problematic. Hraban had a keen sense of the fragility of earthly institutions, of tensions and ambiguities. He understood that some of those who had turned against Louis had been forced to do so. Louis should understand that: not everyone had been out to get him. Forgiveness would therefore help rebuild the community, just as a proper understanding of sin would enable that community and its leaders to understand that 833 had been a mistake.¹⁹²

Although this was addressed to Louis and survives only in one manuscript, surely it was not meant for Louis alone. If the parable of the prodigal son offered Louis a model for forgiving Lothar, it also offered a guide to disobedient sons on how to regain their father's grace and the rewards that would flow from that. Similarly the overwhelming stress in the text on the obedience of sons was surely meant to be overheard by the sons. Louis might have taken righteous satisfaction from Deuteronomy's clear command that rebellious sons be stoned to death, but such a citation was also aimed at the sons. Einhard had already cited it in a letter to Lothar in 830; bishop Jonas of Orléans had also anticipated some of Hraban's citations on filial obedience in his 831 letter to Pippin of Aquitaine.¹⁹³

Hraban's was not the only text on this theme to appear after 833. He himself wrote another letter to Louis in 834 on the obedience due to kings, pointedly referring to Christ as obedient to his parents. Thegan tells us that Abbot Markward of Prüm was sent by Louis in 834 with an 'eloquent letter' to the sullen Lothar that urged him to obey the divine commandment to honour his father and mother. Thegan knew Markward whose letter may have been based on Hraban's text; Thegan also knew the grimly resonant sections of Deuteronomy.¹⁹⁴ Thegan did not simply report such texts; his own work was itself another such text, deeply concerned with this theme and itself intended to influence royal father-son relations, as we shall see shortly.

The massed voices of the bishops assembled at Aachen in 836 also sounded this theme as they repeated the injunctions of the synod of Paris of 829 that the emperor teach his sons to fear God and abstain from sin. Such repetition should not be seen as casual or thoughtless, but rather as a sign of continuing and deepening concern on the part of the bishops, and the aristocracy more generally, with the problematic relations of royal father and sons. How was power to operate over time and across generations?[195] The royal line was not stable.

That line might not even be destined to endure. Something of the aftershock of the events of 833 is also visible in bishop Jonas of Orléans' intriguing dossier of texts touching on such topics as duties of Christian kings, justification for war, the role of kings in war, etc.[196] Jonas probably collected this material as preparation for a tract for Louis the Pious around 836. He here repeats, twice, what had already appeared in his *On the Office of Kingship* and in the synod of Paris in 829:

> Injustice on the king's part not only blackens the nature of his own actual rule but also darkens [the rule of] his sons and grandsons, so that they do not retain the inheritance of the kingdom after him. On account of Solomon's sin, the Lord scattered the kingdom of Israel from the hands of his sons, and on account of David's merit the Lord left the radiance of his seed forever in Jerusalem.[197]

When the bishops at Aachen in 836 turned their attention to Pippin of Aquitaine, their lengthy tract for him included the warning that fathers and sons should fear the 'ruin' of Eli and his sons, the degenerate priestly line that made way for Samuel.[198]

The great churchmen of the realm were counselling the Carolingian rulers to beware the wrath of the Lord. Not all stories from the Old Testament were comforting for kings. Nor need they offer much comfort to their followers. Here we return to Hraban's family letter of 834. Its second chapter set out to show 'how much the dishonouring of parents displeases God'. Referring to stories of the Old Testament patriarchs, Hraban showed that what was at stake was the blessing and favour of the father who could guarantee, or cancel, the prosperity of his sons and their line. These stories were highly charged in the context of 833–4 and after. Sons could lose their father's favour very quickly and it could happen to any of them. The drunken Noah was mocked by 'the middle one of his three sons' who was duly cursed, and his seed also, while his brothers were rewarded with their father's blessing in perpetuity. But of the sons of Abraham, it was Ishmael, the 'first of the sons' who lost out to Isaac and his seed. Of Isaac's sons, it was Esau who may have had the 'honour of the firstborn' but he lost it to the younger Jacob who was loved by his crafty mother and who gained the *paterna benedictio*; the older brother (*senior frater*) lost out. In his turn, Jacob loved 'Joseph his younger son above all his brothers', while David was 'the least among his brothers'.[199]

In such stories, the fate of Esau, the *senior frater*, stood in stark contrast to the glorious status of the beloved firstborn son and *senior frater*, Lothar, over his brothers in the *Ordinatio Imperii*. These shifts of parental favour look all too close to the behaviour of Louis the Pious and indeed to his declaration at the end of the *Divisio* of 831 on his freedom to decide which son had pleased him best.[200] Biblical and Carolingian fathers could favour whomsoever they decided was the most deserving. For the followers of the Carolingians, this meant that instability was the order of the day. Hraban's letter may have comforted Louis and may have worried his sons, but it highlighted the fact that biblical stories provided no clear-cut model of family hierarchy. Obedience to the father could alone offer stability. History showed that sin and disobedience were omnipresent and family arrangements were thus unstable. No-one could ever be sure which son would retain Louis's favour and thus the aristocracy could not be sure which son to back. This was one of the costs of putting the Carolingian family at the centre of politics. Louis's sons fell into disfavour, not because they were seen to be bad rulers, but because they were seen to be bad sons. Here, as Brigitte Kasten has stressed, the political culture was indeed firmly 'patrimonial'.[201]

If Hraban's gaze into the biblical past revealed tensions and problems, other observers saw opportunities. In his biography of the emperor written in 836–7 Thegan, assistant bishop at Trier, cited the same examples of successful younger sons as Hraban had done, but not as a warning. For Thegan, the stories of Isaac, Jacob and David offered hope for the Carolingian family as they pointed it to the right track. Part of Thegan's purpose was to bear witness, to record the fate of the 'martyrs' who had taken risks or suffered for their loyalty to Louis and to preserve the infamy of those who had betrayed him.[202] Recording such infamy was a sensitive matter and Thegan's text was too hot to handle for some contemporaries, judging by Walahfrid Strabo's editorial decision to cut some big names from Thegan's list of 'traitors' of 830.[203]

Thegan intended his text to have an impact on contemporary politics. This is clear in his language of warnings (e.g. on the prospect of the disgraced archbishop Ebo of Reims ever returning).[204] For Thegan, the life of Louis the Pious was a shining example of that triumph of the younger brother at the expense of the older one that Hraban had written about in 833/4. Louis was the youngest of Charlemagne's (legitimate) sons and 'he was the best of his sons, just as from the beginning of the world the younger brother often excels the older brother by his merits' and Thegan backs this up with reference to the sons of Abraham, Isaac and Jesse. But while Hraban saw these stories as warnings, Thegan saw them as a pattern for a positive re-structuring of the royal line. For Thegan, the status of the 'older brother' cut little ice. He knew that the first-born son was not predestined to glory; he recorded the death of Charlemagne's 'first-born son'; he juxtaposed Lothar's status as Louis 'first-born son' with insults for Lothar's associates and a vision of Lothar's imminent treachery to his father.[205]

What counted was the younger son and Louis's status as such anticipated and legitimated the similar status of Louis the German. Thegan makes this explicit in the final sections of his text where Louis the German, the emperor's 'son and namesake' (*equivocus filius eius*) is described as replicating the behaviour 'of those sons mentioned earlier who were the younger by birth'.[206] Here Thegan signals his explicit message, binding the end of the text tightly to its opening just as the younger Louis is bound to the younger sons of the biblical stories. Thegan's narrative is one where the younger Louis is essentially on his father's side and the shared name is a sign of this: the 830 plans of the wicked conspirators against Louis the Pious were frustrated by 'his beloved namesake' (*equivocus*). Thegan was articulating the learned discourse of Carolingian legitimacy. The older Louis is repeated in his younger namesake and thus the dynasty is reproduced. It is no accident that Thegan's text opens with a genealogy. On a more immediate political level, Thegan's bracketing of the father and this particular son screens out the other sons. On Lothar, he is grimly hostile; on Charles the Bald, he is indifferent; on Pippin of Aquitaine, he is relatively neutral but does not go out of his way to exculpate him as he does with Louis the German. Thegan's links to some aristocrats in the younger Louis' circle show that he was not a solitary figure here, and he wanted the older Louis to hear him.[207]

Thegan, however, was to be disappointed. The post-834 world was to remain under the shadow of the early part of the decade. The storms of the early 830s left their mark on contemporaries. Mayke de Jong rightly observes that the rebellions inspired 'an unprecedented wave of public soul-searching', but she also argues that the restored Louis remained a formidable ruler, not essentially damaged by the troubles. As she herself notes, only a full study of Louis's government will deliver a clear verdict on this, but her view of Louis chimes with other revisionist work such as Jinty Nelson's claims that the absence of capitulary texts from 834–40 points to problems of text preservation rather than to a breakdown in governing. The coinage remained strong.[208] Louis took care to reward the loyalty of figures such as count Robert who had stood by him in his troubles.[209] Contemporaries had no wish to repeat the drastic experiments of the early 830s and so Louis could be sure that he would not be abandoned again for the rest of his days, as Nithard put it retrospectively. Nithard's phrasing suggests that people did not necessarily think that Louis's days would be long (he was fifty-six in 834 and the Astronomer thought that the empress worried about his health), but this does not mean that politics went into suspension or that a great calm descended. As revisionist historians have seen, the post-834 Louis was, if anything, all too assertive in his control of patronage.[210]

All Louis's skill and resources, however, bumped against intractable legacies from the troubles. In 836, he and Lothar tried to find solutions to competing claims of those pro-Louis aristocrats who had left Italy in 834 and those pro-Lothar aristocrats now confined there and determined to hang on to the offices that Louis's partisans had lost. Churches north of the Alps also fretted about their properties in Italy being deployed by Lothar as compensations for his followers' losses in Francia.[211] The legacy of 830–4 was a set of time-bombs.

Let us look at three examples of such dangerously unfinished business: count Richard, count Donatus and archbishop Ebo. We begin in the central regions of the empire with Richard, an aristocrat whose family held lands in the Metz region. A holder of high palace office, Richard had strongly backed Lothar in the troubles of the 830s and followed him into exile in Italy in 834. This punishment cost him the rich estate of Villance in the Ardennes which Louis had previously granted him and he wanted this back. His visit to Louis's court in 836 as one of Lothar's trusted envoys shows his continuing importance to rulers but he would surely also have used this northern trip to maintain existing connections among aristocrats and his own family. Confinement to Italy did not make Richard invisible or impotent north of the Alps. Indeed some northerners remembered him all too well. Writing in 836/7, Thegan of Trier included a sombre vignette of Richard's sinister power over the captive Louis in 834, and Thegan's labelling of Richard as 'faithless' (*perfidus*) was echoed by the Coblenz-based continuator of his text around 837, revealing a blasted reputation for Richard in this region.[212] Hostility to Richard, and doubtless to others, did not simply stem from a general culture of scorn for the disloyal but more specifically expressed a fear that powerful exiles such as Richard might return to Francia and disturb post-834 arrangements. Contemporaries thus understood such arrangements to be fragile. Thegan's insistence on Louis the German as the only trustworthy faithful son was not so much a reflection of the latter's secure status as an anxious effort to support the eastern son in the menacingly fluid world of manoeuvrings and resentments among the elite. As Mayke de Jong says, Thegan's text is 'performative' in that its production was an intervention in politics; its very existence is thus itself evidence that contemporaries saw that the 834/5 restoration did not draw a line under the contests of the earlier stormy years.[213]

Louis's eventual forgiveness of Richard in the general reconciliation with Lothar in 839 may not have softened such resentments. And Louis explicitly highlighted Richard's former treachery in the grant returning the estate of Villance to him, a grant issued at the crowded assembly at Worms.[214] Reconciliation came too late for Richard to enjoy its fruits as he died soon after the assembly and he left the estate to the abbey of Prüm, a very Carolingian site. The fact that Lothar I in 842 and Lothar II in 865 both confirmed Richard's bequest for the sake of his soul shows that Carolingian lords knew to pay their debt to their followers. But the fact that the abbey asked these kings to confirm Richard's grant shows some anxiety over Richard's right to hold it. The 830s cast a long shadow that fell not only on Richard. We know that his bequest was carried out by his brother as well as two other counts, a glimpse of the supporting cast that was touched by the disturbances over property lost in revolt, just as the fact that Markward, the abbot of Prüm was close to Richard but also to Thegan, lets us see something of the cross-currents that troubled the aristocracy in these years.[215]

Turning west, to Neuilly, an estate north-east of Paris belonging to the church of Reims, we find another instructive piece of unfinished business after 834 in our second case. Neuilly was a royal grant to the church of Reims in the late eighth century, though kings retained an interest in it. Early in his reign Louis had granted it to count Donatus of Melun. After enjoying it for twenty years, Donatus lost both it and Melun in 834 as punishment for having backed Lothar in rebellion. He never regained either while Louis lived; this suggests that he did not have the influential backers that a figure such as Richard enjoyed. But even if Louis had relented towards Donatus, his own hands were tied; he had given Neuilly to another aristocrat and so to re-endow the rebel Donatus would have been to deprive that loyal follower of a valuable estate. That follower had a vested interest in keeping Donatus out in the cold. Patronage in times of trouble had aspects of a zero-sum game (and that is why Louis did not return Neuilly to Reims). The relentless decades-long struggle of Donatus and, later, his widow and their children to regain Neuilly reveals the hunger of aristocratic families for such plums that offered them economic and social security. The conflicts of the rulers shook that security. Of course, these very quarrels also gave families such as that of Donatus some real leverage. In the kings' war after the death of Louis the Pious in 840, Charles the Bald bound Donatus to his side by granting him Neuilly.[216]

The later efforts of Donatus' widow Landrada to retain Neuilly should remind us that the upheavals of the 830s touched aristocratic women as well as their menfolk. Noble women as well as men were forced into monastic exile and it was women who pronounced the fatally guilty verdict on Gerberga, sister to Bernard of Septimania, in the smoking ruins of Chalon-sur-Saône in 834. And it is the writings from the early

840s of a woman, Dhuoda, wife of that same Bernard, who had herself spent time at Louis's court, which reveal lasting aristocratic anxieties over conflicts of loyalty and security of property stemming from the crises of the 830s.[217]

Our third and final example takes us east, to the abbey of Fulda. This was now a place of confinement and repentance for Ebo, former archbishop of Reims. As a key player in the extraordinary drama of Louis the Pious's penance of 833, a frightened Ebo had to take the fall when Louis was restored to power. In a coldly self-conscious mirroring of the emperor's penitential unmaking of himself, Louis in 835 presided over Ebo's confession of secret guilt and subsequent abandonment of the see of Reims for an existence of penitential contemplation in the monastery of Fulda. While the all too elaborate mechanisms of Ebo's unmaking would later turn out to be problematic, Louis enforced his bishops' participation in these procedures; forty-three bishops dutifully signed a document confirming Ebo's resignation, and many copies of that seem to have been made. Once again, we see that widely circulated documents sought to broadcast and justify actions to an anxiously interested audience beyond the palace. Such an audience was also sceptical; one of Louis's fiercest critics now responded to Ebo's fate by preparing a counterblast in the form of a set of strident texts defending the rights of bishops against overweening rulers.[218]

These later aftershocks do not concern us here. Our focus is on the more immediate political context after 835. Penitential exile in Fulda did not in fact neutralize Ebo. Fulda's abbot was Hraban Maur, who was, as we have seen, actively loyal to Louis during the rebellion. He thus was spared the loss of royal favour endured by his archbishop, Otgar of Mainz, who had backed Lothar in 833–4. Fulda, however, had its own problems. After 834, Fulda belonged to a region in which Louis the Pious and Louis the German both took a harmonious father-son interest, but maintaining aristocratic and institutional networks and properties now became more complicated here under this double royal shadow. Judging by a decline in the recorded grants made to Fulda from the late 820s to 837, the era's political troubles may have discouraged potential donors to the abbey. Abbot Hraban's successful solution to this was to intensify Fulda's holy aura by importing wonder-working relics of holy martyrs from Rome.[219]

Not everything that reached Fulda from south of the Alps was so welcome. Rumours spread from Italy that Lothar was trying to get hold of Ebo in order to make more trouble and this resulted in Hraban being visited by the count of Metz, one of Louis the Pious's hard men, bearing instructions to tighten up Ebo's confinement. Hraban must have found this an uncomfortable and distasteful experience as, despite his loyalty to the old emperor, he was uneasy about the archbishop's fall and began lobbying Louis's wife, brother and son Charles the Bald (as well as abbot Markward of Prüm, once again caught up in the post-835 labyrinth) to intercede for the wretched Ebo. Fulda was obviously not the secure cell that Louis had envisaged for Ebo and he now had to ship him west, to Lisieux in what is now Normandy and then further south to the abbey of Fleury by the Loire. This shows just how radioactive Ebo was; these sites were firmly in the territories assigned to the young Charles the Bald and only there could Louis keep him safely out of the reach of the long arm of Lothar. No wonder that Thegan, as we have seen, campaigned against any return to office by Ebo. Neither the brutal majesty of Ebo's punishment in 835 nor his all too visible disappearing into secure sites had managed to extinguish him. On Louis's death in the summer of 840, the abbot of Fleury turned away from Charles the Bald and whisked Ebo into Lothar's presence so that he could be restored to Reims. The abbot of Reichenau, however, promptly issued a dossier condemning Ebo.[220]

From 835 to 840, Ebo's case had thus embroiled around ten people in its coils, including three kings, an empress and a count; scribes and messengers doubtless formed a sizable supporting cast; places as far apart as Italy, Fulda and Fleury were touched by it. Ebo, Richard and Donatus did not endure their problems in isolation. Many of the wounds of the early 830s were unhealed by Louis's restoration in 834.

Louis, however, was not alone in getting older. Charles the Bald was approaching maturity and his father worked to ensure that he would have a secure grip on his share of the realm. This meant a series of divisions of the empire, proclaimed publicly in assemblies at Aachen in 837, Nijmegen and Quierzy in 838 and Worms in 839.[221] The large numbers of people who attended such assemblies could see that division and inheritance were at the top of the political agenda. We can get a sense of these numbers from the attendance at an emergency meeting summoned by Louis at Aachen in April 838: we know of five archbishops, thirteen bishops, seventeen abbots, twenty-six counts, two counts of the palace, twenty-five royal vassals as well as the emperor, the empress and young Charles.[222] The details of division were on at least one occasion spelled out in a written document so that there could be no uncertainty; we also know that when the old emperor drastically reduced Louis the German's kingdom in 837, he did so with a written judgement; such documents would only have accentuated the solemnity and hoped-for finality of divisions. Aristocrats in the kingdom allocated to Charles had to take oaths to him.[223]

This, however, must have created tensions rather than security as aristocrats knew that the other royal sons would not necessarily accept their father's plans. Louis tried to bind his older sons into his planned future, ensuring that Louis the German and envoys from Pippin of Aquitaine consented to the 837 grant to Charles, while Pippin himself attended and approved the Quierzy assembly of 838 where Charles's coming of age was signalled by his father giving him weapons and a crown. Louis seems to have held back from making grants in the west from 838–40, giving Charles the spotlight there. It is probably in this timespan that Louis released a royal daughter into marriage, an extremely rare event, in arranging for Gisela to marry Eberhard of Friuli, a prominent magnate in Lothar's camp; this was a clear signal of trust in Lothar and his followers.[224] Louis and his sons were at the front of everyone's mind in these years.

Louis's drive and will are impressive and he did all he could to make that apparent to contemporaries. Nithard refers several times to the 'will (*voluntas*)' of the father.[225] It was of course Louis's will that had been seen as the source of the troubles of the earlier years. Not everyone would have approved of Louis's will as Nithard did. Lothar and Louis the German were uneasy about the initial grants to Charles. Louis the German and his father Louis had a ferocious quarrel at the assembly at Nijmegen in 838 which resulted in Louis senior stripping the son of his lands west of the Rhine. The old emperor's ability to impose his authority in east Francia, where his son had been building up power for some years, is striking. But Louis the German was not going to take this lying down and the hostility towards him of the old emperor's agents in the east, count Adalbert of Metz and archbishop Otgar of Mainz, ensured continuing conflict there.[226] Aristocrats were not merely passive observers amidst all these divisions of the realm, but that only meant the ratcheting up of conflict and instability.

Disintegration: 839–43

And everyone, not least Judith and courtiers in Louis's palace, knew that Lothar and his supporters would not stay in Italy forever. At last, Louis summoned his oldest son north, to meet at an assembly at Worms at the end of May 839.[227] Louis the Pious was very much in charge of performance at the assembly. Nithard saw Lothar's appearance as the return of the prodigal son. But Nithard knew that Lothar would later renege on commitments to family harmony and was thus implying that Lothar's penance was not genuine; he cannot have been the only critical observer. Ceremonies such as the embrace between Louis and the penitent Lothar and their subsequent banquet broadcast the reconciliation that they enacted.[228] The earlier stages of the ceremonies presented Lothar's humility: we are told that he 'fell at his father's feet like a suppliant' and we can be sure his forgiveness was conditional; 'on condition that [Lothar and his followers] should never again attempt any action against the emperor with their evil machinations'. The Astronomer's tactful omission of these details points to them being clear signs of Louis's distrust of Lothar and his determination to control him.[229] Stakes were high at Worms and it must have been quite a tense occasion; participants at this assembly saw a stern father setting conditions for his son, but that son was appearing ever more clearly as a prince with a future in Francia.

Lothar, however, was not a free agent at Worms. We are told that his father gave him the choice of dividing up the empire or selecting which portion of it, once it was divided, that he wanted. This choice was illusory. Louis had already allocated a kingdom in the west to Charles in 837, giving him actual control of Neustria in 838; Charles was already exercising patronage there, appointing an archbishop of Sens, and churches were being instructed to pray specifically for him.[230] The death of Pippin of Aquitaine at the end of 838 freed up Aquitaine as a core for Charles's western kingdom. Division and selection were thus a done deal before Lothar got to Worms. In fact it was probably only because these basics were in place that Louis and the court felt secure enough to invite Lothar north. The Astronomer rightly saw that the death of Pippin of Aquitaine was the trigger for Judith and the courtiers to play the Lothar card and to prepare for the latter's reappearance.[231]

Lothar was thus confronted with a ready-made division and choice. References by modern commentators to 'traditional' practice whereby he who makes the division does not make the choice here miss the point of Worms.[232] The three days that were granted to Lothar and his followers to make their fictitious choice were probably part of the time in which final deals about the division were made in the context of the assembly itself. Frisia, for example, awarded to Charles the Bald in 837 now went to Lothar; this would have been one result of the deals made at Worms. Such deals would have been made easier by the fact that Louis had a list of resources in the affected territories, another indication that all had been carefully prepared; such a list could not have been conjured up at a moment's notice.[233] In compelling Lothar and his followers to make a series of choices, Louis was ensuring that they were publicly performing, in front of the assembly's audience, their consent to the division. Lothar had to agree to be seen as choosing his share. He thus could not complain later over what he had freely chosen. The old emperor stage-managed the future by stage-managing the present. Or so he hoped.

But this piece of political theatre had an extra dimension. The key actors in it were predominantly, though not exclusively, the emperor and his sons. Lothar's falling at the feet of his father, the fatherly embrace, the banquet, the drama of Lothar's choice, all this put the royal family centre-stage. This expressed and reinforced the authoritative discourse of Carolingian politics, a discourse of legitimation for the Carolingians. The aristocratic audience at Worms saw father reconciled with son and brothers agree to division of the empire. Our sources are full of affective familial language: 'His son Lothar arrived from Italy and the emperor showed not the slightest reluctance to receive him with fatherly affection … he forgave Lothar with fatherly love and kindness.'[234] Family harmony had made the new settlement possible and only Carolingian family harmony could guarantee its future: 'the father brought the brothers to be of one mind (*unanimes*)'; 'the emperor urged his sons to be of one mind (*unanimes*) and to protect each other, and that Lothar should care for his younger brother, and ought to remember that he was his spiritual father, while Charles should pay due honour to his spiritual father and older brother … mutual love between the brothers'.[235] Familial thinking and family structure were central institutions. Brotherly love, supplemented by bonds of godparenthood, would work towards peaceful filial succession, which guaranteed the reproduction of the Carolingian dynasty as legitimate rulers.

It was precisely here that the problems lay. Familial bonds in the dynasty were not just central institutions, they seemed to be the only ones that mattered at the summit of politics. But contemporaries knew that brotherly love and fatherly benevolence could not be guaranteed. The centrality of the Carolingian family to politics was itself the key problem of the 830s. The equal Carolingian-ness of all the (legitimate) sons of Louis the Pious was the key feature of the political landscape after 829. This meant that there was no way to choose between competing claims except through family agreements and past performance here was not good. The tensions and problems seen by Hraban as inherent in all this were still there. The glory of Carolingian royalty could itself be the source of insoluble problems.

On a more immediately political level, the actual division made at Worms was radically simple. Charles's western kingdom was now to include Aquitaine while Lothar's eastern share was to include what had been Louis the German's east Frankish lands (Louis the German was supposed to remain content with a rump kingdom in Bavaria).[236] Both sons were to inherit lands that had been in the political orbit of their brothers, and the emperor did not give Lothar the chance to grip his new kingdom as the division would only come into effect on the emperor's death. Lothar thus had to depart again for Italy, much as Louis the Pious himself had to leave Francia for Aquitaine when he was promised his inheritance in 813. The theatrical ceremonies at Worms could have hardly succeeded in making the participants forget about other Carolingians, other kings' sons who were very much *not* present at the assembly: Louis the German and the son(s) of Pippin of Aquitaine (who were to lose that kingdom if Louis the Pious had anything to do with it). In fact, the father-son-brother language and ceremonies of Worms, the Carolingian family discourse, could only reinforce the royal status of Louis the German and the line of Pippin of Aquitaine in the eyes of the dynasty's followers. Worms drew attention to these tensions. In holding the assembly at Worms, Louis the Pious was asserting that this region was his, and would become Lothar's; it did not belong to Louis the German.[237]

The very site of the assembly proclaimed the demotion of one son; there were limits to fatherly clemency. But there were also limits to the father's power. Louis the Pious did not use the Worms gathering to abolish the kingship of Louis the German. Indeed, in January of 839, in his spectacular winter campaign against his son, the old emperor had contented himself with humiliating Louis the German by driving him back into Bavaria, but not actually pursuing him into there. The emperor seems to have felt unable to cancel his son's kingship. Annalists' picture of the emperor staying his hand because he 'was deeply worried about spilling the blood of a people who felt themselves one' shows the emperor's yearning for mercy as a way of subduing conflict as well as other contemporary realities: interconnected aristocratic supporters with little appetite for a final showdown while the old emperor still lived.[238] In sending envoys from Worms to Louis the German commanding him to stay within the confines of Bavaria, the emperor was proclaiming to the assembly that Bavaria remained untouchably the kingdom of Louis. The emperor could thus not help but conjure up the figure of absent and aggrieved Louis. No wonder the emperor's palace annalists wrote of the father's mercy, the father's righteousness, the father's commands, the son's disobedience. All this, like the eastern annalist's picture of Louis the German recognizing in that winter campaign that it was 'wicked' (*nefas*) for a son to resist his father, contributed to the discourse of familial kingship while masking political calculations of strength and weakness as recognitions of the moral hierarchy of father and sons. But this could only remind everyone that Louis the German might be a fallen son, but he was still inescapably a son, and a king.[239]

Worms ended with another declaration of such limits. Louis called another assembly for the start of September, but this one was to be held in the west, near Chalon(-sur-Saône). This was to be the muster point for troops to be sent against Pippin II and his supporters in Aquitaine and the proclamation of this assembly at Chalon means that news of Pippin II's rising must have broken during the assembly at Worms. A ghost had come to the feast. For Louis, Worms and Chalon were places where his particular view of the structure of the royal family could be imposed. Objectively, however, they were points on a map that displayed the all too widely generalized distribution of Carolingian charisma and claims across this world. The Carolingians had succeeded too well in convincing themselves and aristocrats of their king-worthiness.

Understanding the situation of the kings who were not at Worms, Louis the German and Pippin II of Aquitaine, and the dilemmas of the aristocracies in their orbit, helps us see just how intractable the internal Carolingian competition had now become. In a characteristically vivid image, Jinty Nelson compares Louis the Pious's orchestration of support for his favoured sons to the deft waltzes of Johann Strauss.[240] But the music of the later 830s was more like Maurice Ravel's *La valse*, a nightmarish parody of the waltz, a dance of dissolution. After Louis the German fled from his father's forces back into Bavaria in January 839, those aristocrats who had been too close to the son now had to make their peace with the imperial father in an atmosphere tense with accusation and the prospect of punishment. Even a loyalist such as abbot Hraban of Fulda felt that he had to approach Louis the Pious as he held his stern court in Frankfurt and admit that he now had doubts about the validity of a grant that Louis the German had made to the abbey some years ago. The old emperor declared that his son had indeed been usurping power but he, the emperor, graciously confirmed the grant. As a loyalist, Hraban may not have felt real anxiety that the emperor would turn against him, but others could not be so sure that their acceptance of the son's patronage would be seen as innocent by the father. Such public acting out by the abbot and the emperor of anxiety, anger and grace meant that those aristocrats at Frankfurt, including the powerful east Frankish aristocrat count Poppo and others as well as Hraban, all had to perform the marginalizing of Louis the German.[241]

While our narrative sources tend to keep the spotlight on the imperial father and his sons, they also point to the actions of this aristocratic supporting cast. Louis the Pious's court annalist tells how envoys shuttled between the emperor and Louis the German in the late summer of 839 carrying requests for the return of lands to Louis the German's supporters and demands that magnates of each Louis should swear oaths not to attack father or son.[242] These envoys travelled to kings but they bore the pleas of wider aristocratic communities without whose support kings could not act and whose requests kings had to heed. The quarrels of the great spread ripples precisely because the great had so much to offer; their patronage provided security, but disturbances in the flow and management of such patronage brought troubles. Abbot Grimald of Weissenburg in Alsace, a man with valuable family connections around the Moselle, had bravely balanced loyalty to the emperor with loyalty to Louis the German in 833–4 but the pressures on him from the clash between father and son in 838–40 proved too much. His loyalty to Louis the German meant that the emperor now deprived him of Weissenburg but Louis the German may also have suspected his loyalties for a while.[243] Having spent his prodigiously talented youth turning the tensions of the Carolingian court into poetry, the poet and scholar Walahfrid now found himself, at the age of thirty, in a world of anxious prose. Louis the Pious's 838 grant to him of the plum post of the abbacy of Reichenau in Alemannia meant that he was and would remain inescapably caught up in these eastern father-son conflicts. We possess an urgent letter to him from someone at the emperor's court briefing him on problems faced by counts over their properties in Alemannia and alerting him to a stream of counter-briefings sent out by Louis the German.[244] Figures such as Walahfrid were now in a region criss-crossed by the messengers and warriors of the hostile rulers.

One reason for all this agitated signals traffic was that all the players here knew that the game was not over. Louis the German's fortunes were at their nadir; Eric Goldberg has noted the collapse of his chancery in this period.[245] But neither father nor son could land a knock-out blow and could thus only try to keep aristocrats on their toes, anxious but not so resentful they might feel they had nothing more to lose, hence the strident demands for oaths of good behaviour and the finely calibrated snatchings and returnings of property. But none of this amounted to a solution to competing Carolingian claims to rule in east Francia. In working with magnates such as the relentless count Adalbert of Metz and archbishop Otgar of Mainz who were hostile to Louis the German and supportive of Lothar, the ageing emperor was programming future conflict even while trying to forestall it.[246] The last years of his reign were not a new phase of peaceful settlement.

The emperor's inability to impose a solution was in part due to the sheer size of the empire. He was only compelled to patch up a truce in the east because trouble was erupting in the far south-west, in Aquitaine. The size of the empire mattered – as well as its diversity – as these months of 838–40 demonstrated. The ever-increasing tempo of ruling shook Louis the Pious from a long stay at Aachen in the winter of 837–8 to Nijmegen, the reassuring site of his restoration in 830, and then to such western palaces as Quierzy and Compiègne and then east to sites such as Mainz and Frankfurt, swinging back west in 839 to Chalon-sur-Saône and then deeper west to Aquitaine, with Christmas 839 spent in Poitiers. The year 840 saw the emperor trundling back to the Rhineland. Not every part of these journeys was political fire-fighting; hunting, feasting, pilgrimage and prayer took up significant time too; these were proper activities for a ruler.[247] But no post-834 Carolingian (with the exception of Charles the Fat) had so wide a realm to span and rule, and the fact that Louis had to spend Christmas 839 in Poitiers of all places is very instructive.

But Aquitaine was not as far from the realm's centres as geography might imply; the presence of Pippin I there, a ruling Carolingian, had made Aquitaine a more central zone. The fact that this vast empire was ruled up until 840 by a father and his sons meant that political distances could be massively compressed for contemporaries into the smallness of the royal family itself.[248] And of course aristocrats and churches owned estates across the Frankish world; Reims, for example, had lands in Aquitaine (see post-843 chapter). In December 838, after a noteworthy lunar eclipse, king Pippin I of Aquitaine died. Even in winter, this news must have travelled fast to his father Louis the Pious as he was heading to Mainz on the Rhine to confront Louis the German. The emperor's court annalist was well-informed: he recorded the precise date of Pippin's death as well as the fact that he left two sons, and the annalist also knew their portentously royal names: Pippin and Charles.[249]

Pippin was around fifteen, the same age as his uncle Charles the Bald, while the Aquitanian Charles was about ten.[250] What happened next to these two youngsters illustrates very clearly just how Carolingian royalty was simultaneously inborn and socially constructed, by the Carolingians themselves and by their aristocratic partners and rivals. At first, and this is significant, nothing happened. Louis froze the succession. The fact that by summer of 839 some Aquitanian aristocrats were no longer prepared to wait for Louis to decide the succession indicates that waiting is what they had been told to do. For Louis, Judith, Charles the Bald and his supporters, Aquitaine's sudden availability was a bonus that could now equip Charles with a kingdom substantial enough to balance the one now being contemplated for Lothar in Louis the Pious's fantasy world.[251]

In brushing aside the claims of his grandsons, Pippin's children, Louis was ignoring the stipulations of 817's *Ordinatio Imperii* which envisaged father-son succession to the kingdoms of the empire, but was also asserting his own will as emperor, acting as wise and caring head of the Carolingian line, in his supporters' eyes.[252] This was doubtless a loyal echo of the case Louis had made for swallowing Aquitaine.

The fact that a case had to be made is significant. Writing around 900, the chronicler Regino tells a bizarre story of Pippin I's abandonment of a spiritual calling for a life of alcoholic madness; this may stem from Metz and be a product of its bishop, Louis' loyal brother Drogo, joining in the older generation's attempt to control the younger.[253] Building on existing Frankish prejudices against Aquitanian society, all this was part of a contemporary effort to discredit the young Pippin (II), but this actually testifies to the strength of Pippin's supporters and of the Frankish expectation of father-son succession. It is true that Pippin I had ruled Aquitaine very much under the shadow of his imperial father and that his royal title in his diplomata highlights his regional rather than untrammelled Frankish authority ('king of the Aquitanians'). This should not make us scale him down as some sort of lowly sub-king. For contemporaries, Pippin I was a real king; the fact that he issued diplomata at all was significant, and he issued coins, even if only to his immediate supporters on his accession to Aquitaine.[254]

Contemporaries had been taught that Pippin I had a future. At the direction of his father in 822, Pippin had married the daughter of the count of Madrie, and Ermold, a contemporary poet, thought it worthwhile in a poem of 826–8 for Pippin to celebrate her as a beautiful queen who took a prominent part alongside the king in great ceremonies at the palaces of Aquitaine. She doubtless also helped bind the wives and daughters of Aquitanian magnates more closely to her husband's court.[255] Pippin's marriage took place in Francia and thus publicly communicated to an audience beyond Aquitaine that he was permitted and expected to be a father. Ermold not only extolled Pippin's royal ancestry in which the name Pippin continually resounded but also hailed his offspring, whom he saw as the centre of Pippin's court.[256]

Pippin I had sons and gave them royal names of Pippin and Charles. And, unusually for Carolingian fathers of his generation, he married off two of his daughters to important aristocrats, binding them to his family.[257] There can be no doubt that Pippin and contemporaries expected his line to continue. But Pippin I died before his own father did and this was what enabled Louis the Pious to re-write the future. No Carolingian son could expect to succeed his father automatically. Nor did a senior Carolingian such as Louis inhabit a political vacuum where he could simply impose his will.

There are two significant points here. First, Aquitaine was not an isolated region; it was very much part of a larger whole. The church of Reims as well as churches in the Touraine had lands in Aquitaine, and could thus not be indifferent about its fate. Pippin I's coinage issue had in fact been a one-off and the coins that circulated in Aquitaine bore the name of Louis, just as the charters issued by Pippin were dated by Louis's years as well as his own. Aquitainians were not to forget the emperor, nor could Francia forget Pippin. He and his aristocratic followers travelled to his father's assemblies, and Pippin issued some of his charters from Francia.[258] Indeed, Pippin was at Quierzy in 838 for the proclamation of Charles the Bald as king in the Neustrian north-west of the realm, and Louis took pains to bind Pippin closely to his younger half-brother there. Bishop Ebroin of Poitiers was also at this Quierzy gathering along with other prominent aristocrats possibly including his relation count Rorico of Le Mans; Ebroin would also have encountered Walahfrid there, whose troubles in Alemannia were to parallel Ebroin's in Aquitaine. It was a small world.[259] The interlocking presence of aristocrats from all regions of the realm at such assemblies meant that this world pivoted on its Carolingian rulers. This made Louis's intervention in Aquitaine possible and credible. Significantly, he did not need to journey to Aquitaine to proclaim its fate. It was at the 839 division of the realm between Charles and Lothar made at Worms that the watching aristocrats heard that Aquitaine was to go to Charles. Louis's court annalist did not even bother to draw attention to this fact but merely listed Aquitaine as one of the items on the menu for the two sons; such was Louis's power and unquestioned right to apportion the Carolingian inheritance.[260]

But Louis's right was in fact sharply questioned, and this is the second point. Pippin II could draw on the same Carolingian family discourse as his grandfather did. The Astronomer's mealy mouthed attempt to defend Louis from the charge of being cruelly bent on robbing his grandson is surely an echo of an urgent effort by Louis to counter such claims.[261] Pippin II could deploy his Carolingian heritage to proclaim the rightness of his kingship. He and his supporters only seem to have activated his rule once they grasped Louis's intentions. His first surviving charter dates from probably the second half of 839 but in backdating the start of his reign to immediately from the death of his father in December 838, Pippin's charters demonstrated that his royal inheritance did not need to wait on pronouncements from grandfather. The fact that this first charter was actually one that had been drawn up for Pippin's own father made that point visually.[262] Pippin also had material resources to lure followers to his cause; it is possible that the dazzling treasures of the Aquitanian abbey of Conques let us glimpse the riches of kings in Aquitaine.[263] He certainly attracted enough followers to make his claim credible. Some may well have felt that they were fighting for justice in backing him; after all, that is what Carolingian hereditary succession taught. Others, however, probably took more calculated decisions about preserving their own status in the face of a new royal patron with his own followers to reward. Shrinking resources concentrated minds.[264]

The aristocracy was under the spell and shadow of Carolingian royalty. Louis's former favourite Bernard could only preserve himself in these years by twisting and turning between rival Carolingians even while his own household breathed a heady air of dynastic loyalty.[265] But even spell-bound aristocrats did not lose consciousness; they remained aware of their own interests and of their own power to endorse Carolingians. Louis the Pious was sufficiently potent to draw bishop Ebroin of Poitiers from Aquitaine to Vlattern near Aachen with his complaints that some aristocrats were backing Pippin II, but this only showed that he could not make these aristocrats accept his definition of the Carolingian line.[266]

For his part, Pippin could find aristocratic supporters and thus become fully Carolingian but he could not take loyalty for granted just because he was his father's son: those counts who had married his sisters now backed Louis, not him. Neither Louis nor Pippin had a trump card and so Aquitanians had to make difficult decisions, and Aquitaine itself was split; it did not act as a coherent region.[267] The process of such decision-making is not made clear in our sources. Pippin II seems to have confined his immediate ambitions, and thus his potential resources, to the limited field of Aquitaine itself with no plans to claim part of Francia. His charters proclaim him to be 'king of the Aquitanians', though the king of Aquitaine's reach had extended into Burgundy earlier in Louis's reign.[268] He had a brother Charles, who got no share of Aquitaine, but who was too Carolingian to vanish. At some stage, he travelled to the court of his uncle Lothar I, a sign that what happened in Aquitaine did not stay confined to Aquitaine. We shall see the sequel of this later.[269]

Pippin II's kingship was so threatening to the emperor's plans that Louis himself had to travel to Aquitaine with warriors, the empress Judith and their son Charles. This was a spectacular show of force as well as a determined effort to redirect aristocratic loyalties to the son of Judith, not the son of Pippin I. Successful sieges of Pippin II's strongholds, extracting oaths of loyalty from local aristocrats and staying for the winter to celebrate Christmas and feast of Epiphany in Poitiers itself show Louis's powers as senior ruler remained great. Participants in Louis's campaign realized, however, that he could not quickly achieve mastery in this landscape broken up by hilly strongholds, woods and rivers. If Louis had strong support, particularly in the northern parts of Aquitaine, Pippin had enough supporters in the south to keep his kingship going. Aristocrats in the west, like those we have seen in the east, had to ensure that what one of Louis's sons had given them was now renegotiated with the imperial father. But time was up. Louis's own health was breaking down with the effort.[270]

The scale of the empire, and its extended communications networks, again exacerbated Louis's troubles. Just as the revolt in the west had called him from the east, so now news reached Poitiers that Louis the German had broken out of Bavaria and was again claiming lands to the Rhine. Louis the German had sufficient support in Bavaria to help him spring over its boundaries; a charter gives us a glimpse of some of these aristocrats, girt with their swords, gathering with contingents near Freising in December 839.[271] The emperor left Charles and Judith in Aquitaine; the presence of the ruler's wife was a sign that the ruler had openly staked prestige on success there. Louis himself rushed back to Aachen in time to celebrate Easter; after displaying this God-fearing dignity, he joined up with the loyal forces already mobilized and drove Louis the German far to the east. This success, however, solved nothing and the emperor's plan to summon Lothar to discuss what to do with the recalcitrant Louis the German shows that he realized that, and he can hardly have been alone.[272]

Louis the Pious eventually ran out of time; we all do. He died in June 840. We possess a vivid account of the emperor's death-bed in the biography of him by the 'Astronomer', a highly placed member of the palace. Probably writing in 840–1 and perhaps writing under the patronage of Louis's half-brother Drogo of Metz who was at the imperial death-bed, the Astronomer certainly had a hard task in closing his biography. No image of smooth succession was available to the Astronomer or to any of his contemporaries in representing Louis's end. One well-informed annalist noted explicitly that the emperor died without his either his wife or his children beside him.[273] The Astronomer turned his account of Louis's dying into an exemplary image of a Christian ruler's end, but this could only reveal the tremendous tensions over the succession that haunted the realm as it awaited change.

The Astronomer presents the dissolution of the ruler as a moral and physical drama in a spiritual community. Louis's bodily and spiritual crisis is resolved by the careful ministrations of the wise bishops who attend upon him.[274] But the bishops' care for Louis's soul only exposed the depths of the fault lines in the royal family as Drogo begged him to forgive Louis the German. Furthermore, the father's eventual forgiveness of his son did not change the fundamental hostility to Louis the German, as the Astronomer's account of this partial reconciliation is preceded by the account of Louis the Pious directing what should go to Lothar and Charles the Bald, thus confirming his will that Louis the German was to be cut out of the (large) succession. Nor could the Astronomer disguise the fact that when Louis sent Lothar a crown and sword these were not simply insignia designating him as an heir but a sign to remind him of his promises to the young Charles the Bald. When the Astronomer wrote this, he knew that these promises had not been kept. Among the bishops too, there was division. The Astronomer presents them as selfless spiritual counsellors but since he notes the presence among them of Archbishop Otgar of Mainz and we know that he was an implacable enemy of Louis the German, we can imagine the politically tense atmosphere among these bishops.[275]

The Astronomer ends with Louis's burial at Metz. On one level, the sonorous music of the general discourse of Carolingian legitimacy resounds here. The funeral is presided over by Louis's brother Drogo; the burial place is the church of St Arnulf, the holy ancestor of the Carolingians; and Louis is buried in the same place as his mother. That past offers a comforting vision of Carolingian succession and dynastic aura. But the problem of Louis's reign, and for much of the period that was to follow, was that that Carolingian aura was at once all powerful and for each generation endlessly negotiated: there was no consensus on how to choose among competing Carolingians. In closing his narrative with death and burial and pointing to the past with no definitive reference to succession, the Astronomer was stating clearly that the future was too dark to be narrated. His picture of Louis's death-bed is no saintly tableau but rather a cry from that messenger 'in old engravings who rushes towards us crying aloud, his hair on end, brandishing a sheet of paper in his hands – a sheet full of war and pestilence, of cries and murder and pain, of danger from fire and flood.'[276]

Louis's death could not bring peace; it could only herald more conflict. For seventy years, ever since Charlemagne took over his brother's kingdom in 771, the Franks had looked to a single senior ruler, no matter how many younger Carolingians held thrones. Now a younger generation of kings had no father's hand over it. Louis as father had not bequeathed Lothar any imperial superiority over his brothers. Lothar may have thought otherwise and evidence suggests that many aristocrats north of the Alps thought so too. But Lothar's brothers had sufficient supporters to challenge this. A contemporary saw Lothar's speedy attempt to claim such superiority and to grab territory in Gaul as a breach of the 'laws of nature'. Lothar was the oldest brother, and also Charles the Bald's godfather, but this did not cancel out brothers' claims.[277]

The result had to be conflict over the inheritance of kingdoms. The royal brothers, and their royal nephew Pippin of Aquitaine, were ready to fight for their inheritance and this meant that their struggle was essentially horizontal. Chroniclers described the clashes as being between brothers, and the same was true of alliances The famous oaths of Strasbourg taken by Charles the Bald and Louis the German in 842 each record their pledge to stand by 'my brother' while their followers promised to support the oaths made by Louis 'to his brother Charles' and by Charles to 'his brother Louis'. Looking back after thirty years, archbishop Hincmar of Reims remembered that Charles and Louis and their supporters believed that of course they matched Lothar and his backers.[278] One brother could not be more equal than others.

Aristocrats must have viewed this prospect with mixed feelings. They could remember that not all the clashes of Louis the Pious's reign had been bloodless. Count Warin of Mâcon, who joined Charles in the winter of 840–1, may have remembered being forced to join Lothar in 834 as Chalon burned around him and his companions were executed. Others, such as count Adalbert of Metz, may have welcomed combat as the best chance to secure their own territories and interests.[279] And no one knew who would win. Nithard's vivid and highly partisan contemporary account of the war makes clear that in its early stages aristocrats and kings waited to see who was going to jump in which direction before joining them. Nor were decisions final. One Eric who decided to back Lothar in late 840 returned to Charles early in the next year. Bishop Drogo of Metz, a loyal supporter of Lothar, found his church in Charles's orbit for some of 842. Such oscillations were common.[280] Bernard of Septimania's wife Dhuoda wrote her book of advice for her son William at precisely this tense time. She says it was begun 'in the second year after the death of the former emperor Louis [the Pious]', and finished on the feast 'of the holy glorious and ever virgin Mary, Christ reigning propitiously *and in hope of the king whom God will give*' (my emphasis). This reveals a Christian aristocrat's understanding of time as marked by great events such as the death of a ruler but also as punctuated by the feasts of the saints. More specifically, it reveals Dhuoda's uncertainty over who would succeed Louis as ruler in her part of the Frankish world (southern France). The fact that she was writing for a son who was effectively a hostage in the entourage of Charles the Bald for her husband Bernard's good behaviour shows how aristocrats tried to grapple with this time of trouble.[281]

Kings' own power was not stable enough now to control such switches but it was strong enough to create insecurity. The sharply observant contemporary Nithard testifies to this. In his account of the build-up to the great battle of Fontenoy in June 841, all three brothers as well as Pippin II and their messengers covered the landscape, uttering threats and promises from Aquitaine to the Rhine, stripping some men of offices, heaping rewards on others, while demonstrating their own kingly status to themselves, their supporters and opponents by celebrating Easter at Aachen (Lothar), praying at St-Denis (Charles), etc.[282]

This was not theatrical posturing. To be stripped of *honores* was to lose valuable resources; to break an oath to one king in order to please another who might keep these resources secure was to lose honour and reputation.[283] Dhuoda's plea to her son William to understand that security lay with God alone and not with evanescent fortunes in this world was advice for a young aristocrat as pointedly relevant as her urging him to grasp family claims to properties and *honores*. Dhuoda had the worldly knowledge and experience of a courtier and she was not the only such woman to raise her voice at this time. The empress Ermengard, wife of Lothar I, wrote to an aristocratic follower of Charles the Bald, probably Adalhard the seneschal, accusing him of betraying Lothar for short-lived rewards, a charge the aristocrat saw as touching his honour and which he hotly denied.[284]

Hard-riding, heavily armed men carried out the bulk of this manoeuvring and threatening. The military 'games' performed by Charles the Bald, Louis the German and their warriors at Strasbourg in early 842 displayed the skill of a fighting elite seldom far from a horse. Louis the German wore a pair of golden spurs. A warrior's bond with his sword was a close one, as displayed in the wall-painting of a ninth-century aristocrat at San Benedetto in Malles, northern Italy; the Ulfberht swords survive to show us something of the quality of these prized possessions. We may sometimes fail to remember the constant presence of weapons for this elite: Louis the Pious was wearing a sword when returning from a church service on Maundy Thursday at Aachen in 817, and it injured him when the palace floor collapsed under him.[285] Such armoury and skills were there to be used. Threats had a real edge. The war of 840–3 was one of clashes and killings as well as menaces and feints.[286] Kings could seldom control the violence that they unleashed; Charles the Bald was only just able to prevent his angry warriors from devastating Laon in the autumn of 841.[287]

The grim climax was that rare thing, a pitched battle, at Fontenoy in Burgundy in June 841. All four royals, Lothar and Pippin of Aquitaine against Charles and Louis the German, fought and it took a heavy toll of their supporters. This battle's terrible slaughter shocked contemporaries and it came to be seen as the reason for Frankish failure against attackers such as Vikings.[288] Yet if Fontenoy was a collective Frankish tragedy, its leading actors nevertheless remained the kings. One contemporary participant, Angelbert (possibly a lay aristocrat, certainly a supporter of Lothar), wrote an anguished poetic lament on the battle, mourning the loss of the blood of the Franks. But the only individuals he picked out by name, apart from himself, were Lothar, Charles and Louis. The non-mentioning of Pippin of Aquitaine is also eloquent.[289]

The kings were not the only actors on the scene. The war opened up divisions in contemporary society; conflict amongst the elite triggered and encouraged a peasant rising in Saxony against aristocratic and royal authority in 841–2.[290] Above all, the aristocracy played a key role. Fontenoy failed to deliver a decisive verdict and most of the significant magnates seem to have survived it. But the prospect of yet more indecisive bloodshed and uncertainty over property and offices (*honores*) drove aristocrats to pressure kings to make peace. Complicated negotiations led to a great settlement made at Verdun in the summer of 843. This was the result of collective effort. One hundred and twenty magnates toured the disputed areas to compile a survey (*descriptio*) of them as a preparation for dividing the realm. The meeting at Verdun to proclaim the division was attended by hundreds, possibly thousands, of aristocrats great and small.[291]

And yet the kings remained at the centre of these aristocrats' world. Bishop Erchanbert of Freising, a follower of Louis the German, took advantage of being at Verdun in August 843 to make a deal over lands with Balderic, a supporter of Lothar. Their transaction turned on their own need to accommodate themselves to the division of lands that Verdun imposed, but the document records its own making as 'near Verdun where a settlement was reached among the three brothers Lothar, Louis and Charles and the division of their kingdom was made'.[292] The fact that the three royal brothers had decided to exclude Pippin of Aquitaine from the settlement, and that they had managed to acquire sufficient resources to establish kingdoms for themselves, but not sufficient to be secure, and that aristocrats now faced potentially even more sharply divided loyalties all meant that Verdun opened as many problematic futures as it closed off. The reign of Louis the Pious had paradoxically masked and highlighted the competitively polycentric nature of Carolingian kingship. The challenge for Louis's sons and descendants was to preserve Carolingian distinctiveness in a world with more Carolingians than ever.

6

Lines of succession and lines of failure 843–79

The Treaty of Verdun in 843 divided up the realm into three kingdoms: the west, under Charles the Bald (d.877); the east, under Louis the German (d.876); and the middle kingdom, under Lothar I (d.855), who retained his imperial title. This middle kingdom, that part of it north of the Alps, disappeared when the emperor's son Lothar II perished in 869, caught up in the throes of the sensational divorce case which had bedevilled his reign. That kingdom survived only as a ghost while the western and eastern kingdoms endured to be recruited by the discourses of modern nationhood as the origins of France and Germany. In 843, however, contemporaries were blissfully unaware of this future and we should forget it too if we want to understand their experience of the post-843 world.

Dividing an empire and rebuilding kingdoms

They did know, however, that 843 marked a break, that it was a real division. An annalist in Cologne in the 860s saw the single realm of Charlemagne as now ruled by several kings, most of whom were useless, fulfilling the biblical prophecy of woe to the land with many rulers; while they postured, their people starved.[1] In the sombre tones of a biblical prophet, the western cleric Audradus Modicus around 850 envisioned a wrathful Christ calling these kings to account for their failings and proclaiming 'Who are these kings? I do not know them'. These kings had survived the chaos of Louis's last years and the war but it was precisely these circumstances that led to their authority being questioned by Audradus who saw that after/with 843 'the constitutional world of the Carolingians began anew', in Paul Dutton's deft summing-up of his complex vision.[2] Audradus was not alone in understanding 843 as marking a fateful new beginning. Around 850, monks at St-Germain-des-Près associated Viking attacks with 'the division of the realm (*regnum*)' of the Franks after which the sins of the people multiplied'.[3] Viking attacks may have made westerners particularly aware of kingly difficulties but they were not alone in their awareness of division. Florus, a churchman in the middle kingdom, lamented the rule of 'petty kings' in a shattered realm where the communities washed by the empire's great rivers now lived apart from each other. Indeed, it was while crossing one of these rivers, the Loire, on a journey from the eastern to the western kingdom that the scholar Walahfrid Strabo drowned, 'a victim of Carolingian diplomacy'.[4]

This was a world of variety and cultural divisions. Churches in an eastern region such as Saxony did not possess the cultural and economic resources of their counterparts in a western one such as Neustria. Travellers from Romance-speaking lands to Germanic ones could carry a phrase-book in case they needed the Old High German for ordinary questions or indeed some basic insults.[5] But such features were not new and were neither cause nor result of political divisions, though the latter could harden them. People in the different kingdoms shared a common Christian culture, common concerns. Count Cobbo from the eastern kingdom sought out the western abbey St-Martin's of Tours as a goal of pilgrimage in the 840s and stopped off on his journey to chat to the monks of St-Germain in Paris about his encounters with Viking leaders who had raided their abbey. While the Rhine rose in the kingdom of Louis the German and flowed through his lands, it also went on to the lands of Lothar, to the profit of merchants in Louis's Mainz and Lothar's Cologne.[6] Florus of Lyons' poetic sadness over the break-up of communities along the Rhine, Loire and Danube may have been an over-reaction, indeed a purposeful one as he actually composed his poem in 842/3 as a tendentious scare-tactic for Lothar's imperial claims.[7] Kings had the skills and will to overcome the difficulties posed to community by, for example, language barriers, as at the famous gathering at Strasbourg in 842. Here Charles the Bald and Louis the German addressed each other's followers in the latter's vernacular language, ensuring that the collective elite remained a unity and incidentally reminding each other's warriors that they, the Carolingian kings, could speak their language. Kings could, however, tailor the use of their kingdom's vernacular to specific occasions, as at Koblenz in 860.[8]

In some ways, the borders that came into existence at Verdun made the separate parts of this world dangerously close; they were not separate enough. Major churches such as the archbishopric of Reims in the western kingdom had lands that stretched eastwards, over the borders of Charles's lands; churches in the middle kingdom such as the abbey of Prüm had lands outside of Lothar's realm.[9] Such landowners had to keep a close eye on kings and magnates in other kingdoms to ensure the security of these landed resources. Kings and magnates could thus put pressure on sensitive spots of institutions outside their own kingdoms. But wariness over the prospect of such painful long-distance squeezing of vital interests was even more deeply present among kings and magnates themselves. Magnates also retained land scattered across all three post-Verdun kingdoms, but rules for office-holding formulated in 806 and repeated in 817 and 831 and doubtless in 843 meant that magnates could only hold offices (*honores*) – more precious now than ever in this competitive world – in one kingdom. A count in the kingdom of Charles might still have some family lands in the kingdom of Louis the German but he could not be a count in Louis's kingdom while he was one in Charles's. Eventually, magnates would generally crystallize around one centre and the complex international connections of land and kin would unravel, resulting in a more regionally rooted aristocracy. But such a change was a long time coming and was not yet fully worked out even forty years later when the Carolingian realm entered its final crisis.[10]

Nor did contemporaries see such a change as inevitably on the horizon, not least because they, kings as well as magnates, did not imagine Verdun as definitive. For now, the high aristocrats continued to hold lands across the frontiers. The best known example is Eberhard duke of Friuli who held office in the realm of Lothar I but possessed land in all three post-Verdun kingdoms and successfully bequeathed it to his children decades after Verdun; other magnates in Italy also maintained their interests north of the Alps for decades after 843.[11] For three decades or so after Verdun, the existence of such connections produced a fluid world of easily crossed frontiers. Magnates driven from one kingdom could find welcome and support in another. In 861, Louis the German exiled duke Ernst and his kin, including a noble relative from the middle kingdom, from his eastern kingdom only to see them make a soft landing in the west where Charles the Bald showed then favour and where they had more kin connections.[12]

All this meant chronic instability. Kings could meddle in their brothers' kingdoms by pressing hard on sensitive aristocratic lands located in their own. Thus, after clashes between kings who had confronted aristocrats with an unpalatable choice of losing lands or offices, aristocrats demanded of kings, once they had grudgingly made peace with each other, that they would not hang on to *honores* and properties confiscated in the heat of conflict. Louis the German's invasion of Charles the Bald's kingdom in 858–9 was such an episode and when peace was restored in 860 Louis, Charles and Lothar II had to publicly soothe anxious aristocrats with elaborate pronouncements, in the vernacular and preserved in Latin, that their grip on lands and offices would now be secure.[13] Aristocrats were also active players here and could deploy similar tactics of menacing pressure. Count Gerard of Vienne in the middle kingdom was able to retaliate against the western king Charles the Bald's threats to his properties in the west by warning a worried archbishop of Reims (in the west) that he, Gerard, would lay hands on those properties of Reims subject to his control in the middle kingdom.[14]

This political landscape of real but fluid internal boundaries was itself bounded by frontiers. Rebellious aristocrats in west Francia begged Louis the German to help them against their king in 853 and 858; otherwise, they would be 'forced to seek help from foreigners and enemies of the faith ... since they could not obtain it from their orthodox and legitimate lords'.[15] The western rebels of 853 and 858 probably meant that they would bring in Viking allies rather than travel to them but some rebels, having backed the wrong horse in conflicts within the Carolingian family itself, did seek refuge across the frontier. In the 860s, Count Gundachar forsook his Carolingian lords for the court of the Moravian ruler Rastislav. A contemporary annalist saw him as a traitor to his 'fatherland' but was particularly outraged at his betrayal of King Louis the German and his sons, that is, the Carolingian royal line. The king marked the slaughtering of this wretched traitor by having all the bells of the royal town of Regensburg rung in proclamation of Carolingian triumph, a triumph also celebrated, more quietly but just as eloquently, by the annalist.[16]

Such threats to withdraw from the Carolingian landscape, to step over a geographical, cultural and political line highlighted what lay on this side of that line: the Christian realm of the Franks and their 'legitimate and orthodox lords'. In other words, the attractiveness of Moravian or Viking leaders was not so much in themselves as in their ability to help rebels put pressure on the Carolingian centre. The relationship with that centre was the one that counted. Having eloped with Judith, daughter of Charles the Bald, in 862 count Baldwin fled from the latter's rage to the court of

Lothar II and begged the pope to plead his case with Charles. The pope duly told the angry father that Baldwin was so desperate that he might enter into alliance with the Vikings. This was probably a way of saying that this was a last chance to negotiate: Baldwin was making a final offer and Charles could show Christian magnanimity in graciously saving Baldwin from association with the enemies of Christendom. In this sort of episode, the Vikings were a sign pointing back to the Frankish realm, not a real landscape on the other side of the frontier.[17]

Such a conceptual frontier simply underlined the dominance of the Carolingians within the Frankish realm. Baldwin's threat was made from the safety of Lothar II's kingdom; Charles complaints about 'our nephew Lothar' thus injuring 'us and our kin (*consanguinitas*)' illustrate the fact that one of the key features of interconnection in this world was that the rulers of these kingdoms were members of the same family.[18]

These rulers were aware of a common dynastic heritage and took care to cultivate this publicly as in, for example, their treatment of the abbey of Prüm. After the treaty of Verdun of 843, this ancestral abbey lay in Lothar's kingdom and he favoured it highly, showering it with gifts of costly books, extraordinarily precious relics and a crown which was hung above the altar. He proclaimed his 'particular love' for it as part of his dynastic consciousness.[19] Prüm's location outside his own kingdom did not stop Charles the Bald from looking on it with favour and requesting prayers for his kingdom from its monks and recalling his ancestor Pippin's eighth-century re-founding of Prüm. Charles's own son, Louis the Stammerer, confirmed Prüm's privileges in 878 after the abbot came to him with the record of these privileges as preserved in the charters of Louis's forebears Pippin, Charlemagne, Louis the Pious, Lothar I, Louis the German and Charles the Bald himself. With the failure of Lothar's line in 869, Prüm passed into the hands of the east Frankish kings and it is striking that Louis the German turned to Prüm for help in restoring the palace complex of Aachen, as well as confirming its privileges granted by his ancestors, including Pippin and Bertrada.[20] Aristocratic patrons of Prüm could not rely on the post-843 political tensions being dissolved in some soup of cosy Carolingian dynastic feelings, as shown by the manoeuvrings around count Heriric's 868 grant to the abbey. Nonetheless, the actions and gestures of all these rulers ensured that aristocrats knew that Prüm was always a special place for the royal dynasty no matter which kingdom its members ruled.[21]

The troubles of Louis the Pious's reign and the conflicts of 840–3 meant that the ruling dynasty had put its followers through a very tough time. We can hear bitter aristocratic resentment at kings' unfulfilled promises and unjustified accusations of treachery in surviving texts from the early 840s by Adalhard the seneschal and Nithard. Later, the scholar Haimo of Auxerre drew the attention of count Conrad to a passage in Quintus Curtius's history of Alexander the Great where a nobleman had to deny false accusations of conspiring against the king.[22] The twists and turns of royal quarrels bred aristocratic resentment and anxieties.

Kings could live with this. But they worried if such resentments drove aristocrats out of a Carolingian orbit. The uneasy peace established by the 843 treaty of Verdun made little difference to a long-running struggle on the lower Loire and sensitive Breton frontier in the far west of Charles the Bald's kingdom. Here count Lambert and Breton allies struck down supporters of Charles in 843 and 844. These venomous clashes had a momentum of their own that could push kings into the background. Lambert's enemies in the region included count Vivian, whose father had perished at the hands of Lambert's kin in 834.[23] Desire for vengeance and local dominance drove such figures. Similarly, those Neustrian aristocrats who defected from Charles the Bald in 858 stayed actively hostile to him even after Louis the German had retreated from the western kingdom.[24]

But, even in a frontier region, a figure such as Lambert was not really outside a Carolingian framework. Local resentments and rivalries fuelled these ferocious quarrels in the lower Loire but they turned on royal patronage. Lambert and his kin were scrabbling to keep a grip on *honores* as well as local status and it was royal manipulation of patronage that governed much of Lambert's activity here. Significantly, all three brother kings sent a message to Lambert in 844 warning him to obey Charles. They thus shut down his room to manoeuvre since none of them would now pose as an alternative patron to Charles. Obedience to a Carolingian was what they all wanted and they reached over a distance of hundreds of kilometres from their meeting at the palace of Thionville to sharply remind Lambert that he lived in a Carolingian world.[25] Lambert duly returned as a penitent sinner to the fold of loyalty in 846 and Charles graciously granted him office. This did not turn out to be the end of Lambert's discontents but the next time he turned against Charles, the king had him killed by 'a trick'.[26] Carolingian reach was long.

All three kings had to rebuild authority in the jittery post-Verdun world. Louis the German spent Christmas 843 in the palace of Frankfurt, a building that he had last seen in 840 when he fled from his father's warriors there. Now he displayed his own kingship in this majestic setting, ostentatiously wheeling out his aunt Theodrada ('daughter of our grandfather Charlemagne') to associate himself with past dynastic glories, and doubtless encouraging work on the palace church begun under his father but now the palace of another Louis. He also had to defang resentful supporters of Lothar now beached in his kingdom by the boundaries of Verdun. He encouraged the monks of Hersfeld to hold on to revenues that would otherwise have gone to the pro-Lothar archbishop of Mainz; he took care to remind the monks of previous acts of generosity by his royal grandfather and father while asking them to pray for him, his wife and offspring as well as for the realm. He also demonstrated his warrior prowess in campaigns to secure frontiers and consolidate his aristocracy behind him.[27]

Nor could the eldest brother and emperor Lothar I relax. His son Lothar II was to recall his father's worries that the diminished resources of a post-Verdun kingdom deprived him of the wealth needed to reward followers. Indeed the emperor's grants to such followers now included an explicit demand for loyalty from them, part of the complex ninth-century development of socially differentiated oaths. That Lothar I had to journey to Provence in 845 to subdue dissident magnates there shows his need to build authority in his post-843 realm.[28] Like his brother Louis, Lothar I took care to stage his royalty in the appropriate setting of a palace, residing after Verdun at Gondreville (where the nearby bishop of Toul would recall the building work done under Lothar's father) and Aachen where he reminded the western abbey of St-Denis and its abbot Louis his kinsman, of his royal lineage; St-Denis was keen to safeguard its properties in Lothar's lands.[29] Lothar also had his kingship represented on a smaller, more intimate but still luxurious medium: a majestic image of him, crowned and enthroned, wearing a bejewelled robe while gripping sceptre and sword, adorns the Psalter produced for him probably around the time of Verdun (Lothar Psalter, British Library Additional Ms 37768). A formal confession of sin in this book may reflect Lothar's own repentance over his actions against 'my brother… the son of my mother'. He and his spiritual advisers understood only too well that the recent empire-wide conflict had its root within the royal family.[30]

Perhaps Lothar's reference to the 'son of his mother' suggests that he did not feel quite so guilty about his half-brother Charles who faced the most severe problems in re-establishing royal authority. The youngest of the royal brothers, Charles had to deal with unruly magnates, Viking raids, and his own nephew Pippin II who had claims to Aquitaine. He responded in 843–4 with ruthlessness and skill, channelling properties from the conveniently vacant church of Reims to hungry followers, striking down the formidable Bernard of Septimania after taking care to have him found guilty of treason by a group of magnates in an army assembly, and unleashing his warriors against Pippin, though with limited success.[31] All this suggests that the young ruler had been encouraged by, or had not even needed, the advice of abbot Lupus who had written to him urging him to rule as a king and to remember that he could strike down magnates (*potentes*) because he had raised them up. Lupus may have deliberately taken a narrow view of the realities of king-aristocrat relations here but he also presented a wider vision of kingship's responsibilities, reminding Charles of the need to give alms and to glorify God. And kingship did indeed become ever more intensely conceived as a Christian office as the century wore on: only now, after Verdun, did ruler portraits appear in Bibles.[32]

But Charles and his advisers understood that neither ruthlessness nor holy splendour was sufficient for successful rule and so they worked to proclaim a collective identity for the west Frankish elite at a big assembly held at Coulaines soon after Verdun. Aristocrats agreed there to respect the king's authority while he promised not to deprive them of office without good cause. While aristocrats across the entire Frankish world needed such re-assurance after the storms of Louis the Pious's reign and the brothers' war, the western kingdom seems to have developed a particular collective ethos and practice. Whether this was because of the role of capitularies in recording and structuring debate at assemblies or is an optical illusion created for us by exceptional creation and survival of capitularies (thanks in part to archbishop Hincmar of Reims) from that kingdom remains debatable.[33]

Amidst all this, Charles sought to have his inborn royal claims to rule articulated, acquiring a poem celebrating his royal ancestry ('successor of kingly grandparents') and commissioning a history (from his kinsman Nithard) of his struggles in the brothers' wars. Both of these predate the Treaty of Verdun and show how important this sort of textual legitimation was even, or especially, in times of conflict. But they also reveal how ephemeral such exercises could be: the poem was produced in Metz which subsequently slipped out of Charles's hands and Nithard's text became a bitterly disillusioned view of Charles's rule.[34] Of course poets celebrated the ancestors of aristocrats as well as royals but only kings had ancestors named Charles and Pippin and only kings had 'an ancestral throne'.[35] And Charles used his own body to reproduce his dynastic status. Charles had married once peace was established and by the time of the great public gatherings at Verdun and Coulaines in 843 his wife was pregnant. A visibly pregnant queen would have signalled to Charles's rivals as well as to his followers that his line had a future. Confident in his own queen's fertility, Charles could afford to be generous to Lothar I's wife at Verdun, graciously permitting her to have lands that had been held by Carolingian queens decades before[36] Charles thus signalled his belonging to continuing dynastic history and the machinery of prayer for dynastic continuity cranked up into action as he now requested prayers for his offspring. Churchmen in his kingdom worked to show him that they saw him as worthy descendant of his line, in particular of his illustrious namesake Charlemagne.[37]

Keeping it in the family: Rule by brothers

After 843, despite Lothar's imperial status, the Carolingian world was no longer vertical but horizontal; there was no over-arching single ruler as there had been between 771 and 840. There were three kingdoms. But their rulers were not isolated from each other and their meetings reminded the political elite that it still lived under a Carolingian sky. The years 844–70 witnessed some fifty-five meetings of kings of separate kingdoms; at least one kings' meeting took place every year from 846–70. Churchmen from the different kingdoms also tended to meet despite the new boundaries.[38] Such meetings could be very grand affairs; the three kings at Savonnières in 862 were accompanied by around 200 aristocratic followers. This may have been an exceptionally high number; when the same kings had met at Koblenz in 860, we know of forty-five aristocratic followers, though there were doubtless others present. It is clear that kings did not meet alone and they would have mobilized advisers, warriors, hangers-on as well as humbler personnel to deal with accommodation and food, etc.[39] These were occasions for kings to display royal style to an important audience, hosting lavish feasts and welcomes, giving spectacular gifts, participating in solemnly joyful religious ceremonies and showing their masculine authority in hunting together as when Lothar I and Louis the German did so in 850, making aristocrats marvel at their closeness.[40] Many of the same aristocrats probably also had to endure the loud quarrel between these two kings in 854, though the fact that we know that the kings shouted at each other on this occasion tells us something about the public importance of royal deportment and its norms.[41]

Kings wanted aristocrats to follow what was discussed at these meetings. Announcements (*adnuntiationes*) made by kings feature in several of the texts (in Latin) that have come down to us and rulers worked to ensure that the attending aristocrats understood them. We know that in 860 Louis the German and Charles the Bald addressed them loudly and clearly in each other's vernacular, and this must have happened on other occasions. As for the Latin proceedings, they were to be read out to counsellors and then more widely distributed.[42] Charles the Bald arranged for distribution of the 860 Koblenz proceedings and while the eastern kingdom of Louis the German may not have had levels of administrative literacy to match the west, Louis's attempt to block the distribution of the proceedings of the 862 meeting at Savonnières shows that he fully understood the importance of circulation of texts.[43] While the manuscript transmission of these texts can sometimes be rather thin, these texts circulated.[44]

Aristocrats would have been aware of these meetings in advance; kings assumed that they heard rumours and reports of their planning.[45] It was trusted aristocrats who acted as envoys between kings to set up such meetings, swaggering confidently if their master was in the ascendant (Louis the German in 870), or dumb with frustration if their lord was in eclipse (Lothar II in 862).[46] They identified with their royal master's fortunes. They attended these meetings, advised the kings, heard their speeches, approved the final written summaries and sometimes took oaths on their masters' behalf as a handful of highly placed counts and bishops did in 870. They could also modify the kings' proclamations, as count Conrad did in 862.[47]

Aristocrats were active players in these meetings, and these meetings loomed large in aristocratic experience. Magnates and kings from different kingdoms came to know each other; Louis the German and Charles the Bald were confidently able to pick out trusted figures from their brother's entourage as observers of their alliance made when they met in 865.[48] Magnates knew a bigger world than their own kingdom. Louis the German, Charles the Bald and their followers attended eight meetings in the middle kingdom between 844 and 867, and they met twice on the borders of Louis's kingdom (849, 859).[49] These people regularly travelled to and met in other kingdoms; kingdoms were porous. But frontiers mattered. The separate kingdoms did not add up to a bland space of generalized Frankishness. The three meetings between Charles and his brother Louis the German in the middle kingdom between 865 and 867 were not encounters in some neutral space of generalized Frankishness, but a visible demonstration to the aristocracy of their designs on the kingdom of their divorce-shadowed nephew, Lothar II.[50]

The encounters of these kings and their followers were ad hoc gatherings to deal with the problems and tensions of a multi-kingdom world. And while much of the substance of these encounters was not political in a narrow sense, they were occasions for the staging of essentials of Carolingian political culture. A good illustration of this is the meeting of five kings in December 861, probably at Christmas, at the nuns' abbey of Remiremont in the Vosges in the kingdom of Lothar II. The kings met in response to the sabre-rattling of Charles the Bald who had been throwing his weight about in the kingdom of young Charles of Provence. The latter, with his brother Lothar II, his uncle Louis the German and two of Louis's sons, all met to respond to the menaces of the western ruler.[51] But their meeting was also, indeed essentially, a social act. These royal men were accompanied by royal women, including Louis the German's pious and well-connected wife Emma, Lothar's scandal-haunted wife/mistress Waldrada as well as Doda, former mistress to Lothar's father. Accusations of sexual immorality cluster round Waldrada and Doda in narrative sources and ecclesiastics' treatises and letters but here they were, celebrating a major Christian feast among the holy women of Remiremont and duly entered in the abbey's commemoration book. Doda's lowly social origins mattered much less than her closeness to the late emperor; she was part of the royal family for the festivities.[52] This was a real family gathering, displaying different generations of Carolingian royalty, from the senior Louis the German, in his mid-fifties; through his children, in their twenties, and his nephews, about twenty-five and fifteen; to a third generation represented by Hugh, young son (aged perhaps five or six) of Lothar II, and the only grandson of Lothar I. Also present were some fifty aristocrats, including five women, who served as audience for this kingly display, not a passive role as they constituted the community of which these royals were the leading part. The fact that we only know about this gathering from the commemoration book of the abbey highlights gaps in our narrative sources as well as reminding us that this gathering had a religious element as well as a political one. The kings and their entourage had probably gathered at the palace at Remiremont but their names in the abbey's book testify to their desire for the nuns' prayers and to their probable visit to the holy site of the abbey itself.[53]

Among the kings, there were two sons of Louis the German, Louis (the Younger) and Charles (the Fat). As part of his disciplining of his line, their father deliberately withheld the title of king from them in his lifetime but the community at Remiremont recognized and defined these sons' kingliness as immanent; they were titled as *rex*, king, in the list.[54] Remiremont served here as theatre and medium for the further constructing of Carolingian royalty to a level that went beyond what even a senior Carolingian such as Louis the German desired. Such audiences were all too enthusiastic participants in the continual making of Carolingian distinctiveness.

Some of the aristocrats present at Remiremont must have counselled Louis the German and Lothar II as they composed a letter to Pope Nicholas I. This letter complained about the recent menacing behaviour of Charles the Bald, a king who coveted others' kingdoms and who was among those who were deaf to appeals to feelings of brotherly love and kinship.[55] The Carolingians and magnates at Remiremont were very much aware of the shadow of the absent king, Charles the Bald, and thus understood that Carolingian family bonds spanned, defined and threatened the political landscape.

A language of familial relations permeated the post-Verdun meetings of kings. They could not help but use familial language in these meetings, referring to their relationship as brothers, nephews and uncles. At times, this might seem to be stating the obvious, as in the 847 Meersen meeting's reference to 'the three brothers and kings', but it was precisely through hearing such proclamations and attending upon kings visibly meeting 'in brotherly fashion' that the aristocracy learned the relationships among the royal families.[56] This was not new for the Franks; the multiple kingdoms of the Merovingians had witnessed the same phenomenon as we can see in, for example, Gregory of Tours' sixth-century *Histories* which frequently refers to such encounters in this type of familial language. Even the savage conflicts of the Merovingian family generated familial references that would remind hearers and readers of the kinship links among the royal dynasty as well as of its ubiquity, as in king Childebert's demand, through envoys, to his uncle king Guntram to hand over queen Fredegund 'who strangled my aunt, killed my father and uncle and put my cousins to the sword'. These killings occurred across northern Gaul.[57]

In evoking their familial relationships, Frankish kings taught the aristocracy that their royal relatives ruled its world. This teaching was more intense and covered a wider area in the Carolingian era. At Koblenz in 860 Louis the German referred not only to his brother Charles the Bald but also to 'my nephews Louis [II of Italy],

Lothar [II] and Charles [of Provence]'. We know that some forty-five high-ranking churchmen and laymen heard the kings' oaths and statements. These magnates held office in places such as Reims, Hildesheim, Auxerre and Bavaria and might never have encountered Louis II, based in distant Italy, or Charles, confined through illness to his kingdom of Provence. But, in pronouncing these exclusively royal names of his kingly nephews, Louis the German (who may have brought his young grandchildren with him) instructed the magnates gathered in the church of St Castor at Koblenz in the developing Carolingian political-familial geography after 843, which was now broader and deeper than rule by brothers.[58] As such, it pointed to a continuing Carolingian future and aristocrats would have grasped this. It is very likely that some of those in Coblenz in 860 had also been there in 842 during the last stages of the brothers' war and their memories of the making of Verdun would now be supplemented with the vision of new generation of Carolingian kings ruling kingdoms created from yet another familial division.[59]

In uttering this language of kinship, kings could find themselves unavoidably reminding the aristocracy of the Carolingian identity of marginalized figures. Louis the German told the magnates at Meersen in 847 that he and his brothers had sent envoys to their 'common nephew' Pippin (II) in Aquitaine, and the journeying of these envoys to him means that understanding of the web of royal kinship was lived and not just learned through words.[60]

Contemporaries knew that they now lived in a world of distinct kingdoms but also that all these kingdoms were ruled by members of one family. The writer Sedulius Scottus addressed poems to all three post-Verdun royal lines, displaying his knowledge that all three shared common descent from Charlemagne. This saved on inspiration as he could salute all kings interchangeably as descendants of Charlemagne, while the re-use of the name Charles in various kingdoms enabled him to praise different kings in more or less identical terms.[61] But this was not just a poet's economy. Sedulius's playing on the reiteration of the name of Charles across the generation confirms his knowledge not only of Carolingian ancestry but of name-giving as a means whereby the royal family itself transmitted and maintained its unique charisma. If Sedulius's poems were recited at court, then they too were part of the work of transmission. All three post-843 kings named a son Charles. Time passed, but Charles's kept re-appearing so that all could stay the same, whether in the west (Charles the Bald: 'a new Charles') or in the middle kingdom (Charles of Provence: 'a new Charles'). The passing of time brought deeper lustre to the line of Charlemagne: royal ancestors who gazed out of the past onto a constant Carolingian present embodied by the young Charles of Provence: 'His grandfather, his great-grandfather and his imperial father bring honour to him'.[62]

That Louis the German and Charles the Bald were brothers was a public fact and Sedulius's knowledge of this ('Behold the two brothers'), of their relative ages ('Louis, elder king') and of their parentage ('Louis [the Pious] alone deserved to raise such sons') would have been widely shared as would, one assumes, his hope for fraternal harmony. Thus, the bishops of Lothar II's middle kingdom hoped in a public letter that ambitious kings such as Charles the Bald would not flout the norms of kinship (*consanguinitas*), norms evoked by the rulers themselves as we have seen.[63]

To be sure, the political elite was not simply fixated on familial royalty and did not consider kingship to be merely a matter of royal blood. Thinkers such as Lupus of Ferrières in the 840s and Sedulius in the 860s reminded kings that true rulership consisted of exercising justice, caring for the common good, giving alms, etc.[64] Such concepts had real force in the political arena. When western aristocrats rebelled against Charles the Bald in 858, they did not simply turn to his brother Louis the German because he had a family claim to the west. The rebels and Louis justified the case for invasion by denouncing Charles as a capricious tyrant who flouted the norms of rulership while claiming that Louis's godly rule would heal the battered Christian community. The oaths taken in 843 to preserve each brother's kingdom were thus conveniently trumped by higher values.[65] For their part, the western bishops who stayed loyal to Charles in 858 grounded their king's rule, not in his Carolingian descent, but in the fact that they had anointed him as king and they forcefully reminded Louis of Old Testament teaching on the inviolability of the Lord's anointed. After surmounting this crisis, Charles himself publicly proclaimed the special status that his anointing at the hands of the bishops had given him and acknowledged that they alone thus had a right to judge him.[66]

Such rituals, texts, assemblies and exhortations were part of that vast ninth-century effort to build kingship as a deeply Christianized office inaugurated in public gatherings where the acclamations of the spiritual and secular elite were heard. Bishops played a key role here in performing the blessings that inaugurated kings (and queens) to their office, and in then relentlessly admonishing kings to fulfil the duties of that office. All this was not confined to the kingdom of Charles the Bald, and the vulnerability of Lothar II's rule to accusations of unkingly conduct in his divorce case shows some of the impact of such concepts.[67] But we should let neither the mystique of anointing (and east Frankish kings do not seem to have been anointed) nor the crowds of the political community at royal inaugurations obscure the sight of the singularity of the king's figure. He alone was the son of a royal father. In the same text in which he recalled his anointing, Charles stressed that Frankish kingship was hereditary and that he had received his kingdom from his father according to the divine will. After all, his anointing took place in 848, some years after he had become king. Carolingian royalty was socially constructed in that the political elite had to recognize a king, but only Carolingians could be so recognized and their status was inborn, in social terms, and thus an integral and necessary part of their royalty along with the religious aura.[68] Even as the western bishops in 858 articulated the vision of kingship as an office for the maintaining of justice and order under God, they bumped into the centrality of the Carolingian family. Even as they rebuked Louis the German for his invasion, they found themselves inevitably referring to his ancestors and kinsmen as rulers. They pointedly reminded him that he was brother to Charles, who had received his kingdom from his father (*paterna donation*) and that Louis and his followers had sworn to abide by this at Verdun, thus echoing Louis' own unease over his invasion as breach of family relations.[69]

Kings tended to paint these family relationships in glowing colours, perhaps to reassure their aristocrats that conflict was unlikely, as in Charles the Bald's references to his 'most dear brother' at St-Quentin in 857 and to his 'most dear nephew' (Lothar II) at

Koblenz in 860 as part of the peacemaking process between them.[70] At their meetings, kings warned their followers that royal family quarrels disturbed the Christian and political order while re-assuring them that royal family harmony betokened harmony in the realm.[71] And such harmony and unity among the family of kings were a natural norm; rulers assured their followers that their relations with their brothers were good 'as they ought to be among brothers', or that they wished to be to each other 'as brothers ought by right to be to each other, and as we ought to be to our nephew, and he with us, and he with his brothers, our nephews … and we as uncles to our nephews and our nephews to their uncles as we and they ought to be'.[72]

Rulers understood such biological ties to be cultural ones and could thus intensify them in order to deepen relationships between kingdoms understood in terms of family structures. Despite his own disappointing experience of Lothar's qualities as a godfather, Charles the Bald chose him as godfather for his daughter in a splendid ceremony in 853. At a big assembly in 862 attended by his uncles, Lothar II gushingly proclaimed his indebtedness to the kindness of his uncle Louis the German who had effectively adopted him as a son; Lothar thus admitted his own junior status while affirming the intensified familial links amongst the dynasty as well as reminding everyone present of his closeness to his formidable uncle-father.[73] Sometimes, these close bonds could take on a sinister aspect as when royal entourages picked up rumours in 848 that Lothar I was pressuring Louis the German to ally with him as a more authentic brother than their half-brother Charles.[74]

The Verdun kingdoms emerged out of a time of crisis that was in large part triggered by the quarrels within the ruling dynasty itself. And yet contemporaries, buffeted by such dynastic storms, saw that dynasty's rule as part of the natural order of their world. The shell-shocked prelates who gathered at Yütz in 844 in the aftermath of the brothers' war warned the kings, with chilling Old Testament parallels, that, unless they restored the tattered fabric of the church as their father and grandfather had done, a dynastic nightmare might unfold. They must beware lest the kingdom acquired so effortlessly by their fathers and left to them in heredity be taken away from them by Christ. The prospect that the realm of the Franks might no longer be ruled by 'our family' was a Carolingian's nightmare, and contemporaries knew this, indeed they articulated it, as in the pessimistic *Vision of Charlemagne* composed a quarter of a century after Yütz. They could understand such dynastic anxiety because they shared it. The post-843 kingdoms ensured that the ruling family was the structure for the whole Frankish realm.[75]

Rule by fathers

Kings (and aristocrats) may not have seen Verdun as a final settlement but were determined to keep their post-Verdun kingdoms in their own line and to make sure that people knew this. The kings had sworn to respect the deals made in 843, probably as part of the public ceremonies at Verdun itself; they had sent a copy of their oath to the pope in Rome, just as Charlemagne had done with his *Division* of 806.[76] They came to understand that settlement as creating kingdoms, not one kingdom, and wanted these kingdoms to descend to their own sons. The horizontal bonds of kingly brotherhood, of royal uncles and nephews, etc., co-existed with vertical relations of fathers and sons. This co-existence was not always harmonious.

All three brothers publicly agreed at a meeting in Meersen in 847 that 'after them, the kings' sons were to hold on to the legitimate inheritance of their kingdom according to the shares agreed on in the present era' and this was repeated, with varying degrees of detail, by all three in 851, by Lothar I and Charles in 854, and by Charles, Louis the German and Lothar II in 860.[77] Poems by Sedulius on the royals of the middle kingdom celebrated queen Ermingard's fertility, hailed the birth of a son to her and Lothar I and prayed for Lothar II to be 'a grandfather and great-grandfather of kings'. This expressed a commitment by its followers to the continuation of Lothar's line and its kingdom (even if that kingdom was divided by inheritance).[78]

The explicit concern at Meersen in 847 that sons should succeed is striking in light of the extreme youth of several of these boys; Charles the Bald's sons were babies in 847. These arrangements did not repeat the micro-managing of Louis the Pious's failed 817 experiment in succession. This represents a deepening of traditional dynastic identity: all sons should inherit, though this turned out not to be so simple, as we shall see. The post-843 kings developed this urgent sense of their sons' rights and expectations because they were worried about their own brothers' expectations. Proclaiming fraternity helped make the political world Carolingian but that meant that kings had to look nervously over their shoulders at their 'most dear brothers'. Carolingians had to monitor the dangerously potent charisma of their own family. It was no accident that Charles the Bald wanted to have the rights of sons proclaimed at gatherings in 854 in 860, in response to the menace of Louis the German's aggression, and Charles instructed envoys in his kingdom to make sure that people knew this.[79] But Charles was prepared to overlook the rights of another king's sons, as when he pounced on the eastern kingdom after the death of his brother Louis the German in 876. The latter's son sent envoys to tell Charles to back off and not to invade the 'kingdom left to us by our father by hereditary right ... and violate the laws of kinship'.[80]

There was thus rather too much family feeling in the post-843 kingdoms. Kings had to work to limit and control their brothers' and uncles' over-generous expectations and claims if they wanted their sons to succeed them. And they did want this. Older scholarship has sometimes tended to formalize the language of royal brotherhood so widely used by kings after Verdun into a system of rule by brothers that downgraded the role of sons. But kings turned to their brothers, in what looks like the triumph of hope over experience, in order to secure a future for their sons. When Louis the German and Charles the Bald met in 'brotherly love' in 849 and, overcome by this, 'each commended his realm, wife and children to the other, should he outlive him', each wanted his children, not his brother, to succeed him.[81] True brotherly love should be unselfish. They made sure that their watching aristocrats got the message by staging a public event in which each king ceremoniously handed over a staff (*baculum*: a sceptre? a staff of office?) to each other. Symbol and ceremony worked to demonstrate meaning and create memory for the audience, which may well have included some of the office-holders who later travelled to Charles's kingdom on follow-up missions.[82]

One suspects that the queens and children were present, to advertise the point that each line of future kings should be the focus of present aristocratic loyalty. Sons trumped brothers. When Lothar II and Charles of Provence, sons of Lothar I, met in 858, this point still held true. Pressing his thirteen-year-old brother hard, whose illness may have been worsening, Lothar got Charles to agree that 'if he were to die ... Lothar would succeed him by hereditary right'. But in invoking 'hereditary right', Lothar also had to recognize explicitly that this deal would be scuppered if Charles were to marry and have sons.[83]

The death of Lothar II himself in 869 activated his brother Louis II's hopes to inherit the middle kingdom. Louis may have been confined to Italy but his claims were broadcast north of the Alps. Letters streamed north from Pope Hadrian II, sternly urging Charles the Bald, his churchmen and his magnates as well as Louis the German not to lay hands on the middle kingdom since divine and human laws insisted that it fall to Louis II, son of Lothar I. He also made this point in a letter to the now kingless magnates of the middle kingdom, hoping that they would wait for Carolingian inheritance to do its work. The succession of royal son to royal father was thus woven into the fabric of the world order, as the pope's biblical citations showed. In addressing not just Charles the Bald, but also the political elite of his kingdom, the pope knew that this would resonate with his audiences, particularly as it chimed with Charles's own promise of 843 to respect the boundaries of each kingdom agreed at Verdun.[84] These letters were public, delivered and doubtless glossed by a team of envoys, including Louis II's followers, and their arrival was a newsworthy event recorded in contemporary annals which echoed the claims of 'hereditary right'.[85]

But Louis's uncles could play an ace unavailable to him in 869–70: they were on the spot. Charles the Bald jumped on to the middle kingdom, installing himself as ruler in an elaborate ceremony at Metz where he outflanked any claims of Louis II. When archbishop Hincmar reminded the prelates and magnates gathered in Metz cathedral that Charles was the son of Louis the Pious and descendant of St Arnulf of Metz (whose tomb was in the neighbourhood) he was reaching over Louis II's head into a more distant Carolingian past (artificially extended to include the Merovingians), and reminding everyone, king and magnates alike of the deep past of the dynasty.[86] The beautiful surviving fragments of the sacramentary given to Metz at this time by Charles may also depict the king alongside St Arnulf. (Paris BN Ms Latin1141).[87] The depth and breadth of the Carolingian past provided a landing place of dynastic legitimacy onto which a ruler such as Charles could descend. Ancestral crowns thus awaited Carolingians in kingdoms other than their own. Ceremonies, texts and exquisite liturgical objects made Metz into a west Frankish site. Enter Charles; exit Louis II. But warriors as well as ceremonies counted: enter Charles's militarily powerful brother Louis the German in 870; exit Charles. Both these senior brothers needed the resources of the middle kingdom, which they duly gained in dividing it between themselves in 870; the pope's pleading for Louis II could gain no traction.[88]

In situations like this, aristocrats were not passive. There is no reason to disbelieve the east Frankish source that says that many of Lothar II's magnates actively wanted Louis the German as their lord in preference to Charles, and this was to be a stumbling block for Charles.[89] Aristocrats could choose and they could reject. Kings could parachute in but could not be sure of their welcome. But aristocrats could only choose a Carolingian. And they could not always get the one that they wanted. Count Gerard of Vienne, pillar of support for the line of Lothar I, found Charles an ungracious lord when that line evaporated north of the Alps in 869. The bishop of Metz, Adventius, was sufficiently keen on Charles to host his coronation there in 869 but could not prevent himself from ending up in Louis the German's half of the divided kingdom.[90]

Kingdoms after 843: The middle kingdom

Within the three post-Verdun kingdoms, all the rulers had sons by 846, even if some of them were very young. Their existence promised a future for each kingdom. But sons could not take succession for granted. The will of the father, fraternal rivalry and the attitude of the aristocracy all affected a son's prospects. Fathers could forcefully remind sons of this and thus un-nerve them and their aristocratic backers. In 865, in one of his many episodes of disappointment with his son Louis the Stammerer, Charles the Bald deliberately kept his son's status ambiguous: he 'neither restored nor withheld his [Louis'] royal title'. Louis the German in 863 was so furious with his son Karlmann that he declared 'before a great mass of people' that the latter, 'as long as he [Louis] lived and ruled, would never hold public office without his consent'.[91] Furthermore, ninth-century Carolingians shrank the pool of heirs, compared to Merovingian times, by on the whole sticking to Louis the Pious's 817 wish to exclude illegitimate sons, though not all such sons, or aristocrats, saw such a ruling as definitive.[92]

These kings certainly did have a narrower band of resources with which to equip sons for kingship. The reduced kingdoms that emerged from the empire provided fewer resources for kings to reward followers, as they themselves lamented. Their kingdoms' confined boundaries and the problem of finding coherent sub-kingdoms within them also made it difficult to establish sons in their own territories. And sons had to have kingdoms.[93] Such problems fed in to the usual tensions generated by frustrated ambitions of royal sons, and all this was further exacerbated by the ambitions and fears of competitive magnates whose possession of lands across the divided world gave them leverage over kings while also making them vulnerable to kingly pressures. All three post-Verdun fathers sought to exert control over their sons. But royal sons knew their worth. Karlmann assumed a pose of cheerful innocence in his encounter with his father in 863; after a grim interview with his angry father Charles the Bald, young Charles of Aquitaine left 'like a man subdued, but despite his humble words, his spirit was still unbowed.'[94]

In Lothar I's middle kingdom, it is true that his oldest son, Louis II of Italy, was much more prominent than his brothers: crowned king of Italy aged fifteen in 839/40, made co-emperor in 850, Louis energetically busied himself in Italy while also regularly appearing with his father north of the Alps, thus reminding aristocrats and his brothers alike of his importance. Neither of Louis's brothers was promoted with him in 839/40 or 850; the spotlight fell on him alone.[95] But the absence of these brothers from the narrative sources need not mean that they were actually invisible. As we have seen in an earlier chapter, young Lothar (II) rode with warriors at the tender age of five in the brothers' war of 840–3. As king's sons with royal names, young Lothar and his brother Charles would have been carefully supervised and taught by a series of tutors and guardians, and thus entered into aristocratic calculations and networks at an early age.[96]

Bishop Adventius of Metz in the middle kingdom gives a vivid picture of the intensely social world of royal youth in an account of Lothar (II)'s marriage under his father's rule. This is a tendentious account as Lothar II's famous marital troubles mean that we cannot be sure that this marriage (to Waldrada) actually took place at the time indicated (early 850s) but it rings true culturally. The wedding was a grand public affair, attended by bishops and magnates such as Liutfrid, powerful uncle of young Lothar. Lothar's royal father chose and approved the noble bride and ostentatiously granted a substantial marriage gift to his son for his wife. Adventius emphasizes the active role of the father and the passive role of the son who has not yet attained maturity but nevertheless appears as an intensely social figure, son of the emperor, nephew of Liutfrid, cynosure of the bishops' eyes, ward of tutors and governors, in short, a 'future heir to his father'.[97] Thus while neither Lothar II nor his younger brother Charles had a crown like their older brother Louis II, their status at court inescapably meant that magnates would invest in them and that their father could not be a free agent in deciding their fate. In a public encounter with his brother Charles the Bald in February 854, Lothar I together with Charles loudly proclaimed their determination to transmit their kingdoms to their sons.[98] Attentive aristocrats would understand this to mean that Louis II was not the sole heir and Lothar I's subsequent granting of Frisia to Lothar (II) in early 855 was a demonstration of his son's kingly status, not a consolation prize to a second-ranker.[99]

On an ascetic deathbed in the intensely Carolingian monastery of Prüm, Lothar I abandoned the world and gave their own kingdoms to his younger sons Lothar II and Charles of Provence who were there, doubtless with their own aristocratic followings. These new kings must have worked to broadcast this. The news of Lothar I's abdication was known within a week or two in places as distant as Rome from where Pope Benedict III sent messages addressing Lothar's two older sons as ruling and as sons and grandsons of Lothar and Louis the Pious. Significantly, he assumed that Lothar II was ruling immediately on his father's abdication without needing to wait for his crowning.[100]

Equally significant, however, is the fact that Lothar II needed to be whisked away by supportive magnates to the protective patronage of his uncle Louis the German in whose kingdom he could safely be proclaimed king at Frankfurt, where he was probably anointed.[101] The magnates who helped organize this event in September–October 855 were not so much exercising a 'constitutional' right to make a king as helping to construct the kingship bequeathed by their late lord Lothar I. As his son, Lothar II was the heir to a throne, but he needed backers to ensure that the throne materialized. These extra efforts to secure Lothar II's inheritance were a response to some all too intense family feeling on the part of other Carolingian rulers. News of Lothar I's illness in 855 had brought his brothers Charles the Bald and Louis the German closer, that is, with an eye to picking on a kingdom soon to be without a ruler. Getting uncle Louis the German onside at Frankfurt enabled Lothar II and his magnates to restrain uncle Charles as well as Lothar's own brother Louis II who was loudly defining Italy as his grandfatherly inheritance and thus claiming Francia as an inheritance from his father.[102]

The problem for youthful heirs such as Lothar II and their aristocratic supporters in the mid-ninth century was that there were too many Carolingians. There were thus too many credible competing claims. Turning his uncle Louis the German into his protector was expensive; Lothar II had to permit his uncle increasing influence in Alsace after 855.[103] Lothar, however, was able to profit from his relationship with uncle Louis the German, who seems to have stood as adoptive father to him, deploying affective familial language to remind kings and aristocrats of this at Savonnières in 862. Lothar could nestle under his mighty uncle's shadow.[104] If family ties could help Lothar II, they did not help his younger brother Charles of Provence. He had to rely on his own aristocrats to defy his older royal brothers, who wanted his lands, and to insist on a portion of the realm for him. Although their father had granted the ten-year-old Charles a kingdom in 855, Lothar II and the oldest brother Louis II tried to snuff out his claims when all three brothers met in 856 to settle their inheritance. But neither Charles's youth nor his poor health discouraged magnates of Provence from supporting him and forcing his brothers to back down. These aristocrats were a group, led by the magnate Gerard of Vienne, who wanted their own king as patron and protector of their interests. They were, however, under the spell of their own Carolingian line (that of Lothar I) and were working to ensure that Charles was now getting what his father had wanted. Even observers outside the middle kingdom knew that.[105] If it was hard for royal sons to get everything they wanted, it was almost impossible to deny a legitimate royal son any claim at all, not least because Carolingians were not the sole guardians of Carolingian claims.

One royal son, however, was to lose out on a large scale: Hugh, son of Lothar II. The dramatic twists and turns of Lothar's attempt to divorce his queen Theutberga and formally marry this boy's mother Waldrada need not concern us here.[106] Born in the late 850s, Hugh was the son of Waldrada (Lothar's literally bewitching concubine, according to Hincmar of Reims; Lothar's beloved wife, according to Lothar himself).[107] Waldrada's questionable position may have cast a shadow over the boy's status, and Hugh was not a kingly name; a contemporary east Frankish prince used it for his son by a concubine.[108] But Lothar II took care to assert his son's special status: the nuns of Remiremont in 861 were to pray for him (perhaps he was present at the royal gathering there); he entrusted his upbringing to a prominent aristocrat, Wicbert, thus ensuring a network of support for him; he granted him Alsace in 867, possibly as public symbol and training ground for future rule of the kingdom.[109]

Alsace, however, lay under the shadow of Louis the German, to whom Lothar commended Hugh in 867; could he really expect Louis the German to advance the claims of a great-nephew? If Hugh's status is not clear-cut to us, that is partly because we have no contemporary regnal chronicle for the middle kingdom as we do for the west and east and we thus lack detail and perspective. But perhaps Hugh's status was not clear-cut to contemporaries. Eastern and western sources make no mention of him claiming a right to inherit when his father died in 869, though this may be a deliberate cover-up as there are hints of aristocratic resistance in Alsace to Charles the Bald's incursion that year that suggest support for Hugh.¹¹⁰ Perhaps Lothar II, younger than his uncles, thought that he would have plenty of time to secure his son's future. But a summer journey to Italy to advance his divorce case exposed him and his followers to a fatal fever and this suddenly decapitated the middle kingdom's elite. Unsurprisingly, Hugh's voice went unheard in 869, but nor is it surprising that he surfaced ten years later, still able to attract followers in a bid to claim something of his inheritance. Hugh's eventual killing of his old foster-father Wicbert shows how his band of followers disintegrated under pressure; but the fact that Hugh's kingly relatives took care to have him blinded in a spectacular performance at Frankfurt palace in 885, when Carolingian blood had become scarce, shows that he was still potent sixteen years after the death of his father and the extinction of his kingdom. He ended his days in the great Carolingian abbey of Prüm as a broken but living museum piece, demonstrating the limits and potential of a particular kind of king's son.¹¹¹

Kingdoms after 843: The eastern kingdom

A ninth-century story of Louis the German's grip being so strong that he could bend iron swords with bare hands suggests something of the fierce control he exerted over his own line. Unlike Charles the Bald or Lothar I, he gave none of his sons a royal title in his lifetime, and he accompanied his allocating them their future kingdoms some time between 865 and 867 with stern proclamations of his continuing overall control.¹¹² Brigitte Kasten has charted the clear limits to the sons' powers; they could not issue charters; their father publicly contrasted their limited authority with his 'paternal rights' and he, not they, exploited the estates of the fisc.¹¹³

She has also argued that Louis wanted to restrict the main succession to one favoured son, the eldest. His 854 backing of his middle son, Louis the Younger, as a candidate for kingship in Charles the Bald's Aquitaine was thus not so much the expression of some generalized Carolingian sense of family entitlement (though it was that) as a thrifty attempt to find something for a son who would otherwise find only slim pickings in east Francia.¹¹⁴ Louis, however, did not necessarily see Aquitaine in such narrowly instrumental terms; his court's perspective on the whole Frankish world was a broad one, and Louis spent lavishly on the invasion of 854. There was nothing thrifty about this.¹¹⁵ And Professor Kasten herself has shown not only that Louis's arrangements for the succession were not rigid but that his sons' royal status was one of the most prominent features of the eastern kingdom. Louis wanted to limit their rights, but not their status. That was embedded in political culture and Louis himself actively promoted it, as did his sons, who were no passive objects. Louis's two younger sons resented and actively resisted any prospect of their older brother's advancement at their expense, and easily mobilized aristocratic supporters, though the latter were driven as much by their own grudges and ambitions as by indignation at the plight of the younger sons.¹¹⁶ Their own father had actively advanced them and given them chances to forge links with aristocrats, and, unlike Charles the Bald, he did not turn any of them into clerics.¹¹⁷

Louis took care to instruct the aristocracy in the special status of his sons. Indeed, he exhibited striking family feeling, or political calculation, in his offering shelter to damaged members of the Carolingian kin such as his great-nephew the exiled Charles of Aquitaine, and his nephew the paternally blinded Carloman.[118] Like all kings, Louis had to tread carefully with his own aristocrats, who were more than a supporting cast. Louis proclaimed that generosity to his faithful men was a mark of his kingship and if the number of his surviving gifts to lay recipients is fairly low, they reveal something of the public splendour of such grant-making in their account of royal response to confident petitions in great assemblies, as well as the interplay of local and regnal interests in the web of royal patronage.[119] Louis could not always punish the defiance of really great magnates with the severity that he may have desired.[120] His kingdom was not a blank canvas; if he advanced a son at the expense of an aristocrat with good claims, this triggered revolt and disquiet.[121]

That kingdom was, however, one in which the special status of Carolingian sons was on display. Louis's sons were young, probably twelve or in their teens, when they started to go on military campaigns.[122] They accompanied him to assemblies and had their own estates around the palace of Frankfurt with their own separate quarters and household there.[123] They may not have issued diplomas but they alone were special enough to subscribe the diplomas of their father as all three of them did at Bodman, majestically sited on the shores of Lake Constance in 857, participating in a property transaction that touched on the interests of a clutch of aristocratic landowners. Not only Louis's sons were special; his daughter Ermingard swelled the ranks of the royal family on its appearance at this seldom-visited site, deepening the royal presence in this fiscally important landscape.[124] Royal titles and full royal authority may have eluded the sons but they cut regal figures in the territories allocated to them, spreading Carolingian kingship across landscapes, leading armies and forming important relations with aristocrats, including marriage into powerful families in these territories. Karlmann saw his followers in Carinthia as 'his own men'; young Charles the Fat may have been only a count in Alemannia but his status transcended this office.[125]

Aristocrats knew to treat these royal sons carefully even when they rebelled against their father the king; 'fear for (or "of") his son' held Louis the German's supporters back from striking at his rebellious son Louis (the Younger) in 866. Louis the German himself took care to confine the rebellious Karlmann only in 'free custody' at his court, a custody that was so loose that Karlmann was able to escape his father's clutches while out hunting in 864, an episode that suggests that no one dared stop him.[126] Such episodes illuminate the social experience of the aura of these sons. Their special status was also articulated through more formal mechanisms such as oaths being taken to them as well as to their father. A treacherous aristocrat's agonized recognition of the wrath of the saints on whose relics he had sworn these oaths did not save him from death.[127]

Louis the German himself, his wife Emma and his brother Charles the Bald all actively muddied the waters of royal father-son relationships in the eastern kingdom in 870–1, possibly pushing the claims of the oldest son Karlmann at the expense of his brothers. This was not just shadow-boxing. Louis blinded a Saxon follower of his restive sons to intimidate them in 871, only to harden their hostility.[128] It is not surprising that his younger sons, mature men by the 870s, resented the senior generation's manoeuvring and Louis the Younger, aged thirty-eight, and Charles the Fat, aged thirty-four, duly plotted against their father in 873. Charles the Fat seems to have cracked under all this familial and political pressure, but his panicky attempt to display his return to loyalty by collapsing in surrender to him at Frankfurt in January 873 only gave his father the chance to humiliate him and scare his co-conspirator brother into submission. Loyalist churchmen classified Charles's misfortunes as the Devil's triumph and their healing rituals in Frankfurt as well as accounts of the drama written in Reims, Mainz, Cologne and Saxony articulated and transmitted a message of a disobedient royal son.[129] These artful reports show that Charles's collapse in the palace of Frankfurt was widely spread as news of paternal triumph. But the father could not let his triumph obliterate his sons; after Easter, by the end of April the two shaken plotters were back in royal action, publicly judging cases at a great assembly under their father's supervision.[130]

At the political centre of the eastern kingdom was the royal family. Louis' sons did not need the formal title of king; being sons was enough. The pope's writing to Louis sons in 867, urging them to honour their father, testifies to how widespread this understanding was.[131] They represented an inescapably Carolingian future. Louis himself had to recognize this. Political society wanted this too as his sons stood for a secure future in which property holders could be guaranteed security across royal generations.[132]

Ending a line: Aquitaine

In creating only three kingdoms, the 843 treaty of Verdun loftily overlooked the claims of Pippin II of Aquitaine. That south-western region was to form part of Charles the Bald's western kingdom and not to be a separate kingdom for Pippin II, son of Pippin I of Aquitaine and grandson of Louis the Pious. Pippin II fought hard for his claims, but eventually failed. We should not assume that that failure was inevitable, but what interests us here is the nature of that failure: how could a system of Carolingian legitimacy snuff out the claims of a legitimate son of a legitimate Carolingian king? Individual failure illuminates structures; the slow-motion destruction of Pippin II reveals how hard it was to break a royal Carolingian identity and thus casts light on the political discourse and practice that constructed and maintained such identity. Effortful creativity was required to eradicate Pippin's identity.

A striking feature of the kingship of Pippin II is its ending. Looking back from the mid-tenth century a genealogist at Compiègne, that palace of Carolingian memory, saw the line of Pippin I as a line that was stopped in its tracks: 'Pippin [I], king of Aquitaine ..., begot Pippin [II] whom his uncle Charles [the Bald] tonsured in the monastery of St-Medard, and so that line came to an end.'[133] Writing his Chronicle in Trier around 908, abbot Regino also knew about the fate of this line in distant Aquitaine, recording details of Pippin's enforced tonsure and monastic confinement as well as stories of his father Pippin I. Addicted to the pleasures of alcohol, the latter had descended into madness. This was a dreadful failure of masculine royal self-control.[134] Regino's suggestion that Pippin II had an unkingly father may be an echo of the black propaganda spread by Louis the Pious about the vices of his own son and grandson in his effort to discredit that line.[135]

All this makes Pippin II look more marginal and doomed than he actually was. He certainly did face formidable obstacles after the death of his royal father in December 838. First, he could not count on automatic support from Aquitaine, partly because Aquitaine itself was not a coherent polity. Even if pro-Louis the Pious sources exaggerate levels of support for the old emperor, it is clear that the aristocrats of Aquitaine did not simply line up behind 'their' line of kings. Many of the key figures in Aquitaine were Franks with connections and interests that stretched far beyond that kingdom, and these interests stretched not just east back into Francia, but south into the Spanish march. Likewise, off-stage actors in the heart of Francia cast long shadows into Aquitaine; Jane Martindale rightly observes that Lothar I's fluctuating attitude towards Pippin II was decisive in ultimately damaging his chances. Aquitaine's remoteness from the heartlands of Carolingian rule gave some of its aristocracy a sense of distance that was simultaneously enjoyed as freedom and resented as neglect.[136] But Aquitaine was not a closed land with a rooted aristocracy pursuing regional interests. Magnates here looked to the centre of the Carolingian world and that was the dynasty itself. Thus, bishop Ebroin of Poitiers travelled all the way to Francia in 839 to beg Louis the Pious to intervene in Aquitaine, just as members of Ebroin's kin in Aquitaine were to appeal to the geographically distant Louis the German to come there in the 850s.[137]

But in the winter of 838-9 if the splits within aristocratic-Carolingian relations meant that not all of Pippin I's supporters swung behind his son Pippin, this also meant that some aristocrats were willing to take a chance on him. Some aristocrats, doubtless fearing that Louis's pushing of his favourite Charles into Aquitaine might squeeze them out of the charmed circle of royal patronage, acted quickly and proclaimed Pippin II as king.[138] Such men did not need to wait for a fickle senior Carolingian to tell them which member of the family was to be king.

Such support came to Pippin because of his identity as a (potential) king of Carolingian descent. That support enabled Pippin to activate that idenitity. His chancery dated the start of his reign from December 838, that is, immediately after his father's death.[139] Pippin and his entourage clearly understood that his kingship depended on his descent from his father and that they could switch it on themselves without Louis the Pious. As his grandfather prepared to extinguish that kingship, Pippin went to the monastery of Figeac in the south. This had been recently established by his father who had requested the monks to pray for him, his wife and his offspring (*proles*), firmly pointing to the succession of his family.[140] Now that offspring, the fifteen-year-old Pippin II, stood there as king, embodying legitimate filial succession and piety, deftly adapting a diploma drawn up for his father to grant privileges to the holy site at Solignac to insert himself in the dynastic series. This diploma of 838/9 recalls his predecessors while publicly proclaiming his rule's distinctiveness from his father's: the diploma was dated by the reign of the young king himself with no reference to the rule of Louis the Pious, a stark contrast to the dating clauses of Pippin I.[141]

No wonder that Louis the Pious himself had to descend on Aquitaine in force to advertise and push through his claim to define the succession. Again we see how difficult it was for even a senior Carolingian to limit the charisma of the dynasty. Louis travelled with his son Charles the Bald, who was the same age as his cousin Pippin, and demanded oaths to himself and his son but his military superiority faded away in this southern landscape. When yet another family quarrel called Louis away from Aquitaine early in 840, he left Charles and his mother Judith behind in Poitiers with warriors. These warriors and their leaders had travelled from centres outside Aquitaine such as Autun and Ferrières and thus now came to know that they were connected to this region. Such men learned the Carolingian nature of their world in trudging through it.[142] Louis knew that oaths were not enough; he had to make his version of the Carolingian line actively and physically present in Aquitaine and that is why Judith stayed with Charles: this mother and son had to trump Pippin II and his dangerously legitimate late royal father. This was an unwilling public tribute to Pippin's claims.

Louis the Pious's death in 840 meant that there was no longer a single ruler to try and enforce rule and claims and the political landscape of Aquitaine became even more fragmented. The aristocracy suffered splits and tensions, reflecting and exacerbating those within the royal kin. Even a magnate as savvy as Bernard of Septimania could not pick the potential winner, oscillating between Pippin II and Charles. His hesitations simply triggered a rising spiral of royal impatience, with Charles the Bald frightening him in 841 by slaughtering his followers and finally killing Bernard himself in Aquitaine in 844. It was not possible for magnates to stay out of these royal rivalries.[143] Pippin's status as son of his father could not in itself convince aristocrats that he was bound to succeed. Even magnates who had married in to Pippin I's family had turned to Louis the Pious, not Pippin II, on Pippin I's death in 838, paralleling the situation in Italy in 817 when Bernard's revolt against Louis the Pious split the aristocracy that had clustered round Bernard's father.[144]

Magnates' anxiety and uncertainty over the outcome could in fact work in Pippin's favour. Bernard of Septimania hedged his bets but did make some form of agreement with him, sealed with an oath. As we have seen, Bernard eventually ran out of rope, but his desperate twists and turns form an agitated counterpoint to the ideal picture of straightforward fidelity to the king painted by his wife Dhuoda for their son, and other aristocrats must have shared Bernard's dilemma.[145] When Lothar I deliberately muddied the waters – backing Pippin in summer of 840, soft-pedalling his support for him by the winter, allying with him at Fontenoy in 841 and later unswearing oaths to him – all this created uncertainty amongst affected aristocrats.[146] These were not secret negotiations but the public articulating of a (fluctuating) Carolingian identity and status. This uncertainty also created opportunities for regional aristocrats who could profit from rival Carolingians' attempts to outbid each other for support.[147] Carolingian rivalries magnetically attracted the aristocracy. Carolingians had the legitimacy and force to be able to insist that no one could opt out of the grid of loyalty to them. They also had sufficient patronage to make choosing them as lord worthwhile.

Charles the Bald himself now unleashed force against Pippin. He personally led warriors to Aquitaine in 840, 842 and 843 and in 844 he penetrated as far south as Toulouse, issuing a flurry of charters to try to bind people to him. Executing count

Bernard in this same campaign showed Charles's ability to balance favour with terror.[148] He also worked hard to chip away at Pippin's identity as a Carolingian. Holding court at the strategically important town of Bourges in January 841, Charles graciously acceded to the request of a bishop in Burgundy to confirm charters previously issued for his church by earlier rulers, including Pippin I. Charles thus co-opted the late Pippin I to buttress his royal status, a pointed act in Bourges. Charles re-routed the former kingdom of Pippin II onto a different royal track. When Pippin II's appointee to the see of Bourges, archbishop Rodulf, acknowledged Charles as king in 844, Charles showed him favour but took care to request that the church of Bourges now prayed for 'us, our wife, our offspring and our kingdom'. The work of patronage, liturgy and memory was to make Charles present and to render Pippin II absent.[149]

In order to be fully visible as a Carolingian, Pippin II needed to be recognized as such and Lothar I had threatened Charles with this prospect as soon as Louis the Pious, the great denier, had died in 840. It was thus a significant victory for Charles when his brothers eventually supported him in 844 in demanding obedience to his (Charles's) rule from Pippin, as well as from the Breton ruler Nominoë and the rebellious magnate Lambert. This lumped Pippin in with non-Carolingian dissidents, all equally guilty of faithlessness towards their rightful lord Charles. This was a public refusal to recognize Pippin as special and reduced him to the ranks.[150] Even when Charles did have to make a deal with Pippin in 845, Charles's followers were given to understand that he only recognized Pippin as having only lordship (*dominatus*), not kingship. But Pippin remained king in his own eyes and in those of his own followers.[151]

Such struggles actually helped construct Pippin's status as a Carolingian and did so as a public process covering a wide geographical area and played out by rulers, envoys and warriors in meetings, agreements and battles. Pippin was not passive here. He had resources that he could deploy to attract and reward followers, appointing his candidate Rodulf to the see of Bourges some time in 840-1 and granting him fiscal lands.[152] He was able to mint coins, and at some stage had access to the wealthy mint of Melle, though it is difficult to chart his coin issues with precision. These coins circulated through Aquitaine bearing his name and royal title and this clearly marked a new beginning as his father had had no independent coinage.[153]

Pippin's claims were in fact quite modest. In his diplomas, Pippin retained his father's title as 'king of the Aquitanians' and also used this on his coinage. This was an attempt to assert and define a political identity, one based in Aquitaine. He was his father's successor; that was the source of his authority; he thus retained his father's title. He was even willing to rule under a senior Carolingian as shown by the dating clause in a diploma of 840 which referred to the year of Lothar I's rule. But this was only a tactic to ensure Lothar's support and he abandoned that as he abandoned Lothar in the aftermath of Fontenoy in 841, returning to Aquitaine as the only credible source and theatre of his power.[154] This contrasts sharply with Charles the Bald. When Pippin's failures against Viking attacks drove the aristocracy of Aquitaine into the arms of Charles the Bald in 848, the latter marked his rule in Aquitaine in a majestic ceremony of royal anointing packed with his bishops and magnates. While this may have been designed to dazzle the Aquitanians, it was not just to make him king of Aquitaine but to mark a hallowing of his original rule, an intensification of his kingship over all his realm.[155] Charles's own bishops saw this ceremony as an extra dimension of specialness for his kingship and Charles ensured that his anointing in Orléans, which was not in Aquitaine, was liturgically recalled in sacred sites in the very heart of his kingdom such as St-Denis.[156]

Pippin, however, looked inward to Aquitaine and may never have experienced an anointing ceremony such as this. This need not have made him a lesser kind of king in contemporaries' eyes. Charles's anointing was not the expression of his special status but an attempt to make him special. We would do well to recall Michael Wallace-Hadrill's remark on the Orléans ceremony as 'a world of symbols that betray insecurity'.[157] Pippin's claims to rule had a narrow but irreducibly Carolingian base; those tenth-century observers of his rule's end had a clear view of its beginning: his father had left the kingdom to his son.[158]

Pippin II's hold on Aquitaine certainly did not match that of his father and he had no chance, or desire, to lay claim to territories further east promised to his father in 817. But he was a king and this was a great advantage, compared to the cases of, say, Hugh son of Lothar II and Carloman, son of Charles the Bald. His career illustrates what a Carolingian could do in the teeth of determined efforts to suppress him. He was a formidable soldier who had warriors strong enough to impress his uncles in the war after 840 and he annihilated Charles the Bald's supporters in a savage clash in 844. A lament for one of his victims refers to Pippin as king.[159] This defeat forced Charles the Bald to make peace with Pippin in 845 at Fleury. A contemporary account by a follower of Charles, bishop Prudentius of Troyes, loyally takes Charles's line that Pippin was recognized as having only 'lordship', not kingship. Furthermore, Prudentius highlights the family hierarchy: Pippin had to swear oaths to Charles that he would be 'faithful to him as a nephew ought to be to his uncle'. This echoed earlier Carolingian arrangements such as Charlemagne's succession plans of 806; familial language and concepts were themselves a central political institution.[160] Such language, however, was a double-edged sword for Charles as it advertised Pippin's Carolingian identity. Charles was ensnared in the web of Carolingian kinship discourse, inescapable for justification and practice of his own authority. Any ceremony at Fleury that demonstrated Charles's and Pippin's relationship would thus have had a double meaning for the kings and their followers. Bishop Prudentius's denying Pippin kingship in his annals was an attempt to interpret the ceremony 'correctly'.

Unsurprisingly, this was a forlorn attempt. Pippin himself saw his status as unimpaired. Back in Aquitaine, he dutifully acknowledged Charles as his 'uncle and patron' in a charter, but that same charter asserted his independent royalty. Flaunting his title as king and the year of his reign (with no reference to Charles), he referred to his own descent from Louis the Pious and requested the monastic beneficiaries to pray 'for the salvation of ourselves and our people and for the stability of the kingdom granted to us by God'.[161] He continued to mint and distribute coins proclaiming him to be king, and may even have intruded on the rich mint of Melle which Charles had reserved to himself at Fleury.[162]

Neither Pippin nor Charles spoke in a vacuum. Their pronouncements and definitions needed social response to become authoritative. Pippin's kingship retained credibility after 845 as we can see in the career of Joseph, a notary in his service. Joseph himself tells us that he was educated at Tours and evidence from St-Martin's indicates that he was a member of the community there from about 820 on. He witnessed a relic transfer ceremony in Neustria, that is, the kingdom of Charles, in the winter of 846-7.[163] But later that year, Joseph was in Pippin's service in Aquitaine working as a notary producing royal charters for his new master, a task he performed until 848.[164] It looks as if the deal made between Pippin and his uncle in 845 had indeed normalized relations between them. Joseph had seen an opportunity open up in royal service and jumped at the chance. That service, however, was not with his own king. But a transfer to Pippin's kingdom was not an exotic choice for a man like Joseph. At Tours, he would have been aware of the fact that his community had benefited from the patronage of Pippin's father in 828; Tours held property in Aquitaine.[165] A career in Aquitaine was thus a logical move for Joseph. He had already experienced, if indirectly, the patronage of Pippin I; now he was working directly for the son. The presence of Carolingian rulers across the empire guaranteed familiarity. For Joseph, such political-personal structures held firm, despite the divisions made at Verdun in 843 or at Fleury in 845, or indeed despite any later vicissitudes.

After the crisis of Pippin's kingship in the late 840s, Joseph found employment in Charles's service in 856 as tutor to the king's son Louis. He had thus passed from Neustria to Aquitaine and back again; wherever he went, he found a Carolingian ruler; these rulers provided him with a career. Joseph himself summed up this career placidly enough: 'I Joseph, sinner and priest, ... at one time chancellor of the former king of the Aquitanians [the very title in Pippin's diplomas] and now although unworthy, tutor of the renowned king Louis and holding office in the sacred palace.'[166] Joseph's pride in his royal service is noteworthy. Furthermore, his balancing of his service in two kingdoms shows that he saw them as equivalent. He saw Pippin II as a perfectly legitimate Carolingian king, in whose service he drew up charters and upon whom he attended when Pippin, in some style, presided over a transfer of holy relics to the monastery of Mozac early in 848.[167] For Joseph, then, Pippin looked like a valid king. Indeed, Joseph's producing charters and attending royal ceremonies helped make him so.

Pippin's kingship was recognized outside his kingdom, even by trusted agents of Charles. Here again the facts of political geography were important. The church of Reims held property in Aquitaine and sometime between 817 and 833 the archbishop had ensured that Pippin I granted it protection.[168] After the deal of 845, such properties still needed to be looked after. The new archbishop, the formidable Hincmar, appointed by Charles the Bald, wrote to Pippin II about them and, although his letter has survived only in summary, he seems to have referred to Pippin as king. Hincmar 'wrote to Pippin the Aquitanian king ... and got letters of King Charles to be sent to that same Pippin.'[169] Other great churches also held property there. Hetti, archbishop of Trier far away in Lothar I's kingdom, had petitioned Pippin about his church's property in Aquitaine and Pippin graciously responded in a charter issued in July 847.[170] Narrative sources written in other kingdoms did refer to Pippin as king and while this may sometimes have been a way of expressing hostility to Charles the Bald, this was not always the case. Pippin was seen as a king across the Carolingian world.[171]

Charles thus failed to cancel out Pippin's status or to downgrade him significantly. In fact, the maddening result of Charles's 845 concession, as Bishop Prudentius noted sourly, was that 'all the Aquitanians who until then had been with Charles hastened forthwith to attach themselves to Pippin'. Pippin, however, had few reserves; the editor of his charters sees a shaky improvised quality to the work of his chancery by 847 and Pippin failed to convince his aristocracy that he could defend his lands against increasing Viking pressure. When Charles pounced on Aquitaine in 848, Pippin's following drained away and his charters dried up.[172] But Pippin remained a Carolingian. Such figures had a fearsome potential; they carried their own resources with them in their Carolingian-ness.

And another resource of Carolingian-ness was now heading Pippin's way: his younger brother Charles. Born in the late 820s, this Charles of Aquitaine may be obscure to us but he was not so to contemporaries. He would certainly have been well known in Aquitaine. When his father requested churchmen to pray for him and his line, he was surely intending that both his sons would be prayed for in the churches across the kingdom of Aquitaine.[173] Louis the Pious certainly recognized the value of the younger generation of princes in Aquitaine. In 832, in one of the frequent episodes of tension between Louis and Pippin I, the old emperor peremptorily ordered his son to come to him 'along with his wife and children'.[174] Pippin I shrewdly failed to obey his father and his children stayed under his control, and presumably prominently by his side, for the rest of his reign. On his death, aristocrats proclaimed only the older son, Pippin II, as king. His solo kinship was probably due to a hasty deal with his brother, recognizing their limited resources. At some stage, young Charles of Aquitaine (I call him this to distinguish him from Charles the Bald) had gone to the court of uncle Lothar I for safety. Charles's journey west from there in 849 was fraternal support when Pippin's hopes looked dark.[175]

Aquitaine was still volatile; Charles the Bald was still struggling to tighten his grip there in 849 and 850.[176] But what could Charles of Aquitaine do? He had probably not even been in Aquitaine for some years. What sort of support could he give? He had his Carolingian blood, but a spark needs material to kindle, a key needs a lock. In fact, he was known across the Frankish kingdoms. He had enjoyed Lothar I's support and contemporary annalists in the north and west of Charles the Bald's kingdom knew details about him, as did the author of the *Annals of Fulda* in the eastern kingdom.[177] Notker of St-Gall in the 880s still knew his place in the Carolingian lineage.[178] A son of a king stayed on radars. This Charles had followers and Charles the Bald's own followers were on the alert to track and catch them; this prince's journey raised the threat level. One of Charles the Bald's most prominent supporters successfully intercepted the Aquitanian prince and his company and dragged him off to the king. Only a senior Carolingian could deal with him. Charles the Bald's loyal followers saw the case as simple: the young Charles was a traitor to his uncle and that deserved death.[179] Carolingian family hierarchy was stark.

But Charles the Bald deployed mercy to ensure that even a treacherous Carolingian remained special, but not too special. Because Carolingian identity was so dangerously precious, the dynasty could not afford to have it cancelled casually. This prince was to willingly dissolve his own Carolingian identity in a carefully staged ceremony. We have what reads like an eye-witness account of proceedings at an assembly called by Charles the Bald at Chartres in 849. Charles of Aquitaine was brought into a sacred building, a church, and, after the ceremony of the mass, went up to the pulpit and announced 'with his own voice' that 'for love of God's service and under no compulsion from anyone he wished to become a cleric'. His wish was granted and he was tonsured on the spot.[180]

Compulsion was of course strongly present in all of this. But we should not think that Charles the Bald held all the cards or that all participants in the proceedings at Chartres were simply hypocrites; people tend to have some belief in the systems that sustain them, even as they manipulate them. And Charles the Bald would not want any accusations of forced clericalization of a king's son coming back to him as they had done to his father. Sending the son of a king into a monastery was a big step. The perpetual performance of Carolingian specialness could not be easily interrupted just to suit the current political needs of Charles the Bald. Furthermore, Charles the Bald was godfather to his nephew. This relationship dated back to the early 830s and presumably had been intended as much to shore up the wavering bonds of affection between the fathers, Louis the Pious and Pippin I of Aquitaine, as to create any lasting bond between the youthful Charles the Bald and the boy from Aquitaine. But here Louis the Pious had built well. Charles the Bald was able to blaze with righteous indignation in 849 at the outrageous behaviour of his nephew and godson whose challenge to Charles had flouted the bonds of godkinship as well as royal authority, but whom Charles's gracious mercy spared.[181]

Rather than being reduced to passive victimhood, the younger Charles was allowed to retain some dignity in being allowed to perform the dissolution of his political identity by proclaiming it to be his own choice. Charles of Aquitaine had not been a king, so he did not need to undergo some ceremony that stripped him of that office. His status did not depend on office; that status was now changed but perhaps not all lost. Mayke de Jong's penetrating examination of monastic confinements reveals that such confinement could have a *double entendre* for contemporaries: 'monastic exile was perpetual but exiles might be pardoned and leave again'. Monastic confinement could make a challenger disappear while preserving his life and honour. It was a way of coping with fierce pressures.[182] Perhaps this was also a signal to encourage Pippin II to surrender. He did not.

At some stage, probably soon after his tonsuring at Chartres, Charles of Aquitaine was ordained as a deacon, a sign of an increasingly clerical identity.[183] This, however, was not the end of his story. It could be hard to stifle Carolingian charisma by merely sending those who possessed it to a monastery. Charles had been sent to the monastery of Corbie, hundreds of kilometres from that Aquitaine where he was a threat, but Corbie was not secure enough to hold him as he escaped from there in 854.[184] Corbie itself had some grudges against Charles the Bald and was part of the inter-connected Carolingian world through its daughter house located in the kingdom of Louis the German; this may have given Charles of Aquitaine a chance to cultivate another Carolingian court.[185] Charles's escape route duly took him to the eastern court of his uncle Louis the German who publicly recognized him by making him archbishop of Mainz, an appointment that did not go down well with all the clergy. Charles's lack of local connections and wealth may have limited Mainz's usefulness to the king here. This only shows, however, how keen Louis was to be seen to honour his nephew (and thus his own kin). Charles of Aquitaine also had value for Louis in that his Aquitanian heritage could be a weapon to deploy against Charles the Bald. Holding office on the banks of the Rhine, Charles's mere birth still gave him potential leverage in Aquitaine. Louis, however, defined Charles's value carefully; confirming Charles's clerical status prevented him from actually ruling in Aquitaine or destabilizing the east Frankish kingdom with his Carolingian blood.[186] Charles was thus anything but a marginal figure; he had been of absorbing interest to all three surviving sons of Louis the Pious and ended his days as a Carolingian presence in the important centre of Mainz (where he may have intensified the aura of the dynasty if the *Vision of Charlemagne* was written there under him).[187]

The changing of Charles of Aquitaine's status was a dry run for the more formidable task of taming his brother Pippin who fell into Charles the Bald's hands in 852. This gave Charles the chance to cancel out Pippin's dangerously potent identity. Charles had him dragged up to Francia, 'a prisoner', not a kingly figure. Charles took care not to deal with him until he had met with Lothar I, the senior Carolingian. Only then did he have Pippin sent to a monastery, St-Medard at Soissons, site of Louis the Pious's confinement a generation ago.[188] Pippin now left the world of action for the world of contemplation. As Janet Nelson has pointed out, Charles wanted Lothar to approve this course of action as senior brother and as a former supporter of Pippin. This was the sound of doors closing. But, as Nelson has also noted, Louis the German thought little of all this; he was not consulted and east Frankish texts referred to Pippin as king.[189] There was thus no united family front; there was no proclamation here by all three kings about their 'common nephew', as there had been at Meersen. in 847. But Charles's consultation with Lothar operated as part of the Carolingian discourse of politics. Two royal brothers had publicly agreed on Pippin's new destiny. The re-defining of Pippin was punctuated by meetings between Lothar and Charles. Their meeting in 852 was followed by another in early 853 when 'Lothar became godfather to Charles's daughter'.[190] A baby girl, as daughter of one king, and niece and god-daughter of another, shone out as a true Carolingian; such brightness made figures such as Pippin more obscure, harder to see, while still keeping the Carolingian family centre stage and demonstrating to watching aristocrats that Carolingian children, even girls, were not as other children.

But what exactly was Pippin's new status and how was it created? Perhaps Lothar negotiated some concessions. It seems to be only in 853 that Pippin 'donned a monk's habit and promised to observe the monastic rule in the usual way'. Janet Nelson sees this 853 ceremony as Pippin only now being 'further bound by the stricter obligations of a monastic profession'.[191] Perhaps Pippin himself had had a hand in negotiating a softer option of 852, that is, monastic exile without definitive monastic identity; as a Carolingian king, he was not entirely the passive figure of bishop Prudentius's narrative.

But Charles's followers did not care about any such subtle distinctions, if they were made. A group of West Frankish bishops and abbots, between twenty and thirty prelates, assembled at Soissons in 853 and said that Pippin had already put on the monastic habit in 852 when he was tonsured. ('*attonsus et in habitu monachico ad monasterium Sancti Medardi custodiendus et docendus*').[192] The west Frankish churchmen were keen to transmit a clear picture of Pippin. They were doing so as part of a public effort to transform Pippin definitively into a monk.

Pippin himself, however, saw the monastery right from the start as a place to escape from. And he duly tried to do so as soon as he could. The attempt failed and Charles came down hard on it at that synod held in Soissons in 853; he had those monks who had tried to help Pippin defrocked as priests and whisked off to other locations while Pippin himself had to (re)acknowledge his monastic status in public. Prudentius was at Soissons and he gives us a clear account of all this; his text inscribes Pippin's new status.[193]

But another text also does this, the proceedings of the 853 synod, and this text has a higher performative value than Prudentius's narrative. We have already seen that the bishops and abbots assembled there saw Pippin as a full-time monk from 852. Like Prudentius in his annals, the proceedings of the synod do not refer to Pippin as king but they cannot hide his Carolingian identity. This account of him opens by describing him as 'Pippin, son of king Pippin son of the emperor Louis' thus implicitly outlining his claim to Aquitaine by tracing his place in the royal line. This was the last thing that these churchmen wanted to do but they could not suppress the music of Carolingian legitimacy that sounded in such a recitation. Boldly re-writing history as Louis the Pious would have dreamed it, they went on to explain that Pippin had only got Aquitaine with the consent of his uncle 'the glorious king Charles'.[194] This is probably a specific reference to the deal made between Pippin and Charles in 845 but is also part of that more general language of family hierarchy, that is, the subordination of nephews to uncles. Thus even this narrative of Pippin's fall from a position that was carefully described as subordinate could not avoid showing Pippin as a Carolingian.

But this identity dissolved as the bishops went on. In their narrative, Aquitaine had consumed itself in chaos but Pippin was not deposed for bad rule. He was simply abandoned by the Aquitanians, brought into the power of his uncle and 'on the advice of the most reverent pontiffs and notables, tonsured and put in the monastic habit he was led to the monastery of St Medard to be guarded and instructed'.[195] There is no explicit reference to penance or punishment here; what counts is the transformation of Pippin's status and identity in 852, publicly recalled and thus re-iterated in 853.

The bishops went on to fix the mask of this new monastic persona more firmly on Pippin, obliterating his Carolingian features. They did this by dropping him from his own narrative. The story of his monastic confinement turns out to be merely the prelude to the real concerns of the synod with this episode. Two wicked monks at St-Medard, led by greed (*cupiditas*), had tried to free Pippin and disturb the peace of the Christian people. The bishops reeled in horror at this un-monastic behaviour but they focused on the monks, not Pippin. It was these monks who had been brought to the synod on the orders of the bishop of Soissons; it was their punishment that was carried out at the synod and recorded in its proceedings. Their punishment was meant to be a warning to others and, on one level, this was simply designed to threaten anyone else rash enough to help Pippin, but on another level, it was a warning to any monk not to menace the Christian order. The monks had been priests and they were defrocked 'canonically' because they were guilty of clerical conspiracy as defined in church councils. Their behaviour was compared to that of Eutyches, a heretical monk in fifth-century Constantinople. The wicked monks of St-Medard thus appeared in a long perspective of church disorder and discipline. And so, by implication, did Pippin; this was his world now. This was why he was dealt with at a synod that was meeting at

St-Medard itself. He now breathed the air of an ecclesiastical world. This was a world of godly authority in which the king loomed large; the synod unfolded in his smouldering presence, as Prudentius emphasized in his account. But Prudentius also saw that the Pippin episode took its place in the series of ecclesiastical business of the synod.[196] Pippin's Carolingian identity was to be extinguished in a very public ecclesiastical sphere. The great churchmen of west Francia attended it and their recitation of Pippin's fate and their punishing of the monks all acted as a command performance of Pippin's new ecclesiastical identity.

A lot of pressure was thus brought to bear on Pippin to crack his Carolingian identity and to re-mould him. The fact that so much pressure had to be deployed shows how potent that identity was. And in fact that identity survived. Pippin had carried it into the monastery with him. The fact that he had found support in St-Medard speaks volumes.

Pippin did eventually escape from St-Médard in 854 back to Aquitaine, and neither his two years' absence nor his monastic profession prevented him from resuming his Carolingian royalty. All that effort at Soissons could not prevent Pippin from shedding his monastic skin. Prudentius tells us that once Pippin got to Aquitaine, 'most of the people of that land went over to him'.[197] In other words, Pippin himself was enough; his identity could be an essence. His supporters did stage a ceremony for him in which they proclaimed him king. That they needed to do this is significant: his Carolingian claim needed support to become real again and his monastic persona was a problem ('they turned [Pippin] from a monk into someone who looked like a king'). But the ceremony may have taken place some time after his arrival there in 854. Supporters had rallied to him before the ceremony. And the ceremony may have been not so much a necessary changing of Pippin's status as more of a counter-blast to the crowning of young Charles, son of Charles the Bald, as king of Aquitaine the previous year.[198]

Pippin's desperate later struggles to establish a position in Aquitaine do not concern us in detail here. His royal status could not magically dissolve the political realities on the ground in Aquitaine where he was only one player in a complex landscape of conflict involving Charles the Bald and his son Charles, intrusive eastern Carolingians, shifting groups of aristocrats and Vikings. This fragmented landscape of the far west gave the returned Pippin footholds but little more. He had to improvise, temporarily battening on to groups of opportunistic supporters, labelled as Aquitanians, Franks, Bretons and Vikings in our sources, acting less like a king than another troublesome magnate, but without a stable base.[199]

Pippin appears amidst an overwhelmingly male cast of characters but it is hard to imagine that he did not try to seal an alliance with marriage, or that he had not married earlier. There is evidence to suggest that he was married. But the chaotically violent scrabbling for marriage visible in the career of Lothar II's son Hugh a generation later suggests that marginalized Carolingians found little stability there.[200] On the other hand, Pippin was obviously still of some use to these temporary allies whose support gave him significance but which did not create that significance out of nothing. The aftershocks of his struggles against his uncle reverberated widely. The breaking of the marriage alliance between the daughter of count Raymond of Toulouse and count Stephen was one of these consequences for an aristocracy caught up in the chaos. Pippin's struggle for kingship did not consist solely of adventurous escapes or carousing with Vikings. Stephen's problems required the attention of a host of bishops as well as of king Charles of Aquitaine.[201] Perhaps Pippin still styled himself king (but without charters or coins) and we might understand him better if we look at his kingship from a post-888 perspective, that is, as a small scale, fiercely contested but real royal position. Charles the Bald, for all his problems, pursued a broader strategy; he recognized only one king in Aquitaine, namely his son Charles, but kept him on a tight leash, not permitting him to issue charters and staging oath-taking to himself to remind Aquitaine where authority lay.[202]

And yet, Pippin remained a player. In 858, some sort of deal was reached between him and Charles the Bald and the latter's son, Charles king of Aquitaine. Bishop Prudentius's annals deny Pippin a royal title and make him the passive recipient of Charles's patronizing grant of 'counties and monasteries' (probably an attempt to buy him off on the eve of trouble with Louis the German). But what is striking is that Charles had to do this at all; Pippin came to him and went away again freely, and he did so as a 'layman' says Prudentius.[203] This is presumably an acid reference to his previous monastic history but Charles must have had to acknowledge that Pippin was no monk and he had to give him something. Pippin seems to have lived out that grim Shakespearean line 'Simply the thing I am shall make me live'. But by 864 when he was again captured and brought to Charles, Charles was a stronger king and Pippin had run out of rope. His main allies now seem to have been Vikings, who obviously found him useful, significantly, but who dominated the alliance. Vikings, not necessarily allies of Pippin, had attacked Poitiers in the winter of 863–4. Association with such figures may have damaged any chance of a come-back offered him by the serious hunting accident suffered by young king Charles, his replacement in Aquitaine. Kings such as Charles the Bald did make alliances with Vikings when it suited them; Viking-Christian relations were not simply cast in a hostile binary mode. Pippin was not the only marginalized royal in the west to ally with Vikings. But such an alliance helped Charles blast the reputation of Pippin once Pippin was on the ropes. And Pippin may have had to acknowledge pagan Scandinavian gods as part of his compact with the Northmen.[204]

The Aquitanians who captured Pippin sent him north to Pîtres where Charles was holding one of the great show-piece assemblies of his reign. At this gathering of the collective elite, Charles staged exemplary demonstrations of his own royal authority. Bretons who, like Pippin, had defied him now sent silver to Pîtres as solid token of their subject status; the king reformed the realm's coinage, to his own profit; he showed favour to the monks of St-Germain of Auxerre where his son Lothar was abbot; he issued a vast legal text that, among other things, decreed penalties against anyone who smuggled weapons to Vikings, defining such as traitors in terms reminiscent of Roman imperial law.[205] Here was the cue for Pippin's final appearance: a bad Carolingian who had not stayed in God's service, unlike Charles's son Lothar; a rebel who had broken faith, political and religious. In his annals, Charles's close advisor archbishop Hincmar of Reims reproduced the language of Pîtres, which he had helped to compose, in describing how Pippin was found guilty 'by the leading men of the realm as a traitor to his fatherland and to Christianity (*ut patriae et christianitatis proditor*)' and was duly condemned to death by the assembly.[206] This was serious. A few years later, an 'apostate' monk who had defected from the Christian world was captured by Charles's magnates and beheaded, giving rise to the haunting scholarly speculation that this anonymous figure might actually have been Pippin.[207]

A Carolingian, however, even a renegade, had a much higher profile than such a monk and, as far as we know, Pippin was not executed. As a Carolingian, he was special enough to be spared but any mercy that was to envelop him would smother that specialness. We possess a fragmentary text that Hincmar wrote to advise the assembly and the king on how to solve the Pippin problem.[208] While Pippin was condemned as a traitor to his fatherland and to Christianity, what counted for Hinmcar here was Pippin's betrayal of the Christian community within which everything else was subsumed (and in his annals Hincmar did refer to Pippin as an apostate).[209] On this basis, Hincmar could get everybody off the hook.

Hincmar's Pippin had realized that he had to stop being a Carolingian. Polluted by association with Vikings and by his broken monastic vows, Pippin is said to repent and declare that he wants to return to being a monk.[210] Within Hincmar's framework, canonical rulings on apostasy and on associating with pagans dominated. They pointed clearly towards penance and that made the case an urgent one: Hincmar said that he understood Pippin to be ill and so his body was not a royal one but that of an ailing penitent and his case had to be handled quickly lest time run out.[211] Pippin was now on church time. He could thus disappear as a Carolingian to be tonsured and quickly and completely enshrouded in ecclesiastical procedures of penance, reconciliation and repentance. He was to be tonsured and become a monk again and be treated with firm mercy lest he return like a dog to his vomit. Once reconciled with the Christian community, Pippin should be treated kindly, allowed a certain amount of liberty (*sub libera custodia*) but stay under monastic supervision. Pippin of Aquitaine was to vanish and to become a repentant monk.[212]

But in what looks like a postscript to the main body of the text, Hincmar instructed the letter's bearer to take it to the king and read it to him. And here, Hincmar revealed that even the elaborate penitential machinery he had designed could not be trusted to completely eradicate Carolingian identity. He urged that Pippin in fact be kept under very close guard, explicitly recalling his escape from St-Médard and that of his brother Charles from Corbie since 'what has happened can happen again'. In evoking the past, Hincmar evoked a potential return of the repressed. Marginalized Carolingians could indeed vanish, but were also fearfully remembered because of the pressures needed to keep them under. Pippin remained radioactively Carolingian; no porous monastery could contain him; Hincmar's recommendations of mercifully light custody were now trumped by his recommendations of the opposite. Charles saw to it that Pippin vanished into 'strictest custody' (*artissima custodia*) in the heart of the kingdom in the recently renovated royal stronghold of Senlis.[213] Charles marked Lent and Easter there the following year and had the treacherous aristocrat William, his own brother-in-law, executed near there in 866.[214] Senlis was a site for the ceremonial and ruthlessly physical work of exercising true Carolingian rule, a showplace for an active ruler and a place of oblivion for a vanished Carolingian unperson. Pippin's father had died in 838; it had taken a quarter of a century and a lot of effort for Pippin's vanishing to take effect. Such was the potency of a Carolingian identity.

Radical options: The western kingdom after 843

Charles the Bald was not only in conflict with his Aquitanian cousins, he also faced challenges from his own sons. In this, his reign resembled that of his brother, Louis the German, but in some ways, the father-son conflicts of Charles's reign were strikingly distinctive. One reason why Charles the Bald's efforts to shape his family and control the succession triggered conflict was precisely because they went against the grain of the system that sustained Carolingian authority. Charles's attempts to transform the special status of king's sons merely reveal the relentless momentum of the system's operation. In his attempt to change the status of royal sons, Charles had to be extremely creative: sending some of his legitimate sons (and a couple of his cousins) into monasteries, deploying fertility magic to re-activate his wife's exhausted body, building an artificial Carolingian (Boso), commissioning counsellors to advise him on disinheriting a son, Charles was the Dr Frankenstein of ninth-century politics.

Turning a king's son into a cleric was hardly new among the Franks. In the 570s, Chilperic I had his own son Merovech tonsured and ordained as a priest while Dagobert II was tonsured and exiled in the 650s. Generally, such enforced clericalizations, where tonsure publicly signalled a transfer from the secular to the ecclesiastical sphere, were carried out by rivals once the son's father was no longer there to protect his claims.[215] But Charles having his young son Carloman tonsured in 854 and 'dedicated' was strikingly different.[216] Carloman's father was very much alive and Carloman was unlikely to be plotting a conspiracy aged five. While Charlemagne, in the *Division* of 806, had envisaged that royal fathers might tonsure sons, he stressed that this should not be done against the son's will. The year 854 appears to mark the first time that a Frankish king destined an innocent and legitimate son at a young age, with a royal name, for a church career. This strategy became all too familiar later in the Middle Ages as it enabled dynastic fathers to shrink the pool of heirs instead of the pool of resources through endless sub-divisions. But it was not a Carolingian norm and Charles's brothers did not do this to their children.[217]

Charles's resources were finite. Kings had limited freedom of action. Magnates who had lost out in other kingdoms found a ready welcome in Charles's, but this cost him dear in the granting of *honores*.[218] Granting a kingdom to a son was potentially even more expensive, even if the father kept overall control. Kingdoms moreover were special and might be tricky to split amongst all who might have a claim. Magnates such as Hincmar of Reims also feared that kingdoms would become unsustainable if divided into fragments.[219] Louis the Pious's insistence in 817 that only legitimate sons could inherit a kingdom shows that rulers sought to limit the pool of heirs, though the privileging of legitimate sons might make it only harder to deny them their claims. There was also the stark fact of political geography. Professor Nelson has argued that within west Francia there were only two sub-kingdoms, Aquitaine and Neustria, and earmarking them for his first two sons meant that the cupboard was bare for Carloman and other sons.[220] Rulers had to think like this. For Professor Nelson, Charles's clericalization of his young son was thus a reaction to a 'crisis of overproduction'; too many sons for too few kingdoms meant that Carloman's younger brother followed him into the church, leaving thrones for only the two oldest boys.[221]

But more complex factors than practicality were in play. After all, neither of Charles's brothers pushed any of their sons into the church; Louis the German cannot have had significantly more *honores* (or fiscal land) at his disposal than Charles but he carved out kingdoms for three sons, even before he acquired more resources from the middle kingdom in 869.[222] It is hard to believe that such creative accounting was beyond Charles the Bald or that he was hamstrung by untouchable pre-existing territorial units; after all, he effectively agreed to some sort of division of Aquitaine with Pippin II in 858. Resources were finite, as they always are; but ways of distributing resources are not finite. Turning royal sons into clerics did conserve resources but royal sons themselves were a resource. Charles's actions were not just an inheritance strategy, but a dependency strategy: all attention was to be focused on him, father and king.

While Charles, unlike his brother Louis, did allow his sons the title of king, he was like Louis in his strict guarding of royal privileges for himself alone. His sons, Charles in Aquitaine and Louis the Stammerer in Neustria, could not issue charters or mint coins and Charles retained control of distribution of *honores*.[223] Of course, these young men were not mere toys of their father and both of his kingly sons came to defy him, not least by marrying without his permission in 862 when Louis was sixteen and young Charles was about fourteen. Their sister Judith also married without her father's permission in the same year in a spectacular challenge by the younger generation, and its aristocratic supporters, to Charles's royal and paternal authority. Young Charles, an anointed king, quickly had to publicly humble himself to his father, while Louis had to beg forgiveness from bishops and pledge allegiance to his father who replaced his kingdom of Neustria with a mere county, one that had been devastated by Vikings.[224] When Charles sent Louis back into Neustria in 865, his refusal to clarify Louis's status as king there trumpeted to the aristocracy his own power as fatherly king-maker.[225]

His third son Carloman too was meant to be his father's instrument and to transmit the message of his authority. About five or six when he was tonsured and about ten when he was ordained as deacon, he was his father's gift and this was not to be revoked. Prominent ecclesiastics understood that Charles was giving over his son to a life of divine service as an offering to God.[226] Carloman's clerical status was meant to be fixed; looking back on Carloman's later disastrous escape from clerical identity, Regino of Prüm was to characterize him as an apostate, the same serious accusation levelled against Pippin II of Aquitaine.[227]

In 866, Charles reiterated his son's status on a big stage. This was at a great synod attended by over thirty bishops held at the monastery of St-Medard Soissons; we can assume that secular magnates were also present. At the king's request, the bishops performed a spectacular royal ritual here; they anointed and crowned Charles's wife, Ermentrud.[228] The queen's family had been in the news. In 865, the king had stripped her uncle and other kinsmen of their offices after they had failed against the Vikings in 865; her brother was plotting treachery against Charles.[229] Disloyalty to the king and failure as warriors stained the reputation of these men. Ermentrud's status, however, was seen to remain undimmed, with Charles relying on her to smooth relations with his nephew Lothar II.[230] Perhaps she herself suggested the ceremony of anointing at Soissons as a clear statement that she was queen indeed. This would have been a good time for Charles to wear the gem-encrusted silk robe that she had given him.[231] The ceremony at

Soissons was thus, among other things, a declaration that Ermentrude was safe, that the king was determined to keep his queen; he himself helped crown her there.[232]

The ceremony also reminded everyone present of the queen's key dynastic function, the bearing of children. This may strike us as rather strange, and may also have struck contemporaries. Ermentrude had already given Charles many children; she bore eleven in the twenty-seven years of their marriage, most of them probably before the 866 ceremony; six of them were sons. And yet the Soissons ceremony was indeed a 'fertility ritual/spell' created by the bishops to refresh the queen's body.[233] Six sons were not enough: one, Lothar, died in 865, two others probably died in 865/6 and the gathering at Soissons knew that Charles of Aquitaine was failing fast, not least because his father requested prayers for him. Charles may have been particularly unlucky among Carolingians in the early death of so many of his sons, but no dynast could know how many sons he might need.[234] Charles's grim determination to re-animate his wife's body is as comprehensible to us as it would have been to contemporaries.

But what is strange is his equally set determination to keep Carloman fixed to his clerical status. The bishops at Soissons summarized the situation of Charles the Bald's children; this must reflect the king's own views even while the bishops' recital formalized and froze them as part of a providential narrative. Hereditary succession was here the necessary security for the whole kingdom. God had continued the unbroken line of succession from the ancestors to whom He had granted the kingdom by giving sons to Charles, to the relief of all. Charles had given some of them (Lothar and Carloman) as an offering to God. God had taken some early from this world while others had caused distress, a reference to the rebelliousness of Louis the Stammerer and Charles of Aquitaine. This was why Charles had asked the bishops to bless his wife, so that she might bear offspring who would protect church and realm.[235] Perhaps not everyone present understood the Latin that the bishops intoned and perhaps not everyone there believed it. But the message of Charles and his bishops was clear: it was displayed on the body of the queen, blessed, anointed and crowned in St-Medard. And that message was stark and destabilizing: Charles needed new sons because the existing ones were not good enough. This was an extraordinarily disturbing message for the aristocracy, reminiscent of the days of Louis the Pious. How serious was the warning of Soissons to the kingly sons and those who had invested in them? How long would it take for Charles to father and raise a new son? Did he simply plan to live forever? How long could Ermentrud continue to bear children? Soissons proclaimed that all bets were off and that Charles, God willing, would keep everyone guessing about the succession.

Carloman was not the only son turned into a cleric by his father. An epitaph for twin sons of Charles from the monastery of St-Amand suggests that they may have been intended for the church, but this is not certain.[236] We do know that in 861 he commanded that his son Lothar be turned into a cleric in a monastery.[237] Lothar bore a kingly name but he was lame; perhaps this clinched his father's decision to confine him to a clerical career. Lothar's clericalization of 861 was only a year after his brother Carloman's being ordained deacon; each event may have normalized the other, making the spectacle of a king excluding his own legitimate, royally named son from the succession less startling. Charles soon (by 863/4?) made Lothar abbot of the eminent monastery of St-Germain in Auxerre.

But neither his removal from the line of succession nor his early death (865?) could make Lothar vanish from the world. Nor would his father have wanted that. Royal sons were too valuable a resource, even in the unusual family economy of the western kingdom, to be secreted away. In the eighth century, the bishopric of Auxerre had been one of the islands of independent aristocratic power that Charles Martel and his sons had broken up, redistributing its resources among the various churches of Auxerre and to their own associates across the Frankish world. Since then, Carolingian rulers had worked hard, and successfully, to bind Auxerre's bishops, abbots and counts to them.[238] A great abbey such as St-Germain was not monochromatically Carolingian. A talented scholar of the abbey, Heiric, celebrated the benefits which the abbey had enjoyed from the patronage of count Conrad and his family (the Welfs), visible in the very buildings as well as in a strong Welf presence there. But this co-existed harmoniously with the Carolingian connection, and with many others; St-Germain's buildings also included a residence for the king (*domus regia*); Heiric celebrated their closeness to the king as one of the glories of the Welfs.[239] To give, receive and exploit the *honores* clustered around Auxerre were to perform what Carolingian rule meant. Like the abbey of St-Denis, St-Germain was one of the spiritual centres of the western kingdom, particularly close to the king. Monks there had been praying for the continuation of the Carolingian line for decades.[240] In making Lothar abbot there, Charles was not injecting a Carolingian presence into an alien region. But kings had to play to a home audience too; that is what made a centre a centre; only thus could Carolingian royalty be authoritative.

Not everything about Lothar's or Carloman's monastic career was political, consciously designed only for Carolingian legitimation. We need not see all such actions and the relationships that they generated in crudely instrumental terms. Such a perspective flattens out our picture of this culture's richness. It can also make us see contemporaries as passive targets of royal initiatives rather than as active participants in the shaping of perceptions of Carolingian-ness. The scholar Heiric of Auxerre was such a participant; he was probably tutor to young Lothar and he recorded the precise date of the latter's appointment as abbot and of his death in his own personal notices. He may well have been among the monks of St-Germain whose petitioning Charles the Bald after Lothar's death resulted in the king's request for prayers for Lothar.[241] Teaching, liturgy and commemoration were part of the rich texture of life in a great abbey such as this one which was much more than a machine for the reproduction of Carolingian distinctiveness.

And yet it was that too, and that would have been an inescapable part of Heiric's experience of Lothar. Heiric was twenty-two when Lothar, in his teens and lame, became abbot; only an exceptionally high-status individual would have been so young an abbot in such a house and impressed Heiric so much; it was the distinctively royal name of Lothar that Heiric recorded so prominently in his personal record.[242] Close encounters with Carolingians did not hypnotize Heiric into uncritical reverence; he took a much cooler view of Carloman's abrasive style as abbot, as did the monks of St-Médard, though neither Heiric nor the monks could forget that Carloman was a son of the king.[243]

Carloman and Lothar were Carolingians in sacred places and their identity as king's son and abbot was meant to intensify these sites' work for divine favour for the dynasty. Soon after Lothar's death, Charles was asking St-Germain to commemorate the anniversary of the death of his 'most dear son' and to go on to supplement such celebration with commemoration of the death day of himself and of his wife Ermintrud; this was issued at Senlis, not simply a place of imprisonment for recalcitrant Carolingians, but also a place where acts of family commemoration were commanded. Lothar was thus incorporated into the chorus of specifically dynastic commemoration uttered in centres such as St-Germain, a chorus that helped keep the world Carolingian.[244]

But not all Carolingians in Charles's realm were to get the prize of a crown. And Carloman never became reconciled to his clerical status. A very capable troubleshooter for his father, he eventually became impatient for rule and rebelled against him in 870. He did attract support but Charles and his bishops came down hard on him. A perfectly calibrated combination of ecclesiastical discipline on the bad abbot and paternal royal anger at the bad son resulted in his condemnation and blinding in 873. He survived, but had become an unperson.[245]

Charles the Bald's refusal to advance Carloman to a kingdom did not stem from his having full confidence in his eldest son, Louis the Stammerer. Charles's acquisition of the middle kingdom in 869 coincided with the death of his queen, Ermentrud, and he swiftly united with a noble woman of the middle kingdom, Richildis. Richildis's speedy union with Charles brought a powerful family close to the western ruler and this displaced some of the king's close associates.[246] But her arrival heralded deeper disturbances, as she brought Charles an inestimable gift: the prospect of new children. In contrast, when Louis the German's wife died in 876 he had neither inclination nor time to marry again and thus spared his kingdom these tensions.[247] But Charles's intense determination to have new children and to experiment with inheritance threatened the dynastically coherent discourse of filial succession with disruption in the western kingdom after 869–70.

Traces of the new royal couple's hopes are still visible in a remarkable book. This is an extremely luxurious Bible (Bible of San Paolo fuori le mura), created as a gift from Charles to God, probably made at Reims, possibly for Charles's marriage to Richildis. Richildis appears alongside Charles himself in a complex ruler portrait, the only picture of a Carolingian king and queen together, and also in the accompanying poem wishing that 'by her distinguished issue may rightfully be given to the realm' (*proles in regnum*).[248] Such books were for the eyes of God and for the attention of a restricted circle on earth. But they emerged from a more public matrix of patronage and concern. The production of this book at Reims may well have been supported by archbishop Hincmar, who would thus have been in 'dialogue' with Charles and his desire for more children.[249] This is rather surprising as the archbishop disapproved of Charles's hasty union with Richildis, but it shows the contemporary awareness of Charles's dynastic plans, and the need to (be seen to) support them.

The same is true of the king's petitioning the Virgin Mary to grant Richildis children; this appears in a diploma saturated with dynastic feeling issued for the church of Paris in 871, one that re-starts the dynastic prayer requests cut short by Ermentrud's death in 869, and contemporaries would have understood this as simultaneously a prayer to heaven and a public declaration of the king's wishes for his line, wishes that their prayers were to support. The request that the Paris churches celebrate the birthday of any child that Richildis might bear proclaimed Charles's vision of a future of more favoured sons.[250] This grand diploma (the original has survived) issued at the royal palace of Servais was a visible object in a series of public acts that drew contemporaries' attention to the royal bed-chamber: crowded with figures from heaven and earth, it was the womb of the kingdom.

The queen's own body transmitted messages on the potential new line to the elite. Richildis was pregnant when she appeared, glowing with imperial splendour, beside her husband at the synod of Ponthion in 876 while the hypnotic chanting of the *laudes* resounded.[251] All this was disturbing for Louis the Stammerer, now about thirty. Even as Charles designated Louis as successor at an assembly at Reims probably in 876, Louis and his supporters must have been glancing nervously at the pregnant queen and would have flinched at the provocatively kingly name given by Charles to her eventual son.[252] The attention that the aristocracy paid to Richildis's pregnancies and the birth, and early death, of the sons that she did bear Charles is reflected in their being recorded in Hincmar's annals. The body of the baby son, Charles, who died in early 877, was pointedly taken to St-Denis for burial in his father's favoured dynastic holy place.[253] Charles relentlessly signalled his desire to enhance the status of Richildis, and thus of her future children, taking her with him on his spectacular journey to Italy in 877 so that she could be crowned empress by the pope. Charles may also have asked his counsellors for advice on how to exclude a bad son from inheritance, a request that would trigger more ripples of uncertainty within the aristocracy.[254]

Richildis's marriage to Charles meant that her brother Boso also advanced in royal favour. Boso is important because he did in fact become the first non-Carolingian king of the century, but this occurred in 879, two years after Charles's death. In his reign, however, Charles raised Boso so high that it looks as if the king was experimenting with blurring the boundaries between the royal line and an aristocratic line, a dangerous step in a dynastic system. In some ways, Boso was not unique; he was one of a group of supermagnates built up by Charles in his last years to help him run the realm; Carolingian patronage remained creatively active.[255] But Boso was distinctive in the scale of his promotion; in 876, Charles gave him control of Italy after the death of Emperor Louis II. Above all, Boso was intensely close to the royal family. Marrying a royal daughter was a rare privilege for the aristocracy but in 876, Boso did just that; he married Ermengard, daughter of the late emperor Louis II, and sour contemporary comment on this shows its impact. His sister and aunt had married Carolingian kings.[256] His shadow fell over Louis the Stammerer when Charles made him the latter's chamberlain in 872. Charles also appointed other magnates to watch over the adult Louis, but it was only Boso who stood as godfather to Richildis's son born in 877 (the boy soon died).[257] Boso was the only living follower singled out by name by Charles in the elaborately specified liturgical commemoration which he commanded at St-Denis in 875.[258]

What did all this mean? Brother-in-law to a king, husband of a Carolingian woman, liturgically present in the royal abbey of St-Denis, wearer of a ducal crown in Italy and Provence, Boso appears as a sort of honorary Carolingian. Was Charles trying to create an 'artificial' Carolingian as alternative to Louis the Stammerer, or as devoted and invested guardian for any future children of Richilids? The 'natural' bonds of family are in fact cultural bonds and so people can manipulate them creatively. Charles's schooling Boso in the formation of a Carolingian identity was surely one of the factors that helped Boso and others see his own kingship as credible in 879. Charles had set a time-bomb.

But in 877, the situation was not so clear-cut. Even Boso's position in Charles's favour was not securely static as other aristocrats jostled for position. Boso joined the aristocratic refusal to respond to his royal patron's call for help in the ill-fated Italian journey of 877. Boso was not alone in abandoning Charles; he was merely one of a group of the 'super-magnates' uneasy over their ruler's Italian adventure and over changes in the aristocratic pecking-order in key regions such as Burgundy.[259] Neither Charles nor Boso was an isolated free agent; they had to work with and respond to competitive aristocrats with substantial resources of their own. Fortune's wheel was always moving. But Charles's extraordinary favouring of Boso would have triggered anxious speculation about the exact arrangements for the succession. Charles's marriage to Richildis, his promotion of Boso, his questioning of laws of inheritance, his determination to keep his adult son Louis on a short leash all worked to obscure Louis's status as heir. Louis, however, was not simply a passive figure and the discourse of father-son succession continued to speak. All this meant that tensions swirled round the succession but the light that they generate lets us see how contemporaries worked through a particularly problematic father-son succession in this dynastic system.

No matter how high the stakes, Charles could not resist very publicly belittling his son's prestige and thus asserting that his own will alone counted. On the eve of his effortful journey to Italy in July 877, the king held a grand assembly at his palace of Quierzy in the royal landscape in the north-east of his kingdom. The surviving capitulary preserves, in its very distinctive call and response form, something of the elaborate performance of ruler and aristocrats as they articulated a settlement of the kingdom's affairs in Charles's absence. As such, it has attracted much comment, not least in the decisions on succession to office, decisions that reveal the balance between expectations of ruler and followers in the distribution and reception of offices.[260] The July assembly was part of a series of measures from that year that reveal Charles's tight grip on his kingdom and its resources, not least in Charles's realistic expectation that he would raise thousands of pounds worth of silver to pay off Vikings. The loss of such money to the latter is less striking here than Charles's ability to get hold of it in the first place. In May, Charles had celebrated the dedication of his expensive new palace chapel at Compiègne. But not everything about Charles looked secure: in the winter of 876–7, he had been dangerously ill.[261]

The super-magnates, the grandees whom Charles had promoted in the 870s to be the pillars of his rule, had their own concerns, resenting the burden of the tribute to the Vikings which fell particularly hard on their estates and worrying about the royal favour now being shown to another group of aristocrats such as count Adalelm of Laon.[262] A royal palace such as Quierzy was not an echo-chamber in which only the king's voice and name resounded. It was a stage for a collective cast. The names of some thirty aristocrats, clerical and lay, appear in the capitulary's text; a version of the capitulary was read out at the end of the assembly by abbot Gauzlin of St-Denis, and contemporaries remembered this; the Latin text as we have it preserves a script of elaborate exchanges between king and his faithful men.[263]

The king's voice, however, was the dominant one and it harped on at the assembled political community about the need to understand Carolingian dynastic authority in correct terms. In his tense concern over control of communications, as including the prospect of false rumours about his death while he was in Italy, Charles betrayed a lively understanding of how Carolingian-ness was constructed through communication and switches of loyalty (he warned aristocrats on this).[264] Charles vividly communicated his obsession with the succession to them and thus focused their attention on it.[265] In making his distaste for his son Louis absolutely clear, he made the latter's status deeply ambiguous. Drawing attention to the succession while trying hard to leave it unresolved was a political high-wire act that threatened the kingdom's fragile equilibrium.

Charles dared not strip the kingdom of rulership by taking Louis with him to Italy, but he left him in Francia under oppressively close supervision, including that of count Adalhard, Louis's new father-in-law, who was to retain the palace seal. Such close supervision was only fit for a 'young man' (*iuvenis*) as Charles humiliatingly labelled his thirty-year-old son at the assembly.[266] Such measures were not abstractions but shaped the aristocracy's perception of Louis's lived royal identity. Indeed, acting as his watchers involved aristocrats in moulding this role for Louis. Count Adalelm of Laon was to count up Louis's hunting booty and to report this to his father. In commanding this and restricting his son's access to some key palaces and hunting-grounds, Charles was partly being a canny estate owner, but was also ensuring that all could see the father's shadow over the son.[267] Above all, Charles publicly diminished Louis's prospects, hinting that Louis might be confined to an Italian kingdom, or to only part of the realm that might have to be shared with an east Frankish nephew or a future child of Richildis. Magnates may also have worried about Louis's own children; he did have sons but they were by his first wife, whom Charles had forced Louis to abandon, and Louis had had to go on to marry into a family that his father approved. This left the status of his sons open to some doubts. Clouds covered his future.[268]

And yet all this effort by Charles to negate Louis crashed against the rock of royal familial specialness. The king's voice at Quierzy uttered the language of Carolingian identity, but so did the voice of the magnates. We need not think that the capitulary preserves the actual words spoken there, nor that the text as we have it was issued as such, but it preserves something of the real discussions between king and aristocrats there.[269] We can hear kingly and aristocratic voices in a chorus of Carolingian discourse as the king referred to his son, wife, daughters and nephews, and aristocrats echoed these familial terms in their replies.[270] Charles himself was possessed by dynastic thinking; he urged the assembly to honour his foundation of St-Mary at Compiègne, that holy community which his spectacularly elaborate diploma, ceremoniously issued in May 877, required to pray for his ancestors, himself his wife and offspring (*proles*) as well as for the realm.[271] Magnates who had absorbed such dynastic concerns in May would not have forgotten them by July. In their exchanges with the king at Quierzy, they replied to his enquiry about how he and they could have confidence in Louis by acknowledging that this was a matter for him alone: he had fathered Louis and brought him up.[272] Carolingian kingship was a family affair and they could not intrude. But Charles was here caught; he himself could not deny the claims of family. The capitulary's text refers almost obsessively to Louis; characterizing him as 'our son' may have been a way of highlighting his dependence on Charles as senior figure in the relationship but it spelled out that relationship as a natural one. Charles may have tied down Louis's authority but Louis remained his son.[273] Charles could not stem the tide of filial claims to succession within a dynastic system that he himself depended on and had done so much to foster.

Moreover, Charles's exchanges with the assembly were a dialogue. The aristocrats reminded Charles that at Reims (in 876) they had already accepted Louis 'whom by the grace of God and your decision we wish to have as future lord after you'. They further said that at Reims they had also acknowledged that Charles might have another son.[274] And it is here that Charles's plans, Louis's claims and the aristocracy's active role all come together in a crux. For Charles, Quierzy was another chance to broadcast his determination to find a substitute to Louis, but he could not completely cancel his only fit adult son. For Louis, Quierzy was disturbing but not fatal. The aristocracy at Quierzy was neither monolithic nor fatalistically passive. Those who were appointed as Louis's 'minders' were important precisely because they were close to a Carolingian. Aristocrats at Quierzy could not ignore Charles's signals against Louis but they had indeed acknowledged Louis as potential successor at Reims, as Hincmar was to remind Louis after his father's death.[275] This was a retrospective view, but even in July some aristocrats must have bet against Charles surviving long enough to raise a new son to challenge Louis. Furthermore, not all would have been happy to support a son of Richildis, and her own prospects were not glowing; she seems to have lost out to her own brother Boso in some family properties in 877. Louis himself had supporters; those followers on whom he showered *honores* when his father died did not simply spring out of the ground on Charles's death.[276]

Louis's Carolingian-ness existed and made him the successor. But the constructed nature of Carolingian-ness seemed to offer space for leverage to make Louis's claims uncertain. Historians have tended to emphasize the conditional nature of Louis's claims rather than his natural right to succeed. This is partly because the sources seem to highlight that, as does Louis's slow-motion accession to the throne. But, as we shall see, the construction of Carolingian-ness depended on there being a Carolingian element to start with. And this was to be Louis's ace in the pack.

Exhausted and abandoned in Italy, Charles the Bald struggled back over the Alps, but died on 6 October 877 at Briançon. The political situation was the reverse of 814 and 840: then the senior ruler had died 'at home', and his potential successor had to travel to the centre, acquiring authority and generating uncertainty on the way. In the autumn of 877, Louis the Stammerer, the potential successor, was at the centre but found it difficult to activate his kingship. Fatherless at last, he could now freely visit the palaces of Quierzy and Compiègne, but his plan to bury his father at the sacred dynastic centre of St-Denis was frustrated by the fact that Charles's entourage had already buried him at Nantua.[277] If the living son was not able to use the dead father as he wanted, the dying father had worked to smooth his son's path, having a document drawn up declaring Louis's succession. The queen was to carry this text, together with a sword, royal robes, crown and sceptre to Louis in an echo of Louis the Pious's demand in 840 that a crown and sword be delivered to the distant Lothar. The year 840 saw the first appearance of regalia in the context of succession, but by 877, Hincmar's account of the transition reveals contemporary understanding of 'funeral ritual as detaching the individual man from the office'; the king was mortal, but the realm immortal.[278]

Since contemporaries could understand these actions as demonstrating kingship's impersonal existence as an office, they could see Louis's journey to the throne as a slow-motion one, not magically achieved on his father's death. Charles had died on 6 October and Louis would have got this news about mid-October. He jumped the gun, immediately showering his own followers with *honores*. These followers included some of the great men of his father, but others among his late father's magnates banded together with the empress to withhold support, and the regalia, from him. In November, archbishop Hincmar contacted him, urging him to come to terms with the aggrieved magnates and sternly advising him on how to rule well.[279] It was only after Richildis had given Louis the document and the regalia on 30 November that he was crowned on 8 December at Compiègne. And it was only after making deals with his step-mother and the magnates that Louis had managed to get hold of that regalia. And it was only after the coronation that his chancery issued diplomas in Louis's own name.[280] The gradual constructing of Louis's kingship could, it seems, only go at the speed of the messengers galloping back and forth between Louis and the empress and the magnates. Impersonal office was thus product of hard physical and mental work of travel and negotiation, of anger and diplomacy in managing expectations of reward and honour.

All this indicates that Louis's kingship was built over time – from October to December – and space – via Briançon, Quierzy and Compiègne, and that it was constructed by many agents, including the empress. It was on 30 November, before his coronation, that Louis publicly proclaimed to the bishops assembled at Compiègne that he would preserve their rights and confirmed this with a document in which he was styled as king by the mercy of God and 'by the election of the people (*electione populi*)'.[281] An older historiography has stressed the importance of this type of kingship by election/choice, noting that the synod of Paris in 829 warned Louis the Pious that it was God, not his ancestors, who gave him his throne and that contemporaries understood perfectly well that hereditary kingship was only one type of rule. In this historiographical perspective, the aristocracy loom large as active king-makers.[282] Such views, however, can be shaped by knowledge of later historical developments and are too formally constitutional in their isolating the aristocracy as a single coherent body with a defined right and duty to choose a king. Contemporaries, clerical and lay, understood *electio* neither as the germ of later forms of electoral kingship nor as a distinct right of king-making that was separate from the mercy of God but as 'a manifestation of the divine will ... and quite compatible with the *misericordia Dei*'.[283]

But what role could Louis's royal birth play in all this? Recently, Geoffrey Koziol has re-emphasized the importance of contemporary 'ministerial understandings of office' and observed that west Frankish anointing ceremonies in this period, as far as we can reconstruct them, did indeed articulate concepts of continuity, but that continuity was one of office. Explicit statements of hereditary right in these ceremonies only came later; they were 'an add-on'.[284] And indeed in the texts of Louis's coronation ceremony at Compiègne in December 877 we find no trace at all of a claim to rule by hereditary right, in contrast to the explicit reference to 'hereditary right in royal succession' in a prayer in a tenth-century west Frankish anointing ceremony.[285] And, as we have seen, Louis's own chancery only issued diplomas after the coronation in December.

Nevertheless, contemporaries understood Louis as embodying a dynastic identity which was key to his claim to rule. As Brigitte Kasten has put it, no one doubted that Louis would rule, what contemporaries wanted was to have a say in *how* he would rule.[286] Hincmar's annals, his November letter to Louis and the texts that he compiled for the coronation show that contemporaries took the chance to negotiate for specific plums such as *honores* as well as for guarantees of more general rights for church and followers. But they conducted these very negotiations in a language saturated with Carolingian dynasticism. In his letter to Louis, Hincmar lectured him on how kings were raised to their kingdoms by the magnates but his many examples of this were Louis's own ancestors, and he duly labels them as such ('your great-great-grandfather [Pippin III] … your grandfather [Louis the Pious]'). Furthermore, the magnates had defended Charles the Bald ('your father') and Louis the German ('your uncle') from Lothar I's attempts to disinherit his brothers. The magnates had known that not only had the kingdom been divided on oaths but that these kings were all 'brothers' and that Charles and Louis were in no way inferior to Lothar in family (*genus*) or power. As for Louis the Stammerer himself, the magnates had already accepted that he would be king because this is what his father had ordained at Reims and at Quierzy.[287] All these ancestors were pushing Louis towards the throne that they had prepared for him.

Perhaps the actual crowning in Compiègne in December lacked some dynastic elements. Amidst his evocations of the crown and gorgeous robes, Hincmar made no reference to Louis's current wife, and Louis's later forlorn attempt to get the pope to crown her in 878 may suggest that she was not present at the December 877 ceremony, though that is hard to believe.[288] Even if she was absent and even though the ceremony itself made no reference to hereditary right, the actors in it could not help but refer to Louis's ancestors. Louis and the bishops both referred to his father ('the lord emperor Charles your father', 'the lord emperor my father') and the bishops took their oath to the king as 'Louis, son of Charles and Ermentrud' (and the magnates surely uttered a similar formula).[289] They saw Louis as the son of a king and a queen. Hincmar had no problem with hereditary claims; when it had suited him, he had created a ceremony that intoned hereditary right as key to succession, as we have seen at Metz in 869 (see above).

The absence of explicit reference to succession by hereditary right in Louis's coronation documentation does not mean that hereditary right was absent from Carolingian royal liturgy. As kings emerged from the line of their ancestors, they heard the voices of the bishops praying for a dynastic future, and these prayers come to us via texts spanning the Carolingian realms. Prayers for the continuation of the royal line, kings coming forth from royal loins, appear in the sacramentary of Gellone, our manuscript of which was written in Meaux or Cambrai at the end of the eighth century but had travelled far south to Gellone by the early ninth, as well as in the sacramentary of Angoulême and in a Bavarian collection from the second half of the ninth century.[290] The Frankish kingdoms expected and desired their kings to beget other kings, and prayers were to help that dynastic future.

Contemporaries understood that Louis was son of a king and that was his essential claim to succeed; he was born to be king. But they also knew that he had to be made into a king; he could not simply rely on his birth. They knew that kingship was an impersonal office. They did not necessarily separate these elements out into formal constitutional factors as some modern historians tend to do. Contemporaries could combine clear-eyed negotiations on king-making with reverence for the charisma of royal birth. We catch a revealing glimpse of this in the reaction of one prominent contemporary to the succession troubles of autumn and winter 877. This is Adalgarius, member of an aristocratic family in northern Aquitaine. He served in Charles's chancery from 867 on, rising to become bishop of Autun and would have been very familiar with the king's view of Louis the Stammerer. But that view included the need for royal followers to pray for the royal offspring, as Charles's 875 grant of the abbey of Flavigny to Adalgarius' church of Autun made clear.[291]

Adalgarius was with Charles the Bald as he was dying and it may well have been Adalgarius himself who drew up the death-bed document (*praeceptum*) by which Charles gave Louis the kingdom and who brought that document north. He was thus closely involved in the slow-motion transition of the crown to Louis.[292] But he knew that the realm was Charles's to give. In October 879, some months after the death of Louis the Stammerer, Adalgarius looked back in a charter to the beginning of the latter's reign. It had been a time of troubles, not least for the church of Autun, and we see why magnates as strong as Adalgarius wanted the shelter of royal rule. Amidst the upheavals, Louis had succeeded 'by the royal custom of inheritance' (*ex more regio haereditate*) and Adalgarius recognized that he was king 'by election and birth' (*electione et genere*).[293] Both elements existed in harmony. Louis duly rewarded Adalgarius and Autun, taking care to request prayers for himself and his offspring.[294]

The death of Charles the Bald marked the passing of the last of the brothers who had made the settlement of Verdun. The upheavals of the subsequent three and a half decades included the disappearance of one of the three kingdoms, the crushing of lines of succession, fierce conflict among Carolingians, bewildering shifts of aristocratic loyalties. But the dynasty's claims to be the exclusive holders of royal authority had held firm and had, as we have seen, been ever more widely and deeply articulated and maintained. One problem in looking at a successful system of legitimation is that we ourselves might fall under its spell and see its survival as natural and inevitable. But Louis's request that Adalgarius and Autun pray for his offspring did not in fact result in unswerving loyalty to a natural successor. Adalgarius penned his recollections of Louis's hereditary accession on the eve of Boso's bid for a crown, and Adlagarius was to declare for Boso. This, as we shall see in Chapter 9, was the prelude to the dynastic system going into crisis.

7

Universal Carolingians: Masteries of time and space 751–888

Looking back from around 840 to the succession of Louis the Pious in 814, the Astronomer turned to the Bible for a text to illuminate the seamless transfer of royal office from father to son. Death here was no rupture but a trigger for repetition, for the reproduction of a father's royal qualities in a son: 'The just man is dead and yet he is not dead, for he has left behind a son like himself as an heir.'[1] To look back (to Charlemagne) was to look forward (to Louis). The present king thus had roots in the past and would himself generate successors for the future. This chapter examines some of the ways in which contemporary combinings of past, present and future played a key role in the discourse and practice of Carolingian royalty. At the heart of this is the figure of the father, stemming from fathers of the past and producing sons who would in their turn go on to be fathers. But this chapter will also look at sons who were not to be kings, illegitimate sons, as well as those male members of the broader royal kin who were not sons of kings but who could also play a part in representing and disseminating Carolingian specialness. Carolingian women are of course thematically relevant here, but their importance demands a chapter of their own. Rulers in this chapter appear very much as family men; that is what they were and that is how contemporaries saw them. Trying to warn king Charles the Bald in 858 of moral perils, the archbishop of Reims urged him to imagine the inescapable day of judgement when the king would be on his own, 'without the help of your wife and sons'.[2] To be isolated in this way was unthinkably frightening.

One-way street: Genealogies towards the future

We begin with constructed memories of the past designed to explain the present and to suggest a future: genealogies. Family genealogies trace origins in order to justify the continued transmission into the present and future of a special quality, a special status. Since they are concerned with familial identity, genealogies tend to make claims about the shape of the featured family and about the relationship of that family to other groups.[3] As such, they are a rich cultural source for more than political history. For example, we can profitably juxtapose Carolingian royal genealogies with contemporary knowledge and reflection on biblical genealogies to cast light on this society's devotion to Mary, the mother of Christ. And the towering figure of Mary may have cast a shadow back over these royal texts, in the consciousness in some of them of the special role played by the female line in the maintenance and boosting of Carolingian royal descent.[4] It is also worth remembering that contemporaries experienced these texts in a broader way than we tend to. This is clear from the manuscript contexts in which they have been preserved and transmitted. Not only do we find these genealogies in historical and legal manuscripts, we can also find them in collections of poetry or in liturgical manuscripts.[5]

Genealogical texts and thinking were thus part of a rich cultural cluster of history, commemoration and the constructing of identities. They were about more than the kings who featured in them; Carolingian genealogies could also work to define a more general Frankish identity, and the role of the Franks in making kings.[6] My own focus, however, will be on the kings themselves. After all, the Frankish genealogical texts produced in our period only featured royal families. And, while contemporaries did not all have clear Carolingian family trees in mind, or indeed the same family trees, genealogical texts of the 'X begot Y' type tend to say something special about special families. To an extent, these genealogies 'functioned to secularize time by grounding it in biology, transforming the connection between past and present into a real one, seminally imparted from generation to generation'.[7]

Discussion of Carolingian genealogies usually starts with the church of Metz. Between 800 and 814, someone there composed a genealogy that traced Charlemagne's descent from saint Arnulf, seventh-century bishop of Metz. But this reached even deeper into the past to link Charlemagne and Arnulf with the Merovingian royal family itself as well as with the Gallo-Roman senatorial aristocracy. The composition of this earliest surviving written Carolingian genealogy drew on Metz's resources and reflected Metz's priorities. Metz's connections to southern France helped provide the material for creating these venerable senatorial ancestors and the text was composed at a time when the church of Metz was hoping to end a long vacancy in its bishopric. The original title of the genealogy seems to have described it as a list of the ancestors of Arnulf, rather than of Charlemagne.[8]

It did not, however, come out of a vacuum. People in Metz may not have been the only ones among Charlemagne's contemporaries who saw him as descended from the Roman nobility or from the Merovingians. A poem of Alcuin's from the late eighth century connects the king to old Roman families such as the Flavii and Anicii. And Charlemagne himself gave Merovingian royal names to his twin sons born in 778.[9] Nor did Charlemagne always need reminding of the importance of Metz for his dynasty. Writing his *History of the Bishops* of Metz for bishop Angilram of Metz c.784, Paul the Deacon found that his material on Arnulf in the seventh century was richly supplemented by an important source. Paul inserts into his text a story about Arnulf that features a traditional motif of the miraculous return of a lost ring. Paul learned this from Charlemagne himself, not a man usually associated with fairy tales: 'I learned this not from any ordinary person but I got it from that declarer of the whole truth, the outstanding king Charles, who is descended from the line of the blessed Arnulf as his great-great-great-great-grandson (*trinepos*).'[10]

It is worth noting the significance of this. As Donald Bullough says, this is 'the only authentic anecdote from Charlemagne's own mouth' (but we also have Charlemagne's story of how he lost his first tooth, see children chapter). We catch something here of the conversation of the great king and find that he liked to talk about a fish, a ring and a holy ancestor. The story's point was that Arnulf's miraculous recovery of his ring restored him to a state of grace, a conclusion found in similar stories, including one about St Mungo (Kentigern), patron saint of the great city of Glasgow. The story, and reverence for St Arnulf, is not comparable to later medieval more fully articulated and elaborated dynastic cults of holy ancestors. For Paul, this story provided a way to introduce Carolingian genealogical material into his Metz history. Paul's description of Charlemagne as descendant of Arnulf – and surely this filiation also stems from Charlemagne, that is, he believed himself to be a descendant of Arnulf – is followed by an account of Arnulf's descendants up to Charlemagne himself. It is Arnulf's blessing of his own son Anschises that results in 'such vigorous and strong men being born that the kingdom of the Franks was to be deservedly transferred to his line'. Did Charlemagne himself think this? Paul knew that Carolingian royalty depended on the disappearance of the Merovingians, and said so in a different text; but in his Metz text, he was strikingly silent on the Merovingian extinction.[11] Paul does not offer a genealogy of saints, but Arnulf's holiness was part of the glorious Carolingian ancestry. Arnulf's blessing of his son guarantees future Carolingian greatness but also announces that that greatness has already arrived. Paul's subsequent genealogy of rulers (essentially a brief and carefully simplified account of the succession of son to father and their achievements) demonstrates the glittering military triumphs of the Carolingians and projects backward their subsequently acquired inborn right to rule.

Charlemagne did not think of Metz as a site only concerned with the distant past of his family. He commanded Paul to compose epitaphs for the Carolingian women who were buried at Metz, including his sisters, his wife Hildegard and their two young daughters.[12] The Metz genealogy of 800/14 thus comes out of a complex of texts and acts in Charlemagne's reign that we might see as 'genealogical' efforts to enhance the Carolingians' status as a royal dynasty. Charlemagne may have entertained and instructed Paul with the story of Arnulf and his ring, and commissioned epitaphs for Carolingian women buried at Metz, and such now-vanished conversations must have been a common part of the contemporary historical experience. This was after all an aristocratic society, though perhaps as not as obsessively snobbish about ancestors as Jane Austen's Sir Walter Elliot in her novel *Persuasion* (1817). But it was Paul, not Charlemagne, who had written all this down. Carolingian genealogies were not composed by the Carolingians themselves, and that is part of their importance for the argument of this book (though there is an exception discussed below).

That genealogy of 800/14 was continued in Metz and surely intended to reach a wider audience. It duly did so.[13] It may have focussed on the church of Metz, but it was a genealogy of kings. As a genealogy, it offered information on the Carolingian past but, above all, it instructed those who encountered it in a way of looking at that past. The reigning king, Charlemagne, had noble and saintly ancestors and that was part of his title to rule the Franks where kingship was hereditary. But the past is not the only focus of a genealogy, and is not its main concern. Adorno's stricture is instructive: 'the concept "origin" must be stripped of its static mischief'. Genealogies are dynamic and can point towards a goal, not an origin. A great sequence of ancestors implies, by virtue of its being a sequence, continuity into the present and the future. Genealogical form, which views royal families in simplified linear terms, not only justifies the transmission of royal power within a single dynasty but also implies that such power will continue to be successfully transmitted.[14]

Genealogy thus proclaims, by its form, that there will be a future for the dynasty as illustrious and lengthy as the past leading back to its origins (and we will see later in this chapter how devoutly dynastic continuity was prayed for in the Carolingian world). The rosy future implied by the genealogy came true in the Metz genealogical text itself as people copied and continued it across the realm through the ninth century. After Charlemagne's death in 814, the text was continued with his son and successor Louis the Pious and then, in various versions, with all three of his sons and successors.[15]

The fathering of Carolingians by Carolingians is thus a key feature of these genealogical texts as well as of other texts and social practices such as fathers giving exclusive royal names to their sons. Contemporaries noted Carolingian fatherhood. In the collection of laws that Lupus of Ferrières made in the 830s for the aristocrat Eberhard of Friuli, a son-in-law of Louis the Pious, he includes a list of rulers dating from the birth of Christ onwards. Here, Roman emperors from Octavian (Augustus) onwards appear in a bare sequence ('Titus succeeded Vespasian. When Titus died, Domitian succeeded') but this eventually swerves rather surprisingly from the eastern emperor Justinian II (d.711) to Pippin II and then continues with the Carolingians. This swerve appears in earlier texts such as a much-copied 807 text on the ages of the world, following a Bedan model. But in Lupus, the bare listing goes on to be replaced for the first and only time in this section of Lupus's text by father and son relations, that is, birth as a criterion for rule: 'After Pippin [III] Charlemagne was made emperor. After the death of Charlemagne *his son* Louis [the Pious] ruled' (my emphasis). Manuscripts of this text leave space for continuations.[16] And of course even in a bare list such as this the very names of the Carolingians proclaimed dynastic origins and progressions (two Pippins each mentioned twice; two Charleses each mentioned twice).

Conversely, a genealogically patterned text could expose the ending of royal lines, a narrative of an imperilled future. This can be seen in a fascinating tenth-century (954–66) 'Genealogy of the kings of the Franks' from Compiègne which offers a multi-perspective view of the lines of the sons of Louis the Pious. Doing so, however, only brought into focus the fact that all these lines, apart from Charles the Bald's west Frankish line, had dried up by the time of this text's composition. The text's explicit sounding of the knell for each of the post-843 royal lines seems to reveal anxiety among the dynasty's supporters, even if the text also glows with west Frankish pride and confidence as that line alone is shown as still continuing with king Lothar (954–86). Moreover, the relentlessly linear form of this genealogy not only highlights continuity of the west Frankish line, it offers no space in its picture of history for the challenge to that line from the proto-Capetians Odo and Robert whose reigns had actually punctured western Carolingian history after the death of Charles the Fat in 888, but whose un-royal names do not appear in the text's Carolingian sequence. How could such irregularly royal figures have a future? Even after the devastating interruption of Carolingian succession in 888 and after, genealogists could imagine Carolingian continuity based on the security of an indisputably Carolingian royal past.[17]

Compiègne was a centre of active memories about and for the Carolingian line, not least because the canons of the palace chapel of Saint-Corneille, itself richly endowed by King Charles the Bald in 877, prayed for the souls of the royal dead. But they had also been instructed in the details of Carolingian ancestry by no less a personage than King Charles the Simple himself who 'dictated' a version of a Carolingian genealogy to them around 920. They continued to update it with more Carolingians, but at some stage around 960 a writer named Witger, probably a chaplain in the service of the count of Flanders, adapted the text to serve as a genealogy of these counts, descendants of a Carolingian king's daughter. This was neither a rejection nor a hi-jacking of a glorious Carolingian past that no longer had a future – the count of Flanders was an ally of the beleaguered Carolingian ruler at the time – but it does show that the re-iteration of Carolingian genealogical sequences had only limited powers. Reiteration could not in itself guarantee a political order. By this stage in the tenth century, Carolingian kings no longer had an unbroken unique right to the throne, and the counts of Flanders were among the first, but would not be the last, among aristocratic families to have their own genealogies defined in a written text. The proliferation of aristocratic genealogical texts in western Europe from the tenth century onwards marks a break with Carolingian Francia's exclusively royal texts.[18]

The focus of these Carolingian texts on the ancestral royal claims of a single family was a lesson for the aristocracy. The aristocracy was not simply a passive audience. After all, aristocrats were among the authors of Carolingian genealogies. The clerics who wrote them were actively articulating Carolingian claims, though they could be pointed in that direction by Carolingians themselves. The author of a poem on *The Origin of the People of the Franks* versified some of the Metz material at the request of King Charles the Bald himself in the 840s. And aristocrats' own culture included a knowledge of Carolingian ancestry. In the late ninth century in east Francia, the 'Saxon poet' referred to songs circulating that glorified Carolingian ancestors and these poems were possibly in the vernacular.[19] Knowledge of Carolingian ancestry was actively taught to aristocrats within their own family; as a result, aristocratic family identity could include reverence for the row of Carolingian ancestors. Writing in the 830s, Thegan of Trier said that he had learned the ancestry of Charlemagne from 'family tradition' as well as from 'histories' (he knew the Metz material). A few years later Dhuoda told her son that his own ancestors had always been faithful to their royal lords; her son's pride in his own aristocratic descent should inspire loyalty to that line whose sequence was a mirror to that of his own forefathers. But when aristocrats such as Thegan and Dhuoda thought about ancestors, they did not think only about Carolingians. Thegan recited the ancestors of Queen Hildegard who had married into the royal family, although her ancestors had not always been in harmony with those of her husband Charlemagne. Dhuoda listed generations of her own family for her son's contemplation and prayer, including family members who had suffered at the hands of wilful Carolingian rulers.[20]

Absence of formal genealogical texts for aristocratic families in this period does not mean that aristocrats belittled their own ancestors. Carolingian rulers were dominant figures, and their ancestry made them special, but Carolingians were not the only actors to breathe and speak the air of ancestral pride.

Institutions as well as individuals could make their memory dovetail with Carolingian genealogy, but on their own terms. Contemporaries were not passively hypnotized by Carolingian ancestral lines. The wealthy and well-connected abbey of St-Wandrille in Neustria, downriver from Rouen, put together a variety of Carolingian genealogical material in the first decades of the ninth century, drawing on the Metz materials.[21] And yet we would be wrong to think of a community such as this merely as a sort of ventriloquist's dummy, trained to recite Carolingian glories by rote. St-Wandrille had its own traditions and interests and was careful to glorify Carolingian ancestry in particular ways.

Founded in the seventh century, St-Wandrille benefited from the patronage of Merovingian kings but (the Pippinid) mayor of the palace Pippin II took it under his protection in 707 and this, together with the fact that its abbot from 723/5 was Hugh, nephew of Charles Martel, shows some tightening of a Carolingian grip on the west of the Frankish kingdom. But the Carolingian family was no monolith; Hugh was no stooge for Charles Martel and his political conduct there was firmly rooted in the local context. St-Wandrille's memories of Hugh highlighted his maternal (non-Carolingian) family.[22] What is significant for us here is that that local context was long remembered, or imagined, in ninth-century St-Wandrille. The history of its abbots compiled there in the 820s lavishes praise on abbot Hugh's formidable maternal grand-mother Ansfled, a member of the local Neustrian, aristocracy. Much of this praise is lifted straight from a very pro-Carolingian set of annals, but it is presented here in a pro-Neustrian perspective which is hardly that of the annals.[23] This shows that even an encounter with a blazingly pro-Carolingian text did not dazzle all readers into losing sight of their own community's roots and concerns.

The rich hagiographical material from ninth-century St-Wandrille offers valuable insights into this community's historical memory, insights rendered all the more valuable by the fact that the abbey had not initially been a straightforwardly zealous Carolingian supporter. St-Wandrille texts written from the late eighth century onwards tell of two abbots who fell foul of early Carolingian rulers. The first is abbot Ansbert, exiled in the late seventh century by Pippin II, who later permitted him to return, but Ansbert died before he could do so. The journey of the abbot's body to St-Wandrille was punctuated by a series of miraculous cures, one of which was later marked by a church, a 'permanent reminder of Carolingian persecution' in Ian Wood's words. The second case is abbot Wando, exiled by Charles Martel in 717 and later restored by Pippin III. But Pippin's grace backfired. The abbot's triumphally public return became an open rebuke to the memory of Charles Martel, Pippin's father.[24]

What had been awkward events for early Carolingian rulers still had a vivid presence in the memory of this ninth-century monastic community. These memories were not anti-Carolingian as such, but the monks of St-Wandrille did have a very strong historical sense in their understanding of royal dynasties as no timeless features of the landscape but as a strictly timebound phenomenon. The *Deeds of the Abbots* tells us that king Childeric, explicitly described as 'the last of the Merovingians', was deposed and forced to become a monk at St-Bertin and it is the only source to tell us of the similar fate of Childeric's son. It is worth recalling here that Einhard, explicit announcer of the Merovingians' end, was abbot of St-Wandrille from 816 to 823.[25]

Dynasties could come and go and here Carolingians were seen to have ascended the throne in the clear light of history in contrast to the misty penumbra of ancestral royalty which predestined them to a kingly future, as in genealogical texts. If St-Wandrille was nonetheless loyal to the new dynasty, that loyalty did not obliterate the community's sense of its own historical identity which was not to be subsumed into a triumphalist Carolingian account. Local institutional identity and memory remained distinctive within the newly refurbished kingdom of the Franks.

We should not see this kind of material as evidence of festering anti-Carolingian resentment dominating the abbot's communal identity and memory. The service of abbot Gervold to Charlemagne was duly celebrated in the *Deeds of the Abbots*; abbots such as Einhard (816–23) and Ansegis were enthusiastic Carolingian loyalists.[26] In fact, the texts produced in the abbey also worked to make it very close to the Carolingians, inserting the abbey itself into the historical structure of the Carolingian family. In the abbey's texts, Carolingian genealogy was malleable. Abbot Ansbert was recalled from exile by Pippin II because, according to the *Life* of Ansbert written around 800, the abbey's founder, Wandregisel, was a kinsman (*propinquus*) of Pippin.[27] The later *Deeds of the Abbots* echoes this claim which, it asserts, is based on the genuine traditions of the monastery, and the claim is repeated in the second *Life of Wandregisel* written around 830. This claim was in fact not only fiction but recent fiction as an earlier *Life* of the founder makes no reference to it.[28] A Carolingian genealogy composed in the abbey makes the link explicit by assigning a third son to St Arnulf of Metz and he, Walchisus, becomes the father of Wandregisel, founder of the abbey.[29] The monks of St-Wandrille, in generously creating new Carolingians, saw the past of the Carolingian family as something that they could manipulate. In doing so, they exerted some control over that past, or over representations of it, but that Carolingian past also had them in its spell as it was the gravitational pull of the Carolingian genealogical material that had drawn them towards the form of a royal genealogy. They were hooked.

It is worth stressing here, however, that it was only the past that was so open to manipulation. As a royal family, the living Carolingians ran a tighter ship than the Merovingians had done. Living members of the Merovingian family were on occasion challenged by pretenders to the throne who claimed Merovingian blood without actually having it and some also faced challenges to their own Merovingian identity.[30] But the inventing of an extra son for Arnulf of Metz was an alteration of the distant past. No living Carolingian between 751 and the challenge of Boso in 879 had a son grafted on to his line, or subtracted from it, in the public sphere and this does contrast with the more flexibly inventive Merovingian era. In his own bid for a crown, Boso did accuse Carolingian princes of not being true sons of their father, a sign that the system was breaking down, as were the doubts about the paternity of Charles the Simple in 893.[31] The Carolingians could not police their own past as effectively as they policed the political arena of their present. The past, however, was not merely a tabula rasa upon which people such as the monks of St-Wandrille could write whatever they liked. If St-Wandrille negotiated its relationship to the Carolingian past, such negotiations were two-way: it was a royal genealogy that was the textual site of their manipulation. Genealogies acted as time's arrow, pointing from a Carolingian past towards Carolingian futures.

Peopling the realm with Carolingians: The wider ranges of kinship

This section looks at 'marginal' members of the Carolingian family, including illegitimate sons, and how they worked within the system that tried to make the realm Carolingian. We thus move from the straight lines of genealogies to a broader, undulating field. Contemporary notions of the scale and definition of the wider Carolingian kin suggest that, normally, people thought of the royal family in quite broad terms. These are general points that do not always hold true; aristocrats could think about their own families in varying ways depending on what suited them best in a given situation, cashing in on closer bonds rather than acknowledging wider links when necessary. This flexibility can apply to the Carolingian wider family group too. In general, however, when contemporaries used terms such as 'royal stock' (*stirps regalis*) or 'royal line' (*regalis prosapia*), this concept of the royal family was a relatively broad, cognatic one. A term such as kinsman (*propinquus*) could refer to a member of the kin-group in the maternal or paternal line.[32]

This being the case, and given the level of intermarriage in the ninth century between the Carolingians and the great aristocratic families of the realm, it can be tempting to conclude with Régine Le Jan that 'the whole Carolingian nobility could be thought of … as a vast *familia*, arranged around the *stirps regia* and the *domus carolingica*'.[33] This view could, and does, explain much about the way the empire functioned but it misses the centrality of royal distinctiveness in the Carolingian political system. This becomes clear if we look at the rather different post-Carolingian world. In the western kingdom in the 1020s, a bishop could indeed imagine the Capetian king Robert as proclaiming that 'Noble families descend from the blood of kings. Noble birth is a source of praise for kings and nobles'. In the east in the tenth century, as Carolingian rule evaporated there, duke Arnulf of Bavaria could have himself depicted as 'stemm[ing] from the line of emperors and kings', that is, from the Carolingians. But this was a challenge to the old hegemony.[34] These later examples illustrate a sharp contrast with earlier Carolingian exclusiveness. Carolingian genealogies and, as we shall see, prayers for royal lines worked to highlight the fact that kings descended from kings. In the Carolingian era, distinct royal descent, not a common pool of noble origins, was the discourse and that was designed to keep kings special.

If kings were special, their relatives could be special. Significantly, a striking contemporary statement on the honour due to the Carolingian kin-group as a whole comes from a member of the aristocracy, from a woman. In her handbook for her son, written in 841–3, Dhuoda assures him that he will find the royal court to be full of the members of the royal family: 'the famous, glorious and outstanding kinsmen of your lord of royal power, those deriving the illustrious origin of their rank whether from the paternal line or from a marriage alliance'. Dhuoda's vision of the royal kin is quite broad; she sees it as including not only those from the 'paternal line' but also those whose origins are in 'marriage alliance'. She also explicitly states that women enjoy status as members of the royal family; she urges her son to 'be faithful to your lord Charles [king Charles the Bald] … and to his worthy kinsfolk of both sexes and to those sprung from royal family'. Dhuoda's view of the royal kin is exalted, and while her reference to Old Testament examples such as Abraham, Isaac and Jacob and their descendants suggests a linear view of descent in her vision, she sees the royal kin as destined to rule ('God has chosen and predestined them into the realm').[35]

Dhuoda's testimony is important but her vision does not pick out all the details of the complexity of historical experience, even of her own. For Dhuoda herself was very close indeed to the royal kin, broadly defined. She had married the aristocrat Bernard of Septimania, son of William of Gellone who was a loyal follower of Charlemagne and a relative of the great king.[36] And Bernard was not only a member of the royal kin in biological terms; he was a godson of Louis the Pious and such artificial family bonds had some of the force of natural ones. But Dhuoda makes no explicit reference to this royal connection. In fact, she conceptualizes her son William's family identity on an aristocratic level, not a royal one. She never places William among the royal kin but rather in a series of aristocrats whose identity resides in loyal service to a royal lord. Dhuoda instructs him to keep his familial focus on his immediate family.[37] She presents the family of King Charles the Bald as something separate from William. Dhuoda's point of view or position in the kin makes her reticence a contrast to her contemporary, the historian Nithard, a 'marginal' Carolingian who gives an explicit account of his own Carolingian origins.[38]

A Carolingian identity in the sense of belonging to the royal kin according to a broad view of that kin could be valuable, but that value and identity could vary. It needed to be constructed and recognized. In encountering and engaging with Carolingians below the level of kings, contemporaries were confronted with degrees of Carolingian-ness and this helped build up their recognition of Carolingian specialness. There were of course all sorts of qualifications and nuances to this in practice, but Notker's story of a bishop being punched to the ground by Charlemagne, angry that the bishop had failed to recognize an obscure royal relative, is instructive here.[39]

Illegitimate sons of kings form a good group with which to start, simultaneously prominent but shadowed. The term 'illegitimate' is problematic. Contemporary sources were sparing in their use of a term such as bastard (*nothus*). It appears in neither of the biographies of Louis the Pious. Some forty years later in the 880s, Notker does use it, but the fact that he uses it for the probably legitimate Pippin the Hunchback merely shows the problems in a search for terminological and conceptual exactitude. Contemporaries could, however, make sharp distinctions if they wanted to. In 786, a church council in England proclaimed that no king should be the son of a concubine. Louis the Pious publicly drew a clear line between the valid inheritance claims of 'legitimate sons' and those of 'sons by concubines' in his 817 succession settlement. Charlemagne seems to have distinguished between his legitimate sons and his sons by concubines in his will of 811, while his 806 division of his kingdom referred only to his sons by Hildegard, and not to any of his young illegitimate ones. Neither Charlemagne's silence nor Louis' command should, however, be seen as definitive shutting down of contemporary expectations about illegitimate sons' prospects. Political culture could remain fluid here.[40]

While accepting that the definition of illegitimate is tricky, we can list some fourteen illegitimate royal sons (not counting Pippin the Hunchback, see Chapter3) among children of rulers from Charlemagne (d.814) to Charles the Simple (d.929). Charlemagne had three (Drogo, Hugh, Theoderic); Louis the Pious had one (Arnulf);

Lothar I had one (Carloman); Louis II had one (Hugh); Karlmann had one (Arnulf); Louis the Younger had one (Hugh); Charles the Fat had one (Bernard); Arnulf had two (Zwentibold, Ratold); Charles the Simple had three (Arnulf, Rorico, Drogo). Such sons were usually, though not always, marked out by a name that was not one of the key royal names, for example, Drogo, Arnulf.[41] Of these fourteen, only four had a clerical career (Charlemagne's three bastards; Rorico, son of Charles the Simple) but of those four, none seems to have been destined for the church by his father (Rorico became bishop in 949, twenty years after his father's death).[42] This does not mean that fathers fondly desired a crown for all their sons, legitimate or not. There is no evidence that Charlemagne groomed any of his illegitimate sons for a kingdom once his legitimate sons started to die after 810, and Louis the Pious pointedly gave his own illegitimate son Arnulf a mere county when he established the succession in 817.[43] It was hard enough for fathers to find sufficient territory and resources for legitimate sons; they did not have enough to spare for the others. But Carolingian specialness was bigger than Carolingian fathers. Only one king in the period 751–888 forced some of his sons to become clerics; this was Charles the Bald in the 850s and 860s, but these were *legitimate* sons and that did not end well.

Illegitimate Carolingian sons could indeed end up in an ecclesiastical career.[44] But, as we have just seen, one thing that royal fathers of the eighth and ninth centuries did *not* do was to send such sons into the church. Royal blood, when it was the blood of a king, was too precious a resource in this period to be squirreled away in the church. Brothers, uncles and cousins of these sons may indeed have taken a different view but, as fathers, kings tended to want a secular career for their illegitimate sons and sons expected to have one. The expectations of such sons involved expectations of aristocrats too. Royal parentage took its place amongst other precious but finite resources such as offices and lands; not all royal claims could be satisfied and this could generate tensions.

Illegitimate sons thus brought questions of high status, resources and expectations into sharp focus. But it was hard for these sons, their watchful legitimate brothers and the equally alert aristocracy to read the picture. If their father would not put them in the church, where would they go? Did their life as young warriors and hunters give them ambitious aristocratic backers, and if their legitimate brothers came to grief, would they have a chance of a throne? The potential high status of such figures usually only appeared when it was snuffed out, as when Louis the Pious panicked at the prospect of family revolt in 817–18 and had his illegitimate half-brothers tonsured. A Carolingian ruler such as Louis benefited from the special status of his family – Louis had given these brothers a prominent place at his court – but that status could also pose a threat precisely because aristocrats believed in it, and found it useful for their own purposes. Aristocrats could thus be more pro-Carolingian than the ruler. Many contemporaries did not approve of Louis's imposition of clerical status on the sons of Charlemagne; Louis publicly admitted in the penance of Attigny in 822 that he had done his brothers wrong and became reconciled with them, though they were now conveniently fixed in their clerical status.[45]

Illegitimacy did matter; Louis the Pious had stated that explicitly in 817. And churchmen could underline this. In the 880s, Charles the Fat strained every nerve to try and have his illegitimate son Bernard accepted as his successor in the 880s, but bishops blocked this even though the king had no other heir. At least one monk, however, disagreed with the bishops.[46] There was no single 'church' line. On the other hand, secular aristocrats could also be uneasy about illegitimacy. In 889 magnates who had actually recognized an illegitimate royal son as king, Arnulf, still publicly stated that, in general, legitimate sons were preferable.[47] The fact that illegitimate sons only became kings in the 880s, when the dynasty was short of sons, suggests that the throne was effectively barred to illegitimate sons. But notions of illegitimacy could be fluid. The potential claims of such sons might have been vague and not stretched as far as a crown, but they did exist. Lothar II's son Hugh may have ended up blinded and tonsured in a monastery by the 890s, but that would not have seemed his inevitable fate when he was born in the 850s.[48] His royal male body had to be broken before it ceased to transmit charisma. Illegitimate royal sons thus made life more complicated for kings and the political elite. And they did so because they incorporated, in puzzling ways, elements of Carolingian specialness.

But if their brothers and uncles could successfully restrain and redefine them, then they could still be part of a large cast of Carolingians below the rank of king, queen, prince and princess who thickened a Carolingian presence across the realm. Dhuoda's vision of the royal palace as a place full of members of the royal kin is paralleled by the realm as a whole. Carolingian men, of varying degrees of closeness to the narrower royal line, popped up in places far from the palace. And, significantly, contemporaries recognized that they were Carolingian.

There were many more members of the family than simply the sons of kings. Members of this larger Carolingian kin group could be found across the realm in a variety of roles. Charlemagne's (paternal) uncle Bernard served in the Italian campaign of 773 and his kinsman (*propinquus*) Theoderic served in Saxony in the 780s, where his royal familial connections aroused jealousy rather than respect among his aristocratic fellow-warriors, testimony to the potency of his Carolingian kinship.[49] Such men could be particularly useful in making and ruling a far-flung empire. Their family identity, if acknowledged and signalled by the ruler, let them reproduce a version of Carolingian charisma but their separation from the main line of the family meant that they posed no threat to the resources that were so tightly controlled by the inner royal line itself. Uncle Bernard, for example, had been squeezed out of the inheritance of his father, Charles Martel (d.741), and thus the inheritance of Bernard's sons came from his marriage and not from the Carolingian family fortune. But Bernard's second wife was a Saxon and this Saxon connection plus the royal links made the son of this marriage, Wala, a natural candidate for a commanding position in Saxony within Charlemagne's empire.[50] Kings confined inheritance to their own line but could cash in on more distant family connections when looking for reliable followers. They thus got the best of both worlds.

It is not possible to calculate the exact number, location and significance of such figures. Nor are they consistently signalled in our evidence as belonging to the royal kin. A charter of king Louis the German from 867 refers to an Alemannian count as the king's relative (*nepos*) and modern research places this count among the kin of Charlemagne's wife Hildegard, king Louis's grandmother who had died in 783. It is striking that the connection was still 'live', and it is also striking that Louis referred to it: this is the only reference in all his charters to kin outside his own narrow, linear family.[51] But connections that are veiled to us were not always so to contemporaries. A letter from 842 refers to a kinsman (*propinquus*) of Charles the Bald, one Bernus, as a possible bishop of Autun, but we know nothing of this man beyond what this letter tells us.[52] There were more kin of kings on the political scene than we can ever recover and we must listen hard to catch and gauge any of their signals. Contemporaries had to do so because they had to calculate the potential impact of such figures on the political stage. Bernus is totally obscure to us, but abbot Lupus, the writer of the letter, knew that he had been brought up in the palace of Louis the Pious. And Bernus had powerful backers for his candidacy for the see of Autun: Lupus wrote on behalf of an archbishop and a count, and Charles the Bald favoured his candidacy.

Calculating the potential value of a man like Bernus was difficult for contemporaries because there was no certainty that a Carolingian identity was in itself a guarantee of advancement. Resources were finite; they always are. A Carolingian family connection had to be activated and recognized by other people, but even then its value could still remain only potential. Bernus did not get Autun. At pretty much the same time as Lupus was lobbying for Bernus, Charlemagne's grandson Nithard was losing out in the division of the empire by his kingly cousins and thus had to switch his hopes for security to the heritage of his other family, that of his father Angilbert.[53] All members of the Carolingian family were no more guaranteed a place at the top table than were all members of aristocratic families.

And those great aristocratic families that had Carolingian connections did not allow them to obliterate or overshadow their sense of their own family's achievements and claims. The Welfs partly owed their prominence in ninth-century politics to a series of royal marriages. Contemporaries acknowledged this element in the family's exalted status but also celebrated this family's own distinctiveness in, for example, the familial grip on the great abbey of St-Germain d'Auxerre, controlled and beautified by count Conrad and his family from the 840s on. As we have seen, Dhuoda did not instruct her son William in his father's royal connection; she pointed to closer kin, highlighting the role of William's uncle in transmitting his inheritance.[54] Such grandees were not likely to lose out to obscure members of the royal kin, though they could not entirely ignore them. After all, aristocratic archbishop Hincmar simply expected kings to favour their relatives, and felt that he had to warn his own king against this tendency in the 870s.[55]

If the potentially privileged position of royal relatives was a fact of political life, there was a more important feature of such royal relatives' presence. In perceiving them as members of the royal stock, contemporaries were inevitably peering through such occasionally marginal figures to the royal dynasty looming up behind them at the centre of the realm. The central dynasty in its turn shed lustre on the marginal figures who beamed it back to the royal line; all this helped bathe the realm in a Carolingian light.

Some of them were indeed clustered at court, as Dhuoda had expected. Such members of the royal kin can be found spending their youth at court from the time of Pippin III (d.768). Charlemagne (d.814) and Louis the Pious (d.840) had sons who were kings but it was at the courts of the senior ruler that we find the young members of the royal kin. They made the centre a centre. The presence of the branch lines of the royal kin displayed the special status of the Carolingians and the flourishing of the family to the young aristocrats who flocked to the court as well as to the older ones who were experienced in the palace.[56]

If the youth of these royal relatives sharpened the profile of Carolingian distinctiveness, the presence of old and experienced royal kinsmen at the court could have the same function. In the 880s, the aged Hincmar of Reims remembered encountering in his youth the wise old abbot Adalhard of Corbie at the court of Louis the Pious some time in the 820s. Hincmar recalled that Adalhard had held a very prominent position at Charlemagne's court; Hincmar knew that he was a member of the royal kin. Adalhard's own memories stretched back to the days of the first Carolingian king, Pippin III (d.768), and he sometimes explicitly recalled this distant era at Louis's court in the 820s.[57] Adalhard thus incorporated the grandeur of the Carolingian past in the present of the 820s and was recalled as a symbol of that grandeur in a text written by Hincmar six decades later for a young Carolingian king who was thus instructed in ancestral splendour. For such courtiers, kings were trump cards. But the juxtaposing of Adalhard and Hincmar reminds us of the finite historical frame of that grandeur. Adalhard could certainly have met people who remembered, or who had even participated in, the deposition of the last Merovingian king. Hincmar experienced Boso's challenge to Carolingian exclusivity in 879. Adalhard's and Hincmar's two lifetimes were enough to contain all that Carolingian grandeur. That is why it had continually to be asserted.

Royal kinsmen such as abbot Adalhard helped the court assert its Carolingian identity across space as well as time. Back in his native Northumbria in 790 and not enjoying the experience very much, Alcuin fondly looked back to Charlemagne's court in a letter to Adalhard that recognized the important position of Adalhard there. Part of that importance was Adalhard's Carolingian identity; Alcuin explicitly labelled this letter as addressed to Adalhard 'kinsman of Charles'. A few years later, Alcuin fretted that Adalhard's brother Bernarius was enjoying his stay at court a little too much, whereas his letters to Adalhard's sister Gundrada celebrate her strong-minded indifference to the pleasures of the palace, though one reason for writing to her was to ask her to speak to Charlemagne for him.[58] Adalhard was just one of a recognized group of royal kin, including women, at Charlemagne's court at this time.

Charlemagne's court may have been exceptional in degree in that it hosted an exceptionally thick cluster of royal kin but it was not unique in kind: we have seen that Louis the Pious had various members of his kin at his court. Kings also had relatives across their realms. All Louis's sons had Carolingian kinsmen in prominent ecclesiastical positions in the separate kingdoms that came into being after the empire was divided up at Verdun in 843. Lothar I had his uncle Drogo as bishop of Metz; in the east, Louis the German had his nephew Charles as archbishop of Mainz, while in the west, Charles the Bald had his cousin Louis as abbot of St-Denis. After 869, when the middle kingdom broke up, Charles the Bald inherited another kinsman, Franco bishop of Liège, explicitly identified in a poem as a 'Carolingian' (*Karolides*). It is worth noting that Charles was to entrust his heavily pregnant queen to the care of this bishop, among others, at a time of danger for his realm in 876.[59]

The bonds of the royal kin could cross the political boundaries erected by the kings themselves. Abbot Louis of St-Denis held his office in Charles the Bald's kingdom but the latter's brothers happily recognized Louis as their kinsman.

Louis the German asked St-Denis to pray for him and his kingdom and the chimes of an exclusive family identity were clearly sounded in this charter which referred to abbot Louis as 'our kinsman and namesake (*propinquus et aequivocus noster*)'. The rulers of the middle kingdom, Lothar I and his son Lothar II, also acknowledged their kinship with abbot Louis in diplomas of 843 and 860 (written up by scribes of St-Denis itself).[60] For his part, Charles the Bald held the memory of his 'most beloved uncle (*amantissimus patruus*)' Drogo in affectionate reverence in a letter suffused with dynastic identity 'even though he [Drogo] lived in the kingdom of Lothar, our late brother, after the death of our father'.[61] As members of the aristocracy, driven by the shifting winds of political favour, moved from one kingdom to another after 843, they would find among the characteristics of Carolingian kingdoms wherever they went a special prominence for (some of) the king's relatives. Carolingian-ness had no boundaries.

In their turn, these royal relatives, as parts of a larger whole, actively worked within the system of Carolingian distinctiveness. Bishop Drogo of Metz himself is an outstanding example of this. As we have just seen, his own family acknowledged his Carolingian identity, but a range of non-Carolingian contemporaries explicitly recognized and revered that identity too. An 842 letter of Pope Sergius II to the bishops of Francia refers to him in glowing terms as son of Charlemagne and as uncle to the three post-Verdun kings, and thus, in the pope's view, a suitable candidate to be papal legate north of the Alps. West Frankish churchmen gathered at Ver in 844 happily acknowledged Drogo's kinship with their king as part of his authority and stature, and the archbishop of Reims also seems to have highlighted Drogo's relationship to the late Louis the Pious in a letter around this time.[62] Drogo may be associated with the writing of royal histories; at the palace of Louis the Pious he had probably been in charge of the composing of annals and it is possible that he was the patron of the anonymous biographer of Louis. But, like other members of the royal kin, Drogo was active away from the palace. Under him, Metz was a workshop of Carolingian identity. Talented young men were educated there, presumably gaining from Drogo, son of Charlemagne, a proper respect for the aura of the Carolingian family. They then went on to hold high posts across the Frankish church: Aldric as bishop of Le Mans (832–57); Adventius as bishop of Metz (858–75); Franco as bishop of Liege (852–901). These men were all educated in Drogo's Metz; Aldric and Franco themselves had Carolingian blood and so Metz may at times been like a miniature court with a cluster of Carolingian kin. We have already seen in the royal genealogies something of Metz's activities in the articulating of Carolingian royalty and specialness. It is possible that the famous statuette of a mounted Carolingian ruler, now in the Louvre museum in Paris, was the result of Drogo's patronage; it certainly has a Metz connection.[63]

The church of Metz was not alone in such activity. Other Carolingian churchmen also created or loomed behind works that focused on the dynasty's history. It is possible that archbishop Charles of Mainz, the son of king Pippin I of Aquitaine, was responsible for the dramatic dream text, the *Vision of Charlemagne*, a bleak warning of dynastic collapse.

In the post-843 western kingdom, Charles the Bald's cousin Louis became abbot of St-Denis and thus presided over a large community of monks from notable families whose duties in the majestic abbey included commemorating members of the royal dynasty, past and present. A surviving manuscript collection of historical texts (Paris, BnF lat. 10911), including the *Book of the History of the Franks* and the *Royal Frankish Annals* which presented Carolingian rulers as part of the great series of rulers of the Franks, may have connections with the St-Denis of Louis's time there as monk and abbot.[64]

Contemporaries knew that abbot Louis was a Carolingian. Writing towards the end of the 860s, the archbishop of Reims knew that Louis was a grandson of Charlemagne and explicitly recalled the name of his mother, Rotrud, who had died as long ago as 810. Diplomas of Charles the Bald himself drew attention to Louis's identity as royal kinsman (*propinquus noster, consanguineus noster, consobrinus noster*). As Charles's arch-chancellor until his death in 867 (when contemporaries reflected on his glorious descent), Louis was a key figure in filtering and expediting royal patronage and its formal expression radiating out across the kingdom in such diplomas.[65] It is tempting to think that the Vikings, connoisseurs of Carolingian politics, captured him in their 858 raid on St-Denis in the (correct) expectation that the king would pay a heavy ransom for the release of his relative. But Vikings were less concerned with Carolingian identities than the author of this book is; they also seized Louis's non-Carolingian brother; high status was their key value here, not Carolingian-ness in itself. For his fellow Franks, Louis was special because of his prominence in the royal palace, not simply because he had Carolingian blood. In the many letters that abbot Lupus of Ferrières addressed to him from the 840s to the 860s, Lupus made no mention of Louis's Carolingian identity in his frequent flattering references to Louis's many fine qualities. What mattered for Lupus in his petitioning for royal favour was Louis's access to the king. Furthermore, Lupus let Louis know that he had other influential patrons at court, assuring him that count Adalhard 'the seneschal' had promised to lobby the king for him.[66]

Neither Louis' Carolingian blood nor his high rank in the palace could guarantee him a solitary eminence above other powerful patrons from the upper echelons of the aristocracy. The Carolingian kin did not have it all to themselves. But that is precisely why it was important for kings to have such relatives in lofty positions. Their presence at the palace and/or regional centres ensured that the music of Carolingian specialness was played in many variants. Lupus did not need to mention abbot Louis's Carolingian-ness; the special name of Louis did that all on its own. And Louis had spent some of his youth at the abbey of Ferrières among its seventy monks, a connection that Lupus reminded him of when Louis was an intimate of the king. Thus, an abbey some 100 kilometres south of St-Denis had nourished a Carolingian, remembered that and took care to remind Louis of it. Such institutional and personal connections, maintained over space and time, mattered to figures such as Lupus, who was not himself from the top-drawer of the aristocracy. They mattered to the grand Louis himself, who was not some passive, impersonal instrument of an abstract Carolingian discourse; his position as arch-chancellor and abbot of St-Denis enabled him to mould the production of royal diplomas to the advantage of his own abbey.[67] And of course such links mattered immensely to a king as they led back to him; having a safely non-throneworthy relative active in such networks gave kings someone to trust.

In the maintenance of a Carolingian discourse, time was to some extent on the Carolingians' side. Carolingian-ness deepened as the dynasty developed and reproduced itself; this world became ever more Carolingian. The continuing succession of the dynasty only further enhanced the status of non-kingly Carolingians which in its turn fed back into the discourse of Carolingian distinctiveness. We catch a vivid glimpse of this development in the case of Drogo's brother Hugh, also a son of Charlemagne propelled into a distinguished clerical career by Louis the Pious in the 820s. Hugh's special status of birth was widely known and deeply respected among the followers of the Carolingians. Einhard includes him in his roll-call of Charlemagne's children, specifying that he was the son of a concubine; Hugh's name appears in a list of 'illegitimate' Carolingians written up *c*.812/813 at the abbey of St-Gall (see Chapter 3 above); Hugh's illegitimate status was thus known far from the royal court. Contemporaries knew that Charlemagne wanted these illegitimate sons to be honoured by their kingly brother Louis and that Louis's doing so enhanced his own court's honour. Hugh had the status and tastes of a great lord; people knew that he was the sort of man who could be satisfied only with a very fine horse for his journeys.[68] When Hugh died in 844, a bishop described him as 'Hugh, priest and abbot, son of the late emperor Charlemagne, brother of his successor Louis [the Pious], and uncle of the three kings Lothar, Louis [the German] and Charles [the Bald]'. The bishop gives due weight to Hugh's clerical status and rank (members of the dynasty in the sphere of the sacred), but also highlights Hugh's Carolingian blood: Hugh was kin to *five* Carolingian rulers whose line stretched out in history.[69]

Hugh was buried in the abbey of Charroux in Aquitaine which had been founded by a count Roger between 785 and 800 but had then become a royal abbey, as we shall see below. Hugh had been sent there by his brother Louis the Pious in the troubles of 817–18, but he grew attached to it. Geography always matters but Charroux's position on a map, far from the heartlands of Francia, should not obscure the fact that this firmly Aquitanian monastery had important links with the court of Louis the Pious and also with the distant abbey of Reichenau. The presence of Hugh, a prominent member of the Carolingian family, helped to bind it to the conceptual centre of the realm. And Hugh would also have played to a significant internal audience in Charroux. The monastery had some eighty-four monks, a substantial community which was instructed in its place in the Carolingian order through Hugh's presence in its ranks. Such instruction continued after Hugh's death in 844 as he was buried there, as he had wanted to be, thus ensuring that there was a corner of Aquitaine that might be forever Carolingian. In the light of all this, the appearance of an abbot of Charroux as an important actor in the upheavals at the court of Louis the Pious in 830–1 may be partly a result of Hugh's role in the interconnectedness of the vast realm.[70]

Figures such as Hugh and Drogo were exceptionally prominent. They were sons of Charlemagne and they benefited from the patronage of their brother Louis the Pious. Louis the Pious, his father Charlemagne and his grandfather Pippin III were single senior rulers, no matter how much their sons or brothers distracted the aristocracy; the patronage of 'marginal' members of the royal kin by a single centre may have given these members a distinction from 751 to 840 that the post-843 realms could not always match. In other words, not all such members of the Carolingian kin were equally highly visible throughout our period. And those royal kinsmen who did hold positions away from the court did not hold long-term Carolingian monopolies on them. Charles the Bald's sons Lothar and Carloman held the abbey of St-Germain of Auxerre in the 860s, interrupting the hold of the powerful Welf family on it; but the Welfs soon returned, only finally losing their own grip on it in 886.[71]

While these non-kingly Carolingians may not have covered the realm with a comprehensive grid, ubiquitous and constantly radiating Carolingian-ness, they nonetheless did help the realm become more intensively Carolingian. After Charlemagne's reign, they tended to do this more in the ecclesiastical sphere. Throughout the ninth century, we find men signalled as the kinsmen of kings holding bishoprics and abbeys throughout Francia. Some examples: the bishoprics of Le Mans in the far west (Aldric, 832–57), Mainz in the east (Charles, son of Pippin I of Aquitaine, 856–63) and Metz (Drogo, 823–55) and Liège in the centre (Franco, 852–901) were all held once by known members of the royal kin. Three important northern abbeys could all count a Carolingian as abbot at some time in the ninth century, sometimes more than once: St-Riquier (Charlemagne's grandson Nithard 840/2–4, shared with his brother Richbod 840–4; succeeded by Charles the Bald's cousin Louis in 844); Corbie (Charlemagne's cousins Adalhard 781–814, and 821–6, Wala 826–36), and St-Quentin (Charlemagne's son Hugh 822–44).[72] This list is not complete; bishop Aldric of Le Mans, for example, was also abbot of St-Amand on the river Scarpe, while abbot Hugh of St-Quentin held several abbeys including Novalese in north-western Italy, which still recalled his resplendent identity as a Carolingian in the eleventh century.[73] And these were just the men (see chapter on women).

Praying for a Carolingian future

That Italian abbey of Novalese, where Hugh was so warmly recalled, had originally been founded in 726 by a wealthy aristocratic ally of Charles Martel who had properties in the Rhone valley and the Alps. Eventually, it came under Carolingian royal control. Its links to the Carolingian royal house did not just depend on the chance of a Carolingian being abbot there. Novalese appears in a list of some eighty monasteries from around 819 that sets out services to the ruler, Louis the Pious. Novalese's wealth and importance are reflected in the fact that it appears in the first group, monasteries owing military service and 'gifts'; a second group owes only 'gifts', while the third and last group owes neither military service nor gifts, but only prayers. All the monasteries in the list owed such prayers and these were prayers of a specific kind; they were for the 'salvation' (*salus*) of the emperor and his sons and for the stability of the realm'.[74]

This was not a comprehensive list of the realm's monasteries, but the prayers it specifies are dynastic in that they are to include the ruler's sons. A sacramentary from the Paris region of the mid-ninth century gives a glimpse of common practice in churches in its inclusion of prayers for the ruler and his 'most noble offspring (*proles*)'.[75] These prayers were just one part of a vast labour of prayer that sought to make Carolingian rulers secure in a world standing under God's surveillance and threatened by recalcitrant earthly powers such as unruly magnates or plunder-seeking Vikings.

The Carolingians neither invented the idea of prayers for the ruler nor did they cunningly impose it on their gullible subjects. Prayers for the ruler were part of Christian culture. Carolingian rulers were heirs to a system that developed in the Christian Roman Empire, but whose roots pre-date the fourth-century conversion of Constantine. St Paul's first Letter to Timothy in the New Testament obliged Christians to make 'supplications, prayers, intercessions, and giving of thanks, … for all men. For kings, and for all that are in authority; that we may lead a quiet and peaceable life in all godliness and honesty' (I Timothy, 2.1, 2). Such prayers were part of a complex world of Christian thought and practice. They embraced the entire Christian community, the living and the dead, the present and the future, as God was entreated to protect rulers who had themselves to rule and care for their subjects in their earthly kingdom in such a way that these subjects might attain the heavenly kingdom. The rewards for such rulers could be manifest on earth, in the form of prosperous reigns, and in heaven, in the form of blessed reward.[76]

The uttering of such prayers for Carolingian rulers is thus on one level, and an important one, simply part of the nature of prayers for order in Christian society and can be found today in established Christian churches such as the Church of England where 'the queen and her ministers' are prayed for. Historians of liturgy have rightly pointed out that prayers were not primarily political, that Carolingian rulers did not draft prayers for people to say, and that tracing the development of prayers for the ruler requires sensitive and detailed exploration of problematic evidence. And not every church in the Carolingian realms might have possessed a sacramentary that contained masses for kings.[77]

Nor should such prayers be seen as simply timeless and occurring in a political vacuum. They were part of a system of symbolic communication that helped reinforce the ruler's authority, or at least helped make the ruler present across time and space. Many states and rulers have sought to align themselves with the heavens for a variety of reasons and in many different historical contexts. The Anglo-Saxon king Æthelstan (924–39) frequently commanded subjects to pray for him regularly (e.g. 50 psalms for him every Friday). In the pre-Christian Roman world, the emperor Septimius Severus wished to deify his predecessor Pertinax in the year 193; he staged elaborate funeral ceremonies 'and erected a shrine to Pertinax and commanded that Pertinax's name should be mentioned at the close of all prayers and all oaths'. In occupied France in the 1940s, the great saints of France such as Joan of Arc and Clotild (wife of Clovis) were publicly called on to preserve the health of Marshal Pétain. Prayers for the ruler could be woven into the texture of people's lives. In Frankfurt in 1806, Goethe's mother, Catherine, experienced the unravelling of this with the end of the Holy Roman Empire: 'Yesterday, the emperor and the empire were omitted in prayers in church for the first time … It is as if we had one funeral after another.'[78]

While the political conflicts and tensions of early medieval Europe do not match those of the modern era, we should not assume that sacredness of prayers automatically created or expressed blind loyalty to kings amongst those who uttered them or heard them. Each individual who took part in such prayers was not necessarily privately keen on the particular king that history and the dynasty had provided. The sacramentary of Echternach (diocese of Trier) composed between 895 and 898 explicitly names king Zwentibold as the king to be prayed for in masses, but relations between the king and the archbishop of Trier were not good and the king went on to strike the archbishop on the head with the latter's own staff of office, a stormy prelude to Zwentibold's own catastrophic end in 900.[79]

But private reservations are scarcely recoverable by us and what mattered was that the objectively existing task of prayer be performed. Churchmen on whom the burden of prayer fell felt their obligations keenly. In 812 in the abbey of Fulda, when the monks rose in revolt against the harsh rule of their abbot Ratger they complained, in terms that echo familiarly in our own public institutions, that the excessive workload kept them from their true business, business that included daily prayers for the emperor, his children and the Christian people.[80]

The monks of Fulda found a sympathetic hearing at the royal court, for kings knew the value of such prayers. Soon after this Fulda affair, against a background of unease and antagonisms in the royal house over the succession to the aged Charlemagne, church councils met and proclaimed the need for harmony on earth and for God's favour. In these assemblies in Reims, Châlon-sur-Saône and Arles all clergy were instructed to pray for 'our most excellent and most glorious lord king Charlemagne' and his children, with Arles specifying that daughters as well as sons were to be included. The councils of 829, brooding on the misfortunes of the realm under Louis the Pious, ordained that priests and people were to pray for Louis and his sons.[81] In 847, the churchmen gathered at Mainz took care to inform Louis the German that they had ordered prayers for him, his wife and his most noble offspring so that God would preserve the kingdom. The scale of these prayers is impressive: 3,500 masses and 1,700 Psalters. Offerings such as these would have been seen as worthy of a king and his family. And that family's well-being was explicitly linked with the stability of the realm, as prayer formulas stated. These were mighty outpourings of prayer, an extravagant form of liturgical largesse in a culture where spiritual giving was intertwined with substantial material gifts and benefits. Kings thus ensured that monks had the necessary resources to devote themselves to such prayers and to feasts of royal commemoration as revealed, for example, in the admittedly lavish provision made by Charles the Bald for feasts at St-Denis in the 860s, where monks consumed thousands of calories to fortify themselves for their liturgical efforts.[82] Kings also ensured, through grants of immunity and protection that monks, the specialists in prayer, were left undisturbed to carry out their weighty task.

The safety of the ruler, and of the kingdom, depended on prayers as much as on the success of the armies. And the royal line was to be prayed for as an integral part of what kept the kingdom secure. The machinery of prayer was monitored to ensure that it was functioning as it should. Thus, in Bavaria around 760, assembled bishops re-assured duke Tassilo, the last pre-Carolingian ruler, that prayers were said night and day by all priests, monks and clergy for him, his realm and his followers and that if anyone was found not to be carrying out this duty he would be disciplined. Some fifty years later in Bavaria, now under Carolingian management, archbishop Arn of Salzburg preached to his clergy on the need to pray for the safety of the realm and for that of Charlemagne, his sons and his daughters. Charlemagne's angry reaction in 783 to the news that the abbot of San Vincenzo in Benevento had refused to join in that community's regular prayer vividly shows how seriously rulers took the matter of prayers for themselves.[83]

Such prayers were part of an impressive apparatus of liturgy and ceremonial that pivoted around the ruler. We can find dynastic elements in the *laudes regiae*, the sonorous acclamations chanted for the ruler and which invoked heaven's blessing on him and his associates in their governance of their Christian world. These chants, to be found in imperial Rome and Byzantium, seem to have been introduced into Francia by the second half of the eighth century. The help of God and the host of the saints was repeatedly implored for the pope, for the ruler and his sons and for the army. The ruler was not the only Frankish beneficiary here; the Franks themselves were drenched in ceremonial splendour. The Carolingian monarchy was not like a modern-era totalitarian dictatorship where all blessings were to be offered to the ruler alone, though Benito Mussolini was keen to have his own name chanted in an extraordinary attempt to revive the *laudes* in Fascist Italy.[84]

It cannot be denied, however, that the ruler has a key place in these *laudes*. The Franks may appear *en masse*, as it were, as the army but only the ruler and his family stand out as specifically named (apart from the pope and, on occasion, certain bishops). Thus, a text of the *laudes* compiled between 788 and 792 prayerfully wishes for life and victory for the nobles and army of the Franks but singles out for special attention the exalted figures of Pope Hadrian, Charlemagne ('most excellent king … crowned by God'), queen Fastrada, and the king's sons ('Charles and Pippin his most noble sons'). The fact that this text was written down as a formula text on a manuscript that had once been connected to the deposed Bavarian ducal family speaks volumes.[85]

The ritual performance of such invocations could be offered to the ruler himself (and his consort) in public contexts, as when Charles the Bald and his wife Richildis, recently crowned as emperor and empress, were greeted with *laudes* in a carefully staged performance at the synod of Ponthion in 876, where 'everyone rose to his feet, each standing in position according to his rank'. Similarly, the emperor Arnulf enjoyed the thunderous *laudes* from the assembled prelates at Tribur in 895, a ceremony that, as Richard Southern observed, must have convinced all present, and Arnulf not least, that the Carolingian monarchy had many more years to run.[86] A powerful illusion. In such contexts, *laudes* were public and reached a politically important earthly audience.

We cannot be certain about the precise content of texts performed on specific occasions, but the general point holds that kings could be re-assured of their own place and, crucially, that of their dynasty, in the order of things and that all the participants were involved in calling on heaven to maintain that order. The *laudes*, with their mesmerizingly relentless progression and triumphal imagery, seem to express certain confidence in the aid of God and the saints even as that aid is invoked. The Latin of the *laudes* is not complex, and indeed the 788/92 text for Charlemagne and Fastrada includes phrases in Romance vernacular. Even people who had only a shaky grasp of liturgical Latin would surely have been able to pick out the names of the royal family and familiar saints. While gazing at these words on the leaves of manuscripts or in their neat columns in modern editions, we surely need to recall something like the great acclamations of the tsar in Mussorgsky's opera *Boris Godunov* if we are to imagine the nature of the potential impact of these awe-inspiring fanfares on contemporaries.

Laudes could of course be sung as part of ceremonies that took place far from the ruler's presence. King Pippin III was not himself present in Rome in 761 when the pope had *laudes* sung in the presence of Pippin's envoys to mark the dedication of an altar gifted by the king.[87] Such ceremonies made the king liturgically present even when he was far away.

It is these elements – prayer as obligation, the concept of dynasty and the evocation of (absent) royal presence – whose importance we can examine in a set of prayers distinct from those that we have surveyed so far. These prayers are the ones referred to in the 'prayer clauses' of royal diplomas, where rulers requested an ecclesiastical community to pray for himself, his wife and/or children and for the kingdom. Such prayers were inescapably bound up with the future, that is, with looking to, praying for, a continuation of the existing royal line. These requests for prayers have been the object of specific study and this permits us to investigate their significance for exclusive dynastic legitimacy more closely here.[88]

This prayer-clause is a particular formula that occurs in royal diplomas throughout our period. It is usually to be found in charters where the king takes a church under his protection and gives it 'immunity', that is, independence from the jurisdiction and interference of outside agents. Paradoxically, such immunity could in fact bind churches more closely to the king and so we should not see the granting of it as a sign of royal weakness.[89] We can find a typical example of the request for prayer in a formulary (a template for the drawing up of documents). This comes from the 'imperial formulas' drawn up in the reign of Louis the Pious in the 820s: the recipient of the privilege is to pray 'for the safety of ourselves (i.e. the ruler himself) and of our wife and offspring and of the whole realm bestowed on us by God'.[90] These formulas were 'live'. Louis himself requested prayers for himself, his wife, his offspring and the security of the realm in diplomas issued on the eve of the crisis of 833 and in its aftermath.[91]

Historians tend to be cautious in assessing the significance of such formulas, precisely because they are formulas. But if formulas were sometimes copied almost automatically, they were not necessarily copied mindlessly. Furthermore, the repetition of such formulas is itself part of their significance. By that reiteration, they help establish what they request as part of the natural order of things. That such repetition was not mindlessly automatic can be seen from the fact that the formula was regularly adjusted to fit specific circumstances.[92]

We have to be careful in using such documents as evidence of the attitudes and intentions of individual kings. But royal charters were not issued casually and their content was important. As we have seen, prayers as obligation and gift mattered to kings and kings did not miss a chance to ask for them. Even before he became king in 751, Charlemagne's father Pippin III had told the monks of Flavigny that he wished them to pray 'for me as well as for all my present and future offspring'; he granted the monks some fishing rights and sent these instructions and details of the grant on some stylish ivory tablets; this was the request of a prominent leader. The mind-set revealed in this letter is consistent with that found in a charter issued by Pippin, again before he became king, for the abbey of St-Denis in which he requested the monks to pray 'ceaselessly day and night for us and our sons and for the stability of the kingdom of the Franks' as well as to have his name recited daily in the mass.[93] Again, the dynastic accent can be clearly heard and, again, there is stress on repetition and on the future. Prayers for the younger members of the soon-to-be royal line are to become part of the liturgical landscape of the great spiritual centres of the realm.

While this was not essentially new, with the Carolingians a stress on the dynasty becomes clearer.[94] Professor Ewig's figures for the general prayer clause (not all of which referred to children) in the charters of the immediate successors of Louis the Pious after 840 give some idea of the frequency of such requests: it appears in 42 out of Lothar I's 139 charters, in 49 out of Louis the German's 171 and in 140 out of Charles the Bald's 461.[95] To pray for the well-being of the ruler, his wife and children was to pray for a secure future for the Carolingians and for a future that would remain securely Carolingian. This was to pray for the reproduction, in every sense, of a Carolingian realm. Prayers for such reproduction could be urgently personal: Charlemagne's mother Bertrada prayed intensely that she would have a son before he was born; the bishops trying to reactivate the child-bearing capacities of queen Ermentrud at Soissons in 866 knew that their blessings and prayers were important for the fate of the whole realm.[96] The prayer clauses that concern us usually referred to living members of the royal family, but illustrious ancestors could be included and so an element of commemoration was often present. In their requests for the royal family to be preserved, these prayers looked to the present and the future and they defined the shape of that future as dynastic. Kings did not request prayers only for their own family; most of these prayer clauses referred to the kingdom as well, and Charles the Bald's elaborate liturgical arrangements towards the end of his reign explicitly named some favoured aristocrats as included among the prayers for the royals.[97] But such individual non-royal references are very rare indeed.

In requesting such dynastic prayers, kings ensured that they and their line were liturgically present even in distant regions of their realm. Lothar I, for example, never visited Marseille, but he asked the church of Saint-Victor there to pray for him, his wife and his offspring as well as for the whole realm. The fact that he made this request in the palace of Aachen in 834 when he was hoping to rule the whole empire with his father in captivity is striking.[98] In fact, requests for prayers could act as a vehicle for transcending, or blurring, political boundaries of the often-divided Carolingian world. Thus, Louis the German, in confirming immunity and protection for the church of St-Martin in Utrecht in 854, requested that it pray for him, his wife and his children even though Utrecht lay in the kingdom of his brother Lothar, for whose line it had already been asked to pray. Such requests may at times have been a rather sensitive matter.[99] In general, kings tended to focus upon their own kingdoms and their own lines. Generalized royal requests for prayers for a broad section of the Carolingian family were in fact quite rare. Professor Ewig has noted the striking request for prayers 'for the line of our family' (*pro generis nostri prosapia*) in two 881 charters of Carloman, grandson of Charles the Bald, but has seen this as expression of a Carolingian family solidarity at a time of fears over the continuation of the dynasty, a real problem in the 880s.[100]

In focusing on their own line, on their own children, rulers sought to secure the future of their kingdom and thus to re-assure their followers that the political order in which they had all invested so heavily would survive. Although the prayer clauses could be varied and sometimes asked only for prayers for the ruler, nearly all the Carolingian rulers north of the Alps from 751 to the death of Charles the Fat in 888 explicitly asked for prayers for their children.[101] Only four kings have left no explicit requests for prayers for their offspring; they are not known to have fathered any children: the young Charles of Provence (855–63), Pippin II of Aquitaine (838–64), and the youthful brothers Louis III (879–882) and Carloman (879–884) of west Francia.

The vast majority of Carolingian kings thus sought prayers for their children which was a commitment, even if a mechanical one, to the continuation of their line. The dynastic principle could be taken for granted. But kings could be very self-conscious in making these requests, and this would have raised the consciousness of contemporaries who were the target of these requests. It may be surprising to encounter the familiar requests for prayers for the ruler, his wife and his offspring in the charters of Charles the Fat (876–87/8). Notoriously, Charles had no legitimate children. Just as notoriously, his queen, Richgard, claimed that she had remained a virgin throughout the marriage (see Chapter 8). But scholars have noted that a clutch of these charters comes from the period 885–7, that is, precisely when Charles was trying to have his illegitimate son Bernard recognized as his successor. Charles was aware that having prayers said for his son in churches stretching from Langres in Burgundy to Passau on the Danube was a chance to make him acceptable across the realm as a fully fledged member of the royal line. Bishop Geilo of Langres had backed the non-Carolingian Boso in his bid for a crown in 879, but now he was to preside over prayers for the natural continuation of the political order, Carolingian hereditary succession. Prayers did not merely reflect status but were to work to create and define it.[102]

Gender could be an element in this defining of status. The prayers referred to in the 819 *Notitia* are specifically gendered in that the text calls for prayers for the son of the ruler, and kings did sometimes specify that sons were to be prayed for.[103] This is probably how contemporaries generally understood the term *proles* (offspring) that appears in these documents. But the dynastic focus could be broader. Charlemagne sometimes explicitly specified that daughters were to be prayed for, as well as sons, in charters spanning the years 792 to 803, a period of highly charged negotiations about the succession and the imperial title.[104] Charters can be tricky documents, created and preserved in a variety of contexts, but one of these is an original. Charles the Bald also explicitly included his daughters as well as his sons in some of his requests when he asked for prayers for 'offspring of each sex'.[105]

Explicit references to the 'offspring of both sexes' are very much in the minority. But contemporaries could understand *proles* (offspring) as including daughters. Charles's own sister Gisela used the term in 874 to refer to all her children, male and female.[106] The explicit references to daughters in charters of Charlemagne and Charles the Bald evoke gender only to make it vanish in the blazing light of Carolingian-ness: on some occasions and in some contexts, all the children of a king were to be considered equally special, equally worthy of the gift of prayers. The identity that appears here is indeed dynastic, not in the specific sense of inheritance of the throne, since daughters could not do so, but in a broader sense of the specialness of the king, ruler and father. Even Louis II, ruler of Italy (840–75), who had no sons, but only daughters, issued diplomas with requests for prayers for himself, his wife and offspring.[107] One of these, from 865, is modelled on a diploma of his father's from 830, itself drawing on a standard formula as well as on documents issued by Charlemagne.[108] But this seemingly automatic repetition makes Louis II's document more, not less, significant: contemporaries were schooled in the assumption that they should acknowledge, signal and perform the distinction of rulers' children. 'Offspring' in Louis II's requests for prayers, unless referring to hoped-for sons, must be referring to his daughters. His daughters were therefore able to constitute by themselves the category of royal *proles*. It is as if a king *had* to be conceived of dynastically, that is, as having offspring, and if they happened to be daughters then they fitted the bill.

Such requests for prayers were a general phenomenon, but were also made of particular abbeys in particular landscapes. Naturally, Carolingian rulers made specific requests to houses that their own family had founded, for example, Prüm.[109] But the rulers looked beyond their own foundations. These requests, particularly in their association with granting of immunity, could be part of the delicate, and not so delicate, manoeuvrings for influence and authority in local contexts. When the Carolingians extinguished the ducal office in Alsace in the 740s, they treated local aristocratic interests, including those of the ducal family, with relative restraint, but they did ensure that monasteries there such as Murbach and Honau that owed foundation and benefits to the ducal family turned to the new rulers. Fiscal revenues were duly converted into resources for lights for Murbach 'for the stability of our kingdom' and Charlemagne himself controlled Murbach directly for a year.[110]

Further west, in Aquitaine Count Roger of Limoges, a loyal follower of Charlemagne, handed over his own monastic foundation of Charroux to the king some time between 785 and 800. Charlemagne's charter of immunity for the abbey specified that it was to pray for him, his wife and his children. Roger and his wife seem not to have originally thought that they would hand the monastery to the king in their own lifetime, but they had intended that the monks of their foundation were to pray 'for the stability of the lord Charles and his offspring and of the whole Christian people and ourselves'. Aristocrats such as count Roger and his wife approvingly understood the importance of prayer for the royal line, and saw no tension between that and requesting prayer for themselves. A contemporary celebrated the piety of Roger and his wife in a poem and around 840 a biographer of Louis the Pious recalled Roger as one of the wise and brave Franks who served so loyally in Aquitaine.[111] Co-operation was an ideal and a necessary reality for kings and aristocrats, and could be harmonious.

But prayer did not smooth all rough edges. Around 860, when count Gerard and his wife established monasteries including Vézelay in Burgundy, they wanted the monks and nuns to pray for themselves and their family but also for Louis the Pious and both his wives, now dead, as well as the very much alive Charles the Bald and his wife and their sons and daughters. This, however, did not prevent serious conflict breaking out between Gerard and Charles at the end of the 860s. And when Charlemagne and Louis the Pious thought of prayers in Charroux, they thought explicitly and exclusively of prayers for themselves and their line; the confirmations of Vézelay's privileges issued by Charles the Bald in 868 and by his son Louis the Stammerer in 877 likewise referred only to the need for prayers for the royal line. Aristocratic foundations such as Charroux and Vézelay thus passed into the great system of dynastic prayer. On the more tangible level of political geography, Charroux was one of a series of monasteries in south-west Gaul conveyed into the hands of the king, and which thus strengthened royal control of this corner of the realm.[112]

Charlemagne's descendants had to continue to ensure that the realm's future remained Carolingian. Decades after Charlemagne's death and hundreds of kilometres to the east of Charroux, King Louis the German of east Francia can be found hard at work on this. Two examples may illustrate this. In 857, at the palace of Bodman Louis, shortly after the death of his daughter Hildegard, granted to the priest Berold some property and chapels. This property belonged to the abbey of St Felix and St Regula in Zurich where Hildegard had been abbess; Berold had been her priest. This was a reward for his faithful service and the charter is suffused with the memory of 'our dearest daughter'. But it also looks forward, requesting prayers for 'us [i.e. Louis], our wife and our offspring'. Here an individual and an institution were caught up in remembering a familiar figure, a royal abbess, and in praying for the king and his dynasty. This is on a much smaller scale than, say, Louis's brother Charles the Bald's liturgical arrangements in St-Denis, but there is a similar insistence on creating and maintaining an awareness of the dynasty, even in a region where the palace of Bodman and abbeys of St-Gall, Reichenau and Zürich worked to foster such awareness. It was precisely this sort of insistence that ensured that such awareness existed and would continue to do so (and I say nothing of the importance to contemporaries of the prayers themselves).[113]

Our second example catches a bigger political fish. In an 858 charter delivered at Frankfurt, Louis tells how one of his vassals, Wolvene, had lavishly restored the monastery of Rheinau, on a picturesque bend of the upper Rhine in what is now Switzerland. It had been founded by his family but badly damaged by 'enemies', and Wolvene had eventually handed it over to Louis who had granted it back to him for his lifetime, while also taking it into royal protection and offering it immunity. Louis specified that the monastery needed to provide him with a war-horse with shield and lance, while the immunity would ensure that the monks were undisturbed so that they could pray for 'us and our wife and offspring as well as for the whole of the kingdom conferred on us by God'. The 'enemies' who had damaged the abbey were in fact probably members of Wolvene's own family; royal protection offered a way of taking the abbey out of the storms and stresses of family disputes. Wolvene was a member of a potent aristocratic family in Alemannia, and he also had properties in Italy. Envoys from the court of Italy's ruler, Louis II, had seen Wolvene hand over the abbey to Louis the German and what Louis was doing here was asserting his authority and presence in this region, a real presence in his appearances at the new palace of Ulm in 854 and 858, but also a virtual presence in this region. The Rheinau transactions take their place in a sequence of actions by Louis designed to cast his shadow over Alemannia in his own kingdom and impress neighbouring Alsace, in the kingdom of his nephew Lothar II, as well as Italy itself.[114]

The dynastic prayers to be uttered in Rheinau are thus only one element in this picture. And these prayers are not what the Rheinau transactions are 'about'. But they are the thread that we have followed and which has led us to this bigger scene. And they belong in that scene as they would have played their part in the 'presencing' of Louis the German and his line in this region.

It would be wrong, however, to think that this system of prayer mattered only in the 'peripheral' areas of the realm or that this machinery could ever relax. By the time of the reign of Charlemagne's grandchildren, the living memory of the Franks could scarcely recall rule by any other dynasty (not everyone had archbishop Hincmar's recollections), but the Carolingian dynasty and in particular a Carolingian future still had to be prayed for. Levels of Carolingian-ness had to be constantly topped up and they had to be topped up everywhere, including heartland sites. We can see this at its most extreme in the elaborate liturgical arrangements made by Charles the Bald (840–77). Throughout his reign, he issued charters requesting prayers for himself, his wife and his offspring (*proles*).[115] From the 860s onward, he made ever more detailed liturgical arrangements of commemoration and prayer at various great churches and in particular at the abbey of St-Denis near Paris, one of the spiritual and political centres of his kingdom. St Dionysius (St Denis) himself was seen by Charles as his special protector in whose spiritual presence the king wanted his tomb to lie, the abbot was Charles's own cousin Louis and eventually Charles himself became the abbot. But, precisely *because* it was such an important centre, St-Denis could not be taken for granted. Personal and dynastic liturgical arrangements had to be fervently articulated here just as much as in the far-flung corners of the empire, perhaps even more so. St-Denis, like other abbeys, had a variety of aristocratic patrons; it was not exclusively in thrall to the Carolingians.[116]

Such royal requests for prayers were not whispered into a void. St-Denis had well over a hundred monks. One set of arrangements for the commemoration there of Charles's father, grandfather, grandmother and aunt (the presence of women is noteworthy) was made by the king at the major assembly of Pîtres in 862, and a text of these arrangements was subscribed by over forty bishops and abbots there. An important public knew about these dynastic prayers. The fact that we know details of Charles's similar requests in 867/9 for dynastic commemoration at the northern abbey of St-Vaast, not from a surviving royal diploma but from an ecclesiastical document subscribed at a synod in 869 in Verberie near Paris by thirty-two bishops and ten abbots (one of whom was Charles's son) testifies to knowledge of and support for these prayers by the elite aristocracy, or at least its spiritual wing. The bishops and abbots gathered at Verberie affirmed that the king's favours for St-Vaast meant that the monks there were to be free to devote themselves to pray for the well-being of 'our lord [Charles the Bald] and of the royal offspring (*proles regia*)', just as the twenty-four bishops and abbots at the synod of Douzy in 871 knew about similar requests by Charles for prayers and commemoration for his wife and offspring at the abbey of St-Medard in Soissons.[117]

Contemporaries understood that Carolingians stretched back in time so that they could reach into the future. They also knew that they could encounter Carolingians of varying types across the space of the realm, in the palace and far from it. And Carolingian rulers asked for prayers to keep things this way. But the very richness of Carolingian presence meant that there were tensions. Many of these tensions derived from the success of Carolingian claims on exclusive possession of royalty, and from the inability of individual rulers to control a system of Carolingian specialness. Glorious ancestors and prospects of a luminous future were a context for the staging of Carolingian royalty, but were not in themselves guarantees of successful performance.

8

Women's work

At the centre of a poem written soon after 799/800 (as we now have it) is a famous hunting scene and at the centre of the scene is the dazzling royal family: Charlemagne, his queen and the great king's sons and daughters. The oldest boy bears his father's name, Charles, and physically resembles him. His brother Pippin is there too and we are pointedly told that his name recalls that of his grandfather and how his own deeds echo those of his father. Both royal sons ride fine horses and are surrounded by other young men. Their royal names point back to the dynasty's past just as their status as king's sons points forward to a future for the dynasty. Significantly, royal women are also present: the 'group of girls' (*ordo puellarum*). This includes Charlemagne's sister Gisela, whose presence ('golden offspring') sounds the chord of exalted family identity (*aurea proles*).

The women bring glamour to the scene. The word 'maiden' (*virgo*) resounds in the poem, striking a note of purity. Their physical beauty and their bejewelled clothes shine through the text, all the more so in contrast to the comparatively less glittering appearance of Charlemagne and his sons. The royal splendour is displaced onto these glowing women. While Charlemagne, in this poem as in Einhard's famous biography, wears ordinary (aristocratic) Frankish clothes, these women embody a 'to-be-looked-atness', in Laura Mulvey's well-known formulation, and constitute an acceptable face of royal display. Furthermore, Charlemagne's daughter Bertha is picked out as resembling her father in gorgeous drag: 'In her voice, manly spirit, her deportment and shining face, she replicates the mouth, the character, the eyes and the heart of her father … she replicates the appearance and character of her father.' Praising a woman by referring to her manly spirit was a commonplace but what counts here is that Bertha actually looks like a man, and not just any man, but her father.[1] She does not, however, transcend her gender. The point lies in the paradox. Although she is a woman, she looks like Charlemagne. This is a strongly gendered account of Carolingian charisma, a charisma so potent that it is transmitted to and blazes out among sons *and* daughters. Bertha repeats the appearance of her father and thus shows that Carolingian identity is repeatable in this family. The women of the poem are not destined to rule, but like the bustling sons, they embody the specialness of the Carolingians and duly broadcast this to their fellow cast members in the poem as well as to its audience and writer.

This evocation of the beauty and extravagant splendour of these women, in their virgin aura, as they rode to the hunt, is irresistibly reminiscent of the contemporary woman rider in the magnificent Hilton of Cadboll carved stone from Pictish Scotland. These poetic women are more richly dressed and more virginally pure than Einhard's

Charlemagne. Women could display the wealth of their male kin, though they had their own treasures. The bejewelled golden circlet known as the Iron Crown of Lombardy can evoke the precious armbands and coronets worn by the great women of the Carolingian world, though we should not let Einhard persuade us that all kings dressed plainly all the time.[2]

The women of the Carolingian house, those who were born into it and those who married into it, what sort of role did they play in the formation, reproduction and transmission of a Carolingian identity? This chapter will argue that they played a key role. That Carolingian royal women could play an important part on the level of events is amply demonstrated by the careers of such royal wives as Judith, wife of Louis the Pious, and the empress Engelberga, wife of Louis II of Italy. Occasionally, a Carolingian royal woman pops up in the sources to give us a tantalizing glimpse of the sort of power such a figure might wield and the readiness to participate in high politics such a figure might display. The episode in which Charles the Bald's half-sister Hildegard captured one of Charles's followers and tried to barricade Laon against him in the troubles following the death of Louis the Pious in 840 is a case in point.[3] Another combative Hildegard, who made trouble for King Arnulf in 895, appears in contemporary perception as 'daughter of Louis [the Younger], King of the Franks' and 'our [Arnulf's] niece'.[4] This chapter, however, is concerned more with structure than with event, with the role played by the women of the dynasty in legitimating and maintaining the political predominance of that dynasty. In this perspective, what these Hildegards did is of less importance than what they were: Carolingians.

As women, they were a particular kind of Carolingian, just as the men were. Carolingian women played a central role in the politics of the era because they belonged to the most important family in the realm, and they helped make that family so. They were constrained by norms and structures, but in giving these women a chapter of their own, I do not intend for 'Women' to be a marginal category, 'something relative to, something contained by "society" and "culture", [where] the concerns of women are regarded as less than the concerns of society'.[5] The study of Carolingian royal women here is not a study of an exotic sub-group, but of a central element of Carolingian authority and thus of the political history of the period. There already exists a substantial amount of work on Carolingian marriage practices, queenship, etc., as well as on the women of the royal and aristocratic houses of Anglo-Saxon England and Ottonian Germany and their role at court and convents.[6] That literature informs this chapter but the focus here is on the overall system of the reproduction of Carolingian distinctiveness.

The marrying kind: Incomers and women as treasures

A royal marriage could be a showpiece of dynastic glory. The spectacular arrival of high-status brides from exotically distant lands enhanced and signalled the specialness of the home dynasty to dazzled contemporaries. In the sixth century, Visigothic princesses travelled from Spain with immense treasures to marry Merovingian kings; in 929,

Anglo-Saxon princesses journeyed through the German realm of Henry I, displaying themselves as prospective brides for his son Otto as well as distributing treasure as they went. Merovingian kings were themselves no slouches in this department; in 584, king Chilperic sent his daughter to her Spanish marriage with fifty waggons full of treasure.[7] This was not a constant feature of Frankish royal marriage. After the sixth century, Merovingian kings did not opt for marriage to such distant figures. Nor did the Carolingians pursue brides of international glamour. This was partly because the dynasty initially needed to form alliances with important families in Francia and to strengthen the foundation of its own line.[8] The exception here is Charlemagne's marriage around 770 to a daughter of the Lombard king of Italy. Horrified at the prospect of his Frankish protectors allying with his opponents in Italy, the pope forcefully urged Charlemagne and his brother to shun such foreign marriages, evoking biblical commandments against such practices. The papal thunderings were to no avail, however, and these particular Biblical injunctions did not go on to have general application in the early medieval west. Nor was Louis the Pious's 817 prohibition of foreign marriages for his sons a statement of a fixed Carolingian policy[9]

If the appearance of a foreign bride in the Carolingian house was a sign of the new dynasty's ambitions, that particular marriage turned out to be a failure, and Charlemagne's sending his Lombard wife home was something of an embarrassment for his biographer some fifty years later. The Frankish conquest of the Lombard kingdom in 774 and the fact that the Visigothic kingdom of Spain had collapsed in 711 meant that there were now fewer non-Frankish royal brides from which the Carolingians could choose. Anglo-Saxon royal families remained very much on the horizon, but Charlemagne reacted angrily to the possibility of his son marrying an Anglo-Saxon princess.[10] The flatness of the surrounding landscape could only enhance Carolingian prominence, a prominence that Charlemagne further secured when he rounded up the family of duke Tassilo of Bavaria in 788. Foreign women, Tassilo's daughters, did indeed now travel again to Francia along with treasure, but as prisoners, symbols of the dominance of Charlemagne's line. These children of Tassilo were re-educated in Frankish abbeys in paying due reverence to their new Carolingian masters. A small but richly decorated book from Mondsee in Bavaria, probably made for the ducal family, travelled west with that fallen family where between 788 and 792 someone cut out some folios that probably contained dangerous and offensive prayers for the Agilolfings and inserted prayers for the Carolingian line. It is possible that Tassilo's daughter Rotrud was a reader of this book's message of dynastic collapse and had to learn to pray with Carolingian women for the triumphant royal line.[11]

Further east, the tantalizing prospect of marriage alliance with Byzantium never came to fruition for the Carolingians, in contrast to the Ottonians' luck here in the tenth century. But they did have chances. Lothar I's son Louis II of Italy was betrothed to a daughter of the Byzantine emperor in the 840s and early 850s but nothing came of this. Charlemagne himself received an offer of marriage from the empress Irene in 800/1 but she fell from power before anything could be done about this intriguing proposal. Nor was it only Carolingian men who were in the frame for a Byzantine marriage. In the 780s, serious arrangements were made for Charlemagne's young daughter Rotrud to marry the emperor Constantine, son of the imperially flirtatious

Irene. While such an alliance would have exported a Carolingian princess rather than importing an impressively foreign spouse, the prospective alliance would have redounded to the prestige of the dynasty. The betrothal was publicly proclaimed at a charged dynastic ceremony in Rome in 781, when Rotrud was about six. Moreover, Constantine sent experts in the ritual and etiquette of the Byzantine court to Francia to tutor Rotrud. The presence of a eunuch from Constantinople would shed lustre on Charlemagne's family as uniquely privileged in the realm; no other young Frankish girl would have had such a tutor. This is one of the features of Carolingian family arrangements suppressed by Einhard in the 820s, or simply unknown to him, when he painted his picture of a very Frankish empire.[12]

If the shimmering vision of foreign brides remained unrealized, the entry of aristocratic women into formal union with Carolingian men could be a grand public event, though we have no epithalamion such as that composed in sixth-century Francia for the marriage of Brunhild and Sigebert. After the death of his wife in 818, Louis the Pious is said to have selected a new wife in a sort of beauty parade at Aachen from among 'the daughters of the magnates who had been brought in from everywhere'. While our sources may have invented this story and sent scholars on a wild-goose chase for an equally problematic Byzantine bride-show as possible parallel for these antics at Aachen, they do not err in highlighting the keen, almost predatory, interest of aristocrats in Carolingian marriage prospects which were inevitably public business.[13]

We have very little detail about Carolingian weddings but they were not hole-and-corner affairs. A hagiographical text from around 670 gives us a glimpse of the making of marriage plans. This is the *Life* of Gertrud (d.653), daughter of Pippin I and thus an ancestral figure for the Carolingians. The story goes that her father invited the Merovingian king Dagobert to a banquet during which a pushy young aristocrat asked the king to arrange a marriage between him and Gertrud. The point for the hagiographer was Gertrud's defiant refusal of this earthly suitor and her pledging herself to Christ. But I would highlight here the text's evocation of the many courses of the banquet, the splendid clothing of the participants and the starry cast of king, palace nobles, Gertrud, her mother and father and her ambitious suitor.[14] Actual royal weddings may not have been quite as exuberant as the biblical wedding feast at Cana as re-imagined in the ninth-century Old High German poem the *Heliand*, but they were surely not quiet affairs. In ninth-century Wessex, King Alfred's wedding feast was attended by throngs of men and women who witnessed the king's dramatic illness. In Carolingian society, marrying was a public affair in that it involved families, property transactions, etc.[15] Much about weddings and marriage, which may have been an elastic concept, remains hidden from us and to focus on marriage means losing sight of the 'mistresses' of the Carolingian kings, those women who tended to be the latter's sexual partners earlier in the royal male life-cycle before the royal father arranged marriage. The imprecision of the information available to us makes it difficult to draw up tables of the marital stages of the royal male life-cycle but it seems that Carolingian sons did tend to marry later than Merovingian ones (with the knock-on effect of ratcheting up father-son tensions) and that marriage was a sign of social rather than sexual, biological maturity (marked by union with mistresses).[16]

Royal fathers needed an aristocratic audience for the weddings of their sons. Louis the Pious had his sons Lothar I and Pippin of Aquitaine married at important assemblies at Thionville and Attigny in 821 and 822. Contemporaries claimed that Lothar I had his son Lothar II publicly married to Waldrada before 855, and that the union of his other son Louis II to Engelberga in Italy was likewise accompanied by public granting of dowry from husband to wife. While these claims about Lothar's sons are tendentious, they reflect contemporary expectations and experience.[17] Contemporaries had to understand such weddings as episodes in the Carolingian dynastic story. Louis the Pious arranged his sons' marriages in the 820s partly to re-assure them that his own second marriage to the young and fertile Judith did not mean that his sons from his first marriage could not go on to found their own lines. Similarly, Louis the German in the next generation balanced his reluctance to grant his sons the title of king with a willingness to arrange marriages for them in the 860s. The marriage of daughters, as we shall see, was much rarer, but kings could use them also to broadcast messages; in the midst of the war with his brothers in 841, Lothar I celebrated the marriage of one of his daughters at Worms, projecting an image of stability for his line as well as trying to bind followers to him.[18]

Sometimes the wedding of a royal son was a sign that he would now be established in a kingdom of his own.[19] What royal weddings and their aftermath did demonstrate to a watching aristocracy was that the royal line would reproduce itself, and that the aristocratic woman who had married a king or his son had thus become part of a new household within a multi-generational royal family. That family could now have different households across the realm. After Lothar I's wedding at an assembly in 821, his father Louis the Pious went to Aachen for the winter but Lothar went to Worms. In 862, Louis the German's son Charles the Fat was left behind with his new bride at the palace of Frankfurt while his father and his as yet unmarried brothers set off with an army to the eastern frontier. The warriors assembled at Frankfurt would have seen these new familial arrangement click into place. Charles the Bald placed his wedding day in public memory by having it commemorated in prayers, though not all rulers did this.[20]

Aristocrats understood the significance of marriage in the elite life-cycle that they shared with the royal dynasty. Dhuoda could recall the day of her own marriage to count Bernard in the palace of Aachen in 824, a date she calculated by the regnal years of Louis the Pious.[21] Presumably those magnates who attended royal weddings remembered them as significant events. The young Hincmar of Reims was at Attigny in 822 when Louis's son Pippin got married and, although he makes no reference to this, he did recall some thirty years later how a grim case of marital discord had been referred to the lay nobles at that very assembly. When Charles the Bald's son Charles married without his father's consent in 862, his youth (he was only fifteen, a contemporary noted disapprovingly) and his flouting of parental consent did not mean that he lacked expert counsel; he was talked into the marriage by an aristocrat, count Stephen, whose own colourful marital history meant that he was something of an expert in what made a marriage binding and legal.[22]

Much of this chapter devoted to women has so far been about men. To some extent, that is inevitable. Carolingian men ruled. There are no real parallels between 751 and 888 to the rule of women in Ottonian Germany when the formidable grandmother and mother of the child Otto III secured the realm from 985 to 994.²³ Carolingians, both men and women, were bound up in networks of relationships and systems of meaning and only there did their individual history acquire political significance. My focus is on the dynastic system rather than on Carolingian queenship as an evolving institution, or on such topics as queens' roles as political figures, as patrons, intercessors, and on their access to resources, for example, the Italian estates held by Charlemagne's wife Hildegard so carefully surveyed in 781.²⁴ The dynastic role is central: how far did aristocratic women who married kings and their sons become honorary Carolingians themselves, and what was distinctive about their role?

Contemporaries may have puzzled over the precise status of queens and queenship, but they realized that a queen was not an ordinary woman and deserved respect. In his commentary on the monastic Rule of St Benedict written in Italy around 845, Hildemar stated that monks should prostrate themselves on the ground when they greeted a king visiting the abbey; the king thus received the same respect as bishops and abbots. When a monk saw a count, he was only to bow his head, not prostrate himself. But when a queen visited, while the monk was not to prostrate himself, he should go down on one knee, though bowing the head was also acceptable. Hildemar, who had travelled through the Frankish realms, obviously thought it was best to err on the side of showing special respect to queens, a deeper obeisance than to a count.²⁵

Women who married into the ruling family formed a key strand in the web of horizontal alliances that helped hold the realm(s) together and such marriages betray the need of Carolingian rulers for close links with the aristocracy. Before 751, Charlemagne's forebears, as great aristocrats, found such marriages helped give them access to resources and supporters. In the early seventh century, Pippin I's marriage to Itta brought him land around Nivelles and Fosses; Pippin II's marriage to Plectrud before 668/70 anchored support in the Meuse and Moselle region; Pippin III's marriage in the 740s to Bertrada re-united their shared inheritances near Prüm and Bonn.²⁶ As king, Charlemagne showed the same dependence on aristocratic alliance in his own marriages to Hildegard, daughter of the Alemannian ducal line, and to Fastrada with her attractive east Frankish connections. Such marriages could be the product of political circumstance rather than long-term thinking but they were consciously undertaken in the expectation of benefits. There was nothing casual about Charlemagne's choice of wife around 794 for his son Louis in Ermingard, known to the genealogical connoisseur Thegan as 'the daughter of the most noble duke Ingram, who was the son of the brother of the holy bishop Chrodegang [of Metz]'; this marriage deepened links between the royal line and Rhineland aristocrats. The fact that Thegan (writing in the 830s) celebrated the glory of Ermingard's ancestry, as he also did for Hildegard, shows that aristocrats were aware of the lines from which such women came, though not all royal wives were equally exalted.²⁷

These women's consciousness of belonging to such noble natal families was not obliterated by marriage. In the late ninth century, Richildis, widow of Charles the Bald, returned to her own family's centres in her widowhood, while Richgardis, wife of Charles the Fat, not only sought to preserve as many documents as she could about her own family's properties in Alsace but arranged that her foundation, the abbey of Landau, should stay under abbesses only from her family. Richildis and Richgardis both outlived their husbands and are rather special cases. And not every queen advanced her own relatives; the kin of Ermentrud, wife of Charles the Bald, did not enjoy the steady favour shown to the kin of Ermengard, wife of Lothar I.[28] Kings, rather than their wives, may have made the choices here, but contemporaries did not lose sight of the queen's family. The brothers of the empress Judith were targets of the hatred that engulfed her in the early 830s.[29]

These women were not solo players, and the families from which they stemmed were not passive. Carolingian husbands did not control everything. The dowries which they bestowed on their wives frequently consisted of estates near the lands of the wife's own family, deepening royal presence in a region such as Alsace but also testifying to, and enhancing, that family's resources.[30] Aristocrats could push women firmly in the direction of Carolingians. We have seen count Stephen in 862 fixing the attention of Charles the Bald's young son on a bride of Stephen's choosing. Regino of Prüm tells a nasty story of an unscrupulous bishop prepared to do anything to ensure that his niece married a king.[31] The Bosonid family, based in the heart of Francia, became addicted to Carolingian marriage: the young Lothar II was bullied into his ill-fated marriage to Theutberga by her ruthlessly ambitious brother Hubert in 855. This ultimately did neither Theutberga nor Hubert much good; she was consumed in the grisly divorce case unleashed by Lothar while Hubert perished in 864 at the hands of agents of Lothar's brother.[32] The family remained undeterred. In 869, Theutberga's nephew count Boso was quick to ensure that his sister Richildis formed a union with king Charles the Bald. Charles, who had lost his first wife only days before meeting Richildis, saw in her and her family a key to holding the kingdom of the recently deceased Lothar II; Boso rightly saw his sister's marriage to Charles as a sign of imminent and generous royal favour. This all happened very quickly; Charles's wife Ermentrud died on 6 October and this news had to travel some 300 km to him; by 10 October, Charles and Richildis were betrothed and their relationship was consummated soon after that, to some contemporary disapproval at all this haste. The fact that we know all this shows how intensely personal were the bonds among the elite, and how public such personal bonds were. Boso himself went on to marry a Carolingian princess in 876, with momentous results for his future.[33]

Marriage to a Carolingian, however, gave these women an extra identity and one that came to be dominant. A key example of successful incorporation into the dynasty is Charlemagne's wife Hildegard, whom he married in 772 when she was around fourteen and who died in 783. First, Hildegard performed an essential dynastic role. Every Carolingian ruler of the ninth century was descended from her union with Charlemagne. It is not surprising that for those concerned with the dynasty's fortunes, she was 'the great Hildegard, mother of kings and emperors'.[34] Furthermore, the dynasty she did so proud had in fact been an enemy of her own ancestors and part of the Carolingian political achievement was in absorbing such figures and ensuring that their identity was articulated in Carolingian terms. On a dynastic level, Hildegard served the Carolingians well in death as in life. She was buried in Metz, in a burial complex that contained many (predominantly female) members of the Carolingian line; her husband and descendants commemorated her in grants stretching from 783 to 862 for that shrine of the family saint, Arnulf, as well as for Kempten and St-Denis. Hildegard was thus woven into the fabric of the dynasty to become a part of its ancestral glories.[35]

Hildegard's particular contribution can be clearly seen in a story in Notker's 'biography' of Charlemagne written about a century after her death in the region that her ancestors had dominated. Notker has several anecdotes featuring Hildegard that reveal that he did not forget the family from which she herself stemmed but he is also deeply concerned with her role as a Carolingian queen. While Charlemagne is off fighting the Avars, he leaves Hildegard under the protection of a bishop. Puffed up with this closeness to Hildegard the bishop asked if he could borrow, as a substitute for his episcopal staff, the golden sceptre of the uniquely royal Charles. Hildegard played for time by saying that she did not dare give it to anyone, but that she would speak to Charlemagne about it. When Charlemagne returned, he and Hildegarde chuckled over the bishop's request. At a great assembly, Charlemagne rebuked such episcopal ambition, stressing that the sceptre was a sign of his own royal authority (*sceptrum nostrum … pro significatione regiminis nostri aureum*).[36] This story, like all of Notker's stories featuring Hildegard, stresses her closeness to Charlemagne (e.g. their laughter of mutual understanding). But this particular story does more than that; it displays her as a guardian of the dynasty's unique right to rule. Hildegard's story here takes its place in Notker's repertory of stories about the assertion of Carolingian authority in the face of challenge; she acts as a Carolingian, anxious, like Notker, to keep the dynasty special.[37]

These women were figures apart. Queens remained married to the king even if their family fell from a king's favour. Emma, wife of Louis the German, and Ermentrud, wife of Charles the Bald, survived the tremors following the fall of their own brothers in the 850s and 860s. This is partly because divorce was a problematic option at this time, as the storms over Lothar II's case showed everyone. And queens could respond actively to such crises. Eric Goldberg has argued persuasively that the silken belt woven by Emma and bearing an inscription referring to the 'shining and most holy queen Emma' formed part of that queen's public proclamation of her special and holy status (*nitens*, 'shining', suggested purity); she thus shored up her position at her husband's court at a difficult time. As for Ermentrud, her willingness to be blessed by bishops into renewed fertility for her husband in 866 may show her determination to remain as queen no matter what happened to her kin.[38] Political intrigue and gendered questions of fertility and purity could make queens vulnerable but these queens turned them round to make their queenly status more exalted.

Moreover, Carolingian queens had unions only with their husbands. Up until 888, as far as we know, only one Carolingian king married a widow, and this was the young Charles of Aquitaine in 862, an act very much against the will of his father Charles the Bald.[39] This contrasts with the more fluid situation of the subsequent period when, for example, Louis IV married Gerberga, widow of the duke of Lotharingia, in 939, or when Otto I of the German kingdom married Adelheid, widow of Lothar II of Italy.[40] Carolingian queens had known no other men. Nor did they re-marry if they themselves became widows. This is very different from, say, the career of Queen Brunhild in the Merovingian era and is a striking feature of the experience of Carolingian queens. As Pauline Stafford has observed of medieval queens, '[royal] widows, who carried claims from their families of birth and marriage, could be even more desirable than virgins as marriage partners'.[41] But no one dared desire Carolingian widows. Our evidence is limited and it is possible to misread silence of our sources but none of the ten known ninth-century Carolingian widows re-married after the death of their husband.[42]

Again, this contrasts with the post-888 period. When king Zwentibold was killed in 900, one of his killers immediately married his widow Oda. The 951 marriage of Eadgifu, widow of Charles the Simple, to a great magnate of west Francia also illustrates the very differently competitive world of the tenth century.[43] Whether Carolingian widows were strong enough to resist suitors, or were subject to control by their sons, they do seem to have been off-limits to the aristocracy while Carolingian hegemony flourished, and that points to their very special status as Carolingian figures. (Judith, daughter of Charles the Bald is an instructive contrast here.[44]) If a widowed queen did show excessive independence in men's eyes, as Charles the Bald's widow Richildis seems to have done in the 890s, even the offended archbishop who wrote to rebuke her still saw her as a queen. Richildis's grants to abbeys in 910 indicate that contemporaries still saw her as queen.[45] Furthermore, it would have been difficult for Carolingian kings to marry the widows of their brother kings, not least because the bonds of marriage could be supplemented with further created ties of kinship. In the 870s, Louis the German seems to have become a godfather to Engelberga, wife of his nephew Louis II of Italy, and his sons duly referred to her as their 'sister', deploying the 'generic familial idiom in which Carolingian politics was habitually articulated', as Simon MacLean has noted. These woman had become Carolingians.[46]

As such, their main task was to produce more Carolingians. That, however, is not all that queens could do. The Empress Engleberga, wife of Louis II of Italy, was so politically important that her name appeared on coins along with her husband's.[47] This was exceptional and not all queens were prominent all the time; queenship was not a fixed office that automatically conferred powers. But queens could realize the potential of their position. A glance at the careers of, for example, Fastrada in the 780s and early 790s and of Richildis in the 870s reveals formidable political operators at work; the fact that Richildis played a key role after her royal husband's death in passing on royal authority to Louis the Stammerer is particularly significant as Louis was not her son: dynastic reproduction was not only biological.[48] Contemporaries did not see queens simply as machines for producing little Carolingians. The well-known text, *On the Governance of the Palace*, written up by Hincmar of Reims in the 881 but based on a text from earlier in the ninth century, gives the queen several important roles, a key one being responsibility for the 'good order of the palace', a concern echoed in Sedulius Scottus's 860s manual for rulers which highlighted the queen's role in keeping the royal household pure.[49]

But what brought the queen to centrality in the palace, the nerve-centre of the realm, was her union with the king. And at the very centre of the palace was the royal bed. A great aristocratic woman such as Dhuoda was very aware of the pleasures and duties of the marital bed and there is no reason to doubt that queens thought like her: 'The learned doctors of the church do not deny its sacred rites to the marriage bed; they only busy themselves in rooting out lechery and illicit intercourse.' Improper behaviour in the royal bedchamber, however, affronted God and threatened the moral security of the realm, hence the vulnerability of queens to accusations of adultery, though it is important to remember that such accusations could also threaten the king.[50]

Queens had to produce results from their activity in the marital bed. The dynastic role played by the women who had married into the Carolingian family became part of the dynastic mask that covered their own features. When Charlemagne's wife Hildegard died in 783, he had an epitaph composed for her, and it duly celebrated her dynastic contribution: 'Alas, O mother of kings, the glory and the pain!' (Nelson trans). As we have seen, Charlemagne had her buried in the church of St Arnulf, Metz, placing her among tombs of his sisters and daughters. Einhard duly noted Hildegard's offspring but also recruited Charlemagne's mother Bertrada into the royal line, imagining her dynastic happiness at seeing that line extend through her son since she lived to see 'three grandsons and the same number of daughters in her son's household'.[51] Contemporaries could vividly imagine the dynastic triumphs and anxieties of the royal line as they knew what was at stake. They could relay this intensity back to the rulers themselves; in the 770s, Cathwulf, who was not even a Frank, urged Charlemagne to be grateful for the blessed fact of his conception, the result of anxious prayers by his mother (see Chapter 3 above).

This is a general concern of hereditary lines. A late tenth-century text tells of the childless king Conrad of Burgundy and his wife making a pilgrimage to the shrine of St Verena to beseech heaven for a son; they prayed, showered gifts on the shrine, made vows and returned home; that very night, the queen went to her husband and conceived a son who grew up to take up the governance of the realm (*regni gubernacula*). The links connecting the intimate world of bodies and the bedchamber with the stability of the realm were widely understood.[52]

The writers and performers of the liturgical chants for rulers, the *laudes,* acclaimed and prayed for queens as part of a royal line: the king, the queen and their children. The Soissons *laudes* focus on Charlemagne, his sons and Fastrada, even though she was mother to none of the sons. In 847, the churchmen gathered at the synod Mainz assured Louis the German that they had decreed that clergy in every parish of his realm would sing some 3,500 masses and 1,700 Psalters 'for you, your wife and your offspring'. Some prayers could be less public, though the same concerns and associations shine through. In Charles the Bald's own prayer book, we can read 'Deliver me ... together with our wife Ermentrud and our children'.[53] Throughout the period, kings' requests for prayers in return for their granting of immunity to monasteries regularly included their wife along with their offspring (see Chapter 7). One of our rare pictures of a Carolingian queen comes from a Bible made in Reims around 870 where the accompanying poem stresses her dynastic role: 'the noble consort on the left, by whom distinguished issue may rightfully be given to the realm (*proles in regnum*)'.[54] This is a depiction of Charles the Bald and Richildis who may have had particular concerns about children but, as we have just seen, such concerns were widely shared. In rituals of royal consecration clergy could pray for 'kings to come forth from [the new king's] loins' while the first Frankish coronation rite for a queen in 856 beseeched God to bless her breasts and womb.[55]

An inability to produce heirs was thus a potentially fatal flaw in a Carolingian wife. Bodies mattered because bodies always matter; we cannot get far beyond the 'alleged facts' of birth and death. Biology, however, existed within politics.[56] Charlemagne's wife

Fastrada only gave him daughters, but this was acceptable as he had rather too many sons in the 790s. Theutberga's inability to give Lothar II a son can only have added to his determination to get rid of her but was not in itself the cause of the marital crisis in the 860s. Anyway, some contemporaries pointed out that the lack of children could actually be Lothar's fault since sterility might not come from the body's infertility but from the wickedness of the husband.[57] To bodies and politics, we must therefore add Christian thinking and belief if we are to understand the pressures and resources around Carolingian queens. If a husband's wickedness was responsible for lack of children, then the prospect of repentance offered dynastic hope. If the biblical Abraham and Sarah could have a son at the ages of one hundred and of ninety respectively, then Charles the Bald and Ermentrud could still be hopeful after over twenty years of marriage; the bishops at Soissons in 866 explicitly referred to the biblical couple in their address.[58]

Bodies are indispensable, but they are not all there is. The bodies of male rulers needed watching. Louis the Pious 'feared that he might be overcome by the innate heat of his body'. The eighth-century Law of the Bavarians warned that when the duke was too old to mount his horse, it was time for him to be replaced.[59] For the men who controlled families and who defined marriage and its validity or breaking through sin, women's bodies could be problematic, puzzling. In the 860s, Archbishop Hincmar pointed out that bishops did not have experience to give them intimate knowledge about women's bodies, but that should not prevent them from probing the 'virgin secrets of girls and women' in such a case as the divorce of Lothar II.[60] The accusations made against Lothar's wife Theutberga in this case were the most specific and exact, but also the most bizarre, of all the accusations launched against queens in this period. Lothar and his supporters accused her of committing incest through anal intercourse with her brother before her marriage; from this monstrous union she conceived a child which she aborted; she thus presented herself as a virgin to Lothar on their marriage. Ninth-century people were not fools and much of this case turned on the nature of evidence and proofs for claims that seemed as bizarre then as they seem now.

How did contemporaries understand the queen's body? Could a woman conceive in this way and remain a virgin? It is not possible here to follow Hincmar's analysis in detail but it is worth noting his understanding of virginity as a physical state. He cites Deuteronomy (ch. 22) on how to counter a man who falsely accuses his wife of not being a virgin; the women's parents are to take the 'signs of the woman's virginity' to the town elders, that is, the cloth as sign of the loss of virginity. Hincmar's discussion remains physical; he sees virginity as lost through sexual intercourse, pregnancy and childbirth. It is impossible for a woman to have a closed womb or intact flesh once she has borne a child and children are conceived through intercourse. This biologically determined definition of virginity thus crushed the accusations. Hincmar understood that the term 'virgin' applied to man and woman but it was the queen's body that concerned him most here. The divorce case of Lothar and Theutberga was an exceptional process but the attention that it fixed on the royal bedchamber was extraordinary only in degree, not in kind. The union of the king and queen was where the realm was reproduced and was thus of concern to all.[61]

Hincmar's very clarity, however, may mislead us about ninth-century attitudes. His definition is rooted in bodily reality and thus appears as non-negotiable. Virginity appears as something physical that can be lost and not regained. As Jerome said, 'God cannot raise a virgin once she has fallen'. But the Fathers' views on virginity were wider than Hincmar's; virginity could also be an attitude of mind and a form of behaviour. Virginity could be cultural as well as 'natural'.[62] Ninth-century kings and queens could thus supplement their body with cultural options.

This seems to have been precisely what queen Richgard and her husband Charles the Fat did in order to end their marriage. In 887, Richgard was accused of adultery with a courtier bishop. Here I follow Simon MacLean's insightful investigation of the case. The accusations of adultery were a means of blackening the reputation of the bishop but also, paradoxically, of proclaiming publicly that Richgard, and indeed Charles himself, were chaste. At an assembly Charles made what Regino describes as the 'amazing' announcement that 'he had never joined with [Richgard] sexually' and she followed this up by asserting to the same assembly that 'she remained untouched not only by him [Charles], but by all male union, and that she prided herself on the integrity of her virginity'.[63] This surprised contemporaries, as Regino's testimony shows. Richgard had certainly been represented as a full wife of Charles; she appears as his wife in his dioplomas and they do contain requests for prayers 'for us, our wife and our offspring'.[64] In fact, Richgardis had no children, but these diplomas show that the generation of children in a royal marriage was taken for granted. We, and contemporaries, know that Charles the Fat was no virgin and that he could father children; he had an illegitimate son, Bernard. Notker of St-Gall thought that Charles, while still married, might produce an heir.[65] Richgard was thus, up until 887's surprise declaration, present in representations or assumptions about a sexually active royal marriage. She turned back time and recreated herself as a virgin and this, with Charles's claim never to have had intercourse with her, enabled them to have the marriage dissolved. Charles could thus hope for a new marriage and the prospect of legitimate heirs though, as we shall see in the final chapter, this was not to happen. Richgardis could retire with honour from the court to the abbey that she had founded. Her and Charles's bodies were thus central to the marriage and its unmaking but these bodies were malleable.

'The whole crowd of women'

Queens were only some of the Carolingian women. They married in to the family and daughters were the product of such marriages. Most famously, Charlemagne's daughters were understood to form a group of Carolingian princesses. There are well-known descriptions of how these glossy beauties attended their father in the royal household, on the hunt, etc. Louis the Pious's expulsion of 'the whole crowd of women' from his father's court in 814 shows that he too was aware of their group-identity and of the fact that this identity encompassed Carolingian birth, though he also wanted to be seen to be purifying his palace of a crowd of immoral women, not just his sisters. Charlemagne's court in his later years was a very distinctive place and not all rulers were surrounded by women in this way.[66] Even if such set-piece descriptions of Carolingian princesses as group are not encountered later, plenty of material survives to make the point that royal women formed a contemporary category and that their royalness was evident. Charles the Bald publicly reminded his counts in 864 that the monasteries granted to his wife and daughters were to receive the same respectful local treatment as the monasteries granted to his sons.[67] There seems to have been a stock of names for Carolingian princesses, though Constance Bouchard has rightly warned against seeing this as being deployed systematically, noting that names could drop out of use. And women's names would be less exclusive and highly charged than male names such as Charles and Louis. Nonetheless, the names chosen for such women, presumably by their father, tend usually to refer to the father's relatives, rather than the mother's. Frequently appearing names include Gisela (Charlemagne's sister) and Rotrud (Charlemagne's grandmother), but also include Hildegard (Charlemagne's wife); this, however, shows that women who married a Carolingian became Carolingian.[68] As we shall see, the regular succession of such women to particular abbacies such as Chelles and Schwarzach suggests that within the royal family certain plum jobs were reserved for a particular category of person. The lustre of Carolingian ancestry shone on the daughters of the house. Poems by Sedulius addressed to the daughter of Louis the Pious and to the daughter of Lothar I paid respectful homage to that ancestry.[69]

The fact that such women's Carolingian identity was not always referred to in hushed tones of respect shows how lively that sense of identity was. Contemporaries imagined that Carolingian women took an arrogant pride in their heritage, as in the story of how Boso of Vienne was nagged by his Carolingian wife into making a bid for the crown in 879: 'I am the daughter of one emperor and have been betrothed to another; I can't stand to live unless you become a king too.' Behind the stereotype of a domineering wife lies the undoubted fact that Boso did value precisely such ancestral charisma in his wife as a means of legitimating his kingship. It certainly helped legitimate that of his son whose highly charged name, Louis, was the exclusive property of Boso's wife's family, that is, the Carolingians.[70] Alongside the encomia of poets and the ventriloquism of chroniclers, we can place the testimony of Carolingian women themselves. Gisela, daughter of Louis the Pious and Judith, and thus sister of Charles the Bald, married a great nobleman, Eberhard of Friuli in the 830s, but her Carolingian identity was by no means swamped in her marriage. Of her four daughters, three bore names that had Carolingian association and Gisela was not merely a passive transmitter of Carolingian-ness, as a remarkable charter of 874 reveals. In this grant to her husband's family monastery of Cysoing, Gisela requests that the anniversaries of her father and mother, Louis the Pious and Judith, and her brother Charles be commemorated; Gisela's Carolingian consciousness was active.[71] Articulate, self-conscious, prominent, such women were every inch a Carolingian.

As children of kings, they were Carolingian, as we have just seen. Gender, however, debarred royal daughters from royal office; daughters of kings, they could themselves be neither king nor queen. They potentially had a central role in articulating the royal house's identity, but what sort of role? One sign of this centrality is an absence. Carolingian daughters do not generally appear among the wives of the aristocracy. Einhard's claim that Charlemagne never wanted his daughters to marry is not strictly true. As is well known, they did have liaisons with prominent and loyal aristocrats, but these were not marriages. Nor did Charlemagne's sister Gisela marry.[72] This points to a fearful awareness of these women's dynastic charisma. It was too dangerous to allow that charisma to leak out into the aristocracy. Charlemagne and his father were all too aware of what happened when duke Odilo of Bavaria took advantage of the chaos on the death of Charles Martel in 741 to unite with the latter's daughter Hiltrud and go on to produce their dangerous son Tassilo. This was still recalled with a shudder by the dynasty's followers a century later.[73]

Across the whole period, however, the experience of Carolingian daughters was more various than this picture suggests. Louis the Pious was happy to marry two of his daughters into the aristocracy: Alpais, probably illegitimate, married Louis's supporter Count Bego around 806, while Gisela, daughter of Louis and his second wife Judith, married Eberhard of Friuli around 836, a marriage possibly pushed for by Judith herself.[74] And, as we have seen (in Chapters 5 and 7) Pippin I of Aquitaine's daughters married aristocrats before their father's death in 838. But the kings who succeeded Louis after his death in 840 kept their daughters away from marriage, though this control depended on these fathers living long enough to exert it. Of the ten daughters of Lothar I, Louis the German and Charles the Bald, Sylvie Joye has counted only two who married, while seven became abbesses. This does suggest tight dynastic control, possibly stemming not simply from the intention to keep royal blood preciously rare but also from a desire not to favour one aristocratic family at the expense of another in the intensely competitive environment of the post-Verdun rivalries.[75]

Such pressure, however, could drive aristocrats to act, as in count Giselbert's abduction of and marriage to a daughter of Lothar I in 846. Significantly, this unnerved all three brother kings and they proclaimed at a joint assembly in 847 that such abductions were forbidden.[76] But pressures did not lessen and in 862 Count Baldwin abducted Judith, daughter of Charles the Bald; Baldwin was determined to match his rivals in the Flanders region, who had Carolingian ancestry as they stemmed from Eberhard and Gisela, daughter of Louis the Pious. Judith was a very special woman; she had been married with her father's consent to an Anglo-Saxon king and consecrated as his queen in Francia. After his death and various adventures she returned to Francia with treasure. Her father kept her confined at Senlis, one of the secure sites of his realm, where her queenly status was maintained and she could play out her role as widow, wearing widow's clothing and staying under the eye of her father and his men. Judith, however, seems to have played an active role in her escape from Senlis and union with Baldwin, a union that Charles eventually recognized.[77]

Daughters were not always passive; fatherly and kingly control could not be absolute. Generational conflict and horizontal bonds and alliances between royal children and aristocrats could challenge kings, or remind them of the limits of their power.[78] Kings keeping royal daughters away from marriage and aristocrats abducting them to force a marriage both testify to the high value of these Carolingian women. But those daughters who did not marry also worked to display and relay Carolingian specialness. To be in a convent was very far from being invisible and inaudible. Women who married into the royal family also cultivated connections with important abbeys and to examine such connections is to see Carolingian women, wives and daughters, as an active group.

The abbey of Faremoutiers illustrates this well. Founded in the seventh century for the noblewoman Burgundofara as part of the monastic culture generated by the

Irish monk Columbanus, Faremoutiers was favoured by the Merovingian court (it was very close to Paris) and in its early days existed in a landscape where the Arnulfings (Carolingians to be) were far from dominant.[79] By our period, however, this abbey was firmly in Carolingian hands and indeed formed part of an intensely Carolingian landscape, being one corner of what one might see as a rough triangle covering lands rich in estates of the fisc whose other corners were Chelles/St-Denis and Soissons. Faremoutiers had a special link with the inner circle of the Carolingian royal family. Charlemagne's daughter Rothild was abbess there in the reign of her brother Louis the Pious and she gained from him Gy-les Nonains in the Gatinais for the economic upkeep of the abbey. This was a grant that Lothar I was happy to confirm in the autumn of 840, in a charter that stressed the importance of family bonds in referring to 'our beloved aunt Rothildis'. Despite Lothar's efforts, the abbey ended up in the western kingdom of Charles the Bald after the Treaty of Verdun in 843. Such political changes did not disturb Faremoutiers as Rothild remained abbess there until her death in 852. It is worth recalling that the death of Louis the Pious in 840 was not the death of the last of Charlemagne's children. Rothild, like her brother Drogo of Metz, lived on into the 850s, some forty years after the death of her father, a visible living link with the great emperor. She was followed by a succession of abbesses with the Carolingian-sounding names of Bertrada, Judith, Hildegard.[80]

Rothild's Carolingian blood, undiluted by the fact that she was the daughter of a concubine, gave her and Faremoutiers access to the favour of Carolingian kings. Within the community itself, Rothild was a Carolingian presence, and she was not alone. Her successor as abbess was one Bertrada, who has been plausibly identified with Bertha, daughter of Lothar I.[81] A list of nuns of Faremoutiers dating from the 830s or 840s includes Bertrada in a prominent position after the abbess Rothild: *Rodhild abb et mon* (abbess and nun); *Theudenus magis et mo* (master and monk); *Et Irminoldus mo* (monk); *Ada mo* (nun); *Bertrada mo*; *Berta mo*; *Imma mo* (etc.). This prominence probably reflects the high status of Bertrada and the same is true of the Ada here, who is the sister of the magnate Count Eccard of Macon. The worldly criterion of high birth, rather than simply the date of entry to the abbey, played its part in the ordering of this list. Bertrada is the future abbess; as a Carolingian woman, she would have learned from her mistress Rothild the arts of cultivating political connections while being groomed for office herself. Within Faremoutiers, the values of reverence for the ruling dynasty were inculcated partly through an intense Carolingian presence; the list of nuns also includes such possibly Carolingian names as Berta (twice) and (again) Rothild; there may have been a considerable pool of Carolingian women here. A Carolingian identity of Faremoutiers was thus asserted within the house itself. Carolingian women controlled and dominated it. Its links with royalty were recognized by the abbesses' male relatives, the Carolingian kings, in charters such as Lothar's. It is no surprise to find Bertrada, once she became abbess, joining with Charles the Bald's queen, Ermentrud (there is an Ermentrud in the Faremoutiers list; was there a family connection with the house?) in successfully petitioning the king to take Faremoutiers under royal protection and grant it immunity as his predecessors had done. In return, Charles requested the community to pray for him, his wife, his children and for the well-being of the kingdom.[82]

Faremoutiers was not a 'propaganda' centre for the Carolingians. Faremoutiers reinforced the royal family's own picture of itself as royal and the support it offered to these rulers was essentially liturgical. Carolingians were physically present there, in the persons of abbesses and nuns, but they were also liturgically present, in the prayers requested by Charles the Bald, just as the grants of Louis the Pious and Lothar were present in the abbey's memory and archives. To some extent, therefore, we are dealing with a closed system, one that, apart from prayers to God, seems to be communicating primarily with itself, and this together with the liturgical and commemorative elements recalls Ottonian parallels.[83] This is one way in which Faremoutiers acted as an instrument for the continuous construction of Carolingian status.

The abbey also existed within a specific historical and geographical landscape. Among the nuns, there were women from the great aristocratic families of the empire such as that sister of count Eccard of Macon, Ada. While Ada was exposed to Carolingian presence and identity in the abbey, members of her family outside it also had links with it. Eccard was not the first man of this family to have a connection with Faremoutiers; his father had been a patron of the abbey. Such connections were close; Eccard made gifts to Ada and Bertrada the abbess and wished himself and his family to be commemorated there. The list of nuns includes names that point to other aristocratic families being represented in Faremoutiers. The name Madalgardis also appears; this is the name of the concubine of Charlemagne and mother of the abbess Rothild, which suggests that Charlemagne's concubine was of noble origin and that her family also had a connection with Faremoutiers. Such was the network along which Carolingian messages might run.[84]

Faremoutiers lay in the diocese of Meaux and in a region rich in Carolingian abbeys and palaces, hardly an area where the dynasty's grip was loose. But it was precisely this continuous presence, so assiduously worked at, that made this area 'Carolingian'. Charles the Bald's request for prayers for himself and his family was to be handsomely gratified. Abbess Bertrada, after Charles's death in 877, inserted a fulsome obituary notice in the abbey's 'obituary' which recorded the death of the emperor Charles, son of Louis Augustus and grandson of his namesake, the most glorious Caesar Charles (Charlemagne). At Faremoutiers the memory of Charles, on the anniversary of his death, was preserved by his relative (*propinqua*) the abbess Bertrada. Charles was remembered in later Faremoutiers tradition as a generous patron. One can see why he, and other kings, thought that Faremoutiers was worth some generosity. Headed by a Carolingian princess-abbess, it was a school for daughters of the royal family and of the aristocracy, where lessons on the generosity and glorious memory of the ruling family could be learned.[85]

Another aspect of Faremoutiers' importance is that it was not, in fact, unique. It was only one in a series of houses performing similar functions, though some asserted Carolingian identity more forcefully than others. It is not possible here to survey all these houses, or the careers of the women in them, in detail. I survey them under two broad headings: first, their position in the contemporary historical-geographical landscape and secondly, their role as creators, transmitters and repositories of Carolingian identity and authority through ceremonies and texts of commemoration and cult. The distinction between these two headings is artificial to a great extent, and it has been drawn simply to make my material and argument clearer on the theme of the articulation and maintenance of Carolingian-ness.

The distribution of such houses (including those controlled by male members of the dynasty) was uneven, with some concentration in the western parts of Francia. Here were houses controlled by royal women for generations, such as Chelles, Notre-Dame de Soissons, Saint-Jean de Laon, and it was in the region of the Oise valley that estates were often granted to royal women.[86] Such houses do appear, however, in each of the three post-Verdun kindgoms. Charles the Bald had such centres at Argenteuil, Chelles, Faremoutiers, Notre-Dame de Soissons and St-Jean de Laon. In the eastern kingdom of Louis the German lay the houses of Schwarzach and St Felix and St Regula at Zürich. As for the middle kingdom of Lothar I, two of his daughters are known to have been in charge of abbeys: Bertha and Gisela. Bertha, however, was abbess of Avenay, which lay in the kingdom of Charles the Bald, though this did not prevent her from being on good terms with her father. Lothar's wife Ermingard held sway over San Salvatore in Brescia in Italy and his daughter Gisela was present in the abbey.[87] North of the Alps in Lothar's kingdom lay Nivelles, dedicated to a Carolingian saint, together with Remiremont which had had a Carolingian abbess in the eighth century and which retained close links with the dynasty in the ninth (see below for these abbeys). Lothar I's successors, Lothar II and Louis II, who inherited the northern and Italian components of their father's realm (their brother Charles of Provence soon died) thus continued to have such centres in their kingdoms. Each of the post-843 kingdoms, therefore, had its share of such centres, ranging from Brescia to Zürich to the neighbourhood of Paris.

These houses may not have existed in sufficiently high numbers as to form a grid across these kingdoms but their existence and location were important. This is apparent in, for example, the political-geographical role of such abbeys in the eastern kingdom of Louis the German. The 850s saw a flurry of activity on Louis's part in the south-western region of his kingdom, designed to cast his shadow over Alsace which lay in the middle kingdom and upon which he had designs. Among Louis's activities here at this time was the granting of privileges to the abbey of St Felix and St Regula in Zürich, which was under the successive control of his daughters Hildegard and Bertha, and to Buchau where his daughter Ermengard was abbess. The placing and privileging of these royal women here were part of a larger strategy involving grants to St-Gall and a rare visit by the king to the great royal palace in this district, Bodman, designed to give Louis a platform from which to reach out to Alsace. After 855, Alsace was in the kingdom of Louis's wayward nephew Lothar II who, anxious not to provoke hostilities while grappling with his intractable divorce case, made all sorts of concessions to Louis in Alsace. Lothar's desire to please Uncle Louis can be seen not only in these concessions in Alsace but also in his granting of property, in a fulsome diploma, to his cousin Bertha, the abbess at Zürich, whom Lothar saw as a useful mediator between himself and his uncle.[88]

What role do the daughters of Louis the German play in such a narrative? It can be tempting to think of them as passive chess pieces placed on the board by the canny grand master, their father, mere instruments of mediation between the active masculine players. Their appointment as abbess must reflect the will of the king. Carolingian children, whether male or female, did not always have an automatic right to positions of authority. In fact, however, their role is more complex than it might appear in this outline. The presence of Louis's daughters in Zürich and Buchau was active in that they gave a royal presence to an area that the king himself did not often visit but which was rich in royal resources and was strategically important. Furthermore, they cultivated the memory and aura of the dynasty by ensuring that its members were recalled in prayer; Lothar II's grant to Bertha ensured that he was remembered by her after his death in a charter that reveals a sense of common Carolingian identity.[89]

What a Carolingian abbess made of her position depended on a variety of factors, including her own abilities and aspirations. One has only to consider Charlemagne's sister Gisela to gain some sense of the formidable capacity of such women for action in the sphere of political culture. Carolingian women may have had reasonable expectations of access to the sort of 'hereditary' abbeys that are under consideration here. From the time of Charles Martel, Chelles, just outside Paris, was presided over by a series of royal women for a period stretching over a century and a half.[90] The fact that Carolingian women at Chelles included those who married into the family such as Heilwig, the mother of Judith, and Ermentrud, wife of Charles the Bald, may suggest that it lay in the gift of Carolingian men, the rulers into whose families they had married. Certainly the role played by husbands, fathers and brothers in awarding appointments was central and kings kept a close watch on the succession in such houses. If the women were not autonomous individuals, neither were kings; cultural norms affected them, and they had to keep their family special. Daughters could trade on the expectations that certain posts would be reserved for them, as the arrangements made by Charlemagne's daughter Theodrada for the succession at Schwarzach reveal.[91] Furthermore, once appointed, such women could use the abbey as a base for a role of their own in politics: Chelles acted as such a base for Charlemagne's sister Gisela and for Judith's mother Heilwig (see below). Royal women in such positions were not unthinking props of a monolithic royal house.

The location and condition of such houses and the identity of their abbesses were therefore important. These women presided as patrons of building activities in their abbeys. Louis the German's daughter Hildegard (d.856), abbess of St Felix and St Regula at Zürich, built up a new church there. Likewise, Gisela, Charlemagne's daughter, built a new church dedicated to the Virgin Mary during her abbacy at Chelles.[92] Such building activities were noted by contemporaries and enhanced the reputation of these abbesses (our information on Hildegard's work at Zürich comes from a poetic epitaph from St-Gall). The audience for such work could be large and was certainly exalted. Pilgrims may have been drawn to Chelles because of the rich collection of relics housed there and we know for certain that Charlemagne himself visited the abbey in 804. The dedication of the new church at Zürich was presided over by the bishop of Constance.[93] Carolingian energy and generosity were thus manifested in the landscape and directed at an audience.

Royal women at work amongst the aristocracy

Carolingian women also had an important audience within their abbeys which were 'staffed' by women of the aristocracy. We have seen that this was the case at Faremoutiers, but the point can be established for houses across the whole of the empire and in all of the post-843 kingdoms. In the western kingdom, for example, a daughter of Count Baldwin I of Flanders was a nun at St-Jean-de-Laon where Charles the Bald's sister Hildegard was abbess. In the kingdom of Louis the German, a list of nuns at Zürich between 853 and 856 includes such well-known aristocratic names as Richildis and we know that Louis's aunt Theodrada, abbess of Schwarzach, was on good terms with the daughter of an east Frankish count.[94]

Outside the Frankish lands, in northern Italy, the great abbey of San Salvatore/San Giulia in Brescia was a showpiece for Carolingian dynastic specialness. The Lombard king and queen had founded it before Charlemagne's 774 conquest and richly endowed it as a centre for queenly royalty and spirituality, the splendour of which, including the paintings, we can still see. The Carolingians learned from this and gradually adopted and developed the exalted atmosphere of queenship and female royalty in this abbey. The empress Judith held it, thus keeping the authority of herself and her husband Louis the Pious present even though they never visited Italy (except for Judith's journey there under duress in the crisis of 833).[95]

As part of Lothar I's middle kingdom after 843, under the control of his son Louis II, Brescia offered a prominent place to Carolingian women, though not always as abbess. Charters of Lothar I from 848 and 851 refer to his wife Ermengard and their daughter Gisela as being in charge of the abbey alongside the abbess. Lothar himself probably came to Brescia for his daughter's entry into the abbey. Traces of this sort of highly charged event and the special status of Carolingian women within the community can be seen in the abbey's great commemoration book, where the entry of Gisela is recorded in red majuscule lettering and her name, as well as that of her equally Carolingian niece, come before the names of other nuns, whose listing follows the chronology of their entry into the abbey.[96]

The Carolingian grip on the abbey was maintained after Italy became separate from the middle kingdom on Lothar I's death in 855. After Gisela's death in 860, her brother the emperor Louis II saw to it that his daughter and wife controlled the abbey. Something of the special nature of that control emerges from the fact that his daughter was given a prominent position in it even though she was young and sickly.[97] Her individual qualities mattered less than the fact that she was the daughter of a king; her youth and illness were transcended by the charisma stemming from her blood. For a generation, then, royal women dominated an abbey whose personnel of around 140 were drawn from the top-drawer families of Carolingian Italy, including that of Eberhard of Friuli, whose daughter, Gisela's cousin, was a nun here in Gisela's time, as were the daughters of counts Adelbert and Rambertus. Brescia thus functioned as a site of bonding not only between high-born women but between Carolingian kings and their magnates, and its connections reached over the Alps beyond Italy throughout the ninth century. Through the names in its commemoration book, we can also trace lesser figures such as the Manuel who gave his daughter to the abbey and see them grouped with other similar figures, traces of the lived texture of broad Carolingian community. The abbey also contained royal material resources. Louis II's widow Engelberga stored her treasure there; the fact that a Carolingian ruler from north of the Alps grabbed that treasure in 875 shows precise knowledge of the abbey's special role for royal women; it also demonstrates their vulnerability.[98]

San Salvatore and the other houses discussed in this section, their location, their resources, their personnel, could be vehicles of instruction. Across the empire, Carolingian women occupied a series of abbeys that acted as centres for the display of Carolingian power and identity in the geographical location of these centres, the scale of their buildings and their connection with the aristocracy. This represents, however, only one side of the activity of these women as part of a machinery that helped make the political landscape Carolingian. This machinery could also be switched on to generate spiritual help and an aura of specialness for the ruling house.

A key role for women was to pray for and commemorate leading men of the royal house, to utter their significance-charged names and to ensure that others did so too. Such prayer could be relatively private, as in the mid-ninth century prayer for her brothers and other kin recorded by a sister or daughter of Lothar I in the Lothar Psalter (probably produced in Aachen shortly after 842, and now in the British Library). But prayers could be very public, designed to win favour for great royal enterprises, as in the litanies performed for victory over the Avars in 791; from the field, Charlemagne wrote to his queen, Fastrada, instructing her to have litanies performed at the palace, an indication of the important part a strong queen could play in mobilizing divine aid for the king and the realm.[99] Far from the court, its ceremonies and luxury manuscripts, Carolingian women still prayed for their exalted relatives. Gisela, daughter of Louis the Pious and Judith, ensured, as we have seen, that her dead parents and her living brother Charles the Bald were prayed for in her late husband's 'family monastery' of Cysoing. An aristocratic house was thus woven into the web of Carolingian liturgical commemoration and prayer. A particularly striking example of this family piety is the arrangement made for prayers for her late husband by Theutberga, widow of Lothar II (d.869). The brutality of the divorce case did not prevent her from seeing that he was fittingly buried and that prayers were to be offered for his soul where he died, at Piacenza in Italy. Lothar's memory was thus preserved by Theutberga, whose own actions entered the memory of the dynasty; we know of them from a charter of Charles the Fat. This is less a posthumous romantic reconciliation than the committed role-playing of a high-born Christian woman.[100]

Commemorations or liturgical ceremonies such as these were not only triggered by individual initiatives and specific circumstances. Prayers for the royal house took place in a systematic network of monasteries (see Chapter 7). Kings requested that houses presided over by their womenfolk pray for them and their family. This is the motivation behind Louis the German's 853 grant to St Felix and St Regula at Zürich, where his daughter Hildegarde was abbess, and Charles the Bald's 859 grant to Faremoutiers where the Carolingian Bertrada was abbess. The community of San Salvatore at Brescia was also regularly requested to offer prayers for the dynasty; in addition to this, the meetings of Carolingian kings in Italy, for example, at Ravenna 880, triggered the recording of the names of such kings and their families in the abbey's commemoration book.[101]

Prayers for members of the royal house were requested from a wide range of religious establishments across the empire so the work of prayer and commemorations undertaken by Carolingian women fits straightforwardly into such a framework. Their work does have, however, a distinctive quality. First, gender is important because prayers for, and commemoration of, a family by members of that family does often seem to have been the special task of women. This is the case for medieval cultures other than the Carolingian world. Women could be the custodians of memory and thus of an important aspect of identity. This is true of the aristocratic families of the empire. The example of Dhuoda, wife of Bernard of Septimania, illustrates this point; in the moral handbook written for her son in the early 840s, she urges him to pray for the members of his family, alive and dead, but it was she who recorded their names and her urging her son to pray indicates that she was the orchestrator of such family piety.[102] While aristocratic family commemorations and prayer seem to parallel royal family commemoration, there was a difference in that aristocratic commemoration regularly involved praying for specific members of the royal house while the reverse was not usually true.[103] The royal house remained special.

A second point follows. While many religious houses prayed for and commemorated members of the Carolingian family, the religious houses headed by a succession of Carolingians were almost exclusively headed by women. A Carolingian family foundation such as Prüm did not have a member of the royal family as its abbot. Carolingian men could themselves become abbots but it was very unusual for the legitimate son of a king to be one in our period. Where an abbey was held by a succession of men with Carolingian blood, as at St-Quentin where Hieronymus (Jerome), the son of Charles Martel, was succeeded by his son Fulrad, who was followed by Charlemagne's illegitimate son Hugh, such men were not the legitimate sons of kings.[104] To find abbeys ruled or controlled by a lengthy series of family members who were children of kings, we must turn to the women of that family. The prayers offered by Carolingian women were therefore rather different from, or formed a particular category among, the prayers generally requested and obtained by the Carolingian rulers. They were prayers for the royal house supervised by the female members of that house.

The third point that marks the activities of these women as special is that they themselves could be prayed for and their Carolingian identity recalled. Berta, daughter of Charlemagne, was included among Carolingian family members to be prayed for in the charters issued in the 860s by her nephew Charles the Bald for St-Denis and St-Medard, Soissons (to which house Berta herself had made a grant in 823). In 857, Louis the German made a grant to one Berold 'for the love of our most dear daughter Hildegard of good memory'; Berold had been Hildegard's chaplain and it seems that all of Louis's daughters would have had their own chaplain.[105] Among the women listed in the series of Carolingian rulers with their wives and daughters compiled between 869 and 876 for commemoration at Fulda is Theodrada, abbess of Schwarzach. Through her mother Fastrada, she was connected to the east Frankish aristocracy, and Schwarzach was possibly founded by Fastrada's family. Theodrada developed her own friendships there with the daughters of the east Frankish aristocracy. She was buried in St-Alban's, Mainz, where Fastrada had been buried. Through her family connections, her 'career', her place of burial and her commemoration, Theodrada helped make east Francia Carolingian. More precisely, she helped make this area the kingdom of Louis the German. In January 844, six months after the Treaty of Verdun, Theodrada was at Frankfurt to receive a privilege for Schwarzach from her nephew Louis the German in a charter that referred to her as 'our aunt Theodrada, daughter of our most distinguished grandfather of sacred memory'. Theodrada, as Charlemagne's daughter, lent her nephew's assembly the lustre of dynastic continuity, just as his issuing a charter for her and Schwarzach showed that he was now the senior male Carolingian in this area.[106]

While Theodrada's presence in the east Frankish kingdom was important for that kingdom alone, women's contribution to dynastic aura could also be more general. Charlemagne's wife Hildegard was fondly recalled in St-Gall, her tomb lay in Metz and she was prayed for in St-Denis; she was thus 'present' in all three of the post-Verdun kingdoms north of the Alps.[107] Queens, mothers, daughters, abbesses, carriers of memory, living symbols of the Carolingian royal house: these women were not mere vehicles through whom the dynastic system transmitted messages. They were active agents within the Carolingian identity that they embodied and asserted. Wallace Stevens's famous line fits here: 'For she was the maker of the song she sang' ('The Idea of Order at Key West').

Indeed, royal and aristocratic women, unlike their menfolk, actually made things. Skill in weaving and sewing was a praiseworthy attribute for such women, almost a duty.[108] Perhaps not all the work attributed to them was done by their own hands, but this work was prestigious. It could also be eloquent. Emma's belt for bishop Witgar spelt out her queenly status quite literally as well as symbolically, as we saw above. Ermentrud, queen to Charles the Bald, sent a stole to the bishop of Laon on his ordination in 847 along with a letter explaining why she had sent this gift, referring to gifts which the bishop had previously sent her, and asking him to pray for her and for the defenders of the realm. Contemporary poets celebrated Ermentrud's talents but in doing so they explicitly associated her with her husband and offspring, as the objects would themselves have done. The same is true for other women, for example, Ermengard, wife of Lothar I. The glow from the exercise of these womanly talents thus suffused the dynasty.[109] This could be literally true. Ermentrud made a silken, golden bejewelled robe for her husband Charles the Bald.

Admittedly, the royals were hardly the only splendidly dressed family in the empire. Perhaps the lady Gisela had made some of the gorgeous clothing that she and her husband Eberhard of Friuli bequeathed to their children. Gisela and Eberhard also left crowns to their children.[110] Crowns, or some types of them, were not markers of exclusively royal status. Counts Matfrid and Hugh wore crowns when they attended upon Louis the Pious and Judith in great ceremonies at the palace of Ingelheim in 826. But this means that we need not think that queens were the only Carolingian women to sport crowns; Alcuin's famous warning to one of his students to beware of 'the crowned doves' of the palace may mean that Charlemagne's daughters indeed wore them.[111] Contemporaries' references to the splendour of the apparel and ornaments of Carolingian women, wives and daughters show how they displayed their own status as well as that of their husbands and fathers, a classic function of elite women. We can still glimpse something of that splendour in such finds as those uncovered from the grave (c.700) of the young high-status girl buried in Frankfurt cathedral. These women, however, did not carry the whole burden of display. The dazzling garment that Ermentrud made for her royal husband is one piece of a range of evidence that also shows that we should not imagine that Carolingian men were plainly attired.[112]

Contemporaries may not always have been favourably impressed by such trappings. Charles the Bald's fancy Greek costume, reflecting his new imperial status, did not go down well with everyone when he appeared in it at an assembly in Francia in 876. But Charles did not hog the imperial limelight; he made sure that his wife Richildis also made a majestic appearance at the assembly. Distinguished visitors, bishops from Italy, escorted her into the public gaze; she wore her crown; her appearance beside Charles was the signal for all to rise to their feet; the bishops chanted the *laudes* for the pope, emperor and empress. And Richildis was four months pregnant.[113]

Not every day was an imperial celebration. The representation of Carolingian specialness was work over time. Carolingian women performed this work in palaces, but more of them performed it in abbeys which thus shared some of the characteristics of palaces in that they were institutional presences in landscapes working to permanently represent royalty. This was not all they did and it was not their primary function, but it was an important aspect of some houses' role. A couple of specific examples will illustrate this.

In the late seventh century, Queen Balthild established an abbey east of Paris at Chelles, developing a chapel founded on the royal estate there by Clothild, wife of Clovis, in the early sixth century. Balthild herself is a spectacular example of a woman from outside (she was a noble Anglo-Saxon woman) who married into a royal family, enhanced its status and power with her connections and her political savvy at court, and then anchored its charisma in the landscape with the founding of Chelles. She herself retired to Chelles, dying there in an atmosphere of holiness and becoming venerated as a saint. The extraordinary 'chemise' of Balthild has survived, giving us a vivid glimpse of the cult and also, in its embroidered imagery of necklaces, showing how Balthild's former life as bejewelled queen was simultaneously recalled and spiritually transmuted.[114]

The Carolingians could build on this glorious Merovingian heritage. As we have seen, series of royal women presided over this establishment rich in resources both economic and spiritual. The community had 130 members. During the rule of Gisela, Charlemagne's sister, the building was expanded and a vast collection of sacred relics was assembled here, including relics of Petronilla, a virgin martyr, the subject of special devotion by Gisela's family. Later patrons included Queen Ermentrud, wife of Charles the Bald.[115] With its library and scriptorium, Chelles was also a remarkable intellectual centre and it is possible that a major historical text celebrating the rise of Carolingian royalty was compiled here under Gisela.[116] Even if this is not the case, Gisela was herself a political player, no mere transmitter of Carolingian men's specialness. She was at Aachen in the summer of 799 where she brought Charlemagne's kingly sons together at a time of political tensions to witness a gift she made to the abbey of St-Denis. She appears in the charter (the original has survived) as 'consecrated to God ... Gisela the most noble daughter of king Pippin and queen Bertrada (Berta)'; her parents made her special; her presence at the palace as holy abbess helped make it and her family's rule pleasing to God (as did the residing at court of a holy woman such as Gundrada, cousin to Gisela and Charlemagne) and Charlemagne's same-day confirmation of her gift also did so. She was a correspondent of Alcuin, who praised her spiritual qualities, but his advice to her not to be boastful about her noble birth was tempered with awareness of her splendid family. Her presence at Rome for the imperial coronation confirms her as a politically and spiritually prominent member of the royal house.[117] The royal women of Chelles were not mere spectators.

This point emerges even more clearly from some of Chelles' activities in the 830s, when the royal house was divided by fiercer tensions than it had been in the era of Gisela and Charlemagne. In 825 Heilwig, the mother of Judith, the second wife of Louis the Pious, became abbess and indeed was to be buried there. Under Heilwig, the cult of Balthild, saint and queen, flourished. In 833, the body of Balthild was transferred to the church of St Mary within Chelles in a splendid ceremony presided over by Heilwig and attended by Louis and Judith.[118] An account of it that was written up some twenty years later puts a spotlight on the role of royal women. Described as 'the most holy abbess' and 'the venerable abbess … mother of the empress Judith', Heilwig plays a key role in the narrative of the ceremony that itself involves the transfer of the saint to the church of St Mary 'which the lady Gisela had built'. Charlemagne's sister Gisela, Louis's wife Judith and Heilwig all appear in the text in terms reflecting their high status and achievements. The fact that this text may not stem from Chelles itself enhances their status still further as it shows how their power was recognized outside of their own community. The activities of Gisela and Heilwig focus on two very prominent women in Chelles: Balthild and the Virgin Mary.[119] Here gender positively enhances status. Mother of an empress, servant of a holy queen, Heilwig follows up the work of her 'ancestor' in office, who had built a church for Mary.

The work of these women was important for Carolingian kings. It had been Louis the Pious himself who had requested that the transferral take place. When miracles subsequently occurred, Louis and his courtiers were delighted: 'in the palace … Louis was thrilled, the magnates were joyful and everyone rejoiced and in honour of so great a mother praise (*laudes*) was sung'. Desiring the spiritual support of Balthild, Louis went on to make a gift of land to Chelles in return for prayers for the safety of the realm and himself and of his wife and sons.[120] Links between the courts of heaven and earth passed through Chelles.

But what was good news for Louis's court was not good news for all Carolingian courts. These ceremonies took place in early 833, when resentment against Louis was brewing in the courts of his sons. The exalting of a saintly queen in a ceremony in the abbey of Judith's mother was therefore to some extent a political act, though the staging of Judith's piety did not help her. If the so-called *Annals of Metz* were indeed written at Chelles, a later addition to them may well have been made by Heilwig. This addition tells the story of the earlier revolt against Louis and Judith in 830. Not only does this account focus tightly on the figure of Judith, but Louis' sons from his first marriage are very specifically described as *filiastri*, 'step-sons', an infrequently encountered term used here to ascribe an outsider status to the rebellious sons whose actions endangered this texts' narrowly defined family group of Louis, Judith and their son Charles.[121] Heilwig had a precise understanding of the dynamics of royal family conflict and as abbess, historian and mistress of ceremonies in 833, she participated in these rivalries and tried to shape the politics of the family into which her daughter had married.

The sharply contemporary edge to Heilwig's activities does not mean that the religious aura of 833 was merely a mask for earthbound politics. Heilwig's glowing picture of Judith – a glittering empress, a mother of a prince, a 'nun' of outstanding piety in her enforced monastic captivity in 830 – stands with the ceremonies of 833 which glorified the holy queen Balthild. The living abbess and empress are bound up with the dead queen-saint and in this perspective Judith and Balthild seem to offer each other mutual support as the mother of the empress supervises the transfer of the queen-saint's remains into a church dedicated to the queen of heaven. It is as if Judith had acquired a holy ancestor by association. For all that the Carolingian dynasty did not make a coherent cult of its holy ancestors in the way that later dynasties were to do, some very potent chords are being sounded here on its behalf.[122]

Such chords sound more loudly when we turn to consider the site of the cult of St Gertrud of Nivelles, a holy figure who was herself an ancestor of the Carolingians. Founded in the late 640s on family lands in what is now southern Belgium by Gertrud's mother Itta, widow of Pippin I, in association with Gertrud's ill-fated brother Grimoald, the convent of Nivelles was presided over by Itta. She was succeeded by Gertrud, who was succeeded in her turn by her niece. Gertrud became the object of a saint's cult and Nivelles grew into a prestigious complex of buildings and a focus for much pilgrimage. This abbey lay in what was to become the heart of Carolingian territory. It is approximately 150 km from Aachen and was connected with other nearby abbeys such as Fosses and Lobbes which had a strong Carolingian presence, being controlled by members of the Carolingian house from 864 to 881. Its properties included estates stretching up both sides of the Rhine from Bonn to Andernach as well as further west at Düren. It was part of a key network of rich material resources.[123]

The greatest material resource was also a spiritual one: the body and cult of St Gertrud herself. It was this that drew the pilgrims and it was to St Gertrud that churches on the abbey's scattered estates were dedicated. Her sanctity may well have helped enhance the status of the Pippinids amidst the challenges of the later seventh century, just as the transfer of her body to a marble tomb in the eighth century marked progress of her cult and her family.[124] But the spirit of Gertrud stretched beyond her properties. Her relics were placed in his cathedral in 834/5 by bishop Aldric of Le Mans, who was close to Louis the Pious. There were also relics of the saint in Saint-Riquier. She was invoked in litanies in Corvey and in the litany of the 'Psalter of Charlemagne'. In 876, during an assembly at the palace of Ponthion in the Marne valley, Charles the Bald confirmed properties to the abbey 'where the body of holy Gertrud rests' at the intercession of his wife Richildis.[125] St Gertrud, a holy Carolingian woman, thus appeared in buildings, reliquaries, altars and ceremonies across the heart of the empire. She could also reach beyond the exalted circle of those who were particularly close to the kings. In the agony of possession by an evil spirit, a girl working on an estate near the monastery of Holzkirchen in Bavaria called on St Gertrud to save her.[126]

Perhaps such evidence tells us more about Gertrud's perceived sanctity than her perceived Carolingian-ness, but contemporaries did see the Carolingian aspect to Nivelles and Gertrud. The contemporaries who stood to benefit most from this were of course the Carolingians themselves. Nivelles, where the body of a holy Carolingian woman lay, was controlled by Carolingian women. Among the most interesting of these figures is Gisela, daughter of Lothar II and Waldrada, who was born in the 860s and died in 907. Despite the disappearance of her father's kingdom on his death in

869, Gisela retained value as the daughter of a king. The actions of her competing Carolingian male relatives in the 880s in marrying her off to a Viking leader and then having him killed and regaining control over her testify to that. Later she had connections with kings Zwentibold and Louis the Child of east Francia and with the west Frankish king Charles the Simple.[127] Zwentibold's troubles led him to make a point of cultivating Gisela, whose legitimate Carolingian mantle could only enhance his own status. Hence Zwentibold's 896 charter for her wraps himself and Gisela in a common Carolingian heritage: 'our dear kinswoman (*propinqua*) Gisela by name, daughter of the most glorious king Lothar'. This charter was issued at Aachen and Zwentibold can be seen to be here pulling out all the Carolingian stops: despite the dynasty's problems after 888, a Carolingian was again in Aachen, attended by the pious daughter of a royal predecessor. A year later, Zwentibold visited Nivelles itself where he issued a privilege for the community. The fact that Zwentibold's itinerary included monasteries such as Nivelles rather than royal estates has been seen as a sign of his political weakness and diminished resources. But what mattered was to have been so publicly linked with the resting-place of the holy Gertrud.[128] If Gisela was present when Louis the Child confirmed an exchange of properties between one of her vassals and a bishop in 906, then the spirits of the two great Carolingian family saints, Arnulf and Gertrud, both hovered over this transaction as it was issued in St Arnulf's, Metz.[129] But such saintly charisma was now thinly stretched over a structurally weaker kingship, as we shall see in the final chapter.

If Gertrud's sanctity was a source of succour for kings, it was through the women of the royal house that Gertrud was reached. These women, however, did not only live through their relationships with kings. St Gertrud and Nivelles were a resource for these women themselves. Thus Hildegard, Charlemagne's wife, on encountering a crippled girl in the course of distributing alms, thought naturally of sending her to Nivelles, where St Gertrud naturally cured her. It is as a result of the charitable action of the lady queen (*domina regina*) that the lady (*domina*) Gertrud is able to cure the girl; a relationship, even if an indirect one, is thus established between the queen and the saint.[130] But the relationship between Carolingian queens and the lady of Nivelles could be much clearer and stronger than this. In 798, Charlemagne's queen Liutgard and her husband's daughters went to Nivelles to celebrate the feast of the Assumption of the Virgin Mary. Liutgard celebrated the virgin queen of heaven at the shrine of the virgin saint of the royal house. Nivelles was thus the nodal point of a 'women's liturgical network linking earth and heaven', in Professor Nelson's vivid phrase, though her description of this as 'the acceptable face of feminine power' points to limits on royal women. The fact that we know about this highly charged liturgical visit from a letter of Alcuin to archbishop Arn of Salzburg shows that news of the movements and activities of women of the court was broadcast; such visits were not private.[131] Nivelles was a perfect vehicle for the creating and manifesting of Carolingian specialness by Carolingian women; it gave charisma and status to the women; in their turn, they deployed these resources for the benefit of the dynasty of which they were a part.

Contemporaries learned the dynastic lesson that the woman taught. In Alemannia, where the ancestors of Charlemagne's wife Hildegard had been dukes, monks in the abbey of Reichenau entered a list of the royal family into the commemoration book in the 820s. The heart of this list consists of seventeen names and the prominence of women is striking; nine of the figures are women. The women have a different, a more complex identity than the men. All the men are Carolingians; that is, they are sons of a Carolingian father, and all bar one are titled as kings or mayors of the palace. All the women bar one (a daughter of Charlemagne) are non-Carolingian in that they did not have a Carolingian parent: they married into the royal family; three of them do not bear a title. The other six bear the title of queen; intriguingly, this includes Swanahild, wife of Charles Martel who was not a king (his other wives are given no title). The titled women thus parallel their husband rulers. The list format (eight men followed by nine women) seems to separate the royal couples but actually reveals that the women, like their husbands, are parents. The women are listed chronologically in the order of their husbands. The list includes children of the pairs of men and women; for example, 'king Pippin' and 'queen Bertha' appear in the list, as do their children 'emperor Charlemagne' and 'Carloman' (some ranking of rulers goes on in this list).[132] These male children are in fact of course not entirely Carolingian; their mothers come from the aristocracy; but these women are assimilated into the Carolingian kin and so Carolingian-ness appears on both sides. Office and family, a royal family, are the essence of this list and women feature prominently in both elements. Here is the success of Pippin's construction of himself, his wife and children as special in the 750s.

Far to the north of Reichenau, and some five decades later, the monks of Fulda also composed a list of royal names. This is part of a larger list of prominent figures such as bishops and counts connected to the abbey; Carolingians were not the only VIPs in such landscapes. The impulse for the list's composition was probably the urgent visit of King Louis the German to Fulda in 874, deeply disturbed by a dream-vision of his father Louis the Pious in torment in the next world. The list is thus a trace of intense activities and prayer undertaken by the monks of this well-connected abbey and is not a political text. But, like the list at Reichenau and the royal diptych of names at the women's abbey of Remiremont in the Vosges, it reveals contemporary awareness of the special status of royal women and is a trace of the performed and learned veneration of the dynasty that suffused these abbeys and the world beyond them. The core of the Fulda list is of sixteen Carolingians, all dead, and, drawing on earlier lists, is built essentially on the family of Charlemagne.[133] It names eight men, five of whom have a royal a title, and eight women, most of whom are merely named; only the last woman on the list is given a title: abbess Theodrada. In some ways, it is surprising to find women so prominent in Fulda. The male community seems to have been uneasy over the presence of women in royal visits, and had worried over the propriety of saint Boniface's request that his saintly kinswoman Leoba should be buried beside him in the abbey church.[134]

Since the list was built on earlier lists, the monks of the 870s may not have known precisely who all these royal women were, and perhaps did not even have a precise idea of all the men. But these women's presence among such stridently Carolingian male names as Pippin, Charles and Louis emblazoned them as royal. And some monks may themselves have remembered the daughter of Charlemagne and Fastrada, abbess Theodrada of Schwarzach, who died between 844 and 857; we have already observed her connections in east Francia, including to the women of the aristocracy.[135] Much of the knowledge and consciousness of these monks, like that of all the actors in this book, escape the modern historian. Whoever copied the list may not have recognized the Gisela in it as Charlemagne's daughter, but could well have recalled that that woman bore the same name as a daughter of Louis the German. That later Gisela duly appears in an addition to the list. She is a blank to modern scholarship but she was a living Carolingian presence to her Fulda contemporaries, who reproduced her Carolingian identity in the texts and actions that helped make their world Carolingian.[136]

Such reverence was not in itself enough to guarantee these women security and prominence. In the fascinating compilation of texts put together around the mid-ninth century by Louis the German's arch-chaplain, abbot Grimald of St-Gall, and his scribes, there are various texts relating to Carolingian women, including an epitaph for Louis the German's daughter Hildegard, abbess in Zürich, that draws attention to her holiness as well as her glorious paternity. Such epitaphs testify to knowledge of and reverence for Carolingian women. There is also a full death-notice for Judith, wife of Louis the Pious and mother of Charles the Bald ('19 April [843] Judith empress (*Augusta*) died at Tours in the monastery of St-Martin where her body is buried').[137] Among the 'most elegant courtly customs' that Grimald had learned in the service of Charlemagne and Louis the Pious was the paying of due reverence to exalted royals. The acclamations (*laudes*) in his compilation for Louis the German and 'Emma our queen' are not mere reflections of royal status; they help construct it. One would not guess from Grimald's reverent entry on Judith that her own son, Charles the Bald, had had to strip her of her wealth to finance his own household after he got married in 842. Widowhood made even a woman as exalted as the empress vulnerable. Death and honourable burial, however, enabled her to function safely in royal representation, as a frozen link in an ever-lengthening dynastic chain.[138]

Representation is an active force in the world, but the world is more than representation. In generally keeping their daughters away from marriage, Carolingian kings ensured that Carolingian blood would be a rare and thus a precious resource. They themselves, however, eventually paid a price for this strategy. From the middle of the ninth century, by keeping royal daughters off the marriage market the dynasty was no longer enfolding aristocratic families in a web of marriage alliances that had spanned the empire and revolved round the dynasty itself. Louis the Pious certainly approved a marriage for one of his daughters and two or three other royal daughters were married in his time.[139] Silvia Konecny calculates that a third of the thirty-four daughters of rulers after Louis were unmarried and that only a handful, five at most, married with paternal permission, while another eight did marry, but only after the death of their father and possibly in marriages that served local aristocratic interests rather than broader royal strategies, though this may be to underestimate the *ad hoc* elements in royal marriages.[140] The change was indeed serious and was more than fathers being miserly with their daughters' future. Dynastic marriage patterns altered after the time of Louis the Pious, as did dynastic luck. Louis had nine children, most of whom outlived him. He arranged marriages for all his kingly sons, apart from Charles the Bald, and, as we have seen, royal daughters were also permitted to marry.

The marriage of royal sons was also of course important and the next generation of kings still exerted sufficient control to restrain or contain sons as well as daughters. Even such episodes as Judith's defiant marriage to Baldwin or the independent marriage choice of her brother, Louis the Stammerer, were contained or changed by their father Charles the Bald.[141] In fact the problem was not so much that kings after the death of Louis the Pious in 840 were losing control of their offspring's marital futures as that they were exerting too much control. Louis the German did not permit any of his daughters to marry and Judith was the only one of Charles the Bald's daughters to escape their father's grip.[142] Charles's grip on his male children was also very tight. As we have seen, he actually took two of his sons off the marriage market by drafting them into a clerical career. The generation that followed these sons of Louis the Pious was neither as lucky nor productive. The reproduction of Carolingian distinctiveness at the very heart of the dynasty was faltering long before 888. These three sons of Louis the Pious fathered thirty children. But the many sons of that next generation fathered only seventeen. No one could have foreseen this shrinking of the dynasty's future, though it highlights the risky element in Charles the Bald's treatment of his sons: only one of his four sons who reached maturity would go on to father children.

While Régine Le Jan notes the change in its marriage patterns in the second half of the ninth century as a sign of the dynasty's loss of grip on the high aristocracy, she also notes that vestiges of the older pattern still survived as in, for example, the marriage of Louis the Stammerer's daughter Gisela to count Robert of Troyes. But such vestiges themselves illustrate changes in the relationship of the aristocracy to the dynasty, as well as changes within the structure of the aristocracy itself. Gisela's husband Robert belonged to an aristocratic network, visible from the 830s onwards, that spanned a wide region north and east of Paris stretching to Troyes, where he was count. His marriage was one of the connections binding him to the king and thus securing his hold on offices (*honores*) and royal favour, and he may have enjoyed the favour of Charles's queen, Richildis. Such elements percolated through broad family connections across an extensive region to secure the dominance of Robert and his allies. As Le Jan has observed, their power circulated horizontally, through cognatic family structures, and was not yet a type of power that was concentrated territorially.[143]

This sort of aristocratic grouping was not building up a bloc of territorial power with which to challenge the Carolingians; rather, this group relied on Carolingian patronage and structures and in such a world Robert's marriage was beneficial to kings and followers. Here we can see how and why the eastern ruler Charles the Fat was to be acceptable in the 880s as a ruler across the whole Frankish world, even in a western kingdom in which he had probably never set foot before his coronation in 884. Robert and his fellows were among the high aristocracy, who had always enjoyed extensive connections. But Robert's royal connections, cultivated since the reign of Charles the Bald, did not survive long enough to develop deep roots. By 884, his kingly in-laws were dead and there was no longer a west Frankish king for Robert to connect to; Robert does not seem to have had any children by his royal wife and by 886 Robert himself had fallen in battle against the Vikings. Some of the rhythms of Robert's group survived the storms of the 880s; in 893 the count of Troyes was Robert's nephew.[144] But Robert nicely illustrates some key features for us. His horizontal network of kin and alliance conditioned the exercise of royal power in its area but did not challenge it; it was not the sort of block to royal power that would appear just a few years later further west in the concentrated hold on Neustria by the family of Odo of Paris, as we shall see in the next chapter.

In the late 870s and after, the future still looked Carolingian, but it was rooted in a thin soil. Like us all, kings had to make choices about the future without knowing what that future would be. The house could not win all the time. After the death of Louis the German (876) and of Charles the Bald (877) the faltering circulation of women into and out of the dynasty meant a fading of Carolingian presence across the realm. This was not because aristocrats disdained royal sons or daughters as marriage partners. The prominent magnate Boso had arranged in 878 for his daughter to marry the young west Frankish prince Carloman, but the marriage never took place. Neither Carloman (d.884) nor his brother Louis III (d.882) was to live long enough to marry and father children. Louis the German's line was only slightly more productive.[145]

These accidents in the male line paralleled the more deliberate dynastic shutting down of marriages of daughters. And yet the giving of daughters to aristocrats was risky. Charles the Bald's favour towards Boso was never more apparent than in his permitting him to marry a Carolingian woman, Ermengard daughter of Louis II of Italy. Contemporary rumours that Boso had abducted Ermengard, or had secretly married her, and had poisoned his first wife to clear the way for his wicked plans, show something of the surprise such a marriage evoked.[146] Partnered by a Carolingian woman, Boso went on to challenge the dynasty's exclusive right to rule by proclaiming himself king in 879. His revolt showed how dangerous such a marriage could be if the royal men ran into trouble, and Boso claimed that contemporary royal men, the young sons of Louis the Stammerer, were unsatisfactory Carolingians precisely because of their father's marital problems.[147] His challenge to the dynastic system reveals that he knew how it worked. The role of women in a system of Carolingian specialness had worked to keep that system operating, but had also contributed to pressures and tensions. That system was to experience fatal storm and stress in the late 870s and 880s.

9

The loss of uniqueness: 888 and all that

The incredible shrinking dynasty?

It is very difficult to look back at the final decade of Carolingian hegemony without seeing it as simply that, a final phase. When Charles the Bald died in 877, he left a son who had two sons of his own; in east Francia and Italy, three Carolingian brother kings ruled, all of whom had a son, even if some of them were illegitimate. By 888, there was only one fully fledged Carolingian ruler left, Charles the Fat; when he died in 888, non-Carolingian *reguli* ('kinglets') claimed thrones and Carolingian hegemony was deeply wounded. Even contemporaries seemed to see a winding-down of the dynasty before the actual crisis of 888. In 881, Archbishop Hincmar of Reims provided his king with a gloomy count-down to dynastic zero: 'The emperor Louis [the Pious] did not live for as many years as his father Charlemagne; your grandfather Charles [the Bald] did not live for as many years as his father [Louis the Pious]; your father [Louis the Stammerer] did not live for as many years his father.'[1] A year earlier, at the other end of the Carolingian world, the monk Notker of St-Gall had feared lest the line of east Frankish kings was dying out: 'may the light of the great Louis [the German] not be extinguished'.[2]

And the picture does indeed look bleak. After the end of the long reigns of the eastern and western kings in 876 and 877, the dynasty unravelled. By 887, five kings had died, as well as two potential heirs. In 881, Vikings stabled their horses in the palace of Aachen, and that site now fades out from narrative sources. The majestic series of Carolingian capitularies (north of the Alps) ended in 884.[3] In 879, a non-Carolingian, duke Boso, had made a bid for a crown, challenging the dynasty's royal exclusivity while also cashing in on its prestige (he had a Carolingian wife).[4] This was a time of crisis.

But we need to understand the meaning of this crisis, including its meanings for contemporaries who did not have our hindsight. A sense of gloomy inevitability colours much historical witing about this period as historians tick off the fatal symptoms: hereditary illness cutting royal lives short, or weak kings falling under the power of aristocratic factions, etc. Even changes in the format of royal documents are claimed as reflections of the 'general anarchy'.[5]

Such views have been vigorously challenged, particularly in Simon MacLean's convincingly positive re-assessment of the reign of Charles the Fat. The point here, however, is not simply to replace a dark perspective with a sunny one. Scholars such as Nelson and MacLean do not deny that 'momentous' changes happened at precisely this time; they argue that 'change came stealthily, bit by bit'.⁶ Contemporaries did not labour under the same burden of inevitability that afflicted modern historians up to about twenty years or so ago. Their perceptions matter as we need to understand their experience and understanding of this difficult decade as part of its historical meaning. Hincmar's grim tableau of diminishing Carolingian life-spans was not some prophecy of imminent extinction but a moralizing warning of the fragility of earthly power, and life, with a specific polemic purpose in view. Similarly, the well-known episode in Fredegar's seventh-century chronicle where Basina, the wife of king Childeric, enlivens their wedding night with a vision of descendants degenerating from lions into dogs does not really tell us that Fredegar's contemporaries thought that the Merovingians were doomed to decline.⁷

Amidst such warnings, Hincmar's references to the king's father, grandfather, etc. highlighted the ancestry that a Carolingian king possessed, and even his reference to royal tombs at Compiègne was a reference to a majestic ancestral *lieu de mémoire*.⁸ While Notker was worried about the possible fading away of the east Frankish royal line, he took heart from the flourishing of the western line, describing the sons of Louis the Stammerer as 'the hope of Europe'; Notker's horizons were broad because they were still Carolingian.⁹ Contemporaries did not know that the capitulary of 884 was the last to be issued by a western Carolingian; for the archbishop of Sens, who was one of its recipients, it fitted very well into what seemed to be living tradition of legislation.¹⁰ For these contemporaries, the game did not seem to be over.

But decisive change did come, and it did not come out of nowhere. Historians know both more and less than contemporaries did, and have to explain this change. Understanding contemporaries' view of their own times is a vital part of that but such perceptions cannot simply be reproduced as explanation. The key questions in this chapter are what happened to resources of Carolingian-ness in this decade, why and how did the spell of exclusivity break? And what did that mean for contemporaries? How did they understand its significance? Carolingians did not vanish in 888; Carolingians continued to be kings until 987, but they occupied a vastly different landscape. I shall argue that Carolingan resources remained strong up until 888, and indeed, in weakened form, even after that; the discourse of dynastic exclusiveness continued to serve the dynasty well and this explains how one ruler, Charles the Fat, had been able to unite all the kingdoms under his rule by 884. But Charles's reign ended in 887–8 in a dynastic crisis which exacerbated longer-term structural problems that could no longer be ignored.

I begin with some resources, the fiscal estates that were part of royal wealth. Were these Carolingians doomed because they were running out of such resources? Kings had to keep spending; they had to reward their followers. In the agony of his final illness in 879, Louis the Stammerer was still issuing diplomata that uttered the formulae of royal generosity.¹¹ Back in the 820s, Einhard had imagined the Merovingians as having run out of 'the kingdom's wealth and power' and eking out a humble existence on a solitary estate. This seems to find an echo in the fate of Charles the Fat, deposed by Arnulf in 887 and marvelled at by contemporaries as transformed from king to pauper.¹² Such moralizing tableaux are not hard evidence for royal poverty, but some modern historians have thought that the combination of royal extravagance and aristocratic greed led to the Carolingian monarchy beggaring itself.[13] Such older views now appear positively misleading but historians can still think that royal resources were in a very bad way when Charles the Simple succeeded to the west Frankish throne in 898. Chris Wickham has unfavourably contrasted the 'finite' state of west Frankish royal lands in the tenth century with the thriving resources available to English kings.[14]

Rulers such as Odo (888–98) and Charles the Simple (893–929) certainly did not operate on the scale of Charles the Bald. One reason for this was surely a lack of royal resources, and this included a shift in the pattern of their distribution. Great western abbeys such as St-Denis, St Martin of Tours and St Medard of Soissons started losing out on royal donations from the late ninth century onwards; this was because they were now screened from kings by the mediatizing grip of powerful magnates such as the Robertians and Herbertians.[15] Such developments had older roots but did tend to become prominent in the 880s and 890s, that is, during the crisis of Carolingian hegemony. They can thus hardly be said to have caused that crisis. Problems with royal resources are in fact much more likely to have been a result of a crisis in royal power than to have been a cause of it. This is the insightful finding of Jane Martindale whose analysis of fiscal resources in Aquitaine remains compelling nearly forty years after it was published.[16] She was able to show that, while Charles the Bald did make larger grants in Aquitaine than his father and grandfather had done, this was neither a symptom of excessive royal generosity nor in itself a problem. She argued convincingly that such royal grants, in themselves a tool of governance, are only one element in the management of royal resources and that such resources have to be understood as not just static pieces of land but as a broad system whose elements include palaces, itineraries, the performance of estate managers, etc. We also have to realize that charters (themselves not always simply records of grants) do not always give us a secure basis for understanding the fate of royal estates and their fluctuating status; they may give a one-dimensional picture, sometimes too gloomy, sometimes too sunny. So much of our information is limited that systematic analysis and comparison are difficult.[17] Kings had to reward followers and so the distribution of resources was a political necessity, not a weakness and kings still kept an eye on what they had granted and could sometimes re-acquire it and then re-grant it in an evolving pattern of circulation.[18]

More systematic research on such resources is needed. Conclusions are thus rather provisional but the pattern is clear. Carolingian rulers in the last quarter of the ninth century did not simply experience a relentless winding-down of resources. In fact, conquest or inheritance could boost individual rulers' holdings. Kings could lay their hands on all sorts of goodies. The east Frankish ruler Arnulf (887–99) managed to get hold of an extremely luxurious Gospel book originally made for the western Charles the Bald and give it to a church in Bavaria, where it was revered as only one of the spectacular gifts from Arnulf.[19] The aura of royal generosity still radiated from real objects.

Charles the Bald and Louis the German both made significant gains in 870 when the middle kingdom fell to them, while Charles's grandson Carloman II acquired fresh estates to give to his followers when his royal brother died in 882.[20] We should be cautious here, however, as by this logic Charles the Fat in acquiring the whole empire in 884 would have been super-rich. Perhaps he was. Royal resources covered the realm on a scale and in a manner that aristocratic resources could not match.[21] Charles the Fat's arrangements for the fisc by Lake Constance illustrate the care he took to remind beneficiaries that land could revert to the fisc if they did not carry out royal instructions. He was also able to juggle estates in, for example, Alsace and Italy through connections with his wife Richgardis and the empress Engelberga.[22] Fiscal officials could still be quite aggressive in maintaining or over-zealously clawing back fiscal properties but we tend only to see this when it is corrected, as in a case involving some aggressive officials in Burgundy from the time of Charles the Bald. In Alsace on the eve of Charles the Fat's disappearance, fiscal administration still ran smoothly, re-processing and re-possessing properties, ensuring fiscal control of the properties in question for another six decades or so.[23]

Fiscal structures could be resilient. In northern Francia, in a region only recently abandoned by Viking marauders, the youthful western king Carloman succeeded in re-activating the venerable fisc in Tournai in 883–4, a fact that is known, all too typically, from a document recording the granting away of fiscal estate to a count. Carloman was not simply losing estates here; he was granting out this resource in order to re-establish the royal link with it and what was left of the fisc there undoubtedly benefited from subsequent restoration of local economic health.[24] This fiscal repair job can be juxtaposed with Carloman's simultaneous expectation that he would be able to get access to significant sums in order to pay off the Vikings with some 12,000 pounds of silver. And Charles the Fat could go on to fund big payments to Vikings.[25]

Of course, this Tournai case is only one episode and a bigger picture would be more complex: Valenciennes, upriver from Tournai, did not recover so well from Viking attack.[26] If this is a reminder of how difficult it is to assess the whole system's health, it is worth remembering that kings had to distribute resources to get anything done. There is no simple bottom line here; rather there is a complexity that was still a royal success. Royal grants, particularly to the major churches, could be a means of redistributing duties and administrative tasks. Thus, Arnulf in 897 outsourced the organizing and supporting of a group of royal messengers in the Rhine valley to the bishop of Worms, an arrangement that lasted for decades.[27] We do, however, need to take care not to replace narrowly negative views of royal extravagance with airily optimistic ones of royal creativity. Matthew Innes characterizes some of the fiscal actions of Charles the Fat and Arnulf in the 880s and 890s as 'frantic' and 'short term'. Jinty Nelson notes that, for all his political creativity after 888, Odo was not able to exploit royal palaces successfully.[28] Nevertheless, it is clear that the Carolingian rulers of this period were far from bankrupt and a simple disappearance of royal resources did not cause the crisis of 887–8. What did cause it? Or, rather, what sort of crisis was it? It was a crisis of political culture. Its origins and meaning must now be sought by looking at the western and eastern lines of the royal family.

The western line certainly had its problems after the death of Charles the Bald in 877. His son Louis the Stammerer (the nickname is contemporary, a significant point in this world where kings had to address assemblies) had a troubled accession, as we saw in a previous chapter. By the summer of 878, he was already visibly ill and this may well have un-nerved his aristocracy.[29] When he died in 879, the succession of his young sons was a difficult and protracted process and much has rightly been made of the splits within the west Frankish aristocracy of this time, in particular the rivalry between Hugh the Abbot and Gauzlin which culminated in the latter's inviting an east Frankish Carolingian to take over the western kingdom.[30] Both sons eventually succeeded to their respective thrones but their youth worried Hincmar of Reims who beseeched the eastern ruler, Charles the Fat, to help his royal kinsmen ('those youths … orphans without a father'), and feared lest they be corrupted without sober and thoughtful elders such as Hincmar to guide them. These later Carolingians were confronted with a Hincmar whose memory stretched all the way back to the good old days of Charlemagne.[31] Even celebration of royal military victory expressed sympathy for such youthful orphans.[32]

But an excessively worried view of these rulers is not convincing. Louis the Stammerer's death was a rupture in the political fabric but his burial in the great palace complex of Compiègne could only deepen the Carolingian aura of that site.[33] Magnates may have used him as a conduit to further riches but all kings had to reward their great nobles and Louis's court still operated as the centre where the distribution of *honores* was decided. It was Louis who had re-distributed the *honores* of the fallen magnate Bernard of Gothia to a favoured few.[34] His sons did indeed have a troubled accession but aristocratic rivalries around royal heirs were not in themselves new; even the collective action of a group of aristocrats inviting in a 'foreign' Carolingian, as Gauzlin and his allies did in 879, was not new, as events of the 850s show.[35] Furthermore, these rivalries pivoted around Carolingian kings; Boso was a lonely aristocratic exception in 879 in his sensational push for kingship.

Duke Boso, erstwhile favourite of Charles the Bald, seems to have lost patience with the Carolingian game amidst all these conflicts around the young sons. The death of Louis the Stammerer marked another stage in the melting away of Boso's uniquely high eminence as other magnates jostled for prominence. Boso saw that the threats posed to him by emerging rivals were also an opportunity for a daring gamble. He was still a potent magnate and through the spring and summer of 879 he built up more resources, getting hold of the county of Autun and developing links with bishop Adalgarius of Autun, an experienced follower of the west Frankish royal line.[36] As the east-west negotiatins and manoeuvrings dragged on, with Louis the Stammerer's sons staying in the picture, Boso broke away from the group. In July 879, he made a grant to the abbey of Montiéramey, a conventional enough transaction. But he had himself described in the charter as 'Boso, by the grace of God that which I am', a biblical formula pointing to grace and transformation. Boso was preparing to leave the orbit of the Carolingians and establish himself as a royal star. He also burnished his own aura as an honorary Carolingian. The document described his wife as 'imperial offspring', pointing to Boso's intimate royal connections.[37] It was Charles the Bald who had permitted Boso to marry Ermingard, daughter of Louis II of Italy, and it was Charles who had raised Boso on high. Boso had learned from his master; he knew how to make himself royal, kingly, like a Carolingian, even if he was not one. His witnesses to this July transaction were three powerful counts, including his brother Richard. He was assembling an arsenal of material and charismatic resources. Louis the Stammerer's sons were crowned at Ferrieres in September 879, but Boso had gone too far to turn back.

Magnates in Provence and Burgundy were prepared to back him. They sought patronage as well as security from Viking and Saracen raids. They feared this would not be forthcoming from the sons of Louis. At an assembly at Mantaille in southern France in October 879, bishops proclaimed that after the death of Louis the Stammerer, there was no leader. This seems to be an echo of Boso's own line of argument; he shrewdly zeroed in on the problems of Louis the Stammerer's marital troubles and pronounced Louis's sons to be 'degenerate'. The fact that the bishops echoed this idea in their inability to see that Louis had kingly sons shows that Boso was much more in the driving seat at Mantaille than is suggested by the flattering picture of episcopal power painted by the bishops themselves in the document.[38] The assembled bishops and magnates chose him as king, and this was not just as king of Provence. More than regional concerns drove Boso's supporters. He was simply king, and his support from bishop Adalgarius of Autun and Geilo, future bishop of Langres, shows that he could reach north into Burgundy. The bishops themselves looked to a wider world than their region; they referred to Boso's prominence under Charles the Bald and Louis the Stammerer and also to his leadership in Italy. They understood Charles the Bald as Boso's maker.[39]

The daring leap was too spectacular to be ignored. The Carolingian rulers suspended their hostilities with each other to combine against the challenger. They had grasped that this was an existential threat. Boso's support melted away as the Carolingians and their warrriors advanced; his brother Richard abandoned him; Geilo and Adalgarius made their peace with the dynasty.[40] But Boso was never captured. Regino of Prüm, who grasped that Carolingian dynastic exclusiveness was the key to the Frankish polity, nonetheless admired Boso's resistance. But he also saw that the Carolingian rulers could not make any compromise with such a challenge.[41] Boso had learned in a Carolingian laboratory how to make a king out of himself. Carolingians shuddered at this episode. But this turned out to be only a prelude to Carolingian loss of authority.

Boso's scorn was only one of the challenges that Louis the Stammerer's sons, Louis III and Carloman, faced. These kings were not as youthfully incompetent and vulnerable as Hincmar would have had his contemporaries (and us) believe. As Offergeld has pointed out, Hincmar rather gives the game away in his comparing his kings to the biblical king Jehoash who was only seven when he began to reign; this was much younger than Louis and Carloman who were fifteen and twelve in 879. Hincmar was using the image of youthful kings in need of guidance as a tactic to enhance his own influence and so his picture is neither objective description nor necessarily representative.[42] Other contemporaries saw these kings' youth in more hopeful terms, as signs of a great future: 'now in their fresh youth they are growing up and blossoming as the hope of Europe'.[43] Youthful kings did pose problems and Carloman himself recognized his dependence on father-figures such as Hugh the Abbot, though he also defined Hugh as a relative; kinship with the king kept this semi-regency in the royal family.[44] Severe Viking raids tested west Frankish leadership and the magnates may have used the king's relative youth as an excuse for their decision to treat with the Vikings in 884. That decision was taken, however, in the royal palace of Compiègne and the Vikings understood the ensuing deal to be one that was made between them and the king who remained a central figure.[45]

Western kingdom, eastern kingdom and the reunited empire of Charles the Fat

The west Franks may have had to deal with ill and youthful kings but kings remained essential. While the majority of recipients of royal charters from Louis the Stammerer and his sons tended to come from Burgundy rather than from Francia proper, royal generosity was sought after from all over the kingdom, including the south.[46] The year 878 saw a gathering in Troyes to meet the pope, who crowned Louis. Louis issued a substantial series of charters for beneficiaries in Narbonne, Barcelona and Burgundy as well as breaking a disobedient magnate, menacing a dissident Carolingian (Hugh, son of Lothar II) and approving a marriage between his son and the daughter of Boso, though he failed to get the pope to crown his new wife. Thus, the west Frankish elite came together at Troyes and saw itself as a community under a Carolingian king, member of a 'sacred line' as the majestic chant of the *laudes* had it.[47] Royal generosity ensured that followers such as Baldricus who had served Charles the Bald continued to prosper in the reign of his son and grandsons.[48] Louis's son Carloman (879–84) still presided over the circulation of fiscal estates from recipients back to the king and onward to other recipients. Louis's sons also struck down dangerous challenges from the usurper Boso, a figure more threatening to the dynasty than any Viking.[49]

These rulers continued to broadcast and articulate the distinctiveness of their dynasty. Louis the Stammerer followed his father in establishing celebrations of the day of his accession, birthday and future death day as well as requesting prayers for himself, his wife and his offspring.[50] Such prayers and commemorations were liturgical acts, not loyalty oaths. Nor did exposure to performance of this dynastic language, whether in the issuing of the charters or the prayers themselves, necessarily guarantee loyalty. On the other hand, such prayers and dynastic language did not exist in a vacuum. In his charter for the intensely Carolingian abbey of Prüm, which was not even in his own kingdom, Louis referred to four generations of predecessors as well as to his royal uncles while asking the monks to pray for him and his offspring. Louis also ensured that the community of St-Martin's at Tours would commemorate all his brothers, including those who had not obtained crowns. The fact that such charters tended to repeat earlier charters' formulae only enhances their dynastic quality.[51] Such dynastic references are less full and elaborate in the charters of Louis's sons, not least because they had no children, but they are certainly present. One charter breathes the air of broad Carolingian dynastic solidarity with its reference to the 'line of our family' ('generis nostri prosapia'), while another envisages a dynastic future in its request for prayers for the king himself and for his successors.[52]

Kings did not merely look inwards, gazing at a mirror in dynastic self-regard. They publicly proclaimed the dynasty's closeness to the great men of the western kingdom. In the summer of 884, Carloman issued a charter for Hugh the Abbot's monastery of St-Germain d'Auxerre. This was a lengthy confirmation of earlier grants from Charles the Bald as well as from Hugh's father Count Conrad, and several other benefactors. Carloman highlighted the royal family's direct connection with the abbey, recalling the grant made by 'our grand-father Charles [the Bald]' for 'the tomb and eternal memory of his son Lothar, our uncle, former abbot of this place'. Carloman here recalled his uncle, who had died the year before he was born and whose posthumous presence helped make the abbey a Carolingian place. Carloman also singled out Hugh the Abbot and count Conrad as members of the royal kin while acknowledging their own pious commemoration of their own kin, and the charter's references to many other 'noble men' evoke an image of the Carolingians and their followers intertwined around the great abbey in its historical landscape.[53] When the eastern Charles the Fat confirmed this charter in 886, he too was able to play the Carolingian music, referring to Charles the Bald as his uncle (patruus) and re-assuring his west Frankish audience that his predecessor Carloman was 'our adoptive son'; thus, the west Frankish royal line helped prepare the way for the eastern ruler. When the non-Carolingian Odo confirmed all this in 889, he could not reproduce this family language.[54]

The eastern rulers also successfully maintained Carolingian distinctiveness in these years. The death of Louis the German in 876 meant that the eastern kingdom was now divided among his three sons, but their fraternal relationship, even when it was tense, ensured that these parts formed a larger dynastic whole. While we do not know what sort of ceremonies these brothers deployed to inaugurate their reigns, they asserted the dynastic identity of their inheritance when all three met up in late 876 and swore to each other that they would respect their division of 'their father's kingdom'. These oaths were written down in the vernacular and widely distributed around the eastern kingdom(s), thus further broadcasting and preserving the performance, and people did remember it.[55] All three sons bound the dynastic past to their own kingdom's present and future in recalling their father and their ancestors more generally in charters requesting prayers.[56] Louis the Younger's well-connected wife Liutgard, a member of the Liudolfing family in Saxony, bore him a son in 877, thus adding a legitimate heir to the line and several of Louis's charters requested prayers for himself, his wife and his offspring. Queen Liutgard's brothers could now look at this child, as they did in the palace of Frankfurt in 877, and feel that their family's investment in Louis the Younger had paid off.[57] The fact that the boy died young, in the tragic fall from a palace window that we saw in Chapter 1, does not cancel out this 877 event. Carolingian family aura was still being successfully beamed out to audiences. Soon after their sister Liutgard gave birth to this potential royal heir, Brun and Otto requested their royal brother-in-law to take the convent of Gandersheim in Saxony, their family foundation, under his protection. The king did so, graciously confirming the family's hereditary hold on the abbey and also granting it some property. This family thus profited from its closeness to the king, still a valuable asset, but the king reached over the family into Saxony itself to remind the nuns in this Liudolfing foundation that the Carolingian family was part of their care; he made his grant for the sake of the souls of his ancestors as well as for himself, his wife and 'most dear offspring'.[58]

For their followers, Louis the Younger and his brothers began their reign as a hopeful future, not the frail figures of the last act of the Carolimgian show. As Eric Goldberg has pointed out, the biological factor that affected these brothers was not sickliness but the extraordinary vigour of their father. Louis the German simply lived too long and so his sons had used up too much of the time allotted to their ninth-century bodies when they finally succeeded. But this need not have been apparent in 876; Karlmann, the eldest, does not seem to have suffered his first stroke until 877.[59]

Even when illness eventually paralysed Karlmann and the inevitable tensions among the brothers complicated their relations, this had the paradoxical effect of highlighting the Carolingian ties that bound these eastern kingdoms together. Disputes saw envoys riding from one brother's court to another and Karlmann's deteriorating health twice brought his brother Louis to Bavaria to fish in troubled dynastic waters there. Such manoeuvrings mesmerized kings' followers, triggering lively arguments among them and making them hedge their bets by backing all three brothers, thus keeping their attention riveted on the royal family.[60] A charter of count Rudolf, lay abbot of the strategically important St-Maurice d'Agaune, in 879 was dated by all three of 'our lord kings, Karlmann, Louis and Charles'.[61] These Carolingians also contemplated themselves and the destiny of their heritage. Although Louis the German's tomb at the abbey of Lorsch lay in the kingdom of Louis the Younger, all three lines of Louis the German's posterity piously commemorated him there and thus individually recalled their reproduction of their glorious common ancestry: 'three heirs now shine in the kingdom as their father did'.[62]

This re-iteration of their common heritage taught these Carolingians, and their followers, that royal ancestry meant a royal future. The realm was theirs and they were everywhere. Confined to Bavaria through illness, Karlmann ruled Italy, proclaiming to an audience north and south of the Alps his familial links with its former rulers, his cousin the emperor Louis II and his formidable widow the empress Engelberga, whom Karlmann described as his 'sister'.[63] Their family's history in Italy gave Carolingian rulers, western and eastern, a variety of tools to deploy there. When the west Frankish king Charles the Bald was trying to master Italy in the 870s, he picked out two distant kinsmen for Italian duties, possibly because their own ancestors had an Italian connection, one which remained known even though it had snapped in 834.[64]

All this was not just the self-absorption of a once-great family. After all, Karlmann could languish in Bavaria and talk about the Italian branch of his dynasty as much as he liked without that in itself making his rule in Italy any more real. For that, audiences, structures and actions were necessary, and they did still exist. After his stroke, Karlmann was confined to Bavaria but he continued to issue a series of grants and confirmations to a stream of Italian beneficiaries who must have crossed the Alps themselves or sent emissaries in order to elicit such grants from the king in his Bavarian palace.[65] Petitioners and beneficiaries, courtiers, scribes, Bavarian magnates would thus have witnessed Karlmann invoke his family as rulers of Italy, just as he had done in Italy before retreating to Bavaria. Italian royal-watchers were so familiar with the repetition of the limited repertory of exclusively Carolingian royal names that they had to call one claimant Charlie in order to distinguish him from his rival, Charles.[66]

There is no convincing evidence that eastern aristocrats were turning away from the dynasty. Tim Reuter saw some Bavarian nobles' attack on Karlmann in 878 as a sign that aristocrats were getting out of control. But this attack triggered royal punishments which these aristocrats only managed to mitigate by the time-honoured means of travelling to the court of another Carolingian ruler and getting him to lobby their own king on their behalf. Even twenty years later, the count who had been the leading trouble-maker found that the reach of the king was a dangerously long one.[67] Sightings of an aristocracy rising at the expense of kings are often only an illusion.

Some historians have noted that the names of secular aristocrats from the Saxon-Thuringian regions start to flash up on the radar of the necrologies of the great abbey of Fulda increasingly prominently in the 870s; they have concluded that the shadow of the aristocracy was falling over a landscape becoming lost to kings. Others, with cooler heads, have pointed out that Abbot Sigihart of Fulda was a faithful servant of Louis the German's line from 869 to 891 and thus hardly likely to preside over Fulda's turning away from the king, and that when Sigihart did fail to please the king, he was easily replaced, even as late as 891. The clustering of aristocratic names in the necrology entries in fact shows that Fulda was helping to bind this regional aristocracy closer to the kingdom.[68]

Furthermore, aristocrats, like kings, faced the problems of their historical situation and could not simply rely on rising effortlessly, borne aloft on the historical wings of the world-spirit. One of the dead magnates commemorated at Fulda was Brun, whom we have already encountered as brother of an eastern queen and thus uncle of a potential heir to the throne and member of the powerful Liudolfing family in Saxony that was to produce the Ottonian kings of the tenth century. If anyone was rising, it was Brun and his kin. But in 879 Brun's little royal nephew died and that particular future was cancelled; then in 880, Vikings obliterated Brun himself together with his army. Brun's younger brother Otto now had to step up as head of the family and this meant that the brilliant prospects of Brun's own descent-line were now dimmed; as for Otto, he did not now automatically dominate Saxony as duke Henry was parachuted in by the king to take charge of forces there and the defeat of Brun may have dented the reputation of the family for a while. Otto was too busy dealing with crises at this time to make plans for his family to smoothly rise to the kingship, and as late as 897 he was happy to renew a marriage alliance with the Carolingian line.[69] Further west, even a figure as prominent as count Conrad could not rise in the middle Rhine region without real effort.[70]

People continued to understand the bonds and conflicts of their rulers as a family affair and thus maintained belief in the claims of the dynasty which they served. The exclusively royal names still functioned as a means of identifying kings, that is, denoting rightful claims to rule, and contemporaries were well-informed on such names and claims; they continued to understand this Carolingian dynastic language of royalty and to work within its structures. Modern readers may roll their eyes at sentences such as this (from the *Annals of St-Vaast*): 'king Louis, the son of Louis, sent envoys to king Louis'.[71] But such sentences describe an entire political landscape that was ruled only by kings with the same sort of name, often indeed with the exact same name, a point not lost on anyone in this hall of mirrors, including the Carolingians themselves. The eastern king Louis the Younger (876–82) emotionally addressed the western Louis the Stammerer (877–9) as 'my blood and bone, my name' and referred to himself as the latter's 'namesake' ('sanguis et ossa mea, … nomen meum; cognominis vester'). The fact that this letter may in fact have been composed by a monk far from these kings' courts for a collection of model letters only underscores the imaginative intensity of contemporary perceptions of the ties that bound the royal kin together.[72] Even a slip made by an annalist is instructive for us in their mistaken reference to the west Frankish king Carloman as Charles. The detail here was wrong but the substance was correct. Charles and Carloman were both royal names and each functioned equally well as a sign of dynastic identity. This slip thus reveals continuing awareness of the pool of exclusive royal names.[73]

These names still marked off the Carolingian rulers from lesser mortals and bound them together into a royal kin. Of course, names in themselves did not enforce Carolingian hegemony, but they expressed Carolingian royalty and thus functioned as a resource for the dynasty in times of challenge. In the *Annals of St-Vaast*'s account of the common action of the Carolingian kings against Boso, the listing of royal names was not mere narrative; it was a programmatic assertion of Carolingian legitimacy in which Boso's very name marked him out as a usurper: 'king Louis [the Younger] sent one of his leading men, a certain Henry, to proceed against the tyrant [Boso] with Louis and Carloman [the western kings] … And they formed an alliance with king Charles [the Fat] himself, Louis' brother, and blockaded Boso. '[74] Even after 888, when the non-royal names borne by kings were signalling to contemporaries that change was underway, the glorious heritage enshrined in dynastic names was still worth evoking by followers of a Carolingian king.[75]

These royal names were also a sign of family relationship and so all kingdoms were understood to be dynastically connected. In this last decade of full Carolingian hegemony, contemporaries knew that each kingdom was ruled by a member of a family that stretched over the boundaries of individual kingdoms, giving the Frankish world a political unity through royal kin ties. Annalists in east and west knew that their rulers were part of a larger family: 'the [eastern] king [Louis] had a fitting meeting with his nephew Louis in Gondreville'; 'The two [western] kings [Louis III and Carloman] … went … to meet their [eastern] cousins at the assembly fixed for mid-June at Gondreville'.[76] And they knew that rule was transmitted hereditarily within this family; succession was a family matter that could involve Carolingians from several kingdoms.[77]

Well-informed figures still kept tabs on remote Carolingians. Hincmar of Reims knew that distant Bavaria was effectively under the control of the son of the ageing Karlmann in 879, and he knew the son's name as well as the fact that he was illegitimate. Less exalted figures also knew their distant royals. In the east, a Mainz annalist could place a royal daughter from another line in relation to her father (dead for fourteen years) and her brother.[78] Such knowledge was worth having because the claims of the royal family could stretch very far. People still lived under a Carolingian sky. In Italy in 878, the bishop of Brescia in north Italy characterized all the sons of Louis the German as his lords but their relationship with 'their cousin the son of Charles [the Bald]' was also a factor in his anxious calculations about political loyalties. The church of Reims still held properties scattered across the Carolingian world, but archbishop Hincmar knew that in some crucial respects this was a small world, ruled by related royals.[79]

Figures such as Hincmar did not feel uncritical reverence for all Carolingians. Eastern and western annalists snorted in derision at neighbouring kings' antics.[80] Notker of St-Gall was a dynastic loyalist but classified some marginal members of the dynasty as 'tyrants' (i.e. illegitimate rulers) and preferred his own eastern line of rulers to its western counterpart.[81] Nor did aristocrats think that any Carolingian could claim any kingdom. Some discontented western magnates looked to the eastern Louis the Younger in 879 but other westerners such as Hincmar stuck to their own line of the dynasty.[82] Kings in these years did not make vague assertions based on dynastic identity but tended to focus on credible territorial claims, for example on the lands of Lotharingia. The articulation and negotiation of these claims in meetings and embassies reminded aristocrats in each kingdom that high politics was driven by the competition of the royal family.[83] It was an annalist, not a king, who imagined the intensity of royal kinship in the midst of royal conflict when he had the eastern king Louis the Younger plead with his wicked western uncle in 876: 'do not tyrannically invade the kingdom left to us by our father in hereditary right and in consequence violate the laws of kinship which naturally hold between us'.[84]

Contemporaries were realistic; they knew that conflict took place. But they understood, and indeed experienced for themselves, the ways in which the separate kingdoms were linked as well as divided. Some of the great magnates were still 'international' in outlook and family structure. When the eastern count Megingaud, who was count in the middle Rhine region with links to the abbeys of Lorsch and Prüm, arrived as an envoy at the 876 summer court of the western king Charles the Bald, he would not have felt himself to be a stranger there. As a member of the kin-group of Robert the Strong, who had died in Charles's service in 866, he had kinsmen in the west. One of his western relatives, the future king Odo, seems in his turn to have travelled east to enjoy the patronage of Megingaud, who also had connections with the church of Reims.[85]

Members of this aristocracy regularly travelled to the courts of competing rulers and rehearsed the claims of the latter's royal ancestors.[86] The 'faithful men' of Louis the Stammerer and Louis the Younger ('king Louis, son of the Emperor Charles, and the other Louis, son of King Louis') gave their 'favour and consent' to these kings' dynastic settlement made at Fouron in 878 with its resonant references to succession 'by hereditary right', to future Carolingian children and to kings helping each other's children to succeed.[87] The meeting at Fouron was only one of a series of encounters among the eastern and western rulers and their followers, encounters that demonstrated to a watchful aristocracy that Carolingian rulers still formed a masterful family community and one that showed, in its onslaught in Boso, how jealously it guarded its privileges.[88] It was a poem in the language of the east, Old High German, possibly composed in Metz, that celebrated the heroic feats of the western ruler Louis III against the Vikings in 881. The poem celebrates the young king as a worthy ruler of the Franks and its language may have been the chosen medium to proclaim this king as a suitable successor to the heirless eastern ruler.[89]

In the light of all this, the fact that Charles the Fat succeeded to all the Carolingian kingdoms by 884 is unsurprising. But what *is* surprising is that he was by that date the only suitable heir left. Here we approach the heart of the dynasty's problems: failure to reproduce itself biologically meant failure to reproduce itself politically. Family and biology cannot be separated from culture. But this central problem remained and grew ever more urgent between 876 and 888. Hincmar's count-down, with which this chapter opened, turned out to be prophetic. Between 877 and 884, six Carolingian kings died as well as two potential heirs.

Dynasties try to cope with death by turning rupture into a prospect of continuity. Louis the Stammerer's burial at Compiègne in 879 showed that in death, kings could still be a royal presence in a key royal palace complex and give successors something to build on.[90] Kings worked for this in these fateful years. The young child of Louis the Younger, royally named Louis, died in an accident in the palace of Regensburg in Bavaria in 879 and was buried there in the rich monastery of St-Emmeram, shrine of the saint who had protected the east Frankish line. Amidst loss, Louis had thus ensured that his little son would act as a permanent reminder of Carolingian royalty in a key centre far from Louis's own heartlands.[91] A year later, Louis's court convulsed in grief again as his older (illegitimate) son Hugh died in battle against Vikings. Louis had this son buried in the abbey of Lorsch, several hundred kilometres' distance from the battlefield. Lorsch itself was a centre of dynastic memory, as we have seen, and the dynasty had lavished resources on it, the scale of which can still be grasped in the sight of the surviving great arched hall and which may have signalled the path to the royal dead.[92] The primary focus of all this was surely devotional and liturgical but the expense of building up Lorsch and the long journey of the dead prince's body can be understood as public facts broadcasting Carolingian royal identity. The sweat of all this effort was one medium in which Carolingian specialness was still being learned and displayed.

If the burials in Compiègne, Lorsch and Regensburg thus deepened the perspective of a glorious Carolingian past, they also transmitted worrying messages to the kings' followers about the future. The death of Louis's illegitimate son in 880 seems to have shattered the king and his court, and it was swiftly followed by that of Louis's brother Karlmann of Bavaria.[93] Alarm bells now began to ring. Tucked away in the monastery of St-Gall, a loyal follower registered the shockwaves of these deaths. In a short historical text written in 881, Notker lamented the untimely deaths of Karlmann and of the two sons of Louis the Younger, noting that the death of Liutgard's young son had triggered all sorts of rumours, which suggests that these royal deaths were indeed big news. Notker was worried: the line of Louis the German might fail and he hoped that God might grant Charles the Fat, still a young man, an heir. As always, the royal bed was the heart of the kingdom; heirs were born, not made. Notker was also keen on the western kings, the young sons of Louis the Stammer, describing them as the 'hope of Europe' and Europe meant the whole Frankish realm for Notker here. But he did not necessarily see them as the solution to east Frankish problems; he remained focused on Charles the Fat and his wife as the proper solution to dynastic worries in the east.[94]

Notker's specific focus shows that this was not a weightless world; the gravity of the local pulled at the high-orbiting flights of the elite. This means that there were tensions in the structures that permitted Charles the Fat to become ruler of all the Carolingian realms in 884 but which also conditioned and limited the nature of that rule. As we have seen, some members of the elite still had broad, 'international' horizons, though that elite was itself subject to historical change. A good example of this is the family of Eberhard of Friuli. Eberhard was a very grand Frankish aristocrat who married Gisela, a daughter of Louis the Pious, in the 830s. He held office in Italy but continued to possess family land in all three post-Verdun kingdoms. When he and Gisela drew up their will in 863–4, they recognized the realities of a post-Verdun world, channelling land in specific regions to particular sons who would now base themselves in separate kingdoms.[95] But one reason why Eberhard and his family are so instructive is that this shows that regionalization was neither rapid nor straightforward. If it had been, then Charles the Fat's reign could never have happened and the politics of the era would have been very different. When Eberhard died, his widow – a Carolingian born – had his body transported far to the north, to the family's monastery of Cysoing which she saw as the centre of commemoration for the whole family; thirty years of office-holding in Italy failed to diminish the senior generation's interest in Francia.

And the next generation would retain a consciousness of family across distance and frontiers as fostered in the will's instructions about family responses to possible depredations by kings in the west, east or Italy. One son, Berengar, was allocated land in Francia, but the death of his brother, who had been given the Italian lands, opened up new opportunities for Berengar in the 870s and he went on to a spectacular career in Italy. For a great family like this one, family ties and the actions of kings meant that horizons were still broad, as well as regional. Berengar seems to have been equally happy to serve Charles the Fat when the latter was king of Italy and Alemannia and then when he was emperor and spent more time north of the Alps.[96] Bonds of kinship and scattered properties meant that the Carolingian empire was still a reality in the 880s.

Some aspects of it were more real than others, however. Like the family of Eberhard, the family of Robert the Strong was part of the high aristocracy, though Robert had not had Eberhard's rare good fortune to marry a Carolingian woman. After Robert's death in 866 in the service of the western king Charles the Bald, his sons Odo and Robert retained their family connections in the Rhineland. Thus, we find one of them, Odo (the future king of west Francia), back in the Rhineland in 876 in the company of one of his relatives who had stayed there. His brother Robert can be found further to the north and west, holding the county of Namur. Their status and connections gave them access to resources and patronage that enabled them to flit from west to east. By 882, Odo was back in the west but his brother remained for a while in the east, enjoying the favour of Charles the Fat, as can be seen in the charter Charles issued to him in 884. This charter is dated June 884, that is, some months before Charles's succeeding to the western throne. It shows that the great aristocratic families of the west knew Charles before that event. This is how Charles could get traction in the western kingdom.[97]

But not every aristocrat lived at this exalted level. Figures such as Odo could fly across the frontiers of this world; they did not need to build up concentrated territorial principalities. There were, however, other realities beneath their flight-paths, realities on the ground. Odo and his like could travel across the Frankish world, confident that they could track down and activate resources of kinship and properties and thus remain credible candidates for patronage.[98] Presumably they took treasure and followers with them. But they would not take all their followers. Not every element in the Carolingian world was in a state of constant flux. Thanks to their father's creation of a well-rooted support-base in Neustria in the region of the middle Loire, Odo and his brother Robert ultimately established their power in the west, and a number of those supporters have been identified. These men did not have the same opportunities for mobility as their superiors; the great masters came and went but these men stayed, serving and supporting whoever was put in charge of this region. Thus, we find around

Tours one Alcharius as a vassal of Robert the Strong in 865, of Hugh the Abbot in 878 and of Odo in 887.[99] Odo's grip on such local figures made him valuable to Charles the Fat; Charles's patronage made him valuable to Odo. As late as the summer of 887, it was still worth Odo's while to make the long journey to Alemannia to attend upon Charles there.[100] Alemannia, however, was far away; it would have been difficult for Charles to monitor Neustria closely and it is hard to imagine that men such as Alcharius would themselves be able to look to Alemannia for royal patronage. Once the crisis of 888 broke, such Neustrians could form a Robertian bulwark against the Carolingians, though this is to anticipate.[101]

Charles the Fat and towards 888

In the early 880s, belief in Carolingian claims, and self-interested need to maintain the kind of structures discussed above, resulted in contemporaries enabling Charles the Fat to step 'easily, quickly and without conflict or opposition' into the legacy of his brothers and cousins. This process, which culminated in Charles's gaining the western kingdom in the winter of 884–5, impressed contemporaries and thanks to Simon MacLean's superb study of the reign, modern observers can share their admiration.[102] Charles now stands as a capable ruler, and above all a ruler who people wanted. They wanted him because he was a Carolingian. People sought Charles. Political structures, as well as his Carolingian blood, helped him, while they also shaped and conditioned his claims. A sense of regnal identity among the east Franks led them to turn to Charles in 882. The western kingdom also had its own profile. Charles and the men who ran his chancery recognized this: they dated his charters by separate regnal years for Italy and east and west Francia, suggesting that his rule was 'additive', and Charles took care to mark his accession in the west as a particular event.[103]

Charles got his hands on these kingdoms only when their magnates asked him to succeed. Could they have asked anybody else? Actually, there were some candidates. In the west, there was the young Charles the Simple. His youthfulness (he was five) meant that his being passed over in a kingdom fearful of Vikings was explicable, while the succession of Charles the Fat, an experienced and legitimate Carolingian, is both explicable and unsurprising in contemporary terms.[104] What is surprising is that Charles does not seem to have been able to get hold of his young kinsman, unless the boy's appearance in the sources after Charles's death is a sign that he had been confined on Charles's orders, which lapsed on the emperor's death. This is speculation but it would be very rash indeed to assume that the silence of the sources accurately represents contemporary indifference to the fate of the western boy. Further east, there were experienced potential challengers in the person of Hugh, son of Lothar II, and the even more formidable Arnulf, son of Karlmann of Bavaria, but Charles was able to subdue and discipline them.[105]

Charles's Carolingian blood assured him support in parts of the empire in which he had never set foot. In west Francia, his predecessors were his relatives, as he took care to point out in a diploma issued for St Martin's, Autun, in 885, requesting prayers for those kin as well as for himself. His diplomas were suffused with references to his ancestral kin, to be understood as the Carolingian line in a broad sense, not just the eastern branch.[106] If such ancestral connections enabled Charles to reach into west Francia as a familiar figure, they also helped him pull his new western followers into a broader Carolingian sequence, one stretching into a Carolingian future. Thus bishop Geilo of Langres in Burgundy, a shrewd political operator, found himself at the eastern abbey of Lorsch in August 885. Here he would doubtless have seen the royal tombs and witnessed or even participated in the ceremonies honouring Louis's memory. Geilo had backed Boso's bid for a crown in 879 but the fierce Carolingian re-action to that had quickly brought him to his senses and now he fostered the cultivation of Charles's own line in the west. In a charter for Langres issued at Lorsch Charles called for the bishop to commemorate the day of his consecration to rule with a feast and also asked for prayers for him (Charles), his wife, his ancestors and his offspring. Charles thus gathered Boso's erstwhile supporter into an east Carolingian embrace at Lorsch and reached into the west through him, triggering western prayers for the continuation of the (eastern) line.[107]

Figures such as Geilo could not survive on the splendours of dynastic aura alone. The point for Geilo and contemporaries, and for us, is that Charles the Fat showed that Carolingian rulers could still deliver the desired patronage to their followers. In commemorating the day of Charles's consecration, Geilo was commemorating an event that he himself had helped to organize, while Charles's favour brought him more tangible powers on the ground in Burgundy.[108] Charles had to reward and protect followers as his predecessors had done. That was the urgent message of archbishop Fulk of Reims in his 886 letter to Charles urging him to come west and combat the Viking menace at Paris. It is clear that Fulk explicitly evoked Charles's links to the west Frankish Carolingian line as a way of reminding Charles of his obligations as well as of the benefits that dynastic connections brought him.[109] In evoking the exclusive royal name of Charles and the dynastic line, Fulk was speaking Carolingian dynastic language to a Carolingian in order to draw him west. And that Carolingian responded, drawing on empire-wide resources, as MacLean has shown: the troops that he led to Paris in 887 included contigents from Bavaria; the bonds of empire functioned. Other, equally tangible, resources circulated; mints as far from Charles's original power bases as Arles and Marseille produced coins in his name.[110]

Overall, Simon MacLean's positive verdict on Charles the Fat is convincing. He has demonstrated the polemical nature of some contemporary sources' excessively negative view of, for example, Charles's struggle against Vikings, whose raids were not a threat to his hold on the throne. And he rightly warns modern historians against taking a teleological view of the Carolingian empire as doomed to collapse at this time.[111] Nor should we think that the great aristocrats, so-called super-magnates, were impatiently waiting in the wings for their turn to replace an ailing dynasty. Boso's fate was not encouraging. Above all, the great figures such as Odo, Rudolf of Burgundy and Berengar of north Italy, who did fight for crowns in 888, were themselves dependent on royal favour to control the shifting networks of local allegiance on which their own power rested and they recognized this in their desire to hold high office under the king.[112] The fact that Rudolf and Berengar had familial links with the royal house was resonant here.

Despite all this, Charles's reign failed to check a series of developments that were extremely dangerous for the dynasty. Since 876-7, the Franks had experienced a stuttering series of short reigns. New kings needed time to solidify their rule and here the Carolingians faced a remarkable run of bad luck. Brevity of reign meant that roots of royal rule became shallow and turnover of succession could lead to insecurity and conflict among ambitious aristocratic players. Bavaria, for example, had experienced three new kings between 876 and 882, while Arnulf's continuing presence meant possible trouble for his uncle Charles the Fat rather than reassuring continuity.[113]

Without kings and their sons active across the realm, Carolingian presence was now neither broad nor deep. While 879 saw five kings in office (Louis III and Carloman in the west – neither of whom was married–, and Louis the Younger, Karlmann and Charles the Fat in the east and Italy), by 884 that had shrunk to one (Charles the Fat) and there was no new generation in place. Great magnates such as Odo of Neustria, Rudolf of Burgundy and Berengar of north Italy were now the gatekeepers of royal patronage, but this only exacerbated aristocratic tensions and rivalries as royal patronage became even more difficult to access. The ruler was becoming more remote.[114]

Charles the Fat had worked hard to cover his expanding realm, travelling further and faster than many of his predecessors. But his luck turned; serious illness struck him in the winter of 886-7 and confined him to Alemannia. As MacLean has pointed out, his illness did not prevent Charles from undertaking major political initiatives in 887. He was still capable of ruling and great men from all corners of the empire travelled to Alemannia to attend upon him.[115] But the court too was now more physically remote. How long would great men travel to it? The king's illness, even if contemporaries did not know that it marked a stage in his final decline, was an un-nerving phenomenon that brought the succession – always a source of anxiety– into worryingly clear focus.

The succession problem stemmed from the turnover of briefly reigning and childless Carolingians and now the consequences of this were clear. It was not that Charles had no solutions to this problem; it was that he saw the problem from a particular perspective and aggravated it by actively working to redefine and reduce the available pool of Carolingian talent. Such a pool still existed; Charles himself had a son, Bernard, though he was illegitimate; his nephew Arnulf, also illegitimate, was a capable strong man in Bavaria; Lothar II's illegitimate son Hugh was still on the prowl; the young Charles the Simple, posthumous son of Louis the Stammerer, was somewhere in the west. Charles, however, perceived these dynastic resources as a potential challenge rather than support. This was the classic dilemma of the dynasty which had always found it difficult to extinguish the potential of kings' sons. Hugh was a Carolingian too many and no warm blanket of Carolingian-ness was to enfold him. Charles had him condemned as a conspirator with Vikings against the realm. This very public cancelling of his Carolingian-ness took place at a big assembly at Frankfurt in 885 and Hugh was then progressively muffled in ever deeper monastic confinement. This recalls the equally public and effortful cancellation of the claims of Pippin II of Aquitaine and Carloman, son of Charles the Bald.[116] Similarly, Charles marginalized rather than advanced his nephew Arnulf, thus stoking up dangerous resentments and raising alarm amongst such observers of the shrinking pool of Carolingian heirs as Notker of St-Gall who in 885-7 was urging Charles to promote Arnulf. By this date,

Notker was increasingly worried by the looming Carolingian deficit and his portrait of Charlemagne, composed for Charles the Fat, was explicit on this; Notker cannot have been alone in these worries.[117]

Charles, however, also attempted solutions that show how creative a system of dynastic rule could be, even in extremis. One reason for his treatment of Hugh and Arnulf was that he thought he had other resources. He laboured mightily in 885 to have his young illegitimate son, Bernard, declared as legitimate in the teeth of opposition from some bishops who did not see Bernard as a credible choice and used his illegitimate birth as grounds for rejecting him.[118] Kings could not control definitions of Carolingian-ness any more in the late ninth century than they could previously. Magnates such as the anti-Bernard bishops played a key role in defining who was acceptable or not as a Carolingian.

It was high-level support, including that of Carolingian women, that resulted in Charles accepting the young Louis, son of the hated Boso of Provence and his Carolingian wife, as a member of the royal family in the summer of 887. Why, and why then? Louis was not the only candidate for acceptance. A western Carolingian, Charles the Simple, was also waiting in the wings; unlike Louis, he was the son of an indubitably Carolingian king (Louis the Stammerer); born in 879, he was probably a bit older than Louis, Boso's son. But this young Charles seems to have been far away in south-west Gaul and, more important, was in the control, not of the Carolingian ruler, but of count Ramnulf II of Poitiers. How Ramnulf got hold of him is unknown.[119] For the son of a king to remain in the hands of an aristocrat was extraordinary. Royal sons were not always with their fathers; on his death-bed in 879, the western Louis the Stammerer had to send messengers about the succession to 'the men who were with his son'.[120] This, however, shows a royal father's remote control of his absent son. The young Charles the Simple was not under the emperor's control. A legitimate son of a king with the potent name of Charles was a precious resource to which the emperor did not have access.

Perhaps the young western Charles did not have any broad support further east. Boso's son Louis of Provence was a young boy but his connections did give him traction. His mother, Ermingard, and grandmother, the empress Engelberga, held properties and influence in Italy and Lotharingia, sensitive regions for Charles the Fat himself.[121] In Charles's very public encounter with Louis in 887, timing was all. A Bavarian chronicler says that the emperor travelled to Kirchen on the upper Rhine and there met Louis along with his mother and grandmother, and 'received him with honour to be his man, as if he were his adopted son.' Was the emperor thus formally adopting the boy as his successor?[122] Unlikely. Adoption (whatever that term meant here) was a weighty gesture but not sufficiently precise to designate a successor. The adopting of a relative by a king was a high-profile way to (re-)define relationships within the royal family. Kinship was not simply a matter of blood. Carolingian rulers did not hesitate to add cultural ties of kinship to existing natural ones. Such gestures were part of the language in which the Carolingian family talked to itself, enhancing or cancelling the status of its members. This was a language designed to be overheard. Thus, the Carolingians uttered themselves, insisting on heredity, filiation, a dynastic right to rule.

In adopting Louis of Provence in the summer of 887 as a son, Charles was effacing the sinister memory of the boy's non-Carolingian father, Boso. Boso's daring challenge to exclusively Carolingian royalty in 879 had so appalled that dynasty that 'with oaths and curses they [the kings] charged not only the leading men and dukes but even their lesser followers, with his irrevocable removal and death'.[123] This statement in Regino's Chronicle lifts the curtain on Carolingian anxieties as well as describing the dynasty's determination to ensure that everyone, 'even their lesser followers', got the message on Carolingian specialness. Boso's death in early 887 decontaminated his son whose Carolingian features could now shine out. Hence, the important role played by his grandmother Engleberga, widow of the emperor Louis II, and his mother Ermingard in the encounter at Kirchen as well as in its preparations and aftermath. The names of Louis, his mother and his grandmother appear in the commemoration book of the great abbey of Reichenau, the surving score, as it were, of the sweet music of Carolingian togetherness played to Kirchen's distinguished audience. That audience included magnates such as bishop Geilo of Langres, who had backed Boso, as well as count Odo of Paris and marquis Berengar of Friuli. They were being shown that structures of empire still worked, and that Charles was master of that empire and of the family that ruled it.[124]

Accepting Louis added an option to the now very narrow choice for the succession. Charles's continuing determination to exclude Arnulf and to push for a son of his own was matched by his ingenuity in finding ways to do this in 887, including further negotiations with the pope on Bernard's status and the dramatic divorce from his wife Richgardis. Inevitably the divorce created upheavals at court. It offered Charles options; he was now free to marry again and to father legitimate heirs, or possibly to marry Bernard's mother and thus retrospectively legitimate the boy, though the dropping of Bernard's name from dynastic prayers requested in a diploma issued by Charles in September 887 can only have disturbed and puzzled contemporaries further.[125]

Charles's initiatives between 885 and 887 demonstrate the continuing centrality of the royal family to politics as well as how flexible it could be as an institution. Questions of definition, of who was recognizable as a Carolingian, were questions about power. Charles's crushing of Hugh, son of Carolingian king Lothar II, and welcoming Louis of Provence, son of the usurper Boso, into the bosom of the royal family both took place at assemblies; the aristocracy needed to accept such actions for their consequences to become real. Charles was not the only actor able to decide who was acceptably Carolingian. His failure to have Bernard recognized says more about Bernard's lack of support than about the boy's illegitimate status.[126] His determination to keep Arnulf at arm's length was not what figures such as Notker wanted. All this means that Carolingian royal identity could be performed social identity but it was also deeply personal and truly dynastic, being represented and experienced on the intimate stage of the royal body: Hugh was blinded and later tonsured; the empress Richgardis recreated her virginity to facilitate her divorce (see Chapter 8); the young Louis's being a child could only highlight his royal status. But Charles's publicly performed acts of ingenuity from 885 to 887 only drew attention to problems of succession and ranking and could not be brought off indefinitely; too many people could no longer see any security in the future. Such pressures forced Arnulf's hand.

888 and the breaking of the dynastic spell

Charles's weakness in 887, his ill health, and his strength, his political creativity, both worked against him. In the winter of 887-8, events slipped quickly out of his control. Challenged by his nephew Arnulf at an assembly in November 887 in Tribur or Frankfurt, Charles found himself abandoned by his own supporters and replaced as ruler by Arnulf. He withdrew to estates in Alemannia only to die in January 888. With this, Carolingian dynastic hegemony came to an end and a series of non-Carolingian challengers made bids for throne. The political consequences of Charles's removal were thus momentous. This need not mean that the causes of it were equally so. And our knowledge of what happened in that fateful winter is limited. We cannot be entirely sure where the key events took place and the scarcity and contradictory nature of the evidence have naturally generated intense scholarly debate.[127]

As Simon MacLean has rightly observed, these problems of evidence make definitive answers impossible but some observations are in order.[128] First, it is significant that the events took place outside Alemannia. Charles was making a great effort to assert his authority. He had spent much of 887 confined to Alemannia and his ill health now worried people.[129] As we have seen, this does not mean that he was utterly enfeebled or that contemporaries thought he was ignorable, but if he was to push through his plans for the succession he had to be seen to be able to do so on a central stage. Hence, he called an assembly for November 887 in Tribur, a palace near Frankfurt in a rich royal landscape; here, he presumably thought that he could bend his nephew Arnulf as well as the magnates of east Francia to his will on the succession.

Assemblies, however, were not always passive; the collectivity of Frankish politics was real. Arnulf was not prepared to wait obediently upon the emperor's will. He appears to have arrived at the assembly with heavily armed warriors, which suggests preparation on his part. This daring aggressiveness may have taken Charles and his supporters by surprise, though it is hard to imagine that Arnulf had a master-plan.[130] Much of what happened next may have been improvised, spontaneous and rapid. In contrast to the suspension of Louis the Pious's rule in 833, bishops as a body do not seem to have played a key role in dismantling the ruler in 887.[131] There is no reference to a disabling penance being imposed on a Charles deemed to have behaved outrageously as happened to Louis or indeed Tassilo in 788. Nor is there any reference to discussions on the gulf between royal name and royal power as there may have been when Pippin, aided and abetted by bishops and magnates, replaced the Merovingians over a century previously in 751. The ending of Carolingian royal exclusiveness was much less carefully prepared than its making.

It may be that Charles was so visibly ill that Arnulf was able to pose convincingly as a fit and urgently needed successor, but the fact that the sources give us such differing accounts of what happened in the assembly strongly suggests that the assembly itself was divided and the outcome not foreordained. We know that archbishop Liutbert of Mainz, recently restored to Charles's favour, was at the assembly and seems to have acted as negotiator between the emperor and his nephew; perhaps his decision to back Arnulf may have helped tip the assembly against Charles.[132] Amidst all the political manoueverings, an aura of the sacred hung over the assembly. Charles may have hoped that an assembly held around the feast of St Martin (11 November) would enhance his status as God-approved and victorious ruler in people's eyes; contemporaries understood that the cloak of St Martin was a sacred relic that brought victory to the Carolingian kings who possessed it.[133] The Mainz annalist (possibly an eye-witness) tells us that Charles himself deployed a holy object to display his royal authority as irradiated with the sacred. He had archbishop Liutbert take to Arnulf 'the wood of the Holy Cross on which he [Arnulf] had sworn loyalty to him, so that he [Arnulf] might be reminded of his oaths and not behave so cruelly or barbarously to him'. Four decades previously, Charles the Bald had successfully scattered his opponents in the civil wars of the 840–3 by advancing by boat across the Seine towards them displaying on his prow the cross on which they had sworn fidelity. Similarly, the despairing king Charles the Simple in 923 was to attempt to recall the Saxon ruler Henry I to his pledges of help and support by sending him a precious relic from St-Denis.[134] Oaths helped make lordship numinous. Tensions would have been high. An oath was not lightly broken. Arnulf's response was masterly. The Mainz annalist tells us that he wept at the sight of the relic and this, as Matthias Becher has argued, signalled clearly to Charles the Fat's followers that he would hold no grudges against them but would be a good lord to them. He thus graciously recognized the justice of Charles's cause even while unbendingly advancing his own claims to rule.[135]

Was Charles formally deposed? One set of annals does say that he was cast out from the kingdom and that he lost his rule (*imperium*).[136] Perhaps some contemporaries did not care that there was no mechanism for such a step in the Carolingian realm. No-one seems to have wanted to return to the experiment in overwhelming penance unleashed on Louis the Pious in 833. In some ways, the fall of Charles oddly parallels the fall of Childeric III, the last Merovingian, in 751. By 751, Merovingian royalty was not what it had been; by the autumn of 887, Charles was slowing down. But the depositions of 751 and 887 were not necessarily the inevitable result of a groundswell of general dissatisfaction. The key actor in each crisis was a Carolingian facing threats to his security; in 751 Pippin had to outflank rivals within his own close family (see Chapter 2 above); in 887, Arnulf had to respond to Charles's succession plans. Their actions were urgent, not confident expressions of consensus.

Not everyone thought that Charles ceased to be emperor in November. The archbishop of Reims thought that Charles was emperor until he died a few months later.[137] Our sources tend to moralize, depicting a fallen ruler, 'made from an emperor into a beggar', as Regino of Prüm put it twenty years later in a sermonizing entry on the fragility of human greatness. They do not give details of Charles being stripped of office; indeed the Mainz annalist and Regino, like the archbishop of Reims, refer to him as emperor even after the events of November 887. Nor do they say that he was sent to a monastery, even though they tend to wrap him in aura of holiness at this point in their narrative. Charles seems to have retreated to royal estates in Alemannia granted him by Arnulf in order to preserve royal dignity of a dying kinsman; or perhaps Charles was still dangerous, hoping to mobilize support there.[138] Only Charles's death in January 888 could definitively take him from the world of political options into a world of pious memory that came to see him as enduring the trials visited upon him by God and proving himself worthy of 'the crown of [eternal] life'. Or so Regino thought. One annalist, however, thought that Charles had been strangled by his own men. Charles had vanished from the political scene but as a Carolingian ruler he could have meanings and morals projected on him. Centuries later, Charles was the subject of ghost stories told in his old stamping-ground at Neudingen in south-western Germany.[139] For his contemporaries, he had become a ghost before he died. As an abandoned emperor, he was an enigma, a troubling spectre of lost rule. In some ways, his death simplified the political situation drastically.

In asserting himself against Charles at Tribur-Frankfurt, Arnulf had played to an east Frankish audience but had also confronted the centre of the empire in the person of Charles. He was to discover that Charles's death revealed that this world had many centres. Arnulf did not linger around Frankfurt. Instead he headed south-east as he had to show himself to his own supporters in Bavaria and Pannonia. His reach could extend far from there, as a confirmation for an abbey at Trier demonstrates; support from his cousin Hildegard suggests some closing of east Carolingian ranks around him; and he evoked his own Carolingian-ness in referring to Louis the German as his grandfather in a confirmation for Lorsch.[140] But he was playing to a limited audience. The events at Tribur and Frankfurt had focused attention on Charles, not on Arnulf. This was certainly the case outside east Francia. The disappearance of Charles from power was followed by an eerie silence. The great magnates seemed spellbound. They do not seem to have made any move to recognize Arnulf or negotiate with him, and he certainly turned his back on them as he headed south.

The logic of this book suggests that the system of exclusively Carolingian royalty would surely have made power-brokers across the whole realm turn to Arnulf. After all, as Regino of Prüm put it in a famous phrase, Arnulf was the 'natural lord' of the kingdoms that burst out of the old empire in 888: 'After [Charles the Fat's] death the kingdoms which had obeyed his authority, just as though a legitimate heir were lacking, dissolved into separate parts and, without waiting for their natural lord, each decided to create a kingdom from its own guts.' Regino here describes the new kings of 888 as turning away from a 'legitimate heir' who was present ('as though a legitimate heir were lacking') and he is surely referring here to Arnulf rather than to a hypothetical figure or to the young Charles the Simple, who was not, however, completely ignored by the king-makers of 888, as we shall see. By 'natural lord', Regino certainly referred to Arnulf.[141] And what made Arnulf the 'natural lord' was his Carolingian descent. As Regino went on to say, the new non-Carolingian kings of 888 possessed splendid 'equality of descent, authority and power' and 'descent' was the first quality on this list; their equality, however, made conflict between them inevitable.[142] Almost a century later, abbot Folcuin, himself of Carolingian descent, echoed and amplified this view, describing this period as one of upheaval, of 'the failing succession of the natural kings, who, among the Franks, ... were held to be hereditary'.[143] In 893, the archbishop of Reims stated that hereditary kingship was Frankish custom, just as the archbishop of Mainz did in 900.[144]

Perhaps Arnulf himself did not think that he was heir to the whole empire, but only successor to his uncle in east Francia.[145] This, however, left aristocrats everywhere else with the problem of succession to Charles the Fat. What could have been more natural for magnates outside the eastern kingdom than to turn to Arnulf? They certainly knew about him. In the west, some people, such as archbishop Fulk of Reims, thought that that kingdom was Arnulf's by right, though they may only have proclaimed this after looking for alternatives. A Bavarian chronicler thought that the empire was Arnulf's to lose: 'While Arnulf long delayed there [Regensburg] many kinglets sprang up in Europe, that is to say the kingdom of his uncle Charles.'[146] Arnulf's delay cost him what should have been his by right of descent.

These 'kinglets', however, could not wait. Because Charles the Fat had reigned over so many territories, his death left a vacuum. The coup that had so ambiguously ousted him held only for east Francia but Charles's death in January 888 touched everywhere. In Italy, west Francia, Lotharingia, Aquitaine and Provence, at least four magnates (Wido, Berengar, Odo, Rudolf) claimed a kingdom, with two others possibly doing so (Ramnulf in Aquitaine and Louis, son of Boso, in Burgundy-Provence).[147] They thus assailed Carolingian exclusivity, but they did not directly target Arnulf's east Francia. They were responding to opportunity and necessity opened up by the crisis of Charles the Fat. We do not know if Arnulf, or indeed Charles himself, sent messengers to the west and Italy with news of the momentous events of Tribur-Frankfurt. Perhaps they did. East Francia was not a sealed-off world. The western church of Reims, for example, still held estates there and that meant maintaining contacts with the archbishop of Mainz. A westerner such as the annalist of St-Vaast understood, or had been given to understand, that Charles's failing health had triggered the east Frankish action and people in Italy also knew that Charles was seriously ill.[148] It seems to have been the news of Charles's illness that pushed duke Wido of Spoleto into action; he probably left Italy to try his luck in west Francia in December 887, i.e before Charles the Fat's death in January 888.[149]

Putting together a precise chronology of events is difficult; our sources often give us insufficient detail and when they do speak up, we suspect retrospective justification. An epic Latin poem, composed around 915 to celebrate Berengar's exploits, would have us believe Berengar's bid for kingship in Italy was supported by no less a figure than Charles the Fat himself, who rallied sufficiently on his death-bed to nominate him as his successor. But we need believe neither this poem nor those equally retrospective modern historians whose belief in coherent plans and sober forethought tempt them to believe that Charles did indeed nominate Berengar, not on his death-bed, but at the assemblies of Waiblingen-Kirchen in May and June of 887. There is no evidence that Charles contemplated a non-Carolingian successor.[150] What this poem *does* point to is the importance of Charles the Fat. Winter was a time when communications would become more difficult and this could only compound uncertainty about Charles's health or Arnulf's intentions. Our own lack of precise information should help us sympathize with the magnates of 887–8.

And for them the stakes were high. Charles had ruled such a wide stretch of territories that his disappearance, even before his death, left no acceptable regnal framework in which the great men of the realm could work out some compromise. Their sense of honour and entitlement under threat would hardly incline them to that. Ironically, it was Charles himself who had summoned the assembly of November 887 that would be the forum in which his rule collapsed. Outside east Francia, no-one now had the legitimacy or inclination to summon all interested parties to a meeting. This contrasts with the succession crisis of 987 when, again, an assembly met after being summoned by the last Carolingian king before his unexpected death, as we shall see.

Kingship still mattered; indeed it mattered so much that there would soon be several kings, but the magnates could not see an obvious Carolingian successor to Charles. Nor could any of them tower over the others. 'Shall I be the only one to lack glory?' raged Wido in Italy as he contemplated the rise of figures such as Odo and Rudolf. Or so a tenth-century poet imagined him saying; poetry here captures a historical truth.[151] And none of the great men possessed a trump card that could ensure an unchallenged acceptance for themselves. Writing around 892, Abbo of St-Germain celebrated Odo, the heroic defender of Paris against the Vikings, as a king who succeeded immediately to Charles on the latter's death, to the joy of all. This was in fact far from the case; Odo did not convince everyone in west Francia; he had competitors and challengers.[152] Similarly, it is hard to believe that two bitter rivals in north Italian politics, Wido and Berengar, amicably agreed on dividing up spheres of influence, the former to act in Francia, the latter to hold Italy. Not only is the writer who tells us this, Liudprand of Cremona, a late (c. 960) source with his own motives for telling a story of deal-making among aristocrats, but Wido quickly returned to Italy and to fighting Berengar. No-one could enforce consensus. Open competition and rivalry were the order of the day.[153]

Such competition gained an edge from the fact that the would-be kings could not count on territorial stability. These magnates did not operate in a privileged stratosphere, unconcerned by questions of local lordship and patronage; quite the reverse. At the level of kingship, they could not count on ready-made solid regnal or territorial identities being at their disposal. It was not a case of whoever got to press the button marked 'west Francia' thus activated a coherently fixed territory and its resources to back him. To be sure, the kingdoms that these magnates claimed in 888 did not come out of a vacuum, but their fluidity made it hard for the claimants to grip them. It took Odo a year to get Ramnulf of Poitiers to stand down from a claim to kingship in Aquitaine. Rudolf I of Burgundy did not merely want to reign over his powerbase in upper Burgundy but sent messengers 'through the whole of Lothar's kingdom' to assert his claims there. This kingdom of Lotharingia was, however, a work in progress rather than a pre-existing entity that could simply be grasped. And Rudolf quickly encountered powerful counterclaims from Arnulf.[154]

One reason for such fluidity was that 'international' connections of property, kinship and patronage still functioned. Odo certainly knew this since, as lay-abbot of St-Martin's in Tours, he himself in 887 had restored its properties in Italy; in 896, the abbey still thought it worthwhile to have Berengar in Italy confirm its properties there.[155] Wido of Spoleto had support north of the Alps in 888 from figures such as count Anscarius who participated in a fairly humdrum property transaction in Langres in Burgundy in 887. Anscarius later rose in Wido's service in Italy but was still able to exploit his Burgundian connections in 891 to try and prepare for another bid by Wido there.[156] People north of the Alps were all too aware of Wido's reach. In 891, the bishop of Orléans, a supporter of Odo, frantically tried to ascertain if rumours of Wido's imminent appearance in the north were true; in 893, Arnulf himself believed that Wido's highly placed supporters in west Francia were trying to lure him north of the Alps.[157]

Further drives towards conflict and instability stemmed from the fact that the leading magnates themselves were subject to pressures and temptations. In west Francia, Odo had gained the county of Orléans in 886 thanks to his closeness to Charles the Fat, but he then stripped one of his own relatives there of lands that she held. This woman's eloquent protest against Odo's action does not reveal his motives for it, but he was probably taking advantage of her widowed status to grab estates that he could distribute among his followers. Odo's promotion in 886 was thus not good news for all his kin; he accumulated in order to spend; he had to be a good patron to his own followers and that meant alienating some of his other allies. In fact, even his gaining kingly status in 888 did not make tensions within his own kin disappear, as his shocking 892 execution of a kinsman demonstrates.[158] The widow's demand for compensation is itself further evidence for the pressures of patronage.

Behind the prominence of the great magnates lay unceasing tensions and demands; they were not masters of the universe, but then neither were kings. In Italy, Berengar had a solid regional power base in Friuli since the early 870s; his closeness to Charles the Fat further enhanced his patronage network, a network that gave him access to hundreds of warriors. This, however, had not been his family's long-term plan; it was only the death of Berengar's older brother around 874 that finally pushed him into building up his position in Italy and this shift in the family balance disrupted his Carolingian mother's strategy for her children's inheritance.[159] In contrast to Berengar's focus on Italy, his great rival, duke Wido of Spoleto, retained a keen interest in opportunities offered by his kin north of the Alps. Messages from them encouraged him in his bid for a crown in the west in 888, though their support turned out to be wavering.[160] All these factors, however, whether they were pressures or opportunities, contributed to instability and competition among the great men. Such insecurity meant that there was no time to wait and see what happened; none of them could impose himself as a natural replacement for Charles the Fat. Regino's retrospective judgment was accurate. It was inevitable that there would be conflict among them once the shadow of Charles the Fat passed, a conflict between equals.

This conflict marked a fundamental break in the political culture of the Carolingian world. The events of 888 were radical, an emancipation of the dissonance. After all, a striking feature of the great men who tried to leap the gap between magnate and king was their lack of royal fathers. Proclaiming one's prominent father was a marker of aristocratic male identity. Nithard's pride in his father shines out in his *Histories*. The mythic Beowulf answered a guard's questions about himself with 'Well-known was my father among the peoples,/A princely battle-chief, Ecgtheow his name'.[161] The Bavarian annalist's explicit listing of the fathers of the claimants points to the limits of their fathers' status; this was no royal genealogy: 'Berengar, the son of Eberhard ... Rudolf, the son of Conrad ... Louis, the son of Boso, Wido, the son of Lambert ... Odo, the son of Robert ... Ramnulf'. There was not a Carolingian king among these glaringly un-royal names (Louis did bear a royal name and was a son of a king, but of the non-Carolingian Boso, a usurper). The Anglo-Saxon observer noted that none of the claimants 'was born to it [the kingdom] in the male line'. Of these six, two (Odo and Wido) had no Carolingian blood at all and one (Rudolf) had a fairly remote, though real, connection with the royal kin.[162]

Those of them with royal blood possessed it through the female line, as the English chronicler pointed out. This could of course be a source of great prestige. Rudolf descended from a relative of Louis the Pious's wife Judith. Ramnulf of Poitiers may have been a son of a grand-daughter of Louis the Pious.[163] Berengar was a grand-son of Louis the Pious through his mother Gisela and the royal blood thus transmitted to his family glows in contemporary texts, including poetry connected to him and his house before and after 888.[164] But while Berengar's Carolingian heritage may have gleamed out like the gold embroidery on the rich tunic bequeathed him by his father, it did not do him as much good as one might have expected. The poet who composed *The Deeds of Berengar* imagined an intense fellow-feeling for Berengar's Carolingian-ness on the part of Arnulf, but he could not disguise the fact that Berengar's royalty was confined to Italy, nor that his royal ancestry failed to over-awe his rival Wido.[165] In the whirlwind of 888, Carolingian ancestry was neither necessary nor sufficient.

We should see this break clearly for what it was. Contemporary belief that Arnulf exercised some sort of hegemony over these upstarts was a natural reaction and a plausible one, but such belief was not general. The Bavarian annalist's reference to Arnulf delaying, which implies that the empire was his to lose, is part of an entry that seeks to show that Arnulf was the hub around which the new kings submissively revolved, with Odo of west Francia, for example, adopting the 'sensible plan of saying that he would prefer to hold his kingdom in peace by the grace of the king [Arnulf] than to rebel in pride contrary to his fidelity'. This, however, is a composed entry that seeks to conceal the improvisations and uncertainties of 887–8. Those western magnates who turned to Arnulf as rightful king in 888 did so later in that year only as a result of their opposition to Odo. We need not believe, any more than Arnulf did, the later claim of archbishop Fulk of Reims that he had favoured Arnulf as soon as Charles the Fat died.[166]

Fulk's claim does have value, however, as it alerts us to contemporary perceptions that it was the death of Charles in mid-January 888 that triggered events. Arnulf was important in the magnates' calculations; his eastern kingdom was off-limits for them, though he was to show that he did not see himself as confined to that. But Charles, in his evanescence, mattered more. As we have seen, Wido of Spoleto made his way north on hearing that Charles's illness was so serious in late 887/early 888. If Charles was failing, challengers, as we have seen, could not afford to wait. Rudolf of Burgundy may not have been able to wait for bishops to arrive at the sacred site of the abbey of St Maurice d'Agaune, strategically placed by the Alpine pass of St Bernard; Regino says that he 'placed the crown on his own head'.[167] In this thunderous atmosphere of uncertainty and challenge the would-be kings were competing with each other, not with Arnulf. In west Francia, Odo's coronation at Compiègne and Wido's at Langres in Burgundy took place within a few days of each other. This is not a coincidence.[168] Messengers, spies and envoys were surely rushing around the west Frankish landscape, picking up and relaying rumours and information. Odo and Wido were thus racing against each other and Wido's returning to Italy at the news of Odo's coronation shows him acknowledging Odo's victory rather than being surprised by unexpected competition. Wido's own appearance in Langres may have been the trigger for Rudolf to rush to Toul for a (second) coronation at this time and outbid the former for the support of local aristocrats there.[169]

Even in this febrile atmosphere, these coronation rituals could be solemn affairs. Bishop Geilo, master of ceremonies for Wido at Langres, was an experienced and artful master of rituals of royal legitimation, and we know quite a bit about the stately ceremonies and glittering regalia of Odo's king-making at Compiègne.[170] These were not shabby stagings. But in 888 participants could not count on them to work. Wido's coronation at Langres turned out to be a loud-sounding nothing, his new royal aura snuffed out by Odo and Rudolf. Odo's own coronation in February failed to light up the west Frankish landscape. On Odo's own doorstep, Archbishop Fulk of Reims was notoriously unconvinced and he was not alone.[171] Does this mean that these rituals did not matter? On the contrary; they mattered so much that they were repeated. Odo was crowned twice, at Compiègne in February and in Reims in November, while Rudolf of Burgundy followed up his January king-making at St Maurice d'Agaune with another one at Toul. Even Wido may have tried to mount another ceremony at Metz after the one at Langres failed to take off.[172]

These ceremonies mattered, but to whom, and what did they signify? First of all, they mattered to the rawly new rulers themselves. To be anointed with holy oil, as Odo and his queen were at the charged site of Compiègne in February 888 and as Louis of Provence was in 890, was to experience an awe-inspiring ritual that must have impressed the new rulers with the necessary sense of their own specialness. These men and women may well have witnessed previous coronations. We can assume that they received instruction in the significance of the Latin words that they would hear intoned over them as they felt the oil upon their heads. Participants in such rituals were made aware of their exposure to the awful power of the living God; we should recall here the extraordinarily vivid image of William the Conqueror 'trembling violently' during his own coronation in 1066 when it seemed to be going dreadfully wrong. Back in the 750s, popes had urgently reminded Pippin III and his family of the weighty responsibilities to God and the saints that their anointing laid upon them. In 881, Hincmar of Reims had reminded the western king Louis III of the meaning of royal consecration at the hands of bishops.[173] Rudolf I of Burgundy was consecrated by bishops later in 888, but his earlier crowning himself with his own hands vividly illustrates how these ceremonies gave these rulers conviction in their own roles and expressed that new status to the other participants.[174]

The spotlight of such ceremonies, however, could remind people of the disturbing newness of the kinglets. Odo's promise to the bishops to maintain justice for their churches could not play any of the familial chords that had resounded through the utterances made at the coronations of Louis the Stammerer in 877 or his son Carloman in 882. Louis of Provence, however, could have the Carolingian card played at his royal inauguration in 890, as his supporters emphasized his suitability as king because of, among other things, his descent from his maternal grandfather, whose resonant name Louis bore. Even here, however, some jagged edges in the smooth dynastic transmission were all too apparent in the evocation of Louis's father 'the most excellent king Boso', whose name was clearly not Carolingian. People knew that they were in a new world of kings and had to creatively deploy as many legitimating resources as they could lay their hands on.[175]

The site of Rudolf's auto-coronation was the abbey of St Maurice d'Agaune, a holy place where Rudolf himself held the abbacy. These ceremonies followed Carolingian precedent in the leading role played by high-ranking ecclesiastics whose proclamations of God's will and prayers for God's blessing were an integral part of king-making. We have no reason to doubt that contemporaries, secular magnates as well as ecclesiastical, took this element seriously.[176] Like Rudolf, Odo was also an abbot (of St-Martin, Tours) and it is possible that Odo took sacred relics as well as regalia from the abbey of St-Denis as part of the apparatus for his first coronation. All this helped link rulers to the sacred, and rulers needed all the help that they could get. On the eve of the Carolingian dynastic crisis, Notker of St-Gall had celebrated that dynasty's possession of the cloak of Saint Martin, a sacred relic that brought victory to the rulers of the Franks; that relic now disappears from the sources: had the Carolingians lost control of it?[177]

These kings' quests for legitimacy show that people wanted kings. Louis of Provence's supporters lamented the internal disorder of the kingdom after the death of Charles the Fat as well as attacks by Vikings and Saracens; they looked for a protector. Odo promised his bishops that he would provide law and justice, preserving their churches' possessions and privileges against oppressors. The distant bishop of Barcelona, unable to attend the coronation at Compiègne, received a copy of Odo's promise reflecting kings' desire to reach the widest possible circle of potential supporters. But that bishop's metropolitan refused to recognize Odo, showing the difficulties which these new kings faced.[178]

These king-makings did mark attempts to create independent kingships. The known coronation sites of 888 – Compiègne, Langres, Reims, St Maurice d'Agaune and Toul – do not point east, though the last two, located in the old middle kingdom, may have set off alarm bells at Arnulf's court which was also keeping an eye on Italy. In avoiding Arnulf's territories, the 'kinglets' were being careful not to infringe on his authority but also making sure that they were not beholden to him. Rudolf of Burgundy and Berengar of Italy may have ended 888 by making some sort of deal with Arnulf.[179] Confronted by western Franks who preferred Arnulf to him, Odo travelled to Arnulf's court at Worms in summer 888. A Bavarian annalist saw Odo's appearance before Arnulf as a recognition of the latter's superiority, and a western annalist tells us that Arnulf sent Odo a crown once Odo was back in west Francia and preparing for his second coronation at Reims. All this, however, did not mark Arnulf's shadow falling over Odo. Rather, it signalled Arnulf's unresponsiveness to west Frankish appeals. Odo had thus managed to outflank those western Franks who preferred Arnulf to him.[180]

Perhaps it was precisely Odo's non-Carolingian identity that mattered to Arnulf; Odo, probably around the same age as Arnulf, had no Carolingian charisma that could spread east and destabilize his rule. Arnulf understood that these new kings were separate from the Carolingians and from himself. They did not look to him for the origins of their rule. The charters of Odo and Rudolf dated the start of their reign from the death of Charles the Fat.[181] The new kings proclaimed themselves to be kings pure and simple, not deputy kings of a region under Arnulf's sway.

Odo, for one, made a bid for a kingship with a future; he was not presenting himself as a place-holder for Arnulf. His wife, Theodrada, was crowned with him at Compiègne in February 888, and we should see this, as Odo must have meant contemporaries to see it, as a 'clear statement of dynastic intent'; they certainly referred to her as 'queen'.[182] Odo also requested prayers for his offspring in charters issued early on in his reign and this reflects a dynastic conception of kingship. He wanted his followers and enemies to understand that he was only the first in a new series.[183]

Amidst the new rulers, however, two legitimate Carolingian princes still waited in the shadows: Charles (the Simple), son of Louis the Stammerer, was eight in 888 and Louis 'of Provence', son of Boso, was also young, perhaps ten years old. Charles was in the south-west, in the hands of Ramnulf of Poitiers whose defiance of Odo in 888–9 may have had more to do with Charles's Carolingian potential than with any desire for a crown on Ramnulf's own part. In the south-east, Louis may have claimed a crown in 888 but contemporaries' response there seems to have been confused and hesitant.[184] Neither of these boys could take a royal inheritance for granted, but neither of them could be safely ignored, and time was on their side.

There was also a third fatherless royal son with potential claims in 888: the thirteen-year-old Bernard, illegitimate son of Charles the Fat. The dying Charles had commended him to Arnulf, doubtless hoping that this would ensure that Arnulf would not harm him, while Arnulf would have hoped to keep the youth under his supervision. Arnulf, however, had enough trouble establishing his own line of succession in 889. Squeezed out, and now at the age of maturity, his father's favoured region of Alemannia was the stage for Bernard's rising against Arnulf in 890. This failed and Bernard was killed by the Alemannian duke Rudolf in 892.[185] Bernard's case shows that marginalized royal sons could still attract real aristocratic support, if they knew where to find it. It also shows that Arnulf, who presumably approved the killing, was less worried about the diminishing pool of Carolingians than in maintaining his own authority and line. Even after 888, dynastic solidarity had limits. The high status and good connections of Carolingian royal children could be a problem rather than an advantage for Arnulf; he also had to subdue his cousin Hildegard in 895, though all this did keep a Carolingian presence in the east Frankish landscape.[186]

Bernard's violent death at the hands of an aristocrat is striking and suggests that illegitimate royal sons had less of a protective royal aura around them than legitimate ones. Brigitte Kasten has observed that five illegitimate Carolingians died fighting in the ninth century but no legitimate ones suffered this fate. This may show that illegitimate sons were not off-limits in the heat of battle. In 900, Zwentibold, illegitimate son of Arnulf and himself a king in Lotharingia, was killed while battling his own magnates, the only Carolingian ruler ever to meet such a fate. His killing went unavenged and this, with the death of Bernard in 892, suggests a dimming of the Carolingian aura in the post-888 world, a world where some people could believe that Charles the Fat had been strangled by his own followers and that Zwentibold was plotting to kill his royal kinsman Charles the Simple in 895. And yet Zwentibold's death shocked at least one prominent contemporary who saw in it and in the killing, similarly unpunished, of the archbishop of Reims signs of catastrophic disorder. Zwentibold's death points, not to a decline in Carolingian royalty, but to a more general problem of kings now being unable to impose compromise and settlements on disputes, particularly in the unstable landscape of Lotharingia.[187]

The ultimate fates of Charles the Simple and Louis of Provence were also to be grim, but the process of how they became truly royal illuminates the fluctuations of Carolingian dynastic legitimacy and the meaning of 888 for contemporaries. The really striking fact about both boys in 888 is not that they were unable to restore an exclusively Carolingian royalty, but that were present on the political stage at all. A century previously, Charlemagne had bundled his nephews into permanent obscurity, and Louis the Pious had successfully reduced Bernard of Italy's descendants to the ranks after 817–18. In 888, by contrast, neither young Charles nor Louis was under the control of a senior male Carolingian or indeed any other ruler. Odo had encountered Charles in 889 but had not managed to get his hands on the boy. Odo's insistence that Ramnulf swear that Charles would not move against him shows the importance that Carolingian birth gave a nine-year-old boy.[188]

Charles and Louis of course needed other historical forces and actors for their inborn qualities to be realized. Here the boys' mothers played a key initial role. The prominence of women as agents here underlines the distinctive status of Carolingian children: exceptionally important but vulnerable. Louis's mother Ermingard was a Carolingian, a daughter of Louis II of Italy. As we have seen, Boso's death in 887 opened the way for Ermingard and her son to affirm their Carolingian legitimacy and have this approved by Charles the Fat. After the upheavals of 888 Ermingard lobbied hard for support for Louis. She attended upon Arnulf at Forchheim in 889 and again in 890 when she brought 'great gifts and was received with honour'. Arnulf recognized her as kin. She was also accompanied by great aristocrats from Burgundy, though the annalist who noted her visit in 890 focused on her alone, describing her as 'daughter of King Louis' but also as 'widow of the tyrant [i.e. usurper] Boso'.[189] Once Boso was dead, Ermingard could turn a disadvantage (Louis did not have a Carolingian father) into an advantage (Louis did have an impeccably Carolingian mother) and so her son was now welcome in all the best circles. Arnulf, as the keystone of the current Carolingian dynastic arch, could hope that Louis would challenge Rudolf in Burgundy. On the eve of Louis's own crowning in summer 890, we get a clear glimpse of Emingard's prominence in the record of a judgement on a property dispute in Burgundy: she is the 'lady queen' (dominatrix regina).[190]

Charles the Simple's mother, Adelaide, did not operate on this scale. Daughter of count Adalhard, an influential magnate in the last years of Charles the Bald, she was not herself a Carolingian, but she married one: Charles the Bald's son Louis the Stammerer, probably around 876. She was Louis's second wife and some contemporaries worried over the status of both marriages; Boso denigrated the sons of Louis's first wife, while Pope John VIII gave Adelaide a wide berth in 878.[191] Adelaide gave birth to Charles in September 879 after her royal husband had died and she took on a key task in the articulation of royal identity for her son; possibly acting on her husband's wishes, she named him with the royal name of Charles. Adelaide's kin remained close to the west Frankish kings even after her husband died.[192] Neither she nor her kin were able to push the child forward in 884 in the face of the adult Charles the Fat but someone kept the boy safe. When Charles the Simple did surface in 888, he was in the care of count Ramnulf of Poitiers, possibly through Adelaide's own family connections which may have brought Charles to safety in Burgundy after Ramnulf's death in 890. Geoffrey Koziol is surely right to imagine that Adelaide's tough experiences with the young Charles made her one of his teachers in the nature of royal destiny.[193] Similarly, Louis of Provence and his mother were among the audience for their own stagings of Louis's royalty; Carolingian destiny existed for Carolingians because they had been taught about it. The fact that women and boys were so prominently on stage tells us much about both the dynasty's resources and its problems at this time.

Both boys thus survived until changing circumstances gave them a chance to bid for a crown. The actions of magnates and the workings of texts and rituals were all necessary for the boys to realize the potential meaning of their own inborn royalty; being born royal was not enough in itself, but that quality of royalty in turn shaped the workings of the magnates, the texts and the rituals. The sources permit us to glimpse something of the effort that went into preparing Louis's coronation in the late summer of 890. Ermingard's lobbying of Arnulf was paralleled by the archbishop of Vienne's success in winning over Pope Stephen V to publicly support Louis in a stream of letters sent north of the Alps. Powerful aristocrats such as Richard of Autun and Wiliam the Pious gave Louis the necessary credibility and strength.[194] Louis's Carolingian blood was not enough on its own. Yet it was a priceless asset. No-one could more fittingly be king than this 'boy stemming from the imperial line', according to the bishops who gathered at Valence in August 890 to proclaim Louis king.[195]

Far to the north, Louis's Carolingian credentials impressed other influential figures. A presentation of Louis as almost the last link in an intensely imagined dynastic chain appears in the text known as *The Vision of Charles the Fat,* probably produced at Reims in 890.[196] This text offers the support of the saints of Reims for the beleaguered dynasty, reflecting the political attitude of archbishop Fulk of Reims whose desire to challenge Odo motivated these manoeuvrings on Louis's behalf. Fulk mobilized more than Reims' saints; bishop Reculf of Soissons, from Fulk's ecclesiastical province, may have attended Louis's coronation at Valence.[197] For Fulk, a figure such as Louis could cross the porous boundaries of a kingdom such as Odo's. But Fulk's text has impressed modern historians more than it did Louis and his circle. The *Vision* is transmitted to us from the north, not the south, and even Reims writers did not subsequently refer to it. Its impact was limited and it was quickly overtaken by events; if Fulk had hoped that Louis would reach north against Odo, he was to be disappointed.[198]

The bishops at Valence in 890 also invoked Louis's imperial descent as well as the approval of Charles the Fat, yet they differed sharply from Fulk in also celebrating Louis's father, 'the most excellent king Boso'. Their reference to 'this kingdom' suggests a more limited territorial focus than the realm dreamt of at Reims. In evoking Boso as king, the bishops and magnates at Valence added an extra level of royal legitimation to Louis who was actually no more (and no less) of a Carolingian than Berengar of Italy. They also pointed to the attacks by Vikings and Saracens upon a kingdom that had been left leaderless on the death of Charles the Fat, while acknowledging current support from the pope and from Arnulf.[199] There were many elements in this cocktail of royalty; where evidence survives, as here, it lets us see both how much effort it now took to make a king and how badly people wanted one. Louis and his supporters were not making all this effort in order to be Arnulf's or Fulk's instrument. Arnulf's support was important; Ermingard had spent time and money winning him over, and the bishops at Valence, in the presence of his envoys, acknowledged Arnulf's role. Arnulf's own conflicts with Rudolf of Burgundy were what drove his support for Louis as potential counterweight. But Arnulf's blessing was only one element in Louis's claims, and Louis reigned without reference to him. When Louis and his backers did turn to Arnulf for support in 894, the latter could not fully deliver.[200] Even a great magnate such as Richard of Autun, who had worked to make his nephew Louis's royal status a political reality and who was singled out at Valence as a potential pillar of the new realm, soon moved away from Louis into orbit round Odo.[201] All the preparation, effort and splendour that went into Valence could not stabilize Louis's position.

Unsurprisingly, though, contemporaries hoped that even such a young king could do just that. The bishops at Valence described Louis as a 'boy' (*puer*), though one with fine qualities, and admitted that he did not seem to be of suitable age to fight Vikings, etc., but they brushed worries aside by pointing to the experienced skills of Richard of Autun and queen Ermingard.[202] Louis's own suitability for office derived precisely from his birth. Louis would not have been considered as a candidate for a moment if he had not been of Carolingian descent. That descent needed to be socially and publicly recognized by supporters, who thus helped confirm it, but the only child that they would thus work for was a credibly Carolingian child. None of the non-Carolingian claimants of this period were a child; that would have been absurd. Louis's youth worked for him here; ancestry was a child's only innate resource; this meant that Louis's youth was actually a badge of his distinction, not his weakness. His youth broadcast dynastic authenticity.

Fulk of Reims, if he was the author of the *Vision of Charles the Fat*, told a story from the past when Louis was a little child. In presenting Louis as very young, passive, almost helpless, Fulk turned what seemed like a political liability into a strength, drawing on Bible stories to spell out Louis's distinctive qualities: 'This child [Louis] is like the one our Lord set down in the midst of his disciples and said, "The kingdom of heaven belongs to such children"'. Fulk here combined Gospel stories which show Jesus warning his disciples not to exclude children from their privileged place in the divine scheme.[203] Unlike the bishops at Valence, Fulk gave Louis no qualities beyond his Carolingian-ness, and Louis's being a child brought this into sharp focus.

Contemporaries were all too aware of the biblical tag, 'woe to the land whose king is a child' (Eccles. 10, 16). Archbishop Fulk used the youth of the eight-year-old Charles (the Simple) as a credible excuse for his not becoming king in 888, but this was a tendentious argument for a specific set of circumstances, not a general view that child kings were unacceptable.[204] The east Franks were willing to accept the seven-year-old Louis the Child as their king in 900. The youthfulness of kings was a real factor in making the contemporary political scene more complicated, especially as there was no formal institution of regency, but it was also a category that could be bent by contemporaries to their own purposes. The Bavarian annalist described Charles the Simple (aged fourteen!) in 894 as a 'boy of childish disposition' (Reuter) but this served to make Charles look small beside Arnulf, depicted as his senior relative; the assembly at Valence used similar language of the ten- or eleven-year-old Louis ('a boy of good quality') but this was to highlight his acceptability and potential.[205]

Fulk was a tough political operator who was connected to one of the non-Carolingian claimants of 888, his kinsman Wido, but his mind remained full of Carolingians, and he cannot have been alone in this. In the *Vision of Charles the Fat*, he makes dead Carolingians insistently articulate dynastic authority.[206] The narrator,

Charles the Fat, sees 'kings of my dynasty' ('reges mei generis'), suggesting a deep line of ancestors but, more specifically, he refers to eight rulers, five of whom are named with, of course, royal names. Nor is Charles the Fat the only pivot around whom this great familial wheel turned. Fulk also imagines the emperor Louis II tracing his own descent line down to Louis of Provence and, significantly, referring to the boy's mother, 'my daughter Ermingard', the sixth Carolingian and only woman to be named in the text. In uttering the vocabulary of kinship, these resonantly named figures speak of a world ruled in the past, present and future by their family. Fulk's intense evaluation of dynastic identity shows how well the Carolingians had built; their followers could still respond to its spell just when the dynasty needed it most. It was hard for people of Fulk's generation and experience to imagine a non-Carolingian world. Fulk himself had begun his service in the Carolingian palace in the 870s, in the reign of Charles the Bald, whom he knew to be the son of Louis the Pious. He accompanied Charles to Italy for the imperial coronation of 875. Fulk had witnessed the successful sequence of Carolingian royalty.[207]

This kind of dynastic language retained its attractiveness and power after 888 and Fulk was a master of it. As we shall see, in 893 Fulk sent a letter to Arnulf to justify his crowning the young Charles the Simple in January of that year, by arguing powerfully for Charles's claims as a full Carolingian whose Carolingian identity gave him an indisputable claim to a west Frankish throne.[208]

Fulk's eloquence, however, should not deceive us. As with Louis of Provence, circumstances, opportunity and hard work were necessary for the unveiling of innate royal qualities. All those magnates who resented Odo were not simply mesmerized by Charles's inborn qualities. To them, opportunity presented itself in the winter of 892-3 as Odo headed south to tackle dissent in Aquitaine.[209] Winter here brought no suspending of political activities, nor did that year's famine, though it may have fuelled a mood of anger and frustration. The northern rebels met up at Reims in January 893, and without Charles; they manoeuvred in a gathering without a kingly figure present. Significantly, they hesitated between backing the young Carolingian or turning to Wido, whose recent coronation as emperor in Italy marked another public challenge to Carolingian exclusivity.[210] The free market in kingship opened up by the events of 888 was still operative. Aristocrats of Carolingian descent such as Herbert of Vermandois were to be among Charles's supporters in 893 but their acceptance of Odo in 888, their consideration of Wido in 893 and their subsequent oscillation between Odo and Charles show that, as Bernd Schneidmüller has put it, the efficacy of the idea of Carolingian legitimation 'did not drive events but was conditioned by events'.[211]

'The aristocracy' was never a bloc acting purely instrumentally in pursuit of coherent self-interest and able to coolly handle the language of Carolingian legitimacy while remaining unaffected by the power radiating from it. These actors were certainly opportunistic, but violence and instability meant their choices were pressurized. Since the future was ever more menacingly opaque, they scrutinized the resources of past and present for support. Such resources naturally included power and favour, but also authority and stability without which power and favour would not hold. Such choices were difficult, as they always are in times of political crisis. A weakened but continuing Carolingian legitimacy did not vanish in this crucible, but that simply made choices harder and more inconclusive, leading to more instability. Archbishop Fulk knew that his break with Odo in 893 would hurt him in the intense regional struggle with count Baldwin of Flanders, but went ahead anyway with his push for Charles.[212]

The decision to back Charles in 893 gave the young king and his supporters a formidable arsenal of legitimist resources; their deploying of it shows how much store they set by it; their skill in speaking the language of Carolingian royalty shows how deeply it had sunk in. It was still a living language and one, it is worth remembering, that was spoken by Charles's supporters as well as by Charles (we do not have any utterances from Charles himself at this time, though our deafness is not the experience of contemporaries). As with Louis of Provence, Charles had to wait until aristocrats were ready to back him before the full force of his Carolingian royalty could live. Only when figures such as the bishop of Paris and count Herbert of Vermandois were ready to break with Odo could Fulk work to reveal the royal qualities that turned out to have been present all along.[213] Charles's aristocratic supporters decided on Reims as the site of Charles's coronation. It was presumably Fulk who orchestrated the ceremony, doubtless making a pointed contrast with the coronation of the non-Carolingian Odo there in November 888. It took place on Sunday 28 January, the date on which Charlemagne had died in 814, a date deliberately chosen to recall past dynastic glories that could now enfold the young Charles, descendant of his mighty namesake.[214] Such dynastic glories had been glaringly absent in Odo's coronation ceremony.

But glory was not enough. One contemporary annalist in the abbey of St-Vaast gives the wrong date for this ceremony. Perhaps this is a simple error which demonstrates the importance and necessity of these constant processes of instruction in dynastic matters that have occupied so much of this book. It is not hard to see why Charles himself later went on to explicitly recall the correct date but we should remember to be historical in our analysis of such ceremonies; not every monastic chronicler knew the significance of carefully chosen ritual dates, not even a date as widely commemorated as the death of Charlemagne. This annalist was in fact underwhelmed by the return of a Carolingian to the throne; he continued to favour Odo, referring to him as king and withholding that title from Charles until the entry for 895.[215] The annalist was no passive automaton whose Carolingian loyalty could be switched back on by the ceremony at Reims. In its northern region, St-Vaast was an important spiritual and economic centre that had benefited from and been controlled by Carolingian patronage for generations. Odo had also lavished attention on it. This abbey was not the site of a calm academic seminar on choosing a legitimate ruler amidst these competitors. Threatened by Vikings, disturbed by the death of its abbot and a catastrophic fire in the abbey, confronted with famine and fearing takeover by the ambitious count Baldwin of Flanders, the community of St-Vaast yearned for protectors and the annalist thought that Odo continued to fit the bill.[216]

This was a post-Carolingian world, but it still contained Carolingians. Even if the annalist was deaf to the Carolingian music of January 28, he nonetheless could not help reproducing the Carolingian claims of Charles in observing that he was 'the son of king Louis' placed 'on the ancestral throne'.[217]

This dynastic music, however, now sounded different. In the *Twilight of the Gods*, the final opera in Wagner's Ring cycle, returning melodies and themes from the earlier operas lose their innocence in a context of dissolution and collapse. The majestic chords of Carolingian legitimacy now sounded less resonant in a world of non-Carolingian kings. Fulk attempted to sound this music at full blast but it is significant that he played it to a particular audience, another Carolingian. This was Arnulf, who had been disturbed by the news of Charles's coronation and sent some plain-speaking envoys to Reims to find out what Fulk was up to. In the autumn of 893, Fulk replied in a substantial letter.[218] Fulk needed to placate Arnulf, who was a dangerous neighbour with a long reach. The latter's prowling through the great churches of Lotharingia in the immediate aftermath of Charles's coronation may not have struck Fulk as being entirely 'for the sake of prayer', as an annalist put it. His envoys had obviously posed some tough questions and demanded answers which Fulk thought it wise to give; Arnulf's threats against the young king and against the Reims eastern properties were real.[219] Arnulf was more concerned about upheavals in the western kingdom spilling over the border than about creating a pan-Carolingian alliance against the usurpers of 888.[220] Like everyone else, Arnulf was caught in a web of shifting, unstable and contradictory alliances. Fulk and Charles journeyed to Worms in the summer of 894 to re-assure him of their reverence for him, but when he did try and help Charles against Odo in that year, Arnulf's own men recalled their alliance with Odo, not with Charles, and this came to nothing.[221]

Charles's Carolingian birth was not enough in itself to trigger unequivocal support from Arnulf. Fulk lets us see how contemporaries scrutinized Charles's dynastic authenticity and weighed its potential power. Arnulf had publicly doubted that Charles was actually a son of a Carolingian father. Arnulf, although himself illegitimate, may have invoked the problematic marital status of Charles's mother or perhaps even these lost or mislaid Merovingian princes who, as we saw in Chapter 2, tended to inconveniently emerge from obscurity to trouble rulers. He certainly betrays here the uneasiness of a Carolingian ruler who did not have control over Carolingian claimants. But Fulk's key piece of evidence was Charles's physical appearance; no-one who actually saw Charles could doubt his origins: he was the image of his father as anyone who had known Louis the Stammerer could see. To scrutinize was thus to authenticate.[222] Physical appearance was genealogical representation as reproduction of this family was reproduction of the political order. This royal son at the end of the ninth century thus repeated and reproduced the very likeness of the father just as Charlemagne's daughter Bertha had done at the century's start. This reproduction of dynastic authenticity was all the more important in a present populated by kings who were 'strangers to the royal kin', as Fulk told Arnulf. Notker of St Gall's fears had been realized and things might get even worse. Fulk paraded before Arnulf the awful example of the ancient Germanic ruler Ermanric who had followed wicked advice and had had all his family slaughtered; let Arnulf beware such appalling counsel and instead help the faltering royal line.[223]

Fulk wanted Arnulf to see that in a world running out of Carolingians, the bonds of kinship among the surviving members of the dynasty were more important than ever. Surrounded by non-Carolingian challengers, the isolated young Carolingian survivor, Charles, could help Arnulf's own son gain his rightful inheritance. Dynastic loyalty such as Fulk's was not selfless. The bonds of Carolingian kinship were useful to contemporaries precisely because they could cut both ways. Fulk's hopes for Arnulf responding to an appeal couched in family terms were balanced by the prospect of family links opening up the eastern kingdom to western influence. Arnulf may not have found this entirely re-assuring; as Michel Sot has remarked, Fulk was being more Carolingian than the Carolingian.[224] Fulk had become archbishop of Reims in 883 and had thus seen how dynastic claims in 884 had enabled Charles the Fat to come from the east to rule the west. Perhaps he thought that the Carolingian family could still transcend the boundaries of kingdoms. His offer of support to Arnulf was also thus a warning.

In fact the system of hereditary kingship that Fulk was outlining to Arnulf was bigger than Arnulf and was thus not subject to his control. Fulk claimed that Charles's supporters had not needed Arnulf's permission to make the former king as it had always been the custom of the Franks, when a king died, to choose another from the royal stock without needing to consult any other king, no matter how powerful. Echoing Charles the Bald from thirty years previously, Fulk said that this had been known to Pope Gregory I and that in helping his own royal line, Arnulf would be helping the Franks.

Stating that his own forefathers had loyally served Charles's predecessors, Fulk saw his own family history as entwined with that of the royal family; serving the Carolingians was a way of performing aristocratic identity. For all his involvement with Wido in 888, service to a Carolingian king was the default position for Fulk and, he must have hoped, for many others. Fulk's statement of dynastic claims was not uttered by a Carolingian but by a member of the aristocracy.[225] Fulk's letter, like the ancestrally resonant date chosen for Charles's coronation at Reims, shows how contemporaries could still plausibly play Carolingian identity as a trump card. In 895, Fulk hoped to woo power-brokers in Italy to support Charles by reminding them that Charles claimed a kingdom 'by hereditary right'.[226]

All this loud insistence on Charles's rights, however, shows that Charles could not expect automatic acceptance. The genie was out of the bottle. Odo's non-Carolingian kingship did not melt away when confronted with Charles and Charles could not even always count on support from fellow Carolingians such as Arnulf and his son Zwentibold. Nor could Charles be definitively marginalized.[227] No one king could assert dominance. Outside of east Francia, magnates confronted competing royal claims after 888. How far did this matter? Were aristocrats able to extort concessions from beleaguered kings and thus build up their own power?

In fact it was hard to find islands of calm amidst these political storms. Some of the great regnal institutions survived, but they were now operating on a smaller scale. Ecclesiastical institutions could continue to look outside the boundaries of the smaller kingdoms in which they now found themselves, but this was not always the case. In the Burgundian kingdoms, for example, churches in the region between the Jura and the Alps looked further afield than did those in Provence. And if bishops continued to loom large in late ninth-century narrative sources such as the *Annals of St-Vaast*, they now did so as defenders of communities against Vikings and as movers and shakers of a political scene where young and inexperienced kings cut lesser figures.[228] In fact narrative sources themselves seemed to run into trouble now. While abbot Regino of

Prüm hoped in 908 that his great chronicle would help the fifteen-year-old east Frankish king Louis the Child understand what Christian rulership meant, the actual content of Regino's work showed that Carolingian hegemony had been fatally wounded. Regino's work was itself the last in a line of historical writing. The Bavarian continuation of the *Annals of Fulda*, ever more regional in its focus, came to an end after 901. In the eastern kingdom, it would take more than a generation for such writing to resume. As for the west, Geoffrey Koziol has suggested persuasively that the report of furious disharmony in 900 among Charles the Simple and his magnates in the Annals of St-Vaast marked a point of discord beyond which the author could not go. As outraged magnates galloped from court, so too the annalist laid down his pen in despair.[229]

Nor did troubles at the centres enable the aristocracy to calmly build up power in the regions. Manasses, count of Dijon, seems to be a good example of the hard men who built up local power while the soaring structures of the Carolingian empire disintegrated over their heads. His patron was the mighty Richard the Justiciar, the great lord of west Burgundy and brother of Boso. Switching their loyalties from one king to another in the all too richly populated royal landscape after 888 while blinding or imprisoning bishops who stood in their way, Manasses and his family built up power in Dijon, Autun and Auxerre.[230] All this looks like the ruthless self-interest that it probably was.

In fact, however, such men and women could not simply mould their world of challenges to their will. Regional power was often much less settled and secure than it might appear from our perspective. This is particularly true of Burgundy whose political geography was fluid in a complex political landscape where the high aristocracy did not have deep regional roots and where even lesser, seemingly more local, figures found it difficult to entrench themselves. Such elites were highly mobile and that meant that they had to be nimble in their cross-regional moves.[231]

This world was thus not securely regional. It was also still one of broad horizons where men like Manasses learned that distant potentates could cast long shadows. Awareness of this is essential to be able to re-imagine the unnerving range of possibilities that could loom up before these figures; only thus can we understand the historical meaning and significance of their experience. After 888, Manasses and Richard had to cope with a bewildering variety of kings across a landscape much wider than Burgundy. Manasses can plausibly be placed in encounters with five kings (Arnulf of east Francia, Charles the Simple of west Francia, Lambert of Italy, Louis of Provence and Rudolf I of Burgundy). This meant journeys to such non-Burgundian sites as Forchheim and Remiremont. His attacks on bishops meant that Manasses's name flashed up on the papal radar in distant Rome.[232] Manasses would have followed his patron Richard in sudden switchings of loyalty from Louis of Provence to Odo to Charles the Simple. Manasses may have been as keen to establish patterns of regional dominance as historians are to trace them but he could not simply focus on western Burgundy; he had to look to all points of the compass. His political landscape was densely populated with rival power-holders whom he could not be sure would remain safely distant.

His were not detached considerations based on a constitutional preference for weak kings who would permit an inevitable rise of aristocratic principalities and consolidation of regional lordships. If the presence of rival kings meant a weakening of kingship, that meant trouble for everyone. In the ten years or so after 888, events in west Francia moved at a frantic tempo. There were more kings than ever, with shallower claims to authority and their fluctuating strength, not powerful enough to impose lasting settlement, but not so weak as to be safely ignored, meant that their presence merely fuelled instability. Thus, when Charles the Simple and his desperate followers found themselves in Burgundy in 894–5 they could only support themselves by stripping the land of all the resources they could find, a worrying development for Burgundian power holders such as Richard and Manasses.[233] Burgundy's aristocrats may have had to cope with an exceptionally fluid political situation, but it was exceptional in degree, not in type. Far to the north of the melées in which Manasses was involved, we find the formidable figure of count Baldwin II of Flanders (879–918), the very model of a builder of a principality. Those great lordships surfaced in the Carolingian world, east and west, and blunted the edge of royal power and authority in the late ninth and early tenth centuries. Baldwin too found that struggles between rival kings may have given him opportunites for playing one off against another but that they could also burn him. Baldwin's drive to possess St-Vaast encountered a severe check from Odo in 895 while Charles's followers ransacked Baldwin's lands in 896, much as they had ravaged Burgundy in 895. Such desperate weakness of royal followings was as much of a problem for figures such as Baldwin and Manasses as royal strength.[234]

These royal quarrels did not affect only the warriors who rode through disputed landscapes. The bishops who gathered at Valence for the coronation of Louis of Provence in 890 lamented the state of their kingdom, leaderless, disordered and unprotected after the death of Charles the Fat. Nor could women of the aristocracy entirely avoid such conflicts. The uncertainty of one of the great families was expressed in the dating-clause of a charter of Ava, sister of duke William the Pious in late 893: 'the first year when the two kings were struggling over the kingdom'.[235] An aristocratic establishment was not happy to see rulers falter. The great magnates looked to kings for confirmations of their own rights and status. Charles the Simple never visited Aquitaine as king but the magnates there accepted him, wanted charters from him and stayed loyal to the Carolingian dynasty when new challenges came to it in the 920s. Nonetheless, loyalty to the king on this political level did not prevent duke William the Pious from pressuring royal vassals to join his allegiance, and this illustrates a general tendency in eastern and western kingdoms towards polycentric structures where the royal court was only one among many centres of power and authority, a point starkly illustrated in the loss of the royal monopoly of minting coins. For some great aristocrats, and this was probably more true of secular figures than bishops, a remote royal figure could seem desirable, as well as problematic.[236]

Ending

Royal power did not vanish in the west. The concept of kingship and royal authority remained important even in areas that did not see kings any more. Aquitaine and the Spanish March recognized, not just kingship but quite specifically Carolingian kingship, hesitating to recognize Odo and preferring Charles the Simple to his challengers. This may have been due less to some mystical attachment to the aura of the Carolingian dynasty than to, in Geoff Koziol's formulation, 'the desire and need for a monarchy that stood outside and above naked grabs for territorial power by magnates'.[237]

Western kings in the late ninth and the tenth centuries do indeed seem to have ruled with less intensity than their predecessors. But images of the noble monolith of royal authority dissolving into a world of violence unleashed by wickedly self-interested aristocrats depend on now rather outdated scholarly assumptions about the nature of Carolingian royal authority and about the levels of violence in the Carolingian period. Charles West's subtle study of the region between the rivers Marne and Moselle is a sober corrective here, not least in its long chronological perspective that rejects visions of the Carolingian era as self-contained, and in its analysis of Carolingian and post-Carolingian exercise of royal rule in terms of horizontal as well as vertical networks. This does not mean that kingship in the late ninth century was the same as it had been in the days of Charles the Bald and Louis the German. West sees that kings became ever more distant from the Marne-Moselle region, and his remarks on the increasing role of castles as regional nodes of aristocratic lordship in the tenth century point to important changes in the landscape of power.[238]

Violence did erupt in this new landscape, but it is difficult to be sure that this violence was itself new. Changes in the forms and uses of medieval political violence can be hard to measure, and since political violence in the high Carolingian era remains understudied, comparisons are not securely grounded.[239] But the spectacular acts of violence among the great that did occasionally appear now do seem to point to irreconcilable conflicts rather than to imposed settlement of disputes. Baldwin of Flanders had hoped that access to King Charles at the Compiègne assembly of 900 would enable him to successfully plead for the abbey of St-Vaast but he found access blocked by archbishop Fulk. Baldwin's explosive reaction was to have Fulk killed, an act that shocked contemporaries.[240] The eastern kingdom also witnessed disturbing political violence in the lurid 'Babenberger feud' with its murders, revenge killings and battles culminating in the show-piece execution of count Adalbert at an assembly presided over by young Louis the Child in 906. As Matthew Innes has perceptively argued, such violence was not the result of an over-mighty aristocracy flexing its muscles now that it was free of royal control. Rather, these explosions were the result of aristocratic desperation with the changing functions of royal courts which had dwindled and narrowed and were no longer sites for the balancing of competing groups, partly because of the 'increasing monopoly enjoyed by a handful of aristocratic mediators'. The killing of Fulk and Adalbert fits this pattern which recalls similar problems in the royal court structure of the later Merovingian period.[241]

The return of a Carolingian, Charles the Simple, to the western throne on the death of Odo in 898 was thus something of an optical illusion. Charles was not only king in west Francia, he asserted himself in the east (against another Carolingian). Once again, a Charles visited Aachen and Prüm, where abbot Regino may have found himself helping him.[242] Indeed, when Regino completed his Chronicle in 908, not only was Charles still king in west Francia, a ruler with the resonantly Carolingian name of Louis was king in the east. Louis's kingship shows that Carolingian dynastic strength could still pulse through the body politic. For Louis was a six-year-old child, the only legitimate son of Arnulf, as contemporaries stressed, proclaimed as king by the eastern magnates at Forchheim in 900.[243] Only the child of a very special parent could become king. To contemplate the evidence from his reign is to encounter, at the distance of over a thousand years, the inescapable fact of his being a child, just as his contemporaries did. On his diplomas issued before he came of age in 909, one seal depicted him as he was: a beardless boy. And modern experts can see in Louis's personal subscribing of his own diplomata the effort made by the child to authenticate the acts of his regime. Contemporaries worked hard to convince themselves and others that the child Louis was truly a king; the archbishops of Mainz and Salzburg both conceded in letters that he was very young but went on to assert that his ancestry and the virtues bestowed on him by God made him fit to be the ruler.[244]

All this, however, did not change the fact that Carolingian dynastic grip was slipping. In the east, Arnulf had deployed traditional dynastic methods of expanding rulership across the realm by installing his son Zwentibold in a 'sub-kingdom' and arranging his marriage to the daughter of the powerful Saxon aristocratic family that had already provided a wife for Louis the Younger. But Zwentibold's failure in Lotharingia meant that this came to nothing. Louis the Child died before he could marry. In the west, Louis the Stammerer had not delegated any real regional power to his sons before his death in 879 and they both died before they could marry. Charles the Simple did not marry until about 907 when he was twenty-eight, an important marriage for him, but oddly late for a Carolingian with no father alive to control his marriage. While he did have children by mistresses, he only had one legitimate son, from his second marriage, in 920/1. All this contrasts sharply with the practice of Charles the Bald and Louis the German up to the mid-870s; luck and longevity permitted them to deploy sons across regions and make connections with aristocrats. The dynastic narrowing apparent in the 880s was not being remedied, with dangerous consequences.[245]

Regino may have written his chronicle in a landscape once again ruled by kings called Charles and Louis, but no other legitimate Carolingians appeared and other non-Carolingian rulers such as Rudolf I of Burgundy remained present. Regino narrated the history of a post-Carolingian world and so his *Chronicle* itself revealed that the Carolingians could not put the clock back.[246] 'After such knowledge, what forgiveness?' The grand line of ubiquitous Carolingian succession had snapped and people knew this. Indeed, they performed and communicated the breaking of it in actions, representation and structures. Prayers are prayers but they were also expressions of political loyalty; now they also voiced political changes. In northern Italy, the monks of Bobbio had dutifully prayed for the Carolingian Louis II (d.875), his wife and children but by 896 they prayed for the non-Carolingian ruler Lambert. In north-west Gaul in 904, the impeccably Carolingian Charles the Simple found that requesting prayers for past kings now meant prayers for non-Carolingian Odo. In Burgundy, the bishop of Autun in 918 asked the church of St-Nazaire to pray for Charles the Bald and his wife but also for the 'glorious king Odo' and for Odo's brother Robert and his descendants. In the Burgundy-Provence region, prayers to God for the victory of the king became around 900 prayers for the victory of 'thy servants', probably a reference to new regional potentates.[247]

Change had come to stay. By 898, Odo seems to have had no son to whom he could bequeath the kingdom, nor does he seem to have been able or willing to have had his brother Robert succeed him in the face of Charles the Simple's claims. Just like Odo, however, the restored Charles had to work with the new reality of the almost 'vice-regal' power of the great dukes in their own lands within the kingdom, grudgingly coming to accept the authority of Robert, Odo's brother, over even such plum royal abbeys as St-Denis.[248] We can see similar developments in the east, where the efforts of great dukes to stabilize their own principalities hindered kings' access to the regions. On the other hand, some regional potentates such as duke Arnulf of Bavaria found themselves being squeezed out of the charmed circle of aristocrats around Louis the Child because of his court's domination by a narrowly focused elite.[249]

Nevertheless, this eastern realm's elite still possessed a distinctive regnal self-consciousness. When Louis died in 911 aristocrats proclaimed the new king, Conrad I, at Forchheim, the same site where they had acclaimed Louis in 900. As his name suggests, however, Conrad marked a real dynastic break; he was no Carolingian. Looking back from the 960s, eastern figures connected to the new royal dynasty of the Ottonians could see that Louis the Child was 'the last of the Charleses' (*ultimus Karolorum*) and that Conrad became king because 'the royal line had failed'.[250] Easterners knew that the Carolingian line continued in the west but also knew very well that it faced challengers: 'until the present day [960s] there is strife between the line of the Charleses and the descendants of Odo just as there is between the kings of the Charleses and those of the east Franks [i.e. the Ottonian dynasty] over the kingdom of Lothar'. The Carolingians were now just one royal family among others and one that had to fight for its place. Even the Carolingians now acknowledged the potency of these other royal lines. The western king Louis IV d'Outremer (936–54) married a sister of Otto I, and Louis' son Lothar (954–86) named one of his own sons Otto, as did Lothar's brother Charles of Lotharingia. The exalted stock of Carolingian names now needed transfusions of fresher material from the family of the strongest rulers in Europe. That fresh material, however, was not available exclusively to the Carolingians. Their Robertian rivals could also tap into it; duke Hugh the Great (936–56) also married a sister of Otto I and Ottonian names duly appeared in his family. These high-born women did not just possess an important brother; they carried dynastic charisma within themselves.[251]

The detailed history of these later Carolingian rulers in west Francia, for all its interest, is not our concern here. Our focus is on the dissolution of that Carolingian specialness that has been the theme of this book. The exclusive Carolingian hold on kingship was successfully challenged by Odo (888–98), by his brother Robert (922–3) and by Robert's son-in-law Raoul (923–36). What is really striking about the tenth-century Carolingian kings is their resilience and tenacity. They successfully returned to the throne after these challenges.[252] Those who raised their hands against a Carolingian suffered for their treachery. When Odo's brother Robert met Charles the Simple in battle in 923, 'Charles drove his lance so hard into Robert's sacrilegious mouth that it split his tongue and came out the back of his head'. Thus, the mouth that had sworn a false oath of loyalty became the point of entry for death. Later in 923, count Herbert of Vermandois, despite his own Carolingian descent, tricked Charles the Simple into captivity from which he was released only by his death in 929. Herbert, however, died guiltily reliving this treachery, obsessively repeating on his deathbed 'There were twelve of us who swore to betray Charles'. Or so one writer believed a century later, testimony to the darkness visible of Herbert's blasted reputation. In thirteenth-century England, Simon de Montfort's outburst to Henry III – 'You ought to be locked up like Charles the Simple' – testified to common awareness in their culture of the un-nerving fate of this Carolingian.[253]

Ancestral charisma and changing political circumstances, including occasional but self-interested support from the Ottonian dynasty in the east, helped Carolingians to reign as kings of varying degrees of credibility up to 987. They planned to keep this kingship in the family. As it does with Louis the Child in the east, our evidence gives us a vivid glimpse of the physical presence of a youthful ruler in the unpractised monogram mark made by the thirteen-year-old Louis (V) on a diploma issued by himself and his father king Lothar in 979. Here is a surviving trace of an embodied performance of the dynastic principle – rule by father and newly anointed son – played out, where else but at the royally resonant site of Compiègne.[254]

Nonetheless, not all the political manoeuvrings of these years, not even the successful bid for the crown by the Robertian Hugh Capet in 987, turned on the question of dynastic legitimacy. Those aristocrats who backed Hugh against the claims of the Carolingian Charles of Lotharingia that year may have done so not out of conscious hostility to the Carolingians but out of suspicion of the Ottonians whose eastern shadow fell all too heavily over Charles. This suspicion was part of a deepening consciousness of the separateness of eastern and western kingdoms.[255]

In some ways, the dynastic change of 987 paralleled that of 751. On its eve, some magnates thought that the (Carolingian) ruler was king in name only while the towering figure of (Robertian) duke Hugh Capet was the one who wielded real, active power. This echoes complaints made about the later Merovingian kings after their fall in 751.[256] Furthermore, neither in 751 nor in 987 did the old ruling dynasty die out or reach a natural end. Childeric III was very much alive, and had a son, when Pippin bundled him off to a monastery in 751. In 987, the young and childless Louis V had died in a hunting accident, but his uncle, Charles of Lotharingia, politically experienced, in his mid-thirties, and father of at least one son, stood ready to leap onto the stage. The changes of 751 and 987 were not cases of natural extinction but were political crises where ambitious magnates, whether Pippin III or Hugh Capet, were driven as much by uncertainty and the prospect of conflict as by confidence in their own destiny, and thus took the risk of making a bid for the throne.

As for Charles of Lotharingia, he was something of an outsider in the western kingdom, but his Carolingian blood gave him a real claim. That dynastic heritage, however, was also dangerous for him. Opponents could claim that there was a discrepancy between his ancestry and his own character. Rather than being foundational, the weight of Carolingian-ness could be crushing. In 984, Theoderic, bishop of the Carolingian memory of Metz, directed a harsh letter to Charles. It is hard to gauge the purpose or impact of this letter, though it need not be seen as revealing the true character of Charles. Nor need we assume that contemporaries universally held him in the contempt so vividly expressed by this bishop. Indeed bishop Theoderich was not always hostile to Charles; it is just possible that he had supported Charles as a sort of anti-king against king Lothar, Charles's brother, in 978.²⁵⁷ Charles certainly had had to play his own game against his kingly brother and rely on the eastern ruler Otto II for backing.

But the peculiar challenges of tenth-century politics in the westetrn kingdom meant that surprising shifts of loyalty and position were necessary. Not everyone under the last Carolingian kings thought that Charles was damaged goods. But it is clear that Charles's ancestry did not exempt him from criticism; in fact, it could become a rod for his back. The opening address in the bishop's 984 letter highlights the bishop's loyalty to the imperial (Ottonian) line in contrast to Charles whose family connection to the bishop himself falls short of sharing the bishop's virtue of fidelity. Charles has savaged his own family and flouted family bonds in his attacks on 'his own brother [Lothar] the noble king of the Franks'. More lowly men than him have kept their oaths and thus surpass Charles, for all his nobility. In all this, sneers the bishop, Charles has failed to follow the path of his ancestors. Here, the brightness of ancestral heritage simply makes Charles look cheap and nasty.²⁵⁸

The bishop systematically takes him apart, turning him into a ghastly parody of the great rulers of the past. I am not claiming that the bishop had read Einhard's *Life of Charlemagne*, nor that there are specific textual echoes of it and other royal biographies in the letter; ideals of good rulership could exist in living political culture as well as in texts. The juxtaposition is mine, not the bishop's. But, the bishop's letter, viewed in the light of Einhard and other biographies, shows how clearly this Charles falls so woefully short of his great ancestors. Contrast his plotting against his brother Lothar with Charlemagne's patient endurance of his brother Carloman's hostility. Contrast Charles's poisonous slanders against his brother's wife queen Emma with Charlemagne's reverence for royal women such as his own mother, his queen Hildegarde and his daughters. Contrast Charlemagne's mastery of such women with Charles's inferiority as a man to a woman (the formidable Beatrice, duchess of Upper Lotharingia and sister of Hugh Capet). Whereas Einhard's and Notker's Charlemagne spoke in a clear voice and said wise and just things, and Thegan's Louis the Pious never let his voice become distorted with raucous laughter, Charles's voice was a hiss that required silencing: 'how often have I had to restrain your shameless mouth with my finger while you, with a snake-like hiss, uttered disgusting things about the archbishop of Reims and even more disgusting things against the queen'.²⁵⁹

Charles's response to this scorching denunciation reveals fearful levels of dynastic anxiety. He claimed that it was actually the bishop who had pushed him into acting against his own brother so that 'our entire royal family' (*omne genus nostrum regium*) would tear itself apart and true kings would be replaced by usurpers (*tyranni*) who would occupy their empty palaces in company with this outrageous bishop. This reads as a nightmare version of Einhard's vision of Charlemagne's ancestors keeping good order in the palace while striking down 'usurpers' (*tyranni*). Significantly, some of Louis V's followers in 987 urged him to retain his grip on his palaces.²⁶⁰

This operatic exchange of 984 need not mean that Carolingian dynastic charisma was running low. The king, Lothar, was a Carolingian and a wily political operator;

he would be succeeded by his son Lous V in 986; and bishop Theoderic's thunderings against Charles seem to have had little impact on contemporaries.²⁶¹ Nevertheless, the letter reveals a dark side to a glorious ancestry and how contemporaries could think about the meanings of royal lineage, and of qualities of rule. This does not mean that they questioned the hereditary principle as such. The aristocrats of 987 were, after all, aristocrats; birth and lineage mattered greatly to them. Back in 829, the same bishops who told Louis the Pious that kings received their kingdom from God, not their ancestors, also proclaimed that all in the kingdom were to pray for the life of Louis, his wife and their offspring.²⁶²

In the summer of 987, at an assembly at Senlis, and thus in the heart of Hugh Capet's power, as it had been of Charles the Bald's, west Frankish magnates recognized Hugh as king, favouring him at the expense of Charles of Lotharingia. Charles did not attend this meeting, but did make his own case to supporters and opponents before and after the assembly. And the archbishop of Reims, no friend to Charles, had to deal with these claims during the assembly itself. Or so Richer tells us. Richer was a monk of St-Remigius in Reims who, in the 990s, wrote a colourful history of the 'conflicts of the Gauls'. While he himself acknowledged a debt to earlier histories produced at Reims by Hincmar and Flodoard, his explicit grappling with the narrative of a post-Carolingian world makes him a worthy successor to Regino of Prüm. Most modern historians have tended to highlight his failings as a reliable source, but like Regino on 888, Richer's extended account of 987 shows his grasp of something deeply significant at stake then.²⁶³

We are dependent on Richer's *Histories* for an account of what happened in 987 and we need to remember that the speeches of the claimants and participants, replete with the language of ancient historians such as Sallust, are not transcripts of what people actually said. Hugh and the archbishop did not engage in discussion of principles of heredity, suitability and election in an academic seminar-style format calmly mirroring modern historiographical concerns with such principles. People at Senlis spoke about such urgent topics because these were rooted in pressing and clashing arguments about power. Assemblies were venues for collective consideration of claims as well as more general consideration of the well-being and structure of the realm. Contemporaries were as capable of political thought as well as hard-faced political intimidation and self-interested calculation of odds of success.²⁶⁴

Richer's text itself shows us this. Writing in the 990s, and fully appreciating the potency of hereditary claims, he was no mouthpiece for Hugh Capet, nor was he an unthinking advocate for the good old cause of the Carolingians.²⁶⁵ His account of the competing claims is evidence that one contemporary tried to understand the situation from various angles, each representing differing claims to rule by interested parties. The speech that Richer gives to Adalbero, the archbishop of Reims, for rejecting Charles reveals that, to exclude a Carolingian in favour of a non-Carolingian, contemporaries had to confront Carolingian dynastic claims. For Richer's Adalbero, Charles's dynastic inheritance was simultaneously not enough and too much: 'I have often heard that when emperors of the most distinguished lineage (*clarissimi generis*) fell from office through weakness of character, they were sometimes succeeded by equals and sometimes by those who were inferior.'

Dynastic inheritance could thus not guarantee that a ruler would be good or that he would be smoothly succeeded. Adalbero recognized that Charles had supporters who argued that his claim was founded in his birth but, he went on, 'a kingdom cannot be acquired by hereditary right, nor should anyone be elevated to the throne unless he is distinguished not only by nobility of body but also by wisdom of mind'.[266] Such points were not radically new. Contemporaries may have agreed with this view of royal suitability in the circumstances of 987, but that did not mean that they rejected dynasties. Hugh quickly followed his own coronation with the coronation of his son Robert.[267]

The curtain had not come down abruptly on the Carolingians, nor risen serenely on the Capetians. These actors were living from moment to moment. It would take some time before Capetian dynastic security would come to be a natural feature of the political landscape. And 987's events did not crush Charles of Lotharingia's dangerously potent claims. Charles successfully mobilized support to resist Hugh, though he does not seem to have proclaimed himself king. The fact that he was able to find some sympathy at the Ottonian court and to temporarily attract figures such as the scholar-politician Gerbert testifies to his resources and credibility.[268] Hugh Capet recognized this. When he finally got Charles in his clutches in 991, he imprisoned him, his wife and those of his children whom he could get his hands on, including Charles's resonantly named son Louis. He also worked to depose Charles's nephew Arnulf, Archbishop of Reims. But Charles's individual case and the general aura of Carolingian royalty still continued to flicker.[269]

Richer's vivid portrayal of Arnulf of Reims emotionally backing Charles as the last hope for restoring their family's honour casts Charles in a tragic light as the last Carolingian. Richer himself may have been a supporter of Charles in 991. Jason Glenn has argued that Richer's sudden departure from Reims on a difficult journey to Chartres just before Charles and Arnulf were captured may have had more to do with involvement with their plight than with an urgent desire to conduct some scientific research that Richer gives as his reason.[270] High politics did not affect only the highest in the realm. Still, Charles's disappearance from the political scene did make Richer's task as a historian easier in one respect. In his Prologue to his *Histories*, he singled out the profuse repetition of the names Charles and Louis as a source of potential confusion for his reader. Such Carolingian royal names vanish from the later chapters of Richer's *Histories* as their bearers vanished from the stage. No Charles or Louis appears in the last eleven chapters of Richer's work. The final chapter mentions the death of Hugh Capet in 996 and describes Robert (II) as succeeding his father. Hugh and Robert themselves did not shy away from invoking the old royal names, but their grants and privileges did so in order to refer back to a royal history whose mantle of continuity and legitimacy now enfolded them, newly royal father and son.[271]

Charles of Lotharingia's tomb is in the church of St Servatius in Maastricht, in what is now the southern tip of the Netherlands, nestling between modern national borders. During the heyday of Carolingian rule, Maastricht lay in a landscape rich in royal estates. It is close to Aachen, one reason for Einhard becoming abbot of St-Servatius there.[272] The tomb of the Charles in Maastricht is a quieter, much less visited spot than the tomb of Charlemagne in Aachen. To contemplate the tomb of Charles of Lotharingia in a church once held by the biographer of Charlemagne is to re-imagine the shifts in Carolingian history. The simple repetition of the name Charles was not enough to guarantee the reproduction of the dynasty's power. It never had been. But that repetition of exclusively royal names was part of the elaborate apparatus that had generated an aura of dynastic specialness that was the hallmark of that dynasty's rule. Eventually, of course, that magic failed, and the Carolingian chorus fell silent. The silence around Charles's tomb in Maastricht is the end of an old song.

Notes

Chapter 1

1. Beaune (1997), 625–36; Beumann and Braunfels (1965–1968), vol. 4.
2. Davies (1996), 306; Pohle, van den Brink and Ayooghi (2014).
3. Morrissey (2003), 278–84.
4. Braunfels (1965), ix; Airlie (2012), vii–viii.
5. Ganz (1995), 267.
6. Borgolte (2014); Airlie (2012), vii–x.
7. Morrissey (2003), 294–7.
8. Morrissey (2003), 294–7; Grau (1992), 117–18; Ganz (1995); Morrrissey (1992), 670; Kerner (2004), 94–6; Blanc and Naudin (2015).
9. *Liber Historiae Francorum*, *c*.43, ed. B. Krusch, MGH SRM 2, pp.315–16, trans. Fouracre and Gerberding (1996), 88; *AMP*, a.714, pp.18–21, trans. Fouracre and Gerberding (1996), 354; Wood (1994), 222; Ewig (1995), 22.
10. *Codex Carolinus*, no.67, MGH Ep. KA 1, p.595. McCormick (1984), 3–4; Brunner (1983); Airlie (1999).
11. Wallace-Hadrill (1967), 185.
12. *AF*, a.888, p.116, trans. Reuter (1992); Leyser (1994), 6.
13. Capitulary no.273, MGH Cap.2, pp.310–28; Nelson (1992), 207–8.
14. Wallace-Hadrill (1978), 1; Einhard, letter no.17, MGH Ep. KA 3, p.119; Smith (1992), 81–2.
15. Freise (1984), 527; Prinz (1972), 294, 300.
16. Dutton (1994); *Epitaphium Berthae*, MGH PLAC 4.3, p.1008; Leyser (1994), 10. Rudolf of Fulda, *Miracula sanctorum in Fuldenses Ecclesias Translatorum*, c.12, MGH SS 15, p.338; Bosl (1969), 123; Prinz (1976), 336; Löwe, Watenbach and Levison (1990), 799.
17. Regino, *Chron.*, a.888, p.129; trans. MacLean (2009), 199, on which my version is based. Leyser (1979), 15; Löwe (1973), 152–3, 162–71; Airlie (2006c). *AF*, a.888 (Bavarian continuation), p.116; Goetz (1987), 143–4.
18. Leyser (1979), 15; Reuter (1991), 121; Brühl (1990), 10–11; Airlie (1992); Airlie (2006c).
19. Airlie (2006c); Kortüm (1994), 511–12. On Justin's work and Regino's use of it, see Löwe (1973), 152–3, 162–71; MacLean (2009), Introduction, 14–15, 30 (second century); McKitterick (2004), 404 sees Justin as third century. Löwe, Wattenbach and Levison (1990), 903–4; Nelson (2001b), 44–5.
20. Justin, *Epitoma Hist*, ed. O. Seel, XII, 18, p.120; XIII, 1, pp.122–3 ('si non inter se concurrissent … nisi fortuna eos aemulatione virtutis in pernitiem mutuam armasset').
21. Alcuin, poem no.9, lines 35–6, MGH PLAC 1, p.229; McKitterick (2004), 28, 43–4; Contreni (2002), 48.

22 Thompson (1974), 389, quoted in Brown (1992), 33; Agamben (2011); Jallinoja (2017), 10–13.
23 Hopkins (1978a), 180.
24 I borrow this from Pohl and Reimitz (1998).
25 Gramsci (1971), 12–13, 323–5; Joll (1977); Lukes (2005), 7–9; Nelson (2008d), 2–4.
26 Gramsci (1971), 327; Lukes (2005), 49–50; Daldal (2014), 152–4.
27 Nelson (1986), 290; Lukes (2005), 50.
28 Gramsci (1971), 340.
29 Bourdieu (2001), cited in Lukes (2005), 139, and see Lukes (2005), 139–44; Bourdieu and Passeron (1977), 31; Jenkins (2002), 103–27.
30 Lukes (2005), 97, 106; Brown (2006), 75–80.
31 Foucault (2001), 123.
32 Foucault (2001), 120; Garland (1990), 138; Brown (2006), 70–2; Foucault (1978), 92–8.
33 *Divisio Regni*, c.18, MGH Cap.1, pp.129–30; Bernard: *AB*, a.844, trans. Nelson (1991a), 57 and see contrasting account *AF*, a.844, pp.34–5. Dhuoda, *LM*.
34 Gregory I, *Homelia in Evangel.*, X, 5, PL 76, col. 1112B, as cited in capitulary no. 300, MGH Cap.2, p.450, also in Council of Savonnières, no.47, B, MGH Concilia 3, p.464.
35 *The Chronicle of Theophanes*, ed. Turtledove, pp.94–5. Fouracre (2001), 376; cf. Offergeld (2001).
36 Lynn Hunt on the French Revolution, cited by Dixon (2001).
37 Franks as *gens sancta*: *Codex Carolinus*, no.39, MGH Ep. KA 1, p.552, Paul I to the Franks, quoting 1 Peter 2:9; also addressed to Charlemagne and Carloman by Stephen III, *Codex Carolinus*, no.45, p.561. On the Petrine phrase, Pohl and Heydemann (2016), 20 and passim; on the phrase as applying to a holy place (Metz), Claussen (2004), 249. See also Nelson (1995), 423–5, and Garrison (2000), 123–9, 144–5. Letter of Theotmar of Salzburg, ed. Losek, p.146: 'Progenitores … senioris nostri Hludouuici, videlicet imperatores et reges, ex christianissima Francorum gente proierunt'.
38 Duindam (2015), 60, and see Duindam (2016); Weber (1968), 237; see also Nelson (1994a), 59; and Weber (1968), 226–51, 1006–15, 1025–8; on Weber, see Steinmetz (1999).
39 For stimulating thoughts on a later medieval political context, see Watts (2009), 1–42.
40 Scott (2015); Geveers and Marini (2015); Bouchard (2015), 106–25.
41 Einhard, *VK*, c.1, pp.2–3; Widukind, *Res Gestae Saxonicae*, I, c.29, and see also I, c.16. Lot (1891b); Schneidmüller (1997); Bouchard (2015), 106–7; Reimitz (2015), 170, 244–5.
42 Louis II, Letter to Basil I, MGH Ep. KA 5, pp.385–94, at pp.388–9.
43 Reynolds (1994), 13. On family, Le Jan (1995); Bouchard (2001); Bouchard (2015).
44 Sedulius, Poem 33, line 16, MGH PLAC 3, p.199; Werner (1967), 454–5. Contrast Ermold on Louis the Pious as 'Carolides', Ermold, Book I, line 155, ed. Faral, p.16; Noble (2009), 131 translates this as 'son of Charles'.
45 Wood (2003), especially 157–71; Wood (2004a). For Boso on sons of Louis, see this book, Chapter 9.
46 Hincmar, *De Divortio Lotharii regis*, Interrogation 6, ed. L. Böhringer, MGH Concilia 4, supplementum 1, pp.246–9. Anton (1968), 295; Nelson (1986), 138; Airlie (1998b).
47 Council of Paris, II, c.5, MCH Concilia 2.2, p.655; Jonas of Orléans, *De Institutione Regia*, c.7, ed. A. Dubreucq (1995), p.216, and see Dubreucq's introduction, p.90; Leyser (1979), 78.

48 Anton (1968); De Jong (2009).
49 Paris, I, c.5, MGH Concilia 2.2, pp.612–13. See this book's Chapter 7 on prayer.
50 Jonas, *De Institutione Regia*, c.1, pp.148, 160–4.
51 Prayer 'Prospice', trans. Nelson (1994a), 58; text in Jackson (1995), Ordo no.IIA, pp.58–9.
52 *De unctione Pippini regis*, MGH SS 15, p.1, and edition by Stoclet (1980), 2–3; McKitterick (2004), 140–1; McKitterick (2008), 292–3; Drews (2009), 141–6.
53 See, for example, Patzold (2008a); De Jong (2009); Airlie (2012).
54 For example, Nelson (1994a); Nelson (1995). Some important studies of regions and specific landscapes include Innes (2000a); Hummer (2005); and West (2013).
55 Reuter (1997), 182.
56 Hincmar translated and commented on by Nelson (1998b), 229; Reuter (2006), 193–216. See also the group terms in the capitularies, for example, 'bishops, abbots, counts and the more powerful men (*potentiores*)', Capitulary no.80, De iustitiis faciendis, c.2, MGH Cap.1, p.176.
57 Dhuoda, *LM*, III.4, p.150 on the loyalty always shown by William's kin.
58 On Gerard and Bertha, see Chapter 7; on Gerard as *nutritor* for Charles of Provence, see Chapter 4. Innes (2000a), 82–5; Costambeys, Innes and MacLean (2011), 271–323.
59 Depreux (1997), 153, 292; Ermold, Book III, lines 1688–9, p.128.
60 *Traditionen des Hochstifts Freising*, ed. T. Bitterauf, no.661; Goldberg (2006a), 115–16; Nelson (1995), 417–22; Airlie (2003a).
61 Davis (2015); Airlie (1998a); Airlie (2006a); Innes (2000a).
62 Barbier (2009); Fouracre (2009); and Innes (2009). Gravel (2012a).
63 Fried (1982); Nelson (1994a), 65; Davis (2015). See also general engagement with Fried in Goetz (1987); Airlie, Pohl and Reimitz (2006); and Pohl and Wieser (2009).
64 Hopkins (1978b), 197.
65 Tellenbach (1979), 241; Dixon (2001), chapter 1; Drews and Höfert (2016), 239–40.
66 Tischler (2001); Ganz (2003); and Ganz (2005). A good summary is provided by De Jong (2009), 67–9.
67 McKitterick (2004), especially 84–155; Reimitz (2015).
68 Tischler (2001); Ganz (2003).
69 De Jong (2009), 248; Airlie (2010); Booker (2009).
70 See, for example, Schramm (1954–6) and Schramm (1983); Garipzanov (2008); Mersiowsky (2000); Koziol (2012).
71 Airlie (2000a); Airlie (2014); Schramm (1954–6); Scharer (2011), 39–45.
72 Text in Esders (1999); Nelson (2008c), 228–9; Davis (2015), 274–5.
73 Reuter (2006), 236–43; Le Jan (1995), 85–6; Innes (2000a), 153–60. Gifts: *AB*, a.832, a.833, trans. Nelson (1991a), 27.
74 Brown (2006), 71.
75 Date: MacLean (2003a), 201–4; see also Löwe, Wattnbach and Levison (1990), 753; Innes (1998a). Notker, *Notatio de viris illustribus*, ed. Rauner (1986), p.64, lines 159, 173.
76 Notker, *GK*, II, c.15, pp.79–80, trans. Ganz (2008), 106. Contrast Notker's characterization of the Merovingian Childeric, *GK*, I, c.10, p.13. Throne: *GK*, II, c.6, p.56; throne, swords and authority, *GK*, II, c.18, p.88; weapons and authority, *GK*, II, c.10, p.66.
77 Notker, *GK*, II, c.9, and II, c.15, pp.62–5, 80; Halphen (1918), 282–3; Nees (1991), 238, 272–3. See *AMP*, a.688, pp.1–2 on Pippin I as David.

78 *Vita Arnulfi*, Acta Sanctorum, Juli4, pp.440–4; Löwe, Wattenbach and Levison (1953), 126; and Löwe, Wattenbach and Levison (1990), 883–4 and 886 for Metz-St Gall links; see also Heidrich (1990), 144–5. Ferrieres: Astronomer, *VH*, c.19, at *p.338, and Tremp's Introduction to Thegan, *GH*, 140, modifying Tremp (1991), 91–4; Hamann-Maclean (1983), 126–38; Nelson (2000), 144–5. MacLean (1998), 195–9 and Henderson (1998), 135–40.

79 Eckhard's will, *Recueil des chartes de l'abbaye de Saint-Benoît-sur-Loire*, eds Prou and Vidier (1900), no.25 ('Adane germanae meae, succincta aurea et sigillo de amatexto, ubi homo est sculptus qui leonem interfecit …'); the date of the will is 870. Kornbluth (1995), 5–7; Bishop (1918), 365.

80 Notker, *GK*, II c.14, p.78, trans. Ganz (2008), 105; see also *GK* II, c.11, p.68 and II, c.12, p.74; Löwe (1973), 142–3; MacLean (2003a), 218–22.

81 Notker, *GK* I, p.1; *GK* I, c.10, pp.12–13; Ganz (1989), 174–5, MacLean (2003a), 226–7 but cf. Nelson (1994a), 72; see also Freculf below.

82 Notker, *GK*, II, 12, pp.70–1; Löwe (1973), 145–7; Goetz (1987), 152–3; MacLean (2003a), 220–1.

83 *Visio Karoli Magni*, ed. Jaffé, and also in Geary (1987), 293–4; Dutton (1994), 200–8.

84 *Epistolae Variorum*, no.14, MGH Ep. KA 3, pp.319–20 (829), 'velut in speculo … quid agendum vel quid vitandum sit'; Freculf, *Histories*, II, 5, 17, p.707 (Rome) and II, 1, c.3, 'depulsos esse a regno Judaeorum vel ducatu ex semine Juda et principes'. Allen (1996), 69 and see Allen's Introduction to his edition of Freculf, pp.16–17. Staubach (1995), 179, 182, 188–90 and 199; Ward (2015), especially 70–2. There was a copy of Freculf's text in Notker's St-Gall, St Gallen Stiftsbibliothek, Cod. Sang. 622; see Allen (1996), 70 and Allen's Introduction to his edition of Frechulf, vol. 1, pp.58*–78*, especially. pp.68*–71*.

85 Einhard, *VK*, c.1, pp.2–4. See, for example, Wood (1994), 102; Wallace-Hadrill (1962), 231–2; Nelson (1994a), 56–7; Fouracre (2005), 5–6; Barnwell (2005). Dates of *VK*: Innes and McKitterick (1994) and McKitterick (2008), 11–14 for an early date, soon after death of Charlemagne in 814; for a date in the mid-820s, see the persuasive summary of scholarship in De Jong (2009), 67–9.

86 Thegan, *GH*, c.1, pp.174–6. Tremp (1988), 28, 55–63; Airlie (1998a), 136–7. Fredegar, Chronicle, III, c.9, ed. Krusch, MGH SRM 2, pp.94–5, and see the dynastically structured prophecy of Merovingian decline at III, c.12, pp.97–8; Moisl (1981), 224–6; Murray (1998); Wood (2003), 149–55, 170–1; Collins (2007), 53; Reimitz (2015), 170–1. Asser, *De rebus gestis Aelfredi*, c.1, c.2, ed. Stevenson, pp.2–4; Tremp (1988), 130–2.

87 Thegan, *GH*, c.1, pp.174–6; Tremp (1988), 26–7, 44. See this book's Chapter 7.

88 Wallace-Hadrill (1962), 232; Bund (1979), 383–4; Airlie (1998a); Fouracre (2005), 6–7. *AF*, a.887 (Bavarian continuation), pp.115–16; Regino, *Chron.*, a.887, a.888, pp.128–9.

89 Einhard, *VK*, c.2, pp.4–5. On the conflict-rich reality, see Chapter 2.

90 Paul the Deacon, *Gesta episcoporum Mettensium*, MGH SS2, pp.264–5, 267; Eberhardt (1977), 240.

91 Einhard, *VK*, Preface, pp.1–2; and see Chapter 4 on children. On Einhard's own family and his experiences at court, Patzold (2013), 23–127. On the royal reception of the text, Ganz (2005), 41, and Tischler (2001); Schneidmüller (1979) for later impact.

92 *Chronicon Laurissense breve*, I, III, 12 (a.750), ed. Schnorr von Carolsfeld, *NA*, 36 (1910), pp.23, 27–8; possibly intended for a wide audience, not just for Lorsch itself, Kaschke (2006), 260. *AMP*, a.688, a.689, a.690, pp.4–12, trans. Fouracre and

Gerberding (1996), 355-59. Fouracre (2005), 6-7; Affeldt (1980), 121-5; Reimitz (2015), 367-8, 370.
93 Letter of bishops to the rebels, Synod of Savonnières, 859, MGH Concilia 3, no.47, text G, pp.482-5; Le Jan (2006), 411-17; Airlie (2009b), 490-1.
94 Capitulary of Pitres, MGH Cap.2, pp.305-6; Wallace-Hadrill (1978), 172; Nelson (1986), 97; Nelson (2001b), 42-5.
95 Notker, *GK*, I, c.19, p.25.
96 *AB*, a.879, trans. Nelson (1991a), 215-19; *AF*, a.879, 92-4; *AV*, a.879, pp.43-6. *The Triads of Ireland*, Triad 75, as cited and discussed in Power (1986), 18 and Kelly (2004), 6.
97 Regino, *Chron.*, a.882, pp.118-19; on date and Regino's errors of chronology, Dümmler (1887-8), vol. 3, 120.
98 Notker, *Continuatio Erchanberti*, MGH SS 2, 330; the child is not named but it is obviously the young Louis.
99 Dip. Louis Y., no.2. Orth (1985-1986), 212-13.
100 *AB*, a.878, trans. Nelson (1991a), 214; Kasten (1997), 543 n.171.
101 Dümmler (1887-8), vol. 3, 120 and see Schieffer (1990b), 156-7.
102 Regensburg: Brühl (1990), 225, 248. Litanies: Bischoff (1981a), 187; Kantorowicz (1946), 106. Löwe, Wattenbach and Levison (1990), 799 n.490. Goldberg (2006a), 51-2.
103 Arnold, *Liber de s. Emmeram*, c.6, MGH SS 4, p.551. Schmid (1976), 351-6; Freise (1986), 83; Löwe, Wattenbach and Levison (1990), 799. See also Geary (1994), 171-2.
104 Orth (1985-1986), 212-13.
105 Benjamin (1972), 94-5; Airlie (2006c).

Chapter 2

1 *ARF*, a.749, a.750, pp.8, 10.
2 Gregory VII to Hermann of Metz, in *Das Register Gregors VII*, IV, 2, ed. E. Caspar MGH Epistolae selectae, 2.1 (1920), pp.293-7; Melve (2007), vol. 1, p.258.
3 Airlie (2003b).
4 Büttner (1952).
5 Ewig (1956); Hlawitschka (1975); Nelson (1986), 283-307; Enright (1985); Schieffer (2004b).
6 Becher (1993); McKitterick (2004).
7 *Cont. Fredegar*, c.33, p.102; McKitterick (2004) 138-9; Collins (2007), 89-92.
8 Buc (2001a), especially 51-87 and 248-61.
9 Latham (1985), 129-33.
10 See below n.24 on *AMP* and *Chronicon Laurissense Breve*.
11 Wood (2004b).
12 Fouracre and Gerberding (1996), 1-26.
13 Wood (1994), 222; Fouracre and Gerberding (1996), 18-19; Wood (2004a), 15-16, 27-30. Bouchard (2015), 108-9 sees the boy as a Merovingian son adopted by Grimoald.
14 ChLA XIV, no.581; Wood (1994), 255-72; *Die Urkunden der Merowinger*, no.149, ed. T. Kölzer, MGH Diplomata regum Francorum e stirpe Merovingica (2001).
15 *AMP*, a.714, p.20, trans. Fouracre and Gerberding (1996), 366; Jarnut, Nonn and Richter (1994); Fouracre (2005).

16 Collins (1994), 235–41; Fouracre (2000), 1; Blanc and Naudin (2015).
17 Wood (1994), 267–72, 286–7, 290; Fouracre (2000), 156–8, 168.
18 *Die Urkunden der Arnulfinger*, no.14 (741), ed. Heidrich, dated by years after the death of king Theuderich; *Die Urkunden der Arnulfinger*, ed. Heidrich, no.17 (743) dated by Pippin's rule; but contrast for example *Die Urkunden der Arnulfinger*, ed. Heidrich no.18 (748); Heidrich (1965/1966), 156–7.
19 *UB St Gallen*, nos 8, 9; Heidrich (1965/1966), 157; Fouracre (2000), 157; Offergeld (2001) 266–7; Reimitz (2015), 306–7.
20 *Cont. Fredegar*, c.28, p.100; Reimitz (2015), 324–5.
21 Wood (2004a), 31; Wood (2003); Ewig (1995).
22 *Gesta Sanctorum Patrum Fontanellensis Coenobii*, X, 4, eds F. Lohier and J. Laporte, p.77; Wood (1994), 362.
23 *Liber Historiae Francorum*, c.43, ed. B. Krusch, MGH SRM 2, pp.315–16, trans. Fouracre and Gerberding (1996), 87–8; Fouracre (2000), 37–8; Wood (2004a), 15–16, 28–30.
24 Einhard, *VK*, c.1, pp.2–4; *Chronicon Laurissense Breve*, a. 750, ed. Carolsfeld, pp.27–8; *AMP*, a. 691, p.12, a.692, pp.14–15 (trans. Fouracre and Gerberding (1996), 359, 360–1).Wood (1994), 267–8; Wood (2004a); Kölzer (2004), especially 33–8 and 58–60; Schneider (2004), 266–7; Fouracre (2005); Barnwell (2005).
25 *Liber Historiae Francorum*, c.52, MGH SRM 2, pp.325–6, trans. Fouracre and Gerberding (1996), 95; Wood (1994), 267–8; Wood (2004a), 26.
26 *Erchanberti Breviarium*, MGH SS 2, p.328. Werner (1973), 504; Wood (1994), 285; Geuenich (2004), 129–39.
27 *Lex Alamannorum*, c.26, c.27, in *Leges Alamannorum*, ed. K. Lehmann, revised K. A. Eckhardt, MGH Leges nationum Germanicarum, 5.1, p.86; Jarnut (2002), 117–18; Geuenich (2004), 130–1; Wood (1994), 117–18.
28 *Lex Baiwariorum*, title I, ed. E. von Schwind, MGH Leges nationum Germanicarum 5.2, p.267 and see also references to the king installing the duke, title II.1, p.291 and see title III, p.313; Wood (1994), 116–17, 285; Airlie (1999), 97. But see Werner (1973), 505–6, on Bavarian bishops thanking God, not the Frankish king, for having given them a prince. On such laws as assertion of ducal legitimacy in the face of Carolingian challenges at this time, see Reimitz (2015), 328–30.
29 Werner (1973).
30 Geary (1985), 126–48; Fouracre (2000), 95–8; NB Wickham (2005a), 196–7.
31 Wolfram (1995b), 237–45; Geary (1985), 138–9; Innes (2000a), 175–8.
32 *Cont. Fredegar*, c.32, p.98; Airlie (1999).
33 Airlie (2004), 112–21.
34 Fouracre (2005), 167; Wood (1994), 290.
35 Fouracre (2000), 79–120, 137–54. General survey in Halsall (2003), while Bachrach (2001) tends to see matters in terms of clear-cut institutions.
36 *Cont. Fredegar*, c.24, 25, 26, 27, 28, 29, pp.97–100; see also *AMP*, a.741, a.742, a.743, a.744, a.745, a.746, a.747, pp.30–40. On non-army years: *ARF* a.745, p.4; cf. *Cont. Fredegar*, c.32, p.102 and c.38, p.108.
37 Fouracre (2000), 137–54; Hummer (2005), 76–104; Wood (2006), 211–35. Alemannia: *Cont. Fredegar*, c.29, p.100; *AMP* a.746, p.37; Collins (2004), 84–5; Fouracre (2000), 169. Aquitaine: Halsall (2003), 137–40; McCormick (2004), 228–30, 236; Innes (2009) questions the conventional picture of conquest of Alemannia.
38 *Cont. Fredegar*, c.41, p.109.
39 *Gesta Episcoporum Autisiodorensium*, c.32, ed. G. Waitz, MGH SS 13, p.395. Semmler (1975), 95–7, and note letter of Auxerre monks later praying for Pippin and Bertada at p.97 n.96; Semmler (1966).

40 *Cont. Fredegar*, c.45, p.114, c.51, p.119.
41 *Cont. Fredegar*, c.42, pp.110–11, c.43, p.112; the text's triumphalist tone is instructive.
42 Nelson (2008c).
43 *Cont. Fredegar*. c.43, p.112; Pippin charter no.16 in Dip. Karol. 1, and see below. Papal envoys, *Codex Carolinus*, nos 22–30, MGH Epistolae Merowingici et Karolini Aevi 1, pp.525–37.
44 *Cont. Fredegar*, c.51, pp.118–19; Capitulary no.18, MGH Cap.1, pp.42–3. Bachrach (2001), 216.
45 Reuter (2006), 230–50; Halsall (2003), 90–1; Airlie (2005), 95–6; Bachrach (2001), 26.
46 *Cont. Fredegar*, c.18, p.93; c.19, p.93; c.20, p.95; c.22, p.96; c.24, p.97; c.25, p.98; c.28, p.100; c.31, p.101; c.32, p.102; c.35, p.103; c.36, p.104; c.37, pp.106–7; c.38, p.108; c.40, p.109; c.42, p.111; c.43, p.112; c.44, p.113; c.45, p.114; c.47, p.116; c.48, p.116–17; c.51, p.119; c.53, p.120. Compare Gerberding (1987), 165.
47 Individuals: *Cont. Fredegar*, c.44, p.113; Franks: *Cont. Fredegar*, c.20, p.95; c.31, p.101; c.36, p.104; c.37, p.107; c.43, p.112.
48 *Cont. Fredegar*, c. 48, p.116. And see note 46 above.
49 Gerberding (1987), 76–7, 167–8; Fouracre and Gerberding (1996), 69, 133. Reimitz (2008), 54; McKitterick (2004), 114–15; Reimitz (2015), 295–304.
50 Nelson (1994a), 54–5, and Nelson (1995), 423–5; Hen (2004). But see also Garrison (2000).
51 Semmler (2003), 17–21.
52 *Lib. Pont.*, life of Zacharias, c.21, p.433, trans. Davis (1992), 46. Collins (1998), 35; Schneider (2004), 253; in general, McKitterick (2004), 142–5.
53 Theophanes, *Chronicle*, trans. Turtledove, p.95; Collins (1998), 35; Semmler (2003), 21–3; McKitterick (2004), 144.
54 Boniface letter no.83, *Die Briefen des heiligen Bonifatius und Lullus*, ed. M. Tangl, MGH Epistolae selectae in usum scholarum separatime editi (1916), pp.184–7. Airlie (2004), 123; McKitterick (2004), 143.
55 Theophanes, *Chronicle*, trans. Turtledove, 94–5.
56 Nelson (1986), 289–91; Bautier (1989), 7–17; older literature in Affeldt (1980); Enright (1985); Stoclet (1980a);.Collins (1998), 36; Angenendt (1992); Angenendt (2004); Semmler (2003), 46–57.
57 *ARF*, a.750, pp.8, 10.
58 McKitterick (2004), 150; Claussen (2004), 19–28.
59 *Cont. Fredegar*, c.33, p.102; Angenendt (2004), 190.
60 Collins (1998), 36.
61 Collins (1998), 36.
62 *Cont. Fredegar*, c.33, p.102, but I use the translation in Nelson (1994a), 54. On traditions, Hack (1999) and Semmler (2003), 30–1, but see Erkens (2004), 497–8.
63 Nelson (2004b), 101; Erkens (2004), 498.
64 Collins (1998), 36; McKitterick (2004), especially 151–5; Semmler (2003), 17–21. See Schneider (2004), 245–51 on minor annals referring to anointing, but more work is needed on such texts.
65 Büttner (1952).
66 Becher (1993) and McKitterick (2004). See Buc (2001a) on the difficulty of reconstructing ritual.
67 Pippin charter no.22 dated June 751, still dated by Childeric, *Die Urkunden der Arnulfinger*, ed. Heidrich and see also no.23. Semmler (2003), 4–5, 12; Collins (1998), 35 on locations.

68 *Cont. Fredegar*, c.33, p.102; Angenendt (2004), 191; Reimitz (2015), 295–304; Nelson (1986), 290–1; Nelson (1995), 424.
69 Paul the Deacon, *Historia Langobardorum*, VI. 16, ed. G. Waitz, MGH Scriptores rerum Langobardicarum, p.170; dated to mid-780s, McKitterick (2004), 77; Kölzer (2004), 36. *Chronicon Laurissense Breve*, a.750, ed. Carolsfeld, pp.27–8; *AMP*, a.691, p.12, a.692, pp.14–15; *ARF*, a.749, a. 750, pp.8, 10; Fouracre (2005); Schneider (2004), 266–7.
70 Theophanes, *Chronicle*, trans. Turtledove, 94; Fouracre (2005), 8.
71 Reimitz (2004), 298–9, 304–12; McKitterick (2004), 121–8; Ganz (2005), 41.
72 Goffart (2007). Genealogies: *Genealogiae Karolorum. II. Commemoratio genealogiae domni Karoli gloriosissimi imperatoris*, ed. G. Waitz, MGH SS 13, pp.245–6; Reimitz (2004), 297–8. See Chapter 7.
73 St Gallen, Stiftsbibliothek, Cod Ssng. 731, pag.294 and pag.342 (online at: https://www.e-codices.unifr.ch/en/csg/0731/bindingA/0/Sequence-653); MGH SS 2, pp.307–8, text 2; Mordek (1995a), 670–6; McKitterick (2008), 70.
74 *Cont. Fredegar*, c.33, p.102; Collins (2007), 91; Reimitz (2015), 299–308, 313.
75 *Cont. Fredegar*, c.10, c.16, pp.89, 92; Reimitz (2015), 295–6.
76 Airlie (2004).
77 De Jong (2001a), 325–6; Diesenberger (2003).
78 *Gesta Sanctorum Patrum*, X, c.4, p.77; De Jong (2001a), 326.
79 Airlie (1999).
80 Wood (2004a); Wood (2004b).
81 Kasten (1997), 113.
82 *Vita S. Arnulfi*, ed. B. Krusch, MGH SRM 2, p.429; Kasten (1997), 106 and 119.
83 Airlie (2004), 112–15; Collins (2004), 76–8.
84 Collins (2004), 77–9; De Jong (2001a), 323–7.
85 *ARF*, a.745, p.4.
86 Drogo in Carloman charter no. 15, *Urkunden der Arnulfinger*, ed. Heidrich; Boniface, letter no.79, ed. Tangl, p.171; *Cont. Fredegar*, c.30, p.100. Becher (1989), 136–8; Airlie (2007a), 259; Collins (1998), 32.
87 Airlie (2004), 116–17.
88 Cathwulf, Letter to Charlemagne, ed. Dümmler, MGH Ep. KA 2, p.502; Becher (1992), 45; Nelson (2004b), 100–1.
89 *Epistolae Aevi Merowingici collectae*, no.18, ed. W. Gundlach, MGH Epistolae Merowinigici et Karolini Aevi, 1, pp.467–8; Becher (1989), 151; Airlie (2004), 118–19.
90 *Annales Petaviani*, a.751, ed. G.H. Pertz MGH SS 1, p.11 and in Werner (1975), 135.
91 Collins (1998), 32–3.
92 Airlie (2004), 119.
93 *Lib. Pont.*, Life of Stephen II, c.27, p.448, trans. Davis (1992), 64; *Annales Petaviani*, a.753, MGH SS 1, p.11. Becher (1989), 140–2; Nelson (2004b), 102–3, whose chronology I follow here.
94 *ARF*, a.755, p.12; Nelson (2004b), 104. *Codex Carolinus*, no.11, p.507.
95 Pohl (2004) on complexity; McKitterick (2004), 60–83.
96 Buc (2005). *Clausula de unctione Pippini*, ed. G. Waitz, MGH SS 15.1, p.1; Stoclet (1980a); Nelson (2004b), 102 and McKitterick (2004), 140–1 are cautious about this text, though Schneider (2004), 254–5 and 268–75, is more optimistic.
97 *Cont. Fredegar*, c.36, p.104; *Lib. Pont.*, Life of Stephen II, cs 25, 26, 27, pp.447–8, trans. Davis (1992), 63–4.

98 McKitterick (2004), 148-9.
99 *Cont. Fredegar*, c.36, p.104; *Lib. Pont.*, Life of Stephen II, c.27, p.448. Airlie (2004), 124.
100 *Lib. Pont.*, Life of Stephen II, c.27, p.448 is explicit on the anointing, and see below for later papal references; Angenendt (2004), 196-207. *Codex Carolinus*, no.11, p.505 on Bertrada with Nelson (2004b), 100; *Clausula de unction Pippini*, p.1.
101 *ARF*, a.745, p.4; *Annales Petaviani*, a.750, p.11. Reimitz (2004), 291.
102 Mayor: Goetz (2004), and Fouracre (2000), 173-2; estates, Ewig (1965) and Fouracre (2000), 47-8 with Fouracre (2009).
103 *Annales Petaviani*, a.755, MGH SS 1, p.11; *Cont. Fredegar*, c.48, p.116; Garrison (2000), 135-6; Halsall (2003), 145-6.
104 Barbier (1990), 284-90. Capitulary no.13, c.5, Cap.1, p.32; Grierson and Blackburn (1986), 139, 204 and plate 33, p.521; Story (2002), 23-5; Garipzanov (2008), 169-72.
105 *Traditiones des Hochstifts Freising*, no.7, ed. Bitterauf; Jahn (1988), 92-3. *Lib Pont*, Life of Stephen II, c.20, p.445, trans. Davis (1992), 60-1; Pohl (2004), 160.
106 *Cont. Fredegar*, c.36, p.104; *ARF*, a.754, p.12; Angenendt (2004), 190-1, 198-9.
107 Angenendt (1980).
108 *Codex Carolinus*, pp.469-657.Garrison (2000), 123-9; McKitterick (2008), 37-8, 66-7.
109 Garrison (2000), 126.
110 *Codex Carolinus*, no.17 (758), p.517.
111 Boniface, Letter no.74, ed. Tangl, pp.155-6 (a letter to Herefirth about delivering a letter to king Aethelbald of Mercia; my thanks to Mary Garrison for reminding me of this). *Codex Carolinus*, no.8, p.497 and no 9, p.500.
112 *Codex Carolinus*, nos 3, 5, 9, 10 and 39, pp.479-88, 498-503, 551-2. Airlie (2004), 123-4 which I here recapitulate and develop.
113 *Lib. Pont.*, Life of Stephen II, c.24, p.447, trans. Davis (1992), 62-3; Borgolte (1986), 230, 232; Schieffer (2000), 288-9.
114 *Codex Carolinus*, nos 4, 5, 6, 7, 8, 9, 11, 12, 14, 16, 17, 19, 20, 21, 22, 26, 28, 34, 37, 41, 43, pp.487-500, 504-17, 519-26, 530-3, 540-2, 547-50, 553-4, 557-8; Pippin's brother Remedius of Rouen is in nos 19 and 40; his brother Jerome is in *Lib. Pont.*, Life of Stephen II, c.38, at *, trans.Davis (1992), 68.
115 *Codex Carolinus*, no. 21, pp.522-4; Schieffer (2000), 288.
116 *Codex Carolinus*, no.14, pp.511-12. McKitterick (2004), 146-8; Angenendt (1980).
117 *Codex Carolinus*, nos 14, 26, 37, pp.511-12, 530-1, 547-50; *Cont. Fredegar*, c.45, p.114; Airlie (2004), 124.
118 *Codex Carolinus*, nos 14, 21, 24, 29, 32, 42, 43, pp.511-12, 524, 528, 533-5, 539, 556, 558.
119 *Codex Carolinus*, for example, nos 12, 14, 17, 28, 35, 38, pp.508, 512, 517, 533, 542-3, 551. Franks: *Codex Carolinus*, no.8, p.496.
120 *Codex Carolinus*, no.6 (755), pp.488-90.
121 See, for example, *Codex Carolinus*, no.7, pp.490-3; Angenendt (2004), 200-7 for other examples.
122 *Codex Carolinus*, no 11, p.505, and see, for example, nos 17 and 28, pp.517, 533 for other references to her; Nelson (2004b), 102; Schneider (2004), 273.
123 Son: *Codex Carolinus*, no.18, p.519; see *ARF*, a.759, p.16 and *Annales Petaviani*, s.759, MGH SS I, p.11; Werner (1975), 123. Dynastic future: *Codex Carolinus*, nos 11, 26, 35, pp.505, 531, 543.
124 *Clausula de unctione Pippini*, MGH SS 15.1, p.1, translation in Dutton (2004), 13-14; McKitterick (2004), 140-1; Schneider (2004), 268-75.

125 *Codex Carolinus*, no.5, pp.487–8; Airlie (2004), 123.
126 Hen (2004), 176; Reimitz (2015), 323.
127 *The Cartulary of Flavigny*, no.3, ed. C. B. Bouchard (1991), 33–4; *Urkunden der Arnulfinger*, ed. Heidrich, no.24; Hen (2004), 176.
128 Airlie (2007a); Claussen (2004), 55–7.
129 Airlie (1995); Hummer (2005).
130 Pippin charter no.8, MGH Dip Karol. 1, and see also *ChLA* XV, no.599; Airlie (2004), 121–2.
131 Semmler (2003), 58–86, especially 86.
132 Airlie (1995); Airlie (2006a) for general studies; Innes (2000a) a model regional study.
133 *Urkunden der Arnulfinger*, no.18 (a.748), ed. Heidrich; Hennebicque-Le Jan (1989), 248–9; Fouracre (2000), 163–4; Levillain (1941).
134 Le Jan (1995), 189–90, 255; Levillain (1941).
135 Pippin, charter no.8, in Dip. Karol. 1; Airlie (2004), 121. In general, Innes (2000a), 28–9, but see also Hummer (2005), 60–1; Innes (2009), 305–7.
136 Innes (2009), 307. See also Innes (2000a), 18–19, 27–9, 179–80; Airlie (2004); Hummer (2005), 59–71.
137 For 'special patron', see, for example, charter of king Theuderic III from 679, *Urkunden der Merowinger*, no.122, ed. Kölzer. For a rash king, *Liber Historiae Francorum*, c.44, ed. Krusch, pp.316–17, trans. Fouracre and Gerberding (1996), 89; Gerberding (1987), 148–9; Wood (1994), 157.
138 Charters nos 166–168, 170, 173, *Urkunden der Merowinger*, ed. Kolzer. Semmler (1989), 91; see Wyss (2001) on the scale of buildings.
139 Charter of king Theuderic IV, *Urkunden der Merowinger*, no.187, ed. Kölzer; Semmler (1989), 91–3. *Urkunden der Hausmeier*, no.14, ed. Heidrich; *Cont. Fredegar*, c.24, p.97; Semmler (1989), 91–3; Dierkens (1996), 41.
140 Pippin, charter no.12, in Dip. Karol. 1 (= *ChLA*, XV, no.600); Kasten (1997), 107.
141 Brown (1989), chapter 1 and Appendix.
142 Dierkens (1996), 41. Pippin, charter no.23, *Urkunden der Hausmeier*, ed. Heidrich; Brown (1989), 310.
143 Semmler (1989), 94–5; Airlie (2004), 121–2.
144 Pippin, charter no.6, in Dip. Karol. 1 (= *ChLA*, XV, no.598); on Grimoald, Wood (1994), 263.
145 752: Pippin, charter no.1, in Dip. Karol. 1. 759: Pippin, charter no.12, in Dip. Karol. 1. Pre-751: Pippin, charter no.18, *Urkunden der Hausmeier*, ed. Heidrich. Airlie (2004), 125.
146 *ChLA* XV, no.601 (a.766); Brown (1989), 422.
147 *Descriptio basilicae sancti Dyonisii*, as in Bischoff (1981b) and Stoclet (1980b) with English translation in Parsons (1987), 42–3; Dierkens (1996), 47–8 and in general; Jacobsen (1989), 180–4.
148 *Cont. Fredegar*, c.53, pp.120–1; Pippin, charters nos 25–28, in Dip. Karol. 1. Dierkens (1996), 38.
149 Dungal, poem no.14, ed. E. Dümmler, MGH PLAC 1, p.405; Hoffmann (1985), 30; Hoffmann (1986), vol. 1, 6.
150 *Translatio Sancti Germani*, c.2, MGH SS 15, pp.5–6; Nelson (2005), 24–8.
151 *Ep. Variorum*, no.19, MGH Ep KA 3, pp.325–7. Hauck (1985), 25; Brown (1989), 283–7, and see p.287 for 'authentic voice'; Dierkens (1996), 39, 41–4.
152 Nelson (2004b), 96; Werner (1982); Zielinski (1989), 102–9; Heidrich (1990), 139–41.

153 Pippin, charters nos 3, 16, in Dip. Karol. 1; Zielinski (1989), 103–4. Charlemagne, charter no.180, in Dip. Karol. 1.
154 Zielinski (1989), 102–9; Merta (1992), 125–7; Garrison (2000), 131–3; Smith (2010), 78–80.
155 *Cont. Fredegar*, c.43, p.112; Halsall (2003), 137–8; Reimitz (2015), 320–8, especially 327.
156 Hauck (1967), 88; Merta (1992), 126. On prayers for king and army, see McCormick (1986), 344–9 and 379; Hen (2004), 172–5. On papal concern for victory for Pippin, including explicit reference to campaigns in Aquitaine, *Codex Carolinus*, nos 20, 21, 24, 27, 28, pp.520–4, 527–9, 531–3.
157 Pippin, charter no.16, in Dip. Karol. 1. Nelson (2004b), 96; Merta (1992), 126.
158 Zielinski (1989), 99; Smith (2016).
159 Pippin, charter no.16, in Dip. Karol. 1; translation from Garrison (2000), 131, and see 131–4.
160 *Lex Salica*, longer prologue, ed. K. A. Eckhardt, MGH Leges nationum Germanicarum 4.2, pp.2–9. Wormald (1999), 41; Garrison (2000), 129–32; Merta (1992), 126–7; Garipzanov (2008), 267–9; Reimitz (2015), 326–34; Claussen (2004), 48 n.160 suggests Chrodegang of Metz as author, but he too was a supporter of Pippin.
161 Airlie (2004), 124–5.
162 *Gesta Aldrici*, fragmentum 6b, in *Actus pontificum Cenomannis degentium und Gesta Aldrici,* ed. M. Weidemann, vol. 1, and commentary, p.163. Airlie (2011b), 235–6.
163 *Die Urkunden, Actus pontificum Cenomannis degentium und Gesta Aldrici,* ed. M. Weidemann, vol. 2, nos 26, 27A and B, 28, 29, 30, 31; on the genuine elements in these documents, see commentary in Weidemann, vol. 2, pp.255–66. See Airlie (2004), 126, on formulas in Alsace and Alemannia.
164 Fouracre (2000), 64–75.
165 *Actus pontificum Cenomannis degentium*, XV, ed. Weidemann, vol. 1, pp.90–3, with commentary, p.99.
166 Names of bishops as in Pippin, charter no.16, in Dip. Karol. 1 and in the Attigny prayer bond, MGH Concilia 2.1, no.13, p.73; Merta (1992), 128; Claussen (2004), 55–7 on Attigny.
167 Pippin, charter no.16, in Dip. Karol. 1. Merta (1992), 126–8; Airlie (2004), 124.
168 Hauck (1967), 88; Merta (1992).
169 *Cod. Lauresh.*, no.6a; Innes (2000a), 189–90.
170 Kuchenbuch (1978); Airlie (2006c).
171 Pippin, charter no.14, in Dip. Karol. 1. Brunterc'h (1989), 143; Merta (1992), 128; Kasten (1997), 128.
172 Pippin, charter no.14, in Dip. Karol. 1, to be compared with *Marculfi Formulae*, I, no.24, ed. K. Zeumer, MGH Formulae, p.58. Heidrich (1973); Merta (1992), 128–9.
173 ARF a.761, p.18; McKitterick (2008), 74.
174 Gellone: *Liber sacramentorum Gellonensis*, ed. A. Dumas, vol. 1 section 330, no.2094, p.298; also in *Ordines Coronationis Franciae* ed. R. Jackson, no.I, p.54; Semmler (2003), 94–5. *Prospice*: Ordo II, Jackson (1995), pp.58–9, and translation and commentary Nelson (1994a), 57–8.
175 *Cont. Fredegar*, c.52, 53, pp.120–1.
176 *Cont. Fredegar*, c.54, p.121. See opening of Chapter 3.
177 Brothers: see above. Sister and daughter: Nelson (1996a), xxv, 232.

Chapter 3

1. Cathwulf, letter to Charlemagne, MGH Ep. KA 2, p.502; *Visio Wettini*, ed. Dümmler; *Visio pauperculae mulieris*, ed. Houben.
2. Contrast *ARF*, a.778, pp.68, 70 with the revised version, a.778, p.51, p.53 and cf. Einhard, *VK*, c.9, pp.12–13, and Astronomer, *VH*, c.2, pp.286–8. *ARF*, a.785, a.810, p.68, p.131; Einhard, *VK*, c.6, c.14, pp.8–9, 17.
3. Mobilization: see, for example, Capitulary no.74, c.8, MGH Cap.1, p.167; Halsall (2003), 75–8. Hostages and captives: see, for example, Einhard, *VK*, c.7, p.10; Capitulary no.115, MGH Cap.1, pp.233–4; Nelson (2008c); Kosto (2012), 66–7.
4. Alcuin, letter no.200, MGH Ep. KA 2, p.332.
5. Saxons: Alcuin, letter no.43, p.89, and see also no.44, pp.89–90 and no.150, p.246. Itinerary: Alcuin, letters nos 146, 147, 151, 152, pp.235–6, 237, 246–8; on Charlemagne's itinerary, McKitterick (2008), 171–86. Winter: Alcuin, letter, no.50, pp.93–4 and Bullough (2004), 434.
6. Alcuin, letters nos 84, 121, 145, pp.127, 177, 231–5; Airlie (2014).
7. Alcuin, letter no.107, p.153–4; Bullough (2004), 468.
8. Alcuin, letter no.100, p.146; no.96, p.140 (with Bullough (2004), 451 n.60); no.84, p.127; no.190, p.317.
9. Alcuin, letter, no.15, p.41; no.50, pp.93–4 (see Bullough (2004), 434). See also, for example, Alcuin, letters nos 32, 72, 84, 195, 196, 213, 214, 216, pp.73–4, 114–15, 127, 322–5, 354–8, 359–60; Nelson (1998b), 185; Nelson (1991b), 209.
10. Alcuin, letter no.33, p.75.
11. Alcuin, letter no.111, pp.159–62 see also, for example, no.110, pp.156–9; Bullough (2003), 373–4.
12. Alcuin, letter no.211, p.351.
13. Esders (1999); Nelson (2008c), 228. See also the King's College London project on Charlemagne's Europe http://www.charlemagneseurope.ac.uk/
14. *Admonitio Generalis*, eds Mordek, Zechiel-Eckes and Glatthaar, MGH Fontes Iuris XVI; Brown (2003), 434–61.
15. This is the perspective in Nelson (2019); I am very grateful for advance sight of much of it.
16. Einhard, *VK*, c.31, pp.35–6, trans. Ganz (2008), 40.
17. *ARF*, a.775, p.42; Collins (1998), 63; Davis (2015), 136–9.
18. Garipzanov (2008), 123–5. *ARF*, a.774, and *ARF*, rev., a.774, pp.38–40, followed by Einhard, *VK*, c.6, pp.8–9. Nelson (1998a), 187, and cf. McKitterick (2008), 109–14.
19. Erchempert, *Historia Langobardorum Beneventanorum*, c.4, MGH SRL, 236; Grierson and Blackburn (1986), plate 51, 576–7. *Codex Carolinus*, no.67, MGH Ep KA I, p.595. West (1999), 351–3, 358–9, 363; Garipzanov (2008), 3, 44–5, 130; McCormick (1984), 3–4. Beneventan dynastic pride visible in epitaph of duke Grimoald, MGH PLAC 1, pp.430–1.
20. *ARF*, a.777, p.48; Collins (1998), 49–51; Balzer (1999), 116–18; Gai (2001), 73–7.
21. *ARF*, rev., a.778, pp.51, 53; *Annales Petaviani*, a.778, MGH SS 1, p.16; Collins (1998), 65–8; Balzer (1999), 118.
22. Airlie (1999).
23. Airlie (2004); Airlie (2005).
24. *ARF*, a.781, p.56; *AnnalesMosellani*, a.781, MGH SS 16, p.497; Kasten (1997), 138–9; Collins (1998), 69–70; McKitterick (2004), 62.

25 Collins (1998), 3–7; McKitterick (2004), 3–5, 84–155; McKitterick (2008), 27–49; Reimitz (2008).
26 Nelson (2008b).
27 McKitterick (2004), 121–3; Reimitz (2000); McKitterick (2008), 27–31.
28 *AMP*, a.688, pp.1–2, trans. Fouracre and Gerberding (1996), 350–1, and see their comments at 334. Hen (2000); Reimitz (2015), 368–75 highlights broader, collective Frankish elements.
29 Reuter (2006), 231–50, and Chapter 2 above.
30 Lombards: *ARF*, a.774, p.38. Avars: Einhard, *VK*, c.13, p.16 (trans. Ganz (2008), 27); *ARF*, a.796, p.98; *Annales Laureshamenses*, a.795, a.796 MGH SS 1, pp.36–7; Theodulf, poem no.25, MGH PLAC 1, pp.483–9, trans. Godman (1985a), 150–63; Wood (2013), 324–5. On Carolingian treasure, Wamers (2005).
31 See, for example, Verhulst (2002); Costambeys, Innes and MacLean (2011), 223–378; Loveluck (2013), 98–150; Mayr-Harting (1996); McCormick (2001), 702, 732–3.
32 Halsall (2003); Nelson (1996a), xxviii–ix; Airlie (2005), 95.
33 Curta (2006), 687–90, 696–9; Nelson (1995), 412–13; Airlie (1995), 443–7.
34 Campbell (2010), especially 258–9 and 260–4; Costambeys, Innes and MacLean (2011), 329.
35 Astronomer, *VH*, c.6, c.7, pp.302–4; Boshof (1996), 56–9; Kasten (1997), 344–5; Depreux (1997), 362.
36 Capitulary no.28, c.5, MGH Cap.1, p.74. Grierson and Blackburn (1986), 206; Witthöft (1994).
37 Capitulary no.28, c.5, MGH Cap.1, p.74; Alcuin, letter no.96, MGH Ep. KA 2, p.140. Garipzanov (2008), 128–36; Coupland (2005), 220–1.
38 Capitulary no.52, c.7, MGH Cap.1, p.140; Grierson and Blackburn (1986), 207; Coupland (2005), 213, 221; Garipzanov (2008), 131–2.
39 Capitulary no.273, c.11, MGH Cap.2, p.315; Garipzanov (2008), 36–7, whose translation I follow. Grierson and Blackburn (1986), 213, 219, 223–7, 230–5, and see plates 34–44, pp.525–51. On the cult of coin portraits, Coupland (2005), 227 and Garipzanov (2008), 214–15.
40 'cum consensu Francorum', *Cont. Fredegar*, c.53, p.121.
41 Pippin, charter no.16 for Prüm, in Dip. Karol. 1; *Cont. Fredegar*, c.45, c.51, pp.114, 119. Kaschke (2006), 122; McKitterick (2008), 74.
42 Nelson (2008a), 40–2.
43 *Cont. Fredegar*, c.54, p.121; *ARF*, a.768, p.28; on the start of the reigns, Mühlbacher's introduction to Dip. Karol, 1, pp.61, 77.
44 *Cont. Fredegar*, c.54, p.121.
45 *Cont. Fredegar*, c.53, p.121; Carloman, charters nos 43, 44, in Dip. Karol. 1; Charlemagne, charter no.55 (769), in Dip. Karol. 1; *ARF*, a.770, p.30. Nelson (2008a), 42; McKitterick (2008), 79–80.
46 McKitterick (2008), 75–88; Capitulary no.45, c.4, MGH Cap.1, pp.127–8. *Codex Carolinus*, nos 44 and 47, MGH Ep. KA 1, pp.558–60 and pp.565–7. Nelson (1998a), 180–1; Kaschke (2006), 106–7; Werner (1975), 135; Settipani (1993), 186, 203.
47 *Codex Lauresh*. I, no.10; *ChLA* XV, no.609; Innes (1998b), 309.
48 Airlie (2005), 97–8.
49 *ARF*, a.771, p.32; Cathwulf, letter to Charlemagne, MHG Ep. KA 2, p.502; Einhard, *VK*, c.3, p.6. Astronomer, *VH*, c.20, pp.340–2.
50 Nelson (1991b), 198.

51 On such knowledge, see, for example, *ARF*, a.773, p.36, and the reviser's *ARF*, a.773, p.37, and *ARF* (reviser), a.782, pp.61, 63. Settipani (1993), 341–6; Kasten (1986), 13–41.
52 *Cont. Fredegar*, c.37, c.38, pp.105–8; Jarnut (1975), 271–5. *Annales Laureshamenses*, a.802, MGH SS 1, pp.38–9, trans. King (1987), 144–5; Davis (2008), 240; Innes (2005), 83–4.
53 *ARF* (reviser), a.782, pp.61, 63; Airlie (2005), 90–1; Hlawitschka (1965), 76–8, challenged by Settipani (1993), 174–6.
54 Bullough (1984); Innes (2005), 83–4.
55 Innes (2005), 79–84; Davis (2015), 117.
56 Charlemagne, charters nos 65, 73, in Dip. Karol. 1. Innes (2000a), 56, 180–2, 189–90; Nelson (2009), 15–20; Hummer (2005), 76–129; Davis (2015), 176–7.
57 Capitulary no. 40, c.14, MGH Cap.1, p.116. See also Hincmar, *De Ordine palatii*, c.vi, eds T. Gross and R. Schieffer, pp.82–4, and Louis the Pious' 829 reference to 'bishops, abbots and counts who should always come to our assemblies', Capitulary no.187, MGH Cap.2, p.9. In general, Nelson (1995), 417–20 and Airlie (2003a).
58 Nelson (1986), 91 for the Wallace-Hadrill quote. Herstal: Capitulary no.20, MGH Cap.1, p.47; McKitterick (2008), 229. 870s collection: Ansegis, *Collectio Capitularium*, ed. G. Schmitz, MGH Capitularia regum Francorum, nova series (1996), p.433. Relevant here is a legal manuscript from the 870s, New Haven, Yale University, The Beinecke Rare Book and Manuscript Library, MS 413; see Schmitz's introduction to his edition, pp.109–10 and p.258, and the University of Cologne capitulary website: https://capitularia.uni-koeln.de/en/mss/newhaven-bl-413/
59 Ansegis, *Collectio*, ed. Schmitz, pp.432–3; Pössel (2006), 268–74; McKitterick (2008), 230–3; Nelson (1995), 409–10; Airlie (2009a).
60 *Epitaphia VI*, MGH PLAC 1, pp.109–10; see also Einhard *VK*, c.9; Astronomer, *VH*, c.2, p.288: 'vulgata … nomina'; cf. *ARF*, a.782, p.60; Airlie (2005).
61 *ARF* (revised) a.785, p.71; *Annales Nazariani*, a.786, MGH SS 1, pp.40–3; McKitterick (2006a), 68–89 and McKitterick (2006b). See also Brunner (1979), 48–53; Innes (1998b); Le Jan (2001), 112–13; Le Jan (2006); Nelson (2009), 13–14.
62 Nelson (2009), 13; Davis (2015), 140–9; Hummer (2005), 109–15.
63 Airlie (2005), 99; Le Jan (2006), 410, 419–20. The capitulary of 789 refers to the plot as being on Charlemagne's life: capitulary no.25, MGH Cap.1, p.66.
64 *Annales Nazariani*, a.786, MGH SS 1, pp.41–3, trans. King (1987), 154–5; *ARF*, a.785, p.71; *Annales Laureshamenses*, a.786, p.32 refers to it as in Austrasia; Einhard, *VK*, c.20, pp.25–6. McKitterick (2006b), 272; Nelson (2009), 13; Le Jan (2006).
65 *Annales Nazariani*, a.786, pp.41–3. Innes (1998b), 313–15; Le Jan (2006), 406–7; Le Jan (2001), 111. On the Hedenen, Fouracre (2000), 110–12; Mordek (1994), especially 345–7. Bad reputation, Willibald, *Vita Bonifatii*, c.6, ed. W. Levison, MGH SRG, pp.32–3; *Passio Killiani martyris*, cs 12–14, ed. W. Levison, MGH SRM 5, pp.726–7. Wood (2001), 62–3, 160–1, 248; Palmer (2009), 100–3.
66 Charlemagne, charter no.116, in Dip. Karol. 1; *Urkundenbuch der Kloster Fulda*, no.83, ed. E.E. Stengel, vol. 1 (1956); Wood (2000), 156–8; Fouracre (2000), 62, 114–15; Palmer (2009), 102.
67 *Annales Nazariani*, a.786, p.42; Innes (1998b), 313–15; Innes (2000a), 186; Le Jan (2006), 409–10; Palmer (2009), 102–3.
68 Innes (2001), 419–26; Nelson (1997a), 150–1.
69 Einhard, *VK*, c.18, c.20, pp.22–3, pp.25–6; Thegan, *GH*, c.2, p.176. *ARF*, a.783, p.66; Nelson (1997a), 154.

70 Innes (2000a), 180–6; Le Jan (2006), 408–10; Nelson (2009), 16–20; Davis (2015), 140–9.
71 Charlemagne, charter no.40, in Dip. Karol. 1. Hussong (1986), 143; Nelson (2009), 18–19.
72 *Annales Nazariani*, a.786, p.41. Nelson (1997b), 154; Le Jan (2001), 110–13; Palmer (2009), 102. Cf. Davis (2015), 143–6.
73 *ARF* (reviser), a.785, p.71; *Annales Nazariani*, a.786, pp.41–3; see also *Annales Laureshamenses*, a.786, MGH SS 1, p.32.
74 Capitulary no.25, c.1, MGH Cap.1, p.66; on the date, Becher (1993), 78–87, 195–6. Later sources' use of the term *coniuratio* points to 'a swearing-together', Nelson (2009), 8, 21–6; McKitterick (2006b), 268–77.
75 Capitulary no.20, c.14, c.16, MGH Cap.1, pp.50, 51, trans. King (1987), 204; context in Mordek (2005), 42–3.
76 Capitulary no.20, c.16, MGH Cap.1, p.51; Mordek (2005), 9–14, 50; Le Jan (1995), 126–30; Becher (1993), 78–212; Innes (2005), 80–1; McKitterick (2008), 268–70.
77 Capitulary no.44, c.10, MGH Cap.1, p.124; Nelson (2001b), 37.
78 Capitulary no.23, c.26, MGH Cap.1, p.64; trans. King (1987), 221.
79 Hauck (1950), 191–2; Ganshof (1971), 115; Becher (1993), 182–3; Contrast Diesenberger (2003), 189; Nelson (2001b), 36–8.
80 Capitulary no.23, c.18, MGH Cap.1, p.63; trans. King (1987), 221; Becher (1993), 120–1.
81 *Annales Nazariani*, a.786, pp.41–3; Becher (1993), 84. Capitulary no.34, MGH Cap.1, pp.101–2; Becher (1993), 91–2, 192; Innes (2005), 81; Davis (2008), 235–6; Davis (2015), 352–3.
82 Ganshof (1971), 114–16; Becher (1993), 139, 143.
83 Nelson (2001b), 38; Nelson (2009), 24–5; Nelson (2008c), 230–1; Davis (2008); Depreux (2002), 221–3, 293–9; Davis (2015).
84 Airlie (1995); Airlie (2005); Le Jan (2001), 109–13.
85 Einhard, *VK*, c.20, p.25. Kasten (1997), 139–40, 146; Winter (2005); Nelson (2009), 8–9.
86 *Codex Carolinus*, no.45, p.561. Le Jan (1995), 274; Nelson (2009), 9; McDougall (2016), 80–3.
87 McDougall (2016), Chapter 3.
88 Classen (1972), 117–18; Nelson (2005), 32–3 and Nelson (2009), 10; Goffart (1986) is too schematic.
89 Classen (1972), 113–18; Kasten (1997), 139; Nelson (2009), 9–12.
90 Paul the Deacon, *Gesta Episcoporum Mettensium*, MGH SS 2, p.265; Kempf (2004); Airlie (2016), 216–20; McDougall (2016), 80–2; Nelson (2009), 10–12, pushes the evidence on Pippin's mother as far as it can go.
91 *Gesta Episcoporum Mettensium*, pp.264–5; Oexle (1967), 299; Hauck (1970), 147–60.
92 Salzburg: *Das Verbrüderungsbuch von St. Peter in Salzburg: Vollständige Faksimile-Ausgabe*, ed. K. Forstner (1974), pag.10 of facsimile. Soissons: text of *laudes* in Appendix to *VK*, ed. Holder-Egger, p.47. Classen (1972), 118; McKitterick (2004), 179; Nelson (2009), 10; Airlie (2016), 210–11.
93 *AMP*, a.790, p.78; Kasten (1997), 141–2; Classen (1972).
94 *Gesta Sanctorum Patrum Fontanellensis Coenobii*, XII.2, eds F. Lohier and J. Laporte, pp.86–7. Kasten (1997), 143; McKitterick (2008), 282–4.
95 Hammer (2008); Nelson (2009), 10; Airlie (2016). See Chapter 6 of this book on Charles the Bald and Carloman.

96 *Annales Laurashemenses*, a.792, p.35. Schieffer (1997), 87; Airlie (2016).
97 Hammer (2008); Airlie (2016).
98 Nelson (2009), 8–12.
99 Hammer (2008); Airlie (2016). Wala: Paschasius Radbertus, *Epitaphium Arsenii*, I, c.6, ed. Dümmler, p.28; Weinrich (1963), 16; Nelson (1991b), 200–1; Davis (2015), 149–52.
100 *Annales Laureshamenses*, a.792, MGH SS 1, p.35.
101 *Chronicon Laurissense breve* (Fulda version), IV, 43, ed. von Carolsfeld, p.38.
102 *Annales Laureshamenses*, a.793, MGH SS 1, p.35; Leyser (1979), 77; Nelson (2009), 22.
103 Bishop of Verdun: capitulary no.28, c.9, MGH Cap.1, p.75; *Gesta Episcoporum Virdunensium*, c.14, MGH SS 4, p.44; Patzold (2008a), 427. Theodold: Charlemagne, charter no. 181, in Dip. Karol. 1 and see the charter of Theodold in *ChLA* XVI, no.638; Brown (1989), 146–8, 162–3; Stoclet (1988), 100–2; Nelson (2009), 10–11.
104 *ARF* (revised), a.792, pp.91, 93; McKitterick (2008), 27–8.
105 *Annales Laureshamenses*, a.792, p.35, cf. Judges, chapters 8, 9. Nelson (2002), 277.
106 Nelson (2002); Nelson (2009), 22–3.
107 Nelson (1996a), 227; Settipani (1993), 208–10; names in Einhard, *VK*, c.18, pp.22–3.
108 *ARF*, a.800, p.110.
109 Charlemagne charter no.319, in Dip. Karol. 1, and *ChLA*, XVI, no.636; the grant was confirmed by Charlemagne charter no.190, in Dip. Karol. 1. Nelson (2002), 279.
110 Airlie (2005), 93; Fried (2016), 402–05.
111 See, for example, *Cod. Dip. Fuld.*, nos 278, 281, 282; Wickham (1995), 519–23; Innes (2000a), 22–3.
112 Capitulary no.33 (*Capitulare misorum generale*), c.2, MGH Cap.1, p.92; capitulary no.34, MGH Cap.1, pp.101–2. Eckhardt (1956); Innes (2005), 81; Davis (2015), 350–7; Fried (2016), 453–4.
113 Ermold, Book I, lines 146–94, ed. Faral, pp.16–20.
114 Alcuin, letters nos 241, 309, pp.386–7, 473–8; Kasten (1986), 47–58.
115 First capitulary of bishop Gerbald of Liège, c.7, ed. P. Brommer, MGH Capitularia Episcoporum, I (1984), p.7; Pokorny (1983), 391–2; Charlemagne, charter no.188, in Dip. Karol. 1.
116 Airlie (2005); McKitterick (2008), 99–102.
117 Einhard, *VK*, c.22, p.26 ('white hair', trans. Ganz (2008), 34; Dutton (2009), 156. Theodulf, poem no.32, line 45–6, MGH PLAC 1, p.524; Alcuin, letter no.164, p.266.
118 Alcuin, 'Dialogue with Pippin', in *Altercatio Hadriani Augusti et Epicteti philosophi*, eds Daly and Suchier (1939); trans. Dutton (2004), 141.
119 Ermold, Book I, lines 600–35, pp.48–50; *Vita Alcuini*, c.15, MGH SS 15, pp.192–3.Godman (1985b), 263–4; date of Alcuin biography, Bullough (2004), 21–2, 27–33; Depreux (1993), 315; De Jong (2009), 20.
120 Ermold, as previous note.
121 Ermold, Book I, lines 604–5, 612–13, p.48; *De Karolo rege et Leone papa*, lines 451–3, ed. F. Brunhölzl, p.40.
122 Kasten (1997), 246–9, 272–377; McKitterick (2008), 154–5.
123 Wandalbert, *Miracula S. Goaris*, c.11, MGH SS 15.1, p.366; Brunner (1983), 5; Kasten (1997), 261; Hammer (2012), 5–6; Airlie (2016), 217.
124 Charles the Younger: Angilbert, poem no.2, line 35, MHG PLAC 1, p.361, trans. Godman (1985a), 114–15; Pippin of Italy: Paderborn Epic, line 200, ed. Brunhölzl, pp.74–5. For family crowd scenes, see, for example, Angilbert, poem 1, MGH PLAC 1, pp.358–60; Theodulf, Carmen 25, MGH PLAC 1, pp.483–9, trans. Godman (1985a),

150–63; Paderborn Epic, ed. Brunhölzl, lines 179–267, lines 440–504, pp.74–9, pp.90–5; Alcuin, poem no.26, MGH PLAC 1, pp.245–6, trans. Godman (1985a), 118–21; Contrast Hibernicus Exul, poem no.2, MGH PLAC 1, pp.396–9, partial trans. in Godman (1985a), 174–9 and see Godman (1987), 61–96.
125 Garrison (1994); McKitterick (2008), 139–42.
126 Alcuin, letters, no.188, and nos 215–17, MGH Ep. KA 2, pp.315–16, 359–61; on the date of no.188, Kasten (1997), 211.
127 Charlemagne charter no.203, in Dip Karol. 1.
128 *ARF*, a.806, p.121; capitulary no.44, c.4, c.10, MGH Cap.1, pp.122–3, 124; Nelson (1998b), 181; Davis (2015), 406.
129 *Divisio regnorum*, capitulary no.45, MGH Cap.1, pp.126–30; Tischler (2008) on text and historiography. On the 806 plans, Classen (1972); Kasten (1997), 151–60; Kaschke (2006), 298–323; Becher (2008a), 313–15; McKitterick (2008), 96–9; Hammer (2012); Davis (2015), 415–23.
130 Thedoulf, poem no.35, MGH PLAC 1, pp.526–7; Godman (1985b), 244–5; Kasten (1997), 157; Hammer (2012).
131 Nelson (1996a), 191–3; Nelson (2002), 279, but cf. Kaschke (2006), 207–8; Davis (2015), 419–20.
132 *AMP*, a.781, p.71; Charles's crowning: *Lib. Pont.*, Life of Leo III, c.24, vol. 2, p.7, trans. Davis (1992), 191. *AMP*, a.789, p.78 is the last reference to him as 'first-born' in that text; see Kaschke (2006), 216–19; contrast Nelson (1996a), 193 and Nelson (2002), 279. *Divisio regnorum*, c.4, MGH Cap.1, p.127; Kaschke (2006), 308 n.53, and cf. 196. Cathwulf: letter to Charlemagne, MGH Ep KA 2, p.502. Sceptical views in Hammer (2012) and Davis (2015), 418–20.
133 Nelson (1996a), 193–4; Kaschke (2006), 203–48; Reimitz (2015), 368–75, 383–4.
134 *AMP*, a.741, a.768, pp.32, 55–6; Kaschke (2006), 223–5, 243. *Chronicon Laurissense breve*, IV, 38, p.35; Kaschke (2010), 121–2; Reimitz (2015), 382–6.
135 Settipani (1993), 211–12, 259, 275; Nelson (1998b), 182; Nelson (2002), 278–9; Innes (1997), 842.
136 *Divisio regnorum*, c.5, MGH Cap.1, p.128. Spain: Collins (1995), 277–8; Wessex: Higham and Ryan (2013), 296–7.
137 See, for example, *Divisio regnorum*, c.6, 7, 8, 9, 10, 11, 12, 13, 14, MGH Cap.1, pp.128–9. Contrast Davis (2015), 359–60.
138 *ARF*, a.806, p.121; *Divisio regnorum*, preface, and c.6, MGH Cap.1, pp.126–7, p.128, trans. King (1987), 251, 253; Kaschke (2006), 196–7, 300.
139 *ARF*, a.806, p.121; capitulary no.46, c.2, MGH Cap.1, p.131; Nelson (1998b), 181; Kaschke (2006), 300.
140 Names in capitulary no.85, MGH Cap.1, pp.183–4, to be dated to 806, see Kasten (1986), 60; Tischler (2008), 199, 201–8, 232. Einhard: *ARF*, a.806, p.121 and Patzold (2013), 86–8.
141 Nelson (1991b), 203.
142 *Divisio regnorum*, c.19, MGH Cap.1, p.130; Kasten (1997), 156. Contemporary view: *Chronicon Laurissense breve*, IV, 38, p.35; *ARF*, a.806, p.121; Kasten (1997), 155; Kaschke (2006), 308–10; Hammer (2012); Davis (2015), 418–20.
143 Kasten (1997), 155; Innes (1997), 835–6; McKitterick (2008), 98; Tischler (2008), 208–9, 228; Reimitz (2015), 375–82.
144 *Divisio regnorum*, c.17, MGH Cap.1, p.129 and see Chapter 8. Daughters and Gisela: Nelson (1996a), 238–41; Wala: Nelson (1991b), 201; Adalhard: Tischler (2008), 199, 201–8, 232.

145 *Divisio regnorum*, preface, c.3, c.4, c.15 (Charles), c.2, c.4, c.15 (Pippin) MGH Cap.I, pp.127–8, 129; familial terms: *Divisio regnorum*, preface, c.1, c.2, c.3, c.4, c.5, c.6, c.11, c.13, c.14, c.15, c.17, c.18, c.19, c.20, pp.127–30.
146 *Divisio regnorum*, c.18, c.20, MGH Cap.1, p.129, 130, trans. King (1987), 255; Kasten (1997), 220; Kaschke (2006), 313.
147 Dhuoda, *LM*, III, 1, pp.134–40; Nelson (2007), 109–10; in general, Kasten (1997), 199–238.
148 *Divisio regnorum*, preface, MGH Cap.1, p.126–7; see also Ermold, Book II, lines 668–73, pp.52–3.
149 *Divisio regnorum*, c. 18, MGH Cap.1, pp.129–30, trans. King (1987), 255.
150 *Divisio regnorum*, c.5, c.18, MGH Cap.1, pp.128, 129–30. Kasten (1997), 159, 402 n.77; Kaschke (2006), 319.
151 Alcuin, letters nos 143, 144, MGH, Ep. KA 2, pp.224, 228.
152 Dip Louis P, no.1; Boshof (1996), 54–70; Depreux (1997), 42–6; McKitterick (2008), 53–4.
153 Davis (2015), 278–89. Pippin is called simply 'king': for example, *ARF*, a.787, p.78 but he is called 'king of Italy' in *ARF*, a.796, p.98. His epitaph calls him 'king of Italy' (*rex Hesperiae*), MGH PLAC 1, no.15, p.405.
154 Kasten (1997), 330–5, 348; Fleckenstein (1959), 67, 113. Image survives in later copy: Steigmann and Wemhoff (1999), vol. 1, pp.54–6; Münsch (2001), 84.
155 *Versus de Verona*, MGH PLAC 1, pp.119–22, trans. Godman (1985a), 180–7; Books: McKitterick (2004), 80–1 and see below on Waldo for use of books to forge bonds. *ARF*, a.810, p.130, death on p.132.
156 Alcuin, letter no.29, MGH Ep. KA 2, p.71 (790–95), and see also Alcuin, letter no 11 (to Angilbert), p.37; Kasten (1997), 211.
157 *ARF*, a.796, p.98, p.100. Kasten (1997), 357–8; Nelson (2002), 27; Airlie (2016).
158 Airlie (2016), 210–15.
159 Bullough (1962), 633 citing chronicle of Gallus Ohem from c.1500.
160 Tellenbach (1957b), 48–9; Bullough (1962); Borgolte (1986), 46–8; Ludwig (1999), 130–1.
161 Alcuin, letter no.119 to Pippin, and no.188 to Charles with reference to letters to Louis, MGH Ep. KA 2, p.174, pp.315–16. Bullough (1962), 634 n.2 sees *mulier* as 'wife' as does Fried (1998), 94; La Rocca (2002), 511, seems to see this as a reference to illegitimate union; see also Kasten (1997), 357–8; McDougall (2016), 83–4 is sceptical that Alcuin is referring to a wife here, but does see the contemporary ambiguity.
162 *De Pippini regis victoria Avarica*, stanza 14, MGH PLAC 1, p.117; trans. Godman (1985a), 191.
163 Thegan, *GH* c.4, pp.178–80; Kasten (1997), 249–50, 260; Depreux (1997), 298.
164 Angilbert, poem no.1, MGH PLAC 1, pp.358–60; Kasten (1997), 269; Hammer (2012), 14.
165 *Lib. Pont.*, Life of Leo, c.16, vol. 2, p.5; *De Karolo rege et Leone papa*, lines 445–62, ed. F. Brunhölzl, pp.40–3. Nelson (2002), 279.
166 Astronomer, *VH*, c.10, 12, 13, pp.308–10, 312–20, with rather confused chronology.
167 Contrast *ARF*, a.801, p.116 with Ermoldus, Book I, lines 640–7, p.50; see also Astronomer *GH*, c.13, pp.312–14. Airlie (2006a), 138–9.
168 Alcuin, letter no.216, MGH Ep. KA 2, pp.359–60; *Lib. Pont.*, Life of Leo, c.24, vol. 2, p.7. Nelson (1996a), 239; Nelson (2002), 279–80.
169 Kasten (1986), 42–53; Nelson (1996a), 239.

170 Alcuin, letter no.217, MGH Ep. KA 2, pp.360–1; Hammer (2012), 2. *ARF*, a.800, p.110; a.801, p.114 (for citation).
171 *ARF*, a.801, p.116; West (1999), 363–4; Airlie (2006a), 104.
172 *Miracula S. Genesii*, c.2, ed. G. Waitz, MGH SS 15.1, pp.170–1. Zotz (1990), 282; Borgolte (1986), 238–9. *UB St Gallen*, nos 191, 197, 197, 199, 201, 202; I am here indebted to Schmid (1976/1983), 503–7.
173 *Divisio regnorum*, c.2, c.3, MGH Cap.1, p.127; Schmid (1976/1983), 506.
174 *UB St Gallen*, no.187; Wolfram (1995a), 144–6; Innes (2008), 256–9; Davis (2015), 277–8.
175 Astronomer, *VH*, c.13, p.320; Kasten (1997), 280, 293. Pippin's epitaph: Hibernicus Exul, poem no.15, line 5, MGH PLAC 1, p.405; Kasten (1997), 269.
176 *ARF*, a.810, 131–2, a.811, p.135; *Chronicon Laurissense breve* (Fulda recension), IV, 43, p.38.
177 *VK*, c.32, p.36; *ARF*, a.810, pp.131–3.
178 Dungal, letter no.1, MGH Ep. KA 2, pp.570–8, see especially pp.576–7. Werner (1990), 28–9, less optimistic than Nelson (1998b), 182–3; Eastwood (1994), 131–2. Einhard, *VK*, c.32, pp.36–7; Astronomer, *VH*, c.58, pp.518–22.
179 Dungal, letter no.1, MGH Ep. KA 2, pp.577–8.
180 See Chapter 4 on children. Einhard, *VK*, c.19, p.24; Nelson (1998b), 188–9; Depreux (1992), 5.
181 Smith (2003); *Chronicon Laurissense breve* (Fulda version XLI), IV, 41, ed. von Carolsfeld, p.37; Patzold (2000), 105; Innes (2000a), 22–3 on networks visible in grants of 811–13. Prayers and royal family: *Epistolae variorum (Supplex Libellus)*, no.33, MGH Ep. KA 2, p.548; Raaijmakers (2003), 39–40. *Epistolarum Fuldensium fragmenta*, MGH Ep. KA 3, p.517 for monks interceding.
182 *Epistolae variorum*, no.32, MGH Ep. KA 2, pp.546–8 (early 811); Kasten (1986), 68. Charlemagne charter nos 211, 214, in Dip. Karol. 1.
183 The will is in Einhard, *VK*, c. 33, pp.37–41, and is seen as being genuine, Innes (1997); Brunner (1979), 69–95; McKitterick (2008), 99–102.
184 Einhard, *VK*, c.33, p.37. Innes (1997), 837 n.4 and 844–6. Nelson (1996a), 239–42.
185 *ARF*, a.810, p.131, 132, a.811, p.135; *Chron. Laurissense Breve*, IV, 43, p.38. Leyser (1979), 86.
186 Einhard, *VK*, c.19, p.24 on grief; Astronomer, *VH*, c.20, p.342 with note 257 at p.343; Depreux (1997), 215–16 on Gerricus.
187 Gravel (2012a).
188 Wendling (1985). Ermold, Book II, lines 652–703, pp.52–6; Charlemagne's envoys to Louis in 808, Astronomer, *VH*, c.15, pp.324–6, and in 809 and 811, *VH*, c.16, c.17, p.330. Louis' followers and their connections, Airlie (2006a), 101–9; Theodulf: Depreux (1997), 383–4.
189 809: Astronomer, *VH*, c.16, p.330; 813: *ARF*, a.813, p.138; both Astronomer, *VH*, c.20, pp.340–4 and Thegan, *GH*, cs 5 and 6, p.180, elide this gap of years. See BM, nos 519, 519 a–b for Louis' movements 809–13.
190 Einhard, *VK*, c.19, p.24; Astronomer, *VH*, c. 21, p.346.
191 Einhard, *VK*, c.19, p.25. *Divisio regnorum*, c.17, MGH Cap.1, p.129.
192 Nelson (1996a), 239–42, with family tree on p.227; Nelson (1998b), 184–91. On aristocratic tensions, Werner (1990), 28–37, and see above, and also below on Adalhard, Wala and Angilbert.
193 Astronomer, *VH*, c.29, p.382, and c.20, p.342.
194 West (1999); Delogu (1995); Roach (2018), 355–62.

195 Davis (2015), see especially pp.364–77 and 415–23.
196 Nelson (1996a), 227; Settipani (1993), 255–6 on children of Louis the Pious.
197 Werner (1990), 35; Kasten (1997), 160–1; Becher (2008a), 314–15. But cf. Innes (1997), 842–5.
198 *Divisio regnorum*, c.5, MGH Cap.1, p.128; *ARF* a.806, p.121; Becher (2008a), 310–19.
199 Foucault (2001), 337; Foucault (1978), 92–8, cited in Wickham (2001), 5.
200 Foucault (2001), 337–9.
201 Kasten (1986), 42–7 (and see above), 68–84; Depreux (1992), 5.
202 *Translatio Sancti Viti*, III, ed. Schmale-Ott (1979), p.38; Becher (1996), 119–21; Davis (2015), 370–2.
203 *Translatio Sancti Viti*, III, ed. Schmale-Ott, pp.37–8 and this source sees Wala as having similar status of provincial governor in Saxony; for date, Schmale-Ott (1979), 11–12 and Löwe, Wattenbach, Levison (1990), 6, p.855.
204 *Chronicon Laurissense breve*, IV, 44, ed. von Carolsfeld, p.36; date: Lowe in Watt-Lev 2, pp.264–5; McKitterick (2004), 35–6; Kaschke (2006), 249–76, especially 249–53.
205 'ipse piisimus Karolus constituit Barnardo, filio Pippini, regem super Italia in loco patris sui', *Chronicon Moissiacense*, a.810, MGH SS 2, p.258. Fried (1998), 84; Kaschke (2006), 260–1.
206 Einhard, *VK*, c.19, p.24; Thegan, *GH*, c.12, p.192 and c.22, p.210, and see Walahfrid's table of contents to Thegan, *GH*, p.170 at XII; Astronomer, *VH*, c.23, p.354, c.26, p.366, c.29, p.382.
207 See above for Adalhard, and for Angilbert; Wala: *ARF*, a.812, p.137.
208 Thegan, *GH*, c.22, p.210. Pro-illegitimacy: Werner (1990), 34; Le Jan (1995), 204; Innes (1997), 843 n.1, and Kasten (2002), 34–5; sceptical: Fried (1998) and Offergeld (2001), 314 n.48. For a general relevant survey of illegitimacy, see McDougall (2016). For the list, see below.
209 Settipani (1993), 212, 255.
210 Capitulary no.136, *Ordinatio Imperii*, c.14, c.15, MGH Cap.2, pp.272–3. Kasten (1997), 163–5, 175; Kasten (2002), 32–8, 51; cf. Le Jan (1995), 204; Innes (1997), 837, 845–6; Kasten (1997), 163–4.
211 The list is in Schmid (1976/1983), 487–90, and Autenrieth (1975), 220, but NB correction to Autenrieth by Schmid (1976/1983), 484 n.16; for the date, I follow Fried (1998), 90–1.
212 *ARF*, a.768, a.771, a.772, a.781, a.782, a.785, a.786, a.796, a.799, a.802, a.807, a.808, a.809, a.810, a.811, a.812, a.813, a.814, pp.26, 32, 58, 60, 70, 72, 98, 104, 106, 117, 123, 127, 128–30, 132, 133–4, 137, 141. Airlie (2007b); Davis (2015), 199–201.
213 Schmid (1976/1983), 485 n.19.
214 Schmid (1976/1983), 500; Autenrieth (1975), 220 n.24; see plate 1 in Schmid (1976/1983), 487. On names in second entry, Schmid (1976/1983), 492–4 and 499 on special nature of this group in the structure of the list.
215 *Miracula S. Genesii*, as above; Borgolte (1986), 238–9. In general, Schmid (1976/1983), 493, 496 and Kasten (1997), 361–2.
216 Udalric: *UB St Gallen*, no.197 and no.202 and in the entry at Schmid (1976/1983), 489 and see 494–6; Borgolte (1986), 248–54; *Ub St Gallen* no.202 is a grant by Scroto and it is just possible that this is count Scrot, Borgolte (1986), 239–40. Richuin: *UB St Gallen*, no.191, and in the entry at Schmid (1976/1983), 489; Borgolte (1986), 206–9; Innes (1997), 844.
217 Schmid (1976/1983), 493, 496, 501; Borgolte (1986), 206; and see Chapter 5 on 817.
218 Schmid (1976/1983), 500; Werner (1990), 44.

219 Fried (1998), 93.
220 Fried (1998), 71–5.
221 *ARF*, a.812, pp.136–7.
222 *ARF*, a.813, p.138.
223 *Chronicon Moissacense*, a.813, MGH SS 2, p.259, and Buc (2000), 205; Thegan, *GH*, c.6, pp.182–4; Wendling (1985); Boshof (1996), 89.
224 MGH Concilia 2.1, Arles, council no.34, c.2, MGH Concilia 2.1, p.250; Reims, council no.35, c.40, MGH Concilia 2.1 p.257; Mainz, council no.36, prologue, MGH Concilia 2.1, p.259; Chalons, council no 37, c.46, MGH Concilia 2.1, p.285; Tours, council no.38, c.1, MGH Concilia 2.1, pp.286–7 (prayers just for Charlemagne). Fried (1998), 78.
225 *Planctus Karoli*, MGH PLAC 1, p.436; trans. Godman (1985a), 207–11.

Chapter 4

1 Burke (1992), 39; Bradbury (1998), 1–3.
2 Airlie (2014), 260; McEvoy (2013).
3 De Jong (2001b), 76; Nelson (1992), 75; a nuanced view in Schieffer (1990b), 155–6; see also Borst (1996).
4 Dhuoda, *LM*, Pref, p.84.
5 Schieffer (1990b); Kasten (1997); Offergeld (2001); Duindam (2016), 57–70.
6 Nelson (2004b), 99–100; Cramer (1993), 149–53.
7 Astronomer, *VH*, c.3, pp.290–9; Nithard, I, c.2, c.3, p.8. Charles's birth appears in neither Thegan nor the Royal Frankish Annals.
8 Schieffer (1990b), 155–6.
9 778: Astronomer, *VH*, c.2, c.3, pp.286–90; 822–3: *ARF*, a.822, a.823, pp.159–61; Settipani (1993), 204–5; Orth (1985–6), 160–7, 183–8. Note also the presence of the heavily pregnant queen Richildis in Charles the Bald's army in 876, *AB*, a.876, trans. Nelson (1991a), 196–8.
10 Froissart/Brereton.
11 Jarnut (1984); Werner (1990), 20–1; Ewig (1995), 12.
12 Charters: Collins (2002), 311; Fouracre (2005).
13 *Epitaphium Chlodarii pueri regis*, MGH PLAC 1, pp.71–3; Paul the Deacon, *Gesta Episcoporum Mettensium*, MGH SS 2, p.265; Kasten (1997), 269.
14 'nomen et ornat avi', Ermold, Book IV, line 2413, p.184; trans. Godman (1985a), 257; Nelson (1992), 80. See also Walahfrid's *De Imagine Tetrici*, ed. Herren and the later celebration of Charles's name in the *Carmen de Exordio Francorum*, lines 85–111, MGH PLAC 2, pp.143–4.
15 Nithard, II, c.1, c.2, pp.38, 40; Astronomer, *VH*, c. 60, pp.530–2; on the tensions revealed by such arrangements, see Nelson (1995), 398–9.
16 Letter of Charles the Bald in Council of Troyes 867, MGH Concilia 4, pp.239–41; Airlie (2000b), 13.
17 *Codex Carolinus*, no.33, MGH Ep. KA 2, pp.539–40; Angenendt (1992), 109; Cathwulf, letter to Charlemagne, MGH Ep KA 2, p.502; Nelson (2004b), 100–1.
18 Stafford (2001a), 261, 263. *Codex Carolinus*, no.18, MGH Ep KA 1, p.519.
19 Einhard, *VK*, c.4, pp.6–7; Becher (2003), 41; Becher (1989).
20 Schieffer (1990b), 157–8; Nelson (1994b), 105–7; Kasten (1997), 240–2; Offergeld (2001), 10–11.

21 Einhard, *VK*, c.19, p.23; Stafford (2001a), 262.
22 *Translatio S. Germani*, MGH SS 15(1), pp.6–8; Nelson (2005), 24–8.
23 Astronomer, *VH*, c. 4, pp.294–6; Thegan, *GH*, c.3, p.178.
24 Notker, *GK*, II, c.12, p.74 (little Bernard), II, c.14, p.78; for the young Louis the German, see *GK*, II, c.10, pp.65–6 and see below.
25 Nelson (1994b), 88–90; Offergeld (2001), 42–3.
26 *Cont. Fredegar*, c.87, p.73–6; Offergeld (2001), 244–5.
27 Astronomer, *VH*, c.4, 294–6; Nelson (1994b).
28 Le Jan (2000), 282–5; Effros (2003), 124–6. Astronomer, *VH*, c.6, p.300.
29 Ermold, Book IV, lines 2400–10, pp.182–4. Nelson (1992), 80; Le Jan (2000).
30 Nelson (1998c).
31 *Ordinatio Imperii*, c.14, c.15, c.16, MGH Cap.1, pp.272–3; *Divisio Regnorum*, c.5, MGH Cap.1, p.128; Kasten (1997), 159, 180, 257–9; Offergeld (2001), 16–17, 301, 312–13.
32 *Ordinatio Imperii*, c.14, c.15, c.18, MGH Cap.1, pp.272–3. McDougall (2016), 77.
33 Schieffer (1990b), 160–1; Kasten (2002); Becher (2008b); McDougall (2016), chapter 2.
34 Treaty of Fouron (clause 3), in *AB*, a.878, trans. Nelson (1991a), 214. Louis the Stammerer seems, however, to have changed his mind soon after this, *AB*, a.879, trans. Nelson (1991a), 215–16.
35 Gregory of Tours, *Decem Libri Historiarum*, V, c.20, ed. B. Krusch and W. Levison, MGH SRM 1.1, p.228. But such status was only a starting point, Wood (1994), 58; Wood (2004a), 22–3; Kasten (1997), 20; McDougall (2016).
36 Offergeld (2001), 300–1; Schieffer (1990b).
37 Kasten (1997), 243–8.
38 Kasten (1997), 250–4, 257–9.
39 Miller (2014).
40 Offergeld (2001), 20–1, 34–40.
41 Nelson (1998b), 7–8.
42 Walahfrid, *De Imagine Tetrici*, ed. Herren, lines 152–61; De Jong (2009), 94–5.
43 Goldberg (2006a), 26–7, 44, 47; contrast Hartmann (2002), 24–8.
44 Offergeld (2001), 20–1, 319 n. 67.
45 Goldberg (2006a), 47 n. 84 and 52–4.
46 *Ordinatio Imperii*, Preface and c.2, MGH Cap.1, pp.270–1; *ARF*, a.817, p.146: 'caeteros reges appelatos'; Kasten (1997), 170–1 sees 817 as ambivalent, that is, taking place at once or dealing with the future, but in a way, that is the point.
47 Ermold, Book IV, lines 2004, 2011, p.152; *ARF*, a.824, p.165.
48 *ARF*, a.761, p.18; McKitterick (2008), 74.
49 *AF*, a.841, p.32; Kasten (1997), 381–2.
50 *AF*, a.841, pp.31–3. On Lothar I's attempts to control this region in the war, Innes (2000a), 207–10.
51 Kasten (1997), 30.
52 *Vita Erminonis*, c.9, MGH SRM 6, pp.468–9; Fouracre (2000), 63 on it as from Pippin's reign. Kasten (1997), 106, 107, 238–9. *Codex Carolinus*, no.18, p.519.
53 Alcuin, *Vita Willibrordi*, c.23, MGH SRM 7, pp.133–4; on this text's links with Echternach, see Wood (2001), 81 and Alberi (1998), 3–4.
54 See above n.7. On the birth of Charles the Simple, Schieffer (1990b), 155 and see Kasten (1997), 238–9 for general comment. NB births in *Annales Petaviani*, MGH SS 1, p.11, see Werner (1975), 135 and Nelson (2004b). On report of the birth of Charles the Fat, MacLean (2003a), 84 n.8.

55 Einhard, *VK*, c.4, pp.6–7; Borst (1996), 33; Becher (1992).
56 *Annales Weissemburgenses*, a.823, MGH SS 1, p.111, with new edition in Hofmeister (1919), 419; Freise (1984), 520; Glansdorff (2003), 945–50. Astronomer, *VH*, c.35, c.36, pp.406, 414–16.
57 Hofmeister (1919), 415–16; Freise (1984), 519–20. Note also the simultaneous promotion of the courtier Hucbert to the bishopric of Meaux and his memory of that time in Frankfurt, Airlie (2000a) 12–13.
58 Werner (1967), family tree.
59 *ARF*, a.759, p.16; *Annales Petaviani*, a.759, p.11; Werner (1975), 122–3; Becher (1992).
60 *AB*, a.854, trans. Nelson (1991a), 77; Kasten (1997), 387.
61 McDougall (2016), 72–86.
62 *AB*, a.853, trans. Nelson (1991a), 77. In a diploma of 855 Lothar I acknowledged her role in soliciting a grant from him and referred to her closeness to him, Dip. Lo. 1, no.138 and see also no.113 for her being freed by Lothar. She appears among the royal women at the meeting of kings at the abbey of Remiremont in 861, *Liber Memorialis von Remiremont*, fol. 43r, eds Hlawitschka, Schmid and Tellenbach, MGH Libri Memoriales, vol. 2, and Schmid (1968), 103.
63 Ermold, Book I, lines 78–85, p.10; Le Jan (1995), 193–4.
64 Le Jan (1995), 52–4, 180–223. See Chapter 9 for the introduction of Ottonian names into the Carolingian family; for names of Carolingian daughters, see Chapter 8.
65 Dhuoda, *LM*, Praefatio, I, 7, pp.84, 116; Wood (2001), 79, 94.
66 *Annales Petaviani*, a.759, p.11 and see n.54 above. Astronomer *VH*, c.3, c.37, pp.290, 422. Regino, *Chronicon*, a.880, p.116.
67 Regino, *Chronicon*, a.878, p.114.
68 Notker, *GK*, II, c.12, p.71, trans. Ganz (2008), 100–1.
69 Nelson (1994b), 95; Stafford (2001a), 263–4.
70 Dhuoda, *LM*, Praefatio, p.84, and I, 7, p.116; Smith (1995), 656–60.
71 Richildis: *AB*, a.876, a.877, trans. Nelson (1991a), 198–9; Kasten (1997), 455, 459, 462. Hildegard: Astronomer, *VH*, c.3, pp.288–90 though he makes a slip here: Jarnut (1984), 650–1.
72 *Codex Carolinus*, no.18 (759), pp.518–19, no.47, pp.565–6; for Lothar as Charles's godfather, Nithard, II, c.1, p.38; Lothar was at court from the summer of 823 until 824, Geiselhart (2002), 11.
73 'Karolus ad catezizandum vocitatus est', Flodoard, *Annales*, a.945, ed. P. Lauer, *Les Annales de Flodoard* (1905), pp.95–6; translated as 'named Charles for the purpose of instruction', in Fanning and Bachrach (2004), 41; this 'instruction' should be understood as part of the preparations for baptism. The father, king Louis IV, was not at Laon for the birth but returned there quickly, see Flodoard, *Annales*, a.945, p.96 and Lauer (1900), p.124. Cramer (1993), 143–4, 149–53.
74 Alcuin, *Vita Willibrordi*, c.23, ed. W. Levison, MGH SRM 7, pp.133–4; Fouracre (2000), 62.
75 *AF*, a.893, p.122; this annalist tells us that the bishops named the child but this can only refer to the baptism ceremony; the name had surely been chosen by the king when he had visited the queen shortly before she gave birth; Dip. LC, nos 4, 9 and 65. Offergeld (2001), 538–40.
76 Boso was godparent at the baptism of Charles the Bald's son Charles, *AB*, a.877, trans. Nelson (1991a), 199.
77 *AF*, a.893, p.122; Schieffer (1990b), 155.

78 Werner (1967), 418. On the Farfa Pippin, see Bullough (1970), 80.
79 Werner (1967) has a comprehensive family tree; some modifications are needed, for example, tree in Nelson (1992) and Hyam (1990).
80 Kasten (2002); Becher (2008b), 665–70; McDougall (2016), 77–84.
81 Regino, *Chronicon*, a.880, p.116; Poeta Saxo, Book V, lines 123–36, PLAC 4.1, p.58. Cf. Notker, *Continuatio Erchanberti Breviarium*, MGH SS 2, pp.329–30 and Notker, *GK*, II, c.14, p.78.
82 Le Jan (1995), 274–7.
83 Sources do tend to label the mothers of these sons as concubines. An example from the earlier period: Louis the Pious' son Arnulf, *Chronicon Moissacense*, a.817, MGH SS 1, p.312; Werner (1967), 443–4 and Le Jan (1995), 275. An example from the later period: Karlmann's son Arnulf, probably born around 850, Notker, *Continuatio Ercanberti*, MGH SS 2, p.330; this liaison did predate Karlmann's marriage, Goldberg (2006a), 264–7.
84 Charles the Fat: MacLean (2003a), 85, 130; Offergeld (2001), 467; sons of Charles the Bald: *AB* a.862, trans. Nelson (1991a), 99–100.
85 Notker, *GK*, II, c.14, p.78; *AB*, a.878, trans. Nelson (1991a), 214.
86 Einhard, *VK*, c.18, pp.22–3.
87 Theodulf, On the court, trans. Godman (1985a), 150, line 29.
88 Notker, *GK*, II, c.14, p.78; Notker's fairly positive view of Bernard (see also *GK*, II, c.12, p.74) contrasts with the hostility of other contemporaries, *AF*, a.885, p.103. MacLean (2003a), 129–34 and 219–20; Kasten (1997), 237, 378, 488 ff., 570 ff.
89 Notker, *GK*, II, c.14, p.78; the story about Pippin is discussed in Chapter 1 above.
90 Notker, *GK*, II, c.11, p.68; see also his *Continuatio Erchanberti*.
91 Notker, *GK*, II, c.14, p.78 and II, c.16, p.81; compare Regino on Arnulf and his ancestor Arnulf of Metz, n.81 above.
92 Sedulius, no.23, lines 5–6, MGH PLAC 3, p.189; Godman (1987), 157; Kasten (1997), 271; Offergeld (2001), 330.
93 Poet Saxo, p.58, lines 131–6; lines 141–8, at pp.58–9 and lines 415–16 and 420–1, p.65. Bischoff (1981a), 256; Penndorf (1974), 158–65; MacLean (2003a), 63; Becher (1996); Rembold (2013), 190–1.
94 Thegan, *GH*, c.1, pp.174–6.
95 Dhuoda, *LM*, III.4, p.148; Le Jan (1995), 56.
96 Poeta Saxo, Book V, lines 117–20, p.58, trans. adapted from Godman (1985a), 342; Becher (1992), 49. Note also the Poeta Saxo's knowledge of the resonance of the name of Arnulf, Book V, lines 123–48, pp.58–9.
97 Innes (2000b), 240–1 and see Chapter 9.
98 Ermold, Book IV, lines 2412–13, p.184; trans. Godman (1985a), 257; Nelson (1992), 80; De Jong (2009), 89–95.
99 'puerile decus', Ermold, Book IV, line 2412, p.184.
100 Astronomer, *VH*, c.59, pp.524–6; contrast the silence on the ancestral parallel in Nithard, I, c.6, p.26 and *AB*, a.838, trans. Nelson (1991a), 39; Werner (1967); Nelson (1992), 149–56.
101 *Annales Mosellani*, a.781, MGH SS 16, p.497. The boy may have been given his original name without being baptized, as baptism was a sacrament and could not be 'revised', Smith (1995), 657, unless the rules were bent for Charlemagne; on the annals, Collins (1998), 6.
102 Le Jan (1995), 203; Collins (1998), 69; Kasten (1997), 138, over-rates the pope's contribution.

103 Bullough (1965), 99, 134; Goffart (1986), 61; Henderson (1994), 255–6; McKitterick (2008), 332–3, who stresses the importance of Hildegard's presence.
104 *Annales Mosellani*, a.781, p.497; *ARF*, a.781, p.56; on Rotrud and Gisela, see Chapter 8.
105 Thegan *GH*, for example, c.36, p.222 and in his finale, c.57, p.252.
106 Schieffer (1990b), 155.
107 *Annales Petaviani*, a.747, a.751, a.759, MGH SS 1, p.11; *ARF*, a.759, p.16; Werner (1975). On Laon annals that mention the birth of Louis the Pious, see Löwe, Wattenbach and Levison (1973), 543 and Löwe, Wattenbach and Levison (1990), 893–4; on annalistic notice of Charles the Fat's birth, see MacLean (2003a), 84 n.8. See also the Weissemburg annals above.
108 Nelson (1994b), 106.
109 Alcuin, letter no.217, MGH Ep. KA 2, p.361.
110 Bayless (2000), 165–6, written for Pippin, probably when he was between thirteen and sixteen.
111 Hincmar, *De Ordine Palatii*.
112 '… ab infantia seu pueritia inter feminas conversatus', Lothar II at council of Aachen, April 862, MGH Concilia 4, p.75.
113 Frantzen (1998), 92; Nelson (2003), 45–6; Nelson (2004a).
114 Einhard, *VK*, c.19, pp.23–5; Innes (2003), 66–8; Duindam (2016), 68.
115 Freculf, letter to Judith, *Epistolae variorum*, no.14, in MGH Ep. KA 3, p.319; Allen (1996), 69, 70; McKitterick and Innes (1994), 212–13; De Jong (2000), 198–9.
116 Ermold, Book IV, lines 2238–365, pp.170–80, and see Charles's prominent position in the procession in Walahfrid, *De Imagine Tetrici*. Nelson (1992), 82–6.
117 Asser's confidence about Alfred's promisingly kingly beginnings is certainly retrospective, see Campbell (1986); on the fourteenth-century emperor Charles IV's view of his own royal beginnings as first-born, etc., see Borst (1996).
118 Notker, *GK*, II, c.10, p.66, trans. Ganz (2008), 97; Penndorf (1974), 155; Kasten (1997), 234–5.
119 Notker *GK*, I, c.34, p.47; MacLean (2003a), 221.
120 Goldberg (2006a), 265; Einhard, *VK*, c.18, c.19, pp.21–5.
121 Duindam (2016), 62–7.
122 *Lib. Pont.*, no.97 (Hadrian I), c.9, c.23, vol. 1, pp.488, 493; Airlie (2005), 97–8.
123 *Lib. Pont.*, no.97 (Hadrian I), c.28, c.31, vol. 1, pp.494, 495; Nelson (1998b), 181; Nelson (2004b), 104.
124 Einhard, *VK*, c.3, p.6.
125 Paul the Deacon, *Historia Langobardorum* I, c.23, c.24, pp.61–2; Le Jan (2000), 291, although she does not refer to this case.
126 Paul the Deacon, *Historia Langobardorum*, VI, c.53, p.183; Kasten (1997), 106; Diesenberger (2003); Bartlett (1994).
127 Le Jan (2000), 292–3; Althoff (1990), 77–84; Le Jan (1995), 77–81.
128 For example, Boso for the son of Charles the Bald, *AB*, a.877, trans. Nelson (1991a), 199; on Charles Martel and Willbrord as godfather for Pippin III, see above. For Charlemagne's son Pippin/Carloman, see above.
129 Smith (1992), 108–15; Louis the Pious and Danes at Ingelheim, Ermold, Book IV, lines 2238–89, pp.170–4; Louis the German and Slav princes, Airlie (2001).
130 *AB*, a.849, a.853, trans. Nelson (1991a), 68, 76; Nelson (1992), 156; Nelson (1995), 396.
131 Dhuoda, *LM*, VIII, 15, p.320; Theoderic does not appear to have been William's uncle, as scholars have often thought: Bouchard (2001), 139–40.

132 Regino, *Chronicon*, a.890, p.132; Kasten (1997), 547.
133 See Chapter 9.
134 Offergeld (2001), 642; Foot (2011), 46–7.
135 Kasten (1997), 107; Innes (2003), 62–3.
136 Paschasius Radbertus, *Vita Adalhardi*, c.7, PL 120, col.1511; Kasten (1986), 15; Kasten (1997), 242. Einhard, *VK*, c.19, p.23.
137 Kershaw (2007).
138 Einhard, *VK*, c.19, p.23.
139 BM, no. 841; Depreux (1997), 398.
140 Astronomer, *VH*, c.4, p.294, c.6, pp.302–4.
141 Einhard's reference to Charlemagne as his *nutritor* is warm, *VK*, Preface, p.1, and see Le Jan (1995), 343; on such terms, see Bullough (1962); Schieffer (1990b), 158; Offergeld (2001), 38 n. 121; Koziol (2012), 288.
142 Gerard: Charters of Charles of Provence, nos 1 and 9, in *Recueil Provence*; Louis the Child, Dip. LC, nos 4, 9, 65 and 66. Offergeld (2001), 332–4, 542–4; Airlie (2006c), 112.
143 Regino, *Chronicon*, a.883, p.121; Hlawitschka (1969), 367–8; Airlie (2011a).
144 *AB*, a.861, trans. Nelson (1991a), 96; Nelson (1992), 201, 205.
145 Regino, *Chronicon*, a.883, p.121.
146 Lupus, letter no.31, ed. Levillain, vol. 1, p.142; Nelson (1992), 129.
147 Goldberg (2006a), 33, 89; Nelson (1992), 97; Innes (2000a), 207.
148 *Epistolae Variorum*, no.2, MGH Ep KA 4, pp.131–2, with corrections in Werner (1990), 77 n.275; Nelson (1992), 97–9.
149 Nelson (1992), 97; Bernard: *AB*, a.879, trans. Nelson (1991a), 216.
150 Depreux (1997), 155–6.
151 Flodoard, *HRE*, II c.19, p.175; Council of Troyes, MGH Concilia 4, pp.239–41; Airlie (1990); Airlie (2000a) 12–13; De Jong (2009), 253.
152 Patzold (2008a), 232–5.
153 See Chapter 2 above for Pippin; Charles the Bald: Lupus, letter no.83, ed. Levillain, vol. 2, p.68, and Depreux (1997), 328–9.
154 *Epistolarum Fuldensium fragmenta*, MGH Ep. KA 3, p.517.
155 C. Manaresi, *I Placiti del 'Regnum Italiae'*, I (1955), no.45; Borgolte (1986), 46–8; Depreux (1997), 92–3.
156 Manaresi, *I Placiti del 'Regnum Italiae'*, I, no.45, pp.149–50, with suggested emendation in Borgolte (1986), 46; Balzaretti (2006), 17–26.
157 Le Jan (1995), 342; Stafford (2001a), 259, 264, 266–7.
158 Innes (2003); Airlie (2007a), 264.
159 Paschasius Radbertus, *Vita Adalhardi*, c.7, PL 120, col.1511; Kasten (1986), 15; Airlie (2004), 125.
160 Dhuoda, *LM*, III.9, p.170, III.8, p.166, '… cum commilitionibus infra aulam regalem'; Nelson (1994a), 62; Nelson (2007), 115–16. Asser, *Life of Alfred*, c.76.
161 *Gesta Aldrici*, c.2, ed. Weidemann, vol. 1, p.119; Depreux (1997), 97; Bullough (1985), 281.
162 Hincmar, *De ordine palatii*, c.v, ed. Gross and Schieffer, p.82; Innes (2003), 72–3.
163 *Gesta Aldrici*, c.2, ed. Weidemann, vol.1, p.119; *Gesta Episcoporum Autisiodorensium*, c.36, MGH SS 13, p.397; Depreux (1997), 97, 241.
164 Cubitt (2003).
165 Bullough (1984).
166 Letter of Pope Hadrian I, no.2, MGH Ep. KA 3, p.7.

167　Frothar, letter 6, ed. Parisse, p.100.
168　Stafford (2001a), 261; Bullough (1984), 89–90. Astronomer, *VH*, c.4, p.296, 'cum coaevis sibi pueris'.
169　McKitterick (1990), 326. Albuin: *AB* a.864, trans. Nelson (1991a), 112, and Regino, *Chronicon*, a.870, p.101, Kasten (1997), 436.
170　See letters of his kinsman abbot Theoto of Fulda, *Epistolarum Fuldensium Fragmenta*, MGH Ep. KA 3, p.532; Kasten (1997), 436 n.31.
171　Dhuoda, *LM*, III.8, p.166; Le Jan (1995), 342; Nelson (2003), 45; see Nelson (2007), 115, on this as Pauline term.
172　Airlie (2006a); Airlie (2000a); Airlie (2007a).
173　Dhuoda, *LM*, III.4, p.148, III.9, p.170, III.10, p.174. *AB*, a.848, a.850, trans. Nelson (1991a), 66, 69.
174　Einhard, *VK*, Preface, pp.1–2, trans. Ganz (2008), 17–18; Smith (2003); Patzold (2013).
175　'ei coeveus et connutritus', Astronomer, *VH*, Prologue, p.284; Airlie (2006a), 106–7.
176　Nelson (2004a), 194–5.
177　Bullough (1984); Bullough (1985), 285 and passim; McKitterick (2008), 137–213.
178　Depreux (1997), 22.
179　Nelson (1992); in general Kasten (1997); see, for example, *AB*, a.856, trans. Nelson (1991a), 81–2.
180　Kasten (1997), 436.
181　Dhuoda, *LM*, III.9, p.170. For general picture, Cubitt (2003).
182　Dhuoda, *LM*, Pref, p.84; Nelson (2007), 118–19; Nelson (2004a), 194–5.
183　Dhuoda, *LM*, III.8.34–62, pp.168–70.
184　Martindale (1977), 21; but NB Innes (2003), warning on the problems of evidence.

Chapter 5

1　*AF*, a.874, 81–2; Dutton (1994), 219–24; see Chapter 6.
2　For example, Godman and Collins (1990); Boshof (1996); Depreux (1997); Kölzer (2005); De Jong (2009); Booker (2009); Gravel (2011); Dip. Louis P.
3　*De Karolo rege et Leone papa*, lines 94–136, ed. F. Brunhölzl (1999), 16–18, and trans. Godman (1985a), 202–5; von Padberg (1999), 71–2, 77–9, but cf. McKitterick (2008), 141; Nelson (2001a), but see also McKiterrick (2008), 165–71.
4　Einhard, *VK*, cs.31, 32, 33, pp.34–41; Ermold, Book II, lines 810–17, p.64; Nelson (2000), 149–50.
5　Astronomer, *VH*, c.63, p.548.
6　Astronomer, *VH*, c.20, p.344; Martindale (1990), 125; Depreux (1994), 261; Nelson (2000), 149.
7　Einhard, *VK*, c.19, pp.24–5.
8　Nelson (1996a), 227.
9　Kasten (1986), 68–71, 103; Nelson (1996a), 236, 240; Fried (1998), 88–9; De Jong (2009), 20–1.
10　Nelson (1996a), 241.
11　Astronomer, *VH*, c.21, p.348, and p.349, n.281.
12　Nelson (1996a), 240; Nelson (2000), 146–9.
13　Louis: Astronomer, *VH*, c. 63, c.64, pp.546–54; Lothar II: *AB*, a.869, trans. Nelson (1991a), 156; Charles the Bald: *AB*, a.877, trans. Nelson (1991a), 202–3; Louis the

Stammerer, *AB*, a.879, trans. Nelson (1991a), 215–16; Louis II: Andreas of Bergamo, *Historia*, c.18, c.19, MGH Scr Lang., p.229; Nelson (2000) and Geary (2012).
14 Nelson (2000), 153–5 and below.
15 Nelson (2000), 166–9; Keller and Althoff (2008), 313–15.
16 Nithard, I, c.2, p.6; Nelson (1996a), 239–40; Nelson (1998b), 184–5; Costambeys, Innes and MacLean (2011), 196.
17 Astronomer, *VH*, c.21, pp.348–50.
18 Nelson (2000), 147.
19 De Jong (2009), 20.
20 *ARF*, a.813, p.138; Einhard, *VK*, c.30, p.34; *ARF*, a.806, p.121; Ermold, Book II, ed. Faral, lines 681–97, p.54. Innes and McKitterick (1994), 206–7, though I disagree on their dating of *VK*.
21 Ermold, Book II, lines 672–3, p.52; trans. Noble (2009), p.143.
22 Capitulary no. 45, prologue, MGH Cap.1, pp.126–7.
23 *Chronicon Moissiacense*, a.813, MGH SS 2, 259; Buc (2000), 205.
24 *Chronicon Moissiacense*, a.814, MGH SS 2, 259; Buc (2000), 206. Astronomer, *VH*, c.20, p.344.
25 Thegan, *GH*, c.6, pp.182–4; *Episcoporum de poenitentia, quam Hludowicus imperator professus est, relatio Compendiensis*, Capitulary no.197, c.1, MGH Cap.2, p.54, trans. De Jong (2009), 275; *Chronicon Moissiacense*, a.813, MGH SS 2, 259, and Buc (2000), 205 with Buc (2001b), 197–8; cf. *ARF*, a.813, p.138 and *Chronicon Laurissense breve*, ed. Carolsfeld, 36, 38.
26 Dip. Karol. 1, nos 174, 179, 187, 202, 208, 209, 217.
27 Buc (2001b), 197–8.
28 Wendling (1985).
29 Depreux (1997), 42–6; Airlie (2006a), 100–7.
30 Depreux (1994), 261–2; McCormick (2001), 479; Gravel (2012a), 87.
31 *Planctus de obitu Karoli*, ed. Dümmler, MGH PLAC 1, pp.435–6. *Translatio S. Viti*, c.III, ed. I. Schmale-Ott (1979), 38; Kasten (1986), 45; Depreux (1994), 263.
32 Depreux (1994), 267.
33 Astronomer, *VH*, c.21, p.346 and Depreux (1997), 383–4; contrast Brunner (1979), 96 and De Jong (2009), 20; for 774: McCormick (1986), 358; Theodulf, poems nos 37, 39, 70, 76, 77, ed. E. Dümmler, MGH PLAC 1, pp.529, 531, 560, 577–8, and McCormick (1986), 365 n.163, 371–2.
34 Ermold, Book II, lines 770–89, pp.60–2; trans. Noble (2009), 145; Depreux (1997), 420.
35 Astronomer, *VH*, c.21, p.346 and cf. c.63, p.548 (message to Lothar) and Nithard, II, c.1, p.36.
36 Nithard, I, c.2, p.6.
37 See maps in Périn and Feffer (1985), 446–53; Atsma (1989); Depreux (1997), 272–3. On St-Denis, Oexle (1978), 15–34, 103–19 and Bullough (1962); Stephen: Hennebicque-Le Jan (1989), 264 and Le Jan (1995), 250; Airlie (2005), 93.
38 Nelson (2000), 141–2; Le Jan (1995), 250; guiding visitors: Hincmar, *De villa Novilliaco*, ed. H. Mordek; Louis' letter to Hilduin (835), no.19, MGH Ep KA 3, pp.325–7.
39 Astronomer, *VH*, c.21, pp.346–8; Nelson (1996a), 240.
40 Joris (1973).
41 *ARF*, a.814, 140; Ermold, Book I, lines 802–21, pp.62–4; Astronomer, *VH*, c.21, c.22, pp.348–52; see BM 519i.

42 Nelson (2000), 149–50; McKitterick (2008), 158; Gravel (2012a), 60–1.
43 Astronomer, *VH*, c.23, p.352; Nithard, I, c.2, p.6. Kasten (1986), 102–5; Nelson (1996a), 240–2; Nelson (1998b), 189–91; Depreux (1997), 390–1; De Jong (2009), 190–3.
44 Depreux (1997), 246–7, 287–8.
45 Depreux (1997), 120–9; Airlie (2006a), 100–9; De Jong (2009), 21–2.
46 Depreux (1997): survivors: Adalung, 84–6; Albgarius, 92–3; Aldric (I), 94–6; Aldric (II), 97–9; Ansegis, 104–6; Arduin, 109; Bernarius, 133–4; Bernard(I), 134–7; Bonifrid, 144–5; Cadola, 149–50; Clemens, 155–6; Drogo, 163–7; Einhard, 177–82; Fridugisus, 199–203; Gerold (I), 210–11; Hasitulf, 229–30; Heito, 234–5; Hildebrand, 248; Hitto, 260–1; Hugh (I), 262–4; Hugh (II), 264–8; Hunfrid, 268; Ibbo, 269; Ingobert, 271–2; Johannes, 274–5; Jeremy, 275–6; Paul, 341; Rampo, 355–6; Ratold, 358–60; Robert (I), 366–7; Sicardus (I), 374; Theoderic, 382–3; Theodulf, 383–5; Theotharius, 385; Willibert, 398. Losers (or discounted as possibly being with Louis before 814): Adalhard (I), 76–9; Warnarius, 206; Gauzhelm, 207; Hildebold, 246–7; Leidrad, 287–8; Lambert, 288–91; Leo, 293–6.
47 Depreux (1997), 410–11.
48 Astronomer, *VH*, c.21, pp.346–8 and cf. Einhard, *VK*, c.19, pp.24–5; Heito, *Visio Wettini*, c.11, ed. Dümmler, MGH PLAC 2 (1884), 271; Walahfrid, *Visio Wettini*, lines 446–65, ed. Dümmler, MGH PLAC 2 (1884), 317–18; Nelson (2000), 148.
49 *ARF*, a.814, 141; Kasten (1997), 165–8; Depreux (1997), 298–300, 341–2.
50 Godman and Collins (1990); Gravel (2011).
51 Reuter (2006), 231–67; Costambeys, Innes and MacLean (2011), 154–60.
52 See, for example, *Admonitio ad omnes regni ordines*, MGH Cap.1, no.150, pp.303–7; Mersiowsky (1996); Airlie (2009a); Patzold (2008a), 140–6; De Jong (2009).
53 *ARF*, a.817, p.146; Goldberg (2013).
54 Kasten (1997), 165–74.
55 Capitulary of Charlemagne, c.2, eds Mordek and Schmitz (1987), pp.399–400, and also Mordek (1995a), no.12, pp.981–9; Council of Mainz, c.5, MGH Concilia 2.1, p.261; Fried (1998), 73, 82–3. *Ordinatio Imperii*, prologue, MGH Cap.1, pp.270–1; Agobard, *De Divisione Imperii*, c.4, ed. van Acker (1981), p.248; Erkens (1996), 447, 483; Patzold (2006a), 57–62; Kaschke (2006), 325–7; De Jong (2009), 23–4.
56 *Ordinatio Imperii*, prologue, MGH Cap.1, p.271; *Chronicon Moissiacense*, a.817, MGH SS I, p.312; Agobard, *De Divisione Imperii*, c.4, p.248; Ganshof (1971), 276; De Jong (2009), 145.
57 *ARF*, a.821, 155, 156; Kasten (1997), 182; Kaschke (2006), 325–6.
58 Dip. Louis P., nos 124 (Alemannia), 129 (Cruas), 126 (Tours).
59 Einhard, *VK*, c.33, p.37; *Ordinatio Imperii*, cs 14, 15, 18, MGH Cap.1, no.136, 272–3; *Chronicon Moissiacense*, a.817, MGH SS 1, 312; Kasten (1997), 175–6; Kasten (2002), 32–8; Kaschke (2006), 343; Depreux (1997), 416–17.
60 *Ordinatio Imperii*, c.16, MGH Cap.1, p.273; Kasten (1997), 257–9; Goldberg (2006a), 27–32.
61 Theodulf, poem 34, MGH PLAC 1, 526; *Divisio Regni*, c.5, MGH Cap.1, p.128; *Ordinatio Imperii*, prologue, c. 14, MGH Cap.1, pp.270, 272–3; Godman (1985b), 246–8; Kasten (1997), 159, 180–2; Kaschke (2006), 344–5.
62 Ermold, Book II, lines 668–9, and lines 1092–111, pp.52, 84–6; *Divisio regni*, prologue, MGH Cap.1, p.127; Einhard, *VK*, cs 18, 19, pp.21–5; Leyser (1979), 86.
63 *Recueil Aquitaine*, no.14 and see also no.17 (a.831, refers to *liberis*); Dip. Lothar I, no.6; Dip. Louis G., no.20.

64 Dip. Louis P., no.94; Depreux (1997), 376–7.
65 Thegan, *GH*, c.21, p.210.
66 Kaschke (2006), 324–53.
67 *Ordinatio imperii*, c.9, MGH Cap.1, p.272. Smaragdus, *Via regia*, c.22, PL 102, col. 961; Kaschke (2006), 353; Bovendeert (2006).
68 Kasten (1997), 170–5; Kaschke (2006), 331–3.
69 *Ordinatio Imperii*, prologue, MGH Cap.1, no.136, p.270; Patzold (2006a); Kaschke (2006), 325–6; De Jong (2009), 27.
70 Agobard, *De divsione imperii*, ed. van Acker, p.249; Airlie (2010), 178–9; Patzold (2006a), 62–4.
71 Kasten (1986), 85–91, 100–3; Werner (1990), 36–48; Depreux (1992), 13.
72 *ARF*, a.814, p.141; Innes (1997), 846–7. *Formulae Imperiales*, no.8, ed. K. Zeumer, MGH Formulae, p.293; Kasten (1997), 166; Depreux (1992), 9.
73 Kasten (1986), 68–9; cf. Depreux (1992), 11–12.
74 Thegan, *GH*, c.12, p.192; Depreux (1992). Contrast Kasten (1997), 166–7 and Innes (1997), 846. Capitularies: Kasten (1986), 72; Mordek (1995b), 1005; Wormald (1999), 67.
75 *Translatio S. Viti*, c.III, ed. Schmale-Ott, p.38; Kasten (1997), 250.
76 Cunegonde's will is in *Codice Diplomatico Parmense*, ed. U. Bassi (Parma 1910), no.II, pp.101–6; La Rocca (2002), 511–12; Nelson (2001a), 227 n.47.
77 Hincmar, *De ordine palatii*, c.v, eds T. Gross and R. Schieffer (1980), MGH Fontes Iuris Germanici, 72–4; Kasten (1986), 79; cf. Nelson (2001a), 227; Settipani (1993), 213–14; Bougard (2006), 386–7.
78 Pippin appears as her son in her will, as at n.76 above, ed. Bassi, p.103; see also Regino, *Chron.*, a.818, p.73; Depreux (1997), 413–14; Settipani (1993), 214.
79 *ARF*, a.815, p.142; *Chronicle of Moissac*, ed. in Buc (2000), 206–7; *Chronicon Laurissense breve*, p.32; Innes (1997), 847 n.1.
80 Depreux (1992), 16–21.
81 Capitulary no.172, MGH Cap.1, pp.352–5; Boshof (1996), 139–41.
82 *Ordinatio Imperii*, c.17, MGH Cap.1, p.273, trans. Dutton (2004), 202; Jarnut (1990), 350; Depreux (1992), 15; Innes (1997), 847.
83 *Chronicle of Moissac*, ed. Buc (2000), 208; Jarnut (1989), 640; Depreux (1992), 14–15.
84 *Chronicle of Moissac*, ed. Buc (2000), 208; Thegan, *GH*, c.22, pp.210–12.
85 *ARF*, a.817, p.147.
86 Jarnut (1989), 640–4; Innes (1997), 847.
87 Letter of Archbishop Hetti of Trier to Bishop Frothar of Toul, Ep. no.2, MGH EpV Ep KA III, pp.277–8 and in Parisse (1998), 136–7; *ARF*, a.817, pp.147–8; Werner (1990), 35–7, and see Chapter 3 above.
88 *ARF*, a.817, 148; Astronomer, *VH*, c.29, pp.382–4; on Isimgrim and Amingus, see below.
89 Dip. Louis P., no.138; Sprandel (1958), 52; Borgolte (1984a), 225, 254.
90 *UB St Gallen*, no.191; Schmid (1976/1983); Borgolte (1986), 206–9.
91 Borgolte (1984a), 227–8.
92 *Translatio Sanguinis Domini*, c.15, c.16, MGH SS 4, p.448; Borgolte (1984a), 221–9; Wolfram (1995a), 143–6; Jarnut (1989), 645 n.40 dismisses this source.
93 Astronomer, *VH*, c.29, p.382; Fleckenstein (1959), 65; Hlawitschka (1960), 292 n.2.
94 *ARF*, a.817, pp.147–8; Thegan, *GH*, c.22, p.212; Astronomer, *VH*, c.29, pp.382–4; Airlie (1998a), 132–3; Depreux (1997), 325–6, 419–20; McKitterick (2004), 117.
95 Capture: *Chronicle of Moissac*, a.817, ed. Buc (2000), 208 and see also Werner (1990), 44 n.142; surrender: *ARF*, a.817, pp.147–8 echoed by later sources, Thegan, *GH*, c.22, p.210; Astronomer, *VH*, c.29, p.382.

96 Thegan, *GH*, c.22, p.210.
97 *Chronicon Moissiacense*, a.817, MGH SS 1, pp.312–13; Thegan, *GH*, c.22, c.24, pp.210–12, 214; Nithard, I, c.3, p.8. Depreux (1997), 384.
98 Fulda: *Epistolarum Fuldensium Fragmenta*, MGH Ep. KA 3, p.517; *Divisio regnorum*, c.18, MGH Cap.1, pp.129–30; *Episcoporum Relatio*, c.1, MGH Cap.2, p.54; Thegan, *GH*, c.6, p.182.
99 Contemporary developments in Italy and Byzantium were also relevant: Werner (1990), 43; Bührer-Thierry (1998), 79–86; Nelson (2009), 20–1.
100 Depreux (1997), 136; *Divisio Regnorum*, c.18, MGH Cap.1, pp.129–30.
101 *ARF*, a.818, p.148; *Chronicle of Moissac*, a.817, ed. Buc (2000), 208; Thegan, *GH*, c.22, p.212; Astronomer, *VH*, c.30, p.384.
102 Astronomer, *VH*, c.30, p.386; Werner (1990), 46, and see *Chronicle of Moissac*, a.817, ed. Buc (2000), 208.
103 *AB*, a. 834, trans. Nelson (1991a), 30; Nithard, II, c.3, p.44; Depreux (1997), 413–14.
104 *ARF*, a.821, 822, pp.154–9; Thegan, *GH*, c.23, p.214; Astronomer, *VH*, cs 34, 35 pp.402–6; *Formulae Imperiales*, no.8, MGH Formulae, p.293; Borgolte (1986), 140; De Jong (2009), 35–6, 122–31.
105 Airlie (2003a); Eichler (2007), 86–106. *Episcoporum relatio*, c.1, MGH Cap.2, p.54; Booker (2009), 169–70; De Jong (2009), 122–31, 238–9.
106 Text in Houben (1976), 41–2; Dutton (1994), 70–4.
107 Costambeys, Innes and Maclean (2011), 205–6.
108 Ward (1990a); Nelson (1992), 87–8; Hummer (2005), 160–3; De Jong (2009), 41; Costambeys, Innes and MacLean (2011), 214, 217–19; Contrast Boshof (1996), 178–80.
109 Nithard, I, c.10, p.10; Zotz (1997a), 1490; Kasten (1997), 187.
110 *Annales Weissenburgenses*, a.829, in Hofmeister (1919), 419; Hummer (2005), 162–3; contrast Zotz (1997a), 1491 and NB a later echo of this in Charles the Fat being made *rector* of Alemannia by his father Louis the German, MacLean (2003a), 84–5.
111 Ermold, Book IV, ed. Faral, lines 2300–1, 2397–415, pp.176, 182–4; Nelson (1992), 78–80.
112 Goldberg (2006a), 55–6.
113 Walahfrid, *De Imagine Tetrici*, text and translation in Herren (1991), 125–8, 134–7; Nelson (1992), 86–7; Goldberg (2006a), 57; Costambeys, Innes and MacLean (2011), 217.
114 *Epistolae variorum*, no.14, MGH Ep KA 3, p.319; M. Allen, edition of Freculf, pp.16*–17*, and see Chapter 4 above. De Jong (2009), 68–9, 130–1.
115 See Chapter 4 above on children; on Lothar as godfather, Astronomer, *VH*, c.60, 530 and Nithard, II, c.2, p.38.
116 Depreux (1994), 352; Ermold, Book IV, ed. Faral, lines 2300–7, p.176.
117 830: *UB St Gallen*, no.330; 829: *UB St Gallen*, no.326 (issued at Worms); McKitterick (1989), 96, 113; Zotz (1997a), 1492. Here I differ from Hummer (2005), 162.
118 Agobard, *De divisione imperii*, ed. van Acker, p.249; Patzold (2006a), 62–4; Booker (2009), 149; for date of text, 829–30, pre-revolt, De Jong (2009), 145. See also Paschasius Radbertus, *Epitaphium Arsenii*, II, c.17, ed. Dümmler.
119 Wormald (1999), 33; Münsch (2001), 11–12; Geiselhart (2002), 26.
120 Walahfrid, Poem no.64 and no.63, MGH PLAC 2, pp.405–6; Walahfrid, *De Imagine Tetrici*, ed. Herren; Godman (1987), 154; Zotz (1997a), 1493. Thegan, *GH*, passim.
121 Nelson (1992), 87; Zotz (1997a); Hummer (2005), 157–65; Goldberg (2006a), 60, but this to be modified in light of Pokorny (2010), 41–3.

122 Council of Paris, MGH Concilia 2.2, no.50, II, c.25, pp.678–9, and II, c.5 on ancestors, p.655; Worms: *Episcoporum ad Hludowicum imperatorem Relatio*, c.60, MGH Cap.2, no.196, pp.49–50; Anton (1968), 209; on Worms text, Patzold (2008a), 166–7 and De Jong (2009), 176 with Lukas (2002a), 539–41 on the manuscript, and see also Lukas (2002b), 68. On the Paris statement on ancestors, office and God, see Chapter 1 above. Walahfrid, *De Imagine Tetrici*, ed. Herren, line 140, p.127 and 135.
123 Council of Paris, I, c.5, MGH Concilia 2.2, no.50, pp.612–13.
124 Agobard, *De divisione imperii*, c.3, c.4, ed. van Acker, p.248; Boshof (1996), 180; De Jong (2009), 145–6.
125 Thegan, *GH*, c.35, p.220; Nithard, I, c.3, p.10.
126 *ARF*, a.827, a.828, pp.172–5; Einhard, *Translatio et miracula sanctorum Marcellini et Petri*, ed. G. Waitz, III, c.14, MGH SS 15, p.253, trans. Dutton (1998), 104. Key texts on the councils: *Constitutio de synodis anno 829. In regno Francorum habitis*, no.50.A, MGH Concilia 2.2, pp.596–7; *Hludowici et Hlotharii Epistola Generalis*, no. 50.B, MGH Concilia 2.2, pp.597–601; Council of Paris, no.50.D, MGH Concilia 2.2, pp.605–80; *Episcoporum ad Hludowicum imperatorem Relatio*, c.60, MGH Cap.2, no.196, pp.26–51. Ganz (2000); Ganz (2007), 43; Patzold (2008a), 135–84; De Jong (2009), 38–40, 148–84; Booker (2009), 232–3.
127 Thegan, *GH*, c.28, p.216; Costambeys, Innes and MacLean (2011), 213–14.
128 *ARF*, a.829, p.177; Agobard, *De divisione imperii*, ed. van Acker, p.249; Depreux (1997), 308–9; Patzold (2006a), 62–4; De Jong (2009), 41; Costambeys, Innes and MacLean (2011), 214–18.
129 Ward (1990b).
130 *AB*, a.832, trans. Nelson (1991a), 25; Thegan, *GH*, c.55, p.250; Depreux (1994), 362–6.
131 Agobard, *De Inusticiis (Ad Matfredum)*, ed. van Acker, pp.225–7; *Capitulare missorum* (829) c.3, MGH Cap.2, no.188, p.10; Depreux (1994), 362; Airlie (2006a), 109–10; De Jong (2009), 144.
132 Ermold, Book 3, lines 1530–1, pp.116–18; Boso: *AB*, a.878, trans. Nelson (1991a), 212. Ermold, Book 4, lines 2294–306, p.176. Depreux (1994), 344–5; Dutton and Kessler (1997), 73–9.
133 Depreux (1997), 137–8, 191; Airlie (2000a), 8–9; Innes (2000a), 198.
134 Hennebicque (1981), 302–5, 312–13; Le Jan (1995), 212–13, 291, 315, 318, 410; Werner (1997), 21.
135 *Cod Dip Fuld.*, nos 395, 429; Levillain (1941), 196; Gockel (1970), 245–6; Hennebicque (1981), 313; Airlie (2000a), 8–9. Adrevald of Fleury, *Miracula S. Benedicti*, c.20, MGH SS 15, pp.487–8; Werner (1997), 23; Airlie (1995), 443–8.
136 Astronomer, *VH*, c.44, c.45, pp.456, 460.
137 *AB*, a.834, trans. Nelson (1991a), 30; Astronomer, *VH*, c.52, pp.492–4; Nithard, I, c.5, pp.20–2; Adrevald, *Miracula S. Benedicti*, c.20, c.21, pp.487–9.
138 Smith (1992); Brunterc'h (1989), 51–74.
139 *AB*, a.834, trans. Nelson (1991a), 30–1; Thegan, *GH*, c.52, p.244; Astronomer, *VH*, c.52, pp.494–6; Nithard, I, c.5, pp.20–2; Dhuoda, *LM*, l, X.4 and X.5, pp.348–50, 354, with Innes (2008), 250–1, and Le Jan (2010), 215–19. Booker (2009), 152–3; De Jong (2009), 200–5.
140 Adrevald, *Miracula S. Benedicti*, c.20, p.487; Werner (1997), 23; Innes (2000a), 198–210; Innes (2008), 264 and passim.
141 Astronomer, *VH*, cs 43, 44, pp.452–4; Radbertus, *Epitaphium Arsenii*, II, cs 7–9; Hofstadter (1964).

142 Agobard, *De Divisione Imperii*, ed. van Acker, 247–50; De Jong (2009), 145–6, 200–1; Airlie (2010).
143 Thegan, *GH*, c.36, c.52, pp.222, 244. *Liber Historiae Francorum* c.45, ed. B. Krusch, MGH SRM 2, p.318, trans. Fouracre and Gerberding (1996), 90, with commentary 21–3; Wood (2004a), 19–20, 29–30; Hartmann (2012), 33–5; Robb (2010), 406.
144 Dip. Louis P., no.283; Depreux (1997), 138–9; Kölzer (2005), 24–5.
145 Hincmar's bleak view of the long dead Bernard: *AB*, a.864, trans. Nelson (1991a), 119. Wallace-Hadrill (1981), 47–8; *Gesta Dagoberti*, c.5, c.6, ed. Krusch, MGH SRM 2, pp.402–3; Levillain (1921), 103–9; Wood (1994), 148; Diesenberger (2003), 202–4.
146 Radbertus, *Epitaphium Arsenii*, II, cs 8, 9, 10, p.72; Agobard, *Liber Apologeticus*, I, c.4, ed. van Acker, p.311. Booker (2009), 151–2; De Jong (2009), 196–7.
147 Thegan, *GH*, c.36, p.222; Nithard, I, c.3, p.10; Radbertus, *Epitaphium Arsenii*, II, cs 7, 8; Depreux (1997), 138–9; De Jong (2009), 199–200.
148 *ARF* (rev.) a.792, pp.91–3; *Annales Laureshamenses*, a.792, ed. G.H. Pertz, MGH SS 1, p.36; Radbertus, *Epitaphium Arsenii*, I, c.6,; Leyser (1994), 57.
149 *AB*, a.830, trans. Nelson (1991a), 21–2; *AMP*, a. 830, pp.95–6; Astronomer, *VH*, c.44, pp.454–6; Boshof (1996), 182–4; Patzold (2006a), 71–2; Booker (2009), 26–9; De Jong (2009), 85–7, 152–3.
150 Astronomer, *VH*, c.44, p.456; Kasten (1997), 204–5.
151 *AB*, a.830, trans. Nelson (1991a), 21–2; Astronomer, *VH*, cs 44, 45, pp.456, 460.
152 Depreux (1997), 309–10, 346.
153 Einhard, letter 11, ed. K. Hampe, MGH KA 3, pp.114–15, and trans. Dutton (1998), 145–7; Kasten (1997), 228–9.
154 Thegan, *GH*, c.36, p.222; Astronomer, *VH*, c.44, pp.456–8; Nithard, I, c.3, p.10; Kasten (1997), 204.
155 Thegan, *GH*, c.36, pp.220–2; and Nithard, I, c.3, p.10.
156 Astronomer, *VH*, c.45, c.46, 460–6; *AB*, a. 830, a.831, trans. Nelson (1991a), 22–4.
157 Booker (2009), 129–82; De Jong (2009).
158 Buc (2001a); Buc (2001b); MacLean (2006).
159 De Jong (1992); De Jong (2009), 34–6, 122–31.
160 Thegan, *GH*, c.38, p.224; Astronomer, *VH*, c. 45, pp.460–2; c.49, p.480; c.51, pp.488–90; c.54, 500; *AB*, a. 834, a.835, trans. Nelson (1991a), 29–33. Booker (2009), 34–9, 186–7; De Jong (2009), 209–13, 249–50.
161 De Jong (2009), 217–59; Booker (2009), 91–4, 129–82.
162 Astronomer, *VH*, c.51, p.486.
163 *AB*, a.831, trans. Nelson (1991a), p.23; *AMP*, a.830, pp.97–8; De Jong (2009), 211–12.
164 *AB*, a.831, trans. Nelson, 23; Nithard, I, 4, pp.18–20 on 833–4 but this must refer to events of 831.
165 Thegan, *GH* c. 37, p.224; De Jong (2004); De Jong (2009), 195–203, 229–30.
166 Agobard, *Liber Apologeticus*, I, c.2, pp.309–10; c.5, p.311, and II c.3, p.316; De Jong (2009), 211–12. Thegan, *GH*, c.36, p.222.
167 Thegan, *GH*, c.38, p.224; Astronomer, *VH*, c.46, p.466; less detail in *AB*, a. 831, trans. Nelson (1991a), 22–3; *Ann Xant.*, a.830, a.831, pp.7–8.
168 Astronomer, *VH*, c.47, p.470.
169 *AB*, a.831, trans. Nelson (1991a), 22; cf. Astronomer, *VH*, c.45, p.461; Nithard, I, 3, p.12.
170 Astronomer, *VH*, c.46, pp.464–6.
171 Walahfrid, Poem no. 38, MGH PLAC 2, 388–90, trans. Godman (1985a), 216–21; Dutton (1994), 104–5, 146.

172 *AB*, a.832, trans. Nelson (1991a), 24; Astronomer, *VH*, c.46, p.468 and c.47, p.470 and see Chapter 6 on sons of Louis the German.
173 *Regni Divisio*, MGH Cap.2, no.194, pp.20–4; Mordek (1995a), 834–5; Boshof (1996), 187–8; Kasten (1997), 191–2; Kaschke (2006), 354–67; Hägermann (2008); Goldberg (2006a), 61–2. Assemblies in 831: Eichler (2007), 112.
174 *Divisio Regnorum* (806), c.15, MGH Cap.1, p.129; *Regni Divisio* (831), c.11, MGH Cap.2, p.23.
175 *Regni Divisio* (831), c.1, MGH Cap.2, p.21; contrast with *Divisio Regnorum* (806), c.4, MGH Cap.1, p.127 which does go into detail; and contrast also with 817's *Ordinatio Imperii*, c.14, MGH Cap.1, p.272 which forbids further division. 831's *Regni Divisio*, c.4, MGH Cap.2, p.22 is an amplification of 806's *Divisio Regnorum*, c.8, MGH Cap.1, p.128; 831's *Regni Divisio*, c.2 and c.3, MGH Cap.2, p.22 repeat 806's *Divisio Regnorum*, c.7 and c.8, MGH Cap.1, p.128 on not invading another kingdom etc., but such clauses would now sound more urgently in the aftermath of 830.
176 *Regni Divisio* (831), c.13, MGH Cap.2, p.23; Kasten (1997), 191–2; Hägermann (2008), 297–8; cf. Kaschke (2006), 361–2, 36–7.
177 *AB*, a.831, a.832, trans. Nelson (1991a), 22–6; Thegan, *GH*, c.41, pp.226–8, Astronomer, *VH*, c.47, pp.468–72; Nithard, I, c.4, p.14; *Cod. Lorsch*, nos 2050 and 3512. Collins (1990), 383–5; Nelson (1992), 90–1; Innes (2000a), 198–9; Goldberg (2006a), 66–8; De Jong (2009), 44–6.
178 Depreux (1998), 227; Eichler (2007), 74, 112.
179 Einhard, letters nos 20, 21, 22, MGH Ep. KA 3, pp.120–1; Innes (2000a), 198–9.
180 Astronomer, *VH*, c. 47, p.470; *AB*, a.834, trans. Nelson (1991a), 24.
181 Booker (2009) and De Jong (2009), from a large literature.
182 Depreux (1997): Adalbert, 69–72; Adalgarius, 73–4; Adalhard (III), 80–2; Adalung, 84–6; Adrevald, 88–90; Aldric (II), 97–9; Ansfrid, 106–7; Badurad, 116–18; Berengar (I), 131–2; Bernard (II), 137–9; Bernold, 140–1; Boniface, 143–4; Boso (II), 148; Burgarit, 148; Charles the Bald, 150–3; Conrad, 156–7; Donatus, 160–2; Ebbo, 169–74; Ebroin, 174–6; Einhard, 177–82; Erchanrad, 185–6; Odo (II), 191; Fulco, 194–6; Freculf, 197–8; Gauzhelm, 207; Gebhard, 208; Guntbald, 218–20; Grimald, 221–2; Wido, 223–4; William (II), 225–6; Helisachar, 235–40; Heribald, 241–2; Heribert, 242; Hetti, 244–6; Hildi, 249–50; Hilduin, 250–6; Hincmar, 257–8; Hitto, 260–1; Hucbert, 261–2; Hugh (I), 262–4; Jonas, 276–7; Judith, 279–86; Lambert, 288–91; Landramnus, 292; Leo, 293–6; Lothar I, 298–314; Louis the German, 315–22; Marcward, 327–9; Matfrid, 329–31; Meginarius, 332–3; Modoinus, 333–4; Nominoe, 335–7; Otgar, 339–40; Pippin I of Aquitaine, 341–8; Prudentius, 349–50; Hraban Maur, 350–2; Rudolf, 358; Ratold, 358–60; Richard (III), 363–5; Richuin (II), 366; Robert (I), 366–7; Rorigo, 368–9; Rothad (II), 371; Ruadbern, 371–2; Theoto, 387–8; Wala, 390–3; Walahfrid, 393–4; Warin (I), 394–6; Warin (II), 396–7.
183 Depreux (1997): Adalhard (I), 79; Adalhard (II), 80; Adaloch, 82–3; Alcuin 93–4; Arnoldus, 110; Atto, 114–15; Bego, 120–2; Benedict, 129; Bernarius, 134; Bernard of Italy, 134; Borna, 147; Cadola, 149–50; Choslus, 153–4; Claudius, 154–5; Dado, 157; Erlaldus, 186–7; Irmingard, 188–9; Warnarius, 206; William (I), 224–5; Haistulf, 229–30; Halitgarius, 231; Hildebold, 247; Immo, 269; Jeremy, 276; Lupus Santio, 323; Mauringus, 331; Odlio, 338; Smaragdus, 378; Theodulf, 385; Theuthardus, 386–7.
184 Depreux (1997), 406–11.
185 Paschasius, *Epitaphium Arsenii*, II, c.14, c.16, ed. Dümmler, p.84; Weinrich (1963), 79–80. Einhard, Letters, nos 13, 14, 15, 16, 17, 18, 25, 27, 28, 29, MGH Ep. KA 3, pp.116–19, 122, 123–4; Kasten (1997), 308–9; Innes (2000a), 200.

186 *Cartulaire de Redon*, ed. de Courson (1863), no.6, no.23 and see also no.2; Smith (1992), 81–2; Depreux (1997), 336.
187 *Episcoporum de poenitentia, quam Hludowicus imperator professus est, relatio Compendiensis*, MGH Cap.2, no.197, c.8, p.55; Agobard, *Cartula de Ludovici imperatoris poenitentia*, ed. van Acker, 323–4; *AB*, a.835, trans. Nelson (1991a), 32. Patzold (2006b), 349; Booker (2009), 129–82; De Jong (2009), 234–59.
188 Booker (2005); Booker (2008); Booker (2009), 91–4. Synod of Soissons, 853, no.27 in MGH Concilia 3, p.292.
189 *AB*, a.834, trans. Nelson (1991a), 31; Astronomer, *VH*, c.49, p.482; Thegan, *GH*, c.52, p.244.
190 Kölzer (2005), 21; Goldberg (2006a), 72–4. For Lothar I's changes, see Depreux (1997), 314, though Pippin of Aquitaine remained formally under his father's authority, Depreux (1997), 345–6.
191 Kasten (1997), 214–15.
192 Hraban, letter no.15, c. 1, c.9, c.12, MGH Ep. KA 3, pp.404–5, 412–15; Innes (2000a), 201; Patzold (2008a), 192–3; De Jong (2015), 92–4.
193 Hraban, letter no.15, c.11, c.12, MGH Ep. KA 3, pp.413–14; Einhard: letter no.11, MGH Ep KA 3, pp.114–15, trans. Dutton (1998), 145–6 with Kasten (1997), 228 for date as start of 830. Jonas: letter to Pippin accompanying his text of *De Institutione regia*, ed. Dubreucq (1995), 162, citing Exodus 20:12 and Ecclesiasticus 3:14, both cited in Hraban, letter no.15, c.1, MGH Ep. KA 3, pp.404, 405.
194 Hraban, letter no.16, MGH Ep KA 3, pp.416–20; De Jong (2000), 206–7 on other relevant texts by Hraban. Thegan, *GH*, c.53, p.246; Tremp, Introduction to his edition of Thegan, *GH*, p.10.
195 Council of Aachen, MGH Concilia 2.2, no.56, c.53, pp.720–1.
196 Wilmart (1933), 219–32, on Paris BNF nouv. acq lat. 1632; Anton (1968), 221–31, especially pp.224 and 230; Anton (1979), 79; Dubreucq, Introduction to Jonas, *De Institutione regia*, 121–3, especially p.123.
197 Wilmart (1933), 224 (dossier, cap. xx on folio 86, from Pseudo-Cyprian); it is also in the earlier part of the dossier, fols 72–8, Wilmart (1933); Anton (1968), 222 for contents and 224 for list of chapters in the collection of texts fols78–89; Jonas, *De Institutione regia*, c.3, ed. Dubreucq, p.190, and of course, in its turn, this is from the council of Paris, II.1 (MGH Conc., 2.2, pp.649–51).
198 Council of Aachen 836, c.45 (VII), MGH Concilia 2.2, pp.749–50; Kasten (1997), 225 n.95.
199 Hraban, letter no.15, c.2, MGH Ep KA 3, p.406; Kasten (1997), 225.
200 *Ordinatio imperii*, Prologue and, for example, c.6, c.14, c.15, etc., MGH Cap.1, pp.271, 272, p.273; *Regni divisio*, c.13, MGH Cap.2, p.20.
201 Kasten (1997), 212–15.
202 Thegan, *GH*, for example, c.44, c.47 (contrasting Gebhard and Richard), c.52, pp.232–8, 240, 244.
203 Thegan, *GH*, c.36, p.222; Walahfrid omits Helisachar and Gottfried, Tremp (1988), 123–4.
204 Thegan, *GH*, c 20, c.50, c.56, pp.208, 242, 252; Patzold (2008a), 231–5.
205 Thegan, *GH*, c.3, c.5, c.28, pp.178, 180, 216.
206 Thegan, *GH*, c.57, p.252, referring to c.3, p.178.
207 Thegan, *GH*, c.4, c. 35, c.36, c.37, c.39, c.45, c.47, c.48, c.54, c.57, pp.180, 220, 222, 224–6, 238, 240, 248; Tremp (1988), 49–55, 79–81; Goldberg (2006a), 76–7.
208 De Jong (2009), 261; Nelson (1996a), 37–50; Costambeys, Innes and MacLean (2011), 221–2.

209 Dip. Louis P., vol. 2, no.361, but see Kölzer, Introduction to his edition, pp.xxv-xxvi on low survival of charters for lay recipients; Innes (2000a), 200–2.
210 Nithard, I, c.6, p.24; Astronomer, *VH*, c.54, p.504; De Jong (2009), 261; Nelson (1996a), 42–4; Costambeys, Innes and MacLean (2011), 221–2.
211 *AB*, a. 836, trans. Nelson (1991a), 35; Kasten (1997), 208, 328–9.
212 Thegan, *GH*, c.47, p.240 and continuation to *GH*, p.254, and Tremp (1988), 19–21 and 100–12; contrast *AB*'s neutral view of him, *AB* a.836, trans. Nelson (1991a), 34.
213 Louis the German: Thegan, *GH*, for example, c.45–8, 57, pp.238–42, 252–4; Tremp (1988), 79–81; Goldberg (2006a), 76–7. Ebbo: Thegan, *GH*, c. 20, c.43, c.44, c.50, pp.204–10, 230–8, 242–4; Tremp (1988), 70–9; Patzold (2008a), 231–5; De Jong (2009), 76–9.
214 Dip. Louis P., vol. 2, no.401.
215 Dip. Lo. I, no.40; Dip. Lo. I, no.23; Depreux (1997), 363–5; Devroey (2011), 181–8; Tremp (1988), 50–2.
216 Hincmar, *De villa Noviliaco*, ed. H. Mordek; Costambeys, Innes and MacLean (2011), 319.
217 *Concilum Ingelheimense*, MGH Concilia 2.2 p.795 (exile); Thegan, *GH*, c.52, p.254; De Jong (2009), 201. Dhuoda, *LM*, III.4, p.150, VIII.14 and 15, pp.318–20; Innes (2008), 249–52; Nelson (2007), 118–20; Le Jan (2010).
218 Patzold (2008a), 196–9, 315–59; De Jong (2009), 252–9; Booker (2009), 186–90; Zechiel-Eckes (2002).
219 Innes (2000a), 200–5; Raaijmakers (2012), 228–30.
220 *Epistolarum Fuldensium fragmenta*, MGH Ep KA III, pp.520–1; *Narratio clericorum Remensium*, in *Concilium Ingelheimense*, MGH Concilia 2.2, p.808; Airlie (2009b), 497–8; Booker (2005); Booker (2008), 5–6; Booker (2009), 191–2.
221 *AB*, a.837, a.838, a.839, trans. Nelson (1991a), 38–48; Nithard, I, c.6, c.7, pp.24–32; Astronomer, *VH*, c.59, c.60, pp.524–32. Nelson (1992), 94–101.
222 Eichler (2007), 43–4.
223 *AB*, a.837, trans. Nelson (1991a), 38; Nithard, I, c.6, pp.24–6; *AF*, a. 838, p.29; Kasten (1997), 379.
224 *AB*, a.838, trans. Nelson (1991a), 39; Nithard, I, c.6, p.26. Kölzer (2005), 32–3; Nelson (1992), 100.
225 Nithard, I, c.6, c.7, pp.26, 28, 30.
226 Innes (2000a), 202–7; Goldberg (2006a), 88–92.
227 Astronomer, *VH*, c. 59, c.60, pp.528–30; Eichler (2007), 84–5.
228 Nithard, I, c.7, p.30; Althoff (1997), 118, 238; Kasten (1997), 217, 227; De Jong (2009), 99–100.
229 The quotations are from *AB* a.839, trans. Nelson (1991a), 45, and see Nithard, I, c.7, p.30; but NB Astronomer, *VH*, c.59, p.528 on Judith making Lothar promise to protect Charles before the meeting at Worms. Astronomer, *VH*, c.60, pp.530–2.
230 *AB*, a.839, trans. Nelson (1991a), 45–6. Astronomer, *VH*, c.60, pp.530–2 and Nithard, I, c.7, pp.30–2 all basically agree here; see also Nithard, I, c.4, p.130 on similar choice pre-Verdun. Nelson (1992), 96. Prayers for Charles: *Gesta domni Aldrici Cenomannicae Urbis epsicopi*, c.29, c.30, ed. M. Weidemann, vol. 1 (2002), pp.142–3; Kasten (1997), 197.
231 Astronomer, *VH*, c.59, p.528.
232 Editor's note at Nithard, I, c.7, p.31 n.3 and editor's note at Astronomer, *VH*, c.60, n. 912, p.531, both following J. Grimm; Boshof (1996), 241.
233 *AB*, a.839, trans. Nelson (1991a), 45; Nelson (2011).

234 *AB*, a.839, trans. Nelson (1991a), 45. Compare the Astronomer, *VH*, c.60: 'Quem pater cum alacritate suscepit', p.530; and Nithard, I, c.7: 'ad pedes patris coram cunctis ... ut pius ac clemens pater', p.30. Kasten (1997), 217, 227.
235 Nithard, I, c.7, p.32; Astronomer, *VH*, c.60, pp.530-2.
236 *AB*, a.839, trans. Nelson (1991a), 45-6; Kasten (1997), 197-8.
237 Innes (2000a), 207; Goldberg (2006a), 90-1.
238 *AB*, a.839, trans. Nelson (1991a), 41.
239 *AB*, a.839, trans. Nelson (1991a), 41, 46; *AF*, a.839, pp.29-30, with Reuter translation p.16 for 'wicked', and Kasten (1997), 209.
240 Nelson (1996a), 152.
241 *AB*, a.839, trans. Nelson (1991a), 41, 46-7; Dip. Louis P., vol. 2, no.395. Orth (1985-6), 192-3; Goldberg (2006a), 91; Haarländer (2006), 41-2.
242 *AB*, a.839, trans. Nelson (1991a), 46; Kasten (1997), 209, 231; Goldberg (2006a), 92.
243 Depreux (1997), 221-2; Hummer (2005), 178-9.
244 *Formulae Augienses*, no.7, MGH Formulae, pp.367-8; Schmid (1957), 286-8; Glansdorff (2011), 82.
245 Goldberg (2006a), 90.
246 Airlie (2007b), 53, 69-71.
247 BM, nos 968b to 974, and 977 to 1014; *AB*, a.838, 839, 840, trans. Nelson (1991a), 38-49.
248 Gravel (2012a) emphasizes distance, political as well as geographical.
249 *AB*, a.839, trans. Nelson (1991a), 40; Astronomer, *VH*, c.59, p.528.
250 Settipani (1993), 278, 281.
251 Astronomer, *VH*, c.59, p.528, c.61, p.534; Nithard, I, c.8, p.32.
252 Astronomer, *VH*, c.61, pp.536-8.
253 Regino, *Chronicon*, a.853, pp.76-7; Collins (1990), 365, 386.
254 Levillain in *Recueil Aquitaine*, Introduction, p.cliv takes a hard line; Kasten (1997) on limits, Koziol (2012), 99-105 is more optimistic; Coupland (1989), 199; cf. Garipzanov (2008), 143-5.
255 *ARF*, a.822, p.159; Ermold, *Ad Pippinum Regem* I, ed. Faral, lines 13-38, pp.202-4; Nelson (2004a), 194-5.
256 Ermold, *Ad Pippinum Regem* I, lines 65-8, ed. Faral, p.20; Ermold, *Ad Pippinum Regem* II, lines 63-4, lines 143-200 and lines 207-14, ed. Faral, pp.206, 222, 232.
257 Astronomer, *VH*, c.61, pp.534-6; on these men as Pippin's sons-in-law, not brothers-in-law, Nelson (1986), 234, and Le Jan (1995), 300 and Settipani (1993), 278-81.
258 Koziol (2012), 129, and see Chapter 6. Martindale (1990), 122-3, and NB references there.
259 *AB*, a.838, trans. Nelson (1991a), 39; *Gesta Aldrici*, Fragments, c.6, c.7, ed. Weidemann, vol. 1, pp.154-66 and p.166 for Walahfrid. Oexle (1969), 163-4, 180; Depreux (1997), 175-6.
260 *AB*, a.839, trans. Nelson (1991a), 45.
261 Astronomer, *VH*, c. 61, pp.536-8.
262 *Recueil Aquitaine*, no.49, with Levillain's Introduction, pp.clix-x. Oexle (1969), 165-6; Koziol (2012), 103-5.
263 Gaborit-Chopin and Taburet-Delahye (2001), 30, 32-43, 50-3; Koziol (2012), 100-1.
264 Astronomer, *VH*, c.61, pp.534-6; Nithard, I, c.8, p.32; Oexle (1969), 165-6 and 179 on Emenus; Martindale (1990), 119.
265 Astronomer, *VH*, c.47, pp.468-71; Nithard, II, c.5, p.50; Dhuoda, *LM*, III, 4, pp.148-53, III, 8, pp.168-9; Nelson (1992), 102-3 and Le Jan (2010), 216-19.
266 Astronomer, *VH*, c.61, p.534.

267 Astronomer, *VH*, c.61, pp.534–6; on these brothers-in-law, see Martindale (1990), 118–22; Collins (1990), 386–8. Gravel (2012a).
268 Collins (1990), 374–5, 387.
269 Martindale (1990), 119–21.
270 *Recueil des chartes de l'abbaye de Saint-Benoît-sur-Loire*, eds Prou and Vider, nos 20, 21; Innes (2008), 252–6. *AB*, a.839, trans. Nelson (1991a), 47–8 and see Nelson (1991a), 48 n.14 for the annalist Prudentius possibly being on the campaign; Lupus, letter 17, ed. Levillain vol. I, pp.98–100. Nelson (1992), 102–3. Oexle (1969), 165–6.
271 *Traditionen des Hochstifts Freising*, ed. Bitterauf, no.634; Goldberg (2006a), 92–3 (though the charter is dated by Louis the Pious as well as by Louis the German).
272 *AB*, a.840, trans. Nelson (1991a), 48–9; *AF*, a.840, pp.30–1; Nithard, I, c.8, p.34; Astronomer, *VH*, c.62, pp.540–4; Goldberg (2006a), 92–3.
273 *Ann. Xant.*, a.840, p.11.
274 Geary (2012), 14–17.
275 Astronomer, *VH*, c.63, c.64, pp.546–64.
276 Benjamin (1999), 433.
277 *AB*, a.840, trans. Nelson (1991a), 49; Anton (1979), 99; Screen (2003).
278 *AB*, a.840, trans. Nelson (1991a), 48–9; *AF*, a.840, a.841, a.842, pp.30–4; *Ann. Xant.*, a.840, a.841, p.11; Nithard, II, c.5, pp.102–8; Hincmar, *Ad Ludovicum Balbum*, c.4, PL 125, col.985.
279 Nithard, I, c.5, II, c.5, II, c.7, pp.20–2, 50, 58; Airlie (2007b), 69–71.
280 Nithard, II, c.3, II, c.5, pp.44–6, 52; *Receuil Charles II*, vol. 1, no.9; Classen (1963), 7.
281 Dhuoda, *LM*, X.2, pp.368–70; Le Jan (2010).
282 Nithard, II, pp.36–78; Nelson (1986), 205–7; Nelson (1992), 112–16.
283 Nelson (1986), 220–3; Airlie (2007b).
284 Dhuoda, *LM*, V.9, VIII.14, VIII.15, pp.284, 318–22; Innes (2008), 249–52; Nelson (2007). *Epistolae variorum inde a morte Caroli Magni usque ad divsionem imperii*, no.27, MGH Ep. KA 3, pp.343–5; Airlie (2007b), 57–9; on Ermengard, Screen (2011), 265–8.
285 Nithard, III, c.6; Goldberg (2006a), 189; Coupland (1990); Stiegemann and Wemhoff (1999), vol. 1, 281–311; Astronomer, *VH*, c. 28, p.374.
286 For example, Nithard, II, c.1, c.3, c.5, c.9, c.10, pp.38, 44, 50, 66, 68–78; *AF*, a.841, pp.32–3.
287 Nithard, III, c.4, 96–8.
288 Nelson (1992), 117–21; Goldberg (2006a), 102–3.
289 *Versus de bella quae fuit acta Fontaneto*, MGH PLAC 2, 138–9, trans. Godman (1985a), 262–5.
290 Wickham (2005), 586–8.
291 *AF*, a.842, a.843, pp.33–4; *AB*, a.842, a.843, trans. Nelson (1991a), 52–6; Nithard, IV, c.4, p.134; *Traditionen des Hochstifts Freising* I, no.661, ed. Bitterauf. Airlie (1985), 116–27; Goldberg (2006a), 113–16; Nelson (2011).
292 *Traditionen des Hochstifts Freising* I, no.661, ed. Bitterauf; Goldberg (2006a), 115–16.

Chapter 6

1 *Ann. Xant.*, a.869, pp.26–7, citing Proverbs, 28:2; Kasten (1997), 524.
2 Audradus, *Liber Revelationum*, ed. L. Traube, p.383, trans. Dutton (2004), 354; Dutton (1994), 128–56.
3 *Translatio Sancti Germani*, MGH SS 15, p.10; Nelson (1992), 151.

4 Florus, poem no.28, MGH PLAC 2, pp.559–64, translation Godman (1985a), 268–9; Dutton (1994), 120–3; Nelson (1992), 158.
5 Saxony: Carroll (1999); Neustria: Périn and Feffer (1985). Phrase-book: Edwards (1994), 143.
6 *Translatio Sancti Germani*, c.17, p.14. Dümmler (1887–8), vol. 1, 347; Nelson (1992), 152; McCormick (2001), 653–69; Innes (2001).
7 Nelson (1996c), 101–2.
8 Nithard, III, c.5, pp.102–8. Koblenz: capitulary no.242, MGH Cap.2, pp.157–8; Goldberg (2006a), 261.
9 Devisse (1975), vol. 1, 34–40, 52–3; Staab (1975), 417–18, 435–6; Büttner and Kaschke (2006).
10 Classen (1963), 19; Airlie (1993).
11 La Rocca and Provero (2000); Hlawitschka (1960), 60–6, 170–1, 276.
12 *AB*, a.861, trans. Nelson (1991a), 94–5; *AF*, a.861, p.55. Nelson (1992), 200–1; Goldberg (2006a), 268–9; Hennebicque (1981).
13 Capitulary no.242, c.7, MGH Cap.2, pp.156–8; see also Capitulary no.270, MGH Cap.2, pp.297–301.
14 Flodoard, *HRE*, III, c.26, p.333.
15 *AF*, a.853, pp.43–4, trans. Reuter (1992), 5; *AF*, a.858 p.49 uses similar wording.
16 *AF*, a.869, p.68; Wolfram (1995a), 320.
17 Nicholas I in *Epistolae ad divortium Lotharii II. regis pertinentes*, no.7, ed. Dümmler, MGH Ep. KA 4, pp.272–4; capitulary no.243, c.5, MGH Cap.2, pp.160–1; Nelson (1992), 203; Heidecker (2010), 102; Stone (2011), 253.
18 Capitulary no.243, c.5, MGH Cap.2, p.161; on the term, Le Jan (1995), 162.
19 'erga prefatum coenobium more predecessorum nostrorum specialem dilectionem servantes'; Dip. Lo. I, nos 130, 122; for the crown, Schramm (1957), 165.
20 *Recueil Charles II*, vol. 1, no.73 and vol. 2, no.425; *Recueil Louis II*, no.7; Dip. Louis G., nos 133, 134.
21 For Heriric, see *Urkundenbuch zur Geschichte*, vol. 1, no.110, ed. H. Beyer (1860); Innes (2000a), 218–20; Goldberg (2006a), 296; overall survey, Kuchenbuch (1978).
22 Contreni (2002), 46–8; Airlie (2007b).
23 *AB*, a.843, a.844, trans. Nelson (1991a), 55–60; Nithard, I, c.5, p.20; Nelson (1996a), 157–8.
24 Council of Savonnières, no.47 (section G), in MGH Concilia 3, pp.482–5.
25 Nelson (1996a), 157–8; Nelson (1992), 135–9, 142–3; *AB*, a.844, trans. Nelson (1991a), 59–60.
26 Lupus, letter no.81, ed. Levillain, vol. 2, p.60; *AB* a.852, trans. Nelson (1991a), 74 ('trick' is her translation). Nelson (1992), 147, 165–6; Smith (1992).
27 Frankfurt: Dip. Louis G., no.34, and Orth (1985–6), 164–5, 194, 195–6; Hersfeld: Dip. Louis G., no.32 and Goldberg (2006a), 159 and Glansdorf (2009), 170–2; see also Goldberg (2006a), 119–46.
28 Dip. Lo. II, no.9; loyalty demand: see, for example, Dip. Lo. I nos 66, 69, 70, 83 and Brunner (1979), 15. Provence: *AB*, a.845, *AF*, a.845, p.35; Brunner (1979), 127–8; Esders (2008).
29 Gondreville: Dip. Lo. I, nos 75, 76, 77 and Airlie (2006a), 108; Aachen: Dip. Lo. I, nos 80, 81, 82.
30 Prayer as edited in Screen (2003), 50–1 and see also there 43–5, and Lowden (1993), 223; Garipzanov (2008), 239–41; Lafitte and Denoel (2007), 102–3.
31 *AB*, a.843, a.844, trans. Nelson (1991a), 55–9; *Regesten Karls des Kahlen*, ed. I. Fees (2007), no.372; Nelson (1992), 140.

32 Lupus, letter no.31, ed. Levillain, I, pp.140–7; Nelson (1992), 128; Krah (2004), 170; Bibles: Kessler (1992), 653; Garipzanov (2008), 235–60.
33 Coulaines: no.3 in MGH Concilia 3, pp.14–17; Nelson (1996a), 155–68; and see Mordek (1995a), 58–60.
34 *Carmen de Exordio gentis Francorum*, line 125, MGH PLAC 2, p.145; Oexle (1967), 263–6 on Metz origin and see Löwe, Wattenbach and Levison (1973), 512; Nithard: Airlie (2007b).
35 *Carmen de Exordio gentis Francorum* at, for example, lines 84–90, 144, MGH PLAC 2, pp.143–4; contrast Sedulius' address to Eberhard of Friuli on aristocratic ancestry as glorious (but not royal), Sedulius, poem no.53, line 20, ed. L. Traube, MGH PLAC 3, p.212. But Eberhard's royal wife shed royal lustre on Eberhard's children, Sedulius, poems nos 37, 38, pp.201–2.
36 *Recueil Charles II,* vol. 1, no.26 and no.196; *Regesten Karls des Kahlen*, ed. Fees, nos 369 and see no.399 for birth of Charles's daughter between September and December 843.
37 Jonas of Orléans, *Epistolae variorum*, no.32, MGH Ep. KA 3, pp.353–5; Paschasius Radbertus, poem no.4, MGH PLAC 3, pp.52–3. For dynastic prayers see, *Recueil Charles II*, for example, vol. 1, nos 30, 31, 37.
38 Bauer (2011), 377–80; Hartmann (2011), 297–9.
39 Nelson (1992), 192–3; Nelson (1995), 419–20.
40 *Ann. Xant.*, a.850, p.17; see also *AF*, a.846, p.36 and *AB*, a.852, a. 853, trans. Nelson (1991a), 74, 76.
41 *AB*, a.854, trans. Nelson (1991a), 79; Goldberg (2006a), 240.
42 Capitularies no.204, MGH Cap.2, pp.70–1; no.205, MGH Cap.2, p.74; no.206, MGH Cap.2, pp.75–6; no.207, MGH Cap.2, pp.76–8; no.270, MGH Cap.2, pp.297–301; no.242, MGH Cap.2, pp.153–8; no.243, MGH Cap.2, pp.163–5; synod of Yütz (844), no.6 in MGH Concilia 3, p.29. Nelson (1986), 150–1.
43 Post-Koblenz: capitulary no.270, pp.297–301; Savonnières 862:*AB*, a.862, p.103 Nelson and capitulary no.243, MGH Cap.2, pp.159–65. For an optimistic view of use of the written word in the east, see Goldberg (2006a), 210–11; on the west, Nelson (1992), 167–8.
44 Hartmann (2011), 289–95.
45 Capitulary no.244, MGH Cap.2, p.166.
46 870: *AB*, a.870, trans. Nelson (1991a), 166; 862: Prinz (1965), 262–3 and Airlie (2011a), 345–8.
47 Oaths: Aachen 870, capitulary no.250, MGH Cap.2, p.192; *AB*, a.870, trans. Nelson (1991a), 166. On Conrad, *AB* a.862, trans. Nelson (1991a), 103.
48 *AF*, a.864, p.62 and see also the joint envoys in *AB*, a.865, trans. Nelson (1991a), 121–2.
49 Bauer (2011), 377–9; on 849, Nelson (1992), 157.
50 *AB*, a.866, trans. Nelson (1991a), 136; Airlie (2011a), 347–8.
51 *Liber Memorialis Remiremont*, ed. Hlawitschka, Schmid and Tellenbach, vol. 1, entry A1 for fol.43r, p.93; Schmid (1968), 113 for identification of the kings.
52 Schmid (1968), 103; Airlie (1998b), 15.
53 Schmid (1968).
54 *Liber Memorialis Remiremont*, vol. 1, entry A1 for fol.43r, p.93; Schmid (1968), 126–7; Kasten (1997), 220–37, 508; cf. MacLean (2003a), 85–6.
55 *Epistolae ad divortium Lotharii II*, no.3, MGH Ep. KA 4, pp.212–13; Schmid (1968), 118–23; Heidecker (2010), 101.

56   Capitulary no.204, c.1, MGH Cap.2, p.69; *AB*, a.851, trans. Nelson (1991a), 70.
57   Gregory of Tours, *Decem Libri Historiarum*, eds Krusch and Levison, pp.329–30 (based on translation in Murray (2000), 376); see also the treaties in Gregory's book VII, c.6, pp.328–9 and book IX, c.20, pp.434–9.
58   Capitulary no. 242, MGH Cap.2, p.154; Bauer (2011), 367 n.36; Goldberg (2006a), 265.
59   Capitulary no. 242, p.154. For 842, Nithard, III, c.7, pp.112–14 and IV, c.4, pp.134–6; *Regesten Karls des Kahlen*, ed. Fees (2007), no.297.
60   Capitulary no.204, p.70.
61   For example, Charlemagne as ancestor of Charles the Bald, Sedulius, poem no.12, MGH PLAC 3, pp.180–1, as ancestor of Lothar I, poem no.59, p.216 and of Louis the German, poem no.30, pp.195–7.
62   Sedulius, poems nos 14 (to Charles the Bald) and 23 (to Charles of Provence), MGH PLAC 3, pp.182–3, 189.
63   Sedulius, poem no.15, p.183, trans. Doyle (1983), 116–17; *Epistolae ad divortium Lotharii II*, no.13, MGH Ep. KA 4, p.230.
64   Lupus, letter no.31, ed. Levillain, vol. 1, pp.140–7; Sedulius, *De Rectoribus Christianis*, ed. S. Hellman (1906); Anton (1968); Kershaw (2011).
65   *AF*, a.858, pp.49–50; Louis' claims are visible in the letter sent him by the western bishops from the council of Quierzy, no.41, cs 1–2, MGH Concilia 3, p.408.
66   Council of Quierzy, no.41, c.15, MGH Concilia 3, p.424; council of Savonnières, no.47 (section B), c.3, MGH Concilia 3, p.465; Nelson (1986), 142.
67   See, for example, Liutbert of Mainz's letter to Louis the German, *Epistolae variorum*, no.18, MGH Ep KA 4, pp.165–6. In general, see, for example, Wallace-Hadrill (1975), 181–200; Nelson (1986); Nelson (1996a), 99–131; Nelson (1997b); Goldberg (2006a), 52–4, 308–9; Airlie (1998b).
68   Council of Savonnières, no. 47 (section B), cs 1–2, MGH Concilia 3, p.464; Erkens (2006), 110–55.
69   Council of Quierzy, no.41, c.4, c.5, c.7, c.8, c.15, MGH Concilia 3, p.410, 411, 413, 417, 418, 424, 426.
70   St-Quentin: capitulary no.268, MGH Cap.2, pp.293–4; Koblenz: capitulary no.242, p.153.
71   Savonnières 862: capitulary no.243, MGH Cap.2, pp.159–65; Tusey 865, capitulary no.244, MGH Cap.2, pp.165–7.
72   Capitulary no.268, *adnuntiatio* of Charles, c.4, p.294; capitulary no.242, *adnuntiatio* of Louis c.2, c.3, p.157; see also capitulary no.243, *adnuntiatio* of Louis, c.2, p.163.
73   *AB*, a.853, p.76; capitulary no.243, *adnuntiatio* of Lothar II, c.1, p.164; Kasten (1997), 385.
74   'sibi germanitatis iure sociaretur', *AF*, a.848, p.37, trans. Reuter (1992), 27; Anton (1979), 98–9, 101–2 and Le Jan (1995), 169–70.
75   Council of Yütz, no.6, MGH Concilia 3, pp.29–35.*Visio Karoli Magni*, ed. P Jaffé (1867), pp.701–4; Dutton (1994), 200–8.
76   John VIII, letter no.41, MGH Ep. KA 5, p.297; Dümmler (1887–8), vol. 1, p.209 n.1; Bauer (2011), 358–9.
77   Capitulary, no.204, c.9, p.69; no.205, c.3, p.73; no.207, p.78; no.242, c.3, p.155; Kasten (1997), 401–7; Goldberg (2006a), 153; Hartmann (2011), 289; Bauer (2011), 358–9, 365.
78   Sedulius, poems no.20, line 41, p.187; no.23, p.189; no. 24, lines 45–6, p.190; no.25, line15, p.191 (trans. Doyle 1983), 125.

79 854: *AB*, a.854, trans. Nelson (1991a), 78; capitulary no.207, p.78; Kasten (1997), 406. 860: capitulary no.242, c.3, p.155 and no.270, c.2, p.297.
80 *AF*, a.876, p.87; trans. Reuter (1992), 72.
81 *AB*, a.849, trans. Nelson (1991a), 67; Becher (2008a), 317–18.
82 *AB*, a.849, trans. Nelson (1991a), 67; Nelson (1992), 157–8.
83 *AB*, a.858, trans. Nelson (1991a), 87; Offergeld (2001), 334–5.
84 Hadrian II, letters nos 16, 17, 18, 19, 21, 22, 23, 24, 25, 26, MGH Ep. KA 4, pp.717–32.
85 *AB*, a.869, trans. Nelson (1991a), pp.164–6; a.870, trans. Nelson (1991a), p.170; *AF*, a.870, p.72.
86 *AB*, a.869, a.870, trans. Nelson (1991a), 156–70.
87 Schramm (1983), 169–70 who goes for Arnulf; Garipzanov (2008), 252–3 is more open; Lafitte and Denoel (2007), 117–18.
88 *AB*, a.870, trans. Nelson (1991a), 165–70; *AF* a.870, p.71. Goldberg (2006a), 297–9; Schneider (2010), 96–7; Bauer (2011), 360–1.
89 *AF*, a.869, p.69; a.870, p.70.
90 Airlie (2011a), 351; Nightingale (2001), 44.
91 *AB*, a.865, trans. Nelson (1991a), 128; *AF*, a.863, p.56, trans. Reuter (1992), 49 and see 50; Kasten (1997), 513–14.
92 Kasten (1997), 378 ff.; in general, see Kasten (2002), Becher (2008b) and McDougall (2016).
93 Kasten (1997), 220–37; MacLean (2003a), 85.
94 *AF*, a.863, p.57; *AB*, a.862, trans. Nelson (1991a), 100.
95 Kasten (1997), 382.
96 *Epistolae ad divortium Lotharii*, no.5, MGH Ep. KA 4, p.215 (trans. Dutton (2004), 387); Kasten (1997), 386–7.
97 *Epistolae ad divortium Lotharii*, no.5, MGH Ep. KA 4, p.215; Kasten (1997), 387; Heidecker (2010), 111–12.
98 Capitulary no. 207, MGH Cap.2, p.78.
99 *AB*, a.855, trans. Nelson (1991a), 80; different view in Kasten (1997), 382–3.
100 *AB*, a.855, trans. Nelson (1991a), 81; *AF*, a.855, p.46; Regino, *Chron.*, a. 855, p.77. *Die Regesten des Regnum Italiae*, no. 138A, ed. H. Zielinski (1991); Kasten (1997), 386.
101 *AF*, a.855, p.46; *AB*, a.856, trans. Nelson (1991a), 82. Dümmler (1887–8), vol. 1, 398; Orth (1985–6), 196–7; Goldberg (2006a), 248–9.
102 *AB*, a.855, trans. Nelson (1991a), 81 and *AB*, a.856, trans. Nelson (1991a), 81–2; *Die Regesten des Regnum Italiae*, no.146. Kasten (1997), 388–91.
103 Hummer (2005), 172–3; Goldberg (2006a), 249.
104 Capitulary no.243, *adnuntiatio* of Lothar II, c.1, MGH Cap.2, p.164.
105 *AB*, a.855, a.856, trans. Nelson (1991a), 81–2; Regino, *Chron.*, a.855, p.77.
106 Airlie (1998b); Heidecker (2010); Airlie (2011a).
107 *AB*, a.862, trans. Nelson (1991a), 102; Dip. Lo. II, no.19 (a.863).
108 Regino, *Chron.*, a.879, p.115.
109 Airlie (2011a), 353–4.
110 *AB*, a.869, trans. Nelson (1991a), 165.
111 MacLean (2003a), 149–52; Airlie (2011a), 353–5.
112 Grip: Notker, *GK*, II, c.18, pp.88–9. Future kingdoms and limits on sons: Notker, *Continuatio Breviarii Erchanberti*, MGH SS 2, p.329; Ado of Vienne, *Chronicon (continuation)*, MGH SS 2, pp.324–5; date of 865 accepted in Hartmann (2002), 70 and Goldberg (2006a), 275–9; date between 866 and 869 argued for in Kasten (1997), 524–5.

113 Kasten (1997), 498–541 especially 503–5 and 509–10.
114 Kasten (1997), 499–501.
115 Goldberg (2006a), 234–5, 238–40.
116 *AF*, a.866, pp.64–5, a.871, pp.72–4; *AB*, 870, trans. Nelson (1991a), 170, but on the translation, Goldberg (2006a), 305 n.2.
117 Kasten (1997), 498–541; Hartmann (2002), 66–76; Goldberg (2006a), 275–9.
118 Kasten (1997), 500.
119 See, for example, Dip. Louis G., nos 99, 104. On issuing of diplomas, Goldberg (2006a), 213–14; Hartmann (2002), 86–7, 162–6; Innes (2000a), 213–14.
120 Innes (2000a), 217–18; Goldberg (2006a), 268–9.
121 Kasten (1997) 505–8, 512–13; Goldberg (2006a), 242–3.
122 842: Nithard, III, c.7, p.112; 858: *AF*, a.853, p.44, a.858, p.49; Kasten (1997), 501; Hartmann (2002), 67.
123 Kasten (1997), 501, 503, 536.
124 Dip. Louis G., nos 81, 83; Borgolte (1986), 38; Maurer (1983), 18–45, especially 28, 33–8.
125 *AF*, a.863, pp.56–7, trans. Reuter (1992), 49; Kasten (1997), 501–3; MacLean (2003a), 84–8; Borgolte (1986), 160–4.
126 Louis the Younger: *AF*, a.866, p.65, trans. Reuter (1992), 55; Karlmann: *AB*, a.864, trans. Nelson (1991a), 120; Kasten (1997), 514, 516–17.
127 *AF*, a.869, pp.67–8, trans. Reuter (1992), 59.
128 *AB*, a.870, trans. Nelson (1991a), 170–1, 174–5; *AF*, a.871, p.73, trans. Reuter (1992), 64–5; Kasten (1997), 533; Airlie (2003a), 40–1; Goldberg (2006a), 305–7.
129 *AB*, a.873, trans. Nelson (1991a), 182; *AF*, a.873, pp.77–8; *Ann. Xant.*, a.873, pp.31–2; *Vita Rimberti*, c.20, ed. G. Waitz, MGH SRG 55, pp.96–7; MacLean (2006).
130 *AF*, a.873, p.78; Airlie (2003a), 39–40.
131 *AF*, a.867, p.66; Kasten (1997), 520.
132 Kasten (1997), 501–2.
133 *Genealogia regum Francorum*, SS 13, p.247; Schneidmüller (1979), 88.
134 Regino, *Chronicon* a.853, pp.76–7. Contrast royal self-control in Einhard, *VK*, c.24, pp.28–9; Thegan, *GH*, c.19, pp.200–4. Reuter (2006), 129.
135 Astronomer, *VH*, c.61, pp.536–8.
136 Astronomer, *VH*, c.61, pp.534–40; *AB* a.839, trans. Nelson (1991a), 46–7; Nithard, I, c.8, p.32. Oexle (1969), 165; Collins (1990), 387–8; Martindale (1990), 118–22; Nelson (1992), 101–3; Chandler (2019), 113–19. But cf. Lauranson-Rosaz (1998), 415–16 and Gravel (2012a), 394–412.
137 Oexle (1969), 189–91; Nelson (1992), 172.
138 Astronomer, *VH*, c.61, p.534; Nithard, I, c.8, p.32.
139 Levillain, introduction, *Recueil Aquitaine*, pp.clix–lx.
140 *Recueil Aquitaine*, no.32; Koziol (2012), 100–1.
141 *Recueil Aquitaine*, no.49 (an original); Koziol (2012), 103–5.
142 *AB*, a.839, a.840, trans. Nelson (1991a), 46–8; Astronomer, *VH*, c.61, c.62, pp.534–44; Nithard, I, c.8, pp.32, 34. Lupus, letter no.17, ed. Levillain, vol. 1, pp.98–100 on personnel.
143 *AB*, a.844, trans. Nelson (1991a), p.57; Martindale (1990), 119–20; cf. Nithard, II, c.5, III, c.2, pp.50, 82–4.
144 Astronomer, *VH*, c.61, pp.534–6. Nelson (1986), p.234; Settipani (1993), 280–1.
145 Nithard, II, c.5, p.50; Dhuoda *LM*. Airlie (2007b).
146 Nithard, II, c.1, p.38; II, c.4, p.48; II, c.10, pp.68, 74; III c.3, p.94.

147 Martindale (1990), 129.
148 Nithard, II, c.3, pp.40–2; *AB*, a.842, a.843, a.844, trans. Nelson (1991a), 53–9; *Recueil Charles II*, vol. 1, nos 36–9, 41, 43–9, 53–5; Nelson (1992), 140. Koziol (2012), 69–74; Gravel (2012a), 344–6.
149 *Recueil Charles II*, vol. 1, no.42; on Rodulf, Gravel (2012a), 403–5 is suggestive.
150 *AB*, a.844, trans. Nelson (1991a), 60.
151 *AB*, a.845, trans. Nelson (1991a), 61; Martindale (1990), 121–2; Nelson (1992), 143–4; Gravel (2012a), 397.
152 *Recueil Aquitaine*, no.50 and Levillain introduction, p.clx; Martindale (1990), 129; Koziol (2012), 102–5.
153 Coupland (1989), modifying Grierson and Blackburn (1986).
154 *Recueil Aquitaine*, no.50; Nithard, III c.4, p.100.
155 *AB*, a.848, trans. Nelson (1991a), 66; Nelson (1992), 154–5; *Regesten Karls des Kahlen*, ed. Fees (2007), no.599.
156 *Recueil Charles II*, no.246 (for St-Denis), no.363 (for Saint-Germain des-Près).
157 Wallace-Hadrill (1978), 163.
158 *Genealogia regum*, MGH SS 13, p.247, and Regino, *Chron.*, a.853, pp.76–7; Martindale (1990), 121.
159 Nithard, II, c.3, c.5, c.10, pp.42–4, 50–2, 68–78; *AB*, a.844, trans. Nelson (1991a), 58–9; *Planctus Ugonis abbatis*, PLAC 2, p.139 calls him *rex*.
160 *AB*, a.845, trans. Nelson (1991a), 61. Levillain, introduction, *Recueil Aquitaine*, pp.clxxviii–ix; Nelson (1992), 143–4; Martindale (1990), 121–3. 806: capitulary no.45, c.18, MGH Cap.1, pp.129–30; Kasten (1997), 429.
161 *Recueil Aquitaine*, no.51 and cf. no.53 (847, an original), which also refers to 'our uncle the most unconquerable Charles', but again in a sequence extolling Pippin's own Carolingian descent.
162 Coupland (1989); Nelson (1992), 144.
163 *Historia translationis Regnoberti episcopi Baiocensis et Zenonis diaconi*, in *Acta Sanctorum*, May III, p.615; Oexle (1978), 35–51; Levillain, introduction, *Recueil Aquitaine*, pp.l–li.
164 *Recueil Aquitaine*, nos 53, 54, 57, 58 and Levillain's introduction, pp.l–li.
165 *Recueil Aquitaine*, no.10.
166 *Historia translationis Regnoberti*, 615.
167 *Recueil Aquitaine*, no.58.
168 *Recueil Aquitaine*, no.19; Flodoard, *HRE*, II, c.19, p.182.
169 Flodoard, *HRE*, III, c.20, pp.267–8; date 845–7; same date in *Recueil Charles II*, vol. 1, no.103.
170 *Recueil Aquitaine*, no.54.
171 *AF*, a.851, p.41; *Ann. Xant.*, a. 844, p.13; Agnellus, *Liber Pontificalis ecclesiae Ravennatis*, ed. O. Holder-Egger, c.174, MGH SRL, p.390; he is also called king in *Planctus Ugonis*, PLAC 2, p.139.
172 *AB*, a.845, trans. Nelson (1991a), 61. *Recueil Aquitaine*, Levillain's introduction, p.clxxxii-iii and *Recueil Aquitiaine*, no. 61; Nelson (1992), 150–1, 154–9.
173 *Recueil Aquitaine*, nos 14, 15, 17, 18, 26, 28, 32.
174 Thegan, *GH*, c.41, p.226.
175 *AB*, a.849, trans. Nelson (1991a), 68; *Chronicon Fontanellense*, a.849, ed. Bouquet, *Recueil* 7 (Paris, 1870), p.41; *AF*, a.851, p.41. Schieffer (1977); Nelson (1992), 156.
176 *AB*, a.849, trans. Nelson (1991a), 68.
177 *AF*, a.851, p.41; *Chronicon Fontanellense*.

178 *Breviarium Erchanberti continuatio*, MGH SS 2, p.329; cf. Liutolf, *Vita et Translatio S. Severini*, MGH SS 15, p.293.
179 *AB*, a.849, trans. Nelson (1991a), 68; count Vivian: *Chronicon. Fontanellense*, ed. Bouquet, pp.40 ff.
180 *AB*, a.849, trans. Nelson (1991a), 68.
181 *AB*, a.849, trans. Nelson (1991a), 68.
182 De Jong (2001a), 319 and passim.
183 *AB*, a.854, trans. Nelson (1991a), 79.
184 *AB*, a.854, trans. Nelson (1991a), 79; *AF*, a.851, p.41; *Chronicon Fontanellense*, ed. Bouquet, pp.41–2.
185 Nelson (1992), 179; Wallace-Hadrill (1978), 161; De Jong (2010), 189.
186 *AF*, a.856, pp.46–7; Schieffer (1977), 49; Hartmann (2002), 85, 175; Goldberg (2006a), 250.
187 *Visio Karoli Magni*; Geary (1987), but cf. Dutton (1994), 202–8 on its being written after the death of Charles of Mainz.
188 *AB*, a.852, trans. Nelson (1991a), 74–5.
189 Nelson (1992), 162, 170.
190 *AB*, a.853, trans. Nelson (1991a), 76.
191 *AB*, a.853, trans. Nelson (1991a), 76 n.6.
192 Synod of Soissons, no.27, c.5, MGH Concilia, 3, p.282; 'docendus' certainly suggests that Pippin needed to be educated, that is, about a new status, cf. De Jong (2001a), 306–7.
193 *AB*, a.853, trans. Nelson (1991a), 76.
194 Soissons, no. 27, c.5, MGH Concilia 3, pp.281–2.
195 Soissons, no.27, c.5, MGH Concilia 3, p.282.
196 Soissons, no.27, c.5, MGH Concilia 3, p.282; *AB*, a.853, trans. Nelson (1991a), 76.
197 *AB*, 854, trans. Nelson (1991a), 79; *AB* a.856 refers to his 'escape', trans. Nelson (1991a), 81.
198 *AB*, 856, trans. Nelson, pp.81–2; Nelson (1992), 173.
199 *AB*, a.856, a.857, a.859, trans. Nelson (1991a), 81–2, 84, 90.
200 Hincmar, letter no.170, MGH Ep KA 6, p.165; Hack (2014), p.46 n.70. Regino, *Chron.*, a.883, pp.120–1.
201 Hincmar, letter no.136, pp.87–107; Nelson (1992), 185, 196–7.
202 *AB*, a.863, trans. Nelson (1991a), 110; Martindale (1990), 125–32.
203 *AB*, a.858, trans. Nelson (1991a), 87–8; Martindale (1990), 122.
204 *AB*, a.864, trans. Nelson (1991a), 119; Hincmar, letter no.170, pp.163–5; De Jong (2009), pp.265–6; Hack (2014).
205 *AB*, a.864, trans. Nelson (1991a), 111, 119; *Recueil Charles II*, vol. 2, no.269; capitulary no.273, c.25, MGH Cap.2, p.321. Nelson (1992), 207–9; Nelson (1996a), 93–8.
206 *AB*, a.864, trans. Nelson (1991a), 119; Nelson (1992), 209. See n.205 above for Pitres reference and see capitulary no.274, c.14 (Tusey, 865), MGH Cap.2, p.332 for another reference to *proditor patriae*.
207 *AB*, a.869, trans. Nelson (1991a), 163; De Jong (2009), 266.
208 Hincmar, letter no.170, pp.163–5; Devisse (1975), vol. 1, 357–9; Hack (2014), 46–7.
209 *AB* a.864, trans. Nelson (1991a), 111, 119.
210 Hincmar, letter no.170, p.163.
211 Hincmar, letter no.170, p.164.
212 Hincmar, letter no.170, p.165.
213 *AB*, a.864, trans. Nelson (1991a), 119; De Jong (2009), 266; Hack (2014), 46–7, 65–6.

214 *AB*, a.865, a.866, trans. Nelson (1991a), 122, 134.
215 Gregory of Tours, *Decem Libri Historiarum*, V, c.14, eds Krusch and Levison, 207–13; De Jong (2001a), 306. *Liber Historiae Francorum*, c.43, p.316; Wood (1994), 222; Wood (2004a); on tonsures, De Jong (2001a), 293–4.
216 *AB*, a.854, trans. Nelson (1991a), 79.
217 Capitulary no.45, c.18, MGH Cap.1, pp.129–30; Nelson (1988a), 109.
218 E.g, *AB*, a.861, trans. Nelson (1991a), 94–5; Nelson (1992), 201.
219 Hincmar to Carloman, 881, PL 125, col.1045; Nelson (1990), 20.
220 Nelson (1988a), 109; Nelson (1992), 174.
221 Nelson (1990), 20; Lothar: *AB* a.861, trans. Nelson (1991a), 94. Two of Charles's young sons, Pippin and Drogo, may have been destined for the church, see their epitaph from St-Amand, MGH PLAC 3, pp.677–8; Nelson (1992), 174.
222 Kasten (1997), 524–5; Goldberg (2006a), 275–6.
223 Martindale (1990); Nelson (1992); Kasten (1997).
224 *AB*, a.862, trans. Nelson (1991a), 99–102; Nelson (1992), 204–6.
225 *AB*, a.865, trans. Nelson (1991a), 128.
226 *AB*, a.854, trans. Nelson (1991a), 79. Hincmar recalls Carloman's being ordained, council of Douzy, no.37, MGH Concilia 4, p.447; Regino, *Chron.*, a.870, pp.101–2 on Charles's presence at the ordaining.
227 Regino, *Chron.*, a.870, pp.101–2, on which see Bührer-Thierry (1998), 87–8; Nelson (1990), 19–20.
228 *AB*, a.866, trans. Nelson (1991a), pp.133–4; council of Soissons, no.23 (section F), MGH Concilia 4, pp.223–5; Ermentrude's coronation *ordo* separately edited in Jackson (1995), 80–6.
229 *AB* a.865, trans. Nelson (1991a), 129, and *AB*, a.866, p.134.
230 Hyam (1990), 158.
231 Garver (2009), 232.
232 *AB*, a.866, trans. Nelson (1991a), 133–4.
233 Wallace-Hadrill (1978), 170; Erkens (1993), 28; cf. Nelson (1997b), 309.
234 *AB*, a.865, trans. Nelson (1991a), 129; epitaphs for Charles's sons Drogo and Pippin in MGH PLAC 3, pp.677–8; for Charles's own reflections, council of Soissons, no.23 (section E), MGH Concilia 4, p.222; Wallace-Hadrill (1978), 169; Hyam (1990), 159. On rates of fertility and survival, Le Jan (1995), 339–40; Nelson (1996d), 53–4; Dutton (2009), 195–8.
235 Council of Soissons, no.23 (section F), MGH Concilia 4, pp.223–5.
236 MGH PLAC 3, pp.677–8; Nelson (1986), 81.
237 *AB*, a.861, trans. Nelson (1991a), 94.
238 Sassier (1991).
239 Heiric, *Miracula Sancti Germani*, II, c.1, PL 124, cols 1247–50; Sassier (1991), 29–32; Airlie (1998a), 134; Auxerre (1990), especially 23–117.
240 See, for example, Dip Louis P., no.355; Sassier (1991), 29, 31.
241 Heiric, *Annales breves*, MGH SS 13, p.80; Freise (1984), 531–2. *Recueil Charles II*, vol. 2, no.288.
242 Heiric, *Annales breves*, a.841; a.863 and a.865, MGH SS 13, p.80; Freise (1984), 529–30.
243 Heiric, *Annales breves*, a.841, 860, 863, 865, MGH SS 13, p.80; Freise (1984), 529–2; see the letter of the monks, *Epistolae variorum*, no.25.II, MGH Ep. KA 4, pp.179–80.
244 *Recueil Charles II*, vol. 2, no.288, and see the later charter of Louis Stammerer, *Recueil Louis II*, no.12.

245 Nelson (1988a); synod of Douzy, no.37, MGH Concilia 4, pp.410–572; I am preparing a study on the end of Carloman's career.
246 *AB*, a.875 (count Engelram), trans. Nelson (1991a), 188; Nelson (1992), 221–2.
247 Goldberg (2006a), 326–7.
248 Poem is in Garipzanov (2008), 256 and see Wallace-Hadrill (1978), 170; Schramm (1983), 55–6, 170–2.
249 Garipzanov (2008), 255, 258.
250 *Recueil Charles II*, vol. 2, no.364; date: Hyam (1990), 159 n.41; Wallace-Hadrill (1978), 170–1; on the series of diplomata, Ewig (1982a), 57; Kasten (1997), 462.
251 *AB*, a.876, trans. Nelson (1991a), 195, and see n.21 there.
252 Hincmar, *Ad Ludovicum Balbum regem*, c.7, PL 125, col.986; Capitulary no.281, c.4, MGH Cap.2, p.281. *Recueil Louis II*, introduction, p.xx; Kasten (1997), 456, 459 suggests between 870 and 875.
253 *AB*, a.875, a.876, a.877, trans. Nelson (1991a), 187, 194–5, 196, 198, 199; Kasten (1997), 468.
254 *AB*, a.877, trans. Nelson (1991a), 201; Nelson (1996d), 61. Alcuin, letter no.132, MGH Ep. KA 2, pp.198–9, redated by Kasten (2004).
255 Airlie (1995), 448–9; MacLean (2003a), 64–80.
256 *AB*, a.876, trans. Nelson (1991a), 190; Regino, *Chron.*, a.877, p.113; Airlie (2000b), 32–3.
257 *AB*, a.872, a.877, trans. Nelson (1991a), 177, 199.
258 *Recueil Charles II*, vol. 2, no.379; Airlie (2000b), 33–4.
259 *AB*, a.877, trans. Nelson (1991a), 201–2; Nelson (1992), 251–2.
260 Capitulary no.281, cs 8, 9, 10, p.358; Nelson (1992), 248–9; Gravel (2012b).
261 *AB*, a.876, a.877, trans. Nelson (1991a), 199; capitulary no.280, MGH Cap.2, pp.353–4.
262 Capitulary no.281, c.15, c.31, p.359, p.361; Nelson (1992), 250–2; MacLean (2003a), 116–17.
263 Names: capitulary no.281, c.12, c.15, pp.358–9, and see the exchanges in cs 1–9, pp.355–8; and cf. Hincmar, *Ad Ludovicum Balbum regem*, c.7, PL 125, cols 986–7. For Gauzlin, capitulary no. 282, MGH Cap.2, pp.361–3 and Nelson (1992), 248.
264 Capitulary no.281, c.11, p.358.
265 Capitulary no.281, c.11, c.21, c. 25, pp.358, 360. Kasten (1997), 457–65.
266 Capitulary no.281, c.15, c.16, c.17, p.359; *Recueil Louis II*, introduction, p.xxi; Kasten (1997), 463; Offergeld (2001), 341–2.
267 Capitulary no.281, c.32, c.33, p.361; Nelson (1992), 249–50; Zotz (1997b), 115–17; Gravel (2012b).
268 Capitulary no.281, c.13, c.14, p.356; Kasten (1997), 461–2; McDougall (2016), 88–9.
269 Nelson (1986), 106–7.
270 Capitulary no.281, c.3, c.4, c.5, c.6, c.7, pp.356–7.
271 *Recueil Charles II*, vol. 2, no.425; Koziol (2012), 112.
272 Capitulary no.281, c.4, p.356.
273 Capitulary no.281, cs 9, 11, 12, 13, 14, 15, 20, 21, 25, 32, pp.358–60.
274 Capitulary, no.281, c.4, pp.356–7.
275 Hincmar, *Ad Ludowicum Balbum*, c.7, PL 125 cols 986–7.
276 *AB*, a.877, trans. Nelson (1991a), 203; Richildis: Maclean (2003b), 15, 34–5.
277 *AB*, a.877, trans. Nelson (1991a), 202–3; Nelson (2000), 163–6.
278 *AB*, a.877, trans. Nelson (1991a), 203; Nelson (2000), 148–8, 158–9, 171–2.
279 *AB*, a.877, trans. Nelson (1991a), 203–4; Koziol (2012), 114. Hincmar, *Ad Ludumicum Balbum Regem*, PL 125, cols 983–90.

Notes to pp.214-219

280 *AB*, a.877, trans. Nelson (1991a), 204–6; *Recueil Louis II*, introduction, pp.xxii–v; Koziol (2012), 112–18.
281 *AB*, a.877, trans. Nelson (1991a), 206; Nelson (1986), 152–3.
282 Schlesinger (1975), 236–8, 242–3; Schneidmüller (1979), 81–92; Nelson (1986), 138; Offergeld (2001), 347–8.
283 Nelson (1986), 153.
284 Koziol (2012), 111–18.
285 Jackson (1995), Ordo XIV, c.8, p.163, cited Koziol (2012), 115; contrast Louis' ordo, Jackson (1995), Ordo VIII, pp.117–23.
286 Kasten (1997), 465.
287 Hincmar, *Ad Ludovicum Balbum Regem*, c.2, c.3, c.4, c.5, c.7, PL 125, cols 985–7.
288 *AB*, a.878, trans. Nelson (1991a), 210; Bautier (1989), 44.
289 Jackson (1995), Ordo VIII, c.2, c.3, c.7, c.10, c.11, pp.117–20; *AB*, a.877, trans. Nelson (1991a), 204–6.
290 Jackson (1995), Ordo I, c 4, p.54; on the manuscript, Lafitte and Denoël (2007), 78; Jackson (1995), Ordo II A, c.1, pp.58–9; Bavaria, Jackson (1995), Ordo IV, c.3, p.71; Nelson (1994a), 57–8.
291 *Recueil Charles II*, vol. 2, no.420; Koziol (2012), 358–9.
292 *Recueil Eudes*, introduction, pp.xxix–xxxi; *Recueil Louis II*, introduction, p.lxix. Koziol (2012), 187–8, 363–4.
293 A. De Charmasse, *Cartulaire de l'église d'Autun* (1865), II, no.1; Koziol (2012), 385n.233 calls it Adalgarius's 'political credo'.
294 *Recueil Louis II*, no.29.

Chapter 7

1 Astronomer, *VH*, c.20, p.344, trans. Noble (2009), 246; from Ecclesiasticus 30:4.
2 Synod of Quierzy, MGH Concilia 3, no.41, c.4, p.410.
3 Fentress and Wickham (1992), 80; Le Jan (1995), 38–41; Pohl (2016).
4 Leyser (2011); see also Wood (2004b); Reimitz (2006); Bouchard (2015), 106–25.
5 History: Reimitz (2000), 51–63; McKitterick (2004), 121–4. Law: Wormald (1998), 36. Poems: Oexle (1967), 253–4; liturgy: Schmid (1994).
6 Reimitz (2000), 53–60.
7 Spiegel (1997), 107; Le Jan (1995), 38. On the variety of genealogical knowledge and perceptions: Bouchard (2015), 106–25.
8 *Commemoratio genealogiae domni Karoli gloriosissimi imperatoris*, MGH SS 13, pp.245–6; Oexle (1967), 252–79; Jäschke (1970), 193–6; Tremp (1988), 33–4; Reimitz (2002), 169–70.
9 Alcuin, poem no.7, MGH PLAC 1, p.226; Oexle (1967), 345–6; Le Jan (1995), 41.
10 Paul, *Gesta Episcoporum Mettensium*, MGH SS 2, p.264; Kempf (2004), 282–3, 286; Nelson (2005), 32–3.
11 Bullough (1991), 136. Paul the Deacon, *Gesta*, p.265; Nelson (2005), 33–4 on another tale told by Charlemagne; Bouchard (2015), 116–17. Later cults: Klaniczay (2002).
12 Paul the Deacon, *Gesta*, pp.265–7; Oexle (1967), 274–5; Le Jan (1995), 41; Kempf (2004), 289–90.
13 Jäschke (1970); Tremp (1988), 33–44; Tischler (2001), vol. 1, 461–2; Reimitz (2002), 170.

14 Adorno (1973), 155-6; Foot (2012), 360-1.
15 *Commemoratio genealogiae domni Karoli gloriosissimi imperatoris*, A, B, C, D, MGH SS 13, pp.245-6; Oexle (1967), 253-4; Jäschke (1970), 193-5; Tremp (1988), 34-5.
16 Münsch (2001), 91, my emphasis, and see pp.94-8 for Bedan material. 'Die ostfränkische Ahnentafel von 807', ed. Borst (2006), 1003-4; Palmer (2014), 156.
17 *Genealogia regum Francorum*, MGH SS 13, p.247, no.V; Schneidmüller (1979), 88.
18 This is contained within the genealogy of count of Arnulf of Flanders: Witger, *Genealogia Arnulfi comitis*, MGH SS 9, pp.302-4, at p.302; see Freise (1989), 216-38; Koziol (2012), 259-61, 391-2, 479-81, 558; West (2012), 510-11.
19 *Carmen de exordio gentis Francorum*, MGH PLAC 2, pp.141-5; Reimitz (2002), 170-1. Poeta Saxo, trans. Godman (1985a), 342-3; Innes (2000b), 240-1.
20 Thegan, *GH*, c.1, c.2, pp.174-6; Tremp (1988), 26-8. Dhuoda, *LM*, III.4, p.150, VIII.14 and 15, pp.318-22, X.5, p.354. Airlie (1998a), 133-4; Le Jan (2010), 216-17.
21 Tremp (1988), 34-41; Reimitz (2002), 176.
22 *Gesta Sanctorum Patrum Fontanellensis Coenobii*, IV, c.1, eds Lohier and Laporte, pp.37-40; date: Howe (2001), 169-70; Gerberding (1987), 138; Wood (1991), 10-11; Fouracre (2000), 48-9, 71.
23 *Gesta Sanctorum Patrum*, IV.1, p.39, and cf. *AMP*, a.693, pp.16-17 (trans. Fouracre and Gerberding (1996), 362); Wood (1991), 11; Wood (2004b), 251.
24 *Vita Ansberti Epsicopi Rotomagensis*, c.34, c.35, MGH SRM 5, pp.639-40; written around 800, Howe (2001), 137. *Gesta Sanctorum Patrum*, VIII, pp.60-1; Wood (1991), 11-12; Bouchard (2015), 145-8.
25 *Gesta Sanctorum Patrum*, X.4, p.77, IV.2, p.42 and cf. VIII.1, p.59 which juxtaposes Charles Martel and Childeric 'the Merovingian king'; on the *Gesta* and Einhard, Tischler (2001), vol. 1, 125 and see also Tischler (2001), vol. 2, 1320; De Jong (2001a), 326 n.102.
26 *Gesta Sanctorum Patrum*, XII, XIII, pp.83-124; Airlie (2009a).
27 *Vita Ansberti*, c. 12, c.22, MGH SRM 5, pp.626, 635; Tremp (1988), 36-7; Wood (1991), 12; on the date Howe (2001), 137-40, whom I follow here rather than Bouchard (2015), 115.
28 *Gesta Sanctorum Patrum*, I.2, p.2. Tremp (1988), 36-7; Howe (2001), 179-80; Wood (1991), 10-12; Wood (2004b), 251.
29 *Domus Carolingicae Genealogia*, MGH SS 2, p.309, column 2; Tremp (1988), 35-6; Reimitz (2002), 176.
30 Wood (2004a) and Wood (2003).
31 Regino, *Chron.*, a.879, p.114; Flodoard, *HRE*, IV, c.5, pp.380-3; see this book's Chapter 9.
32 Costamberys, Innes and MacLean (2011), 308-10. Thegan, *GH*, c.36, 222; Paschasius Radbertus, *Vita Adalhardi*, PL 120, col.1511; Le Jan (1995), 44, 166, 173, 176.
33 Le Jan (2001), 191-2; Le Jan (1995), 294.
34 Adalbero, *Poème au roi Robert*, lines 22-3, ed. and trans. C. Carozzi (1979), p.2; *Fragmentum de Arnulfo duce,* MGH, SS 17, p.570. Airlie (2000b), 32; Le Jan (2001), 192.
35 Dhuoda, *LM*, III.8, pp.166-8; Nelson (1998b), 180.
36 Le Jan (1995), 213, 437; Settipani (1993), 176.
37 Dhuoda, *LM*, III.4, pp.148-56, and IV.8, p.248, X.2, p.344, VIII.14 and 15, X.5.
38 Airlie (2007b), 64-7.
39 Notker, *GK*, I, c.19, p.25. See Chapter 1 above.
40 786 in Alcuin, letter no.3, c.12, MGH Ep KA 2, pp.23-4; Notker, *GK*, II, c.12, p.74, and cf. I, c.4, p.52. Einhard, *VK*, c.18, c.33, pp.22-3, 37; *Ordinatio Imperii*, c.13, c.14, MGH Cap.1, p.237. Kasten (2002); Kaschke (2008), 263-4; McDougall (2016).

41 Werner (1967); Settipani (1993); Le Jan (1995), 204.
42 Settipani (1993), 325.
43 *Chronicon Moissiacense*, a.817, MGH SS I, 312.
44 Le Jan (1995), 244, 399.
45 *ARF*, a.822, p.158; Nithard, I, c.2, pp.6, 8; Thegan, *GH*, c.24, 214; Kasten (1997), 164; De Jong (2009), 35.
46 *AF*, a.885 (Mainz continuation), p.103; Notker, *GK*, II, c.13, c.14, pp.74, 78; MacLean (2003a), 129–34; McDougall (2016), 90–3.
47 *AF*, a.889, p.118.
48 Regino, *Chronicon*, a.885, p.125, trans. MacLean (2009a), 193–4.
49 *ARF*, a.773, p.36; Le Jan (1995), 172, 437. *ARF*, revised, a.782, a.783, pp.61, 93; Nelson (1991b), 198.
50 Nelson (1991), 195–6; Innes (1997), 853; Becher (1996), 119–21, a bit cooler. In general, Le Jan (1995), 398–401.
51 Dip. Louis G., no.124; Glansdorff (2011), 51, 196–7; Glansdorff (2009), 313–15.
52 Lupus, letter no.26, vol. 1, pp.124–6. For other suggestively royal names of unknown individuals, see *Recueil Charles II*, vol. 1, no.100 and vol. 2, no.343 bis. Nelson (1998b), 184 n.37.
53 Nelson (1986), 224–5.
54 Heiric, *Miracula Sancti* Germani, II, c.1, c.2, PL 124, cols 1247–8; Sassier (1991), 29–34; Schneidmüller (2000), 62; Airlie (1998a), 134. Dhuoda, *LM*, VIII.15, pp.320–3; Le Jan (2010), 217.
55 De regis persona et min, c.29, PL 125, col.852 and cf. c.30, col.854.
56 Nelson (1998b), 184–5. See chapter on children above.
57 Hincmar, *De ordine palatii*, ed. Gross and Schieffer, p.54 and n.101, p.55. Agobard, letter no.5, c.3, ed. van Acker, p.122. Boshof (1969), 85–6, 91.
58 Alcuin, letters nos 9, 204, 220, 241, 279, 309, MGH Ep KA 2, pp.34–5, 337–40, 364, 386–7, 435–6, 473–8; Kasten (1986), 50–1; Nelson (1996a), 240; Bullough (2004), 76–7, 92.
59 For Drogo of Metz, Charles of Mainz and Louis of St-Denis, see below. Franco: Sedulius, poem no.33, line 16, MGH PLAC 3, p.199.
60 Dip. Louis G., no.119; Dip. Lo. I no.80; Dip. Lo. II, no.13.
61 Charles to Nicholas I, *Epistolae ad Divortium pertinentes*, no.9, Ep. KA 4, pp.222–3.
62 Pope Sergius, Letter 1, MGH Ep. KA 3, p.583; Synod of Ver, c.11, MGH Concilia 3, p.42; Hincmar: Flodoard, *HRE*, III, c.21, p.279; Oexle (1967), 324, 347–9; Glansdorff (2003), 971–3.
63 Nelson (1991a), 6–7; Tremp (1991); Glansdorff (2003), 982–3; Gaborit-Chopin (1999), 36.
64 Geary (1987), but contrast Dutton (1994), 202–3; McKitterick (2004), 13–19; McKitterick (2008), 47; Reimitz (2015), 428–30.
65 *AB*, a.867, trans. Nelson (1991a), 138; *Recueil Charles II*, Introduction, vol. 3, pp.38–42.
66 *AB*, a.858, trans. Nelson (1991a), 86. Lupus, letter no.36, ed. Levillain, vol. 1, pp.158–60; Noble (1998), 241; see also, for example, letters nos 16, 82, 111, vol. 1, pp.94–6; vol. 2, p.66, pp.154–6.
67 Lupus, letter no.16, ed. Levillain, vol. 1, p.96; Noble (1998), 239–41; Koziol (2012), 167–8.
68 Einhard, *VK*, c.18, c.33, pp.22–3, 37;*Chronicon Moissiacense*, a.813, ed. Buc (2000), 205, and MGH SS 1, p.310; Nithard, I, c. 2, p.6; Kasten (1997), 163–4; Innes (1997), 845–7. St-Gall list: see Chapter 3 above, and Werner (1990), 33–4. Frothar, letter no.22, MGH Ep. KA 3, pp.278–9.

69 *AB*, a.844, trans. Nelson (1991a), 46.
70 *Planctus Ugoni Abbatis*, MGH Poetae Lat 2, pp.139–40; Oexle (1970), 199–204; Depreux (1997), 218–20.
71 Sassier (1991), 29–34; Schneidmüller (2000), 70.
72 Le Mans: *Gesta Aldrici*, c.1, ed. Weidemann, p.118; Mainz: *AF*, a.857, p.46; Metz: *ARF*, a.823, p.161; Liège: Sedulius, poem no.33, MGH PLAC 3, p.199. St-Riquier: Nithard, IV, c.5, pp.138–40, *AB*, a.844, trans. Nelson (1991a), 58; *Recueil Charles II*, vol. 1, no.58; Nelson (1986), 236; Corbie: Kasten (1986), 42–91, 110–44, 166–71; Settipani (1993), 355–6; Depreux (1997), 76–9, 390–3. St-Quentin: *AB*, a.844, trans. Nelson (1991a), 58; *Miracula S. Quintini*, MGH SS 15, p.270; Löwe, Wattenbach and Levison (1973), 544.
73 Depreux (1997), 99. *Chronicon Novaliciense*, III, cs 25, 26, 27, 28, MGH SS 7, p.105; Geary (1994), 121; Depreux (1997), 265–7.
74 *Notitia de servitio monasteriorum*, ed. P. Becker (1963), 493–9; Wagner (1999), 417–20; Garipzanov (2008), 78–9; Kramer (2014), 56–7.
75 *The Gregorian Sacramentary under Charles the Great*, ed. H.A. Wilson (1915), 153 n.5, and see Wilson's Introduction, pp.xxv–xxxvii; Garipzanov (2008), 63.
76 McCormick (1986), 237–8; Tellenbach (1984), 202–3, 206; Garrison (2004).
77 Garrison (2004); Garipzanov (2008), 46–58.
78 In general, Garipzanov (2008), 43–100; Keynes (1990), 237–8 and Foot (2011), 125–6. Rome: Elsner (1998), 29; Vichy France: Rémond (1992), 562–4 and Gildea (2002), 24–5, 166–8. Catherine Goethe cited in Burgdorf (2012), 52.
79 *AF*, a.900, p.134. *Sacramentary of Echternach*, ed. Y. Hen (1996), Introduction, pp.18–23, and text nos 2094, 2098, 2102, pp.404–6.
80 *Supplex Libellus*, *Epistolae variorum Carolo Magno regnante*, no.33, MGH Ep. KA 2, p.548. De Jong (1995), 646–7; Patzold (2000).
81 Council of Arles (813), prologue and c.2; Reims, c.40, p.252; Châlon-sur-Saône, c.66, MGH Concilia 2.1, pp.249, 250; 252; 285; Tours requested prayers for Charlemagne but did not explicitly refer to his children, Tours, c.1, p.287. Fried (1998),76. Council of Paris, c.5, MGH Concilia 2.2, pp.612–13; De Jong (2009), 176–84.
82 Synod of Mainz, letter of archbishop of Mainz, MGH Concilia 3, pp.159–60; Zielinski (1989), 96; Hartmann (2002), 194; Garipzanov (2008), 53; Nelson (1996a), 126; Angenendt (2008).
83 Synod of Ascheim, c.1, MGH Concilia 2.1, p.57; Pokorny (1983), 391–2; Italy: McCormick (1986), 3–4; West (1999), 351.
84 Kantorowicz (1946), with 184–6 on Mussolini; Nelson (1996a), 111–12; Garrison (2000), 140–3;
85 Laudes, appendix to Einhard, *VK*, pp.46–7. Kantorowicz (1946), 13–21, 43–4, 105–9; Diesenberger (2005), 176–8.
86 *AB*, a.876, trans. Nelson (1991a), p.194. Council of Tribur, MGH Concilia 5, pp.319–415. Kantorowicz (1946), 70–1; Southern (1970), 176–7.
87 *Codex Carolinus*, no. 21, MGH, Ep. KA 1, p.524; Schieffer (2000), 288–9.
88 Ewig (1982a); Ewig (1982b).
89 Rosenwein (1999).
90 *Formulae Imperiales*, no.28, ed. K. Zeumer, MGH Forumulae, p.307; see also nos 4, 11, 12, and 29, pp.291, 295, 307–8; Ewig (1982a), 48; Ewig (1982b), 223.
91 See, for example, Dip. Louis P., nos, 331, 346, 335.
92 Ewig (1982a), for example, 51–2.
93 *Cartulary of Flavigny*, no.3, ed. Bouchard; *Die Urkunder der Arnulfinger*, ed. Heidrich, nos 23 and 24.

94 Ewig (1982a), 47–8; Ewig (1982b), 221–3.
95 Ewig (1982a), 49, 55, 70.
96 Cathwulf, letter, MGH Ep. KA 2, p.502; Synod of Soissons, MGH Concilia 4, p.212.
97 *Recueil Charles II*, nos 325 and 379. Ewig (1982b) 226; Airlie (2000b), 33–4.
98 Dip. Lo. I, no.19.
99 Dip. Louis G., no.68 (a.854); based on Dip. Lo. I, no.89 (a.845). Ewig (1982a), 51–2.
100 Carloman: *Recueil Louis II*, no.51, no.55; Ewig (1982a), 62, 51, 75–6, 78.
101 Ewig (1982a), 47–8, 50, 53, 55, 57, 61, 71, 73, 75.
102 Dip. CF, nos 123, 129, 135, 147, 149, 153; see also nos 111 and 117; Ewig (1982a), 75–6; MacLean (2003a), 132.
103 *Notitia de servitio monasteriorum*, ed. Becker, p.496; Charlemagne in Dip. Karol. 1, no.105; Dip. Lo. I, no.25.
104 Dip. Karol. 1, nos 174, 188, 189, 199; no.189 is an original, see facsimile in CHLA, vol. XVIII, no.667 (797/801).
105 *Recueil Charles II*, vol. 2 no.230 for St-Denis in 861 and no.299 for Fosses in 867; *Recueil Charles II*, vol. 2, no.379 for St-Denis in 875 asks for prayers 'pro omni prole nostra vivente seu defuncta'; see also *Recueil Charles II*, vol. 1, no.220, and vol. 2, no.238.
106 Le Jan (1995), 36.
107 Dip. Louis II, nos 35, 36, 44.
108 Dip. Louis II, no.44; Dip. Lo. I, no.6; *Formulae Imperiales*, no.4, pp.290–1.
109 Zielinski (1989), 102–9.
110 See, for example, Pippin III, in Dip. Karol. 1, no.17, and Charlemagne in Dip. Karol. 1, nos 64, 95. Hummer (2005), 58–65; S. Wood (2006), 230–5, 266.
111 Charroux: *Testamentum* of Roger in P. de Monsabert, ed. *Chartes de Charroux*, p.59; Theodulf, poem no.50, PLAC 1, p.550; Astronomer, *VH*, c.3, 290–2. Dip. Karol. 1, no.194; Louis the Pious in Bouquet, *Recueil des historiens de la Gaule*, 6, no.26, pp.474–5. Oexle (1970); Wood (2006), 225–7; Remensnyder (1995), 166ff. on later traditions.
112 Vézelay: *Cartulaire*, no.1 in *Monumenta Vizeliacensia*, Corpus Christianorum, Cont. Med., 42 (1976), pp.243–8, at pp.245–7; *Recueil Charles II*, vol. 2, no.309; *Recueil Louis II*, no.5.
113 Dip. Louis G., no. 82; Zotz (1997a), 1496–8.
114 Dip. Louis G., no.90, with commentary and translation in Glansdorff (2009), 231–9; Borgolte (1984a), 123–4; Geuenich (1989), 52–3.
115 See, for example, *Recueil Charles II*, vol. 1, no.399 (844) and vol. 2, no.441 (877); Ewig (1982a), 56.
116 See, for example, *Recueil Charles II*, vol. 1, no.200 (860), and vol. 2, no.246, no.360 (867).Wallace-Hadrill (1978), 164–6; Ewig (1982b), 225–6; Werner (1988), 44–6; Nelson (1996a), 125–7.
117 862: Synod of Pîtres-Soissons, MGH Concilia 4, pp.106–115; *Recueil Charles II*, vol. 2, no.242. 869: Synod of Verberie, MGH Concilia 4, pp.331–6, quote at p.334; cf. *Recueil Charles II*, vol. 2, no.304. 871: Synod of Douzy, MGH Concilia 4, pp.570–2; *Recueil Charles II*, vol. 2 no.338.

Chapter 8

1 *De Karolo rege et Leone papa*, lines 137–267 (Bertha, lines 220–8), ed. Brunhölzl, pp.18–28; Nelson (1998b), 190–1; Mulvey (1975).

2   Einhard, *VK*, c.23, pp.27–8; contrast, for example, Ermold, Book IV, lines 2270–5, p.174; Schramm (1954–1956), vol. 1, 460–1, 542; Garver (2009), 21–5, 31–7; Carver (2019), 111–12.
3   Nithard, III, c.3, pp.66–8; Airlie (2007b).
4   Nithard, III, c.4, p.98; Airlie (2007b). Dip A, no. 132 (895), issued at Trebur. Hildegard: *AF*, a.885, pp.125–6, trans. Reuter (1992), 13.
5   Strathern (1988), 36.
6   See, for example, Konecny (1976); Nelson (1996a); Nelson (1991b); Nelson (1998b); Garver (2009); Leyser (1979); Corbet (1986); MacLean (2017); Ridyard (1988); Foot (2000); Yorke (2003).
7   Le Jan (2001), 69; Stafford (2000), 61–2; Keller and Althoff (2008), 139.
8   Le Jan (1995), 289–91, 398–9.
9   Kasten (1997), 175, 254–6; Pohl (2014).
10 Einhard, *VK*, c.18, p.22; McKitterick (2008), 282–4.
11 Montpellier, Faculté de Médecine MS 409; Stiegmann and Wemhoff (1999), vol. 2, 805–8; text most easily accessible as an appendix to Einhard, *VK*, pp.46–7; Nelson (1996a), 236; Diesenberger (2005), 176–7; Hammer (2007), 181–98; McKitterick (2008), 338–9; NB Bischoff (1974-1980), vol. 2, 16–18 for the idea of prayer for Agilolfings being removed.
12 *AB*, a.853, trans. Nelson (1991a), 78; Settipani (1993), 267; *Annales Mosellani*, a.781, MGH SS 16, p.497; Einhard, *VK*, c.18, c.19, pp.21–5.
13 *ARF*, a.819, p.150; Astronomer, *VH*, c.32, p.392; De Jong (2004).
14 *Vita S. Geretrudis*, c.1, ed. B. Krusch, MGH SRM 2, pp.454–5, trans. Fouracre and Gerberding (1996), 320.
15 Le Jan (1995), 263–327; Le Jan (2001), 53–88; Le Jan (2003), 72–7; Stone (2011).
16 Le Jan (1995), 274–7; Kasten (1997), 249–52.
17 Sons of Louis the Pious: *ARF*, a.821, a.822, pp.156, 159; Thegan, *GH*, c.28, p.216; Astronomer, *VH*, c.34, pp.402–4; Depreux (1997), 302, 343–4. Lothar II: *Epistolae ad Divortium Lotharii II regis pertinentes*, no.5, MGH Ep. KA 4, pp.215–17; Airlie (1998b), 17. Louis II: Dip. Louis II, no.30; Bougard (2006), 388–9.
18 Kasten (1997), 254; Depreux (1997), 302; Costambeys, Innes and MacLean (2011), 207; MacLean (2003a), 85. *AF*, a.841, pp.32–3; Dümmler (1887–1888), vol. 1, 167, n.2; Settipani (1993), 263.
19 Depreux (1997), 302, 316, 343–4; Kasten (1997), 249–57.
20 *ARF*, a.821, p.156; *AB*, a.862, trans. Nelson (1991a), 102. Dip. Louis G no.108 with commentary in Glansdorff (2009), 280–4; Orth (1985–1986), 200. Ewig (1982a), 60.
21 Dhuoda, *LM*, Praefatio, p.84; Nelson (2007); Le Jan (2010).
22 Hincmar, *De Divortio Lotharii regis et Theutbergae reginae*, Responsio V, ed. L. Böhringer, MGH Concilia 4, sup.1, p.141; Nelson (2005), 20–1. *AB*, a.862, trans. Nelson (1991a), 99–100; Hincmar, letter no.136, MGH EP 8, pp.87–107; Stone (2011), 272–3.
23 Althoff (2003), 40–51; MacLean (2003b), 36–7; MacLean (2017), 166–76.
24 See, for example, Stafford (1983); Konecny (1976); Le Jan (2001); MacLean (2003b); La Rocca (2002), 506. On daughters, Schieffer (1993) and Scharer (2009).
25 Buc (2001b), 201; Hildemar: http://hildemar.org/index.php?option=com_content&view=article&id=104&catid=15&Itemid=102; Coon (2011), 128.
26 Airlie (1995), 432; Fouracre (2000), 44–5; Wood (2004b), 239; Le Jan (1995), 290–1; Nelson (2004b), 96–7.
27 Thegan, *GH*, c.4, pp.180–1; Boshof (1996), 59; Innes (2000a), 185; see also, for example, Hraban epitaph on Lothar I's wife Ermengard: 'nobilis ortu', MGH PLAC 2, p.240.

28 MacLean (2003b), 24–6, 34–5; Hyam (1990), 158; Hummer (2005), 170; Screen (2011), 262–5.
29 Thegan, *GH*, c.36, p.222; Nithard, I, c.3, p.10.
30 Le Jan (2001), 72–8; MacLean (2003b) and Hummer (2005), 170.
31 Regino, *Chron.*, a.864.
32 Adventius, in *Epistolae ad Divortium Lotharii II regis pertinentes*, no.5, MGH Ep KA, 215-17; *Ann. Xant.*, a.864, p.23; Regino, *Chron.*, a.866; *Regesten des Regnum Italiae I*, no.228, ed. Zielinski (1991); Nelson (1992), 198.
33 *AB*, a.869, trans. Nelson (1991a), 164; *Recueil Charles II*, vol. 2, no.355 for October 10. Hyam (1990), 156–7; Nelson (1992), 221–2; Nelson (1996d), 63. *AB*, a.876, trans. Nelson (1991a), 190; Airlie (2000b), 32–3.
34 Notker, *GK*, I, c.13, p.17; Werner (1967), 420.
35 Gaedeke (1987); Schreiner (1975); Dierkens (1991), 161–3.
36 Notker, *GK*, I, c.17, pp.21–2; Goetz (1981), 13–14, 42–4; MacLean (2003a), 208–10.
37 MacLean (2003a) on Notker.
38 Goldberg (2006b), 75–88; Hyam (1990), 158–9.
39 *AB*, a.862, trans. Nelson (1991a), 99–100.
40 MacLean (2017), 51–7.
41 Stafford (2001b), 406; on Brunhild, Nelson (1986), 10–12.
42 Cunigonde, widow of Bernard of Italy; Judith, widow of Louis the Pious; Liutgard, widow of Louis Younger, she died in 885, Settipani (1993), 288; two widows of Lothar II; two widows of Louis the Stammerer, Ansgard, d.880/1 Settipani (1993), 315 while Adelaide d.c.901?, Settipani (1993), 316; Richgardis a special case; Engleberga; Richildis.
43 Regino, *Chron.*, a.900; MacLean (2008), especially 181–7; MacLean (2017), 56–7.
44 Stafford (1990).
45 Flodoard, *HRE*, IV, c.5, pp.386–7; *Cartulaire de l'abbaye de Gorze*, ed. A. d'Herbomez (Paris, 1898), nos 87, 88; MacLean (2003b), 3–4; MacLean (2017), 9, 87; Kornbluth (2003), 169–74.
46 Dip. Louis G., no.171; Dip. Karlmann, no.5; Dip. CF, no.22; MacLean (2003b), 34; Goldberg (2006a), 325; Bouchard (2001), 107.
47 Blackburn and Grierson (1986), 69.
48 Fastrada: Nelson (1997a); Richildis, see Chapter 6.
49 Hincmar, *De ordine palatii*, c.v, ed. Gross and Schieffer (1980), p.72; Sedulius Scottus, *De Rectoribus Chrstianis*, ed. Hellmann, pp.35–7; Nelson (1997b), 304–5, and cf. Nelson (2001a), 226–8 for date of *De ordine*.
50 Dhuoda, *LM*, IV, 6, p.228, trans. Thiébaux (1998), 145; cf. Sedulius Scotus, poem no.79, lines 11–12: 'servasti iura pudica thori', MGH PLAC 3, p.229; on the addressee of this poem, Werner (1967), 449. On clerical discourse and sinful queens, see Airlie (2010), De Jong (2009); Airlie (1998b); Reuter (2006), 217–30; Buhrer-Thierry (1992).
51 Paul the Deacon, *Gesta episcoporum Mettensium*, MGH SS 2, pp.265–7; Nelson (1996a), 234. Notker, *GK*, I, c.13, p.17; Einhard, *VK*, c.18, p.23, trans. Ganz (2008), 32.
52 Cathwulf, Letter to Charlemagne, MGH Ep KA 2, p.502; Nelson (2004b), 96–7. *Miracula S. Verenae*, c.4, MGH SS 4, p.458; Schmid (1977), 104–6, 123.
53 *Laudes*: appendix in Einhard, *VK*, pp.46–7. Prayer book, Schramm (1983), 167–8; Garipzanov (2008), 248 n.158 on the books' prayers as monastic. Mainz: council no.14, in MGH Concilia 3, p.160; Goldberg (2006b), 70.
54 Wallace-Hadrill (1978), 170; Garipzanov (2008), 255.

55 Consecration: the 'Prospice' prayer as in Nelson (1994a), 58, and in Ordo II, in Jackson (1995), 58. Judith: Ordo V, Jackson (1995), p.79, though this is rather a special case (i.e. she is a Carolingian daughter marrying out, not a woman marrying in).
56 Butler (2014), 10.
57 Nelson (1997a); Airlie (1998b), 12, 31.
58 Ordo VI, Jackson (1995), p.83; Stafford (1990), 146.
59 Astronomer, *VH*, c.8, pp.306–8; Störmer (2002), 56.
60 Hincmar, *De Divortio Lotharii*, Responsio 12, ed. Böhringer, p.182; Airlie (1998b), 23.
61 Hincmar, *De Divortio Lotharii*, Responsio 12, ed. Böhringer, pp.177–96; on virginity for man and woman, *De Divortio Lotharii*, Responsio 21, p.220.
62 Bloch (1991) 97–101, Jerome at 97.
63 Regino, *Chron.*, a.887; MacLean (2003a), 185–91.
64 Dip. CF, no.117.
65 Notker, *GK*, II, c.11, c.15, pp.68, 78.
66 Astronomer, *VH*, c.23, p.352; Nelson (1991b).
67 Capitulary no.272, c.5, MGH Cap.2, p.313; Nelson (1986), 80–1.
68 Bouchard (2001), 99–108; Werner (1967), 420.
69 Werner (1967), 417–19, Ewig (1965), 163–6; Carolingian men of course held abbacies, but women did so more frequently. Sedulius, poems nos 38, 61, 78, MGH PLAC 3, pp.202, 217–18, 228.
70 *AB*, a.879, trans. Nelson (1991a), 219; Konecny (1976), 131–3.
71 *Cartulaire de l'abbaye de Cysoing*, no. 6 and see also nos 3 and 4, ed. I. de Coussemaker (1885); Airlie (1995); Nelson (1992), 16, n.32.
72 Nelson (1996a), 232.
73 *Cont.Fredegar*, c.25, p.98; Astronomer, *VH*, c.21, p.348. Nelson (1991b); Schieffer (1993), 128; Airlie (1999), 105; De Jong (2009), 190–1; Joye (2012), 110–11.
74 Boshof (1996), 59, 65; Nelson (2004a), 192 n.34.
75 Schieffer (1993); Joye (2006); Joye (2012).
76 *AF*, a.846, p.36. 847 at Meersen, capitulary no. 204, c.8, MGH Cap.2, p.69. Nelson (1992), 148–9; Schieffer (1993); Joye (2006); Joye (2012).
77 *AB*, a.862, trans. Nelson (1991a), 97; Joye (2006); Joye (2012).
78 See, for example, the marriage plans of Louis the German's son, *AB*, a.865, trans. Nelson (1991a), 128.
79 Wickham (2005a), 193.
80 Dip. Lo. I, no.49; Werner (1967), 445; Ewig (1965), 164, n.125.
81 Werner (1967), 449; Settipani (1993), 263.
82 *Das Verbrüderungsbuch der Abtei Reichenau*, facsimile section, pag.2 at A1, eds J. Autenrith, D. Geuenich, K, Schmid, MGH Libri Memoriales et Necrologia; Schmid (1965), 49–54. *Recueil Charles II*, vol. 1, no.12, to be dated to 859, Werner (1967), 445, 449.
83 Keller (2002), 167–83.
84 *Das Verbrüderungsbuch der Abtei Reichenau*, facsimile section, pag.2, at A3, ed. Autenrieth et al.; Schmid (1965), 50–2.
85 *Annales de Flodoard*, ed. Lauer, Appendix I, p.167 and cf. Lauer's introduction, p.lviii. Settipani (1993), 263.
86 Ewig (1965), 302–9.
87 Dip. Lo. I, nos 118, 124; Brescia: Dip. Lo. I, nos 101, 115.
88 Dip. Lo. II, no.34; Borgolte (1984a), 30–3; Schmid (1968), 104; Hummer (2005), 175–6.

89 Dümmler II, 427–8; Goldberg (2006a), 239; Borgolte (1984a), 33; Borgolte (1986), 25, 99.
90 Nelson (1996a), 157–60; Ewig (1965), 304.
91 Konecny (1976), 150–2 and see, for example, Charles the Bald and Notre Dame, Soissons, *Recueil Charles II*, vol. 1, no.83; Dip. Louis G., no.79.
92 Périn and Feffer (1985), 160–4; Laporte (2012), 128–9.
93 Nelson (1996a), 175; Dümmler (1885–1886), vol. 2, 427.
94 Western kingdom: Freise (1989), 210; Airlie (2007b), 65–6. Eastern kingdom: *Das Verbrüderungsbuch der Abtei Reichenau*, facsimile section, pag.8, ed. Autenrieth et al., see Schmid in the introduction to *Das Verbrüderungsbuch der Abtei Reichenau*, xc–xci; Geuenich (1988), 65; Dip. Louis G., no.34. Schwarzach may have had links with the kin of Theodrada's mother, Fastrada, see Werner (1967), 445, and Bosl (1969), 66–7.
95 La Rocca (1998); La Rocca (2002), 506.
96 *Der Memorial- und Liturgiecodex von San Salvatore/Santa Giulia in Brescia*, eds D. Geuenich and U. Ludwig, MGH Libri Memoriales und Necrologia, nova series 4 (2000), pp.182–3, and facsimile section, fol. 42v. Ludwig (2000), 58, 61; Becher (1983), 308.
97 Dip. Louis II, nos 33, 34; Becher (1983), 311; Ludwig (2000), 61.
98 Becher (1983), 303–5, 337–56, 373–4; Ludwig (2000), 62, 76–88. Manuel and his daughter: *Memorial- und Liturgiecodex von San Salvatore/Santa Giulia in Brescia*, pp.182–3; Ludwig (2000),76, 86. Treasure: Bougard (2006), 393 n.37.
99 British Library, BL Add 37768; Schramm and Mütherich (1981), 124; Schramm (1983), 162; Lowden (1993), 223; Garipzanov (2008), 239; Screen (2018). Letter of Charlemagne: *Epistolae variorum*, no.20, MGH Ep KA 2, pp.528–9; McCormick (1986), 353; Nelson (1997a), 159.
100 *Cartulaire de Cysoing*, no. 6, ed. de Coussemakker. Dip. CF, no. 40; Dümmler (1885–1886), vol. 2, 243; on Lothar's place of burial, Brühl (1968), vol. 1, 420.
101 Dip. Louis G., no.67, and cf. nos 91 and 110, and NB *Recueil Charles II*, vol. 1, no.12. Brescia, see, for example, Dip. Louis II, no.22 and Becher (1983); Dip. Karlmann, no.26, Dip. CF, no.28, and cf. Karlmann's grant, with request for prayers, for the convent founded at Piacenza by Angilberga, Dip. Karlmann, no.27.
102 Dhuoda, *LM*, X, 5, p.354; Garver (2009), 68–121.
103 Leyser (1979), 93; Borgolte (1984b).
104 Nelson (1988a); on Carolingian abbots, Ewig (1965), 303–4.
105 Werner (1967), 444; *Recueil Charles II*, nos 247, 338. Dip. Louis G., no.82; Fleckenstein, Hofkapelle I, p.181.
106 Fulda: Jakobi (1978b), 505–10. Frankfurt: MGH Dip LD no.34; Orth (1985–1986), 194.
107 Gaedeke (1987), 30–3.
108 Einhard, *VK*, c.19, pp.23–5; Garver (2009), 229.
109 Lupus, letter no.66, ed. Levillain, vol. 1, p.244; John Scottus Eriugena Poems, no.2.4, MGH PLAC 3, p.533; see also the *Tituli vestibus intexti*, MGH PLAC 3, pp.687–8. Hyam (1990), 162; Goldberg (2006b), 74; in general, Garver (2009), 224–33; Screen (2011), 267.
110 Garver (2009), 246–9; La Rocca and Provero (2000); Ermold, Book IV, lines 2305–6, p.176. Schramm (1954–1956), vol. 2, 450–79; Schramm and Mütherich (1981), 128.
111 Alcuin, letter no.244, MGH Ep KA 2, pp.392–3. Schramm and Mütherich (1981), 128.

112 Frankfurt: Hampel (1994), 112–51; see also Wamers and Perin (2012). Ermentrud as above; Stafford (1983), 107; Garver (2009), 21–67; Einhard *VK*, c.23, pp.27–8; but see, for example, Theodulf 'on the court' and Ermold lines 2290–313, p.176.
113 *AB*, a.876, trans. Nelson (1991a), p.195 n. 21.
114 Fouracre and Gerberding (1996), 97–118; Nelson (2004a), 188–90; Laporte (2012).
115 Ganz and Goffart (1990), 928–32; Nelson (1991b), 207–8; Hyam (1990), 163; McKitterick (2008), 328.
116 Nelson (1996a), 194–5; McKitterick (2004), 125–6. But cf. Kaschke (2006).
117 Gisela Charter, in Dip. Karol. 1, Appendix, no.319; and see also no.190; Nelson (2002), 279. Gundrada: Alcuin, letter no.241, MGH Ep KA 2, pp.386–7; Nelson (2004a), 191. Alcuin, letter no.15, MGH Ep KA 2, p.41; Nelson (1996a), 238.
118 Ward (1990a), 214–15; Borgolte (1986), 169 is too negative. Sanders (1982), 419–28.
119 *Translatio Sanctae Baltechildis*, MGH SS 15, pp.284–5. Nelson (1996a), 194.
120 *Translatio Sanctae Balthechildis,* pp.284–5.
121 *AMP*, a.830, pp.95–8; Nelson (1996a), 194.
122 Klaniczay (2002).
123 *Vita Geretrudis*, c.2, c.3, c.6, pp.455–61; Fouracre and Gerberding (1996), 308–16; Wood (2004b), 240–2; Dierkens (1985), 70–80, 106–11; Périn and Feffer (1985), 181–2.
124 Effros (1996), 9–10.
125 *Gesta domni Aldrici Cenomannicae Urbis epsicopi*, c.9, ed. M. Weidemann, p.126; Angilbert, *De ecclesia Centulensi Libellus*, MGH SS 15, p.175. Lehmann (1962), 169, 170; Coens (1963), 296–8; *Recueil Charles II*, vol. 2, no.433.
126 Rudolf, *Miracula sanctorum in eccelsias Fuldenses translatorum*, c.12, MGH SS 15.1, pp.337–8; Bosl (1969), 123.
127 Regino, *Chron.*, a.882, a.885; Searle (1988), 20–2; MacLean (2003a), 149–50; Settipani (1993), 273–4. Dip. Zwentibold, nos 11 and 16; Dip. LC, no. 50; *Recueil Charles III*, no. 57. Dierkens (1985), 79–89.
128 Dip. Zwentibold, no.11, no.16; Brühl (1968), vol. 1, 39 but contrast Nelson (1986), 75–90.
129 Dip. LC, no.50.
130 *Virtutum Sanctae Geretrudis continuatio*, c, 4, MGH SRM 2, p.473; Schreiner (1975), 8.
131 Alcuin, letter no.150, MGH Ep. KA 2, p.246; Nelson (1996a), 236.
132 'Karolus maior domus. Pippinus rex. Karlomannus maior domus. Karolus imperator. Karolus rex. Pippinus rex. Bernardus rex. Ruadtrud. Ruadheid. Suanahilt regina. Berhta regina. Hiltikart regina. Fastrat regina. Liutkart regina. Ruadheid. Hirminkar regina', in *Das Verbrüderungbuch von Reichenau*, facsimile section, pag.114, section A1-3; and see the introduction to the edition, pp.lxvii–viii. Hlawitschka (1965), 79; Le Jan (1995), 356–7; Butz and Zettler (2013), 63.
133 Fulda: Jakobi (1978b), 506–17; Raaijmakers (2003), 39–42; Remiremont: Jakobi (1986), 197; Butz and Zettler (2013).
134 Wood (2001), 67–8; Raaijmakers (2003), 179–80; Airlie (2014), 263.
135 Dip. Louis G., no.34 refers to Blutenda, daughter of a count, in connection with Schwarzach; Jakobi (1978b), 509–10.
136 Jakobi (1978b), 510–12; Settipani (1993), 287.
137 Bischoff (1981a), 208–9; Freise (1984), 536–7.
138 Bischoff (1981a), 206–7; Goldberg (2006a), 188. Judith: *Ann. Xant.*, a.843, p.13; Nelson (1992), 130.
139 Le Jan (1995), 293–4; Nelson (2004a), 192 n.34 on Judith as arranging Gisela marriage. Le Jan (1995), 300 on these daughters, seeing Alpais as daughter of Louis the Pious; and the other(s) as sons-in-law of Pippin I of Aquitaine, not of Louis, Astronomer, *VH*, c.61, p.536.

140 Konecny (1976), 150–6; see also Le Jan (1995), 300ff. on daughters and marriages.
141 See above on Judith, etc; Louis the Stammerer: Nelson (1992), 232. Charles Fat's marriage to Richgard, *AB* a.862, trans. Nelson (1991a), 102, with Goldberg (2006a), 294 and he could have arranged Louis the Younger's marriage, for date see Goldberg (2006a), 278. Louis the German's disciplining of Karlmann's father-in-law, Ernst, *AB*, a. 861, trans. Nelson (1991a), 94–5; *AF*, a.861, p.55.
142 See tree in Werner (1967); and Konecny (1976), 150–6; Schieffer (1993).
143 Le Jan (1995), 294, 410–13; Settipani (1993), 317–18; Koziol (2012), 201.
144 Le Jan (1995), 411.
145 *AB*, a.878, trans. Nelson (1991a), 212; Settipani (1993), 287–99, 313–20.
146 *AB*, a.876, trans. Nelson (1991a), 190; *AF*, a.878, pp.91–2. Staab (1998), 376–9.
147 Airlie (2000b), 35–6.

Chapter 9

1 Hincmar, letter 20, c.9, PL 126, col.120; Patzold (2008b), 86–7.
2 Notker, *Continuatio Erchanberti*, MGH SS 2, pp.329–30. MacLean (2003a), 134.
3 *AF*, a.881; Nelson (2001a), 234. Cap.2, no.287, pp.371–5; see Bautier's introduction to *Recueil Louis II*, p.liii; Offergeld (2001), 380.
4 Airlie (2000b).
5 Bruhl (1990), 361–2; Offergeld (2001), 362, 396–7, 407–8, 447; Bautier, introduction to *Recueil Louis II*, p.xliv on weak kings of 'la décadence' in aristocratic power, and see Bautier's assumptions about decline and military power, pp.xli–xlix, lxxxv, ciii and cxi–xii.
6 Nelson (1995), 136; MacLean (2003a).
7 Patzold (2008b), 86–7; Wood (1994), 39; Murray (1998), 110.
8 See Hincmar, letter 20, c. 9, col.120, as cited n.1 above and see the end of it with the references to Compiègne and to tombs of the king's father and grandfather; see also, for example, references to 'consanguineis vestris regibus' in c.8 of the same letter, col.120.
9 Notker, *Continuatio Erchanberti*, p.330; MacLean (2001), 29–30.
10 The text of the capitulary is in the great manuscript of capitulary texts in Vatican MS Pal. Lat. 582 that seems to preserve a Sens collection; see Mordek (1995a), 780–97 and Wormald (1999), 61.
11 *Recueil Louis II*, no.31.
12 Einhard, *VK*, c.1, pp.2–4; Fouracre (2009); *AF*, a.887, p.106; Regino, *Chron.*, a.888, pp.128–9.
13 Thompson (1935); Dhondt (1948).
14 Wickham (2005b), 15–30, especially 28–9; but cf. Nelson (1995), 140–1.
15 Barbier (1999), 595; Nelson (1992), 257–64; Helvétius (1998).
16 Martindale (1985), especially 166–71; Barbier (1989), especially 141; Innes (2000a), 225 n.216; MacLean (2003a), 12 n.14.
17 Rather too optimistic, Bachrach and Bachrach (2009); on sources and difficulty see Barbier (1989), especially 135 and Barbier (2009), 282, with Fouracre (2009), 294–5.
18 *Recueil Louis II*, no.73 (Carloman), and also no.88. West (2013), 42–3.
19 Geary (1994), 172.
20 Goldberg (2006a); Nelson (1992); *Recueil Louis II*, no.88; Barbier (2009), 283.

21 Barbier (1999).
22 Constance: MacLean (2003a), 91 and see 90 n.45; warning to beneficiaries, Nelson (1995), 390; MacLean (2003b), 20–31.
23 *Recueil Louis II*, Carloman, no.6, restoration to St Germain of Auxerre; note the fiscal experience of Gisela and Eberhard, in Airlie (2011b), 226, 229. Alsace: Dip. CF, no.170, Dip. A, no.9; MacLean (2003a), 189. Charles could also reach back into the deep Carolingian past via his grants of property, see MacLean (2003a), 87–8.
24 *Recueil Louis II*, no.86 (Carloman) and see also *Recueil Charles III*, no.2 with its references to activity and to Baldwin – need for the king to confirm the count's transaction. See Pirenne (1925); Verhulst (1999), 10–12, 56–7.
25 *AV*, a.884, p.55.
26 Verhulst (1999), 56–7.
27 Barbier (1999), 588–9; Nelson (1995), 391–2; Innes (2000a), 161–2, 224–5.
28 Innes (2000a), 224; Nelson (1995), 140.
29 *Recueil Louis II*, no.12, no.14; *AB*, a.878, trans. Nelson (1991a), 207.
30 Werner (1979) is classic, if a bit schematic; Offergeld (2001), 349–65.
31 Hincmar, letter to Charles the Fat, PL 125, especially c.1, col.989–90, c.2, col.990–1; Offergeld (2001), 387–92. See also Hincmar, *De ordine palatii*, prologue, eds Gross and Schiffer, p.32.
32 'Ludwigslied', in Dutton (2004), 513.
33 *AB*, a.879, trans. Nelson (1991a), 216.
34 *AB*, a.878, trans. Nelson (1991a), 212.
35 *AB*, a.879, trans Nelson (1991a), 217; for the 850s, see Chapter 6 above.
36 Airlie (2000b); Koziol (2012), 201–3, 381–5; *Die Regesten des Regnum Italiae und der burgundischen Regna 4.1, Fasz. 1: Niederburgund*, ed. Zielinski (2013), nos 2716, 2717, 2728, 2741, 2742, 2743.
37 *Recueil Provence*, no.16 (Boso). Airlie (2000b); Koziol (2012), 203 n.291, 384.
38 Capitulary no.284, MGH Cap.2, pp.365–9, particularly p.368. Boehm (1975).
39 Capitulary no.284, MGH Cap.2, p.368; Koziol (2012), 384–5.
40 Airlie (1998a); MacLean (2001) and MacLean (2003a); Koziol (2012), 385–9.
41 Regino, *Chron.*, a.879, pp.114–15 and see below.
42 Louis born 863/4, Carloman 867, Offergeld (2001), 343, and see 389–92. Hincmar, to Charles the Fat, PL 125, col.991–2.
43 Notker, *Continuatio Erchanberti*, MGH SS 2, p.330; for the 'Ludwigslied' on Louis III's youth as time of hope, Offergeld (2001), 392–4.
44 *Recueil Louis II*, no.77 (Carloman): 'quem pro fidelitate ad nos semper conservta loco patris colimus', and see no.71: Hugh as 'tutor noster'. See also *AV*, a.882, p.53.
45 *AV*, a.884, p.55 and Regino, *Chron.*, a.884, p.122 on the deal; Offergeld (2001), 396–7.
46 *Recueil Louis II*, Introduction, pp.xii–xiv.
47 *AB*, a.878, trans. Nelson (1991a), 207–12 and *AV*, a.878, p.48; *Recueil Louis II*, nos 15, 16, 17, 18, 19, 20, 21, 22, 23 and Introduction, p.xxviii and p.xxxi on *laudes*, with Kantorowicz (1946), 73.
48 *Recueil Charles II*, vol. 2, no.445; *Recueil Louis II*, no.24 and no.56.
49 *Recueil Louis II*, no.73. *AB*, a.880, trans. Nelson (1991a), 221–2, and *AV*, a.880, p.47; MacLean (2001).
50 *Recueil Louis II*, for example, nos 9, 13, 14; Ewig (1982a), 61.
51 *Recueil Louis II*, no.7, no.12 and see also no.20 for wide family; on Prüm, see Chapter 2 above. Formulae: see, for example, *Recueil Louis II*, no.30.

52 *Recueil Louis II*, no.51 for 'prosapia', with no.74 for successors; Ewig (1982a), 61–2; MacLean (2001), 37–8.
53 *Recueil Louis II*, no.77.
54 Dip. CF, no.145. *Recueil Eudes*, no.12.
55 AF a.876, p.89; and see AF, a.879, p.93 for knowledge of this oath. On the clashes of the sons, Kasten (1997), 541–6. The oaths probably contained familial references, as well as territorial ones, to judge by parallel of Fouron, AB, a.878, trans Nelson (1991a), pp.213–15.
56 Ewig (1982a), 73–5.
57 On Louis the Younger's marriage Kasten (1997), 543–4; Liutgard m. 876/7, Settipani (1993), 288, and MacLean (2003a), 85, with 130 on Charles the Fat's son Bernard born c.875; on status of Arnulf, Dip. Karlmann, no.49, and MacLean (2003a), 134. Prayers, Ewig (1982a), 73; Frankfurt, Orth (1985–6), 212–13; Goldberg (2006a), 278.
58 Dip. Louis Y., nos 3 and 4; Ewig (1982a), 74.
59 Goldberg (2006a), 338–9 and see Dutton (2009), 195–8 on life-spans. AF, a.879, pp.92–3, and see trans. Reuter (1992), 83 n.9 and 86 n.1.
60 AF, a.878, a.879, pp.91–3.
61 Dip. Rudolf, no.1; MacLean (2003a), 134–5; MacLean (2001), 41.
62 Epitaph on tomb at Lorsch, Goldberg (2006a), 336. Commemoration: Dip. Louis Y., nos 2, 24; Dip. CF, nos 103, 129; Dip. A, no. 150, no.167. Nelson (2000), 166–9; MacLean (2003a), 111, 132–3; in general, Ewig (1982a), 73–8.
63 Dip. Karlmann, no.27, and see also no.26; on Engelberga's power in Italy, MacLean (2003b), 26–32.
64 Pippin and Herbert, grandsons of Bernard of Italy, AB, a.877, trans. Nelson (1991a), 201; Nelson (1992), 247; on knowledge of Bernard's descendants, Regino, *Chron.*, a.818, p.73.
65 Dip. Karlmann, nos 12, 13, 16, 17, 21, 22, 23, 24, 25, 26, 27, 28.
66 Dip. Karlmann, for example, nos 10, 22; Ewig (1982a), 73. Andreas of Bergamo, *Historia*, c.19, MGH SRL, pp.229–30; Goldberg (2006a).
67 *Annales ex Annalibus Iuvavensibus antiquis excerpti*, a.878, MGH SS 30, p.742; Reuter (1991), 116. AF, a.879, a.898, pp.93, 132; Kasten (1997), 546; MacLean (2003a), 134–5.
68 Jakobi (1978a), 842; followed by Althoff (1992), 48, and Airlie (1998a), 139; But see Becher (1996), 148–9, and Goldberg (2006a), 283–4, 312.
69 See Chapter 1 above for death of the nephew (Louis); AF, a.880, p.94; Leyser (1979), 11; Becher (1996), 74–6, 85; Regino, *Chron.*, a.897, p.145.
70 Innes (2000a), 231–2.
71 AV, a.878, p.43.
72 *Formulae Sangallenses*, 2, no.27, MGH Formulae, p.412; the reference to recent treaty is probably to Fouron. Penndorf (1974), 144–5 sees it as possibly composed by Notker himself, but still datable to 878/9; MacLean (2001), 41 n.65 takes it straight.
73 AF, a.884, p.101, trans. Reuter (1992), 96.
74 AV, a.880, p.47, translation is an unpublished version by S. Coupland.
75 Poeta Saxo, Book V, lines 123–48, MGH PLAC 4.1, pp.58–9.
76 AF, a.881, p.96, trans. Reuter (1992), 90; AB, a.880, trans. Nelson (1991a), 220–1 and see also, for other references to kings as cousins, AB, a.878, trans. Nelson (1991a), 212, a.880; trans. Nelson (1991a), 221; a.882, trans. Nelson (1991a), 223. See also AF, a.875, p.84 for eastern and western kings as namesakes.
77 See AB, a.879, trans. Nelson (1991a), 217–18 for western aristocrats negotiating the succession of Louis II and Carloman with Louis the Younger; see also AB, a.882,

78 trans. Nelson (1991a), 223; *AV*, a.879, p.44 with reference to Hugh the Abbot as royal cousin; and see the brief tableau of east Frankish hereditary royal line at *AF*, a.884 (Bavarian continuation), p.111; NB Fulk's letter to Arnulf below.
78 *AB*, a.879, trans. Nelson (1991a), 218. Lothar II's daughter (Gisela), although the eastern annalist does not seem to know her name in *AF*, a.883, a.884, a.885, pp.100, 101, 103.
79 *Formulae Sangalliensis*, no.39, MGH Formulae, p.421 and see also no.40, pp.421–2; MacLean (2001). Hincmar: see, for example, Flodoard, *HRE*, III, c.20, p.267; *AB*, a.882, trans. Nelson (1991a), 223; Sot (1993), 544–9.
80 *AF*, a.875, p.85 on Charles the Bald as more fearful than a hare; *AB*, a.882, trans. Nelson (1991a), 225 for Hincmar's scorn on death of Louis the Younger; MacLean (2001).
81 Notker, *Continuatio Erchanberti*, c.11, MGH SS2, p.330; Notker, *GK*, II, c.12, pp.70–1.
82 *AB*, a.879, trans. Nelson (1991a), 216–18.
83 MacLean (2001).
84 *AF*, a.876, p.87.
85 *AB*, a.876, trans. Nelson (1991a), 192–3; Lorsch Charter no.1835; Innes (2000a), 217–19, 226, though Innes makes Megingaud a *nepos* of Odo when the reverse was the case; Werner (1997), 14–15.
86 *AB*, a.879, trans. Nelson (1991a), 217–18; *AB*, a.882, trans. Nelson (1991a), 223.
87 *AB*, a.878, at Pref., c.3, trans. Nelson (1991a), 213–14; MacLean (2001).
88 MacLean (2001).
89 Ludwigslied in Dutton (2004), 512–14; contemporary chroniclers on the victory: *AV*, a.891, pp.50–1 and Regino, *Chron.*, a. 883, p.120. Schneider (2010), 343–423, especially 415–23.
90 *AB*, a.879, trans. Nelson (1991a), 216; Schneidmüller (1979), 101–5; Koziol (2012), 543.
91 Dümmler (1887–8), vol. 3, 120; on burial in Regensburg, Schmid (1976), 351–6.
92 *AF*, a.880, p.; *AV*, a.880, pp.46–7; Regino, *Chron.*, a.879, pp.115–16; Nelson (2000), 168; MacLean (2003a), 133.
93 For Louis's shock see the hostile account in fragment ed. Schieffer (2004a), especially p.967 and fo other sources, 968–70.
94 Notker, *Continuatio Erchanberti*, MGH SS 2, pp.329–30.
95 *Cartulaire de l'abbaye de Cysoing*, no.1, ed. I. de Coussemaker (1885); La Rocca and Provero (2000), especially 235, 245–9; Wickham (2009), 402–4; map in Le Jan (1995), 74. In general on patterns of aristocratic inheritance, Le Jan (1995), 225–62.
96 La Rocca and Provero (2000), 265–7; MacLean (2003a), 70–1, 95–6; Airlie (1993); Le Jan (1995), 296.
97 Dip. CF, no.105, issued at Metz; Werner (1997), 15 and MacLean (2003a), 108–9 with references there to Gauzlin and 102–15 for general relation between Charles and west Franks.
98 Le Jan (1995), 381–427; and see above on Odo.
99 Werner (1959), 171; other examples there.
100 Airlie (1998a); MacLean (2003a), 53–4.
101 Werner (1959), 171 on Wandalbertus; Werner (1997).
102 Regino, *Chron.*, a.888, p.198 of MacLean translation; MacLean (2003a).
103 Kasten (1997); Reuter (1991), 115–16; MacLean (2003a), 99–111, 124–9.
104 Offergeld (2001), 403–9.
105 MacLean (2003a), 149–51 and on Arnulf; Airlie (2011a).
106 Dip CF, no.122; see also nos 123 and 124 for Lyon with references to Louis the Pious as his grandfather; in general, Ewig (1982a), 76.

107 Dip. CF, no.129. Airlie (1998a), 142; MacLean (2003a), 110–11, 132–3.
108 MacLean (2003a), 112–15.
109 Flodoard, *HRE,* IV, c.5, p.380; Sot (1993), 131–2.
110 Abbo, *Siege of Paris*, Book II, lines 315–33, ed. Wacquet, pp.88–90; MacLean (2003a), 58, 100–1, 121.
111 MacLean (2003a), especially 1–10, 30–7.
112 MacLean (2003a), 48–80.
113 Reuter (1991), 116–17; MacLean (2003a), 136–44.
114 Reuter (1991), 117; Innes (2000a), 222–33; MacLean (2003a), 78–80, 82 and see section on Baldwin and violence below.
115 *AF* (Mainz continuation), a.886, a.887, p.105 and *AF* (Bavarian continuation), a.887, p.115; MacLean (2003a), 40–1, 81–160.
116 *AF* (Mainz continuation), a.885, p.103; Regino, *Chron.*, a.885, pp.123–6; MacLean (2003a), 149–52; Airlie (2011a).
117 Notker, *GK*, II, c.14, p.78, II, c.11, p.68, II, c. 12, p.74; Notker, *Continuatio Erchanberti*, MGH SS 2, pp.329–30; MacLean (2003a), 143–4, 201–4.
118 *AF* (Mainz continuation), a.885, p.103; MacLean (2003a), 130–4; Offergeld (2001), 465–72; Kasten (2002).
119 If he was indeed a grandson of a daughter of Pippin I of Aquitaine that might have made Charles's mother Adelaide turn to him. Our evidence for this, however, comes from the eleventh-century chronicler Ademar of Chabannes, whose work is notoriously unsafe for the ninth century.
120 Ramnulf: *AV*, a.889, p.67; Settipani (1993), 279–80, 321–2, 376–7; Offergeld (2001), 414; Koziol (2012), 470. Louis' deathbed: *AB*, a.879, trans. Nelson (1991a), 216.
121 See, for example, Dip. CF nos 165, 166; MacLean (2003a), 165; MacLean (2003b), 26–32.
122 *AF* (Bavarian continuation), a.887, p.115, trans. Reuter (1992), 113. Hlawitschka (1978); Offergeld (2001), 472–88; contra, Penndorf (1974), 130–4; MacLean (2003a), 162–7.
123 Regino, *Chron.*, a.879, pp.114–15, trans. MacLean (2009a), 180.
124 *AF* (Bavarian continuation), a.887, p.115; Dip. CF, nos 156, 160, 165, 166; *Das Verbrüderrungsbuch der Abtei Reichenau*, facsimile pag.134 (at A3), eds Autenrith, Geuenich, Schmid, MGH Libri memoriales et necrologia, nova series, 1 (1979); Geuenich (1982), 42; Airlie (1998a), 141–2; MacLean (2003a), 112–13, 162–7.
125 Regino, *Chron.*, a.887, p.127; Dip. CF, no.168; MacLean (2003a), 167–91. See Chapter 8 above on women.
126 See Kasten (2002) and Becher (2008b) on flexibility of illegitimate status.
127 Orth (1985–6), 219–23; MacLean (2003a), 191–8; Keller and Althoff (2008), 45–8, 54–7.
128 MacLean (2003a), 194–5.
129 *AF* (Bavarian continuation), a.887, p.115; MacLean (2003a), 39–42.
130 *AF* (Mainz continuation), a.887, p.106; Althoff (1997), 252; MacLean (2003a), 195.
131 Reuter (1991), 120; MacLean (2003a), 196.
132 *AF* (Mainz continuation), a.887, p.106; *AF* (Bavarian continuation), a.887, p.115; Regino, *Chron.* a.887, p.128; Dip. A, no.1; Fleckenstein (1959), 199–200.
133 Notker, *GK*, I, c.4, p.5.
134 *AF* (Mainz continuation), a.887, p.106; Nithard, II, c.6, 56; Airlie (2007b), 54; Widukind, *Res Gesta Saxonicae*, I, c.33; Althoff (1992), 25–6; Koziol (2006), 385.
135 *AF* (Mainz continuation), a.887, p.106; Becher (2001), 30–1, 47–50.
136 *AV*, a.887, p.64.

137 Flodoard, *HRE*, IV, c.5, p.380.
138 *AF* (Mainz continuation), a.887, p.106; Regino, *Chron.*, a.887, a.888, pp.127–9; MacLean (2003a), 196.
139 Regino, *Chron.*, a.888, p.129; strangled: *AV*, a.887, p.64; *AF* (Bavarian continuation), a.887, pp.115–16. Maurer (1984).
140 *AF* (Mainz continuation), a.887, p.106; *AF* (Bavarian continuation), a.888, p.116; MGH Dip Arnulf, nos 10, 14, 23, and see also nos 5–9, 11–13, 15–22; Bowlus (1995), 230–3; MacLean (2003a), 193; Keller and Althoff (2008), 55.
141 Regino, *Chron.*, a.888, p.129, trans. MacLean (2009a), 199 and I follow his translation of this passage, which is also Hlawitschka's (1968), 65–6, rather than some of the alternatives such as Eggert (1973), 193–4, Nelson (1995), 138–9 and Kasten (2002), 50. We all agree on the identity of the 'natural lord', as does Hlawitschka (1968), 66.
142 Regino, *Chron.*, a.888, p.129, trans. MacLean (2009a), 199; Leyser (1979), 15.
143 'Vacillante rerum statu et regum naturalium, … qui apud Francos semper hereditarii habebantur, deficiente successione', Folcuin, *Gesta Abbatum Lobiensium*, c. 16, MGH SS 4, p.61, my emphasis, and see also c.6, p.58; van Renswoude (2006), 333–4, and 328–9 on Folcuin's view of the Ottonians as 'natural heirs' to the Carolingians. See also Folcuin, *Gesta Abbatum S. Bertini Sithiensium*, c. 93, MGH SS 13, p.623 on Odo as 'non ex regia stirpe'.
144 Fulk of Reims, letter in Flodoard *HRE,* IV, c.v, p.381, lines 17–20 and p.382, lines 28–30; Airlie (2006b), 427–9, 436; Hatto of Mainz, text of letter in Bresslau (1910), 27; Offergeld (2001), 529. See also Keller (2002), 116.
145 Brühl (1990), 376.
146 Hincmar knew of Arnulf back in 879, *AB*, a.879, trans. Nelson (1991a), 218; *AV*, a.888, p.65; Flodoard, HRE, IV, c.5, 380–1. *AF* (Bavarian continuation), a.888, p.116, trans. Reuter (1992), 115.
147 *AF* (Bavarian continuation), a.888, p.116; *AV*, a.888, pp.64–5; Regino, *Chron.*, a.888, pp.129–30. Brühl (1990), 368–72; Keller and Althoff (2008), 45–8.
148 Sot (1993), 222, 551, 598–9; *AV*, a.887, p.64; Erchempert, *Historia Langobardorum Beneventanorum*, ed. G. Waitz, MGH SRL, p.263.
149 *AV*, a.887, p.64; Erchempert, *Historia*, p.263; *Regesten.Regnum Italiae*, ed. Zielinski, no.857.
150 *Gesta Berengarii imperatoris*, I, lines 32–40, MGH PLAC 4.1, p.359 with *Regesten. Regnum Italiae*, ed. Zielinski, no.858; but cf. MacLean (2003a), 168.
151 *Gesta Berengarii imperatoris*, I, lines 78–95, MGH PLAC 4.1, pp.361–2.
152 Abbo, *Siege of Paris*, Book II, lines 442–8, ed. Wacquet, pp.98–100; Guillot (1989), 218; MacLean (2003a), 57–8.
153 Buc (2001a), 25–6.
154 *AF*, a.888, p.116; Ramnulf: *AV*, a.889, p.67; Koziol (2012), 223–6. Regino, *Chron.*, a.888, p.130. Airlie (2011a); Ripart (2011), 437–8.
155 *Recueil Eudes*, no.55; Airlie (2006b), 431. Baccou (2003).
156 Dip. CF, no.155 (a.887); MacLean (2003a), 112; Pokorny (1985), 619–20; Hlawitschka (1988), 196.
157 Letters in Bischoff (1984), 135, with date proposed by Hlawitschka (1988), 195. Flodoard, *HRE*, IV, c.5, pp.380–3; Airlie (2006b), 427.
158 See letters in Bischoff (1984), 131–2. *AV*, a.892, p.72; Regino, *Chron.*, a.892, pp.139–40. Koziol (2012), 227.
159 La Rocca and Provero (2000), 245–6, 252–3, 267–9; MacLean (2003a), 70–1.
160 Erchempert, *Historia*, p.263; *AV*, a. 887, a. 888, pp.64–5. Hlawitschka (1988), 192–5; Sot (1993), 125–6, 133–4.

161 Nithard, IV, c.5, p.138; *Beowulf*, trans. Morgan (1952), 8; Orchard (2003), 170–1.
162 *AF* (Bavarian continuation), a.888, pp.116–17, and a.890, p.119 on Boso, trans. Reuter (1992), 115–17, 120; compare Regino, *Chron.*, a.888, pp.129–30; *Anglo-Saxon Chronicle*, a.887, trans. Whitelock (1979), 199; Brühl (1990), 370–1; Rudolf called one of his sons Louis, Schneidmüller (2000), 81–2.
163 Brühl (1990), 371, n.110; Settipani (1993), 278–81, 322.
164 See Sedulius on his brother Unroch, Sedulius, poem no.38, lines 19–20, MGH PLAC 3, p.202; La Rocca and Provero (2000), 239; *Gesta Berengarii imperatorisi*, I, line 33, MGH PLAC 4.1, p.359 and see also book III, lines 4–20, p.384; *AF* (Bavarian continuation), a.883, a.886, pp.110, 114.
165 *Gesta Berengarii*, III, lines 3–14, p.384; Dümmler (1887–8), vol. 3, 373; Rosenwein (1999), 141–2; gold tunic: La Rocca and Provero (2000), 251.
166 *AF* a.888, pp.116–17, trans. Reuter (1992), 115–16 and see the accounts of Berengar and Rudolf in the same entry; *AV*, a.888, pp.64–5; Flodoard, *HRE*, IV, c.5, 380–1; Sot (1993), 132–5, 138–46.
167 *AF*, a.888, pp.116–17; Regino, *Chron.*, a.888, p.130, trans. MacLean (2009a), 201; Schieffer, IntroductIon to Dip. Rudolf, 6; Schneidmüller (2000), 78; Rosenwein (2001), 272–4; Ripart (2011), 437–8.
168 *AV*, a.888, p.64; Guillot (1989), 207–12; Hlawitschka (1988), 192–5; *Regesten. Regnum Italiae*, no.863.
169 *AV*, a.888, pp.64–5; Hope (2005), 119–22.
170 Airlie (1998a), 142; MacLean (2003a), 110–15, 126–9. The *ordo* survives, Jackson (1995), no.XI, pp.133–38, see further below; regalia: Airlie (2006b), 432.
171 *AV*, a.888, p.65; Guillot (1989), 212–13.
172 *AV*, a.888, pp.64, p.67; Hope (2005); Schneidmüller (1979); *Regesten. Regnum Italiae*, no.864.
173 Odo and queen: Jackson (1995), Ordo XIA, p.137, and Ordo XIII A, p.151; Nelson (1997b), 310–11, and Bobrycki (2009). Louis: capitulary no.289, MGH Cap.2, p.377. William: Nelson (1986), 385. Pippin: for example, *Codex Carolinus* nos 6 and 8, MGH Ep KA 1, p.489, p.496. Louis III: Synod of Fismes, MGH Concilia 5, pp.178–80. Rudolf: *AV*, a.888, pp.64–5 and Regino, *Chron.*, a.888, p.130.
174 Regino, *Chron.*, a.888, p.130.
175 Louis the Stammerer: capitulary no.283, MGH Cap.2, pp.363–5; Carloman: capitulary no.285, pp.369–70; Odo: no.288, pp.375–6; also in Jackson (1995), no. VIII A, no.X and no.XI, pp.117–19, 132 and 138. Louis of Provence: capitulary no.289, MGH Cap.2, pp.376–7. Boehm (1975), 381–6; MacLean (2003a), 164–5; Offeregeld (2001), 495–505.
176 Regino, *Chron.*, a.888, p.130. Schneidmüller (2000); Jackson (1995), no.XI, pp.136–9; capitulary no.289, MGH Cap.2, pp.376–7.
177 Odo regalia, Koziol (2006), 383–5; Notker, *GK*, I, c.4, p.5; Airlie (2006b), 432.
178 Capitulary no.289, MGH Cap.2, pp.376–7; Jackson (1995), Ordo XIB, c.6, pp.138 and 133–4; Guillot (1989), 210–11; Koziol (2012), 94–5.
179 *AF*, a.888, pp.116–17; Regino, *Chron.*, a.888, p.130.
180 *AF*, a.888, p.116; *AV*, a.888, pp.66–7; Guillot (1989), 213–20.
181 Bautier, introduction, *Recueil Eudes,* pp.ix–x; Schieffer introduction, Dip. Rudolf, p.6.
182 Jackson (1995), Ordo no.XI, pp.133–8, supplemented with Ordo no.XIII, pp.142–53, as argued in Nelson (1997b), 310–11, quote at 311 and see Bobrycki (2009). Theodrada is called 'regina' in *Vita Rigoberti Episcopi Remensis*, c.28, ed. W. Levison,

MGH SRM 7, p.77; Levison's introduction, p.55, says that this text was written between 888 and 894.
183 *Recueil Eudes*, no.5 (June 889); no.6 (June 889). Ewig (1982a), 62–3.
184 Hlawitschka (1968), 87.
185 *AF*, a.889, p.118 on Arnulf's succession plans. Offergeld (2001), 488–92 and nb 492 on contemporaries' flexible view of illegitimacy and youth; see in general Kasten (2002).
186 *AF*, a.895, pp.125–6, trans. Reuter (1992), 130 with references at his n.2; Regino, *Chron.*, a.894, p.142.
187 Kasten (2002). *AF*, a.900, p.134 is suggestively tight-lipped on Zwentibold's death; Regino, *Chron.*, a.900, p.148 is more explicit; MacLean (2009b). On Lotharingia, Le Jan (2001), 210–12, and Innes (2000a), 227–9. *AV*, a.887, p.64 (on grim rumours about Charles the Fat), and a.895, p.76 on fears about Zwentibold. Radbod, poem I.1, ed. Winterfeld, MGH PLAC 4.1, pp.161–2; Airlie (2000b), 30.
188 *AV*, a.889, p.67; Offergeld (2001), 414–16; Koziol (2012), 223–6.
189 Dip. A, no.49; *AF*, a.890, p.119, trans. Reuter (1992), 120; *Liber Memorialis Remiremont*, ed. Hlawitschka, MGH Lib Mem, p.3 v; Hlawitschka (1968), 84–8, 95–6, 241–9; Offergeld (2001), 487; Koziol (2012), 336–7.
190 *Recueil Provence*, no.28, and Dip. Rudolf, no.14 and editor's comments there. Hlawitschka (1968), 96, Offergeld (2001), 508; see also Lauranson-Rosaz (1998).
191 Nelson (1992), 232; Pope John: *AB*, a.878, trans. Nelson (1991a), 210–11; Boso on children of first marriage, Regino, *Chron.*, a. 879, p.114. Offergeld (2001), 345–58.
192 Regino, *Chron.*, a. 878, p.114. Settipani (1993), 321; Offergeld (2001), 370 and see Le Jan (1995), 406–7.
193 A later tradition that Fulk of Reims looked after Charles is not reliable, Sot (1993), 142. Offergeld (2001), 314–15, 406–7, 415, 422–3; Koziol (2012), 470–6.
194 Capitulary no.289, MGH Cap.2, p.377; Hlawitschka (1968), 87; Boehm (1975); Hlawitschka (1968), 96, 241–9; Offergeld (2001), 493–4.
195 Capitulary no.289, MGH Cap.2, p.377; date, Hlawitschka (1968), 88.
196 *Visio Karoli*, MGH SS 10, p.348; translated in Dutton (2004), 537–40. Date: Hlawitschka (1968), 100–6, followed by MacLean (2003a), 166 and Offergeld (2001), 500–5; Dutton (1994), 233–51 suggests 888.
197 Hlawitschka (1968), 99; Sot (1993), 135; Offergeld (2001), 503.
198 Hlawitschka (1968), 105–6; Sot (1993), 180; Dutton (1994), 245–7.
199 Capitulary no.289, MGH Cap.2, pp.376–7; MacLean (2003a), 164–5.
200 Hlawitschka (1968), 89–95. 894: Regino, *Chron.*, a.894, p.142, trans. MacLean (2009a), 217–18; Schneidmüller (2000), 80–81.
201 Hlawitschka (1968), 106.
202 Capitulary no.289, MGH Cap.2, p.377.
203 *Visio Karoli,* MGH SS 10, p.458; Dutton (2004), 540; Offergeld (2001), 504; Dutton (1994), 225–51.
204 Fulk, letter in Flodoard, *HRE*, IV, c.5, pp.380–3; on this as tendentious, Offergeld (2001), 417.
205 *AF*, a.894, p.125, trans. Reuter (1992), 128; Offergeld (2001), 453; Louis: Valence, capitulary no.289, MGH Cap.2, p.377.
206 *Visio Karoli*, MGH SS 10, p.458; Dutton (1994), 234–51.
207 Flodoard, *HRE*, IV, c.1, c.4, pp.363–4, 379; Sot (1993), 125–6; Koziol (2012), 476–9.
208 Flodoard, *HRE*, IV, c.5, pp.380–83. Guillot (1989) and Sot (1993), 132–5, 138–46.
209 *AV*, a.892, a.893, pp.71–3; Sassier (1987), 59–60; Offergeld (2001), 420–1.

210 *AV,* a.893, p.73; Flodoard, *HRE,* IV, c.5, p.382; Sot (1993), 144, 147–8; Hlawitschka (1988), 197–8.
211 Werner (1960), 87–119; Schneidmüller (1979), 122–3; Offergeld (2001), 425.
212 Airlie (1993), 159–60; Airlie (2006b), 427–8; Koziol (2012), 477–9.
213 Schneidmüller (1979), 124; Werner (1960), 95; Offergeld (2001), 420–22.
214 *Recueil Charles III,* no. 93; Schneidmüller (1979), 123–4.
215 *AV,* a.893, a.894, a.895, pp.73–7; Schneidmüller (1979), 15–23.
216 Fleckenstein (1959), 237; Helvétius (1998), 290, 295–7. *Recueil Charles II,* vol. 2, no.304; *Recueil Eudes,* no.12 and no.20. *AV,* a.892, a.893, pp.70–3; Koziol (2012), 218, 223, 477–9.
217 *AV,* a.893, p.73, and see also a.894 and a.895, p.74, p.76 on Arnulf and Zwentibold as Charles's kinsmen.
218 Flodoard, *HRE,* IV, c. 5, pp.380–3; Schneidmüller (1979), 125–6; Offergeld (2001), 417–18, 428–32; Sot (1993), 138–46, 197–8; Airlie (2006b), 427–9, which I draw on here.
219 *AF,* a. 893, p.122; Hlawitschka (1968), 120; Sot (1993), 143, 161.
220 Hlawitschka (1968), 129–32; Offergeld (2001), 433–4. Regino saw Charles as a 'usurper', *Chron.,* a.893, p.141.
221 *AV,* a.894, pp.74–5; *AF,* a. 894, p.123; Regino, *Chron.,* a.893, p.141; Flodoard, *HRE,* IV, c.5, 383. Offergeld (2001), 435.
222 Flodoard, *HRE,* IV, c.5, p.382.
223 Flodoard, *HRE,* IV, c.5, pp.381–3; Schneidmüller (1979), 125–6; Innes (2000b), 227–9.
224 Flodoard, *HRE,* IV, c.5, p.382; Sot (1993), 145.
225 Flodoard, *HRE,* IV, c.5, p.381, 382; Airlie (2006b), 428; Koziol (2012), 476.
226 Flodoard, *HRE,* IV, c.3, p.376; Sot (1993), 146–8.
227 *AV,* a.895, p.76 for Zwentibold against Charles. For the chaos and crisis, see Koziol (2012) and Koziol (2006).
228 Castelnuovo (1998), 398; Patzold (2008a), 435–9.
229 Airlie (2006c); MacLean (2009b); Keller and Althoff (2008), 31–41; Koziol (2006), 386–7.
230 Hlawitschka (1968), 133–9; Bouchard (2001).
231 Castelnuovo (1998), especially 399–403 arguing that territorialization of power doesn't necessarily lead to dynasticization; Hlawitschka (1968); Bouchard (2001).
232 Hlawitschka (1968), 147–9, 155, 248–9. Letters of Pope Formosus and Fulk of Reims, see Sot (1993), 149–51, 187–8. Teutbold of Langres was blinded at end of 894, Hlawitschka (1968), 135 n.71.
233 *AV,* a.894, a.895, pp.74–7; Hlawitschka (1968), 133 ff. on w. Burgundy from 893 on.
234 *AV,* a.895, a.896, pp.75–8.
235 Capitulary no.289, MGH Cap.2, pp.376–7; charter of Ava, sister of William the Pious, *Recueil des chartes de l'abbaye de Cluny,* no.53, eds A. Bernard and A. Bruel, vol. 1 (1876); Hlawitschka (1968), 118; Offergeld (2001), 427.
236 Nelson (1992), 261 and Zimmerman (1999). Keller and Althoff (2008), 88–94 on parallels in east and west. West (2013), 135–7. Coins, Grierson and Blackburn (1986), 246–7.
237 Koziol (2012), 497–8 and see also 94–5 and 494–500; Schneidmüller (1979), 194–9; Zimmermann (1999), 428–30.
238 West (2013), especially 54–5, 109–38, 142–5.
239 Reuter (2006), 72–88.

240 *AV*, a.899, pp.81–2; Regino, *Chron.*, a.903, pp.149–50; Radbod, Poem I.1, MGH PLAC 4.1, pp.161–2; Flodoard, *HRE*, IV, c.10, pp.402–3. Airlie (2000b), 30.
241 Regino, *Chron.*, a.906, pp.150–3. Innes (2000a), 231 and see pp.225–33; Le Jan (2001), 210–12; for example, Fouracre (2000), 30–1.
242 Regino, *Chron.*, a.898, pp.145–6, and see trans. Maclean (2009a), 223 n.461.
243 *AF*, a. 900, pp.143–4; Regino, *Chron.*, a.900, pp.147–8.
244 Schramm (1983), 63–4; Dip. LC., Schieffer's introduction, pp.75–9; Offergeld (2001), 580–3. Hatto, Letter in Bresslau (1910), p.27; Theotmar of Salzburg, in Lošek (1997), p.148.
245 Kasten (1997), 547–57. Werner (1967), family tree; Settipani (1993), 324–6; Koziol (2012), 517–20. MacLean (2003a).
246 Airlie (2006c); MacLean (2009b).
247 Lambert charter no.5, in *I diploma di Guido e di Lamberto*, ed. Schiaperelli (1906); *Recueil Charles III*, no.49; Autun: appendice, no.51, *Recueil Robert et Raoul*. Airlie (2006b), 432–3; Koziol (2012), 9–11; McCormick (1986), 386–7.
248 Sassier (1987), 61–71; Koziol (2012), 223–47.
249 Airlie (2000b); Offergeld (2001), 612–41; Keller and Althoff (2008), 88–94.
250 Keller and Althoff (2008), 69. Widukind, *Res Gestae Saxonicae*, I, c.16, ed. P. Hirsch, MGH, p.25; Adalbert, *Continuatio Reginonis*, a.911, ed. Kurze, p.155.
251 Widukind, *Res Gestae Saxonicae*, I, c.29, p.42; Schneidmüller (1997). Family tree in Leyser (1979); Settipani (1993), 329–34, 336–9; Kasten (1997), 495.
252 Sassier (1987); Koziol (2012), 87–92, 459–555.
253 Adalbert, *Continuatio Reginonis*, a.922, ed. Kurze, pp.156–7, trans. MacLean (2009a), 236; Flodoard, *Annales* (5G) trans. Fanning and Bachrach (2004), p.8. Herbert: Rodulfus Glaber, *Histroriae*, I, c.13, ed. France (1989), 14–15; Wallace-Hadrill (1975), 201; Koziol (2012), 330–1, 461–7.
254 Koziol (2012), 555–6, and figure 13, 627.
255 Richer, *Histories*, IV, c.11, ed. Lake (2011), vol. 2, pp.218–22; Schneidmüller (1979), 172–3.
256 Letter of archbishop Adalbero of Reims, in Gerbert, letter no.48, ed. Weigle, p.77; Schneidmüller (1979), 172–3.
257 Letter of Charles to bishop Theoderic of Metz, in Gerbert, letter no.32, ed. Weigle, p.59; Brühl (1990), 567.
258 Letter of bishop Theoderic of Metz, in Gerbert, letter no. 31, ed. Weigle, pp.54–7; Lot (1891a), 139; Sassier (1987), 197.
259 Brother: Gerbert, letter no.31, ed. Weigle, p.56, lines 1–4; Einhard, *VK*, c.18, p.22. Slandering and revering women: Gerbert, letter no.31, ed. Weigle, p.56, lines 3–4, 7–8; Einhard, *VK*, c.18, c.19, pp.22–5. Masculine mastery and inferiority: Gerbert, letter no.31, ed. Weigle, p.56, lines 10–11; Einhard, *VK*, c. 18, pp.21–3. Voice: Gerbert, letter no.31, ed. Weigle, p.56, lines 6–8; Einhard, *VK*, c.22, c.25, p.22, p.30; Notker, *GK*, for example, I, c.3, pp.4–5; Thegan, *GH*, c.19, p.204.
260 Charles's letter is in Gerbert, letter no.32, ed. Weigle, pp.57–60, at p.59; Einhard, *VK*, c. 2, p.4; Richer, *Histories*, IV, c.1, ed. Lake, vol. 2, p.198.
261 Leyser (1994), 174 n.45.
262 Council of Paris, c.5, c.59, in MGH Concilia 2.2, pp.612–13, 655.
263 Hoffmann (1998); Glenn (2004).
264 Richer, *Histories*, IV, c.5–c.14, ed. Lake, vol. 2, pp.206–29; Schneidmüller (1979), 170–85; Sassier (1987), 194–8; Leyser (1994), 174–6; Nelson (1999), 124–5; Glenn (2004), 118–23, 241–3.

265 Hoffmann (1998), 476–82; cf. Koziol (2012), 329–30.
266 Richer, *Histories*, IV, c.11, ed. Lake, vol. 2, pp.218–21; I cite Lake's translation.
267 Richer, *Histories*, IV, c.13, ed. Lake, vol. 2, pp.224–5. Schneidmüller (1979), 170–4; Sassier (1987), 210–11.
268 Gerbert, letters nos 168, 172, 173, ed. Weigle, pp.196–7, 199–200; Leyser (1994), 177–8; Glenn (2004), 93–7.
269 Richer, *Histories*, IV, c.49, ed. Lake, vol. 2, pp.302–3; Huth (1994); Glenn (2004), 123–5.
270 Richer, *Histories*, IV, c.32, c.50, ed. Lake, vol. 2, pp.202–3, 304–11; Glenn (2004), 252–66.
271 Richer, *Histories*, Prologus, 2–5, ed. Lake, vol. 1, pp.2–5; *Histories*, IV, c.109, vol. 2, pp.436–7; the last reference to a Louis (son of Charles of Lotharingia) is *Histories*, IV, c.97, vol. 2, pp.408–9. Hugh and Robert charters in Bouquet, *Recueil des historiens de la Gaule*, vol. 10, no.9, p.556; Schneidmüller (1979), 175–6. Coins no longer helped create a Carolingian reality: Grierson and Blackburn (1986), 246–8.
272 Huth (1994), 121; Theuws (2001), 205–13; Patzold (2013), 104–5.

Bibliography

Primary Sources

Abbo, *Le siege de Paris par les normands: poème du IXe siècle*, ed. H. Wacquet (Paris, 1942).
Actus pontificum Cenomannis degentium, ed. M. Weidemann, *Geschichte des Bistums Le Mans von der Spätantkie bis zur Karolingerzeit. Actus pontificum Cenomannis degentium und Gesta Aldrici*, 3 vols, Römisch-Germanischen Zentralmuseum Forschungsinstitut für Vor- und Frühgeschichte, Band 56 (1, 2 and 3) (Mainz, 2002) in vol. 1, pp.115–79.
Adalbero, *Poème au roi Robert*, ed. and trans. C. Carozzi (Paris, 1979).
Adalbert, *Continuatio Reginonis*, ed. F. Kurze, in Regino, *Chronicon cum continuatione Treverensi*, ed. F. Kurze, MGH SRG in usum scholarum separatim editi, 50 (Hannover, 1890).
Die Admonitio Generalis Karls des Grossen, ed. H. Mordek, K. Zechiel-Eckes and M. Glatthaar, MGH Fontes Iuris 16 (Wiesbaden, 2013).
Ado of Vienne, *Chronicon* (and *Continuatio*), ed. G. H. Pertz, MGH SS 2 (Hannover, 1829), pp.315–26.
Adrevald of Fleury, *Miracula S. Benedicti*, ed. O. Holder-Egger, MGH SS 15 (Hannover, 1887), pp.474–97.
Agnellus, *Liber pontificalis ecclesiae Ravennatis*, ed. O. Holder-Egger, MGH Scriptores Rerum Langobardicarum ei Italicarum saec. VI–IX (Hannover, 1878) pp.265–391.
Agobard, *De Divisione Imperii*, Agobard of Lyon, *Opera Omnia*, ed. L. van Acker, Corpus Christianorum, Continuatio Mediaevalis, 52 (Turnhout, 1981), pp.245–50.
Agobard, *De Iniusticiis (Ad Matfredum)*, Agobard of Lyon, *Opera Omnia*, ed. L. van Acker, Corpus Christianorum, Continuatio Mediaevalis, 52 (Turnhout, 1981), pp.223–7.
Agobard, *Liber Apologeticus*, Agobard of Lyon, *Opera Omnia*, ed. L. van Acker, Corpus Christianorum, Continuatio Mediaevalis, 52 (Turnhout, 1981), pp.307–19.
Agobard, *Cartula de Ludovici imperatoris poenitentia*, Agobard of Lyon, *Opera Omnia*, ed. L. van Acker, Corpus Christianorum, Continuatio Mediaevalis, 52 (Turnhout, 1981), pp.321–4.
Alcuin, *Disputatio*, in *Altercatio Hadriani Augusti et Epicteti philosophi*, ed. L. W. Daly and W. Suchier (Urbana, 1939) pp.137–43.
Alcuin, *Epistolae*, ed. E. Dümmler, MGH Ep. KA 2 (Berlin, 1895), pp.1–481.
Alcuin, *Vita Willibrordi*, ed. W. Levinson, MGH SRM 7 (Hannover and Leipzig, 1920), pp.81–141.
Andreas of Bergamo, *Historia*, ed. G. Waitz, MGH Scriptores rerum Langobardicarum et Italicarum saec. VI–IX (Hannover, 1878), pp.220–30.
Angilbert, *Carmina*, ed. E. Dümmler, MGH PLAC 1 (Berlin, 1881), 355–66.
Angilbert, *De ecclesia Centulensi Libellus*, ed. G. Waitz, MGH SS 15 (Hannover, 1887), pp.173–9.

Anglo-Saxon Chronicle, ed. and trans. D. Whitelock, in *English Historical Documents*, vol. 1 (2nd edition, 1979).
Annales de Saint-Bertin, ed. F. Grat, J. Vielliard, S. Clemencet and L. Levillain (Paris, 1964).
Annales ex Annalibus Iuvavensibus antiquis excerpti, ed. H. Bresslau, MGH SS 30.2 (Leipzig, 1934), pp.727-44, 742.
Annales Fuldenses, ed. F. Kurze, MGH SRG in usum scholarum separatim editi 7 (Hannover, 1891).
Annales Laureshamenses, ed. G. H. Pertz, MGH SS 1 (Hannover, 1827), pp.22-39.
Annales Mettenses priores, ed. B. von Simson, MGH SRG in usum scholarum separatim editi, 10 (Hannover and Leipzig).
Annales Mosellani, ed. I. M. Lappenberg, MGH SS 16 (Hannover, 1859), pp.491-9.
Annales Nazariani, ed. G. H. Pertz, MGH SS 1 (Hannover, 1827), pp.40-4.
Annales Petaviani, ed. G. H. Pertz MGH SS 1 (Hannover, 1827), pp.7-18.
Annales Regni Francorum, ed. F. Kurze, MGH SRG in usum scholarum separatim editi, 6 (Hannover, 1895).
Annales Weissemburgenses, MGH SS 1 (Hannover, 1827), p.111, and in Hofmeister (1919), pp.418-20.
Annales Xantenses et Annales Vedastini, ed. B. von Simson, MGH Scriptores rerum Germanicarum in usum scholarum separatim editi (Hannover and Leipzig, 1909).
Ansegis, *Collectio Capitularium, Die Kapitulariensammlung des Ansegis*, ed. G. Schmitz, MGH Capitularia regum Francorum, nova series (Hannover, 1996).
Arnold, *Liber de S. Emmeramo*, ed. G. Waitz, MGH SS 4 (Hannover, 1841), pp.543-74.
Asser, *De rebus gestis Aelfredi, Asser's Life of King Alfred: Together with the Annals of St Neot's Erroneously Ascribed to Asser*, ed. W. H. Stevenson, revised by D. Whitelock (Oxford, 1959).
Astronomer, *Vita Hludowici imperatoris*, ed. E. Tremp, MGH SRG 64 (Hannover, 1995).
Audradus Modicus, *Liber Revelationum*, ed. L. Traube in L. Traube, *O Roma nobilis. Philologische Untersuchungen aus dem Mittelalter*, Abhandlungen der philologischen Classe der königlich Bayerischen Akademie der Wissenschaften, 19 (1892), pp.378-91.
Bouquet, M., ed., revised by L. Delisle, *Recueil des historiens des Gaules et de la France*, vol. 10 (Paris).
Die Briefen des heiligen Bonifatius und Lullus, ed. M. Tangl, MGH Epistolae selectae in usum scholarum separatim editi (Berlin, 1916).
Capitularia Episcoporum, I, ed. P. Brommer, MGH Capitularia Episcoporum (Hannover, 1984).
Capitularia Regum Francorum, vol. 1, ed. A. Boretius, MGH Legum Sectio 2, Capitularia (Hannover, 1883).
Capitularia Regum Francorum, vol. 2, ed. A. Boretius and V. Krause, MGH Legum Sectio 2 (Hannover, 1897).
Carmen de Exordio gentis Francorum, ed. E. Dümmler, MGH PLAC 2, pp.141-4.
Cartulaire de l'abbaye de Cysoing, ed. I. de Coussemaker (Lille, 1885).
Cartulaire de l'abbaye de Gorze, Ms. 826 de la bibliothèque de Metz, ed. A. d'Herbomez (Paris, 1898).
Cartulaire de l'abbaye de Redon en Bretagne, ed. A. de Courson (Paris, 1863).
Cartulaire de l'église d'Autun, ed. A. de Charmasse (Paris, 1865).
The Cartulary of Flavigny, ed. C. B. Bouchard (Cambridge, Mass, 1991).
Cathwulf, Letter to Charlemagne, ed. E. Dümmler, MGH Ep. KA 2 (Berlin, 1895), p.502.
Chartae Latinae Antiquiores, ed. H. Atsma and J. Vezin, vol. XIV (Zürich, 1982).

Chartae Latinae Antiquiores, ed. H. Atsma and J. Vezin, vol. XV (Zürich, 1986).
Chartae Latinae Antiquiores, ed. H. Atsma and J. Vezin, vol. XVI (Zürich, 1986).
Chartae Latinae Antiquiores, ed. H. Atsma, R. Marichal, P. Gasnault, and J. Vezin (Zürich, 1985).
Chartes et documents de l'abbaye de Charroux, ed. P. de Monsabert (Poitou, 1910).
The Chronicle of Theophanes, ed. and trans. H. Turtledove (Philadelphia, 1982).
Chronicon Novaliciense, ed. L. C. Bethmann, MGH SS 7 (Hannover, 1851), pp.73–133.
Chronicon Fontanellense (Fragmentum), in *Recueil des historiens de la Gaule et de la France*, vol. 7, ed. M. Bouquet, revised L. Delisle (Paris, 1870), pp.40–3.
Das Chronicon Laurissense breve, ed. H. Schnorr von Carolsfeld, *Neues Archiv der Gesellschaft für ältere deutsche Geschichtskunde*, 36 (1910), pp.11–39.
Chronicon Moissiacense a saeculo quarto usque ad a.814 et a.840, ed. G.H. Pertz, MGH SS 1 (Hannover, 1826), pp.280–313, and *Ex Chronicone Moissiacense*, ed. G. H. Pertz, MGH SS 2 (Hannover, 1829), pp.257–9.
Codex Carolinus, ed. W. Gundlach, MGH Epistolae Merowingici et Karolini Aevi 1 (Berlin, 1892), pp.469–657.
Codex Diplomaticus Fuldensis, ed. E. F. J. Dronke (Kassel, 1850).
Codice Diplomatico Parmense, ed. U. Bassi (Parma, 1910).
Codex Laureshamensis, ed. K. Glöckner, vols. 3 (Darmstadt, 1929–36).
Commemoratio genealogiae domni Karoli gloriosissimi imperatoris, ed. G. Waitz, MGH SS 13 (Hannover, 1881), pp.245–6.
Concilia Aevi Carolini 1.1, ed. A. Werminghoff, MGH Concilia 2.1 (Hannover and Leipzig, 1906).
Concilia Aevi Carolini 1.2, ed. A. Werminghoff, MGH Concilia 2.2 (Hannover and Leipzig, 1908).
La Correspondance d'un éveque carolingien. Frothaire de Toul (ca 813–847), ed. and trans. M. Parisse (Paris, 1998).
Die Konzilien der karolingischen Teilreiche 843–859, ed. W. Hartmann, MGH Concilia 3 (Hannover, 1984).
Die Konzilien der karolingisichen Teilreiche 860–874, ed. W. Hartmann, MGH Concilia 4 (Hannover, 1998).
Die Konzilien der karolingischen Teilreiche 875–911, ed. W. Harmann, I. Schröder, G. Schmitz, MGH Concilia 5 (Hannover, 2012).
De Karolo rege et Leone papa, ed. F. Brunhölzl, Beiheft to W. Hentze, ed., *De Karolo rege et Leone papa. Der Bericht über di Zusammenkunft Karls des Grossen mit papst Leo III. in Paderborn 799 in einem Epos für Karl den Kaiser* (Paderborn, 1999).
De unctione Pippini regis, ed. G. Waitz, MGH SS 15, p.1.
Dhuoda, *Manuel pour mon fils*, ed. P. Riché, trans. B. de Vregille and C. Mondésert, Sources Chrétiennes 225 (Paris, 1975).
Domus Carolingicae Genealogia, ed. G. H. Pertz, MGH SS 2 (Hannover, 1829), pp.308–12.
Einhard, *Epistolae*, ed. K. Hampe, MGH Ep. KA 3 (Berlin, 1889) pp.105–45.
Einhard, *Translatio et miracula sanctorum Marcellini et Petri*, ed. G. Waitz, MGH SS 15 (Hannover, 1887), pp.238–64.
Einhard, *Vita Karoli*, ed. G. Waitz, MGH Scriptores rerum Germanicarum in usum scholarum separatim editi (Hannover and Leipzig, 1911).
Epistolarum Fuldensium Fragmenta, MGH Ep KA 3 (Berlin, 1899), pp.517–32.
Epistolae ad divortium Lotharii II. regis pertinentes, ed. E. Dümmler, MGH Ep. KA 4 (Berlin, 1925) pp.207–40.

Epistolae Aevi Merowingici collectae, ed. W. Gundlach, MGH Epistolae Merowinigici et Karolini Aevi, 1 (Berlin, 1892),pp.434–68.
Epistolae variorum Carolo Magno regnante scriptae, ed. E. Dümmler, MGH Ep. KA 2 (Berlin, 1895), pp.494–567.
Epistolae variorum inde a morte Caroli Magni usque ad divsionem imperii, MGH Ep. KA 3 (Berlin, 1899), pp.299–360.
Epistolae variorum inde a saeculo nono medio usque ad moerm Karoli II. (Calvi) imperatoris collectae, ed. E. Dümmler, MGH Ep KA 4 (Berlin, 1925), pp.127–206.
Ep. KA 1, MGH Epistolae Merowingici et Karolini Aevi, 1 (Berlin, 1892).
Ep. KA 2, MGH Epistolae Karolini Aevi 2 (Berlin, 1892).
Ep. KA 3, MGH Epistolae Karolini Aevi, 3 (Berlin, 1899).
Ep KA 4, MGH Epistolae Karolini Aevi, 4 (Berlin, 1925).
Ep. KA 5, MGH Epistolae Karolini Aevi 5 (Berlin, 1928).
Erchanberti Breviarium, ed. G. H. Pertz, MGH SS 2 (Hannover, 1827), p.327.
Erchempert, *Historia Langobardorum Beneventanorum*, ed. G. Waitz, MGH Scriptores rerum Langobardicarum ei Italicarum saec. VI–IX (Hannover, 1878), pp.231–64.
Ermold, *Ad Pippinum Regem* [I and II], ed. and trans. E. Faral, *Ermold le Noir, Poème sur Louis le Pieux et épitres au roi Pépin* (Paris, 1964).
Ermold, *In Honorem Hludowici Pii*, ed. and trans. E. Faral, *Ermold le Noir, Poeme sur Louis le Pieux et épitres au roi Pépin* (Paris, 1964).
Flodoard, *Annales*, ed. P. Lauer, *Les Annales de Flodoard* (Paris, 1905).
Flodoard, *Historia Remensis Ecclesiae*, ed. M. Stratmann. MGH SS 36 (Hannover, 1998).
Folcuin, *Gesta Abbatum Lobiensium*, ed. G. H. Pertz, MGH SS 4 (Hannover, 1841), pp.52–74.
Folcuin, *Gesta Abbatum S. Bertini Sithiensium*, ed. O. Holder-Egger, MGH SS 13 (Hannover, 1881), pp.607–35.
The Fourth Book of the Chronicle of Fredegar with Its Continuations, trans. J.M. Wallace-Hadrill (London, 1960).
Forumula Imperiales, ed. K. Zeumer, in Formulae Merowingici et Karolini Aevi MGH Formulae (Hannover, 1886), pp.285–328.
Formulae Sangallenses, ed. K. Zeumer, in Formulae Merowingici et Karolini Aevi MGH Formulae (Hannover, 1886), pp.378–437.
Freculf of Lisieux, *Histories*, ed. M. I. Allen, *Frechulfi Lexoviensis episcopi opera omnia*, 2 vols, Corpus Christianorum, Continuatio Mediaevalis, 169–169A (Turnhout, 2002).
Fredegar, *Fredegarii quae dicuntur Chronicarum libri IV*, ed. B. Krusch, MGH SRM 2 (Hannover, 1888), pp.1–193.
Genealogiae Karolorum, ed. G. Waitz, MGH SS 13 (Hannover, 1881), pp.242–50.
Gerbert *Die Briefsammlung Gerberts von Reims*, ed. F. Weigle, MGH Die Briefe der deutschen Kaiserzeit 2 (Weimer 1966).
Gesta domni Aldrici Cenomannicae Urbis epsicopi, ed. M. Weidemann, *Geschichte des Bistums Le Mans von der Spätantkie bis zur Karolingerzeit. Actus pontificum Cenomannis degentium und Gesta Aldrici*, 3 vols, Römisch-Germanischen Zentralmuseum Forschungsinstitut für Vor- und Frühgeschichte, Band 56 (1, 2 and 3) (Mainz, 2002) in vol. 1, pp.115–79.
Gesta Berengarii imperatoris, ed. P. Winterfeld, MGH PLAC 4.1 (Berlin, 1899), pp.354–403.
Gesta Dagoberti, ed. B. Krusch, MGH SRM 2 (Hannover, 1888), pp.396–425.
Gesta Episcoporum Autisiodorensium, ed. G. Waitz, MGH SS 13 (Hannover, 1881), pp.393–400.

Gesta Episcoporum Virdunensium, ed. G. Waitz, MGH SS 4 (Hannover, 1841), pp.36–51.
Gesta Sanctorum Patrum Fontanellensis Coenobii (Gesta abbatum Fontanellensium), ed. F. Lohier and J. Laporte (Rouen and Paris, 1936).
Gregory I, *Homelia in Evangelia*, PL 76 (Paris, 1852).
Gregory of Tours, *Decem Libri Historiarum*, ed. B. Krusch and W. Levison, MGH SRM 1.1 (Hannover, 1951).
Hadrian II, *Epistolae*, ed. E. Perels, MGH Ep. KA 4 (Berlin, 1925), pp.691–765.
Hatto of Mainz, letter, in H. Bresslau, 'Der angebliche Brief des Erzbischofs Hatto von Mainz an Papst Johann IX, in *Historische Aufsätze Karl Zeumer zum 60. Geburtsatg dargebracht* (Weimar, 1910), pp.9–30.
Heiric, *Annales breves*, ed. G. Waitz, MGH SS 13 (Hannover, 1881), p.80.
Heiric, *Miracula Sancti Germani*, PL 124 (Paris, 1852), cols 1207–70.
Heito, *Visio Wettini*, ed. E. Dümmler, MGH PLAC 2 (Berlin, 1884), pp.267–75.
Hildemar, *Commentary on the Rule of St Benedict* http://hildemar.org/index.php?option=com_content&view=article&id=1&Itemid=102
Hincmar, *De Divortio Lotharii regis et Theutbergae reginae*, ed. L. Böhringer, MGH Concilia 4, supplementum 1 (Hannover, 1992).
Hincmar, *Epistolae*, ed. E. Perels, MGH Ep. KA 6 (Berlin, 1939).
Hincmar, *Ad Ludovicum Balbum*, PL 125, cols 983–90.
Hincmar, *De ordine palatii*, ed. T. Gross and R. Schieffer, MGH Fontes Iuris Germanici Antiqui 3 (Hannover, 1980).
Hincmar, *De regis persona et ministerio*, PL 125, cols 833–66.
Hincmar, *De villa Novilliaco*, ed. H. Mordek, 'Ein exemplarischer Rechtsstreit: Hinkmar von Reims und das Landgut Neuilly-Saint-Front', *Zeitschrift der Savigny Stiftung für Rechtsgeschichte*, 114, *Kanonistische Abteilung*, 83 (1997), pp.86–112.
Historia translationis Regnoberti episcopi Baiocensis et Zenonis diaconi, Acta Sanctorum 17 May, vol. 3 III (1618), pp.615–24.
Houben, H., '*Visio cuiusdam pauperculae muieris*: Überlieferung und Herkunft eines frühmittelalterlichen Visionstext (mit Neuedition)', *Zeitschrift für die Geschichte des Oberrheins* 124, NF 85 (1976), 31–42.
Hraban, *Epistolae*, ed. E. Dümmler, MGH Ep. KA 3 (Berlin, 1899), pp.379–516.
Jackson, R.A., *Ordines Coronationis Franciae. Texts and Ordines for the Coronation of Frankish and French Kings and Queens in the Middle Ages*, vol. 1 (Philadelphia, 1995).
Jonas of Orléans, *De Institutione Regia*, in Jonas d'Orléans, *Le metier de roi*, ed. A. Dubreucq (Paris, 1995).
Justin, *Epitoma Historiarum Philippicarum Pompei Trogi*, ed. O. Seel (Leipzig, 1935).
Lex Alamannorum, ed. K. Lehmann, revised K. A. Eckhardt, MGH Leges nationum Germanicarum, 5.1 (Hannover, 1966), pp.35–157.
Lex Baiwariorum, ed. E. von Schwind, MGH Leges nationum Germanicarum 5.2 (Hannover, 1928), pp.197–473.
Lex Salica, ed. K. A. Eckhardt, MGH Leges nationum Germanicarum 4.2 (Hannover, 1969).
Liber Historiae Francorum, ed. B. Krusch, MGH SRM 2 (Hannover, 1888), pp.215–328.
Liber Memorialis von Remiremont, ed. E. Hlawitschka, K. Schmid, G. Tellenbach, MGH Libri Memoriales, nova series 1, 2 vols. (Dublin and Zürich, 1970).
Le Liber Pontificalis, ed. L. Duchesne, vol. 1 (Paris, 1886).
Liber sacramentorum Gellonensis, ed. A. Dumas, Corpus Christianorum, Series Latina, vols. 159 and 159a (Turnhout, 1981).

Liutolf, *Vita et Translatio S. Severini*, ed. L. de Heinemann, MGH SS 15.1 (Hannover, 1887) pp.289–93.
Lupus, Loup de Ferrièrres, *Correspondance*, ed. and trans. L. Levillain, 2 vols (Paris, 1964).
Marculfi Formulae, ed. K. Zeumer, Formulae Merowingici et Karolini Aevi, MGH Formulae (Hannover, 1886), pp.32–112.
Der Memorial- und Liturgiecodex von San Salvatore/Santa Giulia in Brescia, ed. D. Geuenich and U. Ludwig, MGH Libri Memoriales und Necrologia, nova series 4 (Hannover, 2000).
Miracula S. Genesii, ed. G. Waitz, MGH SS 15.1 (Hannover, 1887), pp.169–72.
Miracula S. Quintini, MGH SS 15, p.270.
Miracula S. Verenae, ed. G. Waitz, MGH SS 4, pp.457–60.
Monumenta Vizeliacensia, ed. R. B.C. Huygens, Corpus Christianorum, Continuatio Mediaevalis, 42 (Turnhout 1976).
Nithard, *Historiae*, ed. and trans. P. Lauer, *Histoire des fils de Louis le Pieux* (Paris, 1964).
Notitia de servitio monasteriorum, ed. P. Becker in *Corpus Consuetudinum Monasticarum I*, ed. K. Hallinger (Siegburg, 1963), pp.483–99.
Notker, *Continuatio Erchanberti Breviarium*, MGH SS 2, pp.329–30.
Notker, *Gesta Karoli Magni Imperatoris*, ed. H. F. Haefele, MGH SRG, n.s. 12 (Berlin, 1959).
Notker, *Notatio de illustribus viris*, ed. E. Rauner (1986), 'Notker des Stammlers "Notatio de de illustribus viris"', *Mittellateinisches Jahrbuch* 21, pp.34–69.
'Die ostfränkische Ahnentafel von 807', in A. Borst (ed.), *Schriften zur Komputistik im Frankenreich von 721 bis 818* (MGH Quellen zur Geistesgeschichte des Mittelalters, 3 vols) (Hannover, 2006), vol. 1, pp.1003–4.
Paschasius Radbertus, *Epitaphium Arsenii*, in ed. E. Dümmler in *Abhandlungen der königlichen Akademie der Wissenschaften zu Berlin, Phil.-Historische Abhandlungen*, 2 (1900).
Paschasius Radbertus, *Vita Adalhardi*, PL 120, cols 1507–56 (Paris, 1852).
Passio Killiani martyris, ed. W. Levison, MGH SRM 5 (Hannover and Leipzig, 1910), pp.711–28.
Paul the Deacon, *Gesta Episcoporum Mettensium*, ed. G.H. Pertz, MGH SS 2 (Hannover, 1829), pp.260–68.
Paul the Deacon, *Historia Langobardorum*, ed. G. Waitz, MGH Scriptores rerum Langobardicarum et Italicarum saec. VI–IX (Hannover, 1878).
Pippini, Carlomanni, Caroli Magni Diplomata, ed. E. Mühlbacher, MGH Diplomata Karolinorum, 1 (Hannover, 1906).
I Placiti del 'Regnum Italiae', ed. C. Manaresi, vol. 1 (Rome, 1955).
Poeta Saxo, *Annalium de gestis Caroli Magni imperatoris libri quinque*, ed. P. von Winterfeld, MGH PLAC 4.1 (Berlin, 1899), pp.1–71.
Radbod, poem I.1, ed. P. von Winterfeld, MGH PLAC 4.1 (Berlin, 1899), pp.161–2.
Recueil des actes de Charles II le chauve, roi de France, ed. G. Tessier, 3 vols (Paris 1943–55).
Receuil des actes de Charles III le Simple, roi de France, 893–923, ed. F. Lot and P. Lauer (Paris, 1949).
Recueil des actes de Pépin Ier et de Pépin II, rois d'Aquitaine, 814–848, ed. L. Levillain (Paris, 1926).
Recueil des actes d'Eudes, roi de France, 888–898, ed. G. Tessier and R. H. Bautier (Paris, 1967).
Recueil des actes des rois de Provence (855–928), ed. R. Poupardin (Paris, 1920).
Recueil des actes de Louis II le Bègue, Louis III at Carloman II, rois de France, 887–884, ed. F. Grat, J. de Font-Réaulx, G. Tessier and R. H. Bautier (Paris, 1978).

Recueil des actes de Robert Ier et de Raoul, rois de France (922–936), ed. R. H. Bautier and J. Dufour (Paris, 1978).
Recueil des chartes de l'abbaye de Saint-Benoît-sur-Loire, ed. M. Prou and A. Vidier, vol. 1 (Paris, 1900).
Recueil des chartes de l'abbaye de Cluny, ed. A. Bernard and A. Bruel, vol. 1 (Paris, 1876).
Die Regesten Karls des Kahlen 840 (823)–877, Erste Lieferung 840 (823)–848, ed. I. Fees, Die Regesten des Kaiserreichs unter den Karolingern 751–918 (987), 2 Die Regesten des Westfrankenreichs und Aquitaniens (Vienna, Weimar, Cologne: 2007 Böhlau Verlag); online edition: http://www.regesta-imperii.de/regesten/1-2-1-karl-der-kahle.html
Die Regesten des Regnum Italiae und der burgundischen Regna I, Die Karolinger im Regnum Italiae 840–887 (888), ed. H. Zielinski (Vienna and Cologn, 1991 Böhlau Verlag); online edition: http://www.regesta-imperii.de/regesten/1-3-1-karolinger.html
Die Regesten des Regnum Italiae und der burgundischen Regna 4.1, Die Regesten der burgundischen Regna 855–1021, Fasz. 1: Niederburgund von 855 bis zur Vereinigung mit Hochburgund (855–940er Jahre), ed. H. Zielinski (Cologne, 2013); oline edition at: http://www.regesta-imperii.de/regesten/1-3-4-karolinger.html
Regino, *Chronicon cum continuatione Treverensi*, ed. F. Kurze, MGH SRG in usum scholarum separatim editi, 50 (Hannover, 1890).
Richer, *Historiae*, ed. H. Hoffmann, MGH SS 38 (Hannover, 2000).
Richer, *Histories*, ed. and trans. J. Lake, 2 vols (Cambridge, MA and London, 2011).
Rodulfus Glaber, *Historiarum Libri Quinque*, ed. and trans. J. France (Oxford, 1989).
Rudolf of Fulda, *Miracula sanctorum in Fuldenses Ecclesias Translatorum*, ed. G. Waitz, MGH SS 15.1 (Hannover, 1887), pp.328–41.
Sacramentary of Echternach (Paris, Bibliothèque Nationale, MS lat. 9433), ed. Y. Hen (Woodbridge, 1996).
Schiaparelli, L., ed., *I diplomi di Berengario I* (*Fonti per la storia d'Italia* 35) (Rome, 1903).
Schiaparelli, L., ed., *I diplomi di Guido e di Lamberto* (*Fonti per la storia d'Italia* 36) (Rome, 1906).
Sedulius Scottus, *Carmina*, ed. L. Traube, MGH PLAC 3 (Berlin, 1896), pp.151–240.
Sedulius Scottus, *De Rectoribus Christianis*, ed. S. Hellman, Sedulius Scottus (Quellen und Untersuchungen zur lateinischen Philiologie des Mittelalters, 1 (Munich, 1906).
Smaragdus, *Via regia*, PL 102, cols 933–70.
Thegan, *Gesta Hludowici imperatoris*, ed. E. Tremp, MGH SRG 64 (Hannover, 1995).
Theodulf, *Carmina*, ed. E. Dümmler, MGH PLAC 1 (Berlin, 1881), pp.437–569.
Theotmar, Epistola, ed. F. Lošek, Die Conversio Bagariorum et Carantanorum und der Brief des Erzbischofs Theotmar von Salzburg (MGH Studien und Texte 15, Hannover 1997) pp.138–57.
Die Traditionen des Hochstifts Freising.I. Band (744–926), ed. T. Bitterauf (Munich, 1905).
Translatio Corporis Sancti Germani, ed. G. Waitz, MGH SS 15.1 (Hannover, 1887), pp.5–9.
Translatio Sanctae Baltechildis, ed. O. Holder-Egger, MGH SS 15.1 (Hannover, 1887), pp.284–5.
Translatio sancti Viti martyris – Übertragung des hl. Märtyrers Vitus, ed. I. Schmale-Ott (Veröffentlichungen der Historischen Kommision für Westfalen 41) (Münster, 1979).
Translatio Sanguinis Domini, ed. G. Waitz, MGH SS 4 (Hannover, 1841), pp.446–9.
Die Urkunden Arnolfs, ed. P. Kehr, MGH Diplomata Regum Germaniae ex stirpe Karolinorum, 3 (Berlin, 1940).
Die Urkunden der burgundischen Rudolfinger, ed. T. Schieffer, MGH Regum Burgundiae e stirpe Rudolfina Diplomata et Acta (Würzburg, 1977).
Die Urkunden Karls III, ed. P. Kehr, MGH Diplomata Regum Germaniae ex stirpe Karolinorum, 2 (Berlin, 1937).

Die Urkunden Lothars I. und Lothars II, ed. T. Schieffer, MGH Diplomata Karolinorum 3 (Berlin and Zürich?, 1960).
Die Urkunden Ludwigs des Deutschen, Karlmanns und Ludwigs des Jüngeren, ed. P. Kehr, MGH Diplomata Regum Germaniae ex stirpe Karolinorum, 1 (Berlin, 1934).
Die Urkunden Ludwigs des Frommen, ed. T. Kölzer, MGH Diplomata Karolinorum, 2, 3 vols (Wiesbaden, 2016).
Die Urkunden Ludwigs II, ed. K. Wanner, MGH Diplomata Karolinorum, 4 (Munich, 1994).
Die Urkunden Zwentibolds und Ludwig des Kindes, ed. T. Schieffer, MGH Diplomata Regum Germania ex stirpe Karolinorum (Berlin, 1960).
Die Urkunden der Arnulfinger, ed. I. Heidrich (Bad Münstereifel, 2001).
Die Urkunden der Merowinger, ed. T. Kölzer, MGH Diplomata regum Francorum e stirpe Merovingica, 2 vols (Hannover, 2001).
Urkundenbuch der Abtei Sanct Gallen, ed. H. Wartmann, vols. 3 (Zürich, 1863–6).
Urkundenbuch der Kloster Fulda, ed. E. E. Stengel, vol. 1 (Marburg, 1956).
Urkundenbuch zur Geschichte der, jetz die preussischen Regierungsbezirke Coblenz und Trier bildenden mittelrheinischen Territorien, ed. H. Beyer (Koblenz, 1860).
Das Verbrüderungsbuch der Abtei Reichenau, ed. J. Autenrith, D. Geuenich, K, Schmid, MGH Libri Memoriales et Necrologia, nova series, 1 (Hannover, 1979).
Das Verbrüderungsbuch von St. Peter in Salzburg: Vollständige Faksimile-Ausgabe im Originalformat der Handschrift A1 aus dem Archiv von St. Peter in Salzburg, ed. K. Forstner (Graz, 1974).
Visio mulieris, see Houben above.
Visio Karoli, ed. G. Waitz, MGH SS 10 (Hannover, 1852), p.348.
Visio Karoli Magni, ed. P. Jaffé, *Monumenta Carolina* (Berlin, 1867), pp.701–4.
Vita Alcuini, ed. W. Arndt, MGH SS 15.1 Hannover, 1887), pp.182–97.
Vita Ansberti Episcopi Rotomagensis, ed. W. Levison, MGH SRM 5 (Hannover and Leipzig, 1910), pp.613–41.
Vita Arnulfi, Acta Sanctorum, Juli4, pp.440–4.
Vita S. Arnulfi, ed. B. Krusch, MGH SRM 2 (Hannover, 1888), pp.426–46.
Vita Erminonis, ed. W. Levinson, MGH SRM 6 (Hannover and Leipzig), pp.461–70.
Vita S. Geretrudis, ed. B. Krusch, MGH SRM 2 (Hannover, 1888), pp.447–74.
Vita Rigoberti Episcopi Remensis, ed. W. Levison, MGH SRM 7 (Hannover and Leipzig, 1920), pp.58–78.
Vita Rimberti, ed. G. Waitz, *Vita Anskarii aucore Rimberto. Accedit Vita Rimberti*, MGH Scriptores rerum Germanicarum in usum scholarum separatim editi, 55 (Hannover, 1884).
Walahfrid, *Carmina* ed. E. Dümmler, MGH PLAC 2 (Berlin, 1884), pp.259–423.
Walahfrid, *De Imagine Tetrici*, ed. and translated M. Herren, 'The *De Imagine Tetrici* of Walahfrid Strabo. Edition and translation', *Journal of Medieval Latin*, 1 (1991), pp.118–39.
Wandalbert, *Miracula S. Goaris*, ed. O. Holder-Egger, MGH SS 15.1 (Hannover, 1887), pp.361–73.
Widukind, *Res Gestae Saxonicae*, ed. P. Hirsch and H. E. Lohmann, MGH Scriptores rerum Germanicarum in usum scholarum separatim editi 60 (Hannover, 1935).
Willibald, *Vita Bonifatii*, ed. W. Levison, *Vitae sancti Bonifatii archiepiscopi Moguntini*, MGH Scriptores MGH Scriptores rerum Germanicarum in usum scholarum separatim editi, 57 (Hannover and Leipzig, 1905).
Wilson, H.A., ed., *The Gregorian Sacramentary under Charles the Great*, Henry Bradshaw Society, vol. 49 (London, 1915).
Witger, *Genealogia Arnulfi comitis*, ed. L.C. Bethmann, MGH SS 9 (Hannover, 1881), pp.302–4.

Secondary Works

Adorno, T. W. (1973), *Negative Dialectics*, trans. E. B. Ashton, London.
Affeldt, W. (1980), 'Untersuchungen zur Königserhebung Pippins', *FMSt*, 14: 95–187.
Agamben, G. (2011), *The Kingdom and the Glory*, trans. L. Chiesa, Stanford, California.
Airlie, S. (1985), 'The Political Behaviour of Secular Magnates in Francia, 829–879', D.Phil. Thesis, Oxford University.
Airlie, S. (1990), 'Bonds of Power and Bonds of Association in the Court Circle of Louis the Pious', in P. Godman and R. Collins (eds.), *Charlemagne's Heir: New Perspectives on the Reign of Louis the Pious, 814–840*, 191–204, Oxford, repr. Airlie (2012).
Airlie, S. (1993), 'After Empire – Recent Work on the Emergence of Post-Carolingian Kingdoms', *Early Medieval Europe*, 2: 153–61.
Airlie, S. (1995), 'The Aristocracy', in R. McKitterick (ed.), *The New Cambridge Medieval History II c.700–c.900*, 431–50, Cambridge.
Airlie, S. (1998a), '*Semper fideles?* Loyauté envers les Carolingiens comme constituent de l'identité aristocratique', in R. Le Jan (ed.), *La royauté et les élites dans l'Europe carolingienne*, 129–43, Lille, repr. Airlie (2012).
Airlie, S. (1998b), 'Private Bodies and the Body Politic in the Divorce Case of Lothar II', *Past and Present*, 161: 3–38, repr. Airlie (2012).
Airlie, S. (1999), 'Narratives of Triumph and Rituals of Submission: Charlemagne's Mastering of Bavaria', *TRHS*, 6th series, 9: 93–119; repr. Airlie (2012).
Airlie, S. (2000a), 'The Palace of Memory: The Carolingian Court as Political Centre', in S. Rees Jones, R. Marks and A. J. Minnis (eds.), *Courts and Regions in Medieval Europe*, 1–20, Woodbridge; repr. Airlie (2012).
Airlie, S. (2000b), 'The Nearly Men: Boso of Vienne and Arnulf of Bavaria', in A. J. Duggan (ed.), *Nobles and Nobility in Medieval Europe*, 25–43, Woodbridge; repr. Airlie (2012).
Airlie, S. (2001), 'True Teachers and Pious Kings: Salzburg, Louis the German and Christian Order', in R. Gameson and H. Leyser (eds.), *Belief and Culture in the Middle Ages*, 89–105, Oxford.
Airlie, S. (2003a), 'Talking Heads: Assemblies in Early Medieval Germany', in P. S. Barnwell and M. Mostert (eds.), *Political Assemblies in the Earlier Middle Ages*, 29–46, Turnhout.
Airlie, S. (2003b), 'Thrones, Dominions, Powers: Some European Points of Comparison for the Stone of Destiny', in R. Welander, D. Breeze and T. Clancy (eds.), *The Stone of Destiny. Artefact and Icon*, 123–36, Edinburgh.
Airlie, S. (2004), 'Towards a Carolingian Aristocracy', in M. Becher and J. Jarnut (eds.), *Der Dynastiewechsel von 751*, 109–27, Münster; repr. Airlie (2012).
Airlie, S. (2005), 'Charlemagne and the Aristocracy: Captains and Kings', in J. Story (ed.), *Charlemagne. Empire and Society*, 90–102, Manchester; repr. Airlie (2012).
Airlie, S. (2006a), 'The Aristocracy in the Service of the State in the Carolingian Period', in S. Airlie, W. Pohl and H. Reimitz (eds.), *Staat im frühen Mittelalter*, 93–111, Vienna; repr. Airlie (2012).
Airlie, S. (2006b), 'Les élites en 888 et après, ou comment pense-t-on la crise carolingienne?' in F. Bougard, L. Feller and R. Le Jan (eds.), *Les élites au haut Moyen Âge. Crises et renouvellements*, 425–37, Turnhout.
Airlie, S. (2006c), '"Sad Stories of the Death of Kings": Narrative Patterns and Structures of Authority in Regino of Prüm's *Chronicle*', in E. M. Tyler and R. Balzaretti (eds.), *Narrative and History in the Early Medieval West*, 105–131, Turnhout; repr. Airlie (2012).

Airlie, S. (2007a), 'The Frankish Aristocracy as Supporters and Opponents of Boniface', in F. J. Felten, J. Jarnut and L. von Padberg (eds.), *Bonifatius – Leben und Nachleben (754-2004)*, 255-69, Mainz; repr. Airlie (2012).

Airlie, S. (2007b), 'The World, the Text and the Carolingian: Royal, Aristocratic and Masculine Identities in Nithard's *Histories*', in P. Wormald and J. L. Nelson (eds.), *Lay Intellectuals in the Carolingian World*, 51-76, Cambridge; repr. Airlie (2012).

Airlie, S. (2009a), '"For It Is Written in the Law": Ansegis and the Writing of Carolingian Royal Authority', in S. Baxter, C. E. Karkov, J. L. Nelson and D. Pelteret (eds.), *Early Medieval Studies in Memory of Patrick Wormald*, 219-35, Farnham.

Airlie, S. (2009b), 'Not Rendering unto Caesar: Challenges to Early Medieval Rulers', in W. Pohl and V. Wieser (eds.), *Der Frühmittelalterliche Staat –Europäische Perspektiven*, 489-501, Vienna.

Airlie, S. (2010), 'I, Agobard, Unworthy Bishop', in R. Corradini, M. Gillis, R. McKitterick and I. Van Renswoude (eds.), *Ego Trouble. Authors and Their Identities in the Early Middle Ages*, 175-83, Vienna.

Airlie, S. (2011a), 'Unreal Kingdom: Francia Media under the Shadow of Lothar II', in M. Gaillard, M. Margue, A. Dierkens and H. Pettiau (eds.), *De la mer du Nord à la Méditerranée. Francia Media, une region au Coeur de l'Europe (c.840–c.1050)*, 339-56, Luxembourg.

Airlie (2011b), 'Security and Insecurity of Status in the Carolingian Elite', in F. Bougard, H. W. Goetz and R. Le Jan (eds.), *Théorie et pratiques des élites au Haut Moyen Âge*, 221-39, Turnhout.

Airlie, S. (2012), *Power and Its Problems in Carolingian Europe*, Farnham.

Airlie, S. (2014), 'The Palace Complex', in J. Hudson and A. Rodriguez (eds.), *Diverging Paths? The Shapes of Power and Institutions in Medieval Christendom and Islam*, 255-90, Leiden.

Airlie, S. (2016), 'Earthly and Heavenly Networks in a World in Flux: Carolingian Family Identities and the Prague Sacramentary', in M. Diesenberger, R. Meens and E. Rose (eds.), *The Prague Sacramentary. Culture, Religion and Politics in Late Eighth-Century Bavaria*, 203-23, Turnhout.

Airlie, S., W. Pohl and H. Reimitz eds (2006), *Staat im frühen Mittelalter*, Vienna.

Alberi, M. (1998), 'The Evolution of Alcuin's Concept of the Imperium Christianum', in J. Hill and M. Swann (eds.), *The Community, the Family and the Saint: Patterns of Power in Early Medieval Europe*, 3-17, Turnhout.

Allen, M. (1996), 'Bede and Frechulf at Medieval St. Gallen', in L. A. J. R. Houwen and A. A. MacDonald (eds.), *Beda Venerabilis: Historian, Monk and Northumbrian*, 61-80, Groningen.

Althoff, G. (1990), *Verwandte, Freunde und Getreue: Zum politischen Stellenwert der Gruppenbindungen im früheren Mittelalter*, Darmstadt.

Althoff, G. (1992), *Amicitiae und Pacta. Bündnis, Einung, Politik und Gebetsgedenken im beginnenden 10, Jahrhundert*, Hannover.

Althoff, G. (1997), *Spielregeln der Politik im Mittelalter*, Darmstadt.

Althoff, G. (2003), *Otto III*, trans P. G. Jestice, Pennsylvania.

Angenendt, A. (1980), 'Das geistliche Bündnis der Päpste mit den Karolingern (754-796)', *Historisches Jahrbuch*, 100: 1-94.

Angenendt, A. (1992), '*Rex et Sacerdos*. Zur Genese der Königssalbung', in N. Kamp and J. Wollasch (eds.), *Tradition als historische Kraft*, 100-18, Berlin.

Angenendt, A. (2004), 'Pippins Königserhebung und Salbung', in M. Becher and J. Jarnut (eds.), *Der Dynastiewechsel von 751. Vorgeschichte. Legitimationsstrategien und Erinnerung*, 179-209, Münster.

Angenendt, A. (2008), '*Donationes pro anima*: Gift and Countergift in the Early Medieval Liturgy', in J. R. Davis and M. McCormick (eds.), *The Long Morning of Medieval Europe. New Directions in Early Medieval Studies*, 131–54, Aldershot.
Anton, H. H. (1968), *Fürstenspiegel und Herrscherethos in der Karolingerzeit*, Bonn.
Anton, H. H. (1979), 'Zum politischen Konzept karolingischer Synoden und zur karolingischen Brüdergemeinschaft', *Historisches Jahrbuch*, 99: 55–132.
Atsma, H. ed. (1989), *La Neustrie. Les pays au nord de la Loire de 650 à 850*, 2 vols, Sigmaringen.
Autenrieth, J. (1975), 'Das St. Galler Verbrüderungsbuch. Möglichkeiten und Grenzen paläographischer Bestimmung', *FMSt*, 9: 215–25.
Auxerre (1990), *Saint-Germain d'Auxerre. Intellectuels et artistes dans l'Europe carolingienne IXe – Xie siècles*, Musée d'Art et d'Histoire, Auxerre.
Baccou, P. (2003), 'Sur un acte prétendu faux de Bérenger I, roi d'Italie, pour Saint-Martin de Tours', *Mélanges de l'Ecole française de Rome*, 115: 711–26.
Bachrach, B. (2001), *Early Carolingian Warfare: Prelude to Empire*, Philadelphia.
Bachrach, B. and D. Bachrach (2009), 'Continuity of Written Administration in the Carolinigian East', *FMSt*, 42: 109–46.
Balzaretti, R. (2006), 'Spoken Narratives in Ninth-Century Milanese Court Records', in E. M. Tyler and R. Balzaretti (eds.), *Narrative and History in the Early Medieval West*, 11–37, Turnhout.
Balzer, M. (1999), 'Paderborn. Zentralort der Karolinger im Sachsen des späten 8. und frühen 9. Jahrhunderts', in C. Stiegemann and M. Wemhoff (eds.) (1999), *799 Kunst und Kultur der Karolingerzeit. Karl der Große und Papst Leo III. in Paderborn. Katalog der Ausstellung*, 2 vols, vol. 1, 116–23, Mainz.
Barbier, J. (1989), 'Aspects du fisc en Neustrie (VIe–IXe siècles). Résultats d'une recherché en cours', in H. Atsma (ed.), *La* Neustrie. *Les pays au nord de la Loire de 650 à 850*, vol. 1, 129–422, Sigmaringen.
Barbier, J. (1990), 'Le système palatial franc: genèse et fonctionnement dans le nord-ouest du *regnum*', *Bibliothèque de l'École des Chartes*, 148: 245–99.
Barbier, J. (1999), 'Du patrimoine fiscal au patrimoine ecclésiastique. Les largesses royales aux églises au nord de la Loire (milieu du VIIIe siècle – fin du Xe siècle)', *Mélanges de l'école française à Rome*, 111.2: 577–605.
Barbier, J. (2009), 'Le fisc du royaume franc. Quelques jalons pour une reflexion sur l'État au haut Moyen Âge', in W. Pohl and V. Wieser (eds.), *Der Frühmittelalterliche Staat – Europäische Perspektiven*, 271–85, Vienna.
Barnwell, P. S. (2005), 'Einhard, Louis the Pious and Childeric III', *Historical Research*, 78: 129–39.
Bartlett, R. (1994), 'Hair in the Middle Ages', *TRHS*, 6th series, 4: 43–60.
Bauer, T. (2011), 'Die *Francia Media*, ein Land der Begegnung', in M. Gaillard, M. Margue, A. Dierkens and H. Pettiau (eds.), *De la Mer du Nord à la Méditerranée, Francia Media, une region au Coeur de l'Europe (c.840–c.1050)*, 357–80, Luxembourg.
Bautier, R. H. (1989), 'Sacres et couronnements sous les Carolingiens et les premiers Capétiens', *Annuaire-bulletin de la société de l'histoire de France 1987–88*, 7–56.
Bayless, M. (2000), 'Alcuin's *Disputatio Pippini* and the early medieval riddle tradition', in G. Halsall (ed.), *Humour, History and Politics in Late Antiquity and the Early Middle Ages*, 157–78, Cambridge.
Beaune, C. (1997), 'Les sanctuaries royaux. De Saint-Denis à Saint-Michel et Saint-Léonard', in P. Nora (ed.), *Les Lieux de mémoire*, 1, 625–48, Paris.

Becher, H. (1983), 'Das königliche Frauenkloster San Salvatore/Santa Giulia in Brescia im Spiegel seiner Memorialüberlieferung', *FMSt*, 17: 299–392.
Becher, M. (1989), 'Drogo und die Königserhebung Pippins', *FMSt*, 23: 131–52.
Becher, M. (1992), 'Neue Überlieferungen zum Geburtsdatum Karls des Grossen', *Francia*, 19: 37–60.
Becher, M. (1993), *Eid und Herrschaft. Untersuchungen zum Herrscherethos Karls des Großen*, Sigmaringen.
Becher, M. (1996), *Rex, Dux und Gens. Untersuchungen zur Entstehung des sächsischen Herzogtums im 9. Und 10. Jahrhundert*, Husum.
Becher, M. (2003), *Charlemagne*, trans. D. Bachrach, New Haven and London.
Becher, M. (2001), '"*Cum lacrimis et gemitu*." Vom Weinen der Sieger und Besiegten im frühen und hohen Mittelalter', in G. Althoff and V. Epp (eds.), *Formen und Funktionen öffentlicher Kommunikation im Mittelalter*, 25–52, Stuttgart.
Becher, M. (2008a), 'Vater, Sohn und Enkel. Die Bedeutung von Eintritts- und Anwachsungsrecht für die Herrschaftsnachfolge im Frankenreich', in B. Kasten (ed.), *Herrscher- und Fürstentestamente im westeuropäischen Mittelalter*, 301–20, Vienna & Cologne.
Becher, M. (2008b), 'Arnulf von Kärnten – Name und Abstammung eines (illegitimen?) Karolingers', in U. Ludwig and T. Schilp (eds.), *Nomen et Fraternitas. Fests chrift für Dieter Geuenich zum 65. Geburtstag*, 665–82, Berlin.
Benjamin, W. (1972), *Illuminations*, trans. H. Zohn, London.
Benjamin, W. (1999), 'Karl Kraus', in W. Benjamin, R. Livingstone, M. W. Jennings, H. Eiland and G. Smith (eds.), 433–58, Cambridge, MA.
Beumann, H. and W. Braunfels eds (1967), *Karl der Grosse. Lebenswerk und Nachleben*, vol. 4 *Das Nachleben*, Düsseldorf.
Bierbrauer, K. and P. M. Hermes (1999), 'Psalter von Montpellier', in C. Stiegemann and M. Wemhoff (eds.), *799 Kunst und Kultur der Karolingerzeit. Karl der Große und Papst Leo III. in Paderborn. Katalog der Ausstellung*, 2 vols, vol. 2, 805–8, Mainz.
Bischoff, B. (1974–1980), *Die südostdeutschen Schreibschulen und Bibliotheken in der Karolingerzeit*, 2 vols, Wiesbaden.
Bischoff, B. (1981a), *Mittelalterliche Studien. Ausgewählte Aufsätze zur Schriftkunde und Literaturgeschichte*, vol. 3, Stuttgart.
Bischoff, B. (1981b), 'Eine Beschreibung der Basilika von Saint-Denis aus dem Jahre 799', *Kunstchronik*, 97–103.
Bischoff, B. (1984), *Anecdota Novissma. Texte des vierten bis sechzehnten Jahrhunderts*, Stuttgart.
Bishop, E. (1918), *Liturgica Historica. Papers on the Liturgy and Religious Life of the Western Church*, Oxford.
Blanc, W. and C. Naudin (2015), *Charles Martel et la bataille de Poitiers*, Paris.
Bloch, H. R. (1991), *Medieval Misogyny and the Invention of Western Romantic Love*, Chicago.
Bobrycki, S. (2009), 'The Royal Consecration *Ordines* of the Pontifical of Sens from a New Perspective', *Bulletin du centre d'études médiévales d'Auxerre*, 13: 131–42.
Boehm, L. (1975), 'Rechtsformen und Rechtstitel der burgundischen Königserhebungen im 9. Jahrhundert', in E. Hlawitschka (ed.), *Königswahl und Thronfolge in fränkisch-karolingischer Zeit*, 352–98, Darmstadt.
Booker, C. (2005), 'A New Prologue of Walafrid Strabo', *Viator*, 36: 83–105.
Booker, C. (2008), 'The Public Penance of Louis the Pious: A New Edition of the *Episcoporum de poenitentia quam Hludowicus imperator professus est relatio Compendiensis (833)*', *Viator*, 39.2: 1–19.

Booker, C. (2009), *Past Convictions. The Penance of Louis the Pious and the Decline of the Carolingians*, Philadelphia.
Borgolte, M. (1984a), *Geschichte der Grafschaften Alemanniens in fränkischer Zeit*, Sigmaringen.
Borgolte, M. (1984b), 'Gedenkstiftungen in St. Galler Urkunden', in K. Schmid and J. Wollasch (eds.), *Memoria. Der geschichtliche Zeugniswert des liturgischen Gedenkens im Mittelalter*, 578–602, Munich.
Borgolte, M. (1986), *Die Grafen Alemanniens in merowingischer und karolingischer Zeit. Eine Prosopographie*, Sigmaringen.
Borgolte, M. (2014), 'Karl der Große. Ein Global Player?', in Die Stiftung Deutsches Historisches Museum (ed.), *Kaiser und Kalifen. Karl der Große und die Mächte am Mittelmeer um 800*, 16–23, Darmstadt.
Borst, A. (1996), 'Der überlieferte Geburtstag', in R. Schieffer (ed.), *Mittelalterliche Texte. Überlieferung – Befunde – Deutungen*, 1–91, Hannover.
Boshof, E. (1969), *Erzbischof Agobard*, Cologne.
Boshof, E. (1996), *Ludwig der Fromme*, Darmstadt.
Bosl, K. (1969), *Franken um 800*, 2nd edition, Munich.
Bouchard, C. (2015), *Rewriting Saints and Ancestors. Memory and Forgetting in France, 500–1200*, Philadelphia.
Bouchard, C. B. (2001), *'Those of My Blood'. Constructing Noble Families in Medieval Francia*, Philadelphia.
Bougard, F. (2006), 'Les Supponides: échec à la reine', in F. Bougard, L. Feller and R. Le Jan (eds.), *Les élites au haut Moyen Âge. Crises et renouvellements*, 381–401, Turnhout.
Bougard, F., L. Feller and R. Le Jan eds (2006), *Les élites au haut Moyen Âge. Crises et renouvellements*, Turnhout.
Bourdieu, P. (2001), *Masculine Domination*, Cambridge.
Bourdieu, P. and J. C. Passeron (1977), *Reproduction in Education, Society and Culture*, London.
Bovendeert, J. (2006), 'Royal or Monastic Identity? Smaragdus' Via Regia and Diadema Monachorum Reconsidered', in R. Corradini, R. Meens, C. Pössel and P. Shaw (eds.), *Texts and Identities in the Early Middle Ages*, 239–51, Vienna.
Bowlus, C. R. (1995), *Franks, Moravians, and Magyars. The Struggle for the Middle Danube, 788–907*, Philadelphia.
Bradbury, J. (1998), *Philip Augustus, King of France 1180–1223*, London.
Braunfels, W. (1965), 'Vorwort', in *Karl der Grosse. Werk und Wirkung*, Aachen.
Brown, G. (1989), 'Politics and Patronage at the Abbey of Saint-Denis (814–98)', D.Phil. thesis, Oxford University.
Brown, P. (1992), *Power and Persuasion in Late Antiquity*, Madison.
Brown, P. (2003), *The Rise of Western Christendom*, 2nd edition, Oxford.
Brown, W. (2001), *Unjust Seizure. Conflict, Interest and Authority in an Early Medieval Society*, Ithaca.
Brown, W. (2006), 'Power after Foucault', in J. S. Dryzek, B. Honnig and A. Phillips (eds.), *The Oxford Handbook of Political Theory*, 65–84, Oxford.
Brühl, C. (1968), *Fodrum, gistum, servitium regis: Studien zu den wirtschaftlichen Grnudlagen des Königtums im Frankenreich und in den fränkischen Nachfolgestaaten Deutschland, Frankreich und Italien vom 6. bis zur Mitte des 14. Jahrhunderts*, 2 vols, Cologne.
Brühl, C. (1990), *Deutschland-Frankreich. Die Geburt zweier Völker*, Cologne & Vienna.
Brunner, K. (1979), *Oppositionelle Gruppen im Karolingerreich*, Vienna.
Brunner, K. (1983), 'Auf den Spuren verlorener Traditionen', *Peritia*, 2: 1–22.

Brunterc'h, J. P. (1989), 'Le duché du Maine et la marche de Bretagne', in H. Atsma (ed.), *La Neustrie. Les pays au nord de la Loire de 650 à 850*, 1, 29–127, Sigmaringen.
Buc, P. (2000), 'Ritual and Interpretation: The Early Medieval Case', *Early Medieval Europe*, 9: 183–210.
Buc, P. (2001a), *The Dangers of Ritual: Between Early Medieval Texts and Social Scientific Theory*, Princeton.
Buc, P. (2001b), 'Political Rituals and Political Imagination in the Medieval West from the Fourth Century to the Eleventh', in P. Linehan and J. L. Nelson (eds.), *The Medieval World*, 189–213, London.
Buc, P. (2004), 'Noch einmal 918–919. Of the Ritualised Demise of Kings and of Political Rituals in General', in G. Althoff (ed.), *Zeichen – Rituale – Werte*, 151–78, Münster.
Buc, P. (2005), 'Warum weniger die Handelnden selbst als eher die Chronisten das politische Ritual erzeugten – und warum es niemanden auf die wahre Geschichte ankam', in B. Jussen (ed.), *Die Macht des Königs. Herrschaft in Europa vom Frühmittelalter bis in die Neuzeit*, 27–37, Munich.
Bührer-Thierry, G. (1992), 'La reine adultère', *Cahiers de civilisation médiévale*, 35: 299–312.
Bührer-Thierry, G. (1998), '"Just Anger" or "Vengeful Anger"? The Punishment of Blinding in the Early Medieval West', in B. Rosenwein (ed.), *Anger's Past. The Social Uses of an Emotion in the Middle Ages*, 75–91, Ithaca.
Bullough, D. (1962), 'Baiuli in the Carolingian regnum Langobardorum and the Career of Abbot Waldo (†813)', *English Historical Review*, 77: 625–37.
Bullough, D. (1965), *The Age of Charlemagne*, London.
Bullough, D. (1970), '*Europae Pater*: Charlemagne and His Achievements in the Light of Recent Scholarship', *English Historical Review*, 85: 59–105.
Bullough, D. (1984), '*Albuinus deliciosus Karoli regis*. Alcuin of York and the Shaping of the Early Carolingian Court', in L. Fenske, W. Rösener and T. Zotz (eds.), *Institutionen, Kultur und Gesellschaft im Mittelalter. Festschrift für Josef Fleckenstein zu seinem 65. Geburtstag*, 73–92, Sigmaringen.
Bullough, D. (1985), '*Aula renovata*: The Carolingian Court before the Aachen Palace', *Proceedings of the British Academy*, 71: 267–301.
Bullough, D. (1991), *Carolingian Renewal: Sources and Heritage*, Manchester.
Bullough, D. (2003), 'Was There a Carolingian Anti-War Movement?', *Early Medieval Europe*, 12: 365–76.
Bullough, D. (2004), *Alcuin: Achievement and Reputation*, Leiden.
Bund, K. (1979), *Thronsturz und Herrscherabsetzung im Frühmittelalter*, Bonn.
Burgdorf, W. (2012), '"Once We Were Trojans!" Contemporary Reactions to the Dissolution of the Holy Roman Empire of the German Nation', in R. J. W. Evans and P. H. Wilson (eds.), *The Holy Roman Empire 1495–1806*, 51–76, Leiden.
Burke, P. (1992), *The Fabrication of Louis XIV*, New Haven.
Butler, J. (2014), *Bodies That Matter: On the Discursive Limits of 'Sex'*, New York.
Büttner, H. (1952), 'Aus den Anfängen des abendländischen Staatsgedankens', *Historisches Jahrbuch*, 71: 77–90.
Büttner, J. and S. Kaschke (2006), 'Grundherrlicher Fernbesitz und Reichsteilungen am Beispiel des Klosters Prüm', in B. Kasten (ed.), *Tätigkeitsfelder und Erfahrungshorizonte des ländlichen Menschen in der frühmittelalterlichen Grundherrschaft (bis ca. 1000). Festschrift für Dieter Hägermann zum 65. Geburtstag*, 175–96, Stuttgart.

Butz, E. M. and A. Zettler (2013), 'The Making of the Carolingian *Libri Memoriales*: Exploring or Constructing the Past?' in E. Brenner, M. Cohen and M. Franklin-Brown (eds.), *Memory and Commemoration in Medieval Culture*, 79–92, London.
Campbell, J. (1986), 'Asser's *Life of Alfred*', in C. Holdsworth and T. P. Wiseman (eds.), *The Inheritance of Historiography, 350–900*, 115–36, Liverpool.
Campbell, D. (2010), 'The *Capitulare de Villis*, the *Brevium exempla*, and the Carolingian Court at Aachen', *Early Medieval Europe*, 18.3: 243–64.
Carroll, C. (1999), 'The Bishoprics of Saxony in the First Century after Christianization', *Early Medieval Europe*, 8.2: 219–45.
Carver, M. (2019), *Formative Britain. An Archaeology of Britain, Fifth to Eleventh Century AD*, London.
Castelnuovo, G. (1998), 'Les élites des royaumes de Bourgogne (milieu IXe-milieu Xe siècle)', in R. Le Jan (ed.), *La royauté et les élites dans l'Europe carolingienne*, 383–408, Lille.
Chandler, C. (2019), *Carolingian Catalonia: Politics, Culture and the Creation of an Imperial Province, 778–987*, Cambridge.
Classen, P. (1963), 'Die Verträge von Verdun und Coulaines 843 als politische Grundlagen des westfränkischen Reiches', *Historische Zeitschrift*, 196: 1–35.
Classen, P. (1972), 'Karl der Große und die Thronfolge im Frankenreich', in *Festschrift für Hermann Heimpel*, 3 vols, 1, 109–34, Göttingen.
Claussen, M. A. (2004), *The Reform of the Frankish Church. Chrodegang of Metz and the Regula canonicorum in the Eighth Century*, Cambridge.
Coens, M. (1963), *Recueil d'études bollandiennes*, Brussels.
Collins, R. (1990), 'Pippin I and the Kingdom of Aquitaine', in P. Godman and R. Collins (eds.), *Charlemagne's Heir*, 363–89, Oxford.
Collins, R. (1994), 'Deception and Misrepresentation in Early Eighth-Century Frankish Historiography: Two Case Studies', in J. Jarnut, U. Nonn and M. Richter (eds.), *Karl Martel in seiner Zeit, Beihefte der Francia*, 227–47, Sigmaringen.
Collins, R. (1995), 'Spain: The Northern Kingdoms and the Basques', in R. McKitterick (ed.), *New Cambridge Medieval History*, vol. 2, 272–89, Cambridge.
Collins, R. (1998), *Charlemagne*, Basingstoke.
Collins, R. (2002), 'Frankish Past and Carolingian Present in the Age of Charlemagne', in P. Godman, J. Jarnut and P. Johanek (eds.), *Am Vorabend der Kaiserkrönung*, 301–22, Berlin.
Collins, R. (2004), 'Pippin III as Mayor of the Palace: the Evidence', in M. Becher and J. Jarnut (eds.), *Der Dynastiewechsel von 751*, 75–91, Münster.
Collins, R. (2007), *Die Fredegar-Chroniken*, Hannover.
Contreni, J. (2002), '"By Lions, Bishops Are Meant, by Wolves, Priests": History, Exegesis and the Carolingian Church in Haimo of Auxerre's Commentary on Ezechiel', *Francia*, 29.1: 29–56.
Coon, L. (2011), *Dark Age Bodies: Gender and Monastic Practice in the Early Medieval West*, Philadelphia.
Corbet, P. (1986), *Les saints ottoniens*, Sigmaringen.
Costambeys, M., M. Innes and S. MacLean (2011), *The Carolingian World*, Cambridge.
Coupland, S. (1989), 'The Coinage of Pippin I and II of Aquitaine', *Revue Numismatique*, 31: 194–222.
Coupland, S. (1990), 'Carolingian Arms and Armor in the Ninth Century', *Viator*, 21: 29–50.

Coupland, S. (2005), 'Charlemagne's Coinage: Ideology and Economy', in J. Story (ed.), *Charlemagne. Empire and Society*, 211–29, Manchester.
Cramer, P. (1993), *Baptism and Change in the Early Middle Ages, c.200–c.1150*, Cambridge.
Cubitt, C. (2003), *Court Culture in the Early Middle* Ages, Turnhout.
Curta, F. (2006), 'Merovingian and Carolingian Gift Giving', *Speculum*, 81: 671–99.
Daldal, A. (2014), 'Power and Ideology in Michel Foucault and Antonio Gramsci: A Comparative Analysis', *Review of History and Political Science*, 2.2: 149–67.
Davis, R. (1992), trans. *The Lives of the Eighth-Century Popes (Liber Pontificalis)*, Liverpool.
Davis, J. R. (2008), 'A Pattern for Power: Charlemagne's Delegation of Judicial Responsibilities', in J. R. Davis and M. McCormick (eds.), *The Long Morning of Medieval Europe. New Directions in Early Medieval Studies*, 235–46, Aldershot.
Davis, J. R. (2015), *Charlemagne's Practice of Empire*, Cambridge.
Davies, N. (1996), *Europe. A History*, Oxford.
Delogu, P. (1995), 'Lombard and Carolingian Italy', in R. McKitterick (ed.), *New Cambridge Medieval History*, 2, 290–319, Cambridge.
Depreux, P. (1992), 'Das Königtum Bernhards von Italien und sein Verhältnis zum Kaisertum', *Quellen und Forschungen aus italienischen Archiven und Bibliotheken*, 72: 1–25.
Depreux, P. (1993), 'Poètes et historiens aux temps de l'empereur Louis le Pieux', *LMA*, 199: 311–22.
Depreux, P. (1994), 'Wann began Kaiser Ludwig der Fromme zu regieren?', *MIÖG*, 102: 261–70.
Depreux, P. (1997), *Prosopographie de l'entourage de Louis le Pieux (781–840)*, Sigmaringen.
Depreux, P. (1998), 'Lieux de rencontre, temps de négociation: quelques observations sur les plaids généraux sous le règne de Louis le Pieux', in R. Le Jan (ed.), *La royauté et les élites dans l'Europe carolingienne*, 213–31, Lille.
Depreux, P. (2002), *Les Sociétés occidentales du milieu du Vie à la fin du IXe siècle*, Rennes.
Devisse, J. (1975), *Hincmar, archevêque de Reims, 845–882*, 3 vols, Geneva.
Devroey, J.-P. (2011), 'La hiérarchisation des poles habités et l'espace rural. Autour des possessions de l'abbaye de Prüm (893)', in M. Gaillard, M. Margue, A. Dierkens and H. Pettiau (eds.), *De la Mer du Nord à la Méditerranée, Francia Media, une region au Coeur de l'Europe (c.840–c.1050)*, 175–206, Luxembourg.
Dhondt, J. (1948), *Études sur la naissance des principautés territoriales en France (IXe-Xe siècles)*, Bruges.
Dierkens, A. (1985), *Abbayes et chapitres entre Sambre et Meuse (VIIe-Xe siècles)*, Sigmaringen.
Dierkens, A. (1991), 'Le tombeau de Charlemagne', *Byzantion*, 61: 156–80.
Dierkens, A. (1996), 'La mort, les funérailles et la tombe du roi Pépin le Bref', *Médiévales*, 31: 37–51.
Diesenberger, M. (2003), 'Hair, Sacrality and Symbolic Capital in the Frankish Kingdoms', in R. Corradini, M. Diesenberger and H. Reimitz (eds.), *The Construction of Communities in the Early Middle Ages*, 173–212, Leiden.
Diesenberger, M. (2005), 'Spuren des Wandels.Bayersiche Schriftkultur zwischen Agilofinger- und Karolingerzeit', in L. Kolmer and C. Rohr (eds.), *Tassilo III. von Bayern. Großmacht und Ohnmacht im 8. Jahrhundert Regensburg*, 175–89, Regensburg.
Dixon, S. (2001), *Catherine the Great*, Harlow.
Doyle, E. G. (1983), *Sedulius Scottus, On Christian Rulers and the Poems*, Binghamton, New York.

Drews, W. (2009), *Die Karolinger und die Abbasiden von Bagdad. Legitmationsstrategien frühmittelalterlichen Herrscherdynastien im transkulturellen Vergleich*, Berlin.
Drews, W. and A. Höfert (2016), 'Monarchische Herrshaftsformen in transkulturellen Vergleich. Argumentationsstrategien zur Rechtsfertigung von Usurpationen am Beispiel der Karolinger und Abbasiden', in M. Borgolte and B. Schneidmüller (eds.), *Hybride Kulture in mittelalterlichen Europa*, 229–44, Berlin.
Duindam, J. (2015), L. Geevers and M. Marini (eds.) (2015), *Dynastic Identity in Early Modern Europe. Rulers, Aristocrats and the Formation of Identities*, 59–83, Farnham.
Duindam, J. (2016), *Dynasties. A Global History of Power, 1300–1800*, Cambridge.
Dümmler, E. (1887–8), *Geschichte des ostfränkishchen Reiches*, 3 vols, 2nd edition, Leipzig.
Dutton, P. E. (1994), *The Politics of Dreaming in the Carolingian Empire*, Lincoln, Nebraska.
Dutton, P. E. (1998), *Charlemagne's Courtier. The Complete Einhard*, Peterborough, Ontario.
Dutton, P. E. (2004), *Carolingian Civilization. A Reader*, 2nd edition, Peterborough, Ontario.
Dutton, P. E. (2009), *Charlemagne's Mustache and Other Cultural Clusters of a Dark Age*, New York.
Dutton, P. E. and H. Kessler (1997), *The Poetry and Paintings of the First Bible of Charles the Bald*, Ann Arbor.
Eastwood, B. (1994), 'The Astronomy of Macrobius in Carolingian Europe: Dungal's Letter of 811 to Charles the Great', *Early Medieval Europe*, 3: 117–34.
Eberhardt, O. (1977), *Via Regia. Der Fürstenspiegel Smaragds von St Mihiel und seine literarische Gattung*, Munich.
Eckhardt, W. (1956), 'Die capitulare missorum specialia von 802', *DA*, 12: 498–516.
Edwards, C. (1994), 'German Vernacular Literature: A Survey', in R. McKitterick (ed.), *Carolingian Culture: Emulation and Innovation*, 141–70, Cambridge.
Effros, B. (1996), 'Symbolic Expressions of Sanctity: Gertrude of Nivelles', *Viator*, 1–10.
Effros, B. (2003), *Merovingian Mortuary Archaeology and the Making of the Early Middle Ages*, Berkeley.
Eggert, W. (1973), *Das ostfränkisch-deutsche Reich in der Auffassung seiner Zeitgenossen*, Berlin.
Eichler, D. (2007), *Fränkische Reichsversammlungen unter Ludwig dem Frommen*, Hannover.
Elsner, J. (1998), *Imperial Rome and Christian Triumph. The Art of the Roman Empire AD 100–450*, Oxford.
Enright, M. J. (1985), *Iona, Tara, Soissons: The Origin of the Royal Anointing Ritual*, Berlin.
Erkens, F. R. (1993), 'Sicut Esther Regina': Die westfränkische Königin als consors regni', *Francia*, 20.1: 15–38.
Erkens, F. R. (1996), '*Divisio legitima* und *unitas imperii*. Teilungspraxis und Einheitsstreben im Frankenreich', *DA*, 52: 423–85.
Erkens, F. R. (2004), 'Auf der Suche nach den Anfängen? Neue Überlegungen zu den Ursprüngen der fränkischen Königssalbung', *Zeitschrift der Savigny-Stiftung für Rechtsgeschichte*, 121 (*Kanonistische Abteilung*, 90): 494–509.
Erkens, F. R. (2006), *Herrschersakralität im Mittelalter. Von den Anfängen bis zum Investiturstreit*, Stuttgart.
Esders, S. (1999), 'Regionale Selbstbehauptung zwischen Byzanz und dem Frankenreich. Die Inquisition der Rechtsgewohnheiten Istriens durch die Sendboten Karls

des Grossen und Pippins von Italy', in S. Esders and T. Scharf (eds.), *Eid und Wahrheitssuche. Gesellschaft, Kultur und Schrift*, 49–112, Frankfurt.

Esders, S. (2008), 'Fidelität und Rechtsvielfalt: Die sicut-Klausel der früh- und hochmittelalterlichen Eidformulare', in F. Bougard, D. Iogna-Prat and R. Le Jan (eds.), *Hiérarchie et Stratification dans l'Occident medieval (400-1100)*, 239–55, Turnhout.

Ewig, E. (1956), 'Zum christlichen Königsgedanken im Frühmittelalter', in T. Mayer (ed.), *Das Königtum: seine geistigen und rechtlichen Grundlagen*, Vorträge und Forschungen, 3, 7–73, Constance.

Ewig, E. (1965), 'Descriptio Franciae', in H. Beumann (ed.), *Karl der Grosse 1: Persönlichkeit und Geschichte*, 143–77, Düsseldorf.

Ewig, E. (1982a), 'Der Gebetsdienst der Kirchen in den Urkunden der späteren Karolinger', in H. Maurer and H. Patze (eds.), *Festschrift für Berent Schwineköper zu seinem siebzigsten Geburtstag*, 45–86, Sigmaringen.

Ewig, E. (1982b), 'Remarques sur la stipulation de la prière dans les chartes de Charles le Chauve', in R. Lejeune and J. Deckers (eds.), *Clio et son regard. Mélanges d'histoire et d'archéologie offerts à Jacques Stiennon*, 221–33, Liège.

Ewig, E. (1995), 'Die fränkische Königskataog und die Aufstieg der karolinger', *DA*, 1–28.

Fanning, S. and B. Bachrach trans (2004), *The Annals of Flodoard of Reims 919–966*, Peterborough, Ontario.

Fentress, J. and C. Wickham (1992), *Social Memory*, Oxford.

Fleckenstein, J. (1959), *Die Hofkapelle der deutschen Könige 1, Grundlegung. Die karolingische Hofkapelle*, Stuttgart.

Foot, S. (2000), *Veiled Women*, 2 vols, Aldershot.

Foot, S. (2011), *Aethelstan: The First King of England*, New Haven.

Foot, S. (2012), 'Annals and Chronicles in Western Europe', in S. Foot, C. F. Robinson and I. Hesketh (eds.), *The Oxford History of Historical Writing*, 346–67, Oxford.

Foster, S. ed. (1998), *The St Andrews Sarcophagus. A Pictish Masterpiece and Its International Connections*, Dublin.

Foucault, M. (1978), *The History of Sexuality*, vol. 1, trans R. Hurley, New York.

Foucault, M. (2001), 'Truth and Power', in M. Foucault and J. D. Faubion (eds.), *Essential Works of Foucault 1954–1984*, 3, 111–33, London.

Fouracre, P. (2000), *The Age of Charles Martel*, Harlow.

Fouracre, P. (2001), 'Space, Culture and Kingdoms in Early Medieval Europe', in P. Linehan and J. L. Nelson (eds.), *The Medieval World*, 366–80, London.

Fouracre, P. (2005), 'The Long Shadow of the Merovingians', in J. Story (ed.), *Charlemagne. Empire and Society*, 5–21, Manchester.

Fouracre, P. (2009), 'Comparing the Resources of the Merovingian and Carolingian States: Problems and Perspectives', in W. Pohl and V. Wieser (eds.), *Der Frühmittelalterliche Staat –Europäische Perspektiven*, 287–97, Vienna.

Fouracre, P. and R. A. Gerberding eds (1996), *Late Merovingian France. History and Hagiography 640–720*, Manchester.

Fowden, J. (1993), 'The Image and Self-Image of the Medieval Ruler', in A. J. Duggan (ed.), *Kings and Kingship in Medieval Europe*, 213–40, London.

Frantzen, A. (1998), *Before the Closet. Same-Sex Love from Beowulf to Angels in America*, Chicago.

Freise, E. (1984), 'Kalendarische und annalistische Grundformen der Memoria', in K. Schmid and J. Wollasch (eds.), *Memoria. Der geschichtliche Zeugniswert des liturgischen Gedenkens im Mittelalter*, 441–577, Munich.

Freise, E. (1986), 'Der Codex I 2 2 8 der Universitätsbibliothek Augsburg', in E. Freise, D. Guenich and J. Wollasch (eds.), *Das Martyrolog-Necrolog von St. Emmeram zu Regensburg*, 28–95, Hannover.
Freise, E. (1989), 'Die "Genealogia Arnulfi Comitis" des Priesters Witger', *FMSt*, 23: 203–43.
Fried, J. (1982), 'Der karolingische Herrschaftsverband im 9. Jahrhundert zwischen Kirche und Königshaus', *Historische Zeitschrift*, 235: 1–43.
Fried, J. (1998), 'Elite und Ideologie oder Die Nachfolgeordnung Karls des Grossen vom Jahre 813', in R. Le Jan (ed.), *La royauté et les élites dans l'Europe carolingienne*, 71–109, Lille.
Fried, J. (2016), *Charlemagne*, Cambridge, MA.
Gaborit-Chopin, D. (1999), *La statuette équestre de Charlemagne*, Paris.
Gaborit-Chopin, D. and E. Taburet-Delahaye eds (2001), *Le trésor de Conques*, Paris.
Gaedeke, N. (1987), 'Die Memoria für die Königin Hildegard', in P. Riché, C. V. Heitz and F. Héber-Suffrin (eds.), *Actes du colloque Autour de Hildegard*, 27–39, Nanterre.
Gai, A. S. (2001), 'Die karolingische Pfalzanlage. Von der Dokumentation zur Rekonstruktion', in L. Fenske, J. Jarnut and M. Wenhoff (eds.), *Splendor palatii. Neue Forschungen zu Paderborn und anderen Pfalzen der Karolingerzeit* (*Deutsche Königspfalzen* 5), 71–100, Göttingen.
Gaillard, M., M. Margue, A. Dierkens and H. Pettiau eds (2011), *De la Mer du Nord à la Méditerranée, Francia Media, une region au Coeur de l'Europe (c.840–c.1050)*, Luxembourg.
Ganshof, F. L. (1971), *The Carolingians and the Frankish Monarchy*, trans. J. Sondheimer, London.
Ganz, D. (1989), 'Humour as History in Notker's Gesta Karoli', in E. B. King, J. Schaefer and W. B. Wadley (eds.), *Monks, Nuns and Friars in Medieval Society*, 171–83, Sewanee.
Ganz, D. (1990), 'The *Epitaphium Arsenii* and the Opposition to Louis the Pious', in P. Godman and R. Collins (eds.), *Charlemagne's Heir. New Perspectives on Louis the Pious*, 537–50, Oxford.
Ganz, D. (1995), 'Conclusion: Visions of Carolingian Education, Past, Present and Future', in R. E. Sullivan (ed.), *'The Gentle Voices of Teachers'. Aspects of Learning in the Carolingian Age*, 261–83, Columbus, Ohio.
Ganz, D. (2000), 'Charlemagne in Hell', *Florilegium*, 17: 175–94.
Ganz, D. (2003), 'Review of Tischler (2001)', *Francia*, 30.1: 311–14.
Ganz, D. (2005), 'Einhard's Charlemagne: The Characterisation of Greatness', in J. Story (ed.), *Charlemagne. Empire and Society*, 38–51, Manchester.
Ganz, D. (2007), 'Einhardus Peccator', in P. Wormald and J. L. Nelson (eds.), *Lay Intellectuals in the Carolingian World*, 37–50, Cambridge.
Ganz, D. (2008), *Einhard and Notker the Stammerer: Two Lives of Charlemagne*, London.
Ganz, W. and W. Goffart (1990), 'Charters Earlier than 800 from French Collections', *Speculum*, 65.4: 906–32.
Garipzanov, I. H. (2008), *The Symbolic Language of Authority in the Carolingian World (c.751–877)*, Leiden.
Garland, D. (1990), *Punishment and Modern Society*, Oxford.
Garrison, M. (1994), 'The Emergence of Carolingian Latin Literature and the Court of Charlemagne', in R. McKitterick (ed.), *Carolingian Culture: Emulation and Innovation*, 111–40, Cambridge.
Garrison, M. (2000), 'The Franks as the New Israel? Education for an Identity from Pippin to Charlemagne', in Y. Hen and M. Innes (eds.), *The Uses of the Past in the Early Middle Ages*, 114–61, Cambridge.

Garrison (2004), 'The *Missa pro principe* in the Bobbio Missal', in Y. Hen and R. Meens (eds.), *The Bobbio Missal. Liturgy and Religious Culture in Merovingian Gaul*, 187–205, Cambridge.

Garver, V. (2009), *Women and Aristocratic Culture in the Carolingian World*, Ithaca.

Geary, P. (1985), *Aristocracy in Provence: The Rhone Basin at the Dawn of the Carolingian Age*, Philadelphia.

Geary, P. (1987), 'Germanic Tradition and Royal Ideology in the Ninth Century: The "Visio Karoli Magni"', *FMSt*, 21: 274–94.

Geary, P. (1994), *Phantoms of Remembrance. Memory and Oblivion at the End of the First Millennium*, Princeton.

Geary, P. (2012), 'Death and Funeral of the Carolingians', in K. H. Spiess and I. Warntjes (eds.), *Death at Court*, 8–19, Wiesbaden.

Geevers, L. and M. Marini eds (2015), *Dynastic Identity in Early Modern Europe. Rulers, Aristocrats and the Formation of Identities*, Farnham.

Geiselhart, M. (2002), *Die Kapitulariengesetzgebung Lothars I. in Italien*, Frankfurt.

Gerberding, R. (1987), *The Rise of the Carolingians and the Liber Historiae Francorum*, Oxford.

Geuenich, D. (1982), 'Zurzach – ein frühmittelalterliches Doppelkloster?', in H. Maurer and H. Patze (eds.), *Festschrift für Berent Schwineköper zu seinem siebzigsten Geburtstag*, 29–43, Sigmaringen.

Geuenich, D. (1988), 'Beobachtungen zu Grimald von St. Gallen, Erzkapellan und Oberkanzler Ludwigs des Deutschen', in M. Borgolte and H. Spilling (eds.), *Litterae Medii Aevi. Festschrift für Johanne Autenrieth*, 55–61, Sigmaringen.

Geuenich, D. (1989), 'Die politischen Kräfte in Bodenseegebiet', in A. Masser and A. Wolf (eds.), *Geistesleben um den Bodensee im frühen Mittelalter*, 29–56, Freiburg.

Geuenich, D. (2004), '… noluerunt obtemperare ducibus Francorum. Zur bayerisch-alemannischen Opposition gegen die karolingischen Hausmeier', in M. Becher and J. Jarnut (eds.), *Der Dynastiewechsel von 751*, 129–43, Münster.

Gildea, R. (2002), *Marianne in Chains*, London.

Glansdorff, S. (2003), 'L'Évêque de Metz et archichapelain Drogon (801/802-855)', Revue Belge de Philologie et d'Histoire, 81.4: 945–1014.

Glansdorff, S. (2009), *Diplômes de Louis le Germanique (817–876)*, Limoges.

Glansdorff, S. (2011), *Comites in regno Hludouici regis constitute. Prosopographie des détenteurs d'offices séculiers en Francie orientale, de Louis le Germanique à Charles le Gros 826–887*, Ostfildern.

Glenn, J. (2004), *Politics and History in the Tenth Century. The Work and World of Richer of Reims*, Cambridge.

Gockel, M. (1970), *Karolingische Königshöfe am Mittelrhein*, Göttingen.

Godman, P. (1985a), *Poetry of the Carolingian Renaissance*, London.

Godman, P. (1985b), 'Louis "the Pious' and His Poets', *FMSt*, 19: 239–89.

Godman, P. (1987), *Poets and Emperors. Frankish Politics and Carolingian Poetry*, Oxford.

Godman, P. and R. Collins eds (1990), *Charlemagne's Heir*, Oxford.

Goetz, H. W. (1981), *Strukturen der spätkarolingischen Epoche im Spiegel der Vorstellungen eines Zeitgennösisches Mönchs*, Bonn.

Goetz, H. W. (1987), 'Regnum: Zum politischen Denken der Karolingerzeit', *Zeitschrift der Savigny-Stiftung für Rechtsgeschichte, Germanistische Abteilung*, 104: 110–89.

Goetz, H. W. (2004), 'Der fränkische maior domus in der Sicht der erzählender Quellen', in S. Happ and U. Nonn (eds.), *Vielfalt der Geschichte. Lernen, Lehren und Erforschen vergangener Zeiten. Festgabe für Ingrid Heidrich*, 1–24, Berlin.

Goffart, W. (1986), 'Paul the Deacon's *Gesta Episcoporum Mettensium* and the Early Design of Charlemagne's Succession', *Traditio*, 42: 59–93.
Goffart, W. (2007), 'The Name "Merovingian" and the Dating of *Beowulf*', *Anglo-Saxon England*, 36: 93–101.
Goldberg, E. J. (2006a), *Struggle for Empire. Kingship and Conflict under Louis the German, 817–876*, Ithaca.
Goldberg, E. (2006b), '*Regina nitens sanctissima Hemma*: Queen Emma (827–876), Bishop Witgar of Augsburg, and the Witgar-belt', in B. Weiler and S. MacLean (eds.), *Representations of Power in Medieval Germany 800–1500*, 57–95, Turnhout.
Goldberg, E. J. (2013), 'Louis the Pious and the Hunt', *Speculum*, 88.3: 613–43.
Gramsci, A. (1971), *Selections from the Prison Notebooks*, trans. Q. Hoare and G. N. Smith, London.
Grau, C. (1992), 'Planung für ein Deutsches Historisches Institut im Frankreich während des zweiten Weltkriegs', *Francia*, 19.3: 109–128.
Gravel, M. (2011), 'De la crise du règne de Louis le Pieux. Essai d'historiographie', *Revue Historique*, 658: 357–89.
Gravel, M. (2012a), *Distances, rencontres, communications: realiser l'empire sous Charlemagne et Louis le Pieux*, Turnhout.
Gravel, M. (2012b), 'Of Palaces, Hunts and Pork Roast: Deciphering the Last Chapters of the Capitulary of Quierzy (a.877)', *Florilegium*, 29: 89–115.
Grierson, P. and M. Blackburn (1986), *Medieval European Coinage with a Catalogue of the Coins in the Fitzwilliam Museum, Cambridge I. The Early Middle Ages (5th–10th Centuries)*, Cambridge.
Guillot, O. (1989), 'Les étapes de l'accesson d'Eudes au pouvoir royal', in *Media in Francia. Recueil des mélanges offerts à Karl Ferdinand Werner à l'occasion de son 65e anniversaire*, 199–223, Maulévrier.
Guillot, O. (1990), 'Une *ordination* méconnue: Le Capitulaire de 823-825', in P. Godman and R. Collins (eds.), *Charlemagne's Heir. New Perspectives on the Reign of Louis the Pious (814–840)*, 455–86, Oxford.
Haarlander, S. (2006), *Rabanus Maurus*, Mainz.
Hack, A. (1999), 'Zur Herkunft der karolingischen Königssalbung', *Zeitschrift für Kirchengeschichte*, 110: 170–90.
Hack, A. (2014), *Von Christus zu Odin. Ein Karolinger bekehrt sich*, Stuttgart.
Hägermann, D. (2008), 'Divisio imperii von 817 und division regni von 831', in B. Kasten (ed.), *Herrscher- Und Fürstentestamente im Westeuropäischen Mittelalter*, 291–9, Cologne.
Halphen, L. (1918), 'Études critiques sur l'histoire de Charlemagne IV. Le moine de Saint-Gall', *Revue Historique*, 128: 260–98.
Halsall, G. (2003), *Warfare and Society in the Barbarian West, 450–900*, London.
Hamann-Maclean, R. (1983), 'Die Reimser Denkmale des französische Königtums im 12. Jahrhundert. Saint-Rémi als Grabkirche im frühen und hohen Mittelalter', in H. Beumann (ed.), *Beiträge zur Bildung der französischen Nation im Früh- und Hochmittelalter*, 93–259, Sigmaringen.
Hammer, C. (2007), *From Ducatus to Regnum: Ruling Bavaria under the Merovingians and early Carolingians*, Turnhout.
Hammer, C. (2008), '"Pippinus Rex": Pippin's plot ot 792 and Bavaria', *Traditio*, 63: 235–76.
Hammer, C. (2012), 'Christmas Day 800: Charles the Younger, Alcuin and the Frankish Royal Succession', *English Historical Review*, 127: 1–23.
Hampel, A. (1994), *Der Kaiserdom zu Frankfurt am Main. Ausgrabungen 1991–1993*, Nussloch.
Hartmann, W. (2002), *Ludwig der Deutsche*, Darmstadt.

Hartmann, W. (2011), 'Das Reich Lothars II. Zwischen Karl dem Kahlen und Ludwig dem Deutschen', in M. Gaillard, M. Margue, A. Dierkens and H. Pettiau (eds.), *De la mer du Nord à la Méditerranée. Francia Media, une region au Coeur de l'Europe (c.840–c.1050)*, 275–99, Luxembourg.

Hartmann, M. (2012), 'Zwischen Polygamie und Heiligkeit. Merowingische Königinnen', in E. Wamers and P. Périn (eds.), *Koniginnen der Merowinger. Adelsgräber aus den Kirchen von Köln, Saint-Denis, Chelles und Frankfurt am Main*, 18–36, Regensburg.

Hauck, K. (1950), 'Geblütsheiligkeit', in B. Bischoff and S. Brechetr (eds.), *Liber Floridus. Mittellateinische Studien. Festschrift Paul Lehmann*, 187–240, St Ottilien.

Hauck, K. (1967), 'Von einer spätantiken Randkultur zum karolingischer Europa', *FMSt*, 1: 3–93.

Hauck, K. (1970), 'Die Ausbreitung des Glaubens in Sachsen und die Verteidigung der römischen Kirche als konkurrierende Herrscheraufgaben Karls des Großen', *FMSt*, 4: 138–72.

Hauck, K. (1985), *Karolingische Taufpfalzen im Spiegel hofnaher Dichtung* (*Nachrichtung der Akademie der Wissenschaften in Göttingen, I. Phil. Hist. Klasse*), Göttingen.

Heidecker, K. (2010), *The Divorce of Lothar II*, trans. T. M. Guest, Ithaca.

Heidrich, I. (1965/1966), 'Titulatur und Urkunden der arnulfingischen Hausmeier', *Archiv für Diplomatik*, 11/12: 71–279.

Heidrich, I. (1973), 'Die Verbindung von Schütz und Immunität: Beobachtungen zu den merowingisehen und frühkarolingischen Urkunden für St. Calais', *Zeitschrift der Savigny-Stiftung für Rechtsgeschichte, Germ. Abteilung*, 90: 10–30.

Heidrich, I. (1990), 'Die kirchlichen Stiftungen der frühen Karolinger in der ausgehenden Karolingerzeit und unter Otto I', in R. Schieffer (ed.), *Beiträge zur Geschichte des Regnum Francorum*, 131–47, Sigmaringen.

Helvétius, A. M. (1998), 'L'abbatiat laïque comme relais du pouvoir royal aux frontières du royaume: Le cas du nord de la Neustrie au IXe siècle', in R. Le Jan (ed.), *La royauté et les élites dans l'Europe carolingienne*, 285–99, Lille.

Hen, Y. (2000), The Annals of Metz and the Merovingian past, in Y', Hen and M. Innes, 2000: 175–90.

Hen, Y. (2004), 'The Christianisation of Kingship', in M. Becher and J. Jarnut (eds.), *Der Dynastiewechsel von 751*, 163–77, Münster.

Hen, Y. and M. Innes eds (2000), *The Uses of the Past in the Early Middle Ages*, Cambridge.

Henderson, G. (1994), 'Emulation and Invention in Carolingian art', in R. McKitterick (ed.), *Carolingian Culture: Emulation and Innovation*, 248–73, Cambridge.

Henderson, I. (1998), '*Primus inter pares*: the St Andrews Sarcophagus and Pictish Sculpture', in S. Foster (ed.), *The St Andrews Sarcophagus. A Pictish Masterpiece and Its International Connections*, 97–167, Dublin.

Hennebicque, R. (1981), 'Structures familiales et politiques au IXe siècle: un groupe familial de l'aristocratie franque', *Revue Historique*, 265: 289–333.

Hennebicque-Le Jan, R. (1989), 'Prosopographica neustrica: les agents du roi en Neustrie de 639 à 840', in H. Atsma (ed.), *La Neustrie. Les pays au nord de la Loire de 650 à 850*, 1, 231–69, Sigmaringen.

Hentze, W. ed. (1999), *De Karolo rege et Leone papa. Der Bericht über die Zusammenkunft Karls des Grossen mit papst Leo III. In Paderborn 799 in einem Epos für Karl den Kaiser*, Paderborn.

Herren, M. (1991), 'The *De Imagine Tetrici* of Walahfrid Strabo. Edition and translation', *Journal of Medieval Latin*, 1: 118–39.

Higham, N. J. and M. J. Ryan (2013), *The Anglo-Saxon World*, New Haven.

Hlawitschka, E. (1960), *Franken, Alemannen, Bayern und Burgunder in Oberitalien (774-962)*, Freiburg.
Hlawitschka, E. (1965), 'Die Vorfahren Karls des Großen', in H. Beumann (ed.), *Karl der Grosse 1: Persönlichkeit und Geschichte*, 51-82, Düsseldorf.
Hlawitschka, E. (1968), *Lotharingien und das Reich an der Schwelle der deutschen Geschichte*, Stuttgart.
Hlawitschka, E. (1969), 'Waren die Kaiser Wido und Lambert Nachkommen Karls des Grossen?' *Quellen und Forschungen aus italienischen Archiven und Bibliotheken*, 49: 366-85.
Hlawitschka, E. ed. (1975), *Königswahl und Thronfolge in fränkisch-karolingischer Zeit*, Darmstadt.
Hlawitschka, E. (1978), 'Nachfolgeprojekte aus der Spätzeit Kaiser Karls III', *DA*, 46: 19-50.
Hlawitschka, E. (1988), 'Kaiser Wido und das Westfrankenreich', in G. Althoff (ed.), *Person und Gemeinschaft im Mittelalter. Karl Schmid zum fünfundsechzigsten Geburtstag*, 187-98, Sigmaringen.
Hoffmann, H. (1986), *Buchkunst und Königtum im ottonischen und frühsalischen Reich*, 2 vols, Stuttgart.
Hoffmann, H. (1998), 'Die Historien Richers von Reims', *DA*, 54: 445-529.
Hoffmann, K. (1985), 'Zur Enstehung des Königsportals in St-Denis', *Zeitschrift for Kunstgeschichte*, 48: 29-38.
Hofmeister, A. (1919), 'Weissenburger Aufzeichnungen vom Ende des 8. und Anfang des 9. Jahrhunderts', *Zeitschrift für die Geschihcte des Oberrheins*, 73 (NF 34): 401-21.
Hofstatder, R. (1964), 'The Paranoid Style in American Politics', *Harper's Magazine*, November.
Hope, G. (2005), 'The Political Development of the Carolingian Kingdom of Lotharingia, 870-925', Ph.D. thesis, University of Glasgow.
Hopkins, K. (1978a), 'Review Article: Rules of Evidence', *Journal of Roman Studies*, 68: 178-86.
Hopkins, K. (1978b), *Conquerors and Slaves*, Cambridge.
Howe, J. (2001), 'The Hagiography of Saint-Wandrille (Fontenelle) (Province of Haute-Normandie)', in M. Heinzelmann (ed.), *L'hagiographie du haut moyen âge en Gaule du Nord*, 127-92, Paris.
Hummer, H. (2005), *Politics and Power in Early Medieval Europe. Alsace and the Frankish Realm, 600-1000*, Cambridge.
Hussong, U. (1986), 'Studien zur Geschichte der Reichsabtei Fulda bis zum Jahrtausendwende (2)', *Archiv für Diplomatik*, 32: 129-304.
Huth, V. (1994), 'Erzbischof Arnulf von Reims und der Kampf um das Königtum im Westfrankenreich', *Francia*, 21.1: 85-124.
Hyam, J. (1990), 'Ermentrude and Richildis', in M. T. Gibson and J. L. Neslon (eds.), *Charles the Bald: Court and Kingdom*, 154-68, Aldershot.
Innes, M. (1997), 'Charlemagne's Will: Piety, Politics and the Imperial Succession', *English Historical Review*, 112.448: 833-55.
Innes, M. (1998a), 'Memory, Orality and Literacy in an Early Medieval Society', *Past and Present*, 158: 3-36.
Innes, M. (1998b), 'Kings, Monks and Patrons: Political Identities and the Abbey of Lorsch', in R. Le Jan (ed.), *La royauté et les élites dans l'Europe carolingienne*, 301-24, Lille.
Innes, M. (2000a), *State and Society in the Early Middle Ages. The Middle Rhine Valley 400-1000*, Cambridge.

Innes, M. (2000b), '"Teutons or Trojans? The Carolingians and the Germanic past", in Y. Hen and M. Innes (eds.), *The Uses of the Past in the Early Middle Ages*, 227–49, Cambridge.
Innes, M. (2001), 'People, Places and Power in Carolingian Society', in M. De Jong and F. Theuws (eds.), *Topographies of Power in the Early Middle Ages*, 397–437, Leiden.
Innes, M. (2003), '"A Place of Discipline": Carolingian Courts and Aristocratic Youth', in C. Cubitt (ed.), *Court Culture in the Early Middle Ages*, 59–76, Turnhout.
Innes, M. (2005), 'Charlemagne's Government', in J. Story (ed.), *Charlemagne. Empire and Society*, 71–89, Manchester.
Innes, M. (2008), 'Practices of Property in the Carolingian Empire', in J. R. Davis and M. McCormick (eds.), *The Long Morning of Medieval Europe. New Directions in Early Medieval Studies*, 247–66, Aldershot.
Innes, M. (2009), 'Property, Politics and the Problem of the Carolingian State', in W. Pohl and V. Wieser (eds.), *Der Frühmittelalterliche Staat – Europäische Perspektiven*, 299–319, Vienna.
Innes, M. and R. McKitterick (1994), 'The Writing of History', in R. McKitterick (ed.), *Carolingian Culture: Emulation and Innovation*, 193–220, Cambridge.
Jacobsen, W. (1989), 'Die Abteikirche von Saint-Denis als kunstgeschichtlches Problem', in H. Atsma (ed.), *La Neustrie. Les pays au nord de la Loire de 650 à 850*, 2, 151–85, Sigmaringen.
Jahn, J. (1988), 'Bayersiche »Pfalzgrafen« im 8. Jahrhundert?', in I. Eberl, W. Hartung and J. Jahn (eds.), *Früh- und hochmittelalterliche Adel in Schwaben und Bayern*, REGIO, 80–114, Sigmaringendorf.
Jakobi, F. J. (1978a), 'Die geistlichen und weltlichen Magnaten in den Fuldaer Totenanallen', in K. Schmid (ed.), *Die Klostergemeinschaft von Fulda*, 2.2, 792–887, Munich.
Jakobi, F. J. (1978b), 'Zu den Amtsträgerlisten in den Überlieferung der Fuldaer Totenannalen', in K. Schmid (ed.), *Die Klostergemeinschaft von Fulda*, 2.2, 505–25, Munich.
Jakobi, F. J. (1986), 'Diptychen als frühe Form der Gedenk-Aufzeichnungen. Zum Herrscher-Diptychon im Liber Memorialis von Remiremont', *FMSt*, 20: 186–212.
Jallinoja, R. (2017), *Families, Status and Dynasties*, London.
Jarnut, J. (1975), 'Quierzy und Rom. Bemerkungen zu den "Promissiones donationis" Pippins und Karls', *Historische Zeitschrift*, 220: 265–97.
Jarnut, J. (1984), 'Chlodwig und Chlothar. Anmerkungen zu den Namen zweier Söhne Karls des Großen', *Francia*, 12: 645–51.
Jarnut, J. (1989), 'Kaiser Ludwig der Fromme und König Bernhard von Italien', *Studi Medievali*, series 3, 30.1: 637–48.
Jarnut, J. (1990), 'Ludwig der Fromme, Lothar I. und das Regnum Italiae', in P. Godmand and R. Colins (eds.), *Charlemagne's Heir. New Perspectives on the Reign of Louis the Pious (814–840)*, 349–62, Oxford.
Jarnut, J. (1999), *Karl der Grosse-Mensch, Herrscher, Mythos: Ein Rückblick nach 1200 Jahren*, Paderborn.
Jarnut, J. (2002), *Herrschaft und Ethnogenese im Frühmittelalter. Gesammelte Aufsätze von Jörg Jarnut Festgabe zum 60. Geburtstag*, Münster.
Jarnut, J., U. Nonn and M. Richter eds (1994), *Karl Martel in seiner Zeit*, Sigmaringen.
Jäschke, K. U. (1970), 'Die Karolinger Genealogien aus Metz und Paulus Diaconus', *Rheinische Vierteljahrsblätter*, 34: 190–218.
Jenkins, R. (2002), *Pierre Bourdieu*, 2nd edition, Lonodn and New York.

Joll, J. (1977), *Gramsci*, London.
de Jong, M. (1992), 'Power and Humility in Carolingian Society: The Public Penance of Louis the Pious', *Early Medieval Europe*, 1: 29–52.
de Jong, M. (1995), 'Carolingian Monasticism: The Power of Prayer', in R. McKitterick (ed.), *New Cambridge Medieval History*, 2, 622–53, Cambridge.
de Jong, M. (2000), 'The Empire as Ecclesia: Hrabanus Maurus and Biblical *Historia* for Rulers', in Y. Hen and M. Innes (eds.), *The Uses of the Past in the Early Middle Ages*, 191–226, Cambridge.
de Jong, M. (2001a), 'Monastic Prisoners or Opting Out? Political Coercion and Honour in the Frankish Kingdom', in M. de Jong and F. Theuws (eds.) (2001), *Topographies of Power in the Early Middle Ages*, 291–328, Leiden.
de Jong, M. (2001b), 'Exegesis for an Empress', in E. Cohen and M. de Jong (eds.), *Medieval Transformations. Texts, Power and Gifts in Context*, 69–100, Leiden.
de Jong, M. (2004), 'Bride Shows Revisited: Praise, Slander and Exegesis in the Reign of the Empress Judith', in L. Brubaker and J. M. H. Smith (eds.), *Gender in the Early Medieval* World. *East and West, 300–900*, Cambridge.
de Jong, M. (2009), *The Penitential State. Authority and Atonement in the Age of Louis the Pious, 814–840*, Cambridge.
de Jong, M. (2010), 'Becoming Jeremiah: Paschasius Radbertus on Wala, Himself and Others', in R. Corradini, M. Gillis, R. McKitterick and I. Van Renswoude (eds.), *Ego Trouble. Authors and Their Identities in the Early Middle* Ages, 185–96, Vienna.
de Jong, M. (2015), 'Carolingian Political Discourse and the Biblical Past', in C. Gantner, R. McKitterick and S. Meeder (eds.), *The Resources of the Past in Early Medieval Europe*, 87–102, Cambridge.
de Jong, M. and F. Theuws eds (2001), *Topographies of Power in the Early Middle Ages*, Leiden.
Joris, A. (1973), 'Le palais carolingien d'Herstal', *Le Moyen Age*, 79: 385–420.
Joye, S. (2006), 'Le rapt de Judith par Baudoin de Flandre (862): un clinamen sociologique?', in F. Bougard, L. Feller and R. Le Jan (eds.), *Les élites au haut Moyen Âge. Crises et renouvellements*, 361–79, Turnhout.
Joye, S. (2012), 'Carolingian Rulers and Marriage in the Age of Louis the Pious and His Sons', in J. Nelson, S. Reynolds and S. Johns (eds.), *Gender and Historiography: Studiesin the Earlier Middle Ages in Honour of Pauline Stafford*, 101–14, London.
Kantorowicz, E. H. (1946), *Laudes Regiae: A Study in Liturgical Acclamations and Medieval Ruler Worship*, Berkeley.
Kaschke, S. (2006), *Die karolingischen Reichsteilungen bis 831*, Hamburg.
Kaschke, S. (2008), 'Tradition und Adaptation. Die "*Divisio Regnorum*" und die fränksiche Herrschaftsnachfolge', in B. Kasten (ed.), *Herrscher-und Fürstentestamente im westeuropäischen Mittelalter*, 259–89, Cologne.
Kaschke, S. (2010), 'Fixing Dates in the Early Middle Ages: The *Chronicon Laurissense Breve* and Its Use of Time', in R. Corradini, M. Diesenberger and M. Niederkorn-Bruck (eds.), *Zwischen Niederschrift und Wiederschrift*, 115–22, Vienna.
Kasten, B. (1986), *Adalhard von Corbie*, Düsseldorf.
Kasten, B. (1997), *Königssöhne und Königsherrschaft. Untersuchungen zur Teilhabe am Reich in der Merowinger- und Karolingerzeit*, Hannover.
Kasten, B. (2002), 'Chancen und Schicksale unehelicher Karolinger im 9. Jahrhundert', in F. Fuchs and P. Schmid (eds.), *Kaiser Arnulf. Das ostfränkische Reich am Ende des 9. Jahrhunderts*, 17–52, Munich.

Kasten, B. (2004), 'Alkuins erbrechtige Expertise für Karl den Großen?', in P. Depreux and B. Judic (eds.), *Alcuin de York à Tours*, special issue of *Annales de Bretagne et des pays de l'Ouest*, 111, 301–15.

Keller, H. (1975), 'Zum Sturz Karls III', originally published in *DA*, 34 (1966): 333–84 and reprinted in E. Hlawitschka (ed.) (1975), *Königswahl und Thronfolge in fränkisch-karolingischer Zeit*, Darsmstadt.

Keller, H. (2002), *Ottonische Königsherrschaft*, Darmstadt.

Keller, H. and G. Althoff (2008), *Die Zeit der späten Karolinger und die Ottonen 888–1024*, Stuttgart.

Kelly, F. (2004), 'Thinking in Threes: The Triad in Early Irish Literature', *Proceedings of the British Academy*, 15: 1–18.

Kempf, D. (2004), 'Paul the Deacon's *Liber de episcopis Mettensibus* and the Role of Metz in the Carolingian Realm', *Journal of Medieval History*, 30: 279–99.

Kerner, M. (2004), 'Mythos Karl der Große', in *Karl der Große und Europa*, 87–100, Frankfurt.

Kershaw, P. (2007), 'Eberhard of Friuli, a Carolingian lay intellectual', in P. Wormald and J. Nelson (eds.), *Lay Intellectuals in the Carolingian World*, 77–105, Cambridge.

Kershaw, P. (2011), *Peaceful Kings: Peace, Power and the Early Medieval Political Imagination*, Oxford.

Kessler, H. (1992), 'A Lay Abbot as Patron: Count Vivian and the First Bible of Charles the Bald', in *Committenti e produzione artistico-letteraria nell'alto medioevo occidentale*, 647–75, Spoleto.

Keynes, S. (1990), 'Royal Government and the Written Word in Late Anglo-Saxon England', in R. Mckitterick (ed.), *The Uses of Literacy in Early Medieval Europe*, 226–57, Cambridge.

King, P. D. (1987), *Charlemagne: Translated Sources*, Kendal.

Klaniczay, G. (2002), *Holy Rulers and Blessed Princesses: Dynastic Cults in Medieval Central Europe*, Cambridge.

Kölzer, T. (2004), 'Die letzten Merowinger: rois fainéants?', in M. Becher and J. Jarnut (eds.), *Der Dynastiewechsel von 751*, 33–60, Münster.

Kölzer, T. (2005), 'Kaiser Ludwig der Fromme (814-840) im Spiegel seiner Urkunden', in *Nordrhein-Westfälische Akademie der Wissenschaften. Geisteswissenschaften*, 5–34, Paderborn.

Konecny, S. (1976), *Die Frauen des karolingischen Königshaus*, Vienna.

Kornbluth, G. (1995), *Engraved Gems of the Carolingian Empire*, Pennsylvania.

Kornbluth, G. (2003), 'Richilds and Her Seal: Carolingian Self-Reference and the Imagery of Power', in J. L. Carrol and A. G. Stewart (eds.), *Saints, Sinners and Sisters*, 161–81, Aldershot.

Kortüm, H. (1994), 'Weltgeschichte am Ausgang der Karolingerzeit: Regino von Prüm', in A. Scharer and G. Scheibelreiter (eds.), *Historiographie im frühen Mittelalter*, 499–513, Vienna.

Kosto, A. (2002), 'Hostages in the Carolingian World (714–840)', *Early Medieval Europe*, 11.2: 123–47.

Kosto, A. (2012), *Hostages in the Middle Ages*, Oxford.

Koziol, G. (2006), 'Charles the Simple, Robert of Neustria, and the *vexilla* of Saint-Denis', *Early Medieval Europe*, 14.4: 355–90.

Koziol, G. (2012), *The Politics of Memory and Identity in Carolingian Royal Diplomas*, Turnhout.

Krah, A. (2004), 'Anerkennung und Integration – die Basis der Königsherrschaft Karls II', in W. Pohl (ed.), *Die Suche nach den Ursprügen. Von der Bedeutung des frühen Mittelalters*, 159–70, Vienna.
Kramer, R. (2014), 'Great Expectations. Imperial Ideologies and Ecclesiastical Reforms from Charlemagne to Louis the Pious (813–822)', Ph.D. thesis, Freie Universität, Berlin.
Kuchenbuch, L. (1978), *Bäuerliche Gesellschaft und Klosterherrschaft im 9. Jahrhundert: Studien zur Sozialstruktur der Familia der Abtei Prüm*, Wiesbaden.
Lafitte, M. and C. Denoël (2007), *Trésors carolingiens. Livres manuscrits de Charlemagne à Charles le chauve*, Paris.
Laporte, J. P. (2012), 'Grab und Reliquien der Königin Balthilde in Chelles-sur-Marne', in E. Warmers and P. Périn (eds.), *Königinnen der Merowinger. Adelsgräber aus den Kirchen von Köln, Saint-Denis, Chelles und Frankfurt am Main*, 126–44, Regensburg.
La Rocca, C. (1998), 'La reine et ses liens avec les monastères dans le royaume d'Italie', in R. Le Jan (ed.), *La royauté et les élites dans l'Europe carolingienne*, 269–84, Lille.
La Rocca, C. (2002), 'Les cadeaux nuptiaux de la famille royale en Italie', in F. Bougard, L. Feller and R. Le Jan (eds.), *Dots et douaires dans le haut Moyen Âge*, 499–526, Rome.
La Rocca, C. and L. Provero (2000), 'The Dead and Their Gifts: The Will of Eberhard, Count of Friuli, and His Wife Gisela, Daughter of Louis the Pious (853–864)', in F. Theuws and J. L. Nelson (eds.), *Rituals of Power*, 225–80, Leiden.
Latham, R. ed. (1985), *The Shorter Pepys*, London.
Lauer, P. (1900), *Le règne de Louis IV d'Outremer*, Paris.
Lauranson-Rosaz, C. (1998), 'Le roi et les grands dans l'Aquitaine carolingienne', in R. Le Jan (ed.), *La royauté et les élites dans l'Europe carolingienne*, 409–36, Lille.
Lehmann, P. (1962), *Erforschung des Mittelalters. Ausgewählte Abhandlungen und Aufsätze*, vol. 5, Stuttgart.
Le Jan, R. (1995), *Famille et pouvoir dans le monde franc (VIIe-Xe siècle)*, Paris.
Le Jan, R. ed. (1998), *La royauté et les élites dans l'Europe carolingienne*, Lille.
Le Jan, R. (2000), 'Frankish Giving of Arms and Rituals of Power', in F. Theuws and J. L. Nelson (eds.), *Rituals of Power*, 281–309, Leiden.
Le Jan, R. (2001), *Femmes, pouvoir et société dans le haut Moyen Age*, Paris.
Le Jan, R. (2003), *La société du haut Moyen Âge, Vie-IXe siècle*, Paris.
Le Jan, R. (2006), 'Élites et révoltes à l'époque carolingienne: crise des élites ou crise des modèles?', in F. Bougard, L. Feller and R. Le Jan (eds.), *Les élites au haut Moyen Âge. Crises et renouvellements*, 403–23, Turnhout.
Le Jan, R. (2010), 'The Multiple Identities of Dhuoda', in R. Corradini, M. Gillis, R. McKitterick and I. Van Renswoude (eds.), *Ego Trouble. Authors and Their Identities in the Early Middle Ages*, 211–19, Vienna.
Levillain, L. (1921), 'Études sur l'abbaye de Saint-Denis à l'époque mérovingienne', *Bibliothèque de l'école des chartes*, 82: 58–116.
Levillain, L. (1941), 'Les comtes de Paris à l'époque franque', *Le Moyen Age*, 50: 137–205.
Leyser, C. (2011), 'From Maternal Kin to Jesus as Mother: Royal Genealogy and Marian Devotion the Ninth-Century West', in C. Lesyer and L. Smith (eds.), *Motherhood, Religion and Society in Medieval Europe, 400–1400. Essays Presented to Henrietta Leyser*, 21–39, Abingdon and New York.
Leyser, K. (1994), *Communications and Power in Medieval Europe. The Carolingian and Ottonian Centuries*, London.
Leyser, K. J. (1979), *Rule and Conflict in an Early Medieval Society*, London.

Lot, F. (1891a), *Les derniers Carolingiens. Lothaire, Louis V, Charles de Lorraine*, Paris.
Lot, F. (1891b), 'Origine et signification du mot *carolingien*', *Revue Historique*, 46: 68–73.
Loveluck, C. (2013), *Northwest Europe in the Early Middle Ages, c. AD 600–1150. A Comparative Archaeology*, Cambridge.
Lowden, J. (1993), 'The Image and Self-Image of the Medieval Ruler', in A. J. Duggan (ed.), *Kings and Kingship in Medieval Europe*, 213–40, London.
Löwe, H. (1973), *Von Cassiodor zu Dante*, Berlin.
Löwe, H., W. Wattenbach and W. Levison (1953), *Deutschlands Geschichtsquellen im Mittelalter. Vorzeit und Karolinger, Heft 2: Die Karolinger vom Anfang des 8. Jahrhunderts bis zum Tode Karls des Großen*, Weimar.
Löwe, H., W. Wattenbach and W. Levison (1990), *Deutschlands Geschichtsquellen im Mittelalter. Vorzeit und Karolinger, Heft 5: Die Karolinger vom Vertrag von Verdun bis zum Herrschaftsantritt der Herrscher aus dem sächsischen Haus. Das ostfränkische Reich*, Weimar.
Löwe, H. W. and W. L. Wattenbach (1973), *Deutschlands Geschichtsquellen im Mittelalter. Vorzeit und Karolinger, Heft 5: Die Karolinger vom Vertrag von Verdun bis zum Herrschaftsantritt der Herrscher aus dem sächsischen Haus. Das Westfränkisches Reich*, Weimar.
Ludwig, U. (1999), *Transalpine Beziehungen der Karolingerzeit im Spiegel der Memorialüberlieferung*, Hannover.
Ludwig, U. (2000), 'Die Anlage des Liber Vitae', in D. Geuenich and U. Ludwig (eds.), *Der Memorial- und Liturgiecodex von San Salvatore/Santa Giulia in Brescia*, MGH Libri Memoriales und Necrologia, nova series 4, 56–88, Hannover.
Lukas, V. (2002a), 'Neues aus seiner Salzburger Handschrift aus Köln. Zur Überlieferung der Episcoporum ad Hludowicum Imperatorem relatio (829)', *DA*, 58: 539–48.
Lukas, V. (2002b), 'Philologische Beobachtungen zur Rezeption der Relatio Episcoporum ad Hludowicum Imperatorem bis Benedictus Levita', in W. Hartmann and G. Schmitz (eds.), *Fortschritt durch Fälschungen? Ursprung, Gestalt und Wirkungen der Pseudoisidorischen Fälschungen*, 61–88, Hannover.
Lukes, S. (2005), *Power. A Radical View*, 2nd edition, Basingstoke.
McCormick, M. (1984), 'The Liturgy of War in the Early Middle Ages: Crises, Liturgies and the Carolingian Monarchy', *Viator*, 15: 1–23.
McCormick, M. (1986), *Eternal Victory. Triumphal Rulership in Late Antiquity, Byzantium and the Early Medieval West*, Cambridge.
McCormick, M. (2001), *Origins of the European Economy. Communications and Commerce AD 300–900*, Cambridge.
McCormick, M. (2004), 'Pippin III, the Embassy of Caliph al Mansur, and the Mediterranean World', in M. Becher and J. Jarnut (eds.), *Der Dynastiewechsel von 751*, 221–41, Münster.
McDougall, S. (2016), *Royal Bastards: The Birth of Illegitimacy, 800–1230*, Oxford.
McEvoy, M. (2013), *Child Emperor Rule in the Late Roman West AD 367–455*, Oxford.
McKitterick, R. (1983), *The Frankish Kingdoms under the Carolingians, 751–987*, London.
McKitterick, R. (1989), *The Carolingians and the Written Word*, Cambridge.
McKitterick, R. (1990), 'The Palace School of Charles the Bald', *English Historical Review*, 95: 326–39.
McKitterick, R. ed. (1994), *Carolingian Culture: Emulation and Innovation*, Cambridge.
McKitterick, R. ed. (1995), *The New Cambridge Medieval History II c.700–c.900*, Cambridge.

McKitterick, R. (2004), *History and Memory in the Carolingian World*, Cambridge.
McKitterick, R. (2006a), *Perceptions of the Past in the Early Middle Ages*, Notre Dame.
McKitterick, R. (2006b), 'Histoire et mémoire de la crise d'une élite carolingienne: l'année 785 et les *Annales regni Francorum*', in F. Bougard, L. Feller and R. Le Jan (eds.), *Les élites au haut Moyen Âge. Crises et renouvellements*, 267–82, Turnhout.
McKitterick, R. (2008), *Charlemagne. The Formation of a European Identity*, Cambridge.
McKitterick, R. and M. Innes (1994), 'The Writing of History', in R. McKitterick (ed.), *Carolingian Culture: Emulation and Innovation*, 193–220, Cambridge.
MacLean, D. (1998), 'The Northumbrian Perspective', in S. Foster (ed.), *The St Andrews Sarcophagus. A Pictish Masterpiece and Its International Connections*, 179–201, Dublin.
MacLean, S. (2001), 'The Carolingian Response to the Revolt of Boso', *Early Medieval Europe*, 10: 21–48.
MacLean, S. (2003a), *Kingship and Politics in the Late Ninth Century. Charles the Fat and the End of the Carolingian Empire*, Cambridge.
MacLean, S. (2003b), 'Queenship, Nunneries and Royal Widowhood in Carolingian Europe', *Past and Present*, 178: 3–38.
MacLean, S. (2006), 'Ritual, Misunderstanding and the Cintest for Meaning: Representations of the Disrupted Royal Asembly at Frankfurt (873)', in B. Weiler and S. Maclean (eds.), *Representations of Power in Medieval Germany 800–1500*, 97–119, Turnhout.
MacLean, S. (2008), 'Making a Difference in Tenth-Century Politics; King Athelstan's Sisters and Frankish Queenship', in P. Fouracre and D. Ganz (eds.), *Frankland. The Franks and the World of the Early Middle Ages. Essays in Honour of Dame Jinty Nelson*, 167–90, Manchester.
MacLean, S. (2009a), trans. *History and Politics in Late Carolingian and Ottonian Europe. The Chronicle of Regino of Prüm and Adalbert of Magdeburg*, Manchester.
MacLean, S. (2009b), 'Insinuation, Censorship and the Struggle for Late Carolingian Lotharingia in Regino of Prüm's *Chronicle*', *English Historical Review*, 124: 1–28.
MacLean, S. (2017), *Ottonian Queenship*, Oxford.
Martindale, J. (1977), 'The French Aristocracy in the Early Middle Ages: A Reappraisal', *Past and Present*, 75: 5–45.
Martindale, J. (1985), 'The Kingdom of Aquitaine and the "Dissolution of the Carolingian Fisc"', *Francia*, 11: 131–91.
Martindale, J. (1990), 'Charles the Bald and the Government of the Kingdom of Aquitiane', in M. T. Gibson and J. L. Nelson (eds.), *Charles the Bald*, 115–38, Aldershot.
Maurer, H. (1983), 'Bodman', in *Die Deutschen Königspfalzen. Repertorium der Pfalzen, Königshöfe und übrigen Aufenthaltsorte der Könige im deutschen Reich des Mittlelaters*, vol. 3, i, 18–45, Göttingen.
Maurer, H. (1984), 'Sagen um Karl III', in L. Fenske, W. Rösener and T. Zotz (eds.), *Institutinen, Kultur und Gesellschaft im Mittelalter. Festschrift für Josef Fleckenstein zu seinem 65. Geburtstag*, 93–9, Sigmaringen.
Mayr-Harting, H. (1996), 'Charlemagne, the Saxons and the Imperial Coronation of 800', *English Historical Review*, 111: 1113–33.
Melve, L. (2007), *Inventing the Public Sphere: The Public Debate during the Investiture Contest (c.1030–1122)*, 2 vols, Leiden.
Mersiowsky, M. (1996), 'Regierungspraxis und Schriftlichkeit im Karolingerreich: das Fallbeispiel der Mandate und Briefe', in R. Schieffer (ed.), *Schriftkultur und Reichsverwaltung unter den karolingern, Abhandlungen der Nordrehin-Westfälischen Akademie der Wissenschaften*, 97, 109–66, Oplade.

Mersiowsky, M. (2000), 'Towards a Reappraisal of Carolingian Sovereign Charters', in K. Heidecker (ed.), *Charters and the Use of the Written Word in Medieval Society*, 15–25, Turnhout.

Merta, B. (1992), 'Politische Theorie in den Königsurkunden Pippins I', *Mitteilungen des Instituts für Österreichische Geschichtsforschung*, 100: 117–31.

Miller, S. (2014), 'Aetheling', in M. Lapidge, J. Blair, S. Keynes and D. Scragg (eds.), *The Wiley Blackwell Encyclopedia of Anglo-Saxon England*, 2nd edition, 15, Chichester.

Moisl, H. (1981), 'Anglo-Saxon Royal Genealogies and Germanic Oral Tradition', *Journal of Medieval History*, 7.3: 215–48.

Mordek, H. (1994), 'Die Hedenen als politische Kraft im austrasischen Frankenreich', in Jarnut U. Nonn and M. Richter (eds.), *Karl Martel in seiner Zeit*, Beihfefte *der Francia*, 345–66, Sigmaringen.

Mordek, H. (1995a), *Bibliotheca capitulariam regum Francorum manuscripta: Überlieferung und Traditionszusammenhang der fränkischen Herrscherlasse*, Munich.

Mordek, H. (1995b), 'Frühmittelalterliche Gesetzgber und Iustitia in Miniaturen weltlicher Rechtshandschriften', in *La Giustizia nell'alto Medioevo, Settimane di Studio del Centro Italiano di studi sull'Alto Medioevo*, 42, 997–1052, Spoleto.

Mordek, H. (2005), 'Karls des Großen zweites Kapitular von Herstal und die Hungersnot der Jahre 778/779', *DA*, 61: 1–52.

Mordek, H. and G. Schmitz (1987), 'Neue Kapitularien und Kapitulariensammlungen', *DA*, 43: 361–439.

Morgan, E. (1952), *Beowulf*, trans. E. Morgan, Aldington, Kent.

Morrissey, R. (1992), 'Charlemagne', in P. Nora (ed.), *Les Lieux de mémoire. III. Les France. 3 De l'archive à l'emblème*, 631–73, Paris.

Morrissey, R. (2003), *Charlemagne and France*, trans C. Tihanyi, Notre Dame.

Münsch, O. (2001), *Der Liber Legum des Lupus von Ferrières*, Frankfurt.

Mulvey, L. (1975), 'Visual Pleasure and Narrative Cinema', *Screen*, 16.3: 6–18.

Murray, A. C. (1998), '*Post vocantur Merohingii*: Fredegar, Merovech, and "Sacral Kingship"', in A. C. Murrray (ed.), *After Rome's Fall. Narrators and Sources of Early Medieval History. Essays Presented to Walter Goffart*, Toronto.

Murray, A. C. (2000), *From Roman to Merovingian Gaul: A Reader*, Peterborough, Ontario.

Nees, L. (1991), *A Tainted Mantle. Hercules and the Classical Tradition at the Carolingian Court*, Philadelphia.

Nelson, J. L. (1986), *Politics and Ritual in Early Medieval Europe*, London.

Nelson, J. L. (1988a), 'A Tale of Two Princes: Poltics, Text and Ideology in a Carolingian Annal', in *Studies in Medieval and Renaissance History 10*, 105–41, New York.

Nelson, J. L. (1988b), 'Kingship and Empire', in J. H. Burns (ed.), *The Cambridge History of Medieval Poltical Thought c.350–c.1450*, 211–51, Cambridge.

Nelson, J. L. (1990), 'Hincmar of Reims on King-Making: The Evidence of the *Annals of St. Bertin*, 861–882', in J. Bak (ed.), *Coronations: Medieval and Early Modern Ritual*, 16–34, Berkeley.

Nelson, J. L. (1991a), *The Annals of St-Bertin*, Manchester.

Nelson, J. L. (1991b), 'La famille de Charlemagne', *Byzantion*, 61: 194–212.

Nelson, J. L. (1992), *Charles the Bald*, London.

Nelson, J. L. (1994a), 'Kingship and Empire in the Carolingian World', in R. McKitterick (ed.), *Carolingian Culture: Emulatuion and Innovation*, 52–87, Cambridge.

Nelson, J. L. (1994b), 'Parents, Children, and the Church in the Earlier Middle Ages', in D. Wood (ed.), *The Church and Childhood*, 81–114, Oxford.

Nelson, J. L. (1995), 'Kingship and Royal Government', in R. McKitterick (ed.), *The New Cambridge Medieval History II c.700–c.900*, 383–430, Cambridge.
Nelson, J. L. (1996a), *The Frankish World*, London.
Nelson, J. L. (1996b), 'Bad Kingship in the Earlier Middle Ages', *Haskins Society Journal*, 8: 1–26.
Nelson, J. L. (1996c), 'The Search for Peace in a Time of War: The Carolingian *Brüderkrieg*, 840–843', in J. Fried (ed.), *Träger und Instrumentarien des Friedens in hohen und späten Mittelalter*, 87–114, Stuttgart.
Nelson, J. L. (1996d), 'La mort de Charles le Chauve', *Médiévales*, 31: 53–66.
Nelson, J. L. (1997a), 'The Siting of the Council at Frankfurt: Some Reflections on Family and Politics', in R. Berndt (ed.), *Das Frankfurter Konzil von 794*, 1, 149–65, Mainz.
Nelson, J. L. (1997b), 'Early Medieval Rites of Queen-Making and the Shaping of Medieval Queenship', in A. Duggan (ed.), *Queens and Queenship in Medieval Europe*, 301–15, Woodbridge.
Nelson, J. L. (1998a), 'Making a Difference in Eighth-Century Politics: The Daughters of Desiderius', in A. Murray (ed.), *After Rome's Fall. Narrators and Sources of Early Medieval History. Essays Presented to Walter Goffart*, 171–90, Toronto.
Nelson, J. L. (1998b), 'La cour impériale de Charlemagne', in R. Le Jan (ed.), *La royauté et les élites dans l'Europe carolingienne*, 177–91, Lille.
Nelson, J. L. (1998c), 'Monks, Secular Men and Masculinity', in D. M. Hadley (ed.), *Masculinity in Medieval Europe*, 121–42, London.
Nelson, J. L. (1999), 'Rulers and Government', in T. Reuter (ed.), *The New Cambridge Medieval History III c.900–c.1024*, 95–129, Cambridge.
Nelson, J. L. (2000), 'Carolingian Royal Funerals', in F. Theuws and J. L. Nelson (eds.), *Rituals of Power*, 131–84, Leiden.
Nelson, J. L. (2001a), 'Aachen as a Place of Power', in M. de Jong and F. Theuws (eds.), *Topographies of Power in the Early Middle Ages*, 217–41, Leiden.
Nelson, J. L. (2001b), 'Peers in the Early Middle Ages', in P. Stafford, J. L. Nelson and J. Martindale (eds.), *Law, Laity and Solidarities. Essays in Honour of Susan Reynolds*, 27–46, Manchester.
Nelson, J. L. (2002), 'Charlemagne – pater optimus?' in P. Godman, J. Jarnut and P. Johanek (eds.), *Am Vorabend der Kaiserkrönung*, 269–81, Berlin.
Nelson, J. L. (2003), 'Was Charlemagne's Court a Courtly Society?' in C. Cubitt (ed.), *Court Culture in the Early Middle Ages*, 39–57, Turnhout.
Nelson, J. L. (2004a), 'Gendering Courts in the Early Medieval West', in L. Brubaker and J. M. H. Smith (eds.), *Gender in the Early Medieval World. East and West, 300–900*, 185–97, Cambridge.
Nelson, J. L. (2004b), 'Bertrada', in M. Becher and J. Jarnut (eds.), *Der Dynastiewechsel von 751*, 93–108, Münster.
Nelson, J. L. (2005), 'Charlemagne the Man', in J. Story (ed.), *Charlemagne. Empire and Society*, 22–37, Manchester.
Nelson, J. L. (2007), 'Dhuoda', in P. Wormald and J. L. Nelson (eds.), *Lay Intellectuals in the Carolingian World*, 106–20, Cambridge.
Nelson, J. L. (2008a), 'Family Structures and Gendered Power in Early Medieval Kingdoms: The Case of Charlemagne's Mother', in G. Calvi (ed.), *Women Rulers in Europe. Agency, Practice and the Representation of Political Powers (XII–XVIII)*, 27–44, Fiesole.
Nelson, J. L. (2008b), 'Frankish Identity in Charlemagne's Empire', in I. Garipzanov, P. Geary and P. Urbańczyk (eds.), *Franks, Northmen and Slavs. Identities and State Formation in Early Medieval Europe*, 71–83, Turnhout.

Nelson, J. L. (2008c), 'Charlemagne and Empire', in J. R. Davis and M. McCormick (eds.), *The Long Morning of Medieval Europe*, 223–34, Aldershot.

Nelson, J. L. (2008d), 'Organic Intellectuals in the Dark Ages?' *History Workshop Journal*, 66: 1–17.

Nelson, J. L. (2009), *Opposition to Charlemagne*, German Historical Institute 2008 Annual Lecture, London.

Nelson, J. L. (2011), 'Le partage de Verdun', in M. Gaillard, M. Margue, A. Dierkens and H. Pettiau (eds.), *De la mer du Nord à la Méditerranée. Francia Media, une region au Coeur de l'Europe (c.840–c.1050)*, 241–54, Luxembourg.

Nelson, J. L. (2019), *King and Emperor. A New Life of Charlemagne*, London.

Nightingale, J. (2001), *Monasteries and Patrons in the Gorze Reform. Lotharingia c.850–1000*, Oxford.

Noble, T. F. X. (1998), 'Lupus of Ferrières in His Carolingian Context', in A. Murray (ed.), *After Rome's Fall. Narrators and Sources of Early Medieval History. Essays Presented to Walter Goffart*, 232–50, Toronto.

Noble, T. F. X. (2009), trans. *Charlemagne and Louis the Pious. Lives by Einhard, Notker, Ermoldus, Thegan and the Astronomer*, Pennsylvania.

Oexle, O. G. (1967), 'Die Karolinger und die Stadt des heiligen Arnulf', *FMSt*, 1: 250–364, l.

Oexle, O. G. (1969), 'Bischof Ebroin von Poitiers und seine Verwandten', *FMSt*, 3: 138–210.

Oexle, O. G. (1978a), *Forschungen zu Monastischen und Geistlichen Gemeinschaften im Westfränkischen Bereich*, Munich.

Oexle, O. G. (1970), 'Le monastère Charroux au IXe siècle', *Le Moyen Age*, 76: 193–204.

Oexle, O. G. (1978b), *Forschungen zu Monastischen und Geistlichen Gemeinschaften im Westfränkischen Bereich*, Munich.

Offergeld, T. (2001), *Reges pueri. Das Königtum Minderjähriger im frühen Mittelalter*, Hannover.

Orchard, A. (2003), *A Critical Companion to Beowulf*, Woodbridge.

Orth, E. (1985-6), 'Frankfurt', in *Die deutschen Königspfalzen, 1, Hessen* parts 2–4, 131–456, Göttingen.

Palmer, J. T. (2009), *Anglo-Saxons in a Frankish World 690–900*, Turnhout.

Palmer, J. T. (2014), 'The Ends and Futures of Bede's De Temporum Ratione', in P. Darby and F. Wallis (eds.), *Bede and the Future*, 139–60, Farnham.

Parsons, D. (1987), *Books and Buildings: Architectural Description before and after Bede*, Jarrow.

Patzold, S. (2000), 'Konflikte im Kloster Fulda zur Zeit der Karolinger', *Fuldaer Geschichtsblätter. Zeitschrift des Fuldaer Geschichtsvereins*, 76: 69–162.

Patzold, S. (2006a), 'Eine loyale Palastrebellion der "Reichseinheitspartei"? Zur "Divisio Imperii" von 817 und zu den Ursachen des Aufstands gegen Ludwig den Frommen im Jahre 830', *FMSt*, 40: 43–77.

Patzold, S. (2006b), 'Redéfinir l'office episcopal: les évêques francs face à la crise des années 820-830', in F. Bougard, L. Feller and R. Le Jan (eds.), *Les élites au haut Moyen Âge. Crises et renouvellements*, 337–59, Turnhout.

Patzold, S. (2008a), *Episcopus. Wissen über Bischöfe im Frankenreich des späten 8. Bis frühen 10. Jahrhunderts*, Ostfildern.

Patzold, S. (2008b), 'Konsens und Konkurrenz. Überlegungen zu einem aktuellen Forschungskonzept der Mediävistik', *FMSt*, 41: 75–104.

Patzold, S. (2013), *Ich und Karl der Grosse. Das Leben des Höflings Einhard*, Stuttgart.
Penndorf, U. (1974), *Das Problem der 'Reichseinheitsidee' nach der Teilung von Verdun (843)*, Munich.
Périn, P. and L. C. Feffer (1985), *La Neustrie. Les pays au nord de la Loire, de Dagobert à Charles le Chauve (VIIe – IXe siècle)*, Créteil.
Pirenne, H. (1925), 'Le fisc royal de Tournai', in *Mélanges d'histoire du moyen âge offerts à M. Ferdinand Lot par ses amis et ses élèves*, 641–8, Paris.
Pohl, W. (2004), 'Das Papstum und die Langobarden', in M. Becher and J. Jarnut (eds.), *Der Dynastiewechsel von 751*, 145–61, Münster.
Pohl, W. (2014), 'Why Not to Marry a Foreign Woman: Stephen III's Letter to Charlemagne', in V. Garver and O. W. Phelan (eds.), *Rome and Religion in the Medieval World. Studies in Honouor of Thomas F.X. Noble*, 47–63, Farnham.
Pohl, W. (2016), 'Genealogy: A Comparative Perspective from the Early Medieval West', in E. Hovden, C. Lutter and W. Pohl (eds.), *Meanings of Community across Medieval Eurasia: Comparative Approaches*, 232–69, Leiden and Boston.
Pohl, W. and G. Heydemann (2016), 'The Rhetoric of Election: 1 Peter 2.9 and the Franks', in R. Meens, D. van Espelo, B. van den Hoven van Genderen, J. Raaijmakers, I. van Renswoude and C. van Rhijn (eds.), *Religious Franks. Religion and Power in the Frankish Kingdoms: Studies in Honour of Makye de Jong*, 13–31, Manchester.
Pohl, W. and H. Reimitz eds (1998), *Strategies of Distinction: The Construction of Ethnic Communities, 300–800*, Leiden.
Pohl, W. and V. Wieser eds (2009), *Der Frühmittelalterliche Staat –Europäische Perspektiven*, Vienna.
Pohle, P., P. van den Brink and S. Ayooghi eds (2014), *Karl der Grosse/Charlemagne*, 3 vols, Dresden.
Pokorny, R. (1983), 'Ein unbekannter Synodalsermo Arns von Salzburg', *DA*, 39: 379–94.
Pokorny, R. (1985), 'Ein unerkanntes Brieffragment Argrims von Lyons-Langres aus den Jahren 894/5 und zwei umstrittene Bischofsweihen in der Kirchenprovinz Lyon', *Francia*, 13: 602–22.
Pokorny, R. (2010), *Augiensia. Ein neuaufgefundenes Konvolut von Urkundenabschriften aus dem Handarchiv der Reichenauer Fälscher des 12. Jahrhunderts* MGH Studien und Texte 48, Hannover.
Pössel, C. (2006), 'Authors and Recipients of Carolingian Capitularies, 779–829', in R. Corradini, R. Meens, C. Pössel and P. Shaw (eds.), in *Texts and Identities in the Early Middle Ages*, 253–74, Vienna.
Pössel, C. (2009), 'The Magic of Early Medieval Ritual', *Early Medieval Europe*, 17.2: 111–25.
Power, E. (1986), *Medieval People*, London.
Prinz, J. (1965), 'Ein unbekanntes Aktenstück zum Ehestreit König Lothars II', *DA*, 21: 249–63.
Prinz, J. (1972), 'Der karolingische Kalendar der Hs. Ambros. M12 sup8', in *Festchrift für Hermann Heimpel*, 3 vols, vol. 2, Göttingen.
Prinz, F. (1976), 'Zur geistigen Kultur des Mönchtums', in F. Prinz (ed.), *Mönchtum und Gesellschaft im Frühmittelalter*, 265–353, Darmstadt.
Raaijmakers, J. (2003), 'Sacred Time, Sacred Space. History and Identity at the Monastery of Fulda (744-856)', Ph.D. thesis, University of Amsterdam.
Raaijmakers, J. (2012), *The Making of the Monastic Community of Fulda, c.744–c.900*, Cambridge.

Reimitz, H. (2000), 'Ein fränkisches Geschichtsbuch aus Saint-Amand und der Codex Vindobonensis palat. 473', in C. Egger and H. Weigl (eds.), *Text-Schrift-Codex: Quellenkundliche Arbeiten aus dem Institut für Österreichische Geschichtsforschung*, 34–90, Vienna.
Reimitz, H. (2002), 'Anleitung zur Interpretation: Schrift und Genealogie in der Karolingerzeit', in W. Pohl and P. Herold (eds.), *Vom Nutzen des Schreibens. Soziales Gedächtnis, Herrschaft und Besitz im Mittelalter*, 167–81, Vienna.
Reimitz, H. (2004), 'Der Weg zum Königtum in historiographischen Kompendien der Karolingerzeit', in M. Becher and J. Jarnut (eds.), *Der Dynastiewechsel von 751*, 277–320, Münster.
Reimitz, H. (2006), 'Geschlecterrollen und Genealogie in der fränkischen Historiographie', in R. Rollinger and C. Ulf (eds.), *Frauen und Geschlechter. Bilder – Rollen – Realitäten in den Texten antiker Autoren zwischen Antike und Mittelalter*, 335–54, Vienna.
Reimitz, H. (2008), '*Omnes Franci*: Identifications and Identities of the Early Medieval Franks', in I. Garipzanov, P. Geary and P. Urbańczyk (eds.), *Franks, Northmen and Slavs. Identities and State Formation in Early Medieval Europe*, 51–68, Turnhout.
Reimitz, H. (2015), *History, Frankish Identity and the Framing of Western Ethnicity, 550–850*, Cambridge.
Rembold, I. (2013), 'The Poeta Saxo at Paderborn: Episcopal Authority and Carolingian Rule in Late Ninth-Century Saxony', *Early Medieval Europe*, 21.2: 169–96.
Rémond, R. (1992), 'La fille aînée de l'Église', in P. Nora (ed.), *Les lieux de mémoire III, Les France*, 540–81, Paris.
Remensnyder, A. (1995), *Remembering Kings Past: Monastic Foundation Legends in Medieval Southern France*, Ithaca.
van Renswoude, I. (2006), 'Time Is on Our Side', in R. Corradini, R. Meens, C. Pössel and P. Shaw (eds.), *Texts and Identities in the Early Middle Ages*, 323–41, Vienna.
Reuter, T. (1991), *Germany in the Early Middle Ages c.800–1056*, London.
Reuter, T. (1992), trans, *The Annals of Fulda*, Manchester.
Reuter, T. (1997), 'The Medieval Nobility', in M. Bentley (ed.), *Companion to Historiography*, 177–202, London.
Reuter, T. (2006), *Medieval Polities and Modern Mentalities*, ed. J. L. Nelson, Cambridge.
Reynolds, S. (1994), *Fiefs and Vassals. The Medieval Evidence Re-Interpreted*, Oxford.
Ridyard, S. (1988), *The Royal Saints of Anglo-Saxon England*, Cambridge.
Ripart, L. (2011), "Le royaume rodolphien de Bourgogen (fin IXe – début XIe siècle)', in M. Gaillard, M. Margue, A. Dierkens and H. Pettiau (eds.), *De la mer du Nord à la Méditerranée. Francia Media, une region au Coeur de l'Europe (c.840–c.1050)*, 429–52, Luxembourg.
Roach, L. (2018), 'The Ottonians and Italy', *German History*, 36.3: 349–64.
Robb, G. (2010), *Parisians. An Adventure History of Paris*, London.
Rosenwein, B. (1999), *Negotiating Space. Power, Restraint, and Privileges of Immunity in Early Medieval Europe*, Manchester.
Rosenwein, B. (2001), 'One Site, Many Meanings: Saint Maurice d'Agaune as a Place of Power in the Early Middle Ages', in M. de Jong and F. Theuws (eds.), *Topographies of Power in the Early Middle Ages*, 271–90, Leiden.
Sanders, G. (1982), 'Le remaniement carolingien de la *Vita Balthildis* mérovingienne', *Analecta Bollanidiana*, 100: 411–28.
Sassier, Y. (1987), *Hugues Capet. Naissance d'une dynastie*, Paris.
Sassier, Y. (1991), 'Les Carolingiens et Auxerre', in D. Iogna-Prat, C. Jeudy and G. Lobrichon (eds.), *L'École carolingienne d'Auxerre de Muretach à Remi*, 21–36, Paris.

Scharer, A. (2009), 'Charlemagne's Daughters', in S. Baxter, C. E. Karkov, J. L. Nelson and D. Pelteret (eds.), *Early Medieval Studies in Memory of Patrick Wormald*, 269–82, Farnham.
Scharer, A. (2011), 'Objects of Royal Representation in England and on the Continent', in J. Roberts and L. Webster (eds.), *Anglo-Saxon Traces*, 31–45, Tempe, Arizona.
Schieffer, T. (1977), 'Karl von Aquitanien', *Neue Deutsche Biographie*, 11: 238–9, Berlin.
Schieffer, R. ed. (1990a), *Beiträge zur Geschichte des Regnum Francorum*, Sigmaringen.
Schieffer, R. (1990b), 'Väter und Söhne im Karolingerhaus', in Schieffer (1990a), 149–64.
Schieffer, R. (1993), 'Karolingische Töchter', in G. Jenal and S. Haarländer (eds.), *Herrschaft, Kirche, Kultur. Beiträge zur Geschichte des Mittelalters. Festschrift für Friedrich Prinz zu seinem 65. Geburtstag*, 125–39, Stuttgart.
Schieffer, R. (1997), *Die Karolinger*, 2nd edition, Stuttgart.
Schieffer, R. (2000), 'Charlemagne and Rome', in J. M. H. Smith (ed.), *Early Medieval Rome and the Christian West. Essays in Honour of Donald Bullough*, 279–95, Leiden.
Schieffer, R. (2004a), 'Von Saint-Quentin nach Ellwangen: eine Notiz über König Ludwig den Jüngeren', in S. Gouguenheim, M. Goullet et al. (eds.), *Retour aux sources. Textes, études et documents d'histoire médiévale offerts à Michel Parisse*, 965–70, Paris.
Schieffer, R. (2004b), '"Die folgenschwerste Tat des ganzen Mittelalters"? Aspeket des wissenschftlichen Urteils über den Dynastiewechsel von 751', in M. Becher and J. Jarnut (eds.), *Der Dynastiewechsel von 751. Vorgeschichte. Legitimationsstrategien und Erinnerung*, 1–13, Münster.
Schlesinger, W. (1975), 'Karlingische Königswahlen', in E. Hlawitschka (ed.), *Königswahl und Thronfolge in fränkisch-karolingischer Zeit*, 190–266, Darmstadt.
Schmid, A. (1976), 'Die Herrschergräber in St. Emmeram zu Regensburg', *DA*, 32: 333–69.
Schmid, K. (1957), 'Kloster Schienen und seine adligen Besitzer', in Tellenbach (1957a) G. Tellenbach (ed.), *Studien und Vorarbeiten zur Geschichte des großfränkischen und frühdeutschen Adels*, Forschungen zur oberrheinische Landesgeschichte, 4, 282–308, Freiburg.
Schmid, K. (1965), 'Religiöses und sippengebundenes Gemeinschaftbewußtsein im frühmittelalterichen Gedenkbucheinträgen', *DA*, 21: 18–81.
Schmid, K. (1968), 'Ein karolingischer Königseintrag im Gedenkbuch von Remiremont', *FMSt*, 2: 96–134.
Schmid, K. (1976/1983), 'Zur historischen Bestimmung des ältesten Eintrags im St. Galler Verbrüderungsbuch', in *Alemannica. Landeskundliche Beiträge. Festschrift für Bruno Boesch. Alemannisches Jahrbuch 1973/75)*, 500–32, and republished in Schmid, K. (1983), Schmid, K. *Gebetsgedenken und adliges Selbstverständnis im Mittelalter. Ausgewählte Beiträge*, 481–513 (I use the 1983 pagination), Sigmaringen.
Schmid, K. (1977), 'Heirat, Familienfolge, Geschlechterbewusstsein', in *Il matrimonio nella società altomedievale*, 103–37, Spoleto.
Schmid, K. (1983), *Gebetsgedenken und adliges Selbstverständnis im Mittelalter. Ausgewählte Beiträge*, Sigmaringen.
Schmid, K. (1994), 'Ein verlorenes *Stemma Regum Franciae*', *FMSt*, 28: 196–225.
Schneider, J. (2010), *Auf der Suche nach dem verlorenen Reich. Lotharingien im 9. und 10. Jahrhundert*, Cologne.
Schneider, O. (2004), 'Die Königserhebung Pippins751 in der Erinnerung der karolingischen Quellen: Die Glaubwürdigkeit der Reichsannalen und die Verformung der Vergangenheit', in M. Becher and J. Jarnut (eds.), *Der Dynastiewechsel von 751*, 243–75, Münster.
Schneidmüller, B. (1979), *Karolingische Tradition und frühes französisches Königtum*, Wiesbaden.

Schneidmüller, B. (1997), 'Widukind von Korvey, Richer von Reims und der Wandel politisicher Bewußtseins im 10. Jahrhundert', in C. Brühl and B. Schneidmüller (eds.), *Beiträge zur mittelalterlichen Reichs- und Nationsbildung in Deutschland und Frankreich, Historische Zeitschrift, Beiheft*, 24: 83–102.

Schneidmüller, B. (2000), *Die Welfen. Herrschaft und Erinnerung (819–1252)*, Stuttgart.

Schramm. P. E. (1954–78), *Herrschaftszeichen und Staatssymbolik*, 4 vols, Stuttgart.

Schramm, P. E. (1957), *Herrschaftszeichen: gestiftet, verschenkt, verkauft, verpfändet. Belege aus dem Mittalter, Nachrichten der Akademie der Wissenschaften in Göttingen I. Philologisch-Historische Klasse*, 5, 162–226, Göttingen.

Schramm, P. E. (1983), *Die deutschen Kaiser und Könige in Bildern ihrer Zeit, 751–1190*, 2nd edition, Munich.

Schramm, P. E. and F. Mütherich (1981), *Denkmale der deutschen Könige und Kaiser*, 2nd edition, Munich.

Scott, H. (2015), '"The Line of Descent of Nobles Is from the Blood of Kings": Reflections on Dynastic Identity', in L. Geevers and M. Marini (eds.), *Dynastic Identity in Early Modern Europe. Rulers, Aristocrats and the Formation of Identities*, 217–41, Farnham.

Screen, E. (2003), 'The Importance of the Emperor: Lothar I and the Frankish Civil War', *Early Medieval Europe*, 12.1: 25–51.

Screen, E. (2011), 'Lothar I; the Man and His Entourage', in M. Gaillard, M. Margue, A. Dierkens and H. Pettiau (eds.), *De la mer du Nord à la Méditerranée. Francia Media, une region au Coeur de l'Europe (c.840–c.1050)*, 255–74, Luxembourg.

Screen, E. (2018), 'Remembering and Forgetting Lothar I', in E. Screen and C. West (eds.), *Writing the Early Medieval West. Studies in Honour of Rosamond McKitterick*, 248–60, Cambridge.

Schreiner, K. (1975), 'Hildegardis regina', *Archiv für Kulturgeschichte*, 57: 1–70.

Searle, E. (1988), *Predatory Kinship and the Creation of Norman Power, 840–1066*, Berkeley.

Semmler, J. (1965/1976), 'Karl der Grosse und das fränkische Mönchtum', in D. Bischoff (ed.), *Karlder Große. Lebenswerk und Nachleben, II Das geistige Leben*, 255–89, Düsseldorf, and republished in F. Prinz (ed.) (1976), *Mönchtum und Gesellschaft im Frühmitelalter*, 204–64 (I use this 1976 pagination), Darmstadt.

Semmler, J. (1966), 'Zu den bayrisch-westfränkischen Beziehungen in karolingischer Zeit', *Zeitschrift für bayerische Landesgeschichte*, 29: 344–424.

Semmler, J. (1975), 'Pippin III und die fränkischen Klöster', *Francia*, 3: 88–146.

Semmler, J. (1989), 'Saint-Denis: von der bischöflichen Coemeterialbasilika zur königlichen Benediktinerabtei', in H. Atsma (ed.), *La Neustrie. Les pays au nord de la Loire de 650 à 850*, 2, 75–123, Sigmaringen.

Semmler, J. (2003), *Der Dynastiewechsel von 751 und die fränkische Königssalbung*, Düsseldorf.

Settipani, C. (1993), *La préhistoire des Capétiens 481-987. Première partie. Mérovingiens, Carolingiens, Robertiens*, Villeneuve d'Ascq.

Smith, J. M. H. (1992), *Province and Empire: Brittany and the Carolingians*, Cambridge.

Smith, J. M. H. (1995), 'Religion and Lay Society', in R. McKitterick (ed.), *New Cambridge Medieval History II c.700–c.900*, 654–78, Cambridge.

Smith, J. M. H. (2003), 'Einhard, the Sinner and the Saints', *TRHS*, 6th series, 13: 55–77.

Smith, J. M. H. (2010), 'Rulers and Relics c.750–c.950: Treasure on Earth, Treasure in Heaven', *Past & Present*, 206.Supplement 5: 73–96.

Smith, J. M. H. (2016), 'Pippin III and the Sandals of Christ: The Making and Unmaking of an Early Medieval Relic', in R. Meens, D. van Espelo, B. van den Hoven, J. van

Genderen, I. V. R. Raaijmakers and C. van Rhijn (eds.), *Religious Franks. Religion and Power in the Frankish Kingdoms: Studies in Honour of Makye de Jong*, 437–54, Manchester.
Sot, M. (1993), *Un historien et son Église. Flodoard de Reims*, Paris.
Southern, R. W. (1970), *Western Society and the Church*, Harmondsworth.
Spiegel, G. (1997), *The Past as Text: The Theory and Practice of Medieval Historiography*, Baltimore and London.
Sprandel, R. (1958), *Das Kloster St. Gallen in der Verfassung des karolingischen Reiches*, Forschungen zur oberrheinische Landesgeschichte, 7, Freiburg.
Staab, F. (1975), *Untersuchungen zur Gesellschaft am Mittelrhein in der Karolingerzeit*, Wiesbaden.
Staab, F. (1998), 'Jugement moral et propaganda: Boson de Vienne vu par les élies du royaume de l'Est', in R. Le Jan (ed.), *La royauté et les élites dans l'Europe* carolingienne, 365–82, Lille.
Stafford, P. (1983), *Queens, Concubines, and Dowagers: The King's Wife in the Early Middle Ages*, Athens Georgia.
Stafford, P. (1990), 'Charles the Bald, Judith and England', in M. T. Gibson and J. L. Neslon (eds.), *Charles the Bald: Court and Kingdom*, 139–53, Aldershot.
Stafford, P. (2000), 'Queens and Treasure in the Early Middle Ages', in E. M. Tyler (ed.), *Treasure in the Medieval West*, 61–82, Woodbridge.
Stafford, P. (2001a), 'Parents and Children in the Early Middle Ages', *Early Medieval Europe*, 10.2: 257–71.
Stafford, P. (2001b), 'Powerful Women in the Early Middle Ages: Queens and Abbesses', in P. Linehan and J. L. Nelson (eds.), *The Medieval World*, 398–415, London.
Staubach, N. (1995), '*Christiana tempora*: Augustin und das Ende der alten Geschichte in der Weltchronik Frechulfs von Lisieux', *Frühmittelalteriche Studien*, 29: 167–206.
Steinmetz, G. (1999), 'Introduction', in G. Steinmetz (ed.), *State/Culture. State-Formation after the Cultural Turn*, 1–49, Ithaca and London.
Stiegemann, C. and M. Wemhoff eds (1999), *799 Kunst und Kultur der Karolingerzeit. Karl der Große und Papst Leo III. in Paderborn. Katalog der Ausstellung*, 2 vols, Mainz.
Stoclet, A. (1980a), 'La "clausula de unctione Pippini regis": mises au point et nouvelles hypothèses', *Francia*, 8: 1–42.
Stoclet, A. (1980b), 'La *descriptio basilicae sancti Dyonisii*, premiers commentaires', *Journal des Savants*, 103–17.
Stoclet, A. (1988), 'Le temporal de Saint-Denis du VIIe au Xe siècle', in J. Cuisenier and R. Guadagnin (eds.), *Un village au temps de Charlemagne*, 94–10, Paris.
Stone, R. (2011), *Morality and Masculinity in the Carolingian Empire*, Cambridge.
Störmer, W. (2002), *Die Bajuwaren. Von der Völkerwanderung bis Tassilo III*, Munich.
Story, J. (1999), 'Cathwulf, Kingship and the royal abbey of St-Denis', *Speculum*, 74.1: 1–21.
Story, J. (2002), *Carolingian Connections: Anglo-Saxon England and Carolingian Francia, c.750–870*, Aldershot.
Strathern, M. (1988), *The Gender of the Gift: Problems with Women and Problems with Society in Melanesia*, Berkeley, Los Angeles, London.
Tellenbach, G. ed. (1957a), *Studien und Vorarbeiten zur Geschichte des großfränkischen und frühdeutschen Adels*, Forschungen zur oberrheinische Landesgeschichte, 4, Freiburg.
Tellenbach, G. (1957b), 'De Grossfränkische Adel und die Regierung Italiens in der Blütezeit des Karolingerreichs', in Tellenbach (1957a), 40–70.
Tellenbach, G. (1979), 'Die geistigen und politischen Grundlagen der karolingischen Thronfolge', *FMSt*, 13: 184–302.

Tellenbach, G. (1984), 'Die historische Dimension der liturgischen Commemoratio im Mittelalter', in K. Schmid and J. Wollasch (eds.), *Memoria. Der geschichtliche Zeugniswert des liturgischen Gedenkens im Mittelalter*, 200–14, Munich.

Theuws, F. (2001), 'Maastricht as a Place of Power in the Early Middle Ages', in M. de Jong and F. Theuws (eds.), *Topographies of Power in the Early Middle Ages*, 155–216, Leiden.

Thiébaux, M. (1998), *Handbook for Her Warrior Son*, trans. Dhuoda, Cambridge.

Thompson, E. P. (1974), 'Patrician Society, Plebeian Culture', *Journal of Social History*, 7: 382–405.

Thompson, J. W. (1935), *The Dissolution of the Carolingian Fisc in the Ninth Century*, Berkeley.

Tischler, M. (2001), *Einharts Vita Karoli. Studien zur Entstehung, Überlieferung und Rezeption*, 2 vols, Hannover.

Tischler, M. (2008), 'Die *Divisio regnorum* von 806 zwischen handschriftlicher Überlieferung und historiographischer Rezeption', in B. Kasten (ed.), *Herrscher- und Fürstentestamente im west-europäischen Mittelalter*, 193–258, Cologne.

Tremp, E. (1988), *Studien zu den Gesta Hludowici imperatoris des Trierer Chorbishofs Thegan*, Hannover.

Tremp, E. (1991), *Die Überlieferung der Vita Hludowici Imperatoris des Astronomus*, Hannover.

Verhulst, A. (1999), *The Rise of Cities in North-West Europe*, Cambridge.

Verhulst, A. (2002), *The Carolingian Economy*, Cambridge.

Von Padberg, L. (1999), 'Das Paderborner Treffen von 799 im Kontext der Geschichte Karls des Großen', in W. Hentze (ed.), *De Karolo rege et Leone papa. Der Bericht über di Zusammenkunft Karls des Grossen mit papst Leo III. In Paderborn 799 in einem Epos für Karl den Kaiser*, 9–104, Paderborn.

Wagner, H. (1999), 'Zur Notitia de servitio monasteriorum von 819', *DA*, 55: 417–38.

Wallace-Hadrill, J. M. (1962), *The Long-Haired Kings, and Other Studies in Frankish History*, London.

Wallace-Hadrill, J. M. (1967), *The Barbarian West, 400–1000*, London.

Wallace-Hadrill, J. M. (1975), *Early Medieval History*, Oxford.

Wallace-Hadrill, J. M. (1978), 'A Carolingian Renaissance Prince: The Emperor Charles the Bald', *Proceedings of the British Academy*, 64: 155–84.

Wallace-Hadrill, J. M. (1981), 'History in the Mind of Archbishop Hincmar', in J. M. Wallace-Hadrill and R. H. C. Davies (eds.), *The Writing of History in the Middle Ages. Essays Presented to R.W. Southern*, 43–70, Oxford.

Wamers, E. (2005), *Die Macht des Silbers. Karolingische Schätze im Norden*, Regensburg.

Wamers, E. and P. Périn eds (2012), *Koniginnen der Merowinger. Adelsgräber aus den Kirchen von Köln, Saint-Denis, Chelles und Frankfurt am Main*, Regensburg.

Ward, E. (1990a), 'Caesar's Wife: The Career of the Empress Judith, 819–829', in P. Godman and R. Collins (eds.), *Charlemagne's Heir. New Perspectives on the Reign of Louis the Pious*, 205–27, Oxford.

Ward, E. (1990b), 'Agobard of Lyons and Paschasius Radbertus as Critics of the Empress Judith', *Studies in Church History*, 27, 15–25.

Ward, G. (2015), 'Lessons in Leadership: Constantine and Theodosius in Frechulf of Lisieux's *Histories*', in C. Gantner, R. McKitterick and S. Meeder (eds.), *The Resources of the Past in Early Medieval Europe*, 68–83, Cambridge.

Watts, J. (2009), *The Making of Polities: Europe 1300–1500*, Cambridge.

Weber, M. (1968), *Economy and Society. An Outline of Interpretive Sociology*, New York.
Weinrich, L. (1963), *Wala: Graf, Mönch und Rebell. Die Biographie eines Karolingers*, Lübeck.
Wendling, W. (1985), 'Die Erhebung Ludwigs des Frommen zum Mitkaiser im Jaher 813', *FMSt*, 19: 201–38.
Werner, K. F. (1959), 'Untersuchungen zur Frühzeit des französischen Fürstentums (9.-10. Jahrhundert) IV', *Die Welt als Geschichte*, 19: 146–93.
Werner, K. F. (1960), 'Untersuchungen zur Frühzeit des französischen Fürstentums (9.-10. Jahrhundert) V', *Die Welt als Geschichte*, 20: 87–119.
Werner, K. F. (1967), 'Die Nachkommen Karls des Großen bis um das Jahr 1000 (1.-8. Generation)', in H. Beumann and W. Braunfels (eds.), *Karl der Großen. Lebenswerk und Nachleben*, 4, 403–83, Düsseldorf.
Werner, K. F. (1973), 'Les principautés périphériques dans le monde franc du VIIIe siècle', in *I problemi dell'Occidente nel secolo VIII*, 483–514, Spoleto.
Werner, K. F. (1975), 'La date de naissance de Charlemagne', in *Bulletin de la Société des Antiquaires de France*, 1972/1975, and reprinted with same pagination in K. F. Werner, *Structures politiques du monde franc (VIe-XIIe siècles)*, London, 1979, as ch. VII.
Werner, K. F. (1979), 'Gauzlin von Saint-Denis und die west-fränkische Reichsteilung von Amiens', *DA*, 35: 157–224.
Werner, K. F. (1988), 'Saint-Denis et les carolingiens', in J. Cuisenier and R. Guadagnin (eds.), *Un village au temps de Charlemagne*, 40–9, Paris.
Werner, K. F. (1990), '*Hludovicus Augustus*: Gouverner l'empire chrétien – Idées et réalités', in P. Godman and R. Collins (eds.), *Charlemagne's Heir. New Perspectives on the Reign of Louis the Pious*, 3–123, Oxford.
Werner, K. F. (1997), 'Les premiers Robertiens et les premiers Anjou (IXe-début Xe siècle)', in O. Guillot and R. Favreau (eds.), *Pays de Loire et Aquitaine de Robert le Fort aux premiers Capétiens*, 9–67, Poitiers.
Werner, M. (1982), *Adelsfamilien im Umkreis der frühen Karolinger*, Sigmaringen.
West, C. (2012), 'Dynastic Historical Writing', in S. Foot, C. F. Robinson and I. Hesketh (eds.), *The Oxford History of Historical Writing*, 496–516, Oxford.
West, C. (2013), *Reframing the Feudal Revolution. Political and Social Transformation between Marne and Moselle c.800–c.1100*, Cambridge.
West, G. V. B. (1999), 'Charlemagne's Involvement in Central and Southern Italy: Power and the Limits of Authority', *Early Medieval Europe*, 8.3: 341–67.
Wickham, C. (1995), 'Rural Society in Carolingian Europe', in R. McKitterick (ed.), *New Cambridge Medieval History*, vol. 2, 510–37, Cambridge.
Wickham, C. (2001), 'Topographies of Power: Introduction', in M. de Jong and F. Theuws (eds.), *Topographies of Power in the Early Middle Ages*, 1–8, Leiden.
Wickham, C. (2005a), *Framing the Early Middle Ages. Europe and the Mediterranean 400–800*, Oxford.
Wickham, C. (2005b), *Problems in Doing Comparative History. The Reuter Lecture 2004*, Southampton.
Wickham, C. (2009), *The Inheritance of Rome. A Hitsory of Europe from 400 to 1000*, London.
Wilmart, A. (1933), 'L'admonition de Jonas au roi Pépin et le florilège canonique d'Orléans', *Revue Bénédictine*, 45: 214–33.
Winter, M. (2005), '"In Schönheit prangt alles, alles strahlt volles Zier." Der karolingischer Herrscher und sein Körper in den zeitgenossen Schriftquellen', *Frühmittelalterliche Studien*, 39: 101–28.

Witthöft, H. (1994), 'Münze, Maß und Gewicht im Frankfurter Kapitular', in J. Fried, R. Koch, L. Saurma-Jetsch and A. Thiel (eds.), *794 - Karl der Große in Frankfurt am Main*, 124–8, Sigmaringen.

Wolfram, H. (1995a), *Grenzen und Räume. Geschichte Österreichs vor seiner Entstehung*, Vienna.

Wolfram, H. (1995b), *Salzburg Bayern Österreich. Die Conversio Bagoariorum et Carantanorum und die Quellen ihrer Zeit*, Vienna.

Wood, I. (1991), 'Saint-Wandrille and Its Hagiography', in I. Wood and G. A. Loud (eds.), *Church and Chronicle in the Middle Ages. Essays presented to John Taylor*, 1–14, London.

Wood, I. (1994), *The Merovingian Kingdoms 450-751*, London.

Wood, I. (2000), 'Before or after Mission. Social Relations across the Middle and Lower Rhine in the Seventh and Eighth Centuries', in I. L. Hansen and C. Wickham (eds.), *The Long Eighth Century: Production, Distribution and Demand*, 149–66, Leiden.

Wood, I. (2001), *The Missionary Life*, Harlow.

Wood, I. (2003), 'Deconstructing the Merovingian Family', in R. Corradini, M. Diesenberger and H. Reimitz (eds.), *The Construction of Communities in the Early Middle Ages*, 149–71, Leiden.

Wood, I. (2004a), 'Usurpers and Merovingian Kingship', in M. Becher and J. Jarnut (eds.), *Der Dynastiewechsel von 751*, 15–31, Münster.

Wood, I. (2004b), 'Genealogy Defined by Women: The Case of the Pippinids', in L. Brubaker and J. M. H. Smith (eds.), *Gender in the Early Medieval* World, *East and West, 300-900*, 234–56, Cambridge.

Wood, I. (2013), *The Modern Origins of the Early Middle Ages*, Oxford.

Wood, S. (2006), *The Proprietary Church in the Medieval West*, Oxford.

Wormald, P. (1998), *Legal Culture in the Early Medieval West*, London.

Wormald, P. (1999), *The Making of English Law: King Alfred to the Twelfth Century. I: Legislation and Its Limits*, Oxford.

Wormald, P. and J. L. Nelson eds (2007), *Lay Intellectuals in the Carolingian World*, Cambridge.

Wyss, M. (2001), 'Die Klosterpfalz Saint-Denis im Licht der neuen Ausgrabungen', in L. Fenske, J. Jarnut, M. Wemhoff and G. Berndt (eds.), *Splendor palatii. Neue Forschungen zu Paderborn und anderen Pfalzen der Karolingerzeit*, 175–92, Göttingen.

Yorke, B. (2003), *Nunneries and the Anglo-Saxon Royal Houses*, London.

Zechiel-Eckes, K. (2002), 'Auf Pseudoisidors Spur oder: Versuch, einen dichten Schleier zu lüften', in W. Hartmann and G. Schmitz (eds.), *Fortschritt durch Fälschungen? Ursprung, Gestalt und Wirkungen der Pseudoisidorischen Fälschungen*, 1–28, Hannover.

Zielinski, H. (1989), 'Die Kloster- und Kirchengründungen der Karolinger', in I. Crusius (ed.), *Beiträge zu Geschichte und Struktur der mittelalterlichen Germania Sacra*, 95–134, Göttingen.

Zimmermann, H. (1999), 'Western Francia: The Southern Prinicipalities', in T. Reuter (ed.), *The New Cambridge Medieval History III c.900–c.1024*, 420–55, Cambridge.

Zotz, T. (1990), 'Grundlagen und Zentren der Königsherrschaft im deutschen Südwesten in karolingischer und ottonischer Zeit', in H. U. Nuber, K. Schmid, H. Steuer and T. Zotz (eds.), *Archäologie und Geschichte des ersten Jahrtausends in Südwestdeutschland*, 275–93, Sigmaringen.

Zotz, T. (1997a), 'Ludwig der Fromme, Alemannien und die Genese eines neuen Regnum', in G. Köbler and H. Nehlsen (eds.), *Wirkungen europäischer Rechtskultur. Festschrift für Karl Kroeschell zum 70. Geburtstag*, 1481–99, Munich.

Zotz, T. (1997b), 'Beobachtungen zu Königtum und Forst im früheren Mittelalter', in W. Rösener (ed.), *Jagd und höfische Kultur im Mittelalter*, 95–122, Göttingen.

Index

Aachen 64, 116, 130
  bride show at 246
  building of 58
  Charlemagne's family at 71–2, 82, 122–4, 128, 129, 265
  Charlemagne's tomb 55, 91
  as imperial centre 55, 81, 83, 90–1
  Louis the Pious and 122–9, 130
  residences at 118
  Vikings at 273
Adalbero, bishop of Augsburg 104, 114
Adalbert, count of Metz 161, 165, 170
Adalhard, the seneschal 142, 170–1
Adalhard of Corbie, cousin of Charlemagne
  connection with Italy 80, 96–7, 89
  loses royal favour 62
  in royal service 72, 76, 82, 85, 229
Adventius, bishop of Metz 187, 188
Agilolfings, Bavarian ducal dynasty 24, 32
  prayers for 235, 245
Agobard, archbishop of Lyon 133, 140, 144, 145, 148
Albgar, count 79, 115–16
Albuin 117–18, 119
Alcuin
  letters to princes 109
  palace connections 53–4, 229
  royal sons and 73, 74, 78, 79
  royal women and 54, 72, 79–80, 264, 265, 268
Aldric, bishop of Le Mans 116, 117, 233
Alemannia
  aristocracy and Bernard of Italy 89–90, 135, 138
  Charles the Bald and 138–40
  dukes of 31, 268
  links with Italy 79, 81, 135
  and Pippin III 32, 44
Alexander the Great 5, 19, 176, 109–10
Alfred, king of Wessex 30, 116, 246

Alsace
  Carolingian conquest 27, 44, 45, 63
Angilbert, abbot 78, 80, 87, 117, 228
Ansegis, abbot 63, 223
Aquitaine
  attachment to Carolingians 305, 310
  and Charlemagne 94–5, 97
  church lands in 33, 197
  and Louis the Pious 67, 72, 83–4, 90, 91, 95, 97, 114, 122–6
  royal resources in 275
  subdued by Carolingians 29, 33, 47, *see also* Charles of Aquitaine, Pippin I of Aquitaine, Pippin II of Aquitaine
aristocracy
  888 and 294–300, 305
  as collective 62–3, 178–84
  conflict with kings 22–3, 142–6, 152–5, 175, 176–7
  divided loyalties 63–71, 83–91, 146–53
  estates 157–9
  and *honores* 59, 66–7, 143, 148, 170–1
  knowledge of Carolingian ancestry 221, 248
  lands after 843 173–5, 285–6
  opposition to [early] Carolingians 29–33
  as partner of kings 13
  'super-magnates' 211, 288–9
  support for Pippin III 35–7, 40–4, 45–51
  youth spent at palace 111, 113, 116–19, 229
  war 58, 63
Arnulf, king and emperor
  888 and 289, 291–6, 298
  'kinglets' and 294–5, 298, 300, 302–5, 307–8
  name 105, 106, 226
  as 'natural lord' 4, 294

Arnulf, St, bishop of Metz 28, 105, 106, 186
  cult of 30, 38
  genealogies 218–19, 223
Arnulf, son of Louis the Pious 88, 131, 226
assemblies 14, 56, 63, 66
  attendance 63
  numbers at 14, 151, 160, 179
  quarrels at 160, 179
  of royal brothers post-843 179–80, 181–2, 184
  speeches at 72
  timing of 103
Asser, biographer of King Alfred 21
Attigny, 137–8, 147, 226, 247
Atto, *baiulus* of Charles the Bald 114–15
Autchar, follower of Pippin III and Carloman 61
Avars
  Frankish attacks 54, 79
  treasure 54, 58, 79

Baddilo, follower of Pippin III 48
Baldwin I, count of Flanders 175–6, 256
Baldwin II, count of Flanders 306, 310–11
Baturich, bishop of Regensburg 34
Bavaria
  dukes of 34
  Frankish conquest 56, 57
  opposition to Carolingians 31–2
  Pippin the Hunchback 69–70
  support for Carolingians 33, 41
Bego, count 83, 90, 125, 127, 129, 133
Benedict of Aniane 56, 116, 129
Benevento
  conflict with Franks 54, 55, 80
Berengar I, marquis and king 286, 291, 295, 296, 297
  Carolingian blood 288, 298
Bernard, Charlemagne's uncle 62, 227
Bernard, king of Italy 115
  aristocratic support 88–90
  and Charlemagne 82, 85–91
  at Fulda 82
  legitimacy of 79
  Louis the Pious and 129, 133–8
Bernard, son of Charles the Fat 105–6
Bernard of Septimania 141–2, 144–6, 148, 151, 178, 194–5

Bertha, daughter of Charlemagne 243
Bertha, daughter of Louis the German 259–60
Bertha, wife of Gerard of Vienne 19
Bertrada, queen 36, 39
  buried at St-Denis 46
  ceremonies of 751–4 36–7, 40, 42
  family of 47, 50
  mother of kings 39
  and Prüm 47, 50
  as widow 60–1
biblical families 12, 75, 77, 79, 106, 110, 131, 133, 146, 154–6, 253
biblical rulers 54, 58, 71, 124–5, 155, 183, 234, 278
Bodman, palace 191, 241, 259
Boniface, St 24, 41, 43
  king-making of 751 27, 35
Boso of Vienne
  bid for crown 277–8
  denounces sons of Louis the Stammerer 223
  favoured by Charles the Bald 210, 211
  marries Ermengard 272
  threat to Carolingians 279, 283
Bourges 47, 195
Brun, Saxon aristocrat 25, 35, 280, 282

Carloman, king of west Francia 238, 276, 278, 279–80
Carloman, mayor of the palace 24, 29–32
  abdication of 38, 40
  return to Francia 39
Carloman, brother of Charlemagne
  ceremonies of 754 41, 42
  children of 61, 111–12
  death of 56, 61
  relations with Charlemagne 60–2
  tomb 19
Carloman, son of Charlemagne. *See* Pippin of Italy
Carloman, son of Charles the Bald
  clericalisation of 205–9
Carloman, son of Lothar I 101–2
Cathwulf 61, 75, 252
Charlemagne, king and emperor
  accession of 60–1
  ancestral consciousness 218–19
  apprenticeship as king 50

childhood of 40–1, 42, 46, 96–7
Christian kingship 54–5, 91
daughters at court 72–3, 77, 80, 82,
    83–5, 91, 122–3, 243, 255, 264
as father 94–5, 96, 97, 103, 105, 108,
    113, 114
as foster-father 114, 117, 118
last years 81–91
and Prüm 47
reputation of 1–3, 53, 55–6
resources 59, 61–3
revolts against 63–71
and sons of Carloman 111–12
and St-Denis 46, 57, 60, 61, 81–2
succession plans 9, 67–9, 74–91, 124–5
wars 53–7, 63
Charles, archbishop of Mainz 198–200, 230
Charles, king of Provence 106, 107–8, 114,
    180, 182, 186, 188, 189
Charles, son of Pippin I of Aquitaine 112
Charles Martel 29–30, 32, 38, 40
as father 100, 104, 112
prayers for 43
and St-Denis 46
Charles of Aquitaine, son of Charles the
    Bald 117–18, 119, 202, 203, 206,
    207, 247
Charles of Lotharingia 313, 314–18
Charles the Bald
    birth and youth 94, 95, 101, 107, 110,
        138–40
    conflicts with sons 187, 205–10,
        212–13
    control of children 114, 119
    crisis of 830s 138–41, 152, 159–62, 165,
        167–8
    on kingship 9, 22–3
    prayer requests 235, 238, 242
    relations with post-843 kingdoms 174,
        177, 179, 179–87, 192–204, 209
    succession plans 209, 212–13
Charles the Fat, son of Louis the German
    aristocracy and 285–7
    conflict with father 192
    fall of 4–6, 292–5
    illegitimate son 105–6
    prayer requests 239
    reunited empire 285–91
    separation from wife 254

Charles the Simple, king
    Carolingian identity 103, 221, 305,
        307–8
    childhood 103, 113, 287, 290, 301, 302,
        304
    conflicts 309–14
    king-making 305–6
Charles the Younger, son of
    Charlemagne
    crowned in Rome 71–2
    death 83
    gains Neustria 69
    marriage plans 39, 69
    promised Francia 75–7
    royal prospects 71–2, 73–4, 80–1
Charroux, monastery 232, 240
Chelles 75, 260, 265–6
    and Gisela 76
Childebrand, count 28, 36, 37, 43, 51,
    60
Childeric III, last Merovingian king 27,
    28, 30, 31, 32
childhood, royal 94–119
Chilperic II (Daniel), Merovingian king
    31, 38
Chrodegang, bishop of Metz 35, 43
Chunibert, count of Bourges 33
coinage
    Charlemagne's control of 55, 59
    Charles the Fat 288
    non-royal 310
    women and 351
Compiègne 40
    ceremonial centre 143, 147, 153, 211,
        214–15, 285
    memory palace 192, 212, 220–1, 274,
        277, 314
Conrad, count of Auxerre 5, 176, 180, 208,
    228
Conrad I, king 25, 313
crowns 17, 169, 213, 300
    aristocrats and 142, 264
    women and 244, 264
Cunigunda, wife of Bernard of Italy 133

Daniel. *See* Chilperic II
David, biblical king 19–20, 41, 54, 58
Desiderius, king of Lombards
    sons of Carloman 111

Dhuoda
  aristocratic identity 225
  on birth and baptism 93, 102, 103
  crisis of 830s 143, 170
  marriage 247
  respect for Carolingian line 106, 118, 119
Division of the Kingdoms (806) 74–8, 150
Doda, mistress of Lothar I 101–2, 180
Donatus, count of Melun, 158
Doué-la-Fontaine, palace 122, 125, 126
Drogo, son of Carloman 38–9
Drogo, son of Charlemagne and bishop of Metz 101, 229, 230
  relations with Louis the Pious 130, 136, 166, 168–9, 170
dukes
  opposition to rise of Carolingians 29, 31–3, 47, *see also* Alemannia, Bavaria
Dungal, Irish scholar 82

Eberhard of Friuli 160, 175, 256, 264, 285–6
Ebo, archbishop of Reims
  childhood 115
  crisis of 830s 156, 159–60
  given ring by Judith 95
Ebroin, bishop of Poitiers 166–7, 193
Eccard, count of Macon 20, 258
Einhard
  on Charlemagne as foster-father 22
  and crisis of 830s 3, 146, 151, 152, 154
  and *Division* of 806 76
  on Merovingians 10, 21–2, 36
  succession of Louis the Pious 83, 124
Emma, queen 250
Engleberga, empress 247, 251, 261, 281, 290
Ermengard, wife of Boso 210, 272, 290–1, 302, 303–4
Ermengard, wife of Lothar I 170–1, 264
Ermengard, wife of Louis the Pious 90, 248
Ermentrud, queen 264
  fertility ritual 206–7, 238, 250
estates
  administration of 33
  control of 50, 59, 62–3
  and queens 179, 248
  royal 40, 47, 187, 275–6, 279

Faremoutiers, monastery 256–8
Fastrada, queen 64, 68, 69, 262, 263
Flavigny, monastery 43, 237
Florus of Lyon 173–4
Fontenoy, battle 170–1
foster-fathers
  aristocrats 104, 114–16
  kings 111, 114
Franco, bishop of Liège 229
  as a Carolingian 11
Frankfurt
  palace 24–5, 64, 94, 101, 177
  synod (794) 24, 59, 70
Freculf, bishop of Lisieux 110, 139
Fulda, abbey
  commemoration lists 263, 269–70, 282
  connection with Bernard of Italy 82
  prayers 64, 235
  and rebellion 65
  royal patronage 64
Fulk, archbishop of Reims 288, 295, 299, 303–8, 311
Fulrad, abbot of St-Denis 41, 44, 45

Gauziolenus, bishop of Le Mans 49
Geilo, bishop of Langres 239, 278, 288, 291
genealogies 21, 192, 217–23
Gerard, count of Paris 43–4
Gerard, count of Vienne 187, 189, 240
  as foster-father 14, 114
Gerberga, sister of Bernard of Septimania 143, 153
Gerberga, wife of Carloman 111
Gertrud of Nivelles, saint 4, 246, 267
Gerward, librarian of Louis the Pious 5
gifts
  to aristocrats 62, 70
  kings and 17, 18, 34, 41, 42, 46, 54, 70, 179, 233
  queens and 79, 95, 264, 302
  royal women and 54
Gisela, daughter of Charlemagne 57
Gisela, daughter of Louis the Pious 160, 255, 285–6
Gisela, daughter of Lothar II 267–8
Gisela, sister of Charlemagne 42, 51, 54, 265–6
  and Chelles 75

at Rome 800 80
    and royal succession 71–2, 75
Glasgow 219
Gotfrid, duke of Alemannia 31
Gregory I, pope 9
Grifo, son of Charles Martel 32, 38–40
Grimald, abbot 164, 270
Grimoald I, mayor of the palace 2, 29, 30
Grimoald II, mayor of the palace 2, 45
Gundrada, cousin of Charlemagne 229

Hadrian 1, pope 108
Hardrad, conspiracy 63–6, 135
Hartbert, abbot 3–4
Hatto, archbishop of Mainz 104
Hedenen, ducal dynasty 64–5
Heilwig, abbess of Chelles 260, 266–7
Heiric of Auxerre 208
Herbert, count of Vermandois 113, 305, 306, 314
Herstal 63, 65, 128
Hildegard, wife of Charlemagne
    ancestry 221, 249
    buried at Metz 68, 219
    as mother of kings, 67–8, 94, 95, 108
    reputation of 249–50
Hildegard, daughter of Louis the German 241, 244, 260, 262, 263, 270
Hiltrud, daughter of Charles Martel 32, 256
Himiltrud, wife of Charlemagne 67, 103
Hincmar, archbishop of Reims
    capitularies 178, 203
    on kingship 205, 209, 214–15, 228
    Metz coronation 186
    and Pippin II and 197, 203–4
    on royal succession 11–12
    on young kings 109–10
honores 58, 66–7
    after 843 170, 174–5, 205, 206, 277
    crisis of 830s 143, 148, 170, 171
Hraban Maur, abbot 147, 154–6, 159, 164
Hugh Capet, duke and king 314, 316–17
Hugh, count of Tours 137, 141–2, 145
Hugh, son of Charlemagne 130, 136, 232, 263
Hugh, son of Lothar II 114, 181, 189–90, 227
Hugh the Abbot 277, 278, 280

Hugo, nephew of Charles Martel 45
hunting 118–19, 179, 212
    royal children and 96, 98, 113, 117–18

illegitimate sons
    ambiguous status 98, 101–2, 105–6, 225–7, 290–1
    legal status, 98 130–1, 225
Ingelheim 146, 149
    paintings in palace 19
Isimgrim, supporter of Bernard of Italy 135
Istria 17, 55
Italy
    Frankish conquest 55–6
    links with Alemannia 79, 81, *see also* Bernard, Lothar I, Louis II, Pippin of Italy

Jerome, son of Charles Martel 51, 263
Jonas, bishop of Orléans 12, 140, 154, 155
Judith, daughter of Charles the Bald 175, 256
Judith, empress
    crisis of 830s 142, 144–6, 147–9, 152, 161, 165, 168
    as mother to Charles the Bald 94–5, 101, 110, 138–9, 165, 168

Karlmann, son of Louis the German 280–1
    conflict with father 187, 191
'kinglets' of 888, claims to kingship 295–301

laudes (ritual acclamations) 24, 42, 210, 236–7, 252, 279
Lex Salica 48
Liutgard, wife/queen of Charlemagne 54, 71
Liutgard, wife of Louis the Younger 25, 280
Lombards
    clash with papacy 40
    conflict with Charlemagne 55–6
    Pippin III visit 112
Lorsch, abbey
    aristocratic patronage 61–2, 64
    history writing 75, 87
    royal control 62–3
    royal tombs 281, 285, 288

Lothar, son of Charles the Bald 207–9
Lothar twin of Louis the Pious 94–5
Lothar I 100, 101–2
   civil war 840–3 169–72
   crisis of 830s 142, 144–6, 147–9, 157, 161, 165, 168
   godfather to Charles the Bald 95, 112
   prayer requests 238
   relations with post-843 kingdoms 179, 181, 182, 184, 185, 193, 195, 200
   settlement of 817 132–4, 139, 141
   succession plans 187–8
Lothar II 114
   divorce case 180, 183, 188, 189, 253
   relations with post-843 kingdoms 175, 179–84, 186, 188–9
   youth 100, 110, 188
Louis, abbot of St-Denis 229, 230–1
Louis, son of Louis the Younger 24–5
Louis of Provence, son of Boso
   Carolingian identity 290–1, 302, 303, 304
   kingship 303–4
Louis the Child, king 104, 311–13
Louis the German
   control of sons 181, 190–2
   crisis of 830s 142, 148, 151–3, 156, 159–60, 162–5, 168–71
   daughters 269–70, 271
   prayer requests 238, 241
   relations with post-843 kingdoms 175, 179–87, 190, 199, 200
   as young ruler 99, 111, 114
Louis the Pious
   accession of 121–9
   and Bernard of Italy 84, 87, 90–1, 133–8
   as child ruler 23, 114, 117
   crisis of 830s 141–69
   favours Charles the Bald 95, 101, 107, 138–41, 161–8
   king of Aquitaine 57, 67, 72, 83–4, 85, 90, 91
   succession plans 130–4, 150–1, 161–8
   succession to Charlemagne 83–4, 90–1
Louis the Stammerer
   accession of 213–16
   conflict with father 187, 206, 209, 210
   youth 114, 119
Louis the Younger, king 24–5, 280–1, 282, 283, 284–5

Louis II, emperor
   claims to middle kingdom 186, 189
   letter to Basil I 11
   prayer requests 239–40
   San Salavtore and 261
Louis III of west Francia, 278, 284
Louis IV, king 313
Louis V, king, 313–14
Lupus of Ferrières 178, 220, 231

Manasses, count of Dijon 309–10
Markward, abbot of Prüm 154, 158, 159
Matfrid, count of Orléans 139, 141–3, 145, 151, 264
Meersen, meeting (847) 181, 183, 185, 200
Merovingian dynasty 2, 27, 29–31, 34, 36–7, 49
   as ancestors of Carolingians 218
   decline 21–2, 28, 31–2, 36, 37, 274
   loose family structure 10, 11
   marriages 245, 246
   memory of 36–7, 95, 223
   and St-Denis 44–5
Metz
   Carolingian tombs 249, 252
   coronation of Charles the Bald 186, 187
   genealogies 218–20
Murbach, monastery 63, 240

names, royal
   on coins 55
   contemporary awareness of 105–8, 282–3
   distinctiveness 16, 105, 188, 208, 283, 313
   for illegitimate sons 85, 88, 105, 113, 226
   Merovingian 29, 30, 36–7, 95
   newly royal 37, 49
   repetition of 68, 77, 182, 206, 283, 317
   for royal women 255, 257
   system of name-giving 102–8
Neustria 29, 50, 69, 205–6, 222, 286–7, 289
   granted to Charles the Bald 107, 161
Nibelung, count 28, 36, 37, 43, 51
Nithard 228
Nivelles, convent 267–8

Notker of St-Gall
  on Carolingian specialness 23, 111, 250
  fears for Carolingian dynasty 18–20, 105–6, 273–4, 285

oaths
  broken 35, 293, 313
  to Charlemagne 65–6, 72, 76
  conspiracies 65–6
  Louis the Pious and 136, 148, 150, 152, 153, 160, 164, 168
  of Strasbourg 170, 174
  in vernacular 280
Odo, count and king
  Carolingians and 302, 303, 305, 307 310, 313
  as non-Carolingian 295–300, 312, 313
Orléans 126–7, 142–3, 145, 146, 196
Otgar, archbishop of Mainz 54, 59, 65
Ottonian dynasty 84, 245, 258, 287, 313–15

Paderborn 56, 80, 97, 117
palaces
  Carolingian take-over of 40
  centre of purity 251–2
  centre of kingdom 53–4, 72, 82–4
  eastern development of 64
  escaping royal control 276, 315
  impurity in 141–2, 143, 148
  maintenance of 59
  purified by Louis the Pious 128, 254
Paris
  council of 829 12, 140, 154–5
Paul I, pope 42, 96
Pippin, king of Italy
  anointed as king 57
  daughters of 79, 82, 116
  father of Bernard 79, 87
  as king of Italy 73–4, 78–81, 135
  name changed from Carloman 57, 68, 108
  wife 79
Pippin, son of Pippin III 101
Pippin I, mayor of the palace 29
Pippin II, mayor of the palace 29, 58
Pippin III, king
  anointed 754 39–42
  arranges sons' marriages 67
  consecration as king 751 27–8, 34–8, 39,
  childhood 100, 104, 112
  death of 43
  and Prüm 47–9
  reputation of 19
  and St-Denis 40, 44–6
  and young aristocrats 116
Pippin the Hunchback, son of Charlemagne
  alleged illegitimacy of 67, 103, 225
  revolt of 66–71
Pippin I of Aquitaine
  coinage 166
  crisis of 830s 145–6, 248, 249–52, 154–5, 160
  death of 161, 165
  and Jonas of Orléans 12
  marriage 166
  reputation 166, 192–3
Pippin II of Aquitaine
  chancery 193, 197, 198
  civil war 840–3 169–71
  coinage 195, 196
  loss of Carolingian-ness 192–3, 200–4
  nature of kingship 193–8, 202
  resources 195
  succession to father 163, 165–8
  Vikings and 195, 203–4
Pîtres
  assembly of 3, 22–3, 203
Poeta Saxo
  genealogical knowledge 106, 107
Ponthion, palace 40, 210, 236
prayers 39, 42, 47
  for non-Carolingians 300, 312
  for the kingdom 45
  for kings 2, 12, 24
  for the royal family 55–6, 72–3, 74, 78
  for the royal line 42, 45, 49, 50, 132, 140, 177, 189, 193, 234–42, 252, 262, 279,
Prüm, abbey 152, 158
  aristocratic patronage 176
  and Charles the Bald 115
  and Pippin III 47–9
  prayers for rulers 240, 279
  royal patronage after 843 176, 279

Quierzy, assembly 877 211–13

Radbert 144–5, 152
Ratold, bishop of Verona 78, 81, 135
Regensburg
  as Agilolfing palace 24
  as Carolingian palace 24–5, 69–70, 285
Reginhar, supporter of Bernard of Italy 135, 137
Regino of Prüm
  on fall of Charles the Fat 4–6, 293–4
Reichenau, abbey 79, 140, 160, 164
  commemoration list 269
Reims, church
  lands in post-843 kingdoms 165, 166, 174
Remedius, son of Charles Martel 51
Remiremont, abbey 180–1, 269
Rheinau, monastery 241
Richard, count, brother of Boso 303, 304, 309–10
Richard, count, follower of Lothar I 157–8
Richgardis, queen, wife of Charles the Fat 248, 254, 276
Richildis, queen, wife of Charles the Bald 103, 209–10, 214, 249, 251, 252
Richuin, count 89, 135
Robert I, king in west Francia 312, 313
Rotrud, daughter of Charlemagne 57, 81, 245–6
Rudolf I, king of Burgundy 289, 296, 297, 298–9, 300
Rupert, bishop of Salzburg 32
Ruthard, count 41, 44

St-Denis, abbey
  anointings in 754 39–42
  and aristocracy 70
  Carolingian burial site 45–7
  Charlemagne 45, 46
  Historical writing at 57
  Louis the Pious and 46–7, 127, 146, 153
  Lothar I 177
  Merovingian patronage 44–5
  Pippin III 40, 44–6, 60
  prayers 235, 237, 242, *see also* Louis of St-Denis
St-Emmeram, Regensburg 25, 285

St-Gall, abbey 30, 139
  and Bernard of Italy 88–90, 135
  and Pippin of Italy 79, 81
St-Germain, Auxerre 208–9, 228, 233, 279–80
St-Wandrille, monastery 222–3
San Salvatore, abbey 259, 261–2
Saxony
  Charlemagne's wars 30, 53, 54, 56
  Wala as governor 86
Schwarzach, abbey 259, 260, 261, 263–4
Sedulius Scottus
  knowledge of royal names 106, 182
Senlis, royal stronghold 204, 209, 256, 316
Sigibert III, king 97
Smaragdus, abbot 132–3
Stephen, count of Paris 44, 62, 90, 127
Stephen II, pope 35, 37, 39, 42

Tassilo, duke of Bavaria 2–3
  conflict with Charlemagne 56–7
  daughters 245
Thegan
  genealogical knowledge 106
  supports Louis the German 156–7, 158
Theoderic bishop of Metz 314–16
Theoderic, kinsman of Charlemagne 62, 227
Theoderic, son of Charlemagne 89
Theodrada, daughter of Charlemagne 177, 261, 263–4, 269–70
Theodulf, bishop of Orléans 75, 83, 126–7, 131, 136
Theuderic IV, Merovingian king 29–30, 37
Theutberga, queen 253, 262
Thuringia 63–5
treasure
  Aachen 121, 128, 133
  Aquitaine 167
  Avars 54, 58, 59
  kings and 58, 83
  women and 244–5, 256, 261
Tribur, synod 236

Verdun treaty of 14, 171–2, 173–5
Vikings
  Aquitaine 202–4
  threat to kingdoms 278
  tribute 211, 276
virginity 243, 251, 253–4, 268

Waifar, duke of Aquitaine 47
Wala, count and abbot
    at Charlemagne's court 72, 73, 77, 84, 91
    closeness to Bernard 87, 89, 90, 133
    revolt against Louis the Pious 145, 152
Walahfrid Strabo 99
    crisis of 830s 140, 149, 156, 164, 167
    poetry on Carolingians 139–40, 149
Waldo, abbot and bishop 79, 81–2, 127
war
    conquests 53, 55–8
    destructiveness 32–3
    impact of defeat 62, 63, 141
    organisation 32, 40, 53
    plunder and treasure 33–4, 58
    religious aura of 33, 47
    and rise of Carolingians 32–4, 47–50
    weapons 58
Warin, count 50

Welatus, count 49–50
Wicbert, count 114, 189, 190
Wido of Spoleto 295–99, 305
widowhood, of queens 60, 111, 133, 248, 250–1, 256, 262, 270, 302
Widukind of Corvey
    on later Carolingians 10, 313
William of Gellone 56, 62
William, son of Bernard and Dhuoda 116, 117
Willibrord, St 100, 102, 104
Witiza. *See* Benedict of Aniane
Worms, assemblies 138, 140, 158, 160, 161–3
Wulfard, abbot 42, 43
Wulfoald, opponent of Pippin III 43, 44, 45

Zacharias, pope 27, 34–5
Zwentibold, king 113, 251, 268, 301, 312

www.ingramcontent.com/pod-product-compliance
Lightning Source LLC
Chambersburg PA
CBHW052049290426
44111CB00011B/1671